The Life and Letters
of James Henley Thornwell

Eng.d by A H Ritchie

J. H. Moorwell

The Life and Letters
of James Henley Thornwell

D.D., LL.D.

Ex-President of the South Carolina College
Late Professor of Theology
in the Theological Seminary at
Columbia, South Carolina

B. M. PALMER

D.D., LL.D.

The Banner of Truth Trust

THE BANNER OF TRUTH TRUST
3 *Murrayfield Road, Edinburgh* EH12 6EL
P. O. Box 621, *Carlisle, Pennsylvania* 17013, USA

*

First published 1875
*This Banner of Truth Trust edition
published* 1974
Reprinted 1986

ISBN 0 85151 195 3

*

*Reprinted in Great Britain by offset lithography by
Billing & Sons Limited, Worcester*

CONTENTS.

CHAPTER I.

PARENTAGE AND BIRTH.

CHAPTER II.

EARLY BOYHOOD.

CHAPTER III.

HIS PATRONS.

CHAPTER IV.

PREPARATION FOR COLLEGE.

CHAPTER V.

COLLEGE LIFE.

CHAPTER VI.

COLLEGE LIFE CONTINUED.

CHAPTER VII.

HIS CONVERSION.

CHAPTER VIII.

HIS TEACHING AT CHERAW.

CHAPTER IX.

RESIDENCE AT CAMBRIDGE.

CHAPTER X.

First Pastorate.

CHAPTER XI.

First Professorship.

CHAPTER XII.

Voyage to Europe.

CHAPTER XIII.

Letters form Europe.

CHAPTER XIV.

Old and New School Controversy.

CHAPTER XV.

POLEMIC CAREER BEGUN.

CHAPTER XVI.

THE BOARD QUESTION.

CHAPTER XVII.

GENERAL CORRESPONDENCE.

CHAPTER XVIII.

THE ELDER QUESTION.

CHAPTER XXIX.

SEMINARY LIFE.

CHAPTER XXX.

SEMINARY LIFE CONTINUED.

CHAPTER XXXI.

SECOND TRIP TO EUROPE.

CHAPTER XXXII.

THE LATE WAR.

CHAPTER XXXIII.

His Course in the War.

CHAPTER XXXIV.

Organization of the Southern Assembly.

CHAPTER XXXV.

His Death.

CHAPTER XXXVI.

General Review.

APPENDIX.

NOTE.

THE delay in the preparation of this volume is principally due to the fact that, after the papers of Dr. Thornwell were placed in the writer's hands, two years ago, it was still necessary to collect the materials for the early portions of the Memoirs, by extensive correspondence. Valuable memoranda were thus obtained from Gen. James Gillespie, Col. W. L. T. Prince, and the family of Mr. Robbins, of Cheraw, S. C.; Hon. J. A. Inglis, of Baltimore, Md.; Rev. John Douglas, of Charlotte, N. C.; Rev. D. McQueen, D. D., of Sumterville, S. C.; Mr. W. M. Hutson, of Orangeburgh, S. C.; Col. F. W. McMaster, of Columbia, S. C.; Rev. A. A. Morse, of Gainesville, Ala.; Mr. T. E. B. Pegues, of Oxford, Miss.; Dr. Thos. L. Dunlop and Rev. J. N. Craig, of Holly Springs, Miss.; Rev. W. E. Boggs, D. D. of Memphis, Tenn.; Rev. J. M. P. Otts, D. D., of Wilmington, Del.; and Rev. A. J. Witherspoon, of New Orleans, La.; to all of whom a public acknowledgement is herewith most gratefully made by

THE AUTHOR.

THE LIFE AND LETTERS

OF

JAMES HENLEY THORNWELL,

D. D., LL. D.

CHAPTER I.

PARENTAGE AND BIRTH.

INTRODUCTION.—BIRTH.—HIS FATHER'S OCCUPATION, CHARACTER, AND EARLY DEATH.—HIS MOTHER'S LINEAGE.—EARLY SETTLEMENT OF SOUTH CAROLINA.—IMMIGRATION OF A WELSH COLONY.—HIS MOTHER'S CHARACTERISTICS.

HISTORY loves to trace the lineage of those whose lives have been heroic. It seems to add grace to virtue when it descends from sire to son,

> " And is successively, from blood to blood,
> The right of birth."

Even the pride which it begets is shorn of its offence when it becomes the spur to honour, and the legacy of a spotless name is bequeathed, with increasing splendour, to succeeding heirs. The claim of birth is buffeted with scorn only when it stands upon the merit of the past, which it is powerless to reproduce. The rugged sense of mankind discriminates, with sufficient sagacity, betwixt the counterfeit aristocracy and the true. The veneration which is natural to us resents the fraud of an empty name, without the solid worth it was supposed to repre- sent. But if the blood that courses through the veins bears upon its tide the virtues by which it was first distinguished, and the scions of an ancient house give presage of the honour which made their fathers renowned, it bows to such with a deference that seals the legitimacy of their sway. It turns, with a lofty disdain, from those who gild their vices or their weakness with the lustre of a name which is prostituted in the use; but it accepts the blessing coming from ambition itself, when the prestige of birth prompts generations, in their turn,

> " To draw forth a noble ancestry
> From the corruption of abusing time,
> Unto a lineal, true-derived course."

But the longest pedigree must have a beginning; and the whole force of these suggestions goes to show that the chief glory belongs to the founder of a family. It is the impress of his character which honourable descendants are careful to preserve; and though the original dignity may be enlarged, it is by the stimulus derived from his example. The glory of embellishing a name can never be superior to that of first drawing it from obscurity. As, too, a wise government recruits its nobility by timely and gradual accessions from the commons beneath it, so God, in His adorable providence, is continually bringing out the unknown to be princes in the power of their influence over the church and the world. This preeminence is challenged on behalf of the subject of these Memoirs. If his name was never borne with " chant of heraldry " along the aisles of the drowsy past, he has the superior glory, in this respect, of being born only of himself.

> " For being not propped by ancestry, whose grace
> Chalks successors their way ; neither allied
> To eminent assistants ; but spider-like
> Out of his self-drawing web, he gives us note,
> The force of his own merit makes his way :
> A gift that heaven gives for him, which buys
> A place next to the king."

JAMES HENLEY THORNWELL was born on the 9th of December, A. D. 1812, on the plantation of Mr. Christopher

B. Pegues, in Marlborough District, South Carolina. His grandfather, William Thornwell, was an Englishman, who lived in Marlborough District. The family was perpetuated through only one son, James Thornwell, from whose loins sprung the subject of our present story. This son was married on the 25th of June, 1809, to Martha Terrell, daughter of Samuel Terrell and Elizabeth Pearce, being herself born on the 8th of December, 1794. The issue of this latter marriage was as follows: *Elizabeth*, born May, 1810, now living, the widow of William Anderson, in Marlborough District; *James Henley*, and his *twin brother*, born December 9th, 1812, the latter of whom died a few weeks after his birth; *Caroline Jane*, born September, 1815, now living in South Carolina, as the widow of John W. Graham; a *fifth child*, a daughter, who died at two years of age, and *Charles Alexander*, the youngest, born October, 1820, who, after graduating in the South Carolina College, pursued the profession of the Law with considerable distinction, and died in 1855. Of these six children, two sons and two daughters survived the father; who died in the prime of life, on the 30th of December, 1820.

It is unfortunate that so little can be traced of Dr. Thornwell's parentage on the paternal side. Of his grandfather nothing is known but what has been mentioned above. Of his father little can be gathered beyond the fact that he belonged to that important and useful class, so necessary under the partially feudal system which has passed away, who managed the estates of others; serving as middle men between the proprietors, who were often absentees, and the baronial estates, which they managed as their representatives. He is described as generous in disposition, free-handed and hospitable, living always up to his means, and accumulating nothing. Firm in the execution of his purposes, he acquired the reputation of being a good planter and an excellent manager; and to the period of his death held positions of responsibility and trust. When this event occurred he was in charge of the business of a widow lady, Mrs. Bedgewood, afterwards Mrs. Billingsley.

The scene of death is thus described by an eye witness; and it is interesting as bringing, for the first time, distinctly before us the subject of this book. It may lend additional zest to the narrative to say that it is told by one from whom he was separated in birth by only the interval of an hour, in homes which were in sight of each other, upon the same plantation. This surviving friend, sustaining almost the relation of a foster-brother, thus depicts the sensibility and grief of the youthful orphan:

"At that time I lived a great deal with my aunt, Mrs. Bedgewood, and was there when Mr. Thornwell died. Though only some seven or eight years old, I remember the day perfectly. The house was not more than a quarter of a mile from my aunt's; both she and I were there when he breathed his last. It was the first time I had ever seen death face to face. I remember the looks of Mr. Thornwell to this day. After he was laid out, James and myself looked wonderingly on his remains, and then went to the spring, talking, as boys might, of the strangeness of death: I recollect his saying, in almost heart-broken accents, ' *What will mother do ? What will become of us ?*' We remained some time at the spring; he often weeping bitterly, and I consoling him as well as I could. No day of my life is more vividly impressed upon my memory."

It is an artless story like this which most quickly suffuses the eye with tears. It is graphic in its very simplicity. Every line in the picture is sharply cut. Two young boys, just eight years of age, stand together by the side of a corpse, with that strange awe which all remember to have felt when first gazing upon the great mystery of death; then sitting down by the cool spring to appreciate what it imports to the living; then the sudden rush of grief upon the orphan's heart, and the affectionate sensibility which stretches into the desolate future, breaking into the wail, "What will my mother do?" It is the first sign given of the broad and noble nature, which it will be the business of these pages to portray; of that deep affectionateness, which flowed like a majestic stream through a generous life, fertilizing friendships as tender and as lasting as ever gathered around the memory of the dead. It shall be told in due time "what that mother shall do," when we come to see the filial love which bursts forth in the passionate cry of the boy, folding at last her venerable form in his manly embrace, smoothing the pillow under her dying head, and writing her praise in lasting marble over her grave.

These references form an easy transition to the fuller record of his maternal ancestors. It will not be uninteresting here to incorporate a brief chapter of Carolina's early history, upon which a degree of romance is impressed by the dissimilar elements which were fused into her original population. Through a period of sixty years after the first settlement, from A. D. 1670 to 1730, the population of the province increased very slowly. First came a small colony from Barbadoes, and with it the first importation of slaves, in 1671. Then another colony from Nova-Belgia, afterwards called New York, upon its conquest, in 1674, by the English. A considerable emigration of French Protestants flowed in after the revocation of the Edict of Nantz, in 1694; which gave a marked character to the colony, furnishing many of the most honourable names upon the proud roll of this gallant State, even to the present time. In 1696 a further accession was gained by the arrival of a Congregational Church from Massachusetts, which settled in a body at Dorchester, near the head of Ashley river, about twenty miles from the city of Charleston. Dr. Ramsay, from whose history these facts are compiled, proceeds to say, " From 1696 to 1730 no considerable groups of settlers are known to have emigrated to Carolina, though the province continued to advance in population from the arrival of individuals."

It will be remembered that in 1719 the government of the infant province was transferred from the lords proprietors to the crown, a change rendered necessary by the mal-administration of the former, involving them in fatal complications with the occupants of the soil. Under the fostering protection of royalty, a steady impulse was given to the prosperity of the colony, which continued with little abatement to the final disruption of all bonds with the mother country, in 1776. At the period, however, when this change of administration occurred, it was in a condition of infantile weakness, and surrounded with perils on every side. The coast was infested with pirates, who made their captures at the very bar of Charleston. A narrow margin along the sea was all that was settled, not extending fifty miles into the interior. The middle country was held by the aborigines, "tribes of the roving foot," whose incursions penetrated almost within sight of the sea, and who were only less formidable by reason of the destructive wars waged amongst themselves. The accession of the first royal governor was signalized by a more liberal policy towards these. Negotiations were instituted and treaties formed, by which large tracts of land were ceded to the colony, and these troublesome neighbours were removed to a safer distance. The next step, of course, was to fill up this new domain with hardy settlers, whose growing power would prove a surer defence than the rude forts at Dorchester, Wiltown, and other places equally near the coast. Among the salutary measures to stimulate immigration into the new territory, "the governor was instructed to mark out eleven townships, in square plats, on the sides of rivers, consisting each of twenty thousand acres; and to divide the land within them into shares of fifty acres for each man, woman and child that should come to occupy and improve them. Each township was to form a parish, and all the inhabitants were to have an equal right to the river. * * * Each settler was to pay four shillings a year for every hundred acres of land, except the first ten years, during which term they were to be rent free. Accordingly, ten townships were marked out: two on river Altamaha, two on Savannah, two on Santee, one on Pedee, one on Wacamaw, one on Wateree, and one on Black river."*

The offer of such privileges soon attracted the poor and oppressed in other lands, who poured in from Ireland, Holland, Germany, and Switzerland; as well as some from the more Northern American colonies, in search of a more genial clime: so that to Carolina belongs the glory of affording an asylum to the persecuted and distressed of every land, up to the period when a large and fixed population of her own dispensed with the necessity of recruiting her strength by these accessions. And it would be a curious theme for speculation how far the generous character, for which her citizens have always been distinguished, is due to the composition of so many elements in her original society; as well as to trace the operation of those superior influences which melted down their obvious contradictions, and fused them into a consistent and harmonious whole.

The general history intersects just here with our own narrative. The township of Queensborough, located in 1731–2, upon the Great Pedee, a little above the junction of the Little Pedee, was first explored and afterwards settled by a party of Welsh from Pennsylvania. It appears that, as far back as 1701, some Welsh Baptists emigrated from their native country to America, bringing with them their minister, and being constituted regularly into a Church. They first settled in Penepec, Pennsylvania, where they remained a year and six months. In 1703 they removed, and took up lands in Newcastle county, which, by change of boundaries, was afterwards thrown into the State of Delaware; which explains how the branch that found its way to Carolina is differently represented as coming from Pennsylvania and from Delaware. This colony came to the Pedee in 1736, and desiring a larger tract of land, with the privilege of exclusive occupancy, petitioned the Council to that end.

* Ramsay's History of South Carolina, chapter fourth.

The result was a grant of one hundred and seventy-three thousand eight hundred and forty acres of land, part of which lay in the township of Queensborough, the remainder extending up the river a short distance above Mar's Bluff. A second petition, setting forth that the land was not in all respects adapted to their wants, especially in the growth of flax and hemp, was favourably answered in 1737 by running the lines still further up the Pedee, to the fork of the Yadkin and Rocky rivers, beyond the boundary which now separates the two Carolinas. The Welsh seem, however, to have fixed finally upon that rich and compact body of land embraced in the bend of the river opposite the present village of Society Hill, which, stretching over a distance of six miles, was from an early period known as the "Welsh Neck." The actual settlement began in 1736, and by the end of the following year most of the families had arrived from Pennsylvania, and the colony began to assume an organized and permanent character. In 1738 they formed themselves into a church of the Baptist faith, and erected a house of worship, in which they continued to serve God after the manner of their fathers. Rev. Dr. Alexander Gregg, now Bishop of the Protestant Episcopal Church in Texas, in his recently published "History of the Old Cheraws,"* and from which all the above statements have been bodily taken, thus sums up the character of this virtuous, but exceedingly clannish, community :

"Such was the scene presented by this infant band of brothers in the early days of their history, with no court of justice in their midst to which conflicting claims and angry disputes might be referred, and no frowning gaol for the reception of the criminal. Nor were they needed. Few contentions probably were known ; and the voice of society, though newly formed in this Southern home, was potent enough to silence the voice of the blasphemer, and make the evil-minded man

* This work affords a noble illustration of what antiquarian research can accomplish in working up the local traditions in our extended country. It is a mine of historic information, into which few shafts have yet been sunk.

pause in his ways. Simplicity of character appears to have been one of the most marked traits of the people ; a virtue which has been transmitted through succeeding times to their descendants. They were open and sincere, making no profession of feeling which did not exist.

"For sobriety and moderation, also, with what was more essential, as the foundation of all virtue, a deep religious feeling, they were distinguished. These virtues were strongly impressed upon the community they established, presenting in subsequent times a striking contrast to some other neighbourhoods on the Pedee, where dissipation and irreligion so much prevailed.

"The Welsh brought with them to a new country those marked features for which their ancestors had been noted long before. The Welsh are said to have been more jealous of their liberties than even the English, and far more irascible, though their jealousy soon abated."

In the first list of these early settlers occur names which South Carolina has ever delighted to put upon its roll of honour. Allusion need only be made to those of James, Wild, and Evans, conspicuous amongst those she has clothed with the ermine, both in former and in recent days ; whilst others are as household words to those who have traced the fortunes of the State through her chequered history. In the bosom of these names is found that of William Terrell, (originally Tarell), who appears in 1738 taking out titles to land, showing him a man of substance, according to the distribution of property in his day. His son, bearing also the name of William, seems to have been engaged in the public service prior to the Revolution; while the grandson, Captain John Terrell, of Marlborough District, is tersely described as "a worthy descendant of the old Welsh stock, and one of the best men of his day and generation." From this family sprung the mother of Dr. Thornwell, she being the granddaughter of William Terrell, whose name is mentioned above, amongst the first settlers on the Pedee.

She was endowed by nature with an intellect of the highest order, though unimproved by education; possessing great strength of will, and a boundless ambition for the advancement of her sons, in whom she discovered early proofs of mental power. The investigations of science will, perhaps, never interpret to us the law of trans-mission, by which characteristic traits are derived from parent to child, through which a distinct type is impressed upon families and tribes, and by which, more myste-riously still, the intellectual average is preserved in the race at large. This case might, perhaps, be added to hun-dreds of others, which seem to confirm the theory that the *intellectual* qualities come predominantly from the mother, while, perhaps, the *moral* descend more conspic-uously from the father.

This is not the place, nor are we the parties, to discuss a physiological theory like this. But the pages of history will probably be searched in vain for a truly great man who had a fool for his mother. However this may be, the Christian will be delighted to see, in this biography, the fulfilment of those rich promises which the God of grace has made to the widow and the orphan. In how many broken households a feeble and desolate woman lifts her heart to God for strength to bear, not only the burdens of her own sex, but those which should have been borne by her stricken partner! How often does she toil in poverty and sorrow, to support her fatherless children, whom she is permitted to see emerging at length from obscurity and want, to the highest distinctions of society! It was given to this widowed mother to have her proud ambition fulfilled; as this son, clothed with academic honours, sat among the senators and nobles of the land, the noblest patrician of them all, the pride of his native State, the joy and ornament of the Church, and with a fame spread over two continents, the peerless man of his time. It only remains to be added, that Mrs. Thorn-well was, throughout life, an earnest Christian, warmly attached to the doctrines and order of the Baptist Church, in whose communion she remained through seven and thirty years, to the moment of her death. That she im-pressed her own convictions of truth upon those depend-ent upon her care, might be inferred from the massive

force of her character. There is, besides, the affectionate testimony of her son, who, in his Inaugural Discourse, upon assuming the Chair of Divinity in the Theological School at Columbia, South Carolina, openly acknowledged his "thanks to a noble mother, who had
taught him from the cradle those eternal principles of
grace, which that book (the Confession of Faith) contains."

CHAPTER II.

EARLY BOYHOOD.

ORPHANAGE.—EARLY POVERTY.—AN OLD-FIELD SCHOOL.—HIS FIRST
TEACHERS.—ACCOUNT OF MR. MCINTYRE.—ATTACHMENT TO HIS
PUPIL.—HABITS OF STUDY.—EARLY AMBITION.—FIRST IMPRESSIONS
OF HIS GENIUS.—INTRODUCTION TO HIS FUTURE PATRONS.—INDIF-
FERENCE TO PLAY.—MORAL AND RELIGIOUS TRAITS.

WE must return now to the chamber of death, where
the head of a dependent household lies dressed for
the tomb. Alas for the poor! It is one of the hardships
of their lot that they have not leisure even for grief.
The stern necessities of life press at once upon the aching
heart, and they may not indulge the secret luxury of woe.
It is not for them to draw the curtains over the window,
and in the darkened solitude to feed upon the precious
memories of the past. Ye favoured children of fortune,
who find it so hard to break away from sweet communion
with the dead,—so hard, with thoughts flying upward to
their strange world, to take up again the commonplaces
of this poor earth,—think with pity of such as must choke
down their great sorrow even while the parting kiss rests
upon the marble brow, and turn at once to the life-long
struggle for bread!

It was too old a thought for our little orphan weeping
at the spring, "What will become of us?" Yet even he
must pierce the gloom of the future in the sad anticipation of suffering and want. How much darker the
shadow that lay upon the heart of the mother and widow,
was revealed by no passionate cry from her lips. There
was only the "stony grief," the first sickness of a heart
that finds itself alone with its own desolateness. Her

13

strong nature, too, had been already compacted by life's hard discipline, and could better look upon the cloud that blackened the future before her. Yet soon the question must be hers, as well as that of her boy, "What shall we do?" Hath not God other ravens besides those which fed Elijah? Perhaps a voice spoke out of the bosom of that cloud, saying, "Leave thy fatherless children; I will preserve them alive; and let your widows trust in Me." Perhaps a deep but quiet faith responded to the gracious assurance; and the burden was lighter when it had been "cast upon the Lord, who will never suffer the righteous to be moved." It is not for the historian to penetrate these experiences of God's hidden ones; only this we know, "The secret of the Lord is with them that fear Him, and He will show them His covenant."

Some time after the death of her husband, a home was provided for her and her children by Captain John Terrell, her first cousin, an excellent and pious member of the Baptist Church, who removed them near to himself, in a portion of Marlborough district known as Level Green. With only a little money in hand, and the possession of one slave, she was henceforth dependent upon her own industry, and the assistance of this worthy kinsman, for support. A positive and self-reliant character such as hers, would not, however, be likely to tax too heavily the generosity which was so freely extended by him. In the beautiful language of Rudolph Stier, "Man lifts his imploring, empty hand to heaven, and God lays work upon it; thus hast thou thy bread." By weaving, sewing, and such forms of labour as were suited to her sex, she was enabled, not only to "give meat to her household," but to secure to them such elementary education as the neighbourhood afforded. In later days, when a modest refinement graced his own abode, we have heard Dr. Thornwell contrast it with the poverty of those early days. But it was always with that playful badinage so characteristic of his social moods; and no one could tell how far the picture he drew was intended to represent the actual facts, or how far he craved the license of heightening by exaggeration the colours on the canvas. The subject was too delicate to inquire about; and he was never egotistic enough to touch, except by incidental reference, upon details that were simply personal. The difficulty of bridging with scant material the chasm of this early period, has led the writer deeply to regret that he never availed himself of the privilege of friendship in bursting through this reserve, and learning all that he would have freely told of the trials and triumphs of his boyhood. But the opportunity was lost, through mutual delicacy, restraining, on the one side, what might seem a prurient curiosity, prying into the sanctities of life, and on the other, what might be deemed ostentatious vanity in disclosing the disadvantages which had been splendidly surmounted. From the nature of the case, it could not have been a home of plenty in which his youth was nurtured; and it is doubtful if even his unaided strength could have thrown off the oppression which so often stifles the aspirations, as it extinguishes the opportunities, of genius. The worst evil of poverty is not found in the privations it inflicts; for these are, to a large degree, matters of convention and of habit. It is rather the complete engrossment of the mind upon petty and consuming cares, where the exactions of toil yield only to the weariness which buries all in sleep. It is the constant repression of the affections, which have no time for play, and the consequent blunting of the sensibilities, which inflict a wound upon the nature itself, as sad as it is incurable. But perhaps the saddest feature of urgent poverty is, that it allows no childhood. It is but a step from the nursery into the workshop, and heavy care sits upon a heart that has known no mirth. What little of childhood may have been enjoyed in the brief passage goes, too, without a record. No traditions are handed down, when all are too busy to note the changes in the formation of character. Even our illustrious friend is no exception. We look for his boyhood, and there is none. Much of this unquestionably is due to the majesty of his genius, which gave him the strength and thoughtfulness of the man, whilst in stature and in age he was still a child. But in gathering the fragmentary reminiscences from which these pages are compiled, one can scarcely help weeping over that hard necessity of fortune which has left his earliest years without a record.

It must have been during the first portion of the year A. D. 1821 that this widowed mother found herself at Level Green, in the new home provided by her generous kinsman; and here it was that young Thornwell received the rudiments of an English education. He has himself given somewhere an amusing description of an old field school, such as were once common in retired sections of the country, and which may not yet be entirely superseded. The picture was evidently drawn from the life, though we can but faintly sketch the outline from memory. Let the reader then figure to himself a rude building of logs, the interstices being filled with clay or covered by clap-boards, a huge chimney at one end, small windows innocent of glass, and wide doors, which let in the wind together with the light; a slanting shelf, stretching the whole length of the room, answering as a desk, at which the pupils stood to write; benches of a primitive pattern, mere slabs with pins driven in the round side for legs, and the flat side turned upward for the seat, and wholly unsuspicious of any support for the back; and he has before him the usual appointments of an old field school. It would not be safe to say too much as to the gentleman of the birch and ferule, seated before a deal table between the opposite doors. The slender emoluments derived from the State's thin bounty, and the small fees exacted of such as could pay, would scarcely entice men of much culture into these precincts. They were, however, generally equal to the necessities of

the region. They could engineer a boy through Webster's
Spelling-Book and Pike's Arithmetic, rising sometimes
to the dignity of Morse's Geography and Murray's Grammar, and teaching elocution from the Columbian Orator.
Occasionally there appeared teachers of real merit, as we
shall presently see. Yet in these unpretending seminaries
was laid the foundation of scholarship with some of the
best thinkers, who have filled the highest judicial and
legislative positions in the land. It is ascertained that,
between the years 1821 and 1823, young Thornwell was
successively under the discipline of three teachers, whose
names are all that is handed down to us. They were
Eugene Kinnon, an Irish Roman Catholic; Daniel Smith,
who came from Robeson county, North Carolina; and
Levi Lagget, of unknown origin. It is impossible to say
what was his precise indebtedness to these first teachers.
But if the astounding statement is to be received on a
single authority, that he was ignorant of his letters at
nine years of age, we have only to measure backward
from his knowledge at fourteen to be convinced that the
whole intervening period must have been marked by an
astonishing progress.

In 1823 Mr. McIntyre appears as the teacher at Level
Green, a name which deserves to be linked in grateful
remembrance with that of his distinguished pupil, as the
earliest of his benefactors. The debt which the world at
large owes to this gentleman, as being the first to pluck
from obscurity our "mute inglorious Milton," we will seek
in part to discharge by placing his record, so far as it may
be gathered, by the side of the protegé whose merit he
was the first to disclose. Mr. Peter McIntyre came from
a Scotch settlement on Drowning creek, in North Carolina, upon the old stage road from Cheraw to Fayetteville.
The Scotch had a large settlement on this creek, and
persons are still living who remember the annual fair
accustomed to be held among them, at or near a place
called Laurel Hill. Here, too, was an excellent school,

in which were educated such men as the Grahams, the Gilchrists, and others who have made themselves famous in that State. Mr. McIntyre was a member of the Methodist Church, and a local preacher, though he devoted his life to teaching. He married Miss Anna Seals, sister of the Rev. David Seals, long known as a minister in the South Carolina Conference. After finishing his career as a teacher in Marlborough District, Mr. McIntyre removed to Macon, Georgia, where he presided over an academy for some time; and subsequently went to Alabama, where all trace of him has been lost. If still alive, it might prove a solace of his declining age to know how many bless his memory who have profited under the instructions, or have rejoiced in the friendship, of the pupil of his early years. He is represented on every side as a most excellent man, a thorough scholar, with a peculiar tact in imparting knowledge, and a certain magnetic power in drawing persons to him, and of impressing his stamp upon them. These qualities could not fail to make him a successful teacher; whilst a mild and gentle disposition united him in warm friendship, not only with his pupils, but with those whose association was far less intimate.

Young Thornwell's connection with Mr. McIntyre was fortunately continued through a period of at least three years. The dates cannot be fixed with absolute precision. But the year 1823 is generally assigned as the beginning of his teaching at Level Green; and in 1826 Thornwell is still with him, though in a different neighbourhood. His proficiency was so rapid, his habits so studious, and the evidence of his genius so conspicuous, as to enlist the entire professional and personal sympathy of the preceptor. The proof of this is furnished in what occurred when the happy relation between the two was threatened with sudden dissolution. Mr. McIntyre accepted an invitation from the Messrs. Pegues, James and Malachi, and their immediate neighbours, to establish amongst them a select school, composed of their children. Upon removing, however, to his new charge, he said to Mr. Malachi Pegues, that there was a boy of very remarkable talents in the neighbourhood where he had been teaching, with whom he was reluctant to part. He proposed, therefore, to continue his education gratuitously, if Mr. Pegues would afford him a home in his own family. Upon learning that the lad was a son of the Thornwell whom he had familiarly known in former years, he readily consented. The arrangement was duly carried out; and, as the inmate of his house, our little student continued to enjoy the instructions of his old preceptor.

The same diligence and ardour marked his career now as before. In these early years were formed those habits of intense application, which never deserted him to the close of his life. During the long watches of the night, whilst other boys slept, he was poring over the lessons of the succeeding day, digging into the intricacies of obsolete languages, analyzing their structure, and mastering their idioms. The real enthusiasm of the scholar bore him on to understand their genius, and to absorb their spirit. So, too, the hours of recreation, which other boys surrendered to active and healthful sport, were spent by him in threading the mazes of history, or in dallying with the pleasures of literature. It is wonderful that a physical frame, slender from the beginning, did not give way under these severe exactions, at a time when the constitution needs to be consolidated. It is more wonderful still, that the mind itself was not smothered beneath its accumulated load, at a period when the most delicate problem in education is to measure knowledge to the capacity for receiving it. In his case there was a marvellous physical endurance underlying that feeble body, and a mental digestion which assimilated these huge stores, without which the gift of genius would have proved the signature for the tomb. Already he has ceased to be a boy. The attitude and habits of a man have displaced those of the child. He has no relish for the rude sports in which his companions engage; not, as some allege, from the consciousness of his physical inferiority to them, but from that consuming love of study which always made the acquisition of knowledge his supreme delight. His ambition, too, was equal to his powers; and it was exceedingly well defined, even at this early age. Being asked, in later life, what first excited his ambition to be a man of learning, his reply was, that "from his earliest knowledge of himself, he had felt it working as a passion within him."

This will be illustrated by a story, which falls in here as a necessary link in his fortunes. A physician, Dr. Graves, a native of Virginia, and graduate of the Philadelphia School of Medicine, at that time lived in Cheraw, and practised in the surrounding country. In paying a professional visit to the family of Mr. Pegues, his attention was attracted to a pale and diminutive boy, who, in utter indifference to the sports of his companions, was absorbed in the perusal of a book. It turned out, upon inquiry, to be Hume's History of England. In playful banter, the visitor advised the lad to "read something he could understand." Instantly the book was in his hands, with a challenge for examination upon its contents. There was a piquancy in this, which was, to say the least, exciting. The examination was begun and protracted, with a growing wonder at the student's thoughtful familiarity with the volume. The interview was prolonged, and conversation was shifted from subject to subject;

> "And still the wonder grew
> That one small head could carry all he knew."

The profound conviction was riveted upon the mind of Dr. Graves, that he was confronted by one of those intellectual prodigies sometimes thrown up in life, who are to be judged by no ordinary standard. The impression was not transient. Wherever he went he carried the story of this remarkable genius, growing up under the shade of the Pegues settlement. Amongst others, it was told to General James Gillespie, a wealthy planter, who lived about four miles distant, and to William H. Robbins, Esq., a rising lawyer in the town of Cheraw, with the additional remark that "it would not be surprising if this pale-faced youth should one day be the President of the United States." Of course this American hyperbole was simply a compendious expression that, in the speaker's judgment, this obscure lad possessed abilities to achieve the highest statesmanship, and that his present attainments were an augury of brilliant success in any direction. These statements were corroborated by the enthusiastic testimony of Mr. McIntyre himself. General Gillespie, by occasional attendance upon the examinations of the school, had also the opportunity of forming his individual opinion as to the merits of young Thornwell. The combined effect of testimony and observation was such as to lead this gentleman to undertake his entire future education, as soon as he should be discharged from the tutelage of Mr. McIntyre. Stating this purpose afterwards to Mr. Robbins, he came forward with an offer to divide the expenses which should accrue; and the two became henceforth the joint patrons of our young friend.

The institution of these new relations must, however, be reserved for another chapter. What remains of this will best be occupied with a general view of his disposition and character, so far as yet developed. The truth of the old adage will hardly be questioned, "The boy is father to the man." Certainly the moral traits which distinguish childhood, if accurately noted, will be found to be carried over, in a modified form, to mature years. The student life of young Thornwell has, perhaps, been sufficiently depicted. Its special features might doubtless be more fully expanded; such, for instance, as the steady impulse of his ambition, his power of concentration, the thoroughness with which he penetrated beneath the sur-

face of things to their essence, and the royal delight he
felt in knowledge, which spurned all lower joy.   But
they are all comprehended in the description which has
already been given.   One little incident may, however,
be narrated, as illustrating how early he had formed that
almost personal attachment which a true scholar feels for
his books, as though they were living friends, with whom
a living communion is maintained.   Whilst with Mr.
McIntyre, all his books were consumed one night by fire,
with the school house, except those he was at the moment
studying.   His distress was overwhelming; nor could he
refer to the loss without tears, for weeks afterwards.
One can scarcely repress a smile at such grief over the
destruction of a library, which was certainly not of Alex-
andrian proportions.   But beneath it there will lurk a true
sympathy with that scholarly feeling which made him thus
early anticipate the immortal sentiment of Milton, which
he had not yet read: "Books are not absolutely dead
things, but do preserve, as in a vial, the purest efficacy
and extraction of that living intellect that bred them."
Those who recall the look of affection with which, in his
prime, Dr. Thornwell would gaze upon the volumes in
his library, and the pride with which he would exhibit
the best editions, will recognize in these boyish tears one
of his marked characteristics.

His indifference to play whilst a boy must not be construed as a sign of a morose and cynical temper.   He is
described, on the contrary, at this time as eminently
genial and social, warm in his affections, and fond of
talking with others about the books he read and the
studies which he pursued.   He was not simply popular,
but exceedingly beloved by his companions; the best
evidence of which is, that the schoolmates of those early
days clung, with rare devotion, to him throughout life;
and such as still survive cherish his memory with a tenderness which is the best tribute that love can pay to
merit.   Indeed, it could scarcely be otherwise, unless

there had been something in his natural disposition to repel friendship. He came into no rivalry with his companions on the play-ground, and they offered no competition with him in the school-room. Perhaps, through his whole life, no. one was ever pierced less by the shafts of envy. His intellectual superiority was so universally and so cordially conceded, that he was lifted above the jealousy which competition engenders; whilst the *esprit du corps* which belongs to every class, begat in his compeers that feeling of pride, which, unless repelled, easily glides into personal affection. It was his grand fortune through life to be surrounded by friends, whose love was never tainted with envy; who rejoiced in his fame, without the desire to pluck one leaf from the laurels with which he was crowned. It must have been a generous nature which always commanded homage like this.

His habit of late study at night necessitated late rising in the morning. Indeed, whilst a boy, his morning sleep was so profound that he had literally to be pulled out of bed. Doubtless nature was thus at pains to repair the heavy drafts which were made upon her resources. This peculiarity, however, marked his whole career. His studies were prosecuted chiefly at night, and he was habitually a late sleeper. He claimed this, indeed, as an idiosyncrasy; and many were the ingenious arguments he would invent, in playful banter, to prove that the day was intended for rest, and the night for work; and that man, in his perverseness, had wrongfully changed the original and proper arrangement of Providence.

At this early age, no proclivity to any form of vice would be expected. Only once he is represented to have tasted liquor to intoxication; for which, as he richly deserved, he received the severest whipping of his life. He became, however, early addicted to the use of tobacco; commencing to chew at eleven years of age, and a little later, to smoke; both of which habits he indulged freely until his death. Dr. Thornwell was wont to speak of

himself as having been a bad boy, which the surviving
members of his family most affectionately deny. It is a
general expression, used by the two in very different
senses.   Upon his lips, it is just the confession which
would fall from any good man, calling to mind " the sins
of his youth." But from the positive traits which belonged
to him, and which we only knew as modified by Divine
grace, it is easy to understand how his boyhood may have
been distinguished by a certain wilfulness and contradiction of authority, which called for the correction of the
rod. Happily for him, the mother was a woman of
vigorous understanding and strong will, which knew how
to put a curb upon such a temper.   The writer has more
than once heard him refer to these early contests between
insubordination and authority. He would rub his hands,
and tell, with a hearty relish of humour, how some childish
misdemeanour would induce him to take refuge in the
woods, from anticipated chastisement, until the solid
night had shrouded the house in darkness ; then, creeping
softly to his bed, he would lose in grateful sleep all apprehension of the future.   But, alas ! the sure retribution
would come in the morning, when he found a thin sheet
but a poor defence from the long, wiry switch that rained
its cutting rebukes upon the naked limbs.   This is what
he meant by the badness of his youth : that "foolishness
bound up in the heart of a child," which Solomon said,
and his mother believed, "the rod of correction must
drive out."

Beneath all this, there was an outcropping of religious
convictions, rather unusual in a boy of thirteen, and which
we notice here from a still more singular exhibition of
them, which we will meet a little later. He had evidently
imbibed from his mother's teachings and influence a decided predilection for the Calvinistic view of Divine
truth. Always outspoken in his opinions, and ever ready
to sustain them with reasons, he was somewhat of a thorn
in the good Methodist family where he resided. Mrs.

Pegues, especially, who was warmly attached to the doctrines of her church, was often annoyed by the young polemic. Doubtless he was often more irritating than convincing. We can easily fancy how, at unseasonable moments, and in a way more dogmatic than courteous, a disputatious boy might push "the five points" into other people's eyes. It is no small proof of this lady's benevolence, that she could bear the intrusion from this source at all. Though she continued to treat him with a kindness which made no discrimination between him and her own sons, there was always a little soreness in her heart from these disputes. It is of value to us only as the earliest indication of religious thought, throwing light upon an obscure experience by and by.

CHAPTER III.

HIS PATRONS.

THE successive steps by which the subject of these Memoirs was led up from obscurity, exhibit a marvellous adaptation in the agencies employed, to the exigencies of each particular stage. When left an orphan, and the question was one simply of bread, this was provided through the care of a considerate kinsman. After he had stumbled through the rudiments of an English education, and had reached the critical moment for laying the foundation of accurate scholarship, a teacher is furnished exactly suited to this work of drill; under whose instruction he remains, without disastrous change, until this is accomplished. Then, in a way seemingly fortuitous, he attracts the notice of a stranger, who sounds his praise throughout the region; until at length the friends are raised up, who secure to him a complete education, never relaxing their benevolence until he is afloat in life, and able to return to others the benefits received from them. The two gentlemen who now assume the guardianship over him were benefactors, not simply with the purse, but in the distinct impression of their character upon his. A kind Providence has brought him into just such personal relations as were suited to his development. The orphan finds in them more than the father whom, six years ago, he had lost.

To enbalm in this narrative the names of Gillespie and of Robbins, is a legacy silently bequeathed to the biographer of their illustrious protegé; a sort of remainder in trust, to be executed on his behalf, to the memory of those to whom he was so largely indebted. Could his own pen have made the acknowledgment, the throbbing gratitude would only have been equalled by the delicacy of its expression. We can but rudely sketch the portraits, upon which the reader will not be unwilling to look.

We are again indebted to Bishop Gregg's "History of the Old Cheraws," for the first trace of the Gillespie family. The name (originally spelt Galespy) first occurs on the public registry, in A. D. 1743, when James Galespy petitioned the Council, "that, having six persons in his family, a warrant of survey for three hundred acres be granted him in the 'Welsh Tract.'" He was not, however, a Welshman, but came from the north of Ireland. "He was a man of energy and enterprise; and was engaged with General Christopher Gadsden, of Charleston, in boating on the Pedee, many years before the Revolution. He settled at length higher up the river, near to the present site of Cheraw, and entered on a successful career as a trader." Two sons inherited his name, Francis and James. The former died prior to the American Revolution; the latter, Major James Galespy, having at that time reached his majority, took an active part in the struggle, and after the war was over amassed a handsome estate. He left a considerable family, most of whom, before or soon after maturity, died from consumption. Two sons, however, survived to rear families of their own: General Samuel Wilds Gillespie, and General James Gillespie.

The last mentioned is he of whom we are speaking, as the patron with whom young Thornwell was particularly identified; though it is proper to add just here, that after the lad was prepared for College, both brothers were associated with Mr. Robbins in defraying the expenses of his University course. They were both planters, men of large views, generous impulses, and great public spirit.

After the death of the former, which occurred in mid-life, General James Gillespie was left the sole survivor of his father's family; and no one was ever more respected in his native District of Marlborough. He still lives, at a venerable age, a pious member of the Episcopal Church, quietly awaiting the summons to the rest above, upon which his hope and faith have long been fastened.

It is impossible to estimate the influence, upon the plastic mind of a noble-spirited boy, of intimate intercourse with two such men as the Generals Gillespie. They were both eminent types of the Old School Southern gentleman. Quiet and self-contained, with an easy dignity engendered of self-respect, and just a touch of reserve, which sat like a porter in his lodge, to open and shut the gates of intercourse as might be desired; observing with scrupulous exactness all the amenities of life; with a polished education, and that fine sense of honour which shrunk from the very thought of meanness as from the touch of a leper: such were the men in whose cultivated homes and refined society our youthful friend finds himself adopted. The influence upon him may have been as gentle as the light; but like the light, it was absorbed, and tinged his life as plants draw their colour from the sun.

No form of charity, probably, yields as quick and large returns as the education of a promising youth; and some of the brightest gems with which society is adorned were thus rescued from the rubbish, where they would have remained buried for ever. The affection, too, which springs up betwixt the beneficiary and his patron, is often one of the purest that is known on earth. The bonds of kindness on the one hand, and gratitude on the other, bring the two into relations only less endeared than betwixt parent and child. The correspondence shortly to be introduced, will show such to have been the affection between Dr. Thornwell and the friends of his early dependence. It will serve to illustrate that entertained by General Gillespie, to relate an incident which occurred with the

writer of these pages. At one of the commencements of
the South Carolina College, during the presidency of Dr.
Thornwell, the pressure of the crowd thrust the writer
into an uneasy posture, directly behind the chair occupied
by General Gillespie, as a trustee, upon the rostrum. In
one of the pauses between the speeches, when the music
gave the signal for relaxation, and the hum of conversation pervaded the house, he leant forward and whispered
in the ear of his neighbour: " General, I would give a
good deal to drop down into the middle of your heart, and
see exactly how you feel, as you sit there and see and hear
that man, now clothed with the highest dignities of the
State, whom you helped to occupy that post of honour."
Turning round, with eyes brimming with tears, and a
voice tremulous with emotion, he replied: "Mr. Palmer,
you would have to go down into this heart to find it out;
for I have no words in which to express the gratitude and
joy which the recollection gives me." Truly there are
cases in which "it is more blessed to give than to receive;"
and with a generous nature, a gratitude for the privilege
of doing good may rise as high as the gratitude which acknowledges an obligation. Whatever losses may have
accrued from the ravages of war, this venerable benefactor
has an investment in the usefulness of his ward, stretching
along the ages yet to come, of which neither time nor
eternity will ever deprive him.

With his other patron, Mr. Robbins, young Thornwell
was thrown into associations more intimate and constant;
the intellectual and moral impression made upon him was,
therefore, more distinct. We are glad, for this reason,
that the fuller details furnished will enable us to render
this sketch more complete than the preceding.

WILLIAM HENRY ROBBINS was born in October, A. D.
1795, in Hallowell; at that time in a district of Massachusetts, but now in the State of Maine. Prior to his
birth, his parents resided in Plymouth, Massachusetts,
where his grandfather, the Rev. Dr. Robbins, was the

pastor of the First Orthodox Congregation. He appears
to have been religiously trained; his journal, which he
kept from 1810, being largely occupied with the abstracts
of sermons to which he listened in his youth. Most unfortunately for the purposes of this biography, the journal
of Mr. Robbins, which he continued, almost to the time of
his decease, was destroyed in a recent fire. It would have
enabled us to fix with precision some dates which are now
uncertain, and would have contributed valuable facts
known to no other party. His education, begun at Hallowell, was completed at Bowdoin College, Brunswick,
Maine, under the presidency of Dr. Appleton. After his
graduation, he studied law, under Judge Wilde, subsequently upon the Supreme Bench in the State of Massachusetts; and was admitted to practice in the city of
Boston. Finding, however, a Northern clime too severe
for his delicate constitution, he resolved to move South;
a purpose which was delayed two years, in deference to the
opposition of parents and friends. The necessity of change
became only too apparent at the end of this time; and on
January the 2nd, 1820, he sailed from Boston to Wilmington, North Carolina. He studied the laws of this
State, at Fayetteville, taking a few pupils to defray his
current expenses; and in the spring of the same year applied for admission to practice. Most unaccountably, he
was rejected by the Court, as he himself believed, through
the influence of a strong prejudice against men of Northern
birth. It was a crushing blow; not only disappointing
his expectations of providing a comfortable home, but in-
flicting a severe wound upon sensibilities which were
peculiarly alive to that form of suffering. To all this was
added the mortification of being seemingly compelled to
return home, to meet the irritating sympathy of those who
had predicted his failure.

This necessity was averted by one of those trivial incidents, which men term fortuitous, but are so often the
hinge upon which our whole destiny turns. The Hon-

ourable William Lowndes, of South Carolina, happened
just then to be passing through Fayetteville, on his way to
Washington City, to attend the sessions of Congress. To
him Mr. Robbins related his discomfiture, and his purpose
of returning North. "No," responded Mr. Lowndes, "do
not go North, but to South Carolina, where no such prejudice exists." This counsel led to a correspondence with
Mr. Dunkin, of Charleston, also a Massachusetts man,
who subsequently sat upon the Chancery Bench in his
adopted State.

Through the encouragement received from this gentleman, Mr. Robbins removed to South Carolina in the
autumn of 1821, and settled at Society Hill, in Darlington District. After making himself familiar with the
local statutes, he was, in the spring of 1822, admitted
without difficulty to the practice of his profession. His
means were by this time exhausted, while the trials of a
novitiate were still to be encountered. With an independence truly heroic, he accepted the fact of his poverty.
Being unable to purchase a horse, he was accustomed to
walk the whole distance from Society Hill to the county
seats of Darlington, Chesterfield, and Marlborough,—each
being fifteen miles distant,—in his attendance upon court.
As an illustration, not only of his independence, but of
his strict integrity, it may be mentioned that, after one of
these pedestrian tours, a friend tapped at his office window,
and said, "Mr. Robbins, I fear you have not much business, and may be in want of money; I will lend it to you
on your own time." Touched by this unexpected kindness, he could only reply by the pressure of the hand;
but subsequently wrote a note acknowledging the offer,
and saying that, "though his means were indeed small,
he was not willing to take the risk of involving another
in loss, when his success was so uncertain." These self-
reliant qualities seldom fail in the end; and he soon built
up a practice which at least relieved him from the urgency
of pressure. After his removal to Cheraw, his practice

became remunerative; so that, in the course of twenty years, he acquired a handsome competence, and left his family in circumstances of ease at his death. His business was chiefly that of a counsellor in the collection of accounts and the settlement of estates. He was distinguished for system and precision in the duties of his office, and for punctuality and fidelity to his clients. Such was his reputation for legal knowledge and accuracy, that, by the testimony of one of the judges before whom he was accustomed to appear, it was only necessary to know that the papers were drawn by his hand to be assured of their invulnerability; and such were his judgment and skill, that he was never known to lose a case where he himself brought the action.

These facts, together with what remains from his own pen, reveal a mind intensely practical and earnest. He took life as it was, and dealt with it on the principles of vigorous common sense. His determinations were almost judicial in their cast; and a just moderation marked his whole career, both in the opinions he formed, and the policy he pursued. His equipoise was almost perfect. Cautious in the committal of himself, he was inflexible in the decision: one upon whom others could lean, and never disappointing the expectations which he had raised. Such men are rarely demonstrative; but their affections are usually deep and constant. Mr. Robbins had broad sympathies, and unceasing charity; but both were under the control of principle. He felt it a conviction of duty to aid helpless merit; sharpened, doubtless, into a sentiment, by the recollection of his own struggle to gain foothold upon life. He early practised economy and self-denial, in order to fulfil this obligation; for he was only upon the first flood of professional success, when his generous hand was stretched for the relief of our young friend, and whilst he was burdened with the secret support of some of his own kindred at a distance.

The impression has almost universally obtained, that in

his religious views Mr. Robbins was a Unitarian. The charge is warmly repelled by his surviving family, who allege that no trace of this is to be found in the journal where his private thoughts were recorded, nor can their memory recall any admission of it from his own lips. On the other hand, the fact is affirmed by others, without a suspicion of its accuracy; and, what is the most staggering of all, it is stated by those whose spiritual relations to him would afford the best opportunity of knowing his views with certainty. The discrepancy can be explained only in one way. He was educated, as we have seen, in the orthodox faith, and to the period of his removal South sat constantly under an orthodox ministry. But the orthodoxy of New England delighted at this time to be known as a "modified orthodoxy." The term is not ours; and we will allow the distinction to be stated by a clergyman of that region, a near relative, who was consulted on this very point. In a letter, bearing date January 22d, 1873, he writes:

"It is well known that, about the beginning of the present century, there was a very general departure among the churches of Massachusetts from the old orthodox ground. Nearly all the oldest churches along the shores of the Bay, from Cape Cod to Cape Ann, including the churches in Boston, partook of the movement. The objection, as then urged, to the old orthodoxy, was rather to its exclusiveness, and to certain stereotyped dogmatic statements and metaphysical distinctions, which, as was then thought, had been substituted in the place of simple and hearty belief in Jesus Christ as the only ground of salvation, than to any evangelical doctrine stated in Scripture terms. This was very different from what has since appeared, under the name of Unitarians. Its spirit was thoroughly loyal to Christ and the Bible."

It is not difficult, then, to understand how a mind, constitutionally averse to all extreme views, and letting go the sharp distinctions and technical nomenclature, without which neither divine nor any other truth can be scientifically stated, should be involved in perfect confusion and mist upon the subject of the Holy Trinity. If plied, too, with Unitarian books and tracts, as he was by some of his family connexions in New England, he would soon waver in the acceptance of the facts themselves, which could no longer be represented to his own mind in any definite propositions. The truth is apt to slip away from our grasp, as soon as we disallow the necessary terms by which alone it can be defined, and without which it can no longer be reflectively considered. Thus, probably, he became tainted with the Socinian heresy, without formally adopting it as a creed, or abandoning entirely the traditional faith of his youth. These difficulties would naturally be mentioned in confidential intercourse, and, with his religious guides, might well assume the form of polemic discussion, in the effort to escape from the mist of speculation, and to give a palpable shape and body to what flitted before him only as airy abstractions.

We have been thus minute, from a profound respect to the memory of one who has such a just claim upon Presbyterian gratitude. His religious opinions should either not be given to history at all, or the evidence should be produced upon which they are supposed to rest.

But in whatever form this error may have existed, whether floating in the mind as a vague doubt, or crystallized into a fixed opinion, it was squarely abandoned some ten or twelve years before his death, when, under the preaching of the celebrated revivalist, Dr. Daniel Baker, he became the subject of renewing grace. Attaching himself to the Episcopal Church, he remained a consistent and devoted Christian to the end. "His piety," writes the pastor who was with him in his last moments, "was a pervading, steady principle, which imbued his whole life; and he passed calmly and peaceably to his rest, in the full possession of his faculties, and of the testimony of a good conscience; in the communion of the Catholic Church; in the confidence of a certain faith; in the comfort of a reasonable, religious and holy hope; in favour, I doubt not, with God; and in charity with the world. His end was like a peaceful, gradual transfiguration of the mortal into the immortal; like a melting out of our

earthly sight into the invisible world of spirit." The
disease, consumption, which had threatened his early
manhood, returned upon him, after a long suspension.
Through five years the battle was maintained, during
which he was often obliged to leave home; once to take
a sea voyage, as well as to invoke the skill of an eminent
physician in Paris. At length the destroyer triumphed;
and he fell asleep on the 26th of March, 1843, in the
forty-eighth year of his age. His rare modesty, his contempt for the artificial distinctions of life, and the sense
of the littleness of earth, all found characteristic expression in the inscription traced, by his own direction, upon
his tomb :

> " My name, my country, what is that to thee ;
> What, whether high or low, my pedigree ?
> Perhaps I far surpassed all other men ;
> Perhaps I fell below them : what then ?
> Suffice it, stranger, that thou see'st a tomb ;
> Thou know'st its use ; it hides,—no matter whom."

Without name or date, how solemnly this rebuke of
human vanity peals forth in the silent graveyard of St.
David's Church!

Such was the man with whom James Thornwell was
thrown into what may be termed a closet intercourse,
during the most forming period of a boy's life, between
the ages of fourteen and eighteen. There is no calculus
by which to measure the benefit which accrued. But,
surveying the whole of his after career, and knowing all
that Providence designed him to be, it is clear no influence could have better shaped him for the end in view.
Mr. Robbins was an accomplished man; imbued with
the spirit, as well as with the letter, of the ancient
classics, having comprehensive and philosophic views,
thoroughly acquainted with history in its entire range,
and not insensible to what was beautiful in literature and
art. A vigorous and clear intellect like his was nothing
less than a Voltaic battery, waking up the young mind be-

fore it, that was only too capable of absorbing the living energy which thrilled along every nerve, and charged every power with its secret virtue. Here is a lad possessing the ambition to become all that is possible, with a lofty ideal ever beckoning him forward, with a thirst for knowledge which no acquisitions can quench; and here, at his side, is a full fountain, pouring forth its magnetic waters, stimulating the appetite which they seem to fill.

The influence of Mr. Robbins was not less happy in its modifying power. The conspicuous attribute of his mind was its practicalness, which made him an admirable trainer for a genius. It dealt alone with facts and principles; and these were applied with a rigour and precision that estopped all extravagances, and brought one down to sedate and earnest chinking. Truth, in her unadorned majesty, was the touchstone by which every thing was to be tested. The wise cautions, and sometimes the trenchant criticisms, which are to be found in his letters, reveal him as the Mentor of Telemachus to his young ward. And if the genius which he successfully trained did not prove that fatal gift which so often blasts its possessor— if it proved a genius disciplined by culture, and harnessing itself to the practical duties of life, until it wrought a work full of blessing to the world—much of it is due to the moulding influence of this clear, strong, and practical mind, which gave direction to its aspirations, and shaped its development. It is not always given us to trace the agencies and methods by which we have been secretly educated for our work; but the most remarkable feature in this history is, the happy training by which the subject of it was disciplined from the opening of his career.

CHAPTER IV.

PREPARATION FOR COLLEGE.

AS nearly as can be ascertained, Mr. McIntyre ceased
to teach in the Pegues settlement some time in the
year 1826. In accordance with an arrangement previously
made, James Thornwell, then between thirteen and fourteen years of age, went to General Gillespie. The design
to educate him fully does not appear to have been at that
time definitely formed. The new friends were only pledged
at first to advance him in his studies; and they were gradually led forward, by the exhibition of his superior merits,
to complete what had been so auspiciously begun. He
was accordingly sent to Cheraw, and became a private
pupil of Mr. Robbins, and an inmate of his house. Mr.
Robbins was at that period a bachelor, and remained so
during the whole of young Thornwell's dependence upon
him. The solitude of his life was not, therefore, un-
pleasantly broken by the companionship of his pupil,
whilst freedom from domestic care afforded the leisure
for his instruction.

The personal appearance of the youth was almost a
burlesque upon the extraordinary reputation which had
preceded him. Smaller in size than most boys of ten
years, sallow in complexion, and with a general sickliness
of hue, his bodily presence was anything but attractive.
Mr. Robbins, who, with characteristic caution, received

39

him tentatively at first, declares that, upon his introduction, he mentally exclaimed, "Surely, Gillespie must be deceived in taking this boy to be a genius." A few hours' conversation perfectly satisfied him on this point; and in a short time the relations between the two became like those of an elder and a younger brother. Mr. Robbins testifies that, " as a boy he never delighted in the sports of boys, and he was from the beginning a companion to me." Indeed, so much satisfaction did he find in the society of his ward, and so sweetly grew upon him the office of instruction, that the little bed that had been provided for him in another apartment was soon removed to his own chamber, that they might converse to the last moment before falling asleep. Touching friendship between the man of one and thirty years and the stripling of fourteen! It is not the cold guardian, holding himself in stately reserve towards his ward; nor the formal preceptor, contenting himself with a mechanical drill; but an elder brother, taking into his bosom the little one of the household, whom a sad orphanage has placed there, to be nourished with something of a parent's care. It is difficult to say upon which of the two the greater honour is reflected. If it be a proof of the boy's precocity, it was not less an evidence of the patron's generosity. A true benevolence is seen as much in the grace of the conveyance as in the benefit conferred; and it is a kingly heart that knows how to let its charities fall gently as the flakes of snow.

Whilst thus secluded under private tutelage, James was not wholly withdrawn from association with those of his own age. One, who became afterwards his classmate and bosom friend, thus writes: " My first distinct and never-to-be-forgotten impression of this glorious man was in a boys' debating society, connected with the Cheraw Academy, of which he was a member, though not at that time a pupil of the school. The question to be discussed was this: whether, in a particular case, the circumstances of which were specified, it would be right for the Governor to exercise the pardoning power? Young Thornwell made a powerful speech upon the negative side, and carried the vote of the society. He impressed all of us as we never before had been, by his eloquence and the force of his arguments. Pale, swarthy, and sickly in appearance, his voice was strong, and the words flowed from him like a rushing torrent. He quoted Greek and Roman history, and even then showed the logician in a most remarkable manner." This incident is worthy of record, not only in proof of the early possession of those natural gifts by which he was afterwards distinguished, but as illustrating the mould into which he began morally to crystalize. However we may abstractly admit the influence of disposition and temperament upon the opinions we form, few of us appreciate the extent to which this gives complexion to our convictions. The truth which is accepted by one class of men without an effort, can scarcely make its impression upon another class; and this difference results, not so much from a variation in their mental structure, as from the bias of some idiosyncracy of nature. John Foster, for example, wavered upon the doctrine of the eternity of future punishment, not from any weight of evidence which controlled his judgment, but from an excess of sensibility which shrank from its contemplation. The dreadfulness of the thought overwhelmed and crushed him. His reason was put under arrest, and his judgment was suspended. He could not pronounce either way, his faith forbidding its clear rejection, and his morbid sensibility shrinking from its acceptance. It was a clear case of tortured feeling as against reason and faith. "*Non ex quovis ligno Mercurius fit.*"

Men like Calvin and Knox are not made of softly material like Malancthon and Erasmus, and probably no amount of mere intellectual pursuasion could ever convert the one into the other. But our young debater has those robust qualities, which enable him to see a glory in justice as well as in mercy; that if the one be the pillar of

42 LIFE OF JAMES HENLEY THORNWELL.

beauty, the other is the pillar of strength, that stands beside it, in the temple of God. How far this early predilection to vindicate the majesty of law may be due to the Calvinistic teachings of " a noble mother," it is not needful to inquire ; but the shaping hand of an unseen power can be traced all through, preparing the future champion of the truth, who should assert the integrity of the Divine government against the mawkish sentiment that would rob it of its necessary sanction.

James was naturally taken into the office, as well as into the house and chamber, of his patron. Here he studied, and at intervals recited. If business accumulated with unwonted pressure, the boy's leisure might well be employed in copying such legal forms as required nothing beyond attention and care. He wrote at this time a bold, round hand, which was afterwards greatly contracted; always, indeed, neat and clean, presenting to the eye a pleasing regularity, and perfectly legible, but also singularly compact. We have never seen but one person who had the power of putting an equal number of words upon a page; and, strangely enough, he was an eminent lawyer and judge. By gradual practice, James became skilful in drawing up legal papers, such, at least, as the simpler processes required, and soon rose into the position of a useful assistant. He acquired a general knowledge of the office business, and could be safely trusted with its routine, in the absence of Mr. Robbins; sometimes collecting accounts and making the necessary entries and deposits, and sometimes answering the inquiries and letters of clients. The following story illustrates the ardour with which he threw himself into all subjects that attracted his attention, and the ingenious methods of self-discipline to which he resorted: A gentleman passing one day by Mr. Robbins's office, heard voices that seemed to be engaged in loud and earnest discussion. He drew near enough to learn that a flagrant case of hog stealing was upon its trial. Upon looking through the window there

was "little Jimmie" going through the rehearsal alone,
changing his voice as he personated severally the judge,
the jury, the prosecuting attorney, and the counsel for the
defence, not omitting, in his strict impartiality, the criminal himself. In this connection the following anecdote
may be related, not so much for disclosing his capacity, as
illustrating the positiveness of his character and the tone
of his principles: On one occasion, in the absence of
Mr. Robbins, a client entered the office, and made some
inquiries which rendered it necessary to refer to Mr. Robbins's account-book. Having informed himself of what
he desired to know, James left the book open on the desk.
Presently the visitor approached, and was about to make
a personal inspection of its contents, when James promptly
arose, and closed the book in his face, saying that he
would allow no stranger to inspect Mr. Robbins's private
entries. It was, doubtless, inconsiderateness in the party,
for he took no offence, and spoke of it to others with
hearty approval of the boy's spirit. It is through this
instinctive outworking of secret principles, without the
aid of reflection, that character is really disclosed.

It is impossible to determine how long he remained
under the exclusive preceptorship of Mr. Robbins; nor
when he was transferred to the more systematic discipline
of the Cheraw Academy. The reasons for the change
are sufficiently obvious. The growing demands of an
exacting profession must, of course, introduce irregularity
on the part of the teacher, whilst the ripening intellect
and more advanced studies of the pupil would render
important the drill of a regular school. He probably
enjoyed its larger advantages during the better portion
of two years prior to his admission into college; that is
to say, during the years of 1828 and 1829. The Academy
was then under the care of Mr. John G. Bowman and
Dr. Thomas Graham, the latter being from Drowning
Creek, North Carolina, which seems to have been the
nursery of teachers for a large district of country. Both

were excellent instructors, and Mr. Bowman enjoyed the reputation of being a superior Greek scholar. The tradition is still rife in Cheraw, how James Thornwell wore out the tedious night in severe application to study. His proficiency was in proportion to his diligence and enthusiasm combined; and his examination at the final term was so brilliant as to determine his benefactors not to arrest his progress at this stage, but to give him the benefit of a university course. Some idea may be formed, from the following story, of his power of abstraction and concentration in study: A gentleman in Mr. Robbins's office commenced a conversation upon some private and confidential matter, but suddenly paused upon observing the lad sitting there and reading a book. "Oh!" replied Mr. Robbins, "you need not mind him; I will soon convince you that he does not hear a word of what we are saying." Whereupon he began with a loud voice, abusing James in terms well calculated to excite his anger. The unconscious subject of this tirade sat with listless ears, in happy ignorance of the practical joke played off at his expense; and the visitor resumed, and finished the interview with a perfect assurance of its privacy.

He had no love for the study of mathematics, though he pursued it as a duty; but he revelled in the classics, in which he so perfected himself as to become a wonder in the eyes of scholars like himself. He displayed, also, at this period, a fondness for metaphysical studies, in which he afterwards pre-eminently excelled. The writer received from his own lips the following fact, which bears internal evidence of having occurred during the earlier portion of his connection with Mr. Robbins, whilst he was still an undeveloped youth. This gentleman found him poring over Locke's "Essay on the Human Understanding," and badgered him upon the hardihood of attacking a work so abstruse, and so clearly beyond his years. Piqued, as he himself relates, at this implied disparagement of his powers, he resolved at once to master the book; and master it he did, and for all coming time. Shortly after, he happened to light, among the volumes in General Gillespie's library, on Dugald Stewart's "Elements of the Philosophy of the Human Mind." To use his own language, he "felt that his fortune was now made;" and devoured it with the same avaricious delight that he had experienced in the other. Upon what slender contingencies does our destiny often turn! And who can trace up to its source the influence which bears us on to what we afterward become! Dr. Thornwell was accustomed to refer to this incident as having given him the first conscious bias to philosophy. It was doubtless the pivot upon which his whole intellectual history subsequently hinged. The right book, read at the right time, roused a dormant capacity, just when it needed to awake and determine the character of a brilliant and useful career. Thus does Providence watch over its chosen instruments, and a hidden hand touches the secret springs of activity and life.

In the summer of 1828, Mr. Robbins left home upon a visit to New England, while James remained in charge of the office. We give here a portion of a letter, as showing the trust reposed in his business capacity, and also the gentle faithfulness of the guardian in pruning the faults of his ward:

"BOSTON, *June* 30, 1828.

"DEAR JAMES: Your letter of the 18th instant reached me at a time when I was becoming anxious lest the fever, with 'its sequel of evils, had overtaken you. And should this at any time be the case, you will procure my friend, James Gillespie, to write, giving me timely notice of the fact.

"Your letter affords me subject of two-fold remark. *First:* Its matter. I was glad to hear so good report of the corn and cotton crop. From the appearance of the weather I had anticipated the news about the mills; but you do not say how the mill hands are employed. * * * I have written M——— that if I have the mortgage he called for, you will get it; and I think you will find it in the Chesterfield drawer, perhaps enveloped in other papers. I could not have given it him *at the time* I gave him the other release, because I gave him that in Marlborough, where I had not the mortgage. I do not know that my ledger

exhibits all the proper charges against L-•----.   He owes me, &c.   If
he writes again, state these facts, and my other charges.   I hope Jip
will be improved by my return.   You can use him occasionally; it will
assist rather than injure him.   *   *   *   Your account of the ------
business was very satisfactory.   It put H.'s friend in an unenviable
point of view.   It shows, too, how cautious we should be in indulging
too great freedom in our remarks, even when we think ourselves safe
from exposure or misinterpretation.   *   *   *   I was happy to learn that
you were content in your present situation; but as soon as you are
otherwise, you can change it.   I should have no objection to your attending the festival on the 4th; but this letter will meet you too late to
be governed by what I have to say.   There has no production appeared
from Webster or Everett.   I send you regularly the *National Gazette*,
which you will keep on file for me.   I was well pleased with your plan
of a register or diary, and I hope you will keep it regularly.   I went to
Cambridge to-day, and saw a young cousin, who holds a pre-eminent
rank in his class, and could not help thinking, at the time, how much
pleased you would have been to be in his company.   I was much surprised to find, or rather, not to find, a copy of the *Southern Review* in
Boston; and but one or two gentlemen have received it at all.   The book
in greatest demand, just now, appears to be Irving's 'Life of Columbus'; and I mean to bring it out with me.

"I have neither time nor space to notice particularly the *second* ground
of remark suggested by your letter.   But were I called on to point out
the chief fault in the writing, I should say, it is the same I have so often
mentioned to you: a propensity to invest common and occasional remarks in too grave and sober a dress.   An idea of subordinate importance is not to be enveloped in the grave and solemn measure of a
great moral axiom.   It is to assign it a dignity which is not its own; and
not only so, but it affords occasion for the common taunt, "*Montes par-
turiunt*," &c.   Though, on the whole, this perhaps is an error which
time, and increased observation and experience, will correct.

"'Take care of yourself,' referred to your own health, of which you
cannot be too careful.   Most sincerely yours,

W. H. R.

The succession of dates brings us now to a relation,
which may cause the reader to lay down the book and
think awhile before he proceeds further.   The education
of Thornwell, we have said, was undertaken at first with
no definite purpose.   The plan seemed to have been to
give him all the knowledge that could be acquired in the
academy, and then to put him to the study of the Law, in
the office of Mr. Robbins.   James happened to overhear
a conversation in which this purpose was stated.   The

next evening he was missing at tea; but his absence was explained in the following letter, which Mr. Robbins found under his plate:

"CHERAW, *January*, 1829.

"MY DEAR SIR: I have adopted this method of discharging a duty, which I consider due to you in common with my other patrons; as I am incapable of speaking to you on the delicate subject without tears.

"The relation which has hitherto subsisted between us is now to be dissolved. I would to God that this trying scene could have been averted. I would to God that this bitter cup could have passed from me. But His will be done. Though your regard for me should vanish like smoke, and though you should hereafter treat me with the utmost contempt and disdain, yet will I ever love even the very earth on which you tread.

"It is no trivial cause that could induce me to part from one so dear to me. Nothing short of a deep sense of duty could ever have led me to this, especially as you have been at so much trouble and expense on my account. I have laboured hard, but in vain, to reconcile my conscience to the practice of the Law. In selecting a profession, it is certainly the duty of every person to act upon other than selfish motives. He should ever have in view the glory of God and the good of men. Now, the only method, it must be admitted, for him to determine the sphere of action in which he will most contribute to these ends is by scrutiny into the inclination of his particular genius. Now, the greatest difficulty consists in discovering the peculiar turn of his mind. What criterion will you fix for this purpose? Though consultation with his friends may be of considerable service, yet you will not surely contend that he must make their advice the rule of his conduct. I apprehend that the only correct standard is his own feelings. He must not, however, forget to look up to that Being for direction, to whom he must finally render an account for his conduct here.

"In conformity to these views, which appear to me correct, I have determined to adopt theology as my profession. The prospect for an education is as brilliant, I believe, as though I were the son of a gentleman in possession of millions. There is none, however, for wealth, as it is impossible to serve God and mammon at the same time. It is my hard destiny to be placed in a situation where I must determine for life at a very early age. I cannot dogmatically assert that these views will follow me to the grave. But I feel it a duty to act in accordance with them now. It is rational, however, to believe that they will continue by me. I entertained them once before, discarded them, and have resumed them. I cannot well say discarded them; for I smothered them, or rather the conclusion to which they led me, with the hope that farther mental improvement would reconcile me to the Law. As they have come upon me again with increased power, I feel it a duty to reveal them to you. If you think they are erroneous, illustrate their error. If this is not done,

I am compelled to bid farewell, with great heaviness of heart, to a beloved patron, who kindly clothed me when naked, fed me when hungry,
and, above all, has much laboured to dispel ignorance from my mind ;
a beloved patron, whose name is music to my ear, one whom I can
never forget, and of whom I will ever think with the liveliest emotions
of gratitude ; and I humbly hope he will never forget the unworthy
object of his kindness. I do humbly hope his attachment will not
abate, if I have acted in conformity to sound rational principles ; and,
if under the impulse of enthusiasm, I hope he will pity my weakness.
On the word, farewell, my heart lingers, with reluctance to leave you :
and, oh! to think of parting pricks it to the core. But it must be ;
so farewell, my dear friend and respected patron.
                                        J. H. THORNWELL."

This remarkable epistle was read with deep amazement.
Rising instantly from the table, Mr. Robbins found his
ward on the piazza, in the dark, half hidden in the angle
of the chimney, weeping as though his heart would break.
Taking his hand, he led him gently back to the supper
table, and there assured him that he was labouring under
a total misapprehension of his views. It had indeed been
taken for granted that the profession of the Law would be
his choice, both because it gave full scope to his talents,
and promised promotion in the future. At the same time,
nothing was further from the hearts of those who had be-
friended him, than to force his inclination in any degree.
He should be perfectly free hereafter to choose any profession which taste, or prudence, or conscience might suggest ; and that he would enter upon its pursuits with their
good will and blessing ; but that, for the present, he must
lay aside all morbid feelings, and continue to live with
him as his younger brother. The old relations were accordingly resumed, with a better understanding between
the two, and with increased respect and affection.

The delicate sense of honour, which would no longer
accept support from those whose wishes he expected to
thwart, lies so obtrusively upon the face of the narrative,
that there is no necessity for emphasizing it. But under-
neath it lies a mystery which is not easy of solution.
Here is a youth just beyond his sixteenth birth-day, who

has passed through a protracted mental conflict, and settled down into the conviction that he must preach the gospel. All the influences which bore upon him were adverse to such a conclusion. Both his patrons were, at this period, men of the world. The profession of the Law, which he declines, pressed itself upon his acceptance by every motive to which an honourable ambition could respond. And what seals the mystery, this decision is pronounced by one who, as yet, makes no pretensions to personal piety, has given hitherto no evidence of a change of heart, and who did not profess, till several years later, to have become the subject of grace. Upon what principle, then, did this decision turn? Did he regard the sacred ministry as a profession to be chosen, like any other, because it was adapted to one's tastes or mental aptitudes? Men do not ordinarily make costly and painful sacrifices, except upon the altar of duty. Scarcely for anything less than this would he have surrendered advantages and severed ties which were as dear to him almost as life. His letter, too, is pervaded with just such a conviction of duty lying hard upon the conscience ; and though it does not express the high and spiritual views of the ministerial office which he subsequently embraced, there is a general religious tone, which it is hard to explain from one not in a state of grace. The case is fruitful of speculation, which it might not be perfectly safe to indulge. This much seems to be clear. He was from the beginning "a chosen vessel of the Lord, to bear His name before the Gentiles and kings, and the children of Israel;" and to this end, religious truth was made to possess for him a singular fascination. Its earliest indication was that polemic zeal which led him with boyish disputatiousness to

> "Assert eternal Providence,
> And justify the ways of God to men."

Now it assumes the form of a conviction of duty, which throws over him the power of a spell. It is true, this interest in Christianity appears to be thus far rather intellectual than experimental; but it has enlisted the conscience, and it holds him to what we know to have been the ultimate purpose of God, amidst temptations that threatened to swerve him from it. We shall find more of this hereafter, making his religious history something of a puzzle up to a certain date, when the mist is cleared away, and the Gospel is as fully embraced by the heart as by the understanding.

During the summer of 1829, Mr. Robbins again visited New England. We give extracts from several of James's letters, written then, in order that the reader may form his own judgment as to the development of his mind, as well as see the affectionate relations he sustained with his patron. In the first, of date June 30th, 1829, after dispatching certain topics of business, he speaks of a duel which had well-nigh taken place, in the following terms:

"Is it not to be lamented that a squeamish sense of false honour is so prevalent? It is contrary to human dignity, which it should be our pride to support. Every character has motives of the strongest obligation to support it. The parent should consider the interest of his child; the patriot, the welfare of his country; and the philanthropist, the good of mankind."

He then proceeds:

"You ask where I betook myself on the morning of your departure. I attended you to the post-office, and stood by you until you were about to enter the stage. My feelings were such that it was impossible for me to shake hands with you; and as I should have been an object of derision, had I broken forth there into childish lamentations, I thought it more prudent to vent my feelings in private retirement. I wish that I could obtain a proper control of myself on such occasions. If I grieve at a temporary parting, what would be my feelings at a lasting separation?

"I have heard of no sickness since your departure. For myself, during the last week, I was on the very brink of the fever. As soon as I felt the symptoms of disease, I submitted myself to the direction of prudence. With salts for my spear, and moderation of diet for my buckler, I have rushed to the combat, and driven the fever from the field. But so far from being led into hopes of vain security by my victory, I guard myself with more care against his wily attacks.

J. H. T."

The letter which follows discovers his early tendency to moral speculations, though the generalization marks the first awkward effort of an immature mind to use its powers. It is given just as it was written:

"CHERAW, *August* 13*th*, 1829.

"Discontent, how much soever it may be denounced by monks and priests, is not criminal. To possess a mind which storms of fortune or the darkest clouds of destiny cannot ruffle, is indeed desirable. Tranquillity and calmness are qualities, however, which few do or can possess in seasons of adversity. The philosopher and the moralist may prescribe rules for the attainment of these virtues; but the uninstructed peasant, and even they themselves, will forget them in the hour of temptation. It is beyond the power of mankind in general to subject their feelings to the control of their understandings. These turbulent demagogues, like the ancient barons of England, will not submit to the authority of their sovereign. All men repine at what affects their interest. It is a principle of their nature which they cannot subdue, and which must, therefore, have been planted in them by the Deity. These reasons induce me to believe that discontent is not criminal. But there are bounds within which it should be confined, and to exceed which is not justifiable. In these remarks I would by no means depreciate contentment. It is a source, and unfailing source, of happiness, which is worthy of our highest efforts. It is a precious jewel, which too often allures men, as the waters Tantalus, to disappoint; and no man can say that he possesses it until he has passed safely through the furnace of temptation.

"These reflections were suggested to me by the marks of disappointment, which are imprinted on every countenance, in consequence of the late inundation of their crops. None appear to be content; and McN. has converted his blithe boasting into sighs. He has lost, he says, about thirty bales of cotton and half of his corn. He will still make as good a crop as he did last year. I am glad that you will sustain such little damage. Though it is enough to give McN. a rueful countenance * * * * *

"I am diverted at this moment by a warm discussion of a question in political economy between Mr. P. and Major L. The question is, Can the value of gold decrease? P. maintains the affirmative, and L. the negative; and I must think that, though Mr. L. is shrewd and subtle, Mr. P. is superior to him. Mr. L. deals too much in general and indefinite terms. Mr. P. is more precise and explicit. In the course of the discussion, L. granted that an abundance of money depreciated property. P. contended that the money was depreciated, and of course had only a relative value. The general consent of the world has established it as a coin, however, not on account of any superiority to other metals, but on account of its beauty and scarcity. The value of

gold, then, it is clear, can be reduced in three ways: 1. The general
consent of mankind may be changed, and another metal substituted;
2. As the tastes of men sometimes fluctuate, the beauty of gold may
cease to fascinate; 3. A great abundance certainly diminishes its value.
Some such arguments as these might have been employed against Mr.
L., though Mr. P. pursued a different course. I was surprised to hear
Mr. L. argue that gold had an inherent value. He evinced as much
ignorance of the proper meaning of words as the persons who, after a
warm debate on transubstantiation, referred the question to the decision
of an umpire. Being asked what they meant by that long word, one
replied, 'Kissing the saints;' the other, 'Kneeling at the holy altar.'

"The colour of Jip has undergone a great change; he is a chestnut
now, a colour of which, you know, Virgil speaks very favourably. I
should be delighted with an account of the Cambridge Commencement.
                                                          JAMES."

In another letter, written in the same month, he says:

"General Gillespie has given me a new proof of his kindness. He has
resolved to send me to college this year, if he can possibly raise the
money. I do sincerely hope that he may be able to accomplish his design. I am preparing to go to Columbia in October or December."

This hint will appropriately close this chapter, leaving
it to the pages which are to follow to introduce him into
that new and interesting scene.

CHAPTER V.

COLLEGE LIFE.

FIRST APPEARANCE IN COLLEGE.—PERSONAL DESCRIPTION.—REJECTED
ON FIRST APPLICATION.—RECEIVED ON THE SECOND.—HIS OWN AC-
COUNT OF IT.—EARLY IMPRESSION OF HIS GENIUS UPON HIS FELLOW-
STUDENTS.—FACULTY OF THE SOUTH CAROLINA COLLEGE.—INTENSE
APPLICATION.—RANGE OF HIS STUDIES.—SELF-DISCIPLINE.—SECLU-
SION OF THE STUDENT.—HIS EARLY REPUTATION AS A DEBATER.—
POWERS OF INVECTIVE.—CORRESPONDENCE.

EARLY in December, 1829, within a few days of his
seventeenth birthday, James Thornwell made his first
appearance in the campus of the South Carolina College, at
Columbia, the capital of the State. Stunted in his growth,
and with the sallow complexion which has been already
described, his figure was just the kind to excite college
witticism and mirth. The following description, from the
pen of a class-mate, after the lapse of forty years, may
have a slight colouring from the humour with which it is
conveyed; but undoubtedly, in the main, is correct: "In
personal appearance he was, perhaps, the most unpromising specimen of humanity that ever entered such an institution. Very short in stature, shorter by a head than
he became later in life, very lean in flesh, with a skin the
colour of old parchment, his hands and face as thickly
studded with black freckles as the Milky Way with stars,
and an eye rendered dull in repose by a drooping lid, he
looked, to use an Irishism, as he if he was twenty years
old when he was born. His manners were unpolished,
but his air was self-reliant; and though free from boasting, he was evidently conscious of the mental power within
him, which would make him more than a match for most
men, and would throw into the shade his physical defects."

Such is the youth when first seen striding over the campus, arm in arm with a friend six feet high, as if burlesquing his own littleness by the contrast; with a long coat dangling at his heels, rolling a huge quid of tobacco in his mouth, and declaring that he would enter the Junior class or none; sportively adding that, if rejected, he would go up into the town, and apply for admission to the practice of the law. But

> "The best laid schemes of mice and men
> Gang aft agley;"

and this self-appreciation, half serious, half playful, was doomed to experience a sudden but salutary check.

The class which he desired to enter, was the class just rising Junior. Applications were not frequent for admission to this high grade, and the examinations were correspondingly rigorous. Our young friend was pronounced deficient in certain studies, particularly mathematics, and was rejected, with the privilege, however, of another trial at the opening of the new year. The deficiency was more apparent than real; and the unexpected failure was anxiously explained by those who knew his attainments. One says, "the examination in geometry was conducted in a manner unusual to him. In those demonstrations which did not require a good deal of figuring, it was the practice to use no letters, but merely to indicate the side or angle by touching it; and being unaccustomed to this method, he became confused." In his own statement we have no such apology, as will appear from the following letters to his friend, Mr. Robbins:

"COLUMBIA, *December* 5, 1829.

"MY DEAR SIR: I applied for admission into the Junior Class this morning, and was rejected. On Græca Minora, Xenophon, the Odes of Horace, and Cicero, I was admitted, and on part of Mathematics. Homer, and the Art of Poetry, I was rejected on. They say, however, that if I will stand another examination on these, about the first of January, they will admit me. I think it advisable to do so, in preference to joining Sophomore. If I feel myself prepared, I may stand earlier. The difficulty with me, on these books, was not ignorance, but confusion. I was panic-struck as soon as I entered the library-room. The Faculty perceived it. With my examination in Geography, English grammar, and Minora, Dr. Cooper appeared to be well pleased ; and had he continued by me, I should have been successful throughout. Whenever he found that I was embarrassed, he would relieve me. The rest were not so accommodating. They are extremely rigid in their pronunciation ; on that, however, they did not find fault with me. The truth is simply this, that when they placed Homer in my hands, I was in such perturbation that I could scarcely see the letters. As soon as I recovered myself, I read with ease. I recollect to have missed only two words. On Algebra, as far as they examined me, I stood very well. They required one more rule than I had studied ; that I must learn. In Mathematics, or at least in Geometry, where I thought myself safe, I failed. At Mr. Graham's examination, General Gillespie can testify that I was not deficient in it. How it happened that I proved so before the Faculty, I cannot account. I cannot describe my feelings to you. I am overwhelmed with confusion, and ashamed to show my face. I shall keep myself as much secluded as possible, until I redeem my reputation. The three weeks which I must wait will roll heavily on. I shall apply myself with assiduity and attention.

"The students tell me that it has become a custom for the Faculty to reject on the first examination, and grant a second. They tell me there is not the least disgrace in it. It is almost a matter of chance whether they admit or not.—Yours most gratefully,

J. H. THORNWELL."

Fourteen days later, another letter was written to the same party, on the same subject.

"COLUMBIA, *December* 19, 1829.

"MY DEAR FRIEND : I have revised my studies under Mr. McAllily, who was recommended to me by Professor Nott. I shall not apply for admission, however, until the first of January. The Faculty will more willingly receive me then, as they will be apt to judge of my qualifications from the time I have studied. I can keep on studying until that time, and it will not hurt me. * * * There is no being on earth more happy than the student. With all the means of knowledge at his command, what can give him more pleasure than to improve his mind ? He may enjoy, if he wishes, a continual feast of nectar ; and his satisfaction is considerably enhanced when he is esteemed by all his acquaintances. I was never more cordially received by any persons than by my Pedee friends here. They all appeared very glad to see me. I found in College more who knew me than I had any idea of. Some Pedee men, who had heard of me, took the very excusable liberty of introducing themselves, and tendering their friendly services. My rejection they viewed as a matter of chance, since an admission depends so much on luck. The result, they think, might have been more favorable, had I been examined in company, and not alone, as was the case.

"Do write me everything about home. I am anxious to hear from you again, and from General Gillespie, who has not written me since I came here. I fear he is displeased.—Yours truly and gratefully,

J. H. THORNWELL.

"P. S.—You can send by Mr. Mc—— my other vest, my shoes; and, if you think it more advisable to purchase there than here, you can send Locke's 'Essay.' S. G. has the work; if you see him, it will cost nothing."

There is a tone of manliness pervading both these letters, with which the reader cannot fail to sympathize. Mortifying as the discomfiture was to a proud spirit like his—a spirit too untamed by even successful competition in the narrower sphere in which he has hitherto moved— there is not a word of whining complaint, nor boyish re sentment against those who inflicted the disappointment. He accepts it just as it is, with a clear consciousness that his failure was due to an excessive timidity, which had, for the moment, thrown him from his equipoise; and with a steady purpose to retrieve the damage which his reputation may have received. This prepares the way for the more buoyant style of the letter which follows, addressed also to Mr. Robbins:

"COLUMBIA, *January* 4, 1830.

"MY DEAR PATRON: I have now taken my stand in the Junior Class; and so flattering was my examination, that I cannot refrain from giving you a short account of it. I was required to stand first in Homer, in which I was not found wanting. I was then taken on Horace, *De Arte Poetica.* The sentence which was given me Professor Henry thought the most difficult in the book, and said that I read it admirably well. I was then taken in Hutton's Mathematics, in which I demonstrated, without the least difficulty, about twenty theorems; and lastly, I passed with success through logarithms. There were three applicants for the class besides myself; two of whom were admitted; the other was rejected for the third time.

"An unlucky circumstance has occasioned me some uneasiness. Charges greatly derogatory to the character of Mr. —— were communicated to me here, of which I immediately apprised S——. What I wrote, Mr. —— has by some means learned; and he wrote me, requesting the author of that report. I immediately and unhesitatingly complied; as I was bound by no ties of honour not to divulge its author. I should regret to see my name introduced under such circumstances. Mr. G——— knows the whole affair.

All the Pedee students look to me to give her a dignified seat in College. While such hopes are indulged of me, how can I be lax in my exertions?

"College duties not having commenced until to-day, I have attended only two lectures. Professor Henry does honour to Metaphysics and Moral Philosophy. Dr. Wallace is perhaps unequalled in Mathematics; and Professor Nott is not inferior in his department. We have a splendid library, consisting of eight or ten thousand volumes. Indeed, Columbia affords every facility of improvement.

"I found great difficulty in obtaining a room; and my tavern expenses, and the cost of furnishing my room, have reduced my purse to a low ebb. Seventy-five dollars will defray all necessary expenses till June, when I should return. Calculating at this rate, which I think just, two hundred and fifty dollars a year will carry me through College. Should it be inconvenient to send me anything, there is no pressing need. I am not out of money, but have not enough to settle all my College bills.

"Hereafter I shall write to you every other week, and to the General as often. Next Sunday I shall be at leisure to write you a *decent* letter. It is now almost ten o'clock P. M., and I must retire to bed, as I must rise by day-break in the morning, and hie me to the lecture room.

Yours truly,   J. H. THORNWELL."

This letter drew forth a reply so just in its views, and so wise in its counsels, that we shall offer no apology for its introduction. Indeed, all the communications of this noble man deserve to be incorporated in this record of his ward, whose character they contributed so materially to form, as well as for the dignity and weight of the sentiments with which they abound.

"CHERAW, January 9, 1830.

"DEAR JAMES: On my return from Marlborough I received your welcome letter of last Monday, bringing the glad tidings of your admission to the standing in College which your perseverance and good conduct have merited; and I lose no time in offering you my cordial congratulations. If your disappointment shall be attended with no other good, you should feel amply recompensed in the good things it has called from your instructors. But let it teach you that disappointment and mortification attend you at every turn in the path of life; that to be prepared for them is the part of wisdom; and to endure them with manly fortitude, is the way to overcome them. And let it teach you, too, that, when so encountered, they never fail to bring proportionate good in their train. I cannot permit myself to doubt but your future exertions will be commensurate with the expectations of your friends. Your assiduity in the cause of learning gives me assurance that every advantage you now enjoy will be eagerly, and of course successfully, improved. But let me caution you not to suffer your ambition to be bounded by the narrow circle of College honours. To have achieved all that the officers of College can bestow, is distinction dearly bought, if, in the pursuit, you have lost one iota of that purity of character and singleness of purpose with which you commence it; if you shall suffer a conscious superiority to render you uncourteous to an inferior, or indulge one envious reflection at the superiority of a rival. The field of mental exertion is wide enough for all who enter it; there is no need of jostling for a place there. The rewards it holds out are liberal and noble. In their achievement by others we should see the glory of the struggle; and if fairly and honourably won, the head that wears will not disgrace them. To foster these sentiments—to think, to feel, and act, in accordance with them—is to gain a conquest more important and more valuable than all the little distinctions which men can confer upon us. Don't think that I make these remarks because I think you more liable to err in this way than other young men. I know you are not more so: I hope not so much so. I give them that you may fix them as a pole-star in your march through life, and square all your conduct by them.

"I was very sorry to hear that you should have been implicated in an affair like that you mentioned. You did right in surrendering the author; but S——— did great wrong in suffering the affair to escape him. But did you not err, first of all, in communicating the affair at all? 'Tis best to leave these little slanders to the peculiar keeping of those who have no other business or amusement but to search for and propagate them. They are unworthy the notice of a wise man. We should regard them in sovereign contempt; and deem ourselves somewhat tainted in suffering ourselves to think on them, much more so to speak of them; but to *write* them is yet the more imprudent, indiscreet. I have heard it publicly said in the streets here, that *you* had written this story from Columbia. I was sorry to hear it; but as you had written it, you could have done no less than what you did. But, for the future, I hope you will *feel* that to descant on such subjects is to dabble in muddy water. You have nobler objects to achieve in life than the investigation of petty tales, be they true or false.   *   *   *

"Enclosed I send you twenty-five dollars; in my next letter I will send more. I don't like to increase the bulk of letters; and you say you are not out. Your calculation is too small, I think. Recollect what we have told you, and write as often as you can, consistently with other duties; and write fully of your views, and successes too.—Your friend,

W. H. ROBBINS."

This hitch at his entrance into college would not have prejudiced his scholarship in the estimation of his fellow-students, who looked upon it very much as a question of luck. Probably it would not have been noticed at all, but for the extraordinary accounts which had been poured into their ears, and the confident predictions which had been uttered on his behalf. It had been announced by those who knew his earlier history, that " a little, pale boy would come on soon, and bear off the honours of his class." The mortification of these admirers at his rejection was, if possible, greater than his own; for they were obliged to bear the penalty in the laughter which this apparent failure of their champion brought upon their heads. It was not, however, of long duration. We quote again from the same witness who has furnished the preceding description of his person: "The class which he entered was a remarkably ambitious one, and contained among the forty-three young men who composed it many aspirants for the highest honours of the college; but such was the intellectual power displayed by Thornwell, that he had not made more than half a dozen recitations before it was conceded on all hands that the first honour must be *his* beyond all question. This mental pre-eminence was apparent, not only in the class-room, but in debates in the College Society to which he belonged, in social intercourse, and, indeed, wherever there was mental contact with others. There was about his mind, however, nothing of the erratic or impulsive character attributed to genius. His powerful intellect worked with the steadiness of machinery; and its superiority was displayed in the higher reach and wider grasp of thought, with which it advanced, without check, to the attainment of its end, scarcely pausing at obstacles which would have halted others."

In the faculty of the South Carolina College, as at that time constituted, there were at least four gentlemen who could not fail to. impress themselves upon such a mind as here described.

Professor JAMES WALLACE had a rare genius for the Mathematical chair, which he filled; and always im-

pressed his pupils with a conviction of the importance
and value of his favourite studies, as well as the vast
treasures of knowledge which remained for them to explore.   It is to be regretted that his unusual attainments
should be represented only in one work, "On the Globes,"
which, with a few fragmentary disquisitions, is all that
he has left behind him.

Professor HENRY JUNIUS NOTT, to whom was assigned
the department of English Literature, was, beyond dispute, one of the finest Belles Lettres scholars the State
has ever produced, worthy to be the friend and peer of
the gifted Legare.   With a mind enriched by study, and
enlarged by foreign travel; with a memory capable of
reproducing all that he had ever observed or read; with
"a rich humour and a ready wit, which few could turn
to better account;" with a style that is "presented as a
model of easy elegance, and of simple, classic beauty;"
it was impossible to escape the fascination which the brilliant lecturer threw around the beautiful studies in his
department.   The chivalry of his character was mourn-
fully illustrated in his death, upon the wreck of the ill-
fated steamer "Home," in 1837, preferring to sink in
the waters of the Atlantic, by the side of a wife whom
he was too generous to abandon.

Dr. THOMAS COOPER, the President, was, however, at
this time, the Coryphœus of the institution.   His varied
erudition, his trenchant style, his enthusiasm in whatever
he espoused, the boldness and courage with which he
maintained opinions at variance with the popular sentiment, even the restlessness of spirit which had made him
an agitator through the whole of an eventful career,
were qualities exceedingly captivating to the youth under
his charge.   He possessed just the cleverness and the
courage, the dash and the dogmatism, which seem to
the inexperienced the elements of the heroic, and whose
knowledge was not sufficient to estimate the shallowness
of his philosophy, and even of his learning.   That young

Thornwell fell at first under the charm of his influence, appears from an incidental reference in one of Mr. Robbins's letters, where he speaks of Dr. Cooper as "your idol." It is equally certain that this spell was at length broken. It could not be otherwise. The antagonism between the two was complete in the structure of their minds, and in the direction of their favourite studies. The historian of the college records of the President, that "his genius was eminently practical—*utilitarian*. He looked upon man very much as an animal, and believed that the framework of society was designed to provide for his physical wants and necessities. As in man he saw nothing but the animal, so in the objects of nature he saw nothing but external nature. Of man in his higher nature, as a being of immortal powers, with aspirations reaching into a never ending futurity, he had no just conception." From such gross materialism, a mind of such a structure as that of young Thornwell was compelled to diverge, as soon as it should address itself to the solution of these questions at all; and he who was ravished with the charms of philosophy could have no permanent sympathy with one who "held metaphysical and ethical investigations in perfect contempt." Of his fierce opposition to revealed religion we shall have a better occasion to speak hereafter.

But the foremost of them all, in the breadth and permanence of his influence over our friend, was Dr. ROBERT HENRY, who filled, with singular ability, the chair of Philosophy. He was a profound scholar, critically acquainted with the ancient classics, and perfectly familiar with the German, Dutch, Spanish, and French languages. In the studies of his peculiar department he was not less accomplished, having "explored the entire circle of knowledge and speculation, and made the rich fruit of the master minds who had laboured in this field his own." Dr. Thornwell, in later years, always acknowledged his great indebtedness to the classical taste and attainments of Dr. Henry, by whom he was both stimulated and directed in the acquisition of

classic and of philosophic lore.   After his death, the
pupil paid a beautiful tribute to the memory of his preceptor, in the pages of the *Southern Quarterly Review*.
Such were the men, under the influence of whose genius
he found himself placed, upon his entrance into College.

The possession of these advantages stimulated his zeal
to the last degree.   Coupling the assiduity of the German with the fervour of the American, he devoted fourteen hours a day to severe study.   Either his good sense
pierced the fallacy which supposes that genius can win
permanent success without learning as the material upon
which, or the instrument by which, it must work; or else
he was led blindly on by an avaricious love of knowledge,
rendering the toil with which it is gathered itself a delight;
but certain it is, he turned away with the severity of an
anchorite from the blandishments of society; and, like
an athlete of old, with continuous and cruel rigor trained
every muscle and every limb for the Olympic race and
the Olympic prize before him in life.   During his College
career, he omitted no opportunity of discipline, neglected no part of the prescribed curriculum, wasted no
hour in dissipation or indolence; but with elaborate care
prepared himself for every exercise.   In the Literary
Society of which he was a member, the same assiduity
availed itself of every privilege.   Despising the baldness
of mere extemporaneous harangues, he armed himself for
the conflict of debate.   This example, with its attendant
and grand results, stands up in scorching rebuke of the
egotism and folly which would exalt the triumphs of
genius by disparaging the discipline through which its
energies are directed.

His investigations were pushed beyond the text books
of the class room.   They were almost encyclopædic in
their range.   He used the library as no student before
him had ever done, and knocked the dust from ancient
tomes never disturbed but by the brush of the librarian.
He studied subjects as subjects, especially in the depart-

ments to which he had a natural proclivity; and never paused till he had sounded to the bottom. Evidence of this is furnished in the correspondence of this period, and still more in the facts of his religious history, yet to be disclosed. As an illustration of the Herculean labours he would undergo to accomplish some important end, the following achievement may be related; which falls, partially at least, within this period: Being asked by one of his Divinity students what was the best method of improving one's style, he replied: "Language was my great difficulty in early life. I had no natural command of words. I undertook to remedy the defect by committing to memory large portions of the New Testament, the Psalms, and much of the Prophets; also whole dramas of Shakspeare, and a great part of Milton's 'Paradise Lost'; so that you might start me at any line in any drama or book, and I would go through to the end. I regard the above named as exhausting the powers of the English language; and he who masters them, knows his native tongue. It is also the best method of training the memory." In confirmation of this, the writer has frequently heard him, when in a recitative mood, repeat whole pages of Milton without the slightest hesitation; sometimes an entire ode of Horace, or long extracts from Virgil; to say nothing of brilliant passages from Robert Hall and Edmund Burke: all the fruits of this early memorizing. One of his first associates testifies that, before going to College, he could recite entire pages of Dugald Stewart; showing this discipline to have been begun at an early date. This explains, too, what always seemed so wonderful to the writer: that Dr. Thornwell was able, in conversation, to repeat long passages from such rugged writers as Jonathan Edwards and John Owen, without the necessity of recurring to the works themselves for authority. His mind had acquired, through the severe training of his youth, a facility in taking up and retaining the words as well as the thoughts of an

author whom he attentively read. Notwithstanding his
constant depreciation of his own memory, it always appeared to us the most marvellous in its power of retention
and reproduction that we ever met.

As the reader may surmise, such diligence in study did
not comport with free companionship. He was not, indeed, averse from it; for he was constitutionally genial
and sympathetic; and whenever he chose to indulge in its
relaxation, his manner was cheerful, and even buoyant.
Among his young associates he indulged freely in playful
raillery and sarcasm; in which there was not a trace of
bitterness, for he was incapable of malignity. But satire
is a dangerous weapon with which to sport; and to one
who possesses the fatal gift, the temptation to its indiscreet use is often too strong to be resisted. In later
years, Dr. Thornwell was accustomed to acknowledge
that nothing had given him greater trouble than this
propensity to sarcasm. It gleams forth occasionally
through all the passages of his history; and if he had
chosen to indulge it, few could have excelled him in the
power of invective. How sweetly it was controlled, and
finally, by a mellow piety, subdued, can be appreciated
only by those who knew the gentleness of his last years,
when ripening for his translation. But at the period of
which we are now treating, there was little to check the
indulgence of a talent which, however unamiable, is
always an instrument of commanding power. It was
especially in debate that this fearful talent was displayed.
In the language of one of his class-mates, "His words
burned like fire; his sarcasm was absolutely withering."
From this cause, in part, he was not what is called a
popular student in College. "He was admired for his
transcendent abilities, but not loved." This was, however, still more due to his habits of seclusion. He had
something more important to achieve than to court either
the society or the favour of those about him. Indeed,
throughout life, he was a man rather to be sought, than

to be himself a seeker. What he was in later life, he was to some extent in College; and hence he never commanded that shallow popularity which is acquired only by rubbing one's self good naturedly against every man's shoulder.

The polemic character of his mind fitted him to shine in the debating society, which always forms a feature of College discipline. He revelled in the gladiatorial combats that took place. Says one of his class-mates: "He took the most prominent part in the Literary Society of which he was a member, and received all the honours in its gift. His eloquence was unequalled, and his argumentative powers the most amazing. He could detect and expose a fallacy with more dispatch and completeness than I ever witnessed in any other man. The honorary members of the Society, living in Columbia and vicinity, would attend these discussions in large numbers, to hear this wonderful man pour forth torrents of eloquence, and deal, right and left, death-blows to sophistry." Another, in the class below him, thus writes: "On the night I joined the Society, Thornwell rose to make a speech. When he stood up, he was not a great deal higher than the tables. He stepped into the passage between them; and I remember distinctly my reflection, 'Well, you cannot say much till you will have to sit down.' But, to my surprise, without any trepidation or diffidence, he spoke, for twenty or thirty minutes, in a strain of eloquence, and with a flow of language, full of thought. His peculiar gesture was with both arms opened, and raised above his head. He was a ready speaker, and the best debater in the Society. He would sometimes indulge in sarcasm, and was severe in retort." We are careful to quote exactly from these memoranda of eye and ear witnesses, to escape the suspicion of writing a eulogy under the disguise of history. The criticism will be disarmed by remembering that, in a most important sense, the orator, as well as the poet, is born, not made. Culture may be necessary to train the peculiar faculties of both;

but the original creative power, which is their common characteristic, is the immediate gift of God. Germain to this is the following letter, addressed to his patron, General Gillespie:

"COLUMBIA, January 24, 1830.

"DEAR SIR: There is scarcely anything going on here which is worth communicating. A short account of the Society may not be uninteresting. The two last meetings were the best we have had since I became a member. I made my first attempt, concerning 'The justice of punishing the Irish rebels of 1797;' and I justified that measure of the English cabinet with all the arguments that I could muster. Last night I made a second effort, on the question, 'Whether it is probable that the nations of Europe will advance further in refinement than they have done.' I contended that they would not. My argument was this: I first proved, by induction, that it was a law of nature that everything, after having reached a certain point of elevation, must decline. I next showed the method by which we could determine when anything had reached that point; and then made application to the question. The election for monthly orator came off last night, and I was glad to find that I was elected by an almost unanimous vote. There is one difficulty attending the delivery of this oration. The constitution requires that it should be delivered in a gown. Now, the Society's gown is large enough for a man of six feet, and I would be a ridiculous figure in it. Some method must be contrived to obviate this difficulty.

"I am now reading Swift's Works and Hume's Essays. I have finished Berkeley. Swift's 'Tale of a Tub' is a masterly specimen of sarcastic wit; it will distort the gravest muscles. Hume's Essays, which are a compendium of his treatise on Human Nature, I read immediately after Berkeley; because I wish to follow out the train of reasoning by which matter and spirit are proved to be nonentities. And it is ingenious enough, although it depends entirely on a hypothesis, which philosophers have assumed without the slightest evidence, viz., that the mind does not perceive anything but its own ideas. From this assumption the most absured consequences have been rigorously deduced. Matter and spirit are shown to be delusions. Nothing, says Hume, exists but ideas and impressions. There is no mind on which they may be impressed. It is remarkable that men of such sagacity and penetration as Berkeley and Hume should have taken for granted a principle from which such ridiculous consequences flowed. The absurdity of the conclusion should have led them to suspect their premises. Indeed, Berkeley undertakes to prove that his whimsical notion, concerning the non-existence of matter, coincides with the general sentiments of mankind; and that the belief of the existence of matter was the oddest of the two. Hume, however, has the frankness to confess that his opinions contradict the common sense of men. It is amusing to observe into what a labyrinth of perplexities men may involve themselves.

Yours, affectionately,

J. H. THORNWELL."

CHAPTER VI.

COLLEGE LIFE CONTINUED.

IN the following correspondence the letters explain themselves, from the close relation in which they stand:

"DEAR JAMES: Enclosed is eighty dollars, which I wish you to acknowledge the receipt of immediately. Our Court of Equity sits on Monday, and I am too much occupied to write more at present. Use no delicacy, James, in asking for money. If this shall not be enough for you, remember there is more where it came from.

Your friend ever,   W. H. ROBBINS."

"COLUMBIA, February 12, 1830.

"MY DEAR SIR: I have just received your letter covering eighty dollars, for which you have my warmest gratitude. The alacrity and cheerfulness with which you grant my requests render it extremely unpleasant for me to ask anything from you. And it is more unpleasant, since the only recompense which I am capable of rendering you is to be *serviceable to myself.* Common gratitude, did no other motive enter, would require me to prove not unworthy of the confidence which you have reposed in me. Dignified deportment and close application, combined with a proper selection of associates, are the least things you can require. Indeed, so far as regards associates, I am perhaps too fastidious. There are seven in one hundred and twenty with whom I sometimes associate; but only *one* who is in any wise an intimate. * * *

"The last number of the *Southern Review* is, in my opinion, a failure. The review of Stuart's Hebrew Grammar is written by Mr. Michallowitz, the Professor of Oriental Languages in this College. If that work is intended to be read, it should surely lay aside its pompous parade of learning. This number, or at least the article on the Hebrew Grammar, and that on Higgins's Celtic Druids, are fit for nothing but show. A few

67

privileged characters may be let into their mysteries ; but of what benefit are they to the mass of the people ?

" The review of Hoffman's Legal Outlines, in the last number of the
North American, is calculated to add to the merited celebrity which
that journal has obtained. I think it superior to the article which appeared in the *Southern*. By this journal it was termed a misnomer ;
the *North American* has shown it to be otherwise. The article in the
Southern Review, headed ' Louis Courier,' is written by Professor Nott.
I have not read it yet.

"A letter, giving me a full account of things at home, would be like
cold water to a thirsty soul ; for I am homesick. It is some consolation
that I shall see you in May.   Yours affectionately,
                                            J. H. THORNWELL."

                                    " COLUMBIA, *March* 5, 1830.

" MY DEAR PATRON : The metaphysical distinction drawn by Lord
Shaftesbury between what is good and what is virtuous, seems unnecessary. The former, according to him, implies whatsoever promotes the
interests of the general system ; the latter, an *affection* for what promotes that interest. Virtue, therefore, is a quality of the agent ; good,
of the action. A notion of good must be obtained before we can become virtuous. For how can we have an affection for what we do not
comprehend ? Nothing, says this author, can be denominated either
good or ill, unless it promotes or counteracts the interest of the system
of which it is a part. No animal can be called ill unless it is hurtful
to the animal system. No man can be called ill, unless he is hurtful
to the human species. But what sagacity can trace the result of human
actions ? Few men inquire whether their actions promote the weal of
society or not, and yet know whether they are good or bad. How is
this ? Nature has given them a sense of right and wrong. Whatever
pleases this intellectual sense is right ; the contrary, wrong. It is the
character of good actions, however, to promote the interest of the general system.

" This is a summary of Lord Shaftesbury's sentiments, as far as I have
read. To find his meaning in a mountain of useless verbosity is no
ordinary task. I chain myself down to it, however. To give you some
insight into his style, if style it may be called, he expresses in twenty
lines no other sentiment than this : ' That a man, by vice, does himself
as much harm as if he were to wound himself.' Guess from this of his
verbosity. Still his periods are very harmonious. They are delightful
to the ear, but rough to the understanding. His style has the good
effect of concentrating the attention. He never expresses clearly and
distinctly ; but he envelopes everything in a cloud of words. Self-
examination is a clear idea of itself ; but Lord S. makes it a mystery. It is to be a self-dialogist ; to form the dual number with one's
self ; to enter into self-partnership ; to divide one's self into two parties ; and all such nonsense as this. But let us leave this worthy deist.
          Yours, gratefully and affectionately,   J. H. THORNWELL."

"CHERAW, *April* 10, 1836.

"DEAR JAMES: You judged rightly; it has been the pressure of professional business that prevented my writing you before; and I trust you will excuse me, knowing as you do, that it is but rarely, and then only with a good reason, that I suffer even the impatient calls of professional business to interrupt my performance of the duties of friendship. I know you will not accuse me of neglect or indifference to your interest.

"So you think that if you pay '*some* attention' to a book, in the reading, you will find little to do in the review! This expression of yours amused me not a little; and, to say the least, it furnished no evidence of your self-distrust. But I suppose you think it the privilege of great minds to possess, and sometimes to exhibit, a consciousness of superior power. It is so; and it is probably the surest test of a superior judgment, to determine wisely the subject and occasion when to put it forth. To be confident in our opinions and assertions in trivial matters, or too often so in any matters; or even rarely, when the occasion does not require and justify it, is neither more nor less than downright dogmatism. And besides, it is impolitic in another view; by being habitually positive, we multiply the chances of being sometimes in error; and the most fortunate man cannot promise himself that he will never be detected; and whenever caught tripping in this way, in a matter of opinion, distrust in his judgment—in a matter of fact, doubt in his veracity, is sure to follow. Nor will the consequences be restricted in its operations to the narrow circle of those who were personal witnesses of the cause; good report travels at snail's pace, whilst detraction outrides the wind. Such a practice, too, begets suspicion in the minds of intelligent men, that what we lack in reason, we seek to make up in assurance; and this inference is generally a just one.

"But on the contrary, a truly great mind, flinging aside all adventitious props, rising buoyant of its own native energies, and poising itself proudly on the consciousness of its own moral power, is, at the same time, the rarest and most magnificent spectacle in the moral universe. It impresses us with admiration, with wonder and fear. It is a noble daring, which fills us with solemn awe, the highest effort of moral courage; because it is done under the deepest sense of personal responsibility; because it is done at the hazard of everything which such a man holds valuable in life: present mortification, influence, and pride of character. And when we analyze this sentiment, we find that it derives all its sublimity from its rare exercise by such a mind, the importance of the occasion, and the noble reason which prompts and sustains it; take away either, and, instead of sublimity, we shall have a precious specimen of the ridiculous; deprive it of all, and you leave us the antagonist character, in which vanity, rant, and dogmatism are the essential ingredients.

"Now, I would not have you think that these reflections have a personal bearing. They have not, nor were they so intended. They are

general remarks, which have suggested themselves to my mind ; and I
have thrown them out as food for your reflection, and for animadversion
and correction, if you are so inclined, in a future letter.   I should prefer some original speculations of your own, to the general remarks on
authors which you introduce into your letters : and let them be suit-
ably interspersed with any incident of personal interest which may
transpire. I mention this, not in the tone of censure ; but that you
may know that incidents of a personal interest to you will always have
an interest for me. I never thought you extravagant, but suspect that
you deny yourself too much. Have enclosed twenty dollars.

W. H. ROBBINS.

" COLUMBIA, April 14, 1830.

   " MY DEAR PATRON : I received yesterday your letter covering twenty
dollars ; which, although not adequate to my present exigencies, was, I
assure you, a very acceptable boon. Thirty dollars more would be
amply adequate to pay demands until June, when I should need the
same amount again.
   " I am ' strangely oblivious,' as the Dominie would say, if I did not
give you or General Gillespie an account of the late excitement in
College."

(Here follows a long recital of a riot, with the details
of which the reader would not be interested. We pass,
therefore, to the closing paragraph of this letter.)

   "The sentence in my letter which gave rise to the philosophical reflection in yours, was intended as a modest way of telling you that I
studied my lessons the first time, and therefore found little new in the
review. I did not mean to say that, whilst others were compelled to
labour and toil over their lessons, I could learn them with barely ' some
attention.' This was not my idea. If I have not the self-distrust, I
have the discretion, at least, to restrain such bursts of vanity. Your
remarks, however, could not have been personal ; for you would have
been disgusted, and not ' amused.'
Yours gratefully and affectionately,
J. H. THORNWELL."

" COLUMBIA, May 1, 1830.

   " MY DEAR PATRON : Your letter covering thirty dollars has been received, which filled me with emotions of the liveliest character. Indeed,
how could it have been otherwise, unless I had been made of stone.
Your closing sentence in particular aroused the tenderest sentiments of
my heart ; and, my dear sir, as long as I have a heart, as long as I am
myself, the warmest feelings of my nature shall ever be indulged towards you. I entertain a deep, and I hope a noble, sentiment towards
the kindest benefactors that ever relieved the wants of suffering human-

ity. When I consider my former situation, the ignorance and poverty that seemed my inevitable doom, and contrast it with my present state, my bosom glows with the most ardent gratitude and affection towards those generous souls who stretched out the hand of relief, and still hold it out. When old age shall have come upon you, with its attendent miseries, should all others desert you, I will still cling the closer to you, and deem it my greatest satisfaction to rock the cradle of your declining years, and to smooth your bed of death. The evening of your life shall not disappear in clouds, but shall pass off as calmly and as tranquilly as a summer's day; and when the grave shall have closed upon you, I will pay the tribute of affection to your memory. These are the feelings of my bosom. Accept them, I pray you, as all that I can now return for your kindness to me; but remember the day is not far distant, perhaps, when you will find some satisfaction in

J. H. THORNWELL."

The three letters which follow are such as are seldom found in a College correspondence. The instances are rare in which, on the one hand, a parent or guardian has need to urge the child or ward to spend more freely the money which is munificently supplied; whilst the pupil, on the other hand, finds himself driven to philosophy to justify his parsimony. It is equally honourable to both the parties. It is the more remarkable, since Dr. Thornwell was naturally extravagant in all his tastes; and his expenditures were bounded only by his means. The disclosure in these letters fully justifies the testimony of Mr. Robbins, given in later years, when his ward had won his own independent position in the world: "James is lavish with his own means, but careful and honest with that of another." But to the letters:

"CHERAW, November 10, 1830.

"DEAR JAMES: I received last evening your letter of the fourth current; also that of last month, enclosing Dr. Green's receipt for the money. * * * I like and approve a wise economy; but carried too far, as I fear you have done, it ceases to be a virtue; and neither the Generals nor myself desire it, nor can we approve. We wish you to be liberal, not profuse, in your expenditure; and anything short of this we cannot sanction. Your impatience to be earning for yourself is premature. This will do well by and by. Let all your present aims be directed to the laying a solid foundation. The superstructure must await this; and without it, future exertion will be unavailing. Not only endeavour to supply your mind with knowledge, but cultivate a

cool and dispassionate judgment in all things, whether appertaining to
your conduct now, or to your opinions. It is by this, rest assured, that
all human things are to be weighed; and to this, as a test, must and
will all be submitted in the realities of life. Enthusiasm, which naturally recommends itself to youth, is regarded in its proper light by
age and experience. It is a pleasant attendant to solid sense and correct views; but without them, 'tis unsure to stand upon. In all your
reflections, where conduct is the aim, regard human nature as it is, not
as it should be. Man has sought out many inventions, says the good
Book; and if we would influence man, or govern him, we must not
only know, but reckon on, these inventions. The seaman who would
determine by course and distance only, will find himself at fault when
he makes land; the winds and currents must enter into his estimate, too,
if he would fix his true place. When you have gotten your education,
the quality of which depends more on youself than on your instructors,
there will be ample time to devise and pursue the business of life. Before then, we wish you to employ all your thoughts on the cultivation
of mind. Let them not be bounded by the narrow horizon of College
and its honours; these are trivial affairs, and not worth a thought, in
comparison with that general knowledge and cultivation of judgment;
that broad and comprehensive view of *men, subjects,* and *things,* which
alone go to constitute the character of a great mind. 'Tis a good rule,
never to hazard an opinion on a subject until it is wholly before you :
for, by being frequently detected in error, men lose confidence in our
ability and judgment; while, on the other hand, to be *positive* seldom,
and always to be found right, fixes a character which will ensure, because it will merit, the confidence of others. These are a few hasty hints
for your consideration, You said you would send a copy of my last
summer's letters. Do so in your next.

I am, as ever, yours,

W. H. ROBBINS."

" COLUMBIA, *November* 13, 1830.

"MY DEAR PATRON: " I have just received your letter, which affords a
striking illustration of the power of the associating principle. The train
of thought which suggested your philosophical reflections can be easily
traced out. You are particularly anxious to guard me against a dogmatical
spirit. In other words, you think that I had passed an opinion on your
letter, which I had positively asserted to be true, but which turns out to be
false. Taking this for granted, you are desirous of preventing me from
committing future errors of the same kind. Your reflections are just,
and are calculated to be serviceable. It is not to their tendency, or the
spirit which dictated them, that I object. These are noble, and receive
my hearty thanks. But the assumption on which they rest, I cannot
grant. That you may judge for yourself, however, I copy your letter :
' I have time only to enclose you thirty dollars, and to exhort you to
make good use of it. You had better go with others, and deny yourself

no indulgence which does not exceed the limits of a gentlemanly decorum.' It is dated 24th April, 1830. Does this differ from what I stated
to be its import? Can I, by any means, gather the meaning of the
phrase, ' You had better go with others?' It cannot allude to the rebellion, for that took place early in March. Your reflections shall guide
me in other cases, although they do not apply to this. In speaking of
frugality or economy, may I presume to suggest that you had overlooked
a material circumstance? What is economy in one man is parsimony
in another; and *vice versa*. It depends on the circumstances of men.
A man in my circumstances cannot be well charged with meanness or
stinginess; but a rich man can. We must accumulate before we can
spend, and not spend before we accumulate. If these remarks are
wrong, you will please correct me; if right, you can confirm them by
your sanction. I shall endeavour to profit by your remarks on the true
objects of a Collegiate education. They are confirmed by every writer
on that subject, and deserve the attention of all men who are anxious
to improve their minds.

" The examination will take place in about three weeks, and then I
hope to be a Senior. Will you be here then? If you come, do not
forget to bring my French Grammar. I stand greatly in need of it.
In January I commence German. I am very anxious to understand
that language. It is a common acquisition at the North. I am reading Cicero de Legibus in the original, and find little difficulty; also
Stewart's Philosophy. Saturdays I amuse myself with history.

Yours, gratefully and affectionately,

J. H. THORNWELL."

' CHERAW, *November* 20, 1830.

" DEAR JAMES: I have received your last letter; and as I have sur-
mised, you fell into error in the construction you gave my old letter,
by taking too narrow a view of it. I admit that the words ' go with
others,' unqualified by any other expression, do bear the construction
which you gave them. But how it was possible, taking the whole sentence together, for you to have fallen into the error you did, I cannot
imagine. After saying that I enclosed money, and exhorting you to
make a good use of it, I remarked further, that ' You had better go with
others, and deny yourself no indulgence,' etc. Now, it seems to me
that the latter clause confines and explains the preceding, that it would
be impossible to misinterpret it. The meaning was: if you were solicited to go to a supper, regard not the cost, but *go*; if to a ride, regard
not the cost, but *go*. I meant that you must not deny yourself little indulgences, though they might require money; not seclude yourself from
your companions and their amusements, when any demands would be
laid upon your purse; but ' go with them.' And I must think, on a
second view of the sentence, you will wonder how you should have so
marvellously erred. In haste, your friend,

W. H. ROBBINS."

According to his expectations, Thornwell rose Senior
at the opening of the next session, in January, 1831.   It is
to be regretted that there are no remains of the correspondence, which was yet vigorously maintained, as we learn
from the only relic in our possession.   The studies of this
year, so much in unison with the genius and taste of our
young friend, the increased maturity of his own mind, and
the freedom of discussion so generously solicited by his
patron, would doubtless have enriched these pages with
epistles of surpassing interest.   It is singular that the
chances of time should have spared nothing upon either
side, with the exception of a solitary communication from
Mr. Robbins.   This is characterized by the same vigour
of thought, the same justness of discrimination, the same
moderation of tone, and the same elevation of moral
principle, which the reader has perceived in the letters
already given.   His attachment to his ward rendered
him, by no means, blind to the faults from which he was
only effectively delivered by Divine grace, at a later
period.   He perceives them with a perfectly clear eye,
and addresses himself to their correction with a direct-
ness and precision that could not be evaded.   At the
same time, we are filled with wonder at the skill with
which the invidious task is accomplished; and know not
which most to admire, the delicacy which escapes wound-
ing the sensibilities and arousing the resistance of his
protegè; or the wisdom which, under the form of philosophical disquisition, insinuates his criticisms into a mind
that was ravished with the charms of metaphysics.   No
mind could have been better fitted to discharge the office
of a Mentor to such a temperament as that he had undertaken to mould.   And those who recall the prudence of
Dr. Thornwell, in after life, in forming his opinions, and
the caution with which he surveyed a question on every
side, before committing himself, will perhaps trace the
influence of these reiterated suggestions, in framing one
of the wisest counsellors that ever sat in the courts of the

Church. It is thus he deals with certain tendencies in his young ward to dogmatism and intellectual pride:

" CHERAW, May 23, 1831.

"MY DEAR JAMES: Your last very ample letter gave me much pleasure. It went more largely into your own views of future employment than I supposed you had hitherto suffered your mind to stretch itself. There is opened to me such a boundless field of remark, in the different subjects embraced in your letter, that it will not be expected that I shall notice all of them ; indeed, I shall say anything only on one or two. I was glad to find that you appreciated in their proper light, the value of College distinctions ; and the reflections you make all coincide with my own views; and, my boy, if report speaks not falsely, you will bear off some honour in this way. I was glad to hear it ; but I was far more so to hear, from your own pen, the just estimate you attached to all Collegial honours. Your aspirations are fixed on higher, nobler objects ; but be cautious that your attachment to these, and to those employed in achieving them, be not coupled with any sentiment of contempt or detestation for them, occupied in the pursuit of those of humbler sphere. All men are not endued with the faculties of a Newton, Bacon, Locke; nor even with those of Gibbon, Paley, or Stewart. Nature never designed, therefore, that they should act the same parts. And the dispensation is a wise one ; for if all were scholars, where is to be done the vast and important business of the world ? Who is to bid the forest to disappear ? Who to construct edifices for human convenience; to till the earth for human sustenance ; to teach the child, the youth, the man ? Who to administer cures for human ills; the laws, for human safety ? In short, what is to become of the whole machine of civil government, if we are all to wrap ourselves up in ourselves, and write philosophical, moral, and metaphysical disquisitions ? Mark me ! I do not urge these considerations for the purpose of deterring you from the pursuit of a favourite employment; only that they may qualify and check a something of contempt, which I think I discovered in your letter, for every man not employed in similar studies, and not endowed by nature with extraordinary capacities. Recollect, both taste and talent are mainly the gift of nature to man. He is accountable to the Giver only for the proper use of what he has, not for the highest possible endowments. And it ill becomes us, because we have been more liberally dealt with by a kind Providence, to look with scorn or contempt on those to whom less has been given, and of whom less will be required, who perform equally well with ourselves their several offices in life and those offices, perhaps, no less important and necessary than those which fall to our lot, for the use, comfort, and well-being of society.

" But besides all this, methinks you carry your notions on this subject by far too far. An accomplished and elegant scholar, and a profound one too, if you please, is a <i>white swan</i> in our land, I admit : but his fame is confined, after all, to a very limited sphere; and though he may work out for himself a name of celebrity, yet he is of little real practical use in life. Not that I would have you betake yourself to politics; 'tis the curse of our land; but I would have you a well-read and sound lawyer, an elegant and able advocate. We cannot devote all our time to abstract studies of pleasure. Some must be given to the business of life; for by this we earn our support. And in the Law is a source, not only of gain and fame, but, to one of your metaphysical propensities. of real pleasure; and I doubt not but you will be as much taken with its nice distinctions and metaphysical subtleties as you ever were with Reid, Stewart, or Brown. But the attainment of the highest celebrity in this does not preclude the enjoyment of any literary penchant which the lawyer may possess. And more, this very philosophical taste you may have will enable you to read law as a science. Your own enlarged views will prompt you to practice it as a *science*, not as a trade; and so to read and practice it is the infallible road to eminence.

"What I said of your idolatry was said *ironice*. Have you not yet learned to distinguish between irony and taunt? And don't you know, too, that when I rebuke *you*, it is without any ill feeling, but with a sincere desire for your amendment? *Vive et cognosce!*

"I leave this for the North on the 17th of June. I am anxious to see you before I go. I am glad that you have written regularly. You must also write me once a fortnight, and at length, when I am North. Direct to Boston. Let me know when I shall see you.

Yours affectionately,

W. H. ROBBINS."

On the back of this letter is endorsed this criticism: "A general diffusion of science and knowledge would not have the effect ascribed to it in this letter. J. H. T."

From youth to manhood, the moral character of Thornwell was almost irreproachable. In his boyhood, Mr. Robbins writes of him: "He was pure and chaste, I never discovered any want of, or deviation from, integrity and truthfulness, and never was called on to correct any lack of principle." The testimony of his classmates gives almost as clear a record, during his College life. One says: "I have heard it said that Thornwell was dissipated in College. It is a mistake. He was one of the most steady students among us all. He had no bad habits, according to the standard of College morality. I do not remember to have ever heard him use an oath. He never gambled, nor do I think he played at cards, or indulged in any other game for amusement. He but rarely used wines or ardent spirits. I saw him once heated with liquor, and I was much surprised, it being so entirely contrary to his habits." From another, we have the following amusing specifications: "Thornwell was not a professor of religion while at College; but, so far as I know, and I had opportunities for such knowledge, from rooming near him, he indulged in none of the vices common among young men at such institutions; certainly not habitually. I can recall but three instances of deviation from the course of strict morality. One was on the occasion of a College treat on the election of an Anniversary orator, when few, even of the abstemious, left such scenes without having 'got outside,' as the phrase was, of a quantity of wine and cordials; and our friend was not in the minority. Another was on the occurrence of a snow storm in Columbia; when history and tradition informed us it had ever been the practice to disregard all College regulations, suspend all College exercises, and take to hot punch and honey. Considering the weather quite too inclement to permit the classes to reach the recitation rooms, they marched 'up town' for the materials for the punch; and returning, indulged in a wild jollification, our friend acting a prominent part. The third was a nocturnal visit to the strawberry beds in the garden of one of the citizens of the town, without the formality of asking leave. At that time, such depredations by the students were sustained by College public opinion, as not only not disreputable, but as good practical jokes, of the success of which one might boast. But the strawberry expedition was the only instance within my knowledge of his ever yielding to the spirit of fun, in that direction."

The simple fact is, that, independent of the moral principle which he unquestionably possessed, his scholarly tastes and overweening ambition would serve to restrain anything short of an invincible propensity to vice. It is the prerogative of a master passion to root out whatever

contradicts its own supremacy. And the form which depravity would be most likely to assume in such a nature
as his, would be predominantly intellectual, the adoption
of skeptical and infidel views, which would trample upon
the humility of grace, and defy the authority of God.
How near he came to this, leads to the consideration of
his religious history at this period.

Whatever the traditional bias of his mind upon this
subject, one of his speculative turn could not be brought
in contact with opposing views, without subjecting the
whole matter to re-examination. The form of infidelity
which pervaded the College in his day has already been
indicated, and this forced the subject anew upon his attention. He was in little danger of being caught in the toils
of materialism. Every operation of mind, and every conscious emotion of the heart, are an insurrection against
this base usurpation. His metaphysical tendencies offered
protection in this direction, and the very instinct of thought
would be to him an assertion of the spiritual in man. The
writer had from his own lips the substance of the following paragraphs.

The question that first engaged his attention involved
the claim of Deism. Admitting the existence of a Supreme Being, can reason alone gather, from the oracles
of nature, within and without itself, a competent knowledge of his character and will, to enable man to meet the
responsibilities of his condition. He examined with care
the writings of the ablest advocates on both sides, and
rose from the perusal with a clear and unshaken conviction
of the necessity of a Divine revelation.

He next turned to the systems which profess to found
upon the teachings of the Bible. Socinianism had special attractions, in its exaltation of human reason, and its
promise of unbridled liberty of thought. With the knowledge of his after life in our possession, it would be interesting to trace the mental conflict through which he must
now have passed; and did we not know the result, we

might tremble for the decision which is to be rendered. Its destructive criticism strips Christianity of all that is supernatural, and drags its sublimest mysteries before the bar of human reason. It converts "the signs and wonders" of the Bible into the legends of a fabulous age; or into myth and allegory, the mere symbols of philosophy masking its teachings under the guise of fancy; or into the jugglery of nature, beneath which we are to detect only the working of her secret and invariable laws. Shall our student be dazzled with the boldness of a system, which

> "Soars untrodden heights, and seems at home
> Where angels bashful look;"

which professes to subdue things divine under the dominion of reason, and offers up all truth as a sacrifice at last upon the altar of human vanity? Or, on the other hand, shall his earnest soul, longing for the positive and the real, turn away from its endless negations, from the destructive criticism which it offers in lieu of a constructive faith, and which substitutes the abstractions of reason in place of a substantive testimony? Before the fervour of his gaze will not these airy speculations, woven of the mist and sunlight, melt away, like the deceitful mirage upon the distant horizon. Shall not his warm and loving heart find itself chilled, in an atmosphere which offers nothing to the embrace of the affections? Can such a nature as his be content to dwell in the beautiful snow-houses of this polar latitude, shining indeed, with crystaline splendour, but beneath a sun which neither cheers nor warms? The decision trembles not long upon the balance; he turns away from Socinianism, with the indignant sarcasm of Mr. Randolph, "What a Christless Christianity is this!" "I found it," said he to the writer, "a system that would not hold water;" and even reason could not mend the leaks through which its virtue oozed out.

Thus far a purely intellectual examination had con-

ducted him to a recognition of the Scriptures as the revelation of God, and of Christianity as the scheme it
unfolds. Upon the interpretation of this book, he has,
as yet, framed no hypothesis. But the time has come for
casting his traditional belief into an articulated creed.
And here again, an unseen hand interposes for his guidance, and a seeming accident forms the hinge of his future
career. During an evening stroll, he stumbles into the
book store of the town, and finds lying upon the counter
a small volume, entitled, "Confession of Faith." He had
never before heard of its existence; he only saw that it
contained a systematic exposition of Christian doctrine.
It is needless to apprise the reader that it was the Westminster Confession. He bought it for twenty-five cents,
carried it home, and, as he himself testifies, read it entirely through that night.   "For the first time," he adds,
" I felt that I had met with a system which held together
with the strictest logical connection; granting its premises,
the conclusions were bound to follow." He could not
immediately pronounce it true, without a careful comparison of the text with the scriptural proofs at the bottom
of each page. But he was arrested by the consistency and
rigour of its logic. This book determined him as a Cal-
vinist and a Presbyterian; although he had never been
thrown into contact with this branch of the Church of
Christ, and had never been, but once, within any of its
sanctuaries of worship. The circumstance, however, of
most interest in the whole series, is the fact that the chapter which most impressed him in this "Confession," was
the chapter on Justification—the doctrine which is the
key to the whole Gospel, and well styled by Luther, "*ar-
ticulus stantis aut cadentis ecclesiæ.*" How parallel with
the history of Luther himself, and of the great Reformers of the sixteenth century! who, by this clue, ex-
tricated themselves from the toils of Popery, and built
Protestant Christianity upon it as the keystone of the
arch, by which the whole superstructure was supported.

Those who recall the fierce conflict which raged in the Presbyterian Church, at the time our friend was introduced into its ministry, and who remember the distinguished part he was called to bear in defence of the doctrines of the Reformation, which are only the doctrines of grace, cannot fail to recognize here the wonderful method by which he was unconsciously trained for a similar work of reform. None can fail to see, that those who are raised up to be the champions of truth, in an age of defection and strife, and those who are destined to shape the theology of their age, must drink the truth from no secondary stream, but fresh from the oracles of God, and from those symbolical books, in which the faith of the universal Church is sacredly enshrined.

But if these researches led him within the temple of Christian truth, it was only to wonder, and not to worship. He stood beneath its majestic dome, and mused along its cathedral aisles, as before he had wandered through the groves of the Academy, or paused beneath the porch of the Stoic. The gospel was nothing more than a sublime philosophy; and if it secured the homage of his intellect, it failed, as yet, to control the affections of his heart. If he seemed to sit with reverence at the feet of the Great Teacher, it was only as a teacher something greater than Socrates, and more divine than Plato. The seed must lie dead for a time. How soon it was to germinate, and what fruit to bear, we shall shortly trace. There is a statement that he had, in College, moments of deep conviction for sin; and would then resort to the room of a pious student, soliciting his prayers. But most certainly, these convictions did not then ripen to any permanent issue, however they may have served to keep alive the fire of religious feeling, until the moment of God's merciful visitation.

An incident deserves to be recorded, in this connection, not as bearing upon religious experience, but as illustrating the honesty of his character, and the tone of his

moral principles. During his Senior year, the report was
rife throughout the State, that Dr. Cooper was abusing
his position by teaching infidelity in his lectures. A
meeting of the class was called by certain indiscreet
friends of this distinguished man, and resolutions were
introduced repelling the charge, strong appeals being
made to secure a unanimous vote in their favour. It was
a moment of severe trial to young Thornwell, who was a
candidate for the honours of his class, to be awarded by
the very party whom his conscience compelled him to
offend. He resolved to do what he felt to be right, be
the consequences as they may. He opposed the resolutions with such vigour that they were withdrawn; and
the effort to influence public opinion in this way was
abandoned.

It is pleasant to add, that this exercise of moral courage
did not work the forfeiture which he had risked. In fact,
his position had been too cordially and too universally
conceded in his class, to remain unrewarded at last. In
December, 1831, at nineteen years of age, he graduated
with the highest distinction the College could confer, and
pronounced, as usual, the Latin salutatory, on Commence
ment day. He left his *Alma Mater*, followed by universal predictions of his future greatness; and by the path
of these same predictions he returned, six years later, to
be as distinguished amongst its teachers, as before he had
been amongst its pupils.

CHAPTER VII.

HIS CONVERSION.

AFTER obtaining his degree, our friend did not immediately plunge into the great world. Desiring to lay broader and deeper the foundations of scholarship, he proposed to remain within the College halls, as a resident graduate, for the term of one year. Another reason for this course was, his inability to settle down upon the choice of a profession. His repugnance to the Law remains invincible, and he finds himself destitute of the spiritual qualifications necessary to the pulpit. It is evident that he will, if possible, steer clear of both, and live, if the way should open before him, the life simply of a scholar. The difficulty was in the way of support. His independence—we might add, his sense of justice—would not allow him to remain a pensioner upon the bounty which had sustained him thus far. He attempts, therefore, to eke out a subsistence as a private tutor, to such as desired to enter College. But this system of "coaching," as it is termed in English Universities, not being a feature grafted upon our American Colleges, his scheme failed, as might have been anticipated; and he was soon driven from the classic shades he still desired to haunt. His designs, and methods of accomplishing them, will, however, be best unfolded by himself, in the extracts which follow, from a letter addressed to his class-mate, M∴ W. M. Hutson:

"COLUMBIA, *February* 18, 1832.

"DEAR HUTSON: I am going to give thee an epistle truly original in its character, and I will lay thee a wager that, when it is concluded, thou wilt not be able to make head or tail of it.   Imprimis: I am hard engaged in the study of Greek, Latin, and German; I read all sorts of Greek commentators, as Vigerius, Middleton, Mathiæ, and others.   I have commenced regularly with Xenophon's works, and intend to read them carefully.   I shall then take up Thucydides, Herodotus, and then Demosthenes.   After mastering these, I shall pass on to the philosophers and poets.   In Latin, I am going regularly through Cicero's writings.   I read them by double translations; that is, I first translate them into English, and then re-translate them into Latin.   By pursuing this course, I observe the idioms, phrases, and construction of Latin sentences much more accurately than I otherwise would.   In German, I am pursuing Goethe's works, in company with Gladney.   My life, you can plainly see, is not a life of idleness.   There is only one lazy trait in my character, however, of which I cannot divest myself; and that is, sleeping in the morning.   I can no more rise before the sun rises, than I can go to bed before the sun sets.   * * *   I take private scholars, and thereby accumulate a little 'gear.'   If you know of any young men who wish to prepare for College, and can find it in your conscience to recommend me, I would be glad if you would do so.   I cannot bring myself to study law.   It is a good profession to contract the mind and freeze the heart.   Nothing but necessity shall ever induce me to study it.   I find myself most sadly puzzled about selecting a profession; and if I can get along without one, I will never study one.   If I had anything of an ordinary human shape and size, I might marry into wealth enough to support me; but as it is, if I should happen to have a son, it would be a hard matter to distinguish the sire from his issue.   Fancy to yourself what a figure I would cut with a wife, especially if she were fat and portly.

"Burn this scrawl, and believe me your friend,

J. H. THORNWELL."

Whilst he is in the enjoyment of this Academic repose, it may be as well to introduce a letter, written at an earlier date, while still an undergraduate, to one who had been the first companion of his childhood, and who remained his steadfast friend till death.   It not only illustrates the early and constant tendency of his mind to run everything which he observed in life back into the principle on which it rests; but it will serve as the precursor of other letters addressed to the same party:

"COLUMBIA, *October* 7, 1831.
"MR. ALEXANDER H. PEGUES.

"MY DEAR FRIEND: I now sit down, not so much to redeem my promise, as to gratify my own feelings. Though not a votary of Epicurus, I love pleasure; and where can it be found so pure and refined as in the temple of friendship? But I am not about to declaim on this subject in the sickly strains of a school boy, or of a girl just caught in the trap of Cupid. I intend that my letter shall contain, on the contrary, sundry speculations connected with passing events. The first thing that suggests itself is the excitement about the negroes. We have conversed considerably on this subject; but one topic grows out of it, upon which we have never touched. I allude to the singular phenomenon, that frightened men trust to their imagination for their facts, instead of their memories. Our good old metaphysical vocabulary teaches us that the memory is the record of facts; the new vocabulary of fear teaches us that the imagination is. How has this change happened? How comes it to pass that these faculties of the mind have exchanged places, or rather, functions? Has the memory become full, and turned over its surplus to the sister power? I confess that I have thought much on this subject, but I am not satisfied yet. My reflections, such as they are, you are heartily welcome to know.

"Do you remember that beautiful passage in **Shakespeare's** 'Tempest,' where Prospero compares his brother to one,

'Who having unto truth, by telling of it,
Made such a sinner of his memory,
To credit his own lie.'

His brother had told it so often that he was Duke, that, although it was a lie, he came at length to believe it. Here the lie had been so often in his mind as to form a necessary link in the chain of his ideas. It had intermingled itself with all his thoughts. Precisely analogous is the case of those 'sons of terror,' who circulate the most outrageous rumours for serious truth. They have no design to deceive, nor is their false information owing to debility of memory. Where the mind is cool and dispassionate, they remember facts with as much accuracy as other men. But the truth seems to be, that they are alarmed; they naturally turn their attention to the coming danger, and make conjectures about it. These conjectures, however extravagant or erroneous, form, after a while, a necessary part in their trains of thought, and consequently they attach the same credit to their correctness and accuracy. Whenever any facts are afterwards related to them, they, too, are disposed in their own minds, in the same order with their conjectures; and eventually the latter are ascribed to the same author. These remarks will account for the incredible reports, so industriously circulated, about Africa's sooty children. It evidently follows, if this account of the case be correct, that no moral reproach should be fastened on those who give currency to these reports. They believe firmly what they say. They have 'unto truth made such sinners of their memory as to credit their own lie.' I know that many censure them as the propagators of malicious falsehoods; but they should be pitied as the dupes of their fears. But enough of this *black* subject.

I have talked about a subject suggested at home; let me now talk of one suggested on the road. I came to Columbia in company with four jolly fellows, whose minds were never strained with deep thinking. They were constantly whistling, singing, humming tunes, or telling odd stories, which they took to be mighty witty. This circumstance led me to reflect on the various methods which men of empty brains devise in order to kill time. The first I shall notice is music. This seems to remove the languor that hangs over those whose minds are vacancy; and it is used, either for this purpose, or as the natural expression of a pleasing serenity. Have you never observed the negroes at their daily task? They sing; and I can only account for it by supposing that the hours are dull and heavy, and they wish to make them lighter; or they feel very pleasant, and wish to give vent to their agreeable sensations through the channel of music, which is peculiarly fitted for that purpose. You will perceive that I am not speaking of music as an art; but only of those involuntary strains which break forth unobserved. Story-telling is a pastime much akin to music; and methinks, should be ascribed to the same cause. Works of fiction are read by most men for the same purpose. It may be laid down as a general rule, that a vacant mind is always at hard work. In the works of nature there is nothing to amuse him who cannot think. Art has no charms for him. Where, then, shall he look for pleasure, for something to dispel the stupefying languor that hangs over him like a cloud? Shall he turn to his own internal treasures? Alas! all is emptiness within! Poor wretch! what shall he do? Whither shall he turn? In the bitterness of despair, he picks up a novel; but gathers not one solitary idea. He tries poetry, but his brain is empty still. He sings, he whistles; but time flies slowly. He rejoices when dinner comes, and is still gladder to see the approach of night. Employment of some kind, either bodily or mental, is the only cure for that languor of which I have already spoken; and happy is the man who has been inured early to the holy exercise of meditation and thought! Of that man it may be said, 'His mind is his kingdom.' He alone can hold pleasant communion with his own thoughts in solitude and retirement. He possesses an inexhaustible source of entertainment within, when everything without has lost its power to please. When the period shall have passed away in which vivid sensations of pleasure are the sole objects of thought worthy of pursuit; when everything around us shall have lost its charms and fascinations; when we shall have become unable to mingle in business any longer, but must forsake the haunts of men; bitterly will we regret it if we have wasted the morning of life without laying up a rich fund of useful knowledge. I am sorry that an opinion has gone abroad that the acquisition of knowledge is not a moral obligation. To me it appears a matter of incumbent duty. If the love of learning be natural to man; if he has faculties suited to acquire it; if there is sensible pleasure in the discovery of truth, and proportionate pain in mental vacuity; why, then, to improve our minds is surely the voice of nature and of divinity speaking within us. To cultivate those qualities by which any species is distinguished from every other, constitutes, says Aristotle, the peculiar duties of every individual belonging to that species; and man is evidently distinguished from every other animal, no less by his mind than his heart. His intellectual powers form as striking characteristics as his emotions or affections. But the opinion of the world is quite at variance with these propositions. Provided a man is moral, it matters not how uncultivated may be his mind. Ignorance is not followed by disgrace, though vice is attended with opprobrium. For my part, I think it as great a crime to be a fool as to be a knave, provided a man has the means of improving himself in his power; and I think it, too, a very unfortunate circumstance that a different opinion prevails. It is a chief reason that we have so few scholars. Once make it a disgrace to be ignorant, and ignorance will take her flight for ever. But the subject would branch out to infinity, if I stop not now.

"I shall offer for the Librarian's office, but have only a faint hope of success. I came out entirely too late. Under more favourable circumstances the opposition would have been quite sturdy. If I succeed, I shall try to become a respectable scholar.

"Now for the *Southern Review*, No. 14. But, alas, I have no space to say anything of it, except that there is an able article on Bentham and the Utilitarians, written by Legare. I hope to see the downfall of that frigid system of philosophy, which, though not originated by Bentham, it has been the warmest wish of his heart to sustain against truth and reason. Bentham is an atheist, and his philosophy is no better than atheism. It cramps the genius, freezes the vivid and glowing aspirations of a young mind, and clips, with unsparing hand, the lofty flights of intellect. The article on Codification was likewise written by Legare. Professor Nott wrote the article on French Novels. Professor Henry wrote that on Waterhouse's Junius.

"Write to me copiously and openly, as soon as you receive this; and believe me,
Your friend as ever,
J. H. THORNWELL. '

To the same:

"COLUMBIA, *February* 2, 1832.
"MY DEAREST FRIEND: When I reflect upon my dreary and unprotected situation in this world of cares, melancholy and gloom imperceptibly steal upon my mind, and shroud it in its own sable livery. The ship of my fortunes is now launched on the ocean of life; her sails flutter freely in the breeze; but the haven of my hopes is far distant, and I may perish in the storm, before I can reach it in safety. I am now entering on life with all the ardour of youth; but I may soon re-

tire from it, sickened with the treachery of friends, or disgusted with the malignity of enemies. On the other hand, I may succeed in reaching that point of honourable distinction after which my soul panteth, even as the stricken deer panteth for the water-brooks. I may die in the gloomy vale of obscurity, or ascend ' the steep where fame's proud temple shines afar.' I am not foolish enough to dream of passing through a world where good and evil hold a divided empire, without tasting occasionally the bitter, loathsome mixture of vinegar and gall. Sorrows, deep, blighting, withering sorrows, I expect to undergo, and shall, I hope, be prepared to meet them. No matter what form they may assume, I am ready to say, Let them come. If I cannot learn from philosophy how to suffer, I can learn at the foot of the cross. A lamp of consolation burns brightly on Mount Calvary, which has power to cheer and illumine the darkness of woe. To suffer is the lot of all ; to suffer with dignity, is the characteristic of the philosopher ; and it would seem to require something of more than human power to meet death or dire affliction with calmness and tranquillity. But too many instances of philosophical composure, under torturing severity, are on record, to admit of a doubt as to what man can do when he ' screws his courage to the sticking place.' We should draw a distinction, however, between mere obstinacy and moral firmness. The Indian encounters ' the king of terrors' without a flinch or a groan ; but it is only the man of conscious integrity who can meet him with firmness. The difference is this : the one possesses strong nerves and the physical ability to endure pain ; the other is guided by cool reflection and a sound philosophy. The brightest example of unyielding fortitude which ever attracted the wonder of the world, is certainly to be found in the bloody record of its Redeemer's death. He, in truth, died like a God. Guided by His brilliant example, I shall endeavour to bear with dignity all the sorrows with which it may please God to afflict me. Like the oak rent by the lightning from heaven, I may be scathed indeed, but I hope not bent. Let the winds howl and the thunders roar, I shall endeavour to withstand the pelting of the ' pitiless storm,' if not with the grandeur of a philosopher, ' at least with the firmness of a man.'

" But more men are able to endure sorrow with fortitude than bear prosperity with moderation and dignity. Where fortune smiles upon their efforts, men are apt to become maddened by their own success. They manifest their gratitude to a kind Providence, by a dismissal of their understandings. Seat them quietly in the lap of prosperity, and there are some men who will not fail to put on the cap of fools. Intoxicated with unexpected happiness, they sacrifice their reason at the altar of folly. Look upon the world, and see how few can bear to be prosperous ; how few can retain their understandings, when the gale of good fortune blows favourably upon them. It is my wish, therefore, to temper my mind with such discretion, that all shall go well, whether I am rocked in the cradle of prosperity, or chilled with the winter blasts of adversity. I wish to train myself in such a manner, that I can rest undisturbed on

a bed of down or a pillow of thorns. I may fail, however, in my efforts ;
if so, it will be the weakness of humanity. All my hopes, soaring as
they are, may eventually prove to be baseless as a vision's fabric ; if so,
it will be because I cannot use proper means to accomplish my ends.
Happiness is my aim ; it is the object of all men ; they pursue it with
avidity, but most of them catch only a few crumbs as they fall from her
table. I am philosopher enough to know that happiness, like gold, can
never be obtained, if regarded as the primary object of pursuit. We
must seek it through the intervention of some medium, as we seek
money through the medium of labour. None but an alchemist ever
dreamed of getting the precious ore without 'hard toil and spare
meals ;' and none but a downright castle-builder ever thought for a
moment of becoming happy, without placing happiness in some particular object. It does not exist of itself ; it is a mode, a quality of other
things, as heat is a quality of fire, or odour of roses. It exists in them,
and it is to be extracted from them, like oil from a vegetable. It is
plain, therefore, that a preliminary step in our inquiry after happiness,
is to ascertain in what particular things happiness exists ; next, how we
are to obtain these things ; and a third step, of equal importance, is,
after we have obtained the things, how are we to make them subservient
to our happiness. These three preliminary inquiries should be made a
matter of serious, deliberate reflection, by every young man about to
enter on the busy scenes of life. They are all-important, and he who
neglects them is a traitor to his own interests. He cannot be said to
act in life, who proceeds upon no regular, digested system of conduct ;
he does not act, he is *driven* along by the force of circumstances ; and is
entitled to no credit for his actions, how meritorious soever they may
be.

"Some men place happiness in wealth, and consequently strain every
nerve, muscle, and fibre in order to become rich. Others place it in political power ; and some make an awful shipwreck of their fortunes on
the rock of ambition. Some seek it in haunts of dissipation and 'un-
godly glee,' and vex, with their impious mirth, 'the drowsy ear of
night.' The truth is, there are almost as many different opinions on
this subject as there are men in the world. It is plain that there are
three distinct sources of enjoyment—sense, the mind, the heart. There
are, consequently, sensual, intellectual, moral, and religious pleasures. It is in a skilful selection, and a just combination of these, that
the great secret of true felicity consists. Some sensual pleasures are to
be avoided ; some intellectual pleasures are to be enjoyed with care.
Here, judgment and philosophy must come to our assistance ; and he
who trusts to anything but these, builds his house upon a sandy foundation. As to what particular objects are best calculated to afford these
pleasures, every man must be his own judge, and must suit his own particular desires, provided that they be not criminal. Rules may be laid
down ; they may be gathered from experience and reflection. All happiness, then, may be summed up : 1. A sound body ; 2. A sound mind ;

8. A sound heart. Much as I esteem and venerate the awful majesty of virtue, I have not. declaimed so pompously, as some moralists would have done, on the '*mens sibi conscia recti*,' the approving smiles of the conscience ; because there are other pleasures equally indispensable to happiness. I grant that a wicked man cannot be happy ; neither can a man tortured with a fit of the gout. Say what you will, happiness is pleasure. It consists in the possession of agreeable objects ; and twist it as you will, you can make nothing more of it. By arbitrary definitions, you can make it consist in anything ; but I speak of it as it is usually understood ; and I think the remarks I have made on it are just. You can easily conceive, therefore, by what compass I shall direct my course. Such sensual pleasures as my comfort requires, I shall not hesitate to enjoy. My intellectual pleasures shall be as extensive and as elevated as I can make them. My moral pleasures shall consist in unwavering integrity and an ardent love of virtue ; and my religious pleasures, in an humble love of God, a fervent adoration of Him, and a firm reliance on His goodness, and the benevolence of my Redeemer, together with a penitent sorrow for my errors and infirmity. Thus I hope to be as happy as human weakness will permit; and thus, too, I have unfolded to you the general principles by which my life shall be guided.

" At present, I am somewhat cramped for want of money, but hope to struggle through my difficulties. My prospects are not very bright. The season was too far advanced to do much ; next fall will be the time for me to do well. I am halting between two opinions, whether to write or not, for the *Review*. If I succeed, it would be a source of emolument : if I failed, of deep and thrilling mortification. I am so little satisfied with my own composition, that I can hardly persuade myself others would derive from it either instruction or amusement. But whatever I conclude to do, I shall let you know. As to the prize tale, I am by no means enamoured of the idea of being called a *tale-teller* ; yet the money, if I could get it, would be acceptable. I have a notion of writing an article on eccentricity, for the *North American Review*, and on Herschel's philosophy, for the *Southern ;* but like many other projects, may fail to execute them. Have given out all idea of establishing a Literary. In these days of political excitement such an attempt would be hopeless.

" Your friend, as ever,

J. H. THORNWELL."

The experience of three months was sufficient to demonstrate the impossibility of remaining longer a resident graduate in the College, upon the scanty and contingent support upon which he must there rely. In the month of April, accordingly, we find him removed to the town of Sumterville. It is better, however, that the story should

be told in his own words, in the progress of his correspondence with his friend, Mr. A. H. Pegues. In fact,
we have preferred not to curtail the letters written at this
period, in order that the reader may trace the process by
which both his mind and character crystallized into final
shape. Interesting as these letters are, and clearly above
the level of the correspondence usual at his age, they still
bear evident marks of immaturity; in the crudeness sometimes of his generalizations; in the cast of some of the
opinions, which were largely remoulded in after years, and
a certain ambitiousness and egotism of tone, from which
he became subsequently most remarkably free. The
truth is, extraordinary as his powers were from the beginning, Dr. Thornwell in every respect matured slowly.
He was not, at this time, even physically grown; and
there is, perhaps, a closer connexion than we ordinarily
suppose between the complete expansion of the body and
the perfect development of the mind. We shall reach a
period, about three years later, when the whole man undergoes a stupendous transformation, and comes out the
perfect crystal, which he afterwards remained, without any
change beyond the deepening of the channel of his
thoughts, and the constant mellowing of his character.
His present letters are to be read, as exhibiting his period
of growth, of which the change referred to above was the
completing touch. But to the correspondence.

"SUMTERVILLE, *April* 19, 1832.

"MY DEAR FRIEND: About two hours ago, I received your generous
letter; and now am about, not so much to reply to it, as to give a loose
to the current of my own thoughts. You will perceive that I have removed to Sumterville, and will, no doubt, be anxious to know the why
and wherefore. I found that, in Columbia, my prospects waned with
the waning year. So I began to feel tolerably uneasy. Two weeks ago
I was invited here to take charge of a school, but the inducement was
not sufficiently strong. I found, however, that I could get a private
class, yielding me between four and six hundred dollars a year; and Mr.
Richardson, a friend of mine, was anxious for me to stay. He has a
splendid library, and I myself have a very good one. So upon the
whole, I concluded to become a resident of Sumterville. I have not

lost the main benefit which I enjoyed in College, to wit, the conversation of Professor Henry ; for I now correspond with him.

"When I first arrived here, I was seized with a fit of dejection and melancholy, which neither the precepts of philosophy nor the injunctions of religion were able to subdue. I felt myself a solitary hermit amid the humming multitude around me. Poor, desolate and friendless, what could I find to cheer my drooping soul, to rouse my flagging spirits? I felt my situation with a sensitive acuteness that had almost completely prostrated the faculties of my mind. Poverty, disappointment, and misfortune, like the blighting influence of a mildew blast, had withered all my energies and smothered all my hopes. The clear, blue sky was indeed above me, the sun was moving in its majesty, and the day shining forth in its splendour ; but the brilliant prospects of future bliss, which in by-gone days could play before my fancy, had vanished for ever, and, 'like the baseless fabric of a vision, left not a trace behind.' My soul was wrapped in the darkness of midnight, and brooded over its fallen felicity, as the 'vindictive malice of a monk' would dwell upon its schemes of anticipated vengeance. The future seemed enveloped in dark and lowering clouds, those sable precursors of a coming storm ; and from every scathed oak I could hear, in fancy, the ominous croakings of the raven. But there is a balm in Gilead to soothe the agonies of a wounded spirit. There is a holy influence in *Time* to cure the sternest malady of the soul. When philosophy, with all her wisdom, proves of no avail; when religion herself fails, with all her promises of future retribution, to heal our sorrows ; the mercy of heaven has provided a cure in the lapse of *time*. It is the great physician of all our woes. Many a tear has it wiped from the widow's cheek, many a sorrow from the orphan's heart. To its healing influence, the melancholy feelings which have stifled my enjoyment, have at length given way, and 'Richard is himself again.' Time, too, will efface from your bosom the gloomy emotions in which you indulge. Harrowing scenes have recently disturbed the serenity of your mind ; but when their recollection shall have ceased to be so vivid, you will then return to your former tranquillity. This now seems to be beyond the pale of probability ; but consult the experience of your race, and you will no longer be a skeptic. It is an awful thing to part for ever from those whom we love ; and in reading your letter, I felt myself the gloom which overshadowed you, when you bade an eternal farewell to a beloved sister. * * * *

"Since I wrote to you before, I have read Sir James Mackintosh's view of the progress of Ethical Philosophy. It is a work in which a great deal of learning is exhibited ; but still it is exceedingly defective. As a history of Ethical Philosophy, it is quite incomplete, as some very distinguished writers on that subject have been entirely overlooked. On the writers that he does notice, his remarks are sometimes ingenious, but always confused. It is plain that he had no settled and clear ideas of his subject. He wrote in great haste ; and sometimes, it would seem, actually laboured only to fill a certain quantity of paper with a certain quantity of words. His idea that conscience is not a simple, ultimate principle of our nature, but secondary and derivative, is very feebly supported. When he enters on that point he talks in mysticisms. If I had time, I would give you a copious analysis of the book; but must reserve that for another occasion.

"I am a harder student than ever. Day and night I toil at my books, or indulge in my own speculations. I write, too, a great deal in the papers. I have written on various subjects. I wrote a satirical review of the article in the *Southern Review* on American Literature, for the *Columbia Hive.* I wrote one piece on Duelling, and another on Utility, for the *Southern Whig;* and I have now in the press a pamphlet, which will consist of about thirty pages, on Nullification. It will be published in May. Part of it has already appeared in the *Columbia Hive*, in a series of numbers, signed 'Clio.' I shall send you a copy as soon as it is published; but of course you will keep my name, as the author, a secret. I think it contains some strong arguments against Nullification. I do not know the causes that brought about the failure of the *Southern Review.* Write soon.

"Your sincere friend as ever,

J. H. THORNWELL."

To the same:

"SUMTERVILLE, *April* 29, 1832.

"MY DEAR FRIEND: In my last letter, I promised you that my next should contain a general and cursory review of Sir James Mackintosh's 'View of the Progress of Ethical Philosophy.' That promise I shall not now fulfil, inasmuch as I am preparing an article on the subject, which you may have the pain of perusing in print. Richardson and myself design establishing a literary paper in this place, if we can procure a sufficient number of subscribers to warrant the undertaking. If we succeed, the first number will appear in June. It is to be published every fortnight, and each number will contain twenty pages, and all will be original matter, prepared either by ourselves or by our correspondents. Politics, and everything but literature, will be religiously excluded. It will consist chiefly of reviews, essays, moral and philosophical, and original poetry. We propose to call it '*The Southern Essayist.*' It will be printed in octavo form, and on fine paper. The price will be three dollars a year in advance. Richardson owns the press, and of course will be the avowed editor. We will give a grave and dignified tone to our paper, and it will be supported by able correspondents. I think that, if South Carolina could not support the *Southern Review*, she can uphold our literary journal. Literature flows in fountains at the North, and here we have not even a refreshing rivulet. It is a blot on our character, a stain on the fair escutcheon of the South. I have engaged to furnish for each number at least five pages. Sometimes, of course, I will write more. I suppose that I will average two hundred pages a year.   This will be a pretty decent volume.   My first article will be a review of Sir James Mackintosh, which I shall labour with a great deal of care.   The main point to which I shall confine my attention, is the simplicity of the moral sense.   Sir James contends that it is a compound faculty.   I shall attempt to show that his arguments are inconclusive ; and that it is a simple, original ultimate law of the human constitution.   If our paper should not succeed, I will extend the article into a more detailed review of the whole book, and send it to the *North American*.

You will plainly perceive that I have as little relish as ever for a quiet obscurity.   My dreams of hope, and visions of fame, are as airy as they used to be in by-gone days ; and many an aspiration have I poured forth in the lonely forest, or at the dead and solemn hour of midnight.   To die unknown, unhonoured, and unsung, like the wild beast of the field, I hope in God may never be my gloomy fate.   When we walk into our church-yards, among the numberless tombs with which we meet, how few bear any other memorial of their dead than that they lived and died.   They have left us no traces of profound thought, or illustrious achievements, to attract our attention, or inspire our ambition.   They have lived and died ; they have done merely what every brute must do ; and that, too, without their own consent.   If no other monument could have been erected to their memories ; if they have, indeed, derogated from the dignity of their nature, and been silent to the clarion of fame, better, far better, that no stone should point the traveller to the spot of their entombment, than that this worst of satires, which records only the time of their birth and the period of their death, should ever have been imposed on them.   For my own part, I can truly say, that

> " ' With me, nor pomp, nor pleasure,
>   Bourbon's might, Braganza's treasure,
>   So can fancy's dream rejoice,
>   So conciliate reason's choice,
> As one approving word of fame's impartial voice.'

" But by fame I mean the esteem of the wise and good, not the puff of a dunce, or the noisy acclamation of a crowd.   Fame, or rather love of fame, becomes dangerous, when we make *it*, instead of a regard to duty, the ruling principle of action.   It should be always kept in proper subjection to more exalted sentiments.   Let it spur us to generous achievements, but never to a departure from the straight road of moral rectitude.   A permanent reputation must be based on a permanent foundation ; and what is so enduring as real excellence, whether of mind or heart ?   But I am drawing to the bottom of my paper.   I have a dollar which is burning in my pocket ; and which is extremely anxious to be spent for a letter from you, consisting of four or five sheets.   I hope my lonely dollar may not be disappointed.

" Your warm and sincere friend,

J. H. THORNWELL."

The literary projects detailed in this letter, doubtless fell through for want of sufficient patronage, as no reference is made to them in subsequent correspondence. But whilst his mind was occupied with these studies and schemes, the most important event of his life occurred, which changed the whole complexion of his career. On the 13th of May, he united with the Concord Presbyterian Church, a few miles below Sumterville, at that time under the pastoral charge of the Rev. John McEwen. This date is accurately determined by the following brief, but touching prayer, which has floated down to us upon a single leaf, when other and larger productions of his pen have perished through the ravages of time. The prayer is as follows :

"O God! I have to-day made a public profession of my faith in the blessed Redeemer, and taken upon me the solemn covenant of the Church. I would not impute to myself any merit on this account, as I have only done, and that, too, after a long delay, what was expressly enjoined on me in Thy Holy Word. But, O God! I feel myself a weak, fallen, depraved, and helpless creature, and utterly unable to do one righteous deed without Thy gracious assistance. Wilt Thou, therefore, send upon me Thy cheering Spirit, to illume for me the path of duty ; and to uphold me, when I grow weary ; to refresh me, when I faint ; to support me against the violence of temptation and the blandishments of vice. Let me, I beseech Thee, please Thee in thought, word and deed. Enable me to go on to perfection, support me in death, and finally save me in Thy kingdom ; and to the glorious Three-in-one be ascribed all the praise. Amen.

"SUMTERVILLE, *May* 13, 1832."

Not a line more, delineating the spiritual exercises through which he was led to this eventful decision, which involved, as will presently appear, an immediate and unshaken consecration of himself to the work of the ministry.

Happily, however, a ray of light is cast back upon this
portion of his religious history, from words uttered in after
years; which will greatly assist in comprehending what
would otherwise be obscure.   One of his divinity students
relates this conversation, which he was at pains to jot down
within a few hours after it was held.   "Ought we to be
able to point out the exact time of conversion?"   "Not
necessarily ; the substantive change of heart, that is, the
actual change, is probably momentary.   There is a time
in which the man is passive; that is, when the Spirit is
implanting the new nature.   But the *phenomenal* change,
or the *development*, the *manifestation* of that new nature,
is very different in different persons, and in some it is
very slow, and not perceived by the man himself for some
time."   "What, Dr. Thornwell, was your own experience?"   "My own experience," he replied, "was the
most mysterious thing I know of.   From a boy, I was
so constituted that I could rest in no opinion, unless I saw
the first principles on which it hung, and into which it
could be resolved.   I was religiously brought up; but,
even when ten years old, was always trying to reconcile
the difficulties of religion, such as free-agency and the
like.   When at school, this left me to some extent.   When
I went to College, I was under Dr. Cooper ; but read the
Bible through, and became convinced as to the nature of
God's plan of salvation.   In the Senior year, I became
strongly convinced of sin.   But God never had a more
rebellious subject.   Feeling guilty, condemned, and miserable, I was determined to fight it out to the last, that it
was not my fault, and that I was born without any agency
or consent of my own, &c.   Then I thought I had committed the unpardonable sin ; and for three months scarcely
slept, and would sometimes drink liquor for the purpose
of drowning these convictions.   In my childhood, no one
ever suspected that I had such feelings.   At last, light
began gradually to break in upon me; and by degrees I
came out, as I believe, a Christian.   Now I stand firmly

on the Bible; and when bewildered by skepticism, I can still say that I believe God is righteous, and Christ is a Saviour; whether for *me* or not, I sometimes doubt; but never doubt the truth of His word, that 'God is in Christ, reconciling the world unto Himself.'" Recurring again to this subject of his mental conflict, he adds: " I can take you to the very spot, where I stood and gnashed my teeth, and raised my hand, and said, 'Well, I shall be damned, but I will demonstrate to the assembled universe that I am not to blame. God made me as I am, and I can't help my wickedness.' The next thing I knew, when I felt myself a Christian, was that to go to Christ was so simple and easy, that I thought I could show anybody how to do it, and be saved."

The series of facts, thus far developed, seems to be: that he was originally endowed with strong religious susceptibilities; that these were deeply impressed by the influence and teachings of a pious mother; so that, at the age of ten years, he discussed the high problems of "fate and free will," and became the partisan of views against which his heart rebels. This religious interest continues to ebb and flow, until, at sixteen, we find him prepared to surrender advantages and friendships dearly prized, rather than commit himself to a life work other than advocating the claims of Christianity. At College he is brought suddenly in contact with opinions antagonistic to those he had hitherto cherished. Curiosity is aroused. With almost the love of romantic adventure, he rushes into the battle, where a keen and subtle dialectic must supply the weapons of assault and defence. He delivers himself forthwith from the web of materialism, in which he was first in danger of being ensnared by his "idol," Dr. Cooper. He pushes the investigation forward, under an impulse which appears to be, and, doubtless, predominantly was, a purely speculative interest, until his mind is settled. upon the truth of Christianity. With an intellectual conviction which was never afterwards seriously disturbed, he accepts the doctrines of the fall of man, and of recovery by grace alone. We quote again his own language, used of his experience at this period: "Whether man looks within or without himself, the evidences of 'a fall' are overwhelming. But where did he fall? In Adam, as a federal head; for Paul makes death and sin co-extensive, on which theory alone the death of infants can be accounted for. If you take this doctrine from me, I would hold the super-mundane theory, that at some former time, in some former state, now forgotten by us, we each had a trial and fall for himself. Certain it is, that man is a darkened picture of what he once was."

The reader will perceive that, in the terrific conflict which subsequently took place, he does not waver for an instant upon any of these points. When brought under a sense of guilt, both in College and afterwards, he does not dispute the fact of "the fall," nor of the estate of sin and misery, into which the descendants of Adam are introduced. His spiritual conflict turned upon the admission of all this, and his proud will resists the righteousness of the procedure. The precise moment, therefore, of the great change, when, to use his own language, "the new nature was implanted," we suppose to be the moment when, by the gracious work of the Holy Spirit upon his heart, this conflict ceased; and he was enabled to see and appreciate the completeness of redemption by Jesus Christ, and of salvation by faith in His blood. It is of no consequence to determine when, nor how, this was manifested to his own consciousness, or was reflectively placed before him as an object of knowledge. That "phenomenal change" was, doubtless, in his case, very gradually wrought; the truth dawned upon him by degrees. This explains how, at least, he passes quietly and unexpectedly into the Church, without record of any special exercises of soul. The great battle had already been fought, the victory had previously been won by Divine grace, and nothing remained, at this stage, but the dis-

covery of the fact to himself, and the ripening of all into
the final decision. It is the key also to much of his remaining history ; for even now, although in the communion of the Church, his religious experience is but partially developed, and he matures very slowly into the full
proportion of a Christian. His religious impressions, at
this time, were not regarded by others as deep; and his
various addresses delivered now are represented as having
more of the flavour of philosophy than of the gospel. In
his letters, too, of which the reader will presently have a
specimen, there is more of the sentiment of religion than
of its spiritual power over the heart. In fact, the free
Spirit of God chooses His own avenue of approach to
every human soul; and the way by which we are severally
led to Christ forms sometimes an important part of preparation for our future life work. This man was clearly
raised up to be, in his day, an eminent champion for the
truth ; and the sovereign Spirit chose to approach his
heart chiefly through the door of the understanding.
Before any experimental acquaintance was had with the
gospel, it was lodged firmly in his judgment as a glorious
system of truth. This gave to his experience, especially
at the outset, a predominantly intellectual cast. His
convictions as to the truths of Christianity, if they did not
overbear, at least, obscured from view the movements of
the affections. There was not, at first, a proportional
development of the mind and heart. This remained to
be accomplished by and by. The reader will not, of
course, construe these statements into a divorce between
the understanding and the affections, in the act of conversion; only, that in all stages of Christian experience
the two are not always fully co-ordinated, which is the
great business to be achieved in our progress in sanctification.

On this point, there is nothing better than Dr. Thornwell's own analysis of religion, when, in conversation, he
described it as " a state of heart which holds *knowledge*

and *affection* in solution, not successively, but in unity. If you take away the affection, you have only *dogmatism;* if you take away knowledge, you have a mere *spiritualism,* a mere fancy, an *idolatry.* If you preach doctrine to a Christian, the affection springs spontaneously on the apprehension of the doctrine; if you preach the *affection* to him, ·he will immediately, and, perhaps unconsciously, hitch it on the doctrine; and this endorses the maxim that we ought to preach our doctrine practically, and our practice doctrinally." A more formal exposition of the same idea is given by him elsewhere, in these clear and beautiful terms: "The form of Christian knowledge is love; it is a higher energy than bare speculation; it blends into indissoluble unity, intelligence, and emotion; knows by loving, and loves by knowing. The mind sees not only the reality of truth, but its beauty and glory; it so sees as to make it feel; the perceptions are analogous to those of the right and beautiful, in which feeling exactly expresses the intellectual energy."

But we pass from this to his correspondence, in which he reveals the change which has taken place to his friend, Mr. A. H. Pegues.

"SUMTERVILLE, *June* 25, 1832.

"MY DEAR FRIEND: * * * Since you heard from me, a great, yea, an important change has taken place in my condition. I have attached myself to the Presbyterian Church, and shall commence next year the study of Divinity. Two years ago, who would have thought that I would ever have become a Presbyterian clergyman. Religion is but the poetry of the heart, the fair and sublime of the moral world It is an unfailing fountain of elysian enjoyment, from whose streams I heartily wish that all could drink. It is more refreshing than the Nectar poured out by the fair hands of Hebe. Who would not wish to cultivate 'that chastity of moral feeling which has never sinned, even in thought; that pious fear to have offended, though but in a dream; that *pudor* which is the proper guardian of every kind of virtue, and a sure preservative against vice and corruption?' The love of God is a sublime and solemn enthusiasm, counteracting the downward tendencies of self-love; the evidence of a regenerated nature, purified from the contaminations of the world and the body; acting under the influence of grander views, and re-asserting its original glory and perfection.

" Yesterday I delivered an address before the Bible Society, which, I believe, was very well received. Some weeks ago, I gave an exhortation from the pulpit, which had a fine effect; but I am awfully afraid that the orator is too conspicuous in everything I say. My periods are too nicely rounded, and the whole composition too laboured for a miscellaneous crowd. They admire the speaker, but are not made any better; they are delighted as they would be with a Fourth of July oration; but are not persuaded to turn from the error of their ways. They compliment me here very highly, and I am afraid that I sometimes am pleased with their admiration; but I pray fervently to God, to guard me against vanity, and to direct my footsteps by His wisdom. I am still as warmly as ever devoted to the Classics and Metaphysics. I look upon them both as absolutely essential in the education of a clergyman. I have purchased a complete set of Cicero's works, which I have read very attentively.

" Your sincere friend, as ever,

J. H. THORNWELL."

CHAPTER VIII.

HIS TEACHING AT CHERAW.

AT what time, or under what circumstances, his engagement at Sumterville was terminated, we are not informed; but in November, 1832, he is amongst his old friends in the town of Cheraw. The following letter, gloomy as it is, cannot be withheld, as it reveals a phase of character which was temporary; confined, indeed, almost wholly to this period of his life, and of which hardly a trace could be detected by the friends of his later years. It is written to J. Johnston Knox, Esq.

" Cheraw, *November* 22, 1832.

"My Dear Friend : Circumstances, which it is quite useless to mention, have prevented me from writing to you as early as I should otherwise have done. To a mind constituted like my own, the condition in which I find myself placed abounds in subjects of disquietude and sorrow. Naturally of a gloomy temperament, even the brightest objects around me I am prone to clothe in a sombre hue. How dark and forbidding, therefore, must those appear which are really tinged with the darkness of calamity ! My morning dream of hope, my early visions of future bliss, have been sadly obscured by the cloud of disappointment. The friends of by-gone days, the sportive companions of my childhood, are many of them mouldering in the silent grave ; and one whom I love as a father, who has done more for me than millions can repay, is now standing on the brink of the tomb. An incurable disease has, I fear, seized upon his vitals, and I know not how soon I may be called to attend his body to the narrow house appointed for all living. It may be years, or it may be months ; for nothing is so subtle and deceptive as pulmonary consumption. Another of my patrons is just recovering

103

from a severe attack of bilious fever, and I myself have been fixed to the sod. Bring my situation home to yourself, and conceive, if you can, the wilderness of soul to which it has reduced me. I look upon the world with new eyes. I know its vanities, and feel its emptiness. There was a period (and I can hardly revert to it without a tear) when my bosom glowed with the rapture of hope; when the future appeared to me arrayed in the garlands of joy; when my nightly dreams were of bliss, and my waking thoughts of approaching felicity. But the delusion has disappeared, and all the phantoms of beatitude, which once allured me, have faded away. 'Delirium is our best deceiver.' 'Our lucid intervals of thought' only expose to us our real condition. They unveil before us the naked skeletons of misery, and torture our minds with woeful forebodings of disappointment and sorrow.

"But I have no disposition to dwell upon the sad picture of human suffering, which it would require no exercise of fancy to depict. Our calamities are all intended for our good. They are merely chastisements from the hand of a kind and benevolent Father; and we should regard them in the light of instruction, not of wrath. 'Those whom He loveth, He chasteneth,' says the Apostle; and it would be well for us to keep this important truth ever in our view, to prevent us from murmurs, and to secure our improvement. In the garden of life there is indeed placed a sepulchre, but it is placed there for our benefit. In walking among the roses and lilies, it is good for us to stumble occasionally on the sad monument of human decay. From it we could draw instructive lessons concerning the instability of all earthly enjoyment, the delusive nature of all earthly hopes, and the final consummation of all earthly expectations. It would teach us to contemplate our latter end, and to prepare in earnest for appearing before the dread tribunal of our Redeemer and Judge. Skeletons and bones, the coffin and the shroud, the winding sheet and sepulchre, are the most instructive volumes we can possibly peruse. Their lessons are written in dark characters, but they are only the more legible on that account. I love to take a solitary ramble in a church-yard. A sort of gloomy, melancholy pleasure is diffused over my mind as I read the tale that is told by the little mounds which conceal what once was life and health and animation. The mournful tribute of affection to departed worth, the brief history on the gravestone of the dust that lies beneath it, all speak to me in thrilling accents, which find a pensive response from my own bosom. 'Man is like a thing of nought, and his days as a shadow that fleeth away.' But brighter visions open upon us beyond the grave; and thanks be to God, who giveth us the victory over the king of terrors! Jesus Christ has disarmed death of his sting, and hell of its malice. Let us cling to Him, and all will be well with us. Christianity is the best gift of God to man. The Bible is a treasure whose value cannot be calculated. On the darkest midnight of the soul it pours the beams of day. The poisoned arrows of affliction become, under its influence, teachers of virtue; and even prosperity itself grows brighter, when illumined by the 'Sun of Righteousness.' Let us, then, hold fast to this religion. It is precisely adapted to our circumstances; and if we give it up, we plunge into an awful chaos. It is indeed a blessed thing to be a Christian; and I would not surrender the hope that is in me for worlds upon worlds, or systems upon systems. Were it not for the consolations of Christianity, who could bear to drag out a miserable existence on this earthly ball! A wounded spirit would be intolerable without the alleviations of the gospel. Those, therefore, should truly be anathema who would rob us of this blessing. But I must leave this subject.

"My prospects are flattering for the Principal's place in the Academy next year. The salary is $700, payable quarterly.

"Your sincere friend,

J. H. THORNWELL."

This hope was soon realized. In January, 1833, having just passed his twentieth birth-day, he was associated with Mr. Donald (now the Rev. Dr.) McQueen, in teaching the Cheraw Academy, where he had been himself prepared for College. Mr. McQueen resigning in October, he continued, in conjunction with Mr. Thomas E. B. Pegues, in the same important position, until June, 1834; at which time we shall follow him to a different sphere. During these eighteen months he gave unmistakeable proof of those qualities which afterwards distinguished him as a teacher. The same enthusiasm was displayed in imparting knowledge which he had always exhibited in acquiring it. His patience and zeal were unbounded. He would *bribe* the brightest scholars to spend their Saturdays with him in the school-room, and would often protract the exercises of the day, until the gathering darkness drove him, with the class, to the open door for the remains of light left by the setting sun. Laborious and patient with the more docile pupils, in whom he could arouse an interest similar to his own, his temper would break forth sometimes against the indolent. So intense was his own passion for learning, that he failed in sympathy with such as were indifferent to their opportunities. It was something he could not understand; and a feeling of contempt mingled with his anger against the methods of evasion to which the thoughtless would resort. At the same time, he was so companionable with his pupils, so devoted to their welfare, and so much interested in their sports as well as their studies, as to win their respect and love, notwithstanding occasional severity in his discipline. One of these pupils furnishes this sketch: " I went to school to Mr. Thornwell after his graduation. He was very thorough as a teacher, took great interest in all the recitations, neglected nothing, and would complete the exercises, even if the approaching twilight drove him to the door to get light enough to read by. On such occasions, the boys would increase the darkness by closing the window shutters, while he was so absorbed with the class as to be utterly unconscious of it. They would also make all kinds of noises, by scraping their feet on the floor, dropping slates, coughing, clearing their throats, &c. For a time he would seem unconscious of all this ; but would occasionally be aroused, and then what a storm would come! The most cutting sarcasms and withering reproofs, making the guilty shrink away in shame and confusion. These were really, at times, tirades of personal abuse, and exhibited the utmost contempt for the meanness and baseness he was reproving." When it is remembered that he had not yet learned to put a check upon his powers of invective, before which his equals in age and his peers in knowledge always quailed, it is not strange that these boys should cower beneath the flash of his eye, and the overwhelming sneer which he could throw into his tones. But the monotony of the school-room furnishes few incidents for a narrative. Let it give way to his correspondence, which opens again the experience of his inner life. The following, addressed to his friend, Mr. Knox, is tinged with the same melancholy as the preceding ; but it throws light upon his religious history.

"CHERAW, *June* 27, 1833.

" MY DEAR FRIEND : I received your kind and cheering letter some time ago, and would have replied to it immediately, but my attention was so much taken up with the necessary preparations for my examination that I could find no leisure for the calls of friendship. Dream not for a moment that it was from want of disposition; my feelings yet flow generously and freely in their old channels. It was purely the want of time. I have now a vacation, a rest of two weeks; and I propose to visit my 'old stand.' There are many hallowed associations in my mind connected with Sumterville. Many a day of agony I indeed spent there; many a bitter disappointment I experienced there; but my darker hours are now so blended with holier recollections, that the sting is extracted from anguish, and the wormwood from sorrow. I love to think on by-gone days. There are many things presented by a retrospect of the past, over which I would willingly draw the veil of oblivion. Ordinary misfortunes can be cured by time; common sorrows are soon forgotten; or, if they continue to be remembered, they are remembered with a melancholy pleasure. But there is a disease of the heart which preys upon the vitals, and mocks at remedy. It is a canker-worm consuming its finest energies, and destroying its fairest hopes. Wherever it touches, it spreads a moral desolation, and converts the fruitful field into a waste and vacant wilderness. It is *despair*. The sirocco and simoon, the tempest and the whirlwind, are fearful things; but they can and do pass away. But despair is an eternal midnight of the mind. Days, months, and years may roll on; it still remains, a fierce destroyer of all joy, all comfort, all peace.   *   *   *   *

"In Cheraw we have something of a revival of religion. Our good pastor, Mr. Powers, has been labouring hard for the last week amongst us. Many are serious, and others profess to be converted. I confess, for my own part, that I have been mightily revived. The Spirit of the Lord is among us; the hand of the Most High is with us. Men in all quarters are awakening to the importance of the subject, and the millenium is in its morning dawn. I rejoice to see it come. 'Come, Lord Jesus, come quickly.' This is the prayer of every genuine Christian. Would to God that I could be delivered entirely from sin, that I could live entirely and unreservedly to the Lord Jesus Christ. Let us be awake to the importance of the subject; let us remember that the blood of sinners is required at our hands. To be a follower of the Lamb involves a fearful responsibility. Let us all shake off our besetting sins. I know what mine is; it is the *blues;* and would to God that I could get entirely rid of them. They give me much uneasiness. They are partly hereditary, and partly the result of dyspepsia; but they are yet sinful. I have, by the grace of God, almost succeeded in shaking them off; they have lost much of their bitterness. Believe me,

"Your sincere friend,

J. H. THORNWELL."

The three years following his graduation from College, from 1832 to 1834 inclusive, form a clear parenthesis in the life of Dr. Thornwell; during which his character

appears to differ from what it was both before and after
it.   It was, as we have seen, the period of a great religious
change; it was also the season of a great physical transformation.   He grew at least a head taller, and reached to
the ordinary height of men.   His complexion became
clear, throwing off its sallow hue; and though never
ruddy, it was not unduly pale, but wore the appearance
of health.   His hair, which rivalled the raven in its blackness, lay smooth and soft upon a head, which was never
large, but exceedingly well developed.   The expansion
was complete, from the diminutive stature which had
marked him from childhood, to the full proportioned
man; with the spare habit, and carriage of body rather
distinguished by easy negligence than grace, which is so
well remembered by all who knew him in public life.
This change, too, was wrought by the simple force of
nature herself, without the adventitious aids which might
have been supplied.   On the contrary, his habits were
precisely such as should have thwarted this favourable
development.   Sitting up, in severe study, to a late hour
at night, frequently so absorbed as to be arrested by the
morning's dawn still at his desk, indifferent as to food,
negligent of recreation and exercise, thoroughly inattentive
to the demands of nature in all respects, it is not strange
that he became the victim of dyspepsia, which threw its
oppresive gloom over a spirit constitutionally elastic and
buoyant.   The only wonder is, that his frame should
have matured at all, or that it should have possessed any
of the vigour and endurance that marked his future years.

   The prevailing sadness breathed into the correspondence
of this period, had also a moral source, to which we recur
with all the delicacy possible.   His affections had become
seriously entangled; which, like the educational "first-
love" of most men, was destined to issue in disappointment.   The two young hearts would indeed have disposed
of the case differently.   But the stern prudence of older
heads could see little that was promising in the poverty

of the ardent wooer, nor in his unsettled plans, his soaring visions, and his somewhat fitful temper. The attachment, nevertheless, was strong, and runs through the whole of this period. As it came to nought, we have not chosen to bring it into prominence; and would gladly have withheld even this allusion, if it were not the dark thread in the web of his present experience, needed to explain the gloom with which it is distempered. Whether these combined causes are sufficient to explain it or not, a due consideration of all the facts compels us to regard him as being, during this transitional period, in a morbid and abnormal condition. This gloom, for example, was not constitutional; for if he had one characteristic more prominent than any other in his after life, it was the playfulness into which he would relax when unbending his mind from severe study. It was this wonderful elasticity, springing from a native gaiety and joyousness of spirit, that kept him alive amid the exactions of laborious toil. Then, too, the original and deep affectionateness of his nature rendered it impossible for him to be unamiable; he was capable of quick resentments, but never of sour misanthropy. It would, therefore, be severely unjust to take occasional and external exhibitions of fretfulness as the criterion of habitual character. It would be wise to consider whether the natural disposition might not be warped by constraining influences from without, throwing it out of its normal state, and producing the irregularities which are observed.

The friend most intimate with him at this period, and whose heart was knit to him as that of Jonathan to David, writes: "I think he had, at times, the most perverse disposition I ever met with. His prejudices were easily excited; and he could neither see a flaw in those whom he loved, nor a virtue in those whom he disliked. Avaricious of praise, yet too proud to solicit attention, he writhed under any appearance of neglect. Impatient of contradiction, he had a feeling akin to scorn and contempt for those whose opinions differed from his own. His morbid feelings rendered him suspicious of slights which were never intended, whilst his invectives were reckless of those who chanced to displease him. His sensitiveness kept every company uneasy in which he was thrown, lest some unguarded remark should cause an explosion. His eye, which was a little dreamy in repose, glared like lightning when he was aroused ; and the sneer which curled his lip will never be forgotten by such as have withered beneath its sarcasm. His later friends can form no adequate idea of the terror of that countenance, when inflamed by anger. The flash of the eye always remained ; but its inexpressible fierceness was quenched by Divine grace."   The witness, whose language is here given, proceeds to furnish an illustration of this untamed spirit. " I remember that he drove from the Academy a gentleman who had been a former teacher, but was now placed over an institution for females in the town, yet retaining a general supervision of the Academy. He was a reputable scholar, but a complete pedant; in fact, a fair specimen of a Boston public-school teacher. He had notions about discipline, order, and other things, which Thornwell despised. On one unfortunate day, he undertook to examine Thornwell's class in Greek; who sat with an ominous curl of the lip, and an eye darting fire from beneath those drooping lashes. At length, a boy was corrected in his translation. Never did a panther leap upon his prey with more ferocity, than did Thornwell upon his unhappy victim. He fairly shouted, 'the boy is right,' and proceeded to prove it beyond all dispute. The old teacher was perfectly overwhelmed ; and feeling himself degraded in the eyes of the pupils, could never be induced again to cross the threshold of the Academy."

There is, perhaps, a psychological explanation of much of this. We incline to think that most youth of large promise encounter a trying middle passage, just as they enter upon manhood. Conscious of mental power, they

are not able yet to take its exact measure. The successes of their novitiate have sharpened ambition, without
giving the precise gauge of their capacity. Visions of
hope float ill-defined in the air, while life spreads out
before them a vast and unexplored sea. As they stand
upon its shores, and look across its tempestuous billows, a
vague dread seizes upon the spirit, lest it should prove
unequal to the dangerous voyage. Its perils are magnified
by the fear through which they are viewed; and a sick-
ening conflict ensues betwixt the ambition which would
court the trial, and the self-esteem that cannot brook the
anticipation of possible defeat. A feverish irritability is
the result; which, if indulged, becomes excessive and
tormenting. The mind casts round for some presage of
the future, and seeks in the adulation of partial friends a
prophecy of ultimate success. It is challenged, if withheld; and there is a jealous assertion of prerogatives
which are far from being established. The whole condition is one of restlessness and of morbid sensibility, which
renders the party unhappy, and, therefore, unamiable;
but which generally disappears, as soon as the duties of
life are fairly assumed, and the pressure of responsibility
is really felt. More or less of this marks every boy at
"the disagreeable age," when the down first begins to
appear on the peach; and which partly justifies the raillery
of the lady who said, "it is a pity there is not an asylum
where they could all be put till they have passed the
disagreeable age." But it is immeasurably more intense
with youth of real intellect, tortured by ambition, but uncertain of their real strength. If to this we add the other
causes which have been previously named, it will be easy
to account for all that has called for criticism in Mr.
Thornwell's character, at this period; and we can better
understand the completeness of the revolution, as soon as
he took hold upon life, and entered upon its earnest work.
Beneath all these faults, however, there was much that
was truly heroic. He was ardent and generous in his

affections, trustful and confiding in his friendships, artless
and simple in his conduct, high-minded and honourable in
all his purposes and acts. He was honest in his search
after truth, to whose authority he always bowed with absolute docility ; and was incapable of disguise or evasion
in any form. There was no infusion of malignity, even
in his sarcasm, and his explosions of anger were followed
by humiliation and acknowledgment. Even in the affairs
of the heart, where the temptation is so strong to over-
reach opposition, he was the soul of honour, and came
out of these delicate complications, without a stain upon
his integrity. He just needed to be turned upside down,
and to bring the better qualities to their legitimate supremacy.

His religious experience was, of course, alike defective;
the leaven had not yet leavened the entire lump. He
adhered still to the hope he had expressed, and was active in prayer meetings and the like. But his addresses
were lacking in spirituality. They were effective in
demolishing infidelity, and establishing the truth of
Christianity : sometimes directed sharply against the
inconsistencies of professors of religion, whom he would
describe as " needing bells on their necks to distinguish
them from the world." But the sweet savour of the
gospel did not impart unction to his words. The friend
above cited writes of him : " He lacked humility, and did
not feel sufficiently his lost condition as a sinner. All
this was too much a matter of the intellect. He had not
studied God's Word as he studied other books. He got
at his doctrines rather as they were discussed by other
men, and was not pervaded by their spirit." A painful
impression of this sort was made upon the Presbytery of
Harmony, upon his application, in the autumn of 1833,*
to be taken under its care, as a candidate for the ministry.

* The Presbytery met at Winnsborough, Fairfield District, November
29th, 1833 ; and Mr. Thornwell was taken under its care, as a candidate
for the ministry, on the 2d of December.

His examination was so unsatisfactory upon his personal experience, and his views for seeking the sacred office, that the Presbytery hung in doubt what decision to render. The scales were turned at last by the wise counsel of the Rev. Robert W. James, a man eminent for his practical judgment, whose name is still as " ointment poured forth," in all the region where he lived. Said this judicious counsellor : " Notwithstanding the difficulties in the way, I think I descry the root of the matter in this young man. Remember that, in taking him under our care, we are not licensing him to preach. If, hereafter, we shall find him still labouring under these unsatisfactory views, we can then drop him. There is something, however, about him, which impresses me with the idea that he will yet be a man of great usefulness." It is pleasing to know that Mr. James lived long enough to have his rare penetration justified, and to see his hopeful prophecy fulfilled.

An event occurred now which affected considerably the movements of our friend. The Rev. Dr. Ebenezer Porter, of the Theological Seminary at Andover, Massachusetts, spent the winter of 1833–'4 in the South, to which he was driven in feeble health. A considerable portion of it was spent in Columbia, South Carolina, whither he was attracted by the society of his friend, the Rev. George Howe, D. D. In the school of the prophets over which Dr. Howe presided, Dr. Porter delivered the Lectures on Homiletics, subsequently published, and extensively used as a text-book in that department. Upon his return homeward, in the spring of 1834, he took Cheraw in his route, for the purpose of visiting one of his former pupils, the Rev. Urias Powers, the pastor of the church in that town. Mr. Thornwell was here introduced to him, as one having the gospel ministry in view ; to whom Dr. Porter tendered the privileges of the Andover Seminary, without cost, if he chose to avail himself of them. This invitation was accepted, under the urgent persuasion of Mr. Powers, and in the hope of enjoying superior advantages in acquiring the Oriental languages. To this place we shall then follow him, in the next chapter.

CHAPTER IX.

RESIDENCE AT CAMBRIDGE.

Sudden Removal to Andover, Massachusetts.—Thence to Cambridge. —Reasons for the Latter Change.—Letter from Mr. Robbins.— Correspondence.—Amusing Story of a Visit to Boston.—Hears Mr. Everett's Eulogy upon Lafayette.—Contrasts between Different Stages in the Same Life.—Letters.—His Return Home.

ABOUT the middle of the year 1834, Mr. Thornwell, being released by the trustees from his engagement as Principal of the Academy at Cheraw, finds himself at Andover, Massachusetts. He arrived during the vacation of the Divinity School; and not being pleased with the place, or with the advantages it offered, transferred his residence at once to Cambridge. The impression made upon him, and the incidents of his brief sojourn in Massachusetts, will be best exhibited through his own letters; with which this chapter will be exclusively occupied. The first is addressed to his former patron, General James Gillespie :

"Harvard University, *August* 13, 1834.

"My Dear General : You have above an exact representation of the Theological Seminary at Andover. The building which I have marked (A) is Phillip's Hall ; (B) is the Chapel ; (C) is Bartlett Hall ; and (D) is Phillip's Academy. They are all four stories, and made of brick. The trees are large elms. The college-yard is cut into walks, and each walk is lined with trees. The rest of the area is covered with a rich grass, occasionally shaded by a branching elm. Such is the external appearance of Andover. I have left the institution for good, and shall state to you my reasons for this sudden movement. 1. The advantages were not such as I expected. Dr. Robinson has left the institution, and there is neither German, Syriac, Chaldee, nor Arabic teacher. Nothing, in short, is taught there which is not taught equally well at Columbia. Professor Stuart is the only able man in the institution. 2. The Theology taught there is such as I cannot countenance ; it is awfully

115

New School.   3. The habits of the people are disagreeable to me.   4. I
have no idea of settling in this country.   No money could induce me
to do it.   *   *   *

"I came to Cambridge to-day, and shall spend the remainder of the
year here as a resident graduate.   I shall devote myself chiefly to Hebrew and German ; will take a room in Divinity Hall, and attend regularly the lectures of Harvard.   I intend to prepare myself for the Senior
Class in Columbia* next January, being deficient only in Hebrew.

"Yours as ever,

J. H. THORNWELL."

In the following, addressed to him, the reader would
detect, without the signature, the tone and style of his
old Mentor, Mr. Robbins:

"CHERAW, *August* 23, 1834.

"DEAR JAMES : It gave me great pleasure to receive your letter of
the 6th, about a week since, and to find that you had settled down on
your plan of occupation for the year.   I doubt not that the employment
of your mind on subjects of higher importance, will direct it from the
sickly sensibility about those you have left behind you, which ever en-
hances the absent, and minishes the comforts of our present situation.
This, James, is nothing more or less than *home-sickness.*   You may
never have felt it before, but rest assured it is a very common disease.
There is nothing of an alarming character in either its symptoms or results.   'Men have died, and worms have eat them, but not for *home-sick*
love ;' and, for your consolation, I can assure you, (for I have travelled
over every inch of ground you are now treading,) that the first serious
occupation of your mind on any other subject of interest or importance
will infallibly dispel the dark clouds which may now be gathered over
your horizon.   You will find skies as fair, hills as green, and breezes as
soft in the latitude of Massachusetts, as those you leave behind you.   I
was glad to see that you were becoming more at ease than when you
penned your first letter from Baltimore, which A. G. showed me.   Indeed, I could wish you had not written at all, when in that frame of
mind.   It always gives occasion to our enemies to predict evil results,
when they find us early and easily daunted in our projects ; and I confess that pride, more than anything else, contributed to reconcile me to
the absence from my home.   I knew that there were those who would
chuckle at my disappointment and return ; and I resolved, at all hazards,
to disappoint their malice ; and by perseverance I did it.   And you may
be sure it is just so in your case.   I have no earthly doubt but your
perseverance will so disappoint your enemies, and achieve for yourself

* His reference here is to the Theological Seminary, then under the
care of the Synod of South Carolina and Georgia, and located in Columbia, South Carolina.

a reputation, and standing, and situation in life, which will be in every respect enviable. But let me caution you against too great expectation at first. Here you have a degree of reputation for scholarship and attainments, which has not followed you in your new residence. You have got to create such a character *there*, and time is required to do this. No intelligent people, especially those about you now, are captivated at first dash; but they are sure to give credit to talent and learning. And when they find it testified by a sufficient number of manifestations, they will be as proud to foster you, as you will be pleased to receive their patronage.

"My wife often says, 'How much we shall miss James this winter;' and when she heard you were going to return in September, she said, 'For our sakes she should admire to have you; but on your own account, she would have you remain where you are.' In fine, my dear James, take courage. I have only room to say, go to Boston, call on my brother, ask him for letters to Mr. Folsom, Ware, Palfrey, Hedge; call on them occasionally, sit half an hour with them, and give them opportunity to know you. I do not fear for your principles in religion;·they withstood the insidious approaches of Dr. Cooper, and they cannot now give way to error, in a less dangerous form. My dear boy, I will pray for you; and I feel strongly confident that the wise and merciful Being, who overrules all things for our good and His own glory, will give you His power to triumph over every difficulty, and set you at last at His own right hand for ever.

"Yours affectionately,

W. H. ROBBINS."

In the letter which follows, addressed to his friend, Mr. A. H. Pegues, the first portion is occupied by a recapitulation of his reasons for leaving Andover, which have been clearly stated. It is, therefore, omitted. The letter is dated,

HARVARD UNIVERSITY, *August* 14, 1834.

MY DEAR FRIEND: * * * * I am now comfortably settled in this venerable abode of science, literature, and learning. The Library contains thirty-nine thousand volumes, and the Athenæum Library of Boston, sixty thousand; to both of which I have access, besides the privilege of attending all the Lectures of the College. You see, therefore, that the advantages I enjoy, and the facilities for study, are liberal and encouraging. I room in Divinity Hall, among the Unitarian students of Theology; for there are no others here. I shall expect to meet and give blows in defence of my own peculiar doctrines; and God forbid that I should falter in maintaining the faith once delivered to the saints. I look upon the tenets of modern Unitarianism as little better than downright infidelity. Their system, as they call it, is a crude compound of negative articles, admirably fitted to land the soul in eternal misery. The peculiarity of their belief consists in *not believing*. Read over their tracts and pamphlets, and you will find that they all consist, not in establishing a better system, but simply in *not believing* the system of the Orthodox. Ask them to tell you what they *do* believe, and they will begin to recount certain doctrines of the Orthodox, and tell you very politely that they do *not* believe these. The truth is, they have nothing positive; their faith is all negative; and I do not know that the Bible holds out a solitary promise to a man for *not believing*. And yet these *not-believers* talk about Christian charity with a great deal of pompousness, and take it hugely amiss that they are not regarded by pious men as disciples of Jesus. Have you seen "Norton's statement of reasons for *not believing* the doctrine of Trinitarians?" It is a queer book, and should be read just for the curiosity of seeing its absurdity and nonsense. When a difficult passage stares him in the face, he turns it off very nicely, by saying that Paul was mistaken here; that he did not understand the real nature of Christianity, and therefore blundered. Sometimes he makes even Jesus Christ go wrong; because he happened to be busy about something else, and did not have time to correct Himself. Now, a man who can swallow such stuff as this, can swallow anything. It is an open defiance of all the established laws of exegesis; and the doctrines, which need such miserable subterfuges to support them, cannot come from God. No, my friend, we are never safe in departing from the simple declarations of the Bible. Let me entreat you to read Shuttleworth on the consistency of Revelation with reason. It is the ablest work which has issued from the British press since Butler's Analogy. Read it carefully, and you will find philosophy bowing at the altar of religion; read it prayerfully, and you must become a Christian.

"The Unitarian will tell you that experimental religion is all an idle dream; but, my friend, believe not the tale. It is no such thing. The truly pious man walks with God; he is under the influence of the Holy Spirit; the consolations of the Gospel support him in affliction, and cheer him in distress. There is such a thing as holy communion with the blessed Trinity; as a peace of mind which passeth all understanding; as joy in the Holy Ghost, and consolation in believing. There is no fanaticism, no enthusiasm here; it is all sober truth; and those who laugh at these things now, will weep bitterly in a coming day. May God be with us both! May He take us under the shadow of His wing, and save us in the hour of final retribution!

"Yours, as ever,

J. H. THORNWELL."

To General James Gillespie:

"HARVARD UNIVERSITY, *August* 27, 1834.

"MY DEAR GENERAL: As you have always manifested a lively interest in the cause of education, I have taken the liberty of sending you a little volume on the subject, containing many valuable remarks ; but interlarded, I think, with a great deal of error. In regard to the classics, and the principle may be extended to every other study, the question should be, not what is the speediest method of acquiring them, but what is the *best*. By the best method, I mean that which most powerfully developes, employs, and strengthens the faculties of the mind. Childhood and youth are the forerunners of manhood, and are periods of life evidently designed for the attainment of. those *habits* of thought and reflection which will be needed in more advanced years. The great principle which should be kept steadily in view, in every system of education, is that of intellectual *discipline*. You intend your son for a lawyer ; but you certainly would not think of teaching him Law until he became a man. You would give him, however, the *habit* of mind which a lawyer ought to possess. Let knowledge come afterwards. A man's mind is a bundle of *susceptibilities* lying dormant. The aim of education is to call forth and exercise these susceptibilities, and to develope them all fully and harmoniously. You must, therefore, present to the inactive mind some *fit* subject. Any subject will not do. A man possesses the susceptibility of pity ; but sorrow and suffering are the only occasion of its development. So a man possesses the susceptibility of imagination, but only certain subjects will develope it. Who would think of exciting the fancy by a theorem of Euclid ; or of training the discursive faculty by Robinson Crusoe ? It is not enough to develope the powers of the mind ; they must be developed in harmonious and just proportions. Give no one power the preponderance, but train the whole of them fully.

" Taking it for granted, then, that the aim of education is to develope and train all the powers of the mind in just proportions, and bearing in memory that the powers of the mind are a mere bundle of susceptibilities which require *fit* subjects to call them forth, the only practical question seems to be, What are these fit subjects, and what is the best manner of presenting them to the dormant faculties? These questions embrace the whole ground of education ; and on a proper solution of them depends a proper system of intellectual discipline. In so far as boys are concerned, I maintain that the classics are the fit subjects ; but I differ widely from the book which I have sent you, with respect to the best method of teaching them. I keep my eye fixed steadily on the end, discipline ; and I do maintain that the mind is more exercised and more fully developed by thorough grammatical analysis than by any other method. To teach Latin and Greek as spoken languages is no doubt the speediest plan of communicating a knowledge of them. But then it trains the memory in disproportion with the other faculties ; it destroys the harmony and equilibrium of the mind. By the other course, this harmony is sustained. You train the memory in getting the grammar by heart ; you train the judgment by an application of the rules ; you train the power of analysis by the difficulties of etymology. In the reading of the classics with a diction-

ary, I do not know of a single faculty which is not employed, and employed, too, to its full extent. It is the teacher's duty to see that the
instruction is thorough. In our present systems of teaching, the plan
suggested by our author is altogether impracticable. We must have a
large number of scholars to support the school. Mr. Locke suggested
the same method long ago. It did not take then, and I hope it will not
take now. These are my views, expressed as briefly as I am able to do
it. One hint more in regard to your own Academy, and I am done
with the subject. Would it not be well to divide that institution into
two parts, English and Classical? You could then arrange the parts
into classes. This would render the course of instruction more thorough
and accurate. Should you publish your plan, it would give your school
a character, and ensure a liberal patronage. I have thought much on
this subject, for I am warmly interested in the prosperity of the Cheraw
Academy.

" Harvard Commencement took place to-day, and was truly a poor
exhibition of talent and learning. Could old Johnson or Walker have
risen from the tomb, they would have shuddered at the mongrel dialect
of the Harvard scholars; for it was, in truth, neither Latin, Greek, nor
English. The pronunciation of English is most shamefully neglected
here, both by teachers and students; and whenever occasion requires,
they coin words without any compunction. There were, however, four
excellent speeches; the rest were flat enough. The Phi-Beta-Kappa
will be delivered to-morrow; and I shall send you a copy, as soon as it is
published.

" I met Professor Nott here to-day. He told me that he was publishing fictitious tales, having regularly embarked on the sea of novel-writ-
ing. He has relinquished the task of writing Sumter's life. Fiction,
he says, is better suited to his taste than biography. I shall call on him
in a day or two, and spend, for once again, a few happy hours.

" I am myself writing an article on the study of the Greek, or rather
of the classics. It will probably appear in the January number of the
North American Review. I have written about ten pages, but shall not
be able to finish it before the middle of September. I am also collecting materials for an elaborate work, on which I hope to found a reputation. It is a treatise on the philosophy of the Greek language. This
will not appear under a year or two, and Professor Henry must see it, before it comes to light. I wish to establish a literary character in my native State; for I have an eye on a Professorship in the Theological
Seminary at Columbia. That institution is destined to take the lead in
this country.
                " Yours, affectionately and gratefully,
                                J. H. THORNWELL."

From the sound views here expressed, of the object
and methods of academic training, he never receded; and
he based upon them all his later efforts to advance the

educational interests of his native State. He discovers, too, his predilection for a scholastic life, little dreaming of the sphere in which it would be indulged; but it is a singular coincidence that his last labours should have been devoted to that institution, to which his early aspirations had been directed, and that he should there have wrought out the work upon which his permanent reputation will chiefly rest: a work which, though arrested in its progress by the hand of death, attests, even in its incompleteness, the power of his genius and the wealth of his knowledge.

But to his correspondence again.

To General James Gillespie:

"CAMBRIDGE, *September* 6, 1834.

"MY DEAR GENERAL: It is now nearly twelve o'clock at night, and I have determined, with a miserable pen, to give you a short account of the incidents of the day. Early in the forenoon I went into Boston, for the purpose of hearing Edward Everett's eulogy on Lafayette; and a splendid production it was. There were some passages in it unsurpassed by the finest flights of Chatham or of Burke; and throughout, it was a chaste, classical, and elegant composition. I had taken up the impression that Everett was a cold, dull, heartless, and formal speaker, who aimed only to please, and not to arouse the feelings of his auditory; but I was quite in the wrong. He is impassioned and vehement, and exercises as strong a control over the passions of his hearers as Preston himself; and I presume that the secret of his failure in Congress, is an inability to extemporize. He drew tears to-day from the stoutest heart; and was repeatedly interrupted by deafening shouts of applause, which made old Faneuil Hall ring, but which were hardly suitable to the badges of mourning that shrouded the walls. His oration was nearly three hours long, and I was extremely sorry when he got to the close. It will, in all probability, be published; and if it should be, I will send you a copy.

"Mr. Everett is a very small man, about five feet seven inches high, and withal very thin; but his countenance is strongly marked. The most remarkable feature of his face is his mouth; it would attract attention the moment you should lay your eyes upon him; it is exactly like that of Dr. Watts, as exhibited in his portraits. Everett's eyes are a dark blue, and have the cast of thought and study. His forehead is full and finely arched, and the general expression of his countenance is that of calm meditation. I have been thus minute in my description, because I was absolutely charmed with the man, and am determined, by some means or other, to obtain an introduction to him.

" There was an immense concourse of people assembled on the Common ; and the procession, I should think, was a mile and a half long, and averaged five persons in width. There were probably four or five thousand crowded into Faneuil Hall. I was about the head of the procession, and consequently obtained a good seat near the orator. As soon as I got into Boston I found out the order of arrangements. Distinguished strangers were invited to head the procession ; and as this circumstance gave them the choice of seats, Evans and myself took it into our heads to introduce ourselves to the marshal as belonging to this class. We did the thing with such grace that the claim was admitted, and we joined the line with John Quincy Adams, Daniel Webster, and that whole tribe, chuckling all the while over our new bought dignity. I breathed the atmosphere of greatness, and could hardly persuade myself that I was simply James H. Thornwell, once pedagogue in the Cheraw Academy. I was certainly a great man, but had not been fortunate enough to find it out, until I found myself ranked with distinguished strangers. A little impudence is a great help in this world ; and I have called in its aid on several occasions to great advantage, since I have been at the North.

" I am quite cheerful and contented in Cambridge, and have established something of a character. So far as I can learn, they give me credit for a virtue which I was never suspected of possessing by my friends at home, and that is *modesty*. Evans has joined the Law-school, and adds considerably to my enjoyment. I have, besides, a pretty extensive circle of acquaintances in members of College from South Carolina, and am winding my way into the affections of the natives themselves. I am an intense student, and am making rapid progress in Hebrew and Biblical Literature. I average, this week, fifteen hours per day ; but I cannot continue to apply myself at that rate, for I begin to experience already the inconvenience of it, manifested by indigestion and a slight pain in my chest. I shall hereafter study about thirteen hours a day, and exercise freely ; and I have no doubt that I shall be able to escape all ill consequences. I attend the recitations of the Divinity School, and derive the same advantages as if I were a regular member, without being subject to any restrictions.

" I have nearly finished my article for the *North American Review*, and shall probably hand it in about the first of October. It is now quarter past one o'clock, and I must bid you good-night.

" Sincerely and gratefully,

J. H. THORNWELL."

The associating principle, which touches the springs of memory everywhere, and binds together our knowledge and experience—did it bring back the incidents, so pleasantly related in the above letter, at a later day, when, seated by the side of the man here so greatly wondered at, he surprised Mr. Everett by a remarkable citation in the original, from Thucydides, and became in his turn the object of as much admiration and delight? If so, he must have mused upon those strange coincidences, which some-times bring the different stages of our life into such vividness of contrast, as almost to overbear the conviction of our identity, and make us feel as though two different beings are represented in them. The story is thus told by one who participated in the interview: "In the year 1857, Mr. Everett was in Columbia, to deliver his cele-brated oration on Washington; and was the guest of that accomplished gentleman, the Hon. W. F. Desaussure. Dr. Thornwell proposed to me that we should go together to pay our respects to the distinguished stranger. After being introduced, a good many inquiries were made about Cambridge, and the literary men of Boston; when the conversation turned upon the recurrence of certain ideas in different eras of the world. Mr. Everett illustrated it by reference to a passage in Thucydides, which he ren-dered into English. Dr. Thornwell replied by quoting, in the original Greek, a few lines from the same author. Mr. Everett rejoined once more in English, when Dr. Thornwell made a far more extended quotation from Thucydides, in the Greek. All were surprised and de-lighted at the exhibition of learning, so spontaneous as to be free from the suspicion of pedantry. The following day Mr. Desaussure expatiated, in my office, in praise of ' our Southern giant.'" We relate the incident in this connection, that it may enjoy all the light of contrast.

But to resume the correspondence of this period:

"To Mr. Alexander H. Pegues:

"Cambridge, *September* 11, 1834.

"My Dear Friend: Midnight has drawn her sable curtain over half the world; and I seize upon this hour of solemn stillness to renew my intercourse with a cherished friend. There are a thousand ties which link the race in harmony; but the affections of the heart cannot be sat-isfied with expansive action. Like the rays of light centred in a

burning focus, their energies must all be directed to a single point, to
produce the maximum of happiness, and produce the fullest development of which they are susceptible.   It is not enough to love the
species; there must be individuals of the species, whom we cherish
with peculiar fondness.   A candle can give light to a single room, but
it cannot illuminate the world.   I am charmed with the notion of universal philanthropy, and am as anxious as most men to diffuse the
means of knowledge and happiness among my brethren of the earth;
but then I find more real enjoyment and unmingled felicity in the narrower circle of domestic affection and of private friendships.   I am
willing to grant that love to the species should be the main-spring of
all our actions; but then I maintain that love to the species accomplishes its end only through the medium of circumscribed action; that
the greatest happiness is ultimately produced by discharging properly
the humble duties of our social relations.   It is a sad misnomer to call
an unfaithful friend or a cruel husband a genuine philanthropist.   The
man who is careless of his own household is hardly able to take care of
the world; and the man who loves not his own family can hardly be
expected to love the race.   He is the best philanthropist who is the
truest friend, the most faithful husband, the most tender parent, and
affectionate neighbour.

"*September* 18, 1834.

" Some few evenings since, as you observe, I commenced an epistle to
you, but have forgotten entirely the train of thought which was then in
my mind.   You will excuse me, therefore, for beginning *de novo*.   And
I must be in a pretty considerable hurry; for in a few minutes I have
to attend a party, to which I have been invited, and where I shall see
the intelligence and beauty of Cambridge.   I had gotten thus far, and
was interrupted for three hours by company.   Meanwhile, the music
of the party has struck up, and I am rather afraid there will be dancing.
If there should be, I most assuredly shall not go.   You remember the
eloquent declamation of Cicero upon the subject, when a Roman Senator was publicly impeached for the heinous offence of using his legs too
lightly.   There is neither rhyme nor reason in ' capering nimbly over a
lady's chamber, to the lascivious pleasing of a lute.'   I am an open and
avowed enemy to the sport, because I believe that it is an enemy to the
best and most substantial interests of man.   Just think of it soberly, and
at the least, it cannot but appear ridiculous.   And yet, like most other
follies, it is fatally contagious; and men freely indulge in it without
being aware of its enormity.   It is an insult to God, who has made us
beings of intellectual dignity; it is an abuse of our own persons, and a
prostration of our own powers.   It is all nonsense to call it an amusement; it has no claim nor title to the appellation.   That only is properly
amusement which relaxes the mind after laborious toil; which refreshes
its exhausted energies, and preserves it from the listlessness incident to
fatigue.   But is this a characteristic of dancing?   Is it not a mere invention to kill time?   Yours sincerely, as ever,

J. H. THORNWELL."

To the same:

"CAMBRIDGE, *October* 1, 1834.

"MY DEAR FRIEND : I received your letter this afternoon, and was glad to find that you had not entirely forgotten me ; though I had begun to suspect that the probabilities of hearing directly from you were exceedingly faint. You have misapprehended Dr. Whately's object, in in his 'Historic Doubts concerning Napoleon.' His design was to show that the very same arguments which are directed against the miracles of Christianity, can be applied with equal force against the existence of Buonaparte; that the one cannot be admitted or rejected with consistency, without admitting or rejecting the other. The stand which Mr. Hume and his followers have taken in regard to our Saviour's miracles is, that an event, in itself improbable, is incapable of being proved by testimony ; that its inherent improbability is a standing and unanswerable argument against it. On the same grounds, such men must have rejected the existence of Napoleon, as an event in itself improbable; but all men have admitted this fact; and therefore, the conclusion is irresistible, that adequate testimony is sufficient to establish any fact, however improbable it may appear. It was, consequently, Dr. Whateley's object to show that Hume's reasoning proved too much, and consequently proved nothing; that it proved not only that Jesus Christ wrought no miracles, but that Napoleon Buonaparte never lived or died. I look upon the pamphlet as one of the happiest effusions of well-sustained irony that I have ever read. I was delighted with it, and therefore sent it to you.

"The more I examine Hume's celebrated argument against miracles, the more I am satisfied that it is utterly untenable and fallacious. A law of nature is only a compendious expression for uniformity in the appearances of nature. To say, therefore, that anything violates a law of nature, is only to say that it does not conform with the general appearances. Our knowledge of nature's laws depends upon the testimony of our senses ; our knowledge of a miracle depends upon the testimony of the senses of other men. There is, therefore, the same ground for believing in a miracle, as for believing in the laws of nature. One is, the usual appearance of nature ; the other, an unusual appearance. We know both from the evidence of sense. A man, therefore, who denies a miracle, ought, in consistency, to disbelieve the laws of nature; they both rest on the same grounds ; there is no difference between them, except that one is uniform ; the other is not. This uniformity can make no difference, because we know *it* only from the evidence of sense.

"This is a meagre skeleton of the *direct* argument with which I would meet infidelity ; the indirect would be drawn from the nature and attributes of God; but it is quite unnecessary to touch upon it here. I should pay but a poor compliment to your understanding, if I thought you were in danger of being ensnared by the sophisms of Hume, which are now universally abandoned, even by Free-thinkers themselves. The

recorded experience of the world is a living testimony against h... doctrines; and no man who mingles in the world can act upon his principles.

"You do not overrate the advantages of Cambridge, but you certainly
underrate those of South Carolina. There are no more facilities here for
acquiring an education, than there are among us; and I had just as soon
send a son to Columbia as to Cambridge. A large library is far from
being an advantage to under-graduates. They are indiscreet and imprudent in their selection of books; and where there are so many volumes,
they leave the hall very often without knowing what to choose. A large
library is a help to *scholars*, in the way of reference and consultation;
but to no other men, and in no other way.

"On the morning of the 4th of October, I shall set sail for Charleston, and shall be in Cheraw about the 20th or 21st. I regret very much
to leave Harvard; but I am compelled to do so. I am delightfully situated here; and should be exceedingly happy, under other circumstances, to spend two or three years. A physician of Boston has assured
me that it would be certain death for me to try a Northern winter; and
I have already suffered nearly as much from the cold, as I ever did in
South Carolina. The climate, for the last two weeks, has been very
variable; sometimes very piercing, and sometimes pleasant. I have
consequently determined not to risk my health, but to return as early as
I safely can. I start rather earlier than I expected, on account of the
uncertainties of a sea voyage. I am anxious, too, to be present at your
sister's nuptials, and shall bend all my efforts to reach Cheraw in time.

"Your sincere friend,

J. H. THORNWELL."

CHAPTER X.

FIRST PASTORATE.

Licensure.—Settlement in Lancaster.—Spiritual Conflict.—Character of his Early Preaching.—Extraordinary Ascendancy over his Audience.—His Singular Power of Illuminating the whole Gospel.—His Bearing as a Pastor.—Marriage.—Death of his First Child.—Complete Formation of Character.—Development of Piety.—Extracts from his Private Journal.—Confession and Prayer.

MR. THORNWELL was licensed to preach the gospel, by the Presbytery of Harmony, met at Tolerant Church, in the bounds of Beaver Creek congregation, on the 28th of November, 1834: exactly one year from the time he was taken under the Presbytery's care. His examination was eminently satisfactory; and very unusual encomiums were pronounced upon his ability and proficiency, by the members of the court, in rendering their decision upon the parts of trial. The Rev. Dr. Goulding, then Professor in the Theological Seminary at Columbia, is reported as saying, "Brethren, I feel like sitting at this young man's feet, as a learner:" a very sweet expression of humility, on the part of one whom the Church was honouring with an office of the highest responsibility and trust; but also a wonderful testimony to the attainments of the young theologian which drew it forth.

His first settlement was, however, within the bounds of a different Presbytery. Certain gentlemen from the village of Lancaster were present at this examination, and bore away with them such impressions as determined eventually his location. On the 8th of April, 1835, a church was organized in this village, by the Presbytery of Bethel, which immediately made overtures to Mr. Thorn-

well to become its pastor. Accordingly, on the 11th of
June, he was transferred as a licentiate from the Presbytery of Harmony to that of Bethel; and on the following
day he was ordained and installed pastor over the infant
church. His labours were not, however, restricted within
this narrow sphere. The old mother church of Waxhaw,
and the church of Six-Mile creek, in the same District of
Lancaster, enjoyed his occasional, if not his constant,
ministrations; and in April, 1836, having made out separate calls, they were united with the church at Lancas-
terville in a joint pastoral charge; and the installation
services were performed by Rev. Messrs. J. B. Davies and
Pierpont E. Bishop, as a Committee of the Presbytery.

The reader has observed the spiritual conflict through
which our friend passed in his earlier years, and the gradual ascendency which the gospel gained over his character and life. He will not, therefore, be surprised to
find these culminating in one last struggle, which would
seem to terminate the discipline of this preparatory period. The letters, too, which have been given, reveal his
towering ambition, which had been fed by constant and
brilliant success in academic competitions. What more
likely than that this tremendous passion should gather up
all its force, to deter him from a calling in which it may
not lawfully be indulged? What more probable than
that conscience should itself shrink back in alarm, from
the responsibility of the sacred office, not measured in its
awful magnitude until it is about to be assumed? What
more in keeping with the artifice and malignity of Satan,
than that, at such a crisis, he should seize upon all that
is good, as well as all that is evil, within us, and array
them against a decision by which he is discomfited forever? It is a fearful struggle when, once for all, a noble
spirit brings its longing after fame, and lays it down a
perpetual sacrifice to conscience and to God. For though
the pulpit has its honours and rewards, woe! woe! to
the man who enters it under this temptation:

"To gaze at his own splendour, and exalt,
Absurdly, not his office, but himself."

The shadow of a fearful curse falls upon him who "does
this work of the Lord deceitfully:" upon him who cannot
with a purged eye look beyond the meed of human applause, to the benediction of the great Master, as his final
crown.

Dr. Thornwell relates, that such was the apprehension
of his soul in what he was about to do, that he appeared
before the Presbytery with a half-cherished hope they
would reject him; and thus the Church would assume the
responsibility of releasing him from the pressure of the
Apostle's woe. In this apprehension he has, however,
only entered within the shadow of the cloud which was
yet to darken upon him. The authority of the Church
has sent him forth to preach the Word, and a hungry
charge beckons from the distance to come and give it the
bread of life. In his solitary way, as he journeys along,
in the beautiful spring, terrible thoughts settle upon his
mind, which he cannot conjure away. What if, after all,
he should not be a converted man! What, if it should
be a profane touch that he was to give to the ark of God!
What, if he was going up to the place and people of the
Lord, and His presence was not with him! What, if the
ministry should prove to him an iron bondage, and,
having preached to others, he should be himself a cast-
away? And so he journeyed on, like Saul to Damascus,
with the deep midnight upon his soul. At the end of a
day's travel he rested under the hospitable roof of a pious
elder, to whom he opened all the sorrow. But no comfort came from all the comfort that was spoken. The
good elder could succeed only in exacting a promise, at
parting, that he would go on to his appointment; and if
the Lord, in answer to prayer, did not make his duty
plain, why, then, he need not preach. The place is
reached; he enters the pulpit, with "the great horror of
darkness" resting upon him still. It is the garden of

Gethsemane to this young but chosen servant of the Lord,
who must here learn to drink of the Saviour's cup, and be
baptized with His baptism. He rises to preach; and now
the time has come for the revelation of the Saviour's
love. Through a rift in the gloom, there rushes down
upon him such a sense of his acceptance with God as was
overpowering. The assurance and the joy overflowed
into the discourse, which poured the sacred oil over the
assembly; until some gathered unconsciously near the
pulpit, in breathless suspense upon the young prophet's
lips. He was from that moment anointed to a life-work,
which is precious in its record here, and—above.*

His early preaching was not dry and scholastic, as
many predicted it would be. On the contrary, one of
his habitual hearers describes it as "intensely practical
and plain; nothing abstract. The impression in my mind,
now, is that of earnest expostulation with sinners. Now,
to-day, is the day of salvation. He was very earnest; his
eye kindled with intense excitement; his whole frame
quivered. His sermons created great enthusiasm among
the people of all denominations, who crowded into the
little church until it overflowed." Another writes: "Mr.
Thornwell's sermons, from the commencement of his
preaching, were profound, logical, and eloquent. He
gestured more with *both arms* than he did in after life,
and there was more vehemence of action." Indeed, it is
the opinion of many who knew him intimately through
his whole career, that, for popular effect, those early discourses were never surpassed by the riper productions of
his later years. Though his learning became more various and his discussions more profound, yet the first
impressions of his oratory were never transcended. We
suspect, however, that it was largely changed in its char-

---

* The incident is given precisely as it was first related to us. Another
authority places it a little later in his early ministry, and substitutes a
minister for the elder as his adviser and friend. This slight discrepancy
rather confirms, than weakens, the occurrence of the fact.

acter. It was eloquence of a higher order that he afterwards obtained, though less attractive to the multitude.
A severer taste, and a deeper religious experience, led
him to disregard the graces of rhetoric, with which at first
he had charmed a popular assembly. His eloquence dug
for itself a deeper channel than in his earlier years, and
poured itself in a much broader flood; rather overwhelming by its majesty, than attracting by its grace.

In proof of the ascendency he always gained over the
minds of his hearers, the following incident may be related, in the very words given to us: "Soon after he came
among us, the time arrived for the regular semi-annual
communion at the Waxhaw Church. It had always been
customary for neighbouring pastors to assist each other
at these meetings. Our young pastor commenced on
Friday morning, the usual time, without any assistance.
One of our venerable elders, who did not arrive till Sat-
turday morning, was displeased with this course, thinking
it presumptuous in him to suppose the people would be
content without the usual variety, to which, on such occasions, they were accustomed. But after listening to the
morning discourse, the old gentleman approached those
to whom he had expressed his dissatisfaction, and said:
' I am very glad now, that no other minister is here.' The
sermon was from the text, ' A man that hath friends must
show himself friendly; and there is a friend that sticketh
closer than a brother.'" A sermon from this text, doubtless the same, was one of the earliest that the writer himself heard from the lips of his friend; and portions of it
are distinctly remembered at this day, across the interval
of three and thirty years.

His sermons at this period seldom exceeded thirty
minutes in length, though they afterwards stretched to
the orthodox sixty. But he was sometimes borne beyond
himself, as in the case now to be recited, and which affords
a better illustration than the preceding of his immense
power over an audience. We draw upon the same testi-

mony as before : "On Sabbath morning his text was, ' It
is a faithful saying, and worthy of all acceptation, that
Jesus Christ came into the world to save sinners.' It was
one of his finest efforts. When he had been preaching
for an hour and a half, he took out his watch, stopped
suddenly, and apologized to the congregation, saying he
had no idea he had been speaking so long. The cry
rose at once, from all parts of the house, 'Go on! go on!'
And he did go on for nearly an hour more." Remembering how staid a Presbyterian congregation usually is,
and restrained by the sanctities of the sanctuary, this outburst of enthusiasm, breaking over all conventional pro-
prieties, was no slight tribute to the power of the orator.
But the charm of the story remains yet to be unfolded.
"My father," adds the witness, " a very old gentleman,
was present. A few days afterwards he sent for me,
saying, 'I want to talk to you about that sermon. My
son, if you ever had a doubt about the truth and perfection of the plan of salvation, you surely can have none
now. I have been studying that subject all my life, but
I never saw it before as I do now. Now I am ready to
die, that I may enter upon its full enjoyment.' He never
was able to attend church again; and eternity alone will
reveal the comfort and instruction which that one sermon
gave to this aged servant of God; how it smoothed his
pathway to the tomb, and lighted up his future with hope.
Scores and hundreds of others have been similarly profited, as they hung upon the truth from his lips."

   This affecting narrative brings to view one feature of
Dr. Thornwell's preaching, which may as well be signalized here as elsewhere. It was the power he possessed
of sometimes illuminating the whole gospel in a single
discourse. We enter, for example, a chamber at twilight;
and, with a dim, uncertain vision, recognize the furniture
and appointments. Each object is disclosed, but in faint
outline; and the relation of the parts to each other can be
but imperfectly traced. Suddenly a taper is applied to a

single burner, and one jet of flame is sufficient to light up
the whole. Every article in the room presents its clear
profile to the eye; all is brought out from the shadow into
bold relief; and the total effect is taken in at a glance
from the grouping, which discloses the taste and disposition of the occupant. Just so, the truths to which we
have been listening all our lives are disposed in a certain
catechetical order in our mind, yet fragmentary and dis-
jointed. How often will a single paragraph in a book, or
a single utterance of the living voice, light them up with
a new clearness, and show them in the beauty and power
of an organic unity, as parts of a comprehensive and harmonious system. This faculty Dr. Thornwell possessed,
in a degree which marked no other man whom it has
been our privilege to know or hear. His power of
analysis stripped every subject of all that was adventitious or collateral. He removed skilfully every sucker
shooting out from the stem of his doctrine, and exposed
at once the living germ from which all growth and
development sprung. With this ultimate principle in
the grasp, the hearer had the key to unlock the entire
subject; with the thread of Ariadne in his fingers, he was
guided safely through all the intricacies of the longest
discussion into which it might afterwards expand. As
every system, too, however complex, must hang upon a
few cardinal postulates, it was his delight to seize upon
those which were fundamental in Christianity, and, with
amazing constructive skill, build up the grand temple
before the eyes of his audience, laying beam upon beam,
and stone upon stone, and "bringing forth the head-
stone thereof, with shoutings of, Grace, grace unto it." A
good illustration of this tendency of mind is furnished in
his Inaugural Discourse, when inducted into the Theological chair in the Seminary at Columbia, in which he
attempts to denote "the central principle of theology,"
which brings its diversified matter into such "unity of
relation as constitutes it properly a science." This was

a constant attribute of his preaching; which had a value beyond the demonstration of single truths, in supplying the *nexus* which bound them together in unity and completeness. From this cause it happened that, in his various travels, wherever he would tarry for a Sabbath, a single sermon proved to so many a life-event, from which a new Christian experience was developed. Hundreds of such are to be found through this broad land; and not until they shall sit down with him upon the Mount of God, can he know in how many blessed experiences his earthly ministry was blent. There is power in genius; and where it is sanctified by grace, and wielded as an instrument of the Holy Spirit, there is nothing beneath the skies that is half so grand—nothing before which the human soul bows with so much of deference and love.

> "Yes; to thy tongue shall seraph words be given,
> And power on earth to plead the cause of Heaven;
> The proud, the cold untroubled heart of stone,
> That never mused on sorrow but its own,
> Unlocks a generous store at thy command,
> Like Horeb's rock beneath the prophet's hand."

Mr. Thornwell, during his pastorate, resided in the village of Lancaster, where a neat church building was soon erected under his auspices. The Waxhaw Church was distant about eight miles; and the Six-Mile charge, about eighteen miles. These distances, however, were easily covered by a fleet horse, which rejoiced in the soubriquet of "Red Rover," and was habitually driven at the speed of ten and twelve miles an hour. "This was, however, no cruelty to the horse," writes the chronicler of this period; "it was only in keeping with the spirit and mettle of the animal;" but adds he, somewhat quaintly, "it gave our pastor the appearance of being a little fast." Poor Red Rover was before long offered a sacrifice upon the altar of love; for upon the master's marriage, the friends of the lady could by no means consent for her to ride at such break-neck speed, and behind a horse of which all but the owner were afraid. Character is most displayed in little things. It is an illustration of Mr. Thornwell's conscientiousness, that, when compelled to part reluctantly with his favourite steed, though offered fifty per cent. more, he would take only one hundred dollars, which he considered his money value.

Whilst indulging this gossip, it may not be amiss to state, that Dr. Thornwell exhibited through life one mark of extravagance, in always having the best of everything in its kind. Indeed, it was his doctrine that the best was always the cheapest. He always concurred with Carlyle in his denunciation of "the cheap and nasty;" which, like Carlyle, he pushed in many directions, and made it the measure of men and principles, as well as of things. Still, it was with him very much a matter of taste. He always bought the best editions of books; wore clothing of the finest texture; was fond of fine horses; and smoked always the best brands. To illustrate his epicurianism as to the last named, the writer once offered him a cigar, such as he was himself smoking at the time, and as good in quality as he felt he could afford. After drawing two or three whiffs, it was pitched impatiently through the window, with the exclamation, "Any man who will smoke such cigars will steal!" The anecdote will be excused its want of dignity, if it shows the freedom and dash of his raillery towards those whom he loved.

He was scarcely less dear as a pastor to the people of his charge, than admired as a preacher. The morbid sensibility, and recoil upon himself, of past years, have entirely disappeared. The Rubicon is passed; he has grappled with life, and deals with its realities rather than with its dreams. The preliminary fear of the battle has subsided with the first shock of arms, and he feels the stern joy of the encounter. His initiation into life was, too, of the nature of a triumph. Everywhere sought,

admired, caressed; all things conspired to draw out the
original simplicity and guilelessness of his nature. His
constitutional buoyancy of spirits bore him on its flood,
and the native gaiety of his disposition sparkled through
his whole demeanour. Wherever his social visits were
dispensed, he romped with the children, and bantered the
middle-aged with sportive wit; whilst those who needed
comfort and advice were met with genial sympathy, and
with instruction which could not be exceeded in its richness. Men stopped to wonder at him as he passed along
the streets, striving to put together the solemnity of his
pulpit utterances and the exuberant pleasantry of the
private companion. Many, perhaps, had to unlearn some
of the old, stereotyped lessons of cant, and make the distinction between a genuine zeal and the sanctimonious
Pharisaism that hides in the folds of a white cravat, and
in the stiff precision of an artificial saintliness. But
the result was the combined respect and love of all; who
were as much won by the artless demeanour of the week,
as by the stormy eloquence of the Sabbath. In proof,
however, that all this playfulness was but the unbending
of a serious mind, a single question or word was sufficient
to call it back to the earnestness and gravity which were
habitual. Says the friend who has furnished most of
these sketches: " He was an inmate of my family, and I
then knew him intimately. Only those who have enjoyed
a similar privilege can appreciate the delight his society
afforded. My rule was to ask him a question, and, as he
undertook to answer it, his mind would turn fully to the
subject, and his discourse would be intensely fascinating
as well as instructive." The rapidity with which he
could pass from the gay to the severe, and exchange the
play of wit for the most abstract and elaborate reasoning,
all can testify who were ever admitted into his confidence.
The writer has a thousand times admired the self-mastery
thus displayed in the perfect control of his own modes of
feeling and of thought.

On the 3d December, 1835, Mr. Thornwell was united
in marriage with Miss Nancy White Witherspoon, second
daughter of Colonel James H. Witherspoon, of Lancaster
District. Colonel Witherspoon was one of the leading
men in the District, and not without distinction in the
State; having served as Lieutenant-Governor, and was a
candidate for Congress, with every prospect of being
elected, when he was stricken by paralysis, which terminated in death. He was a man of large views, of great
energy and enthusiasm, and possessed an almost unbounded popularity. Mr. Thornwell gained easy admission into his household, not only by his official relations
as a pastor, but through an intimacy with two of his sons
in college, one of whom was his class-mate. Though
Colonel Witherspoon, with the worldly prudence that
guides most men in disposing their daughters in marriage, saw what looked little better than starvation in a
salary of six hundred a year, still, he could not refuse
domestic alliance to a young man whom he openly proclaimed intellectually the equal of Mr. McDuffie or Mr.
Calhoun. From the time of marriage the happy couple
took up their abode in the family mansion, till their removal to a different home. By this union, a true help-
meet was provided for one whose gifts and whose calling
required that he should not be entangled in the things of
this life. Mrs. Thornwell's sound judgment and practical
wisdom were a valuable check upon the ardent temperament and too confiding generosity of her husband.
Her prudence and skilful management released him from
domestic cares, to meet the exactions of his public station; while her womanly grace and cheerful disposition
threw a serene charm about his home, in which his spirits
found always a perfect repose. No man had better reason
to know the truth of Solomon's assertion, that "a prudent
wife is from the Lord." The happiness of these early
years was darkened only by a single sorrow, the death of
their first-born, at the age of three months. This visi-

tation drew from his friend and patron, Mr. Robbins, the
following expression of sympathy and affection:

"My Dear James: I have just received your letter, conveying the
afflictive intelligence of the loss of your dear babe. We are both much
afflicted by this unexpected calamity, and desire to join our sympathies
in the sorrows of the parents. We can do so most deeply and affectionately. We know what it is to watch the gradual unfolding of the
physical and intellectual faculties of a *dear* child, a *first* child, an *only*
child; and in the full flood-tide of our enjoyment, to have the dear object of our love snatched from our presence and our care. Such a loss
is heart-rending indeed; and the mourner is disposed to attach little
value to other blessings of life, for a season, since the greatest has been
withdrawn. But a short time and a little reflection will dispel the blackness of the cloud, and show us a clear and serene sky beyond it. *We
do know*, James, that our heavenly Parent, whose love to us surpasses
that of a woman to the child of her bosom, is the immediate Author of
these bereavements. *We do know* that He never afflicts willingly, or
grieves the children of men; always for some cause—great, good, adequate cause. What this cause is, it is our privilege and our duty to
inquire. Sometimes it is wisely withheld from our search; but frequently, very frequently, it is within the reach of our reflection. It
may be in mercy *to the child*, to rescue it from a more dreadful calamity
which would have attended it in life; it may be in mercy *to the paren.*,
to spare the more acute suffering at beholding an unworthy life, or
an unworthy connection in life. * * * These were some of my own
reflections when called on to mourn, as you now do; but, my dear
James, I believe most men can find—I think I found—some unfaithfulness in myself, for which the visitation befell me; and, with the
blessing of God, I have endeavoured to reform it. Should this be your
case, I pray most devoutly that He, whose grace is sufficient for us,
may enable you to discover and cast it out. Rest assured of the sincere
personal and Christian sympathy of yours,

W. H. Robbins."

From the moment of his settlement in the ministry,
the crystallization of Mr. Thornwell's character appears
to be complete. All mawkishness of sentiment and moo-
diness of temper have vanished for ever. He has become,
in the fullest sense, a man, and has put away these childish
things. His style of writing is more robust, like that of
one who has ascertained his real strength; and it is henceforth discharged of the ambitiousness which perhaps is
but the natural blemish of youthful self-assertion. His

religious experience is amazingly deepened, by more familiar study of the Scriptures and nearer acquaintance
with God. The doctrine of salvation through grace became more precious to himself, as he pressed it upon the
acceptance of others. In this, too, he was greatly profited by his intimacy with the Rev. Pierpont E. Bishop,
one of his co-presbyters: a man not comparable with himself either in learning or genius, but of excellent mind
and of profound piety. He was one of the few, in any
generation, of whom it can be said with emphasis, that
they " *walk* with God." His holiness was rooted in principle; it pervaded his character, and was of that earnest
and controlling type which the Calvinistic view of Divine
truth imparts, when fully received into the heart. This
was precisely the bond which linked Mr. Thornwell to him;
and the affection subsisting between the two, throughout
life, was formed in Christ, their common Lord. "As iron
sharpeneth iron, so a man sharpeneth the countenance of
his friend;" and the sweet savour of Mr. Bishop's piety
penetrated into the life and history of his brother in the
gospel.

A few extracts from his private journal, kept at this
time, but discontinued after a few months, and apparently
never resumed, are given, to show the severity with which
he probed his own heart, and his watchful jealousy of all
tendencies to earthly pride and vainglory.

" *April 2nd*, 1836.—I have this day commenced to keep a journal of
my personal history, with a view chiefly to my growth in grace. Nearly
a year has elapsed since I was ordained and installed the pastor of the
little church in Lancaster ; and what have I done for the glory of God,
the edification of His people, or the conversion of sinners? Unfaithfulness! unfaithfulness! must be written upon my very best efforts.
Great God, give me more largely of the spirit of grace! My mind this
day has been much concerned for the welfare of my little flock.
Some of them manifest the spirit of the gospel; but others are cold
and lifeless, and seem to take no sort of interest in eternal things. O
Lord, revive Thy work! In reviewing my labours, I am quite satisfied,
and I trust am humbled, that my Bible class has been conducted too
much with a view to the head, and too little with a view to the heart; it

has too much criticism, and too little personal application. By the grace of God I am determined to remedy this defect.

"*May* 14*th.*—I returned home to-day, after having been absent for more than three weeks. During my visit to York, I experienced a distressing visitation in the sudden illness of my wife. I feared that she was on the brink of the grave; and was deeply humbled under a heavy sense of my ingratitude to God for so sweet a gift. Her society had not been sufficiently improved for spiritual purposes. I felt that I most richly deserved some decided manifestation of God's displeasure; and in reliance on His grace, I trust I formed the resolution of living more faithfully for the glory of God, and of regarding my wife as a help-mate in spiritual and eternal matters. God has spared her, and restored her to me again. Oh! may the Lord give me grace to fulfil my purposes of renewed obedience.

"During my absence, I attended an adjourned meeting of Presbytery, held at Purity church, in Chester, for the purpose of ordaining Brother Douglas. I was appointed to preach the ordination sermon, and did so from Rom. i. 5. I felt much of the solemnity which the occasion was fitted to inspire; but not half as much as the great interests involved ought to have produced in my heart. It is a source of constant pain and grief to me, that the realities of eternity have no more *sensible* effect upon my mind. I cannot feel them with that force, and power, and depth, which their tremendous importance requires. I can see very clearly how I ought to be affected; but then I am not so affected. O Lord, give me more largely of Thy precious and efficient grace!"

"*June* 2*nd.*—Returned home, after an absence of nearly a week. Attended a sacramental meeting of Brother Bishop's, at Unity. That is a precious and a godly man. I felt much of the evils of my heart, but could not be humbled. I see in my own heart so much selfishness, and pride, and vanity; so much hardness and insensibility; so little affection for the Saviour, or devotedness to the glory of God, that I am often seriously led to doubt whether I am a child of God. It is my sincere and constant desire to make the Lord my portion, to live to Him, and for Him, and on Him. Oh! for a single eye and a simple heart! I enjoy the comforts of religion by fits and starts. They come in occasional flashes; they are not my constant and habitual atmosphere. I have one consolation, the Lord reigneth. I am anxious to serve Him, and to be just in that field of labour which shall most promote His glory.

"*June* 4*th.*—Finished to-day my sermon on 'The Refuges of Lies,' from Isa. xxviii. Felt much mortified, but I am afraid not humbled, in feelings of vanity and self-complacency with which I contemplated the composition. I invoked the Spirit's influence when I commenced the sermon; but at the close I found I was leaning on my own arm, and shamefully feeding my own vanity. Lord, be merciful to me, a sinner!

"Commenced reading this evening the Life of Henry Martyn. I was struck with some coincidences between his early history and character and my own. Oh! that I may ever make the same advances in the divine life, in devotedness to God, and in mortification of sin!

"*July 19th.*—This morning has been set apart for secret fasting and prayer. I have lately been terribly beset with the dark and horrible suggestions of the great adversary of souls. Blasphemous and awful words would be shot through my mind with the rapidity of lightning, when I would engage in secret prayer at night, or undertook to meditate on the Scriptures, or to read them. This day, thus far, has been a day of terrible gloom to me. My soul has been in thick darkness. I have had no enjoyment of God. My heart has been cold and cheerless, and seems utterly incapable of realizing eternal things. I have been reviewing my past life, and am almost driven to despair at the recollection of my sins. My heart seems to be nothing but a sink of corruption, a Gehenna of iniquity. All my services have been selfish. My frames, which used to be pleasant, were, I fear, utterly destitute of spirituality. I am exceedingly desirous to love holiness and hate sin; but I fear that it is a mere selfish desire. I sometimes suspect that my desires for holiness are more for its results than for itself. O Lord, lead me in the paths of truth and purity. Remove from me every darling lust, and enable me to live wholly for Thy glory!

"*July 30th.*—For the last two or three days I have been much engaged in reading close works on experimental religion. Boston on the 'Covenant of Grace' is a luminous exposition of that wonderful transaction. I feel my mind established in that great truth of the gospel; but my heart does not take that deep and abiding interest in them which I earnestly desire, and which their importance demands. I have gloomy and distracting doubts of my own personal acceptance. To-day I set apart for private fasting, humiliation and prayer, with reference to a protracted meeting, to be holden at Six-Mile, and my brother's conversion. But my heart has been cold and stupid. I have had no clear views of any spiritual object. My understanding assents, but my feelings are dead. My religion seems to be all in the head. Would to God it were otherwise!

"*September 5th.*—I have been much hurt this evening, having heard that I had offended some of the Methodists of the village by some rough and unchristian expressions about shouting. I was wrong in saying what I did. I sinned, and sinned grievously; and shall, by the permission of God, make an acknowledgment to-morrow. My tongue is an unruly member, and I often say, under the influence of excitement, what I am sorry for, immediately afterwards. May the Lord give me prudence. My feelings, I am afraid, are too strongly set against the peculiarities of Arminians. There is more of the flesh than the spirit in them. The truth is, I see nothing about myself that is right; I am altogether a sinner. But blessed be God for free grace! That is my only hope.

"*September 6th.*—Formed the design this morning of writing a short treatise on the peculiar doctrines of the gospel. May the Lord grant

that I may be guided by His Holy Spirit, that I may contend for nothing but the truth, and that in the spirit of the gospel; and may the
whole work conduce to His glory! Lord, grant that there may be no
self-seeking, pride, vanity, nor ambition; but may there be a single
eye to Thy glory, and the prosperity of the Church. Aid me, O Thou
Father of lights, by Thy grace; and enlighten me in a saving knowledge of the truth!"

These extracts from his journal will be appropriately
closed by the following confession, evidently drawn up at
this period. Its strong expressions will be understood,
when it is remembered that the instrument is intended to
cover his former unconverted state, as well as his present
penitence and sorrow:

CONFESSION OF SIN.

"I. 'Thou shalt have no other gods before Me.'

"I have broken this commandment, and do continually break it, by
not knowing and acknowledging God to be the only true God, and *my*
God. I have been guilty of *atheism*, in ascribing to chance, or luck, or
fortune, what has been brought about by the dispensations of His providence. I have been guilty of *idolatry* in several respects. 1. In
worshipping self. I have lived for self; I have toiled and laboured and
agonized for self; and, what is worst of all, I have preached self. 2.
In worshipping *fame*. I have sought this as my chief good. While I
was in College, I counted all things but loss for the sake of literary distinction; and since I left College, I have repeatedly worshipped, with
an eastern devotion, at this very altar. 3. My love of self and of fame
has given rise, in my heart, to a third idol, which has robbed God of
His glory—ambition—and that of the most exclusive kind. I have been
anxious, burningly anxious, to be regarded as the *greatest* scholar and
most *talented* man that ever lived. Think, O my soul, upon thine
atheism and idolatry! Thou hast not only denied God, but, even when
compelled to acknowledge His existence, thou hast robbed Him of the
glory which is justly due to His name.

"But I have broken this commandment in a more covert way, by
ignorance, forgetfulness, misapprehensions, false opinions, unworthy and
wicked thoughts of Him. I have looked upon Him as a hard master.
I have taxed Him with injustice, and have dared to plead my cause as a
just one before Him. It is of His tender mercies that I am not consumed. There is still another way in which I have broken this commandment; and that is, by vain credulity, unbelief, heresy, distrust,
insensibility under judgments, trusting in lawful means, carnal delights
and joys, lukewarmness and deadness in the things of God, estrangement
and apostasy from God. I have also consulted the silly practice of

fortune-telling. I have resisted God's Spirit, been impatient and rebellious under the dispensations of His providence, and have ascribed to myself, or creatures, the good that I have received. Again, I have not esteemed, adored, honoured, loved, trusted, and delighted in God with all my heart, as this law requires.

"II. 'Thou shalt not make unto thyself any graven image, or any likeness of any thing that is in heaven above, or that is in the earth beneath, or that is in the water under the earth; thou shalt not bow down thyself to them, nor serve them; for I, the Lord thy God, am a jealous God, visiting the iniquity of the fathers upon the children, unto the third and fourth generation of them that hate Me, and showing mercy unto thousands of them that love Me and keep My commandments.'

"This commandment requires the pure and holy and spiritual worship of God. I have made images of God in my mind, and have broken it. I have forgotten that He is a Spirit, and have broken it. I have not had that zeal for the house of the Lord and the ordinances of the sanctuary which this commandment requires. I have frequently been unwilling to go to His temple, and have often made light of the solemnities of worship. This law requires a *spiritual* worshipper. Ah! Lord, what am I but flesh and blood! These two commandments present me in the awful and hell-deserving light of an atheist, an idolater, a sensualist.

"III. 'Thou shalt not take the name of the Lord thy God in vain; for the Lord will not hold him guiltless that taketh His name in vain.'

"The Lord's name is upon all His works; it is recorded in His word and ordinances of His house, and is written upon all His providences. I have broken this commandment by swearing; by making light of God's word; by not seeing his hand in His works, and by abusing His gifts. I have cast lots, which is an abuse of the lot of the Lord.

"This commandment requires a consistent profession of religion. Mine has not been so. I have been light, and giddy, and vain, and have thus taken the Lord's name in vain. I have, for purposes of argument, and showing my own wit, misapplied and perverted the word, or passages of the word of God I have taken His name in vain in the solemn act of prayer; and too often, at table, my request for a blessing is a mere mockery.

"IV. 'Remember the Sabbath day to keep it holy. Six days shalt thou labour and do all thy work, but the seventh day is the Sabbath of the Lord thy God; in it thou shalt not do any work; thou, nor thy son, nor thy daughter, thy man-servant, nor thy maid-servant, nor thy cattle, nor thy stranger that is within thy gates. For in six days the Lord made heaven and earth, the sea, and all that in them is, and rested the seventh day; wherefore the Lord blessed the Sabbath day, and hallowed it.'

"Every Sabbath finds me in the violation of this law. My thoughts are prone to be away from God; and it is a fearful proof of depravity, that we cannot devote *one* day in seven *entirely* to Him. The sum of the four commandments already noted, is to love the Lord our God with all our hearts, and with all our soul, and with all our strength, and with all our minds.

PRAYER.

" O most holy and righteous God, in reviewing my heart and life, from infancy until the present time, I am constrained to acknowledge that shame and confusion of face belong unto me.

" I have broken Thy holy law; I stand convinced of rebellion, in its worst forms; I have been an atheist, an idolater, a sensual worhipper, and a Sabbath-breaker. The fear of God has not been before my eyes; I have worshipped self, fame and ambition; I have taken Thy holy Sabbath, and profaned it to my unholy uses; and I have dared to make an image of Thine inconceivable majesty, in my own mind; I have been distrustful of thy promises; I have taken Thy name in vain; I have sported with Thy word, Thy gifts, and Thy providences; and altogether, have been an abuser of God's goodness. O Lord, I have sinned against light, and knowledge, and reproofs, and warnings; there is no excuse for me; I deserve hell. O God, my heart is rotten; it is the seat of all my iniquity. O Lord, give me a new heart; a heart to hate sin and self, to love Thy glory in the face of Jesus Christ, and to serve Thee continually. Oh! enable me to love Thee with all my heart, with all my mind, and with all my strength. All I ask is in the name, and for the sake of Jesus Christ. Amen."

Mr. Thornwell's ministry in Lancaster was not of long duration, extending from the middle of 1835 to the close of 1837. A man of his abilities and general reputation could not be retained in a retired country charge; and shortly before his twenty-fifth birth-day, he received information of his election to the Professorship of Logic and Belles Lettres in the South Carolina College, rendered vacant by the recent death of the lamented Nott.

CHAPTER XI.

FIRST PROFESSORSHIP.

Reorganization of the College.—Enters it as Professor.—Intimate Friendship with Others of the Faculty.—Is Appointed to Teach Mental Science.—Enthusiasm and Success in this Department.—His Native Aptitude for these Studies.—Vindicated from the Charge that He was Wanting in the Æsthetic Element.—Scruples of Conscience.—Resigns His Professorship.—Installed Pastor of the Columbia Church.—Author's First Impressions of Him.—He is Recalled to the College.

THE College had been completely reorganized since Mr. Thornwell left it as a graduate, six years before. Under the infidel influence of Dr. Cooper, it had steadily languished, until the force of public sentiment compelled a change of administration. In the language of the College historian, Dr. Cooper "had drunk deep at the fountain of infidelity; he had sympathized with the sneering *savans* of Paris, and sat at the feet of the most skeptical philosophers of England. If there was any feeling of his nature stronger than all the rest, it was the feeling of opposition to the Christian religion. He believed it to be a fraud and imposture; an artful contrivance to cheat fools, and scare little children and old women."* It was not wonderful that the Christian people of the State rose up to defend " the altars which he proposed to subvert," and to "protect their sons against the influence of a false and soul-destroying philosophy, a species of Pyrrhonism, a refined and subtle dialectics, which removed all the foundations of belief, and spread over the mind the dark and chilling cloud of doubt and uncertainty." The issue was slowly but stubbornly joined between the religious faith of

*Dr. La Borde's History of the South Carolina College, pp. 175-7.

145

the masses, on the one hand, and a cold, bloodless Deism on the other, which had enthroned itself upon the high places of intelligence and power, and was poisoning the very fountains of knowledge in the State.

Let the reader pause here, and adore the mystery of that Providence which worketh not after the pattern of human expectation. Who could have dreamed, when this ribald infidelity was in the zenith of its power, that it was even then nourishing in its bosom a champion for the truth, who would soon enter the lists, and take up the gage of battle, and bear it off upon its triumphant lance! Who that, eight years before, saw a half-grown youth sitting at the feet of the great apostle of Deism, and drinking in his counsels as the inspiration of an oracle, could foresee the advocate for Christianity, standing for its defence upon the platform of its evidences, and undoing the work of his own oracle and guide! Who could then have foretold that an infidel philosophy was whetting the dialectics which should unravel its own sophisms, and feathering the arrow by which its own life should be pierced; that Deism itself should be made to train the giant strength by which its own castle should be demolished, and the spell of its foul enchantment be dissolved! Who can understand the ways of God? It was the young Saxon monk, climbing Pilate's staircase upon his knees, who shook the gates of Papal Rome. It was the young man bearing the garments of those who stoned the first martyr, who filled the world with the faith which once he destroyed.

In December, 1835, the *personnel* of the Faculty was entirely changed. The Hon. Robert W. Barnwell was elected to the Presidency, and the Rev. Dr. Stephen Elliott was appointed to the Professorship of the Evidences of Christianity and Sacred Literature, and the Chaplaincy of the College—a chair for the first time created, in obedience to the exactions of public opinion, and of which Dr. Elliott was the first incumbent. And now, two years later, in November, 1837, the Christian influence is strengthened in the College, by the addition of Mr. Thornwell to its staff of teachers. Never did three men work together with greater harmony and efficiency. The ties which bound them in the most intimate fellowship were the purest and the most enduring that can exist on earth: the love of sound learning, and perfect coincidence in their views of evangelical religion. Messrs. Barnwell and Elliott were splendid types of the accomplished gentleman; with those high and honourable instincts, and with that dignity and suavity of address, which are covered by this suggestive term. They were both distinguished for what we are accustomed to express by the word *character;* and withal were men of generous scholarship, broad and public-spirited in their views, accustomed to sustain high trusts, and fully commanding the respect and homage of the citizens of the Commonwealth. With them Mr. Thornwell was soon brought into the fullest sympathy; and a personal friendship was formed which even death has not interrupted, but which, as between two out of the three, is now perpetuated and consummated in the light and glory of heaven. Thus happily were the fears disappointed, entertained by some who were friends of both, that two ministers of different branches of the Church could not be brought together in the Faculty without developing rival and sectarian interests in the College.

The chair which Mr. Thornwell was invited to fill was not, in part at least, the one which he was most fitted to adorn. By a change soon after made, the department of Metaphysics, as more congenial to his tastes, was committed to him. No better opportunity than this will offer itself, to repel a criticism which has been urged against the character of his mind, that it was wholly deficient in the æsthetic element. This will certainly appear to be a superficial judgment, if one will but consider the rythm and flow of his magnificent diction. The allegation will be stranger still to those who know what a purist he was in the selection of words, and the fastidious taste which trammelled him as a writer, and limited the extent of his authorship. His ear was offended with everything not drawn from "the pure well of English undefiled;" and the slightest inaccuracy in the etymological application of words jarred his nerves like the harsh filing of a saw. His acquaintance ranged over the literature of his native tongue, and over much of that to be found in foreign dialects, both ancient and modern; and when in the vein for it, he could adorn his style with the choicest gems gathered from their stores.

It is freely admitted that the reason, rather than the imagination, was the dominant faculty. He sought for Truth herself; was never content unless he could embrace her own fair form. He was a reasoner, and not a dreamer; and his taste led him out of the ideal world into the actual and true. He did not linger in "the chamber of imagery," upon whose walls were traced the pictures of things; but he went forth into the broad fields of knowledge, to find the originals of which these pictures were but the shadows. There could not be ascribed to him, as to his polished predecessor, "*Tantus amor florum et generandi gloria mellis.*" His style was never festooned with tropes and figures, serving only to embellish; but he was more than a logician, fatally entangled in the formulas of that rugged science; or the subtle dialectician,

> "Who could distinguish and divide
> A hair 'twixt south and southwest side."

He was an orator who could soar to the copestone of heaven in his matchless eloquence, the spell of which was never broken but with the cessation of the tones of his voice; and the orator is always a poet, and a fervid imagination is as necessary to the creations of the one as of the other. The shallow criticism, which denies to him all sensibility to the beautiful, is sufficiently refuted by the brilliant eloquence which enchained every audience he addressed; for the sympathies and emotions of men are never controlled, except where a living fancy works as an organizing force, creating and actuating the forms in which truth is painted before the mind.

A couple of incidents, happening, indeed, at a later period, during his second visit to Europe, are singularly appropriate just here, as a part of the vindication we are attempting. The first was related by himself to a friend, who gives this account of it: "We sat in his study, and had been laughing over the Doctor's sad want of musical capacity, when he suddenly broke in with this account of his seeing Raphael's Madonna: 'I had about given it up as a bad case, and accepted the verdict of my friends, that I had no appreciation of the æsthetic, until my visit to the Dresden gallery undeceived me. I had grown weary of the guide's ceaseless prosing about this painting and that, and determined to turn aside to await the return of my friends, after they had made the tour of the gallery. I suppose that a considerable time had elapsed, when I was aroused by their expression of amusement at my deafness. I had been totally absorbed in the admiration of a painting, which proved to be the Sistine Madonna. I had happened upon the right place to show that I had some sense of the beautiful in my composition.'"

A second incident is given by the same friend, upon the authority of one who was a companion of the Doctor's travels, a favourite nephew, who unhappily fell in the second battle of Manassas: "The tourists had been climbing, with much fatigue, one of the Alps, cheered by the confident assurance of their guide that they would soon be rewarded for their toil by a splendid prospect, when the wind should scatter the mist which completely shut them in. At length, the promised relief came. The impenetrable walls of fog began to quiver as the breeze gathered power; and then the vapoury masses were drifted up the mountain's side, like a great white curtain rolled up by the deft hands of invisible spirits. The transition was sudden, as the effect was overpowering. Frightful gorges, smiling valleys, snow-capped summits, frowning cliffs, cascades, and glaciers shimmering in the sunlight, stood revealed, where all was a blank but a moment before. My young friend told me that his attention was withdrawn from the magnificent scenery to the grotesque attitude and movements of his uncle. Every feature of his countenance bespoke the most ecstatic rapture, as he bent forward upon his mule, the past toil forgotten, his hat crushed upon the back of his head, his eye dilating, the under jaw relaxed, while incoherent words burst from his lips. No doubt they expressed adoring worship of the great Creator."

The accession of Mr. Thornwell to the corps of instructors in the South Carolina College, was hailed with pleasure by all who were familiar with his previous career. The peculiar bent of his genius, his scholarly tastes, his rare learning at so early an age, his insatiable thirst for knowledge, and above all, his peculiar facility in imparting these spoils to others—all pointed to academic life as the sphere in which he would acquire most repute, and be also the most extensively useful. These anticipations, both of success and renown, were not shaded by disappointment in the least degree. Within two years from his induction into office, he became so rooted into the very life of the College that, during a period of eighteen years, each successive effort to separate himself from its venerable halls was defeated; until at length, the Church, that had so long lent him to the State, rose in her majesty, and reclaimed the last few years of his invaluable life to her immediate service.

The industry with which he ploughed the field of philosophy is proved by the existence amongst his manuscripts of a course of lectures covering the entire field;

all prepared within the two years in which only he taught in this department. The value set upon these lectures at the time of their delivery, is attested by the melancholy gaps in the series, as they were borrowed by the students and never returned. These breaks it is now impossible to supply; and they so mar the completeness as probably to prevent their publication. Perhaps, too, it would scarcely be just to surrender to public criticism lectures written five and thirty years ago; and therefore, not abreast with the later literature of a science, which has been enriched by the contributions of such scholars and thinkers as Sir William Hamilton and others, who would be the pride and ornament of philosophy in any age of the world. The editors of his works, who hold his posthumous reputation as a sacred trust, cannot fail to remember that these lectures were prepared in haste, at a a very early age, and were but the tentative efforts of one who had just entered upon that branch of study, and were never afterwards subjected to revision.

In contemplating the labours of truly great men, one can scarcely repress the foolish wish that it were possible to split the one man into many, and yet to carry over the whole of him into each severed part. Human life is so short, and the limit of physical endurance is so soon reached, that the subdivision becomes almost painfully minute. The comprehensive genius, which shows an equal facility for every branch of knowledge, we regret to see shut up within any bounds at all. It always seemed to the writer that there was stuff in his friend to make a dozen men; and, in writing these lines, the fruitless sigh will breathe itself out anew, that he could not have occupied all the provinces of human thought at once. His studies were doubtless remanded by Providence to subjects of greater utility than that of speculative philosophy. Yet, if his life could have been spent in this department, his biographer would have been allowed to apply to him the splendid eulogium he has pronounced upon Sir William Hamilton: "In depth and acuteness of mind, a rival of Aristotle; in immensity of learning, a match for Leibnitz; in comprehensiveness of thought, an equal of Bacon." Even as it is, since the days of Edwards, no one has appeared on this continent so natively competent to realize this grand combination, than the impassioned panegyrist himself by whom it was framed. It is unfortunate that, aside from the aroma which breathes through all his writings, the evidence of his large acquisitions can be gathered only from monographs; and these upon topics which rather implicate philosophy than lie wholly within its domain. He was unquestionably master of its history, from its dawn amidst the schools of Greece, through the mid-day slumber in which it dozed with the schoolmen, to the frenzied and fantastic dreams of our modern transcendentalist. Acquainted with every shade of opinion, his own criticism winnowed the chaff from the wheat; and every valuable contribution, made by any school or age, was safely gathered into the chambers of his memory. These stores of knowledge were of course only gradually acquired in the copious reading of after years; but a solid foundation was laid, during the brief period of his first professorship, upon which were accumulated the results of later study.

On the 1st of January, 1838, he found himself transferred from the quiet duties of a country pastorate to the still greater seclusion of academic life. He entered at once, with characteristic ardour, upon the office of instruction, in studies so peculiarly adapted to his taste. Metaphysical science he speedily vindicated from the charge of inutility, showing the application of its principles to the practical pursuits of men, and as implicitly involved in the whole current of human intercourse. His lucid exposition dispelled the haze of uncertainty hanging around themes so abstract and difficult of research. The warmth of his enthusiasm quickened into life, and clothed with flesh, the marrowless bones of what was regarded only as a dead philosophy. The reanimated form, instinct with the beauty which his glowing fancy diffused, invested with the drapery which his varied learning supplied, and speaking with the elevated tone which his eloquence inspired, no longer repelled the embrace of ardent scholars, as when it lay a ghastly skeleton covered with the dust of centuries of barren speculation.   Such was the impulse given to this study, and so paramount the influence he continued to wield in its behalf, during his long connection with the College, that, enthroned among the sciences, its ascendency has never since been disputed.

But congenial as were these pursuits to the young professor, his conscience began to be disturbed with scruples which marred his repose. It has already been shown with what unusual solemnity and depth of conviction he assumed the office of the holy ministry. His ordination vow presses hard upon him. He had covenanted to make the proclamation of God's grace to sinners the business of his life. Did this comport with a life spent in teaching others only the endless see-saw of the syllogism, or even the sublime mysteries of the human mind? The opportunities afforded for the occasional ministration of the Word, how frequent so ever, did not seem to fill up the measure of obligation he had contracted, by the "laying on of the hands of the presbytery." He must preach with constancy and system, as a man plying his vocation. "The word of the Lord was in his heart, as a burning fire shut up in his bones, and he was weary with forbearing." The charms of scholastic retirement had not palled upon his enjoyment; but, with a stronger passion for the salvation of men, he longed for the cure of souls. Under this pressure of conscience, he proffered his resignation to the Board of Trustees, in May, 1839, to take effect at the close of the year; with a view to accept the pastorship of the Presbyterian Church in Columbia, South Carolina, made vacant by the retirement of the Rev. John Witherspoon, D. D., LL. D.   Accordingly, on the 1st day of January, 1840, he was installed by the Presbytery of Charleston in this new relation, and finds himself once more the pastor of a Christian flock.

Dr. Thornwell was, however, no stranger to the Columbia pulpit, as he often, during the preceding year, for consecutive Sabbaths, occupied the place of the pastor, Dr. Witherspoon, when disabled by chronic sickness. It was at this period the writer's acquaintance with his friend began; though his own position as a Divinity student did not warrant the intimacy which was enjoyed a little later, when brought into the relation of a co-presbyter. The impression will never be erased of the first discourse to which he listened, in the year 1839. A thin, spare form, with a slight stoop in the shoulders, stood in the desk, with soft black hair falling obliquely over the forehead, and a small eye, with a wonderful gleam when it was lighted by the inspiration of his theme. The devotional services offered nothing peculiar, beyond a quiet simplicity and reverence. The reading was, perhaps, a trifle monotonous, and the prayer was marked rather by correctness and method, than by fervour or fulness. But from the opening of the discourse, there was a strange fascination, such as had never been exercised by any other speaker. The subject was doctrinal, and Dr. Thornwell, who was born into the ministry at the height of a great controversy, had on, then, the wiry edge of his youth. The first impression made was that of being stunned by a peculiar dogmatism in the statement of what seemed weighty propositions; this was followed by a conscious resistance of the authority which was felt to be a little brow-beating with its positiveness; and then, as link after link was added to the chain of a consistent argument, expressed with that agonistic fervour which belongs to the forum, the effect at the close was to overwhelm and subdue. "Who is this preacher?" was asked of a neighbour, in one of the pauses of the discourse. "That is Mr. Thornwell; don't you know him?" was the reply. Thornwell,

Thornwell! the sound came back like an echo from the distant past, or like a half-remembered dream, which one strives to recover; when suddenly it flashed upon the memory that, eight years before, when a lad of thirteen, he had heard a young collegian say, "There is a little fellow just graduated in my class, of whom the world will hear something, by and by; his name is Thornwell." This and that were put together; the prophecy and the fulfilment already begun. How little did the writer dream, in the wondering of that day, that nearly twenty years of bosom friendship would bind him to that stranger, as Jonathan was knit to David; or that, after five and thirty years, he would be penning these reminiscences in this biography. Let him be forgiven for floating thus a moment upon the flood of these memories.

Dr. Thornwell remained in this, his second pastoral charge, but a single twelve-month. His brief term of service in the College had proved his value as an educator too much to induce a general acquiescence in his withdrawal. An opportunity was soon presented for his recall. The election of the Rev. Dr. Elliott as Bishop of the diocese of Georgia, left the College pulpit without an occupant. The vacant chaplaincy was at once tendered him, in connection with the Professorship of Sacred Literature and the Evidences of Christianity. The conscientious scruples which had withdrawn him from the chair of Philosophy, did not embarrass his acceptance of a new position, where he would be intrusted with the care of souls, and those of a most important class in society. At the opening of the year 1841, he entered upon his duties in the College, amid the lamentation and tears of his deserted charge. Never before or since was the gospel preached to them with the eloquence and power with which it fell from his lips; and in the agony of their great loss, the question was upon every tongue, "What shall the man do that cometh after the king?" The bereavement was only mitigated by the fact that he still re-

mained a resident of the town, and the opportunity would
be frequently enjoyed of listening to the music of his
voice.   In his renewed connection with the College, he
remained, with only slight interruptions, through a period
of fifteen years, which it will be our pleasure to trace in
the chapters that follow.

CHAPTER XII.

VOYAGE TO EUROPE.

SYMPTOMS OF AN ALARMING DISEASE.—ORDERED TO EUROPE.—LETTERS
BY THE WAY.—SAILS FOR LIVERPOOL.—JOURNAL.—REFLECTIONS UPON
THE OCEAN; UPON THE VALUE OF TIME; UPON THE SEA AS A SCHOOL
FOR THE CHRISTIAN GRACES.—DESCRIPTION OF A NEWFOUNDLAND FOG.
—DANGERS.—STORM AT SEA.—ARRIVES IN EUROPE.

THE College session of January, 1841, found Dr. Thornwell, as we have seen, restored to its halls. But his
labours were soon arrested by symptoms of an alarming
disease. Great prostration and several hemorrhages gave
tokens of that wasting consumption, which so often falls
as an early blight upon the most promising and useful
lives. A sea voyage was prescribed as necessary to his
restoration, including, as a motive for it, a visit to Europe. The needful arrangements were completed by the
month of May, which finds him upon the journey.

It was evidently his purpose to keep a minute journal
of his travels, for the gratification of his family, and as a
memorial for himself. The distraction of sight-seeing,
however, prevented its execution, with the exception of
the record kept whilst he was at sea. Besides this, there
are no memoranda to be found among his papers; and we
are left to glean his impressions of the Old World from
the letters addressed to his wife. With copious extracts
from these, the reader will have to be content, affording,
as they do, glimpses into his home life. The first was
written from Charleston, the first stage of his journey:

"CHARLESTON, S. C., May 1, 1841.

"MY DEAREST WIFE: I received your *very, very* welcome letter this
evening, by Mrs. McFie; for I was waiting for her at the depot, anxious
to hear from home. I have now seated myself to give you a long letter;

157

not so much because you have requested, as because it is a source of pleasure to me to write to you, when I am away. How much we owe to letters, and what a glorious invention is the art of writing! In the first place, I send a kiss to your own sweet lips, then one to Nannie, and then another to Jenny, and my best wishes for all the rest of the family. I arrived in Charleston yesterday afternoon, much wearied by the uncomfortable ride in the stage-coach. The wind blew severely on Thursday night; the doors of the coach had neither glass nor curtains, and we had to take the wind as it came. My seat was just by the door, and so I had the full benefit of all the breezes. There were nine passengers, none of whom I knew; and I was much amused with some of their discussions. Among other things, they took up the subject of Foreign Missions, and came to the conclusion that it did more harm than good to send the Gospel to the heathen. They contended that the heathen were happy in their ignorance; and that to give them the Gospel was only to give them the arts, and consequently the wants and desires of civilized life, and thus to make them wretched. I could not but think of the deplorable stupidity of the carnal heart. These men never once adverted to the state of the soul, and the prospects of the heathen for eternity. Poor creatures! they were consistent. They never thought of their own salvation ; and how could they be expected to think of the salvation of others ? Their desires for themselves extended only to the comfort of their bodies and the lusts of their flesh, and it was in this aspect of the matter that they viewed the probable influence of the Gospel upon the dark places of the earth.   *   *   *   *

" I went down with Hall McGee, to see the different ships soon to sail for Liverpool. I went all over the vessel in which Mrs. McFie expects to sail. I think it a poor ship. It is very large, but its accommodations are not good.   *   *   * There is another ship, which sails for Liverpool on Thursday, that it charms the eye to look at. She is called the ' Colombo.' I am almost tempted to go out in her. My present arrangement is to go to Boston ; but if Mrs. M. will go in the ' Colombo,' I am not sure but I will go with her ; but I could not be tempted to go in the ' Thetis.'

" I feel, my dearest, that we are in the hands of God. He has wonderfully sustained me in the bitterness of separation. I feel confident that all is for good, and that I shall be restored to you in health and strength. I can see His hand in the whole matter. Let us endeavour to love Him more and serve Him better. And now, dearest, good night. I feel quite well. May God bless and keep you and the children.

" Your affectionate husband,

J. H. THORNWELL."

To the same :

" BALTIMORE, MD., *May* 11, 1841.

" MY DEAREST WIFE : Although I did not promise to write you until I reached New York, yet having a few hours of leisure in this place, I find my thoughts recurring with fond affection to my dear wife and

children, and the beloved friends I have left behind me. It is a great
satisfaction to think of you all, and to commend you to that God, whose
I am and whom I endeavour to serve. I cannot say that I am distressed
with anxious thoughts about your health and comfort. The Lord has
mercifully preserved me from painful and harrassing apprehensions in
regard to you; but I often throw myself into your company, carry on
an imaginary conversation with you about wnat I see and hear, and
fancy how you would feel and think, and what you would probably say,
if you were along by my side.   *   *   *   If God should preserve me
and keep me, and restore me to you all again, my heart leaps within me
at the rapture of our meeting. The prospect of that joy reconciles me,
in some measure, to the privations and discomforts of our temporary
separation. Let us often pray for each other, and for the dear children,
our sweet, precious little babes.

"Agreeably to your own request, I shall now attempt to give you
some account of what has befallen me since I left Charleston. We had
a fine passage to Wilmington; but the next day were detained on the
road by the cars breaking down. We were left at the house of a good
old Presbyterian family, in which there were some excellent religious
books; such as the 'Confession of Faith,' 'Erskine and Fisher's Catechism,' 'Watts on Prayer,' and so on. I was quite edified and interested in reading these memorials of the piety and faithfulness of a former generation, and consequently did not feel disposed to murmur
at the Providence which detained us. There were two subjects which
bore much upon my mind, while at this house; upon both of which I
intend putting my thoughts to paper when I get out to sea. They were
suggested to me by reading 'Watts on Prayer.' One was the true spirit
and grace of prayer; in what they consisted; how they might be approved; and why they were so little found among the great body of professors of religion. I am satisfied that there is much more formality in
our ordinary prayers than we, ourselves, are generally conscious of;
that in a multitude of instances we do nothing more than mock God, and
deceive ourselves. The other subject which pressed upon my mind, was
the defective spirit in which preaching is listened to, by those who call
themselves the children of God. Hearers are not sufficiently aware of
the true intent and end of the Christian ministry, and, therefore, do not
receive from the ministrations of the sanctuary that comfort and instruction which, under the blessing of the Spirit, they are calculated to
afford. These meditations, coupled with many thoughts of home, and
many prayers for my precious wife and family, occupied my time during my delay upon my journey.

"The next day, we came safely on, and on last Saturday, at about
ten o'clock at night, we reached the city of Baltimore, where I now am.
On Sunday morning I went to Brother Breckinridge's* church, and
heard an excellent sermon. I went home with him, and have been staying with him ever since. The more I see of him, the more I love him.

* Rev. Robert J. Breckinridge, D. D., LL. D.

There is no man in the Church more misrepresented and more misunderstood. He is exceedingly affectionate, kind, and affable in his
family, and among his people. He has some habits like my own. He
loves to sleep in the morning, to smoke cigars, to sit up at night, and to
tell funny stories. He is a very industrious and laborious man. Yesterday he made me write another article † in reply to the Catholic priests,
which will be published in the next *Visitor*. He has furnished me with
some very flattering letters to ministers in Europe, for which I am very
much indebted to him.

"To-morrow morning I leave for New York, and then shall *immediately* set sail for Europe. After much reflection and consultation, I
have determined not to go in a steam packet, but in a sailing ship. The
steam packets are too crowded, and are said to be much more uncomfortable and unsafe than the ships; which, at this season of the year,
are as expeditious as the steamboats. In a few days more I shall be
upon the broad ocean. It is the very best season of the year for a voyage. Everything seems favourable, and I hope to be in Liverpool early
in June. When I reach Europe, I shall keep the journal which you desired, and send it to you regularly. My health seems to be the same as
usual. I have had no return of spitting blood; the weakness in my
chest seems to have disappeared; and if it were not for prudential and
prospective considerations, I had as lief preach as not. The sea, thus
far, has agreed finely with me. And now, dearest, let me exhort you to
be cheerful and happy until we meet again. Go among your friends and
kindred; visit much, and take frequent exercise, and be as hearty, as
strong, and as lovely, as care on your part can make you, when your
dear husband returns to you from abroad. He commits you and the
babes with confidence to God. A kiss for yourself, for Nannie and
Jenny, and love to all.

"Your devoted husband,

J. H. THORNWELL."

At sea there was no opportunity for correspondence,
and we are thrown upon his journal for the current of his
thoughts. We will cite only such passages as reflect his
character and experience, through which the reader will
come into more personal and intimate acquaintance with
him:

"*Wednesday, May 19th*, 1841.—About one and a half o'clock, P. M.,
we left the wharf at New York, in the packet-ship 'Columbus,' and were
towed over the bar at Sandy Hook by the steamboat 'Hercules.' At

† The first article here referred to, was the famous Essay on the
Claims of the Apocrypha, which gave rise to the discussion with Dr.
Lynch, and to his own book, entitled, 'Romanist Arguments Refuted,'
all of which may be found in Vol. 3 of his 'Collected Writings.'

three o'clock the last tie which bound me to my native land was severed, and we were fairly afloat upon the mighty ocean. The weather was so calm that we did not lose sight of the lights upon the shore until three o'clock the next morning. The change in the atmosphere was remarkable; it became so cold after crossing the bar that I was compelled to pull my overcoat closely around me, and would have been delighted at the prospect of such comfortable fires as I left in Columbia. While passing the bar we sat down to dinner. Our captain, a fine, jovial, good natured man, did the honours of the table; and his fare would have done credit to a New York hotel."

Here follows a sketch of the persons who were his companions during the voyage, and the journal continues:

" We were indeed an ill-assorted collection, bound together by no affinities at all; and consequently each pursued, without any especial regard to the comfort and convenience of others, the ' even tenor of his way.'

"*Thursday, May* 20*th.*—When I arose (which, by the way, I did not do until nine o'clock) there was nothing to be seen but sky and water. It was a beautiful morning; the sun shone out in brightness and beauty; not a cloud fringed the sky; the wind was so gentle that we moved at the rate of only two or three miles an hour, and the whole prospect was one of surpassing loveliness. I thought of Byron's beautiful apostrophe to the ocean; but I confess that I cannot enter fully into the spirit of it. One labours under a sense of confinement in gazing upon the sea, when smooth and unruffled. The horizon is too limited; you feel that the waters stretch beyond it, and hence you are conscious of a constant effort to enlarge the sphere of your vision, and to make your view co-extensive with the vast expanse, which you know is spread out before you. The ocean at rest is *beautiful,* but not *sublime; lovely,* but not *majestic;* it *soothes* and *charms* the mind, but does not *elate* and *expand* it. A storm at sea is doubtless a sublime spectacle; but the mere expansiveness of the waters conduces nothing to the impression. It is the rolling and dashing and heaving of the waves, the tremendous roar of the billows, the tossing of the vessel, the threatening aspect of the heavens, the dismal howling of the winds, and the appalling prospect of terror which storm and tempest spread before them. It is not the vastness of the ocean, but the impressions of the moment, the associations of terror, and danger, and awful power; the sense of the Godhead riding forth in vengeance and majesty : these are the things which render a storm so transcendently sublime. 'But the mere extent of the ocean makes a very vague and indistinct impression. You cannot feel as you think you ought to feel. You are disappointed in your own sensations; the prospect is more circumscribed than you had been led to anticipate, and you exhaust yourself in vain attempts to stretch the volume of waters beyond the capacity of your vision. Such, at least, was the

case with myself. After gazing to the full upon the loveliness of a calm
and unruffled sea, reflecting, as a mirror, the bright rays of the sun, I
turned my thoughts, or rather they turned themselves with something
like magnetic attraction, to my own beloved home. Thoughts of home,
under such circumstances, are unutterably sweet. But it were vain to
attempt a description of the imaginary interviews which I held with her
whom I early led to the altar, and to whom I have plighted my faith,
and the precious little babes, the fair fruits of our early love. Though
far away, I can commend them with confidence to the care and protection of the Shepherd of Israel, who never slumbers nor sleeps.

"In walking to and fro upon the deck of the ship, my attention was
arrested by the motly character of the steerage passengers. Some appeared to be decent and respectable people; they were neatly and tidily
dressed, and were quite prepossessing in their carriage and demeanour.
Poverty had doomed them to that quarter of the ship. Others were
the very picture of filth, meanness, and consummate wretchedness.
Dirty and ragged in their apparel, squalid in their countenances, low
and vulgar in their behaviour, the very refuse and off-scouring of the
earth, I was really glad that they were going away from our shores.
Our ship, in its cabin and steerage passengers, its officers and crew, presents no mean picture of the world, in its various divisions and classes
of society.

"I was much struck with the various efforts of my fellow-passengers
to while away the time. Though they would have shuddered at the
thought of death, they evidently had more time than they knew what to
do with. They tried cards, and dice, and chess; they would walk, and
yawn, and smoke, and loll; and, after all, sigh out in awful moans under
the intolerable burden of too much time. Ah me! on a dying bed
these wasted hours will be like fiends from hell, to torture and harass the
burdened soul. How important is the caution of the Apostle, 'Redeeming the time!' Mark that word, redeeming. It implies scarcity;
it teaches that time must be *purchased;* but who, until a dying hour,
now finds time scarce, or feels constrained to buy it?

"*Saturday, May 22d.*—It is now Saturday night, and I must prepare
for the holy Sabbath. My Bible and Confession of Faith are my travelling companions, and precious friends have they been to me. I
bless God for that glorious summary of Christian doctrine contained in
our noble standards. It has cheered my soul in many a dark hour, and
sustained me in many a desponding moment. I love to read it, and
ponder carefully each proof-text as I pass along.

"*Monday, May 24th.*—I begin to feel very strongly the tameness
and monotony of a sea voyage. When your curiosity is gratified, and
the freshness of novelty subsides, you become very much wearied with the
continual recurrence of the same prospects and the same events. Sky
and water, sky and water, morning, noon, and night, are the constant
objects of contemplation presented to the eye. The only variety in the
scene is made by the changes in the wind, the sporting of the fish, the

flying of the sea-gulls, and the curious movements of Mother Carey's chickens; and even these partake, in a few days, of the same general monotony. Calms are the school of patience; storms, of faith; and a voyage, as a whole, a fine school for every Christian grace. And yet the very circumstances by which it is adapted to discipline the graces of the spirit, call out into powerful action the contrary vices of the carnal heart; and hence sailors are proverbially the most wicked and abandoned men on earth. Those who, of all others, have the most to remind them of their dependence upon God, who require His breezes to waft them on their way, and His protection in the perils of the storm, are, of all others, the most forgetful of His claims, and most thoroughly unmindful of His being. What a proof of His goodness when so many ships are spared, manned by blasphemers, and mingling the voice of cursing and imprecation with every murmur of the wind! Surely His tender mercies are over all His works.

"It is now ten o'clock at night. I was forcibly struck to-day with the propensity of my heart to trust in the creature rather than the Almighty. About twelve o'clock we were threatened with a squall; the wind was high, the heavens were gathering blackness; and some of the passengers began to be alarmed. I at once, though I trust I was not wholly forgetful of God, turned my attention to the strength of the ship and the skill of our sailors; and found, I am afraid, full as much quietude of mind, from contemplating the calmness and self-possession of the captain, as from the gracious promises of Him who says to the ocean, 'Thus far shalt thou come, and here shall thy proud waves be stayed.' I pray that God may deliver me from the sin of unbelief. I know its wickedness, but I feel its power. I strive and fight against it, and sometimes am ready to congratulate myself that the victory is won; but in an evil hour I have fresh and mortifying evidence that I am sinful dust and ashes.

"*Tuesday, May 25th.*—We have been nearly becalmed all day, and what little progress we have made has been out of our course. The effects of a calm in crushing the spirits of the passengers were very observable at dinner. We all sat for a long time as mute as mice, until the captain, with his usual good humour and pleasantry, broke the dismal silence with some of his lively jokes. Such is his exhaustless store of anecdotes and bon-mots, that the most austere ascetic would find it difficult to preserve his gravity, or maintain the rigid contraction of his features. He fills up my idea of what a sea-captain should be, in every respect but one. and that is piety. Polite, without affectation; decided, without severity; gay, without levity; and humorous, without buffoonery, he is always pleasant himself, and renders every one pleasant around him. He is a fair specimen of the moral effects which a religious education will produce, even under the most unfavourable circumstances. He was trained among the genuine old Puritans of New England; and though he went to sea very early in life, the habits and impressions of his childhood adhere to him; and he has been preserved, by his early instruction, from the countless temptations and abandoned dissipations of a sailor's life. His external deportment is not only blameless and irreproachable, but to a certain extent, exemplary; and apparently, all that he wants is a new heart. Ah! what a want is that.

"*Wednesday, May 26th.*—At this moment, ten o'clock at night, we have a most convincing illustration of the vanity and folly of trusting in the flesh. We are now on the edge of the banks of Newfoundland, enveloped in a mist so thick and dark that we can hardly see twice the length of the ship ahead; in the very regions of mountains of ice, without the probability of discerning when we approach them, and compelled to sound a constant alarm of bells, to prevent ourselves from coming in collision with other vessels. In such circumstances what can the skill of man accomplish? What can human prudence or sagacity achieve? When we consider the multitude of vessels that pass these banks, shrouded in almost midnight darkness at noonday, and yet preserved from the desolation of the icebergs, how clear is the proof of a guiding hand upon us, and of a superintending Providence above us! Those who have not seen it, can form no conception of the impenetrable thickness of the mists that here overhang the sea. It is like an immense body of smoke lying upon the bosom of the waters, and shutting out every prospect, either of sky or ocean, from the eye of the observer. It is, indeed, awful to witness!

"*Thursday, May 27th.*—We sail to-day amid unseen dangers on every hand. The water is very near the freezing point, an impenetrable fog hangs around the ship, and we know not at what moment we may be dashed against a mountain of ice, and consigned to a watery grave. Already this morning have we met the shattered fragments of some vessel that has recently met her fate in these dreary regions. How awful is a wreck! How solemn and how prayerful should we be, when we pass among the melancholy memorials of those who have been lost—suddenly, unexpectedly, awfully lost—upon the yawning deep! Oh! it is fearful; in the full career of manhood, in health and strength, with all our energies about us, buoyant with hope, away from friends that we love, and a family that we fondly cherish, to meet death riding in terror upon the foaming billows; to die in the full consciousness of death; to die when we feel that we are full of life. Great God! preserve me, preserve us all from this dreadful end!

"About sunset it became so frightfully dark that the captain could not venture to proceed, and accordingly, in sailor dialect, '*lay to.*' In about two hours afterwards the wind shifted to the northwest, and dissipated the fog so that we were able to go on. And here we are now under full sail, with a fine breeze and a clear sky, and the moon reflecting her silver light upon the bosom of the waters. I here record my solemn conviction, that God has favoured us in answer to prayer. My own heart has been going out in humble supplication, and I am sure that others on board have an interest at the throne of grace. Oh! it is a delightful view of the Divine character, which the psalmist gives us in these words: 'Thou that hearest prayer.'

"I shudder to think of the dangers through which we have passed to-day. Every precaution which human skill or prudence could suggest was adopted; but still our limited vision rendered our situation appalling, and our safety must be ascribed to Him who holds the sea in the hollow of His hand. By the grace of God, which marvellously enabled me to trust in His protection, I was calm and composed; and never in my life enjoyed so richly the portion of the Larger Catechism extending from question 178 to the close. The answers there set down, and the various proof-texts, precious jewels from the exhaustless mine of God's holy Word, contain a summary of Christian instruction, and a model of Christian spirit, which cannot be too faithfully studied. I have read the creeds of most Christian bodies; I have been rejoiced at the general harmony of Protestant Christendom in the great doctrines of the gospel; but I know of no uninspired production, in any language, or of any denomination, that, for richness of matter, clearness of statement, soundness of doctrine, scriptural expression, and edifying tendency, can for a moment enter into competition with the Westminster Confession and Catechisms. It was a noble body of divines, called by a noble body of statesmen, that composed them; and there they stand, and will stand for ever, the monuments alike of religious truth and civil freedom.

"*Monday, May 31st.*—To-day we have a rough sea; our vessel is tossing upon the waters like an egg-shell, and most of the passengers are sick. About five o'clock in the afternoon we had a most terrific squall. The waves were rolling like mountains, and every moment it seemed that our gallant ship must be engulphed. She was dashed now upon one side, now upon the other, now plunging her bow under huge billows which broke over her, and seemed as if they would sink her; and then riding the waves as if in defiance of their fury; the sea meanwhile foaming, and dashing, and roaring like constant thunder, and the wind howling through the rigging with deafening violence, while the heavens were scowling in blackness. The whole scene was one of terror and sublimity, which baffles all description. One could hardly resist the impression that the vessel was conscious of her danger. She appeared to prepare herself to meet every wave, and to withstand every gust of wind. Sometimes we would appear to be several feet beneath the general level of the whole body of the sea ahead, which seemed rolling on to meet and crush us; but the vessel, as if instinct with life, would raise her bow and dash forward, as if driven by ten thousand furies, and fleeing for her safety.

"*Thursday, June 3d.*—Wind against us all day. Six weeks this night have rolled around, since I bid farewell to my beloved family. I can see my wife now in the posture of patient resignation and holy sorrow, in which she sat when, with a throbbing heart, I bid her a mournful farewell. I can see my cherub babes, all unconscious as they were that evening of what was taking place; I can see them now smiling before me in the loveliness of infancy, and all the fond endearments of home are crowding around my heart. Well might Cowper say,

> " 'Domestic happiness! thou only bliss
> Of Paradise, that hast survived the fall!
> Thou art the nurse of virtue; in thine arms
> She smiles, appearing, as in truth she is,
> Heaven-born, and destined to the skies again.'

" *Monday, June 7th.*—I preached yesterday. The cabin and steerage passengers, with the crew, made a very good congregation, and they listened very attentively. Wind against us yesterday and to-day."

" *Monday, June 14th.*—After a succession of head-winds we at length have a favourable breeze, which has diffused joy and gladness throughout the ship. We have been sailing to-day along the coast of Ireland, having passed Kensale, Cork, and Waterford.

" *Tuesday, June 15th.*—Sailing to-day along the coast of Wales, and a picturesque coast it is. We took a pilot on board about two o'clock P. M.

" *Wednesday, June 16th.*—We entered the docks at Liverpool early this morning; and I took my breakfast in the Grecian Hotel, devoutly thankful for my safe passage. The Lord's name be praised for all His mercies, and may He continue his loving kindness through all my wanderings, and through all my life."

CHAPTER XIII.

LETTERS FROM EUROPE.

IT is tantalizing that Dr. Thornwell should have made
two visits to Europe, leaving behind no detailed account of what he saw, and of the impressions made upon
his own mind. In both instances, however, he was in
feeble health, and his stay exceedingly brief. Little more
could be accomplished by him than to maintain a regular
correspondence with his family, upon which we are thrown,
in this chapter, for all that is known of his first trip:

"LIVERPOOL, *June* 16, 1841.

"MY DEAREST, MOST PRECIOUS WIFE: Twenty-eight days have
elapsed since I left New York, in the fine packet-ship, 'Columbus,'
under the command of my old friend, Captain Barstowe; and here I
am now in 'merry old England,' safe, sound, and hearty. * * * As
I know that you must be very anxious in regard to my health, I shall
state at once that the voyage has been of immense service to me. I
look fifty per cent. better than I did when I left New York, and a hundred times better than when I left Charleston and Columbia. I am
sorry that you were distressed with the false report of my having had a
hemorrhage on the road. I have had none since I left home. I had a
cold in Charleston, from riding at night, but that passed off before I
left the city. At this time my appetite is *unusually fine;* and, in justice to England, I must say that there is everything to gratify it. My
complexion is clear and healthful, my digestion uncommonly good, and
in every respect I have abundant reasons for thankfulness to the Giver
of all good. I firmly believe that the crossing of the ocean has been

167

the very making of me ; and I now rejoice that the passage was long,
because the sea-air has been so eminently serviceable. You cannot
imagine how it has *strengthened* me.

"You may wish to know something about Liverpool. As a matter
of course, one day's acquaintance is too short for forming a very correct
opinion. The docks, which are about the greatest curiosity here, are
immensely large ; built of stone, and crowded with vessels from all
parts of the world. They extend something like two miles, and for all
that space are literally crammed with ships, their masts pointing to the
skies like huge forests, and their colours gracefully floating to the
breeze. There is nothing in all America like these spacious docks.
The tides in our country do not rise high enough to admit of them ;
and here they rise too high to admit of what we have in all our cities—
wharves. At high tide here the water rises nineteen feet. The public
buildings in Liverpool are on a magnificent scale, much larger and finer
than buildings of the same sort in America ; but they are deplorably
smoky and dingy from the immense quantities of coal consumed here.
The stores and private buildings are not so handsome as they are in
New York or Philadelphia. The streets are narrow and crowded, and,
in some parts of the town, disgustingly filthy. The police is stationed,
a man for about every fifty yards, along every street, so as to be within
a moment's call for the purpose of suppressing mobs, riots, and all disorder. You see an immense poor population here, all ragged and dirty,
and begging for alms at almost every corner you turn. Sometimes
you meet a wretched, squalid woman in ragged clothes, barefooted,
with a sheet, or something like it, tied around her, and two or three
little children fastened in it, begging for bread, or alms of some sort,
and exciting your compassion by pointing to the helpless condition of
her babes. I am told that these children are frequently borrowed, and
carried about fraudulently, for the purpose of touching the feelings of
spectators. I was walking along in a street to-day, in a very dirty part
of the town, and found the cellars, damp, dark, and filthy, occupied by
families poorer than the poorest that I ever saw in America. Sometimes two or three families, amounting to about twenty persons, live in
a single room, several feet under ground, in a hole not larger than our
pantry, with not a single window in it, and pay nearly all that they can
earn by hard labour for their rent. This is *wretchedness*, this is *poverty
indeed.* Those who can get enough to eat have a very healthful, ruddy
appearance. Their faces looked so red and rosy that my first impression was that they *painted.* But I am told it is the natural complexion
of the people.

"I like the plan of the English hotels very much. A man is as private
in them as in his own house. You order whatever you wish for your
meals ; are charged for what you get, and eat it in your own dining
room. There is no such thing as a public table. Every man or family,
eats when and what he pleases. The cooking is superb ; everything is
clean and tidy ; nothing out of place ; and the servants are prompt, and

active, and as polite as French dancing-masters. I have arrived here at the finest season of the year. Strawberries and cherries are just ripe, and Liverpool abounds with them. The strawberries are about four times as large as ours. We have also gooseberries in abundance, but they are dreadfully sour. The beef is delicious; and such coffee as I have drunk here I have not tasted in many a day before. In short, so far as my outer man is concerned, I abound in comforts. * * * I have no difficulty in getting along here. I feel perfectly at home. I hear my own language, see many of the customs with which I am familiar, and cannot realize that I am among strangers.

"I have been amused here with the warmth with which the people discuss politics. They are just as violent as they are in America. You see handbills stuck up along the streets, by the different parties, just as there was in Columbia, during the contest between Van Buren and Harrison. The tories and whigs are equally violent, and equally abusive. They have public meetings, make furious speeches, abuse the Government, curse one another, generally close by raising a mob, and these are scattered by the police. Another wonder to me, was the prodigious size of the dray horses. They are nearly as large as elephants, very muscular, and two of them draw the weight of six or eight with us. They are too large, however, to be active; and hence I have never seen them move faster than a walk. I believe, now, dearest, I have told you all that I have seen during my first day in Europe. There is but one thing which prevents me from being perfectly happy, so far as this world is concerned; and that is, you are not with me. I seldom see anything new, strange, or interesting, without thinking of you, and wishing that you could see it too. May God bless you, and keep you. Have no fears about me; the Lord will preserve me; and I feel every confidence that in His own good time we shall meet again. His hand is visible in my leaving home. Just think of the very little matter upon which all my subsequent movements have turned. Prof. —— failed to fill an appointment, and that sent me to Europe. Two months ago, and who dreamed that I should be in Liverpool to-day? It is the Lord's doing, and it is marvellous in my eyes. I feel that I am a child of a wonderful and mysterious Providence; and I am satisfied that good is to arise out of this matter. I have never enjoyed the Bible and communion with God so much in all my life, as I did upon the ocean. I lived upon the Scripture, and can truly say, that, in a spiritual point of view, my voyage has been of as much service to my soul, as, in a physical respect, it has been to my body. It has been, too, a great comfort to me to think that many of God's people are praying for my prosperity. I wept freely when I read *Coit's* letter. Such a friend is a treasure beyond all price. * * *

"In a day or two, I shall leave Liverpool for Ireland, where I shall visit Dublin, Belfast, &c.: and from Ireland proceed to Scotland, and make a tour of two or three weeks there; and then proceed to London; so that I shall not be in London until the last of July. After finishing the tour of Ireland, Scotland, and England, I shall proceed to Paris; thence to Switzerland; thence to Germany; and, if I have time, to Rome. If not, I shall return to Liverpool, and probably take a ship directly for Charleston. But it is useless to calculate so far ahead; I may change my mind a hundred times. And now, dearest, I must bring this long, hasty scrawl to a close. Kiss the dear little babes for me, remember me to all our friends, and be perfectly at ease about my health, committing me to the care of our Lord and Saviour, Jesus Christ. God bless you with all spiritual blessings in heavenly places in Christ Jesus.

"Your devoted husband,

J. H. THORNWELL."

"LONDON, *June 28th*, 1841.

"MY OWN MOST PRECIOUS NANCY: You will probably be greatly surprised to find that I am in London so soon, having written to you that I purposed visiting Ireland and Scotland first. But two circumstances induced me to change my route. One was the badness of the weather. The day that I had fixed on for going to Dublin was a windy, gusty day, and I did not feel like going to sea in a strong gale. Another inducement for coming to London at once, was my anxiety to witness the ceremony of proroguing Parliament, which was done last Tuesday. After all, however, I did not see it, as I was misinformed about the time, and got there too late. I must now attempt to give an account of myself since I last wrote you.

"From Liverpool I went to *Chester*, about sixteen miles off, one of the oldest towns in England. It is situated upon the river Dee, has a large thick wall built entirely around it, which affords a splendid walk of a summer afternoon, the wall having a balustraded walk on the top, large enough for two persons to go abreast. This wall was built when England was in possession of the Romans. It has several towers, intended originally as stations for watchmen upon the wall, and which now afford very fine views of the country around. Upon one of these towers Charles the First beheld the rout of his army at Marston moor. There is an inscription upon it commemorative of the fact. Most of the houses in Chester are constructed upon a very peculiar plan. 'They are excavated from the rock (Chester being situated on a rocky eminence) to the depth of one story beneath the level of the ground on each side, and have a portico running along their front, level with the ground at their back, but one story above the street. These porticoes, which are called the Rows, afford a covered walk to pedestrians; and beneath them are shops and warehouses on a level with the street.' While you are walking along these Rows, you are walking between shops and stalls. Among the lions of Chester, which, after all, is distinguished for nothing but its antiquities, is the Castle, part of which was built during the time of William the Conqueror, and part in modern times. It is a very magnificent building, comprising an armoury containing nearly thirty thousand stand of arms, tastefully disposed, a gunpowder magazine, the shire hall, with a noble portico, the county gaol. etc.

"Next comes the Cathedral, a huge Gothic pile, parts of which were built nearly twelve hundred years ago. Like all buildings of its class, it is in form of a cross. It contains some curious monuments, the inscriptions upon which have been effaced by the hand of time. Among the illustrious dead deposited within its walls lie the remains of Travis and Smith. The cloisters of the priests and monks, when it was an abbey, in the possession of the Roman Catholics, prior to the Reformation, are very much worn by age. Though the edifice is constructed of solid stone, its huge colossal pillars look as if there had been floods of water constantly but slowly washing them away. The bishop's throne, upon which I had the impudence to seat myself, feeling myself to be as much of a bishop as any body, was formerly Saint Werburgh's shrine. I felt, in traversing its huge nave, and walking under its lofty ceiling, that I was conversing with men of a by-gone age. I could almost hear the monks counting their beads and muttering their idle prayers, as they did in days of yore in this prodigious pile. There is nothing specially to recommend this building, but its hugeness and antiquity. I noticed within it the monument of the venerable Bishop Hall. I attended worship at Chester, in the morning at an Independent chapel, and in the afternoon at Saint Peter's church, where I heard Rev. E. Bickersteth, whose works, you know, I own. Both preachers were evangelical, but their delivery was shocking, a real school-boy whine. Their gowns seemed too much in their way; they were constantly shrugging their shoulders to keep these worthless appendages from tumbling off. Saint Peter's church, like the Cathedral, tells of other days. The hand of time is visibly marked in the wasting of its pillars; its shape and structure also indicate a high antiquity. I was glad to hear the pure gospel preached, however badly preached, where, three centuries ago, the absurd fooleries of Rome held undisputed sway. God grant that every papist chapel on earth may witness the same change. In Trinity church, another ancient edifice in Chester, lie the mortal remains of Matthew Henry, the commentator, and the poet, Parnell. The style of architecture, if bricks apparently thrown together in heedless confusion can be called a style, is evidently ancient. The houses are low, dreadfully smoked, thrown up without taste or elegance, and shockingly crowded together. Nothing but their age redeems them from contempt; and yet the situation of the town is fine. Almost around it flows the river Dee. On one side you have a beautiful view of the mountains of Wales, on the other a commanding prospect of the hills of Cheshire, while all around the country is lovely from its striking undulations. In this city is the famous cheese mart of England. It is a large area enclosed on all sides, where fairs are held of cheese brought from all parts of the country.

"There are still to be seen here the remains of an old Roman hot and cold bath; and some houses with grotesque devices, that might have

been erected in the earlier stages of British history; evidently put up
as early as the Roman invasion. This town, seven hundred years ago,
was the scene of the interview between Henry the Second and Malcolm
the Fourth; and here, more than five hundred years ago, Edward received the submission of the Welsh. It stood out for the King during
the civil wars, but was finally taken by the Parliament, in 1645. Its population is about twenty-two thousand. There are as many buildings now
without as within the walls. The old town is on a rocky eminence;
many of the new buildings are in a valley; and as you walk upon the
old wall, you have these buildings beneath your feet; and the whole de-
clivity, down to their level, is in a rich state of cultivation. About
three miles from Chester is Eaton Hall, the magnificent seat of the Marquis of Westminster, one of the richest noblemen in England. His income is about five thousand dollars a day. His yard, as we would call it,
embraces about thirty square miles, beautifully laid out in forests, gardens, and parks. He has been at immense expense to import every variety
of trees, and flowers, and fruits, from all parts of the world. His hot-
houses cover several acres of ground; and include a fine peach orchard, a
rich grape arbour, thousands of pine-apple trees, oranges, lemons, and
every fruit of every climate; and that, too, in full perfection. In the midst
of his gardens, and just before his door, winds the river Dee; from the
portico of his mansion, on one side, you have a beautiful view of the
mountains of North Wales, and on the other, of the hills of Cheshire.
His park is stocked with deer, grazing about as tame as sheep. I went
all over his building, which has recently been fitted up; but its rich and
gorgeous saloons, its plated furniture, its spacious halls, I am utterly
unable to describe. His stables are fine, rich buildings, with heavy
Gothic arches and windows. They would be a palace for men, much
less for horses. In the gardens is an old Roman altar, with nymphs
and fountains, which the Marquis has preserved.

"I have now gone through my description of Chester; from which I
came on to London, without stopping at any of the intermediate towns.
I reached London the day that Parliament was prorogued by Her Majesty, the Queen, but I did not witness the ceremony. I was in the
Houses of Lords and Commons, however, immediately after; and guess
my surprise to see what little, narrow, contracted halls they were; and
the benches were, for all the world, like school benches, except that they
were cushioned. On expressing my astonishment that the British Legislature should meet in such quarters, I was reminded of what I knew
before, that these were only temporary accommodations, the old ones
having been burnt; and that they were now putting up magnificent
buildings for the purpose. From these halls I went to Whitehall, where
Charles the First was executed; then to Westminster Abbey, where our
noble Confession of Faith was drawn up, and where lie crowded together the mighty dead of many centuries. Thence I went to Westminster Hall, a spacious area, originally built for a banqueting-house;
thence to the Parks—Hyde Park, Saint James', the Palace, and Regent's

Park ; but as I have been here a week, and have seen yet only a corner of London, I must reserve a description of this vast metropolis for another of my *short* epistles. One of my first achievements was to hunt out the book range, the famous Pater Noster Row; and imagine my surprise to find it a little, narrow, dirty lane, where a carriage could hardly pass. The whole region smelt of Popery : Pater Noster, Ave Maria, Amen, &c., being the streets of the square. And now, dearest, I must draw to a close. In about ten days more I leave for Scotland.

" Your most devoted husband,

J. H. THORNWELL. "

His third letter, dated London, July 2d, 1841, is largely occupied with personal and domestic allusions, which would have little interest for the general reader; after which he proceeds to say :

"I have not yet flirted with the Queen, neither have I seen Her Majesty; and as I am not disposed to pay one or two hundred dollars for the privilege of paying obeisance to royalty, I shall not seek the honour of an introduction. You can only be introduced in a court dress ; which consists of knee-breeches, silk stockings, silver buckles, and I know not what trumpery besides. I have been all around and about, though not in, the Palace. I have seen most of the noblemen's houses, and almost all the lions of London. Mr. Trezevant's family, who have shown me great kindness, and Mr. Stevenson, are the only acquaintances I have made. My object has been to *see* ; and hence I have not been anxious to get into society. I have traced out all the leading places in London, rendered illustrious by literary association. I have been in the very cell in the famous tower, where Sir Walter Raleigh was confined, and where he wrote his history of the world. I have stood upon the spot where Anne Boleyn was executed, and have lifted the axe which took off her head. I have seen the armours of kings and knights, from eight hundred years ago to the present time. I have sat in the *great chair* in which all the Kings of England have been crowned for eight hundred years. I have seen the monuments of the mighty dead, extending ten centuries back ; I have stood upon the place where Charles the First was gloriously executed, and have been entranced in the chapel where our noble standards were compiled. I have gazed upon the edifice in which Watts and Owen preached, though it is now sadly dilapidated, and has ceased to be a *church*. I have been in the range where Johnson lived, and where the literary men of his day met their clubs. The inn is still standing where the poet Chaucer and twenty-nine pilgrims, were accommodated on their journey to Canterbury. London is full of literary associations. It has been the scene of great and glorious events, as well as others of a contrary character. I have been in all the villages for ten miles around London, visiting some by land, and others by boats upon the river Thames. It is impossible, in the compass of a single letter, to give anything like a description of this vast metropolis, and of the exquisite loveliness and beauty of the country and villages around. But I often think of Byron's description of it in 'Don Juan :'

> " 'A mighty mass of brick, and stone, and shipping,
> Dirty and dusky, but as wide as eye
> Can reach ; with here and there a sail just skipping
> In sight, then lost amid the forestry
> Of masts ; a wilderness of steeples peeping
> On tip-toe, through their sea-coal canopy ;
> A huge dun cupola, like a foolscap crown
> On a fool's head—and there is London town.'

" The west end of London, always bating the smoke, surpasses the most extravagant conception which a stranger can form of it. Its parks and squares, its crescents and public buildings, are almost like enchanted ground ; and then, the great variety, the astonishing contrasts, which a short walk will present you with, from the Palace to Billingsgate. It is, in fact, a faithful picture of the world. Greenwich Hospital, and Greenwich Park, are themselves worth a trip across the Atlantic to see. They are about three miles from what is called London, though it is built up nearly all the way. I walk, on an average, about ten miles every day, gazing, wondering, and cogitating. I have seen much of the common people, having arrived here at the time of the general elections. I have attended some of their meetings, worming myself through the vast crowds with my hands on my watch and my purse, for there are some prodigiously light-fingered gentry here ; and I have witnessed something of bribery, fraud, and intimidation, which are practised by the rich and great. It is now a time of intense political excitement. I must say, that in all that makes life precious, and exalts, refines, and elevates the mass of the people, America is immeasurably superior to England. Give me my own country forever. I see what is excellent in England ; but I see so much of an opposite character, that I must still sigh for my native land. The tories here have a prodigious prejudice against us, and abolitionism is, if possible, more fanatical here than in America.

" Next week I shall leave London for Scotland. I shall travel leisurely, visiting all the principal places. My health is quite good. I feel as strong as I ever did ; much more elastic, and have not the slightest sensation of weakness in the chest. I feel confident that, by the blessing of God, my health will be quite restored, so that I can return to my duties by the first of December. In regard to *journalizing*, I cannot write anything of interest, from want of time. I could only give a meagre skeleton of names and places, with some general description, that would amount to nothing. My letters, I hope, will be as interesting as a journal, such as I should be compelled to write. And now dearest, precious Nancy, I commend you to God, and the word of His grace; and believe me as ever,

"Your devoted husband,

J. H. THORNWELL."

The next letter is dated,

"GLASGOW, SCOTLAND, *July* 15, 1841.

"MY DEAREST WIFE: It is with heartfelt pleasure that I sit down to hold communication with her whom my soul loves, in the only way which is now left me. I feel that, in your affections, I possess a prize of inestimable value; and I look forward, with interest and delight, to the renewed joys which we shall experience in the society of each other, when God shall bring us together again, after our long and painful separation. I have thought much of the best methods of sanctifying our love, and of being fellow-helpers to each other in our heavenly pilgrimage. I feel a renewed obligation, from God's great goodness to me since I left home, to devote myself wholly, unreservedly, to His service and glory. He has protected me from danger, and has, I trust, entirely restored my health. What can I render to Him but that life which He has preserved, that health which He has restored, and that strength which He has increased? Let us both endeavour to be more holy, watchful and devoted; let us endeavour to build each other up in the most holy faith. I am afraid that, in past times, our intercourse has not been sufficiently of a religious character. We have both been a little shy in communicating our spiritual states, our joys or sorrows, our hopes and fears. If there has been an error of this sort, let us try to correct it hereafter, and delight more in being heirs together of the grace of life. It is my earnest prayer that God may give us grace to glorify His name in all things.

"I have been in Glasgow five days, and have made the acquaintance of several clergymen, who have treated me with the utmost cordiality, and insisted upon my protracting my stay in order to preach for them. I had the opportunity also of attending the meeting of the Presbytery of Glasgow. The leaven of New Schoolism, I am sorry to say, is beginning to work its way, even here. The Presbytery of Kilmarnock, at its last meeting, deposed a man from the ministry for holding sentiments somewhat similar to those of Albert Barnes. Error, however, has yet made little progress; and the prompt steps of the Presbytery, which were confirmed and applauded by the Synod, I sincerely hope may arrest it. The Scotch are indeed a noble race; a little too much inclined to bigotry; but if the spirit of speculation on theological subjects should once become propagated among them, there is no telling where the evil would stop. Some of the fathers of the Church here say that I am exactly right on the subject of Boards and Agencies, and urge me to cry aloud and spare not. They have strong sympathy with the orthodox among us. I am glad to see that they are taking a decided interest in missionary operations; and have really adopted the very plan, so far as I have yet been able to learn their system, which I recommended in my article. These Presbyterians of whom I am speaking are all Seceders. I have made no acquaintances yet among the ministers of the Establishment, though I have heard one of their most distinguished men, Dr. Buchanan, preach; and a very fine preacher he is.

"It is really a treat, after coming out. of England, to see how the Sabbath is observed in Scotland. Everything on the streets is as still as death; no travelling is allowed, and their churches are all full of attentive listeners. The style of preaching among the Seceders is eminently instructive and edifying. They do not allow the minister to *read*. In the Established Church, however, they generally *read* their sermons. I have been much interested in the old Cathedral here, where the famous Assembly of 1638 was held, which deposed the bishops, defied the government, and broke up Episcopacy in Scotland. It was a glorious body, with Henderson at its head; and I could not but pray that the land which had been rendered illustrious by such a body, might always maintain and defend the noble and precious doctrines, for which that Assembly testified and suffered. It is now vacation in the University of Glasgow; all the Professors are out of town, so that I have had no opportunity of becoming acquainted with them. Glasgow is a much larger city than I expected to find it, and much more elegantly built; it is about the size of Philadelphia. I came to Glasgow with the intention of visiting the Highlands of Scotland; but the constant rains and the severe cold, for the season, have led me to abandon the project. It has rained every day since I left London, and there is not the least likelihood of its clearing up soon. I could not go to the Highlands, without being cold and wet all the time, and I shall not suffer my curiosity to lead me into such folly. To-morrow I leave for England again, intending to stop a few days at Edinburgh; and from London shall set out immediately for the Continent. I am extremely anxious to get somewhere where I can see and feel the sun.

"In coming to Scotland I made an extensive and interesting tour through the country. I visited Kenilworth, where are the ruins of the ancient and magnificent castle, where Elizabeth was sumptuously entertained by Leicester for seventeen days. The gorgeous structure is now a mere waste, and part of its former enclosure is now a grazing ground for sheep. From Kenilworth I went to Warwick, where there still exists, in all its original grandeur, one of the finest baronial castles in England. There, among a thousand memorials of ancient times, I saw the bed and bed-room furniture of Queen Anne, which had been presented to the Earl of Warwick by George the Fourth. From Warwick I went to Stratford-upon-Avon, and saw the room in which Shakespeare was born, and trod upon the grave where his ashes repose. The walls of the room are covered with the names of those who have visited the spot, as also are several large albums. Two Americans, in their folly and enthusiasm, had beds made for them in the room, and slept there all night. Probably they thought that they might catch something of Shakespeare's genius. From Stratford I went to Henley, on account of its name, and found it a miserable, dirty little village. From there I went to Birmingham ; thence to Tamworth, Derby, Chesterfield, York (the chief city of the North of England, with the finest Cathedral in the country), Darlington, Durham (another fine Cathedral), and Newcastle-upon-Tyne ; thence I had a dreary ride over the bleak, sterile, and desolate Cheviot hills in Scotland. Here I visited the interesting ruins of Melrose Abbey, the scene of Scott's Monastery. About four miles off, I visited the ruins of Dryburgh Abbey, and saw the grave of Sir Walter Scott, and the monuments of Ralph and Ebenezer Erskine, the Seceder divines. This Abbey is really enchanted ground. It is embowered in a lovely grove of trees, some of which are as old as the Abbey itself (seven hundred years), while the Tweed gently murmurs close by it. After musing at Dryburgh, I returned to Melrose, and then visited Abbotsford, the late residence of Scott. But I found nothing specially remarkable there. The name of Scott gives it all its charm. I then proceeded to Edinburgh, passing through Galashiels and Dalkeith, and passing by Craignuller castle, in which Mary, Queen of Scots, was confined. From Edinburgh I came to Glasgow, passing the ancient palace of Linlithgow, in which the same unfortunate Mary was born.

"Such is the rapid outline of my travels since I last wrote. I have been much charmed with the beautiful, undulating surface of England, and the variegated scenery of Scotland.

"And now, dearest, I must draw to a close. Kiss the children again and again ; and may God be with you and keep you, and restore us speedily to the beloved society of each other.

"Your devoted husband,

J. H. Thornwell."

The last letter from Europe contains little of general interest to the reader. It is dated,

"Paris, *July* 31, 1841.

"Here I am again writing to my beloved Nancy, ten thousand times dearer to me than all the world besides. You see that I am in France, as the French say, 'La belle France.' I had a rough passage across the English channel. The boat did not strike me as being the best in the world ; it was old and small, and we had one hundred and twenty passengers on board. There blew up a severe gale, and we had to put into the most convenient port until the gale was over. I do not think I ever saw so much alarm and sea-sickness. We were about the most weather-beaten set you ever saw when we reached Boulogne, the French port at which we were landed. We were marched up in files to an office, under an escort of a few soldiers, where our passports were examined. Our luggage was all sent to the custom-house, where it was examined ; and if all proved straight, as it did with me, we were permitted to travel on without interruption to Paris.

"The ride from Boulogne to Paris was not particularly interesting. The country was in a high state of cultivation ; some of the towns, such as Montreuil and Abbeville, powerfully and strongly fortified.   On yesterday morning, about 6 o'clock, I reached Paris; and I must confess that I was prodigiously disappointed in the general appearance of the city.   The streets are narrow and dirty ; the buildings tall, dingy, and irregular, and I did think utterly destitute of taste in their arrangements and external appearance ; and then, again, the extent and magnitude of the city were far short of what I had been led to anticipate.   Compared with London, Paris is a mere child in size, richness, and grandeur.   But although I was disappointed in the French metropolis as a *whole*, when I descended to the examination of its particular *parts*, my most sanguine expectations were more than realized.   The public buildings, the Tuileries, with its spacious gardens; the Champs d'Elysees, the cathedrals, the libraries, the galleries of painting and statuary, exceed any description which I could be able to give.   You have heard a great deal of *the Boulevards*.   What do you suppose they are ?   Why, nothing in the world but a long street with trees planted along the sidewalks for shade. It extends about four miles; it is pleasant and beautiful, and that is about all you can say of it.   The gardens of the Tuileries are splendid, and all through the walks are scattered various specimens of statuary. The French have a perfect passion for paintings and statues, and in this respect Paris excels London.   The Elysian Fields are lovely beyond all comparison.   The Chamber of Deputies is a fine Grecian building, and the Madeline is the most magnificent edifice I ever beheld.   The Royal Library, which I traversed through and through, contains eight hundred thousand volumes.   The French hotels are far inferior to the English or American in neatness, elegance, and comfort ; but their servants are much more interesting.   The French, from the lowest to the highest, are naturally polite, and are free from the stiffness and formality of English manners.   *   *   *   *

" Of course there is no such thing as Sunday here.   A tradesman will engage to have your boots or your coat done on Sunday as readily as on Saturday.   Such is the blessed result of Popery.   It is religion enough to have splendid churches, and burn candles all day before doll-baby images.   Nothing more is required to get to heaven.   Alas, for the superstition, the wretched superstition, which in this enlightened age covers so fair a portion of the globe !   But the Protestants are bestirring themselves in France.   God grant them rich and glorious success. * * *

" Next week I intend setting out for Geneva, the scene of Calvin's labours.   I think it doubtful if I shall be able to get to Rome.   If the snows are very heavy in the Alps, I shall not attempt it; but shall go probably into Belgium and Prussia, and then return to England.   If I find, however, that I can go to Rome without any difficulty, and make up my mind to do so, I shall not go into Belgium or Germany at all. It will be too cold by the time of my return from Italy. When I shall direct my steps homeward I cannot positively say *now*. If I were to consult my own feelings instead of my interest, I should set out at once. * * * * My health now is as good as it ever has been in my life ; and I have no doubt that it would have been better still, if I had not staid so long in the trying, cold, and rainy climate of England. I have no cough, no blood-spitting ; a fine appetite, a good digestion. I do not know that I am any fatter than I always was. I belong to the lean tribe, and am afraid there is no prospect of my ever getting much meat upon my bones. * * *

"The General Assembly of Scotland was over before I reached Europe. It was held in May, about the same time with our own. I have seen the proceedings of our own, which really amounted to nothing. Some very important matters were completely slurred over. But still, I think the prospect of a return to the old paths is encouraging, and I thank God for what He has already done for us. I have gathered some important facts about the state of religion in England and America, which I shall be able to use to advantage when I get home. You will be delighted to hear that the religious condition of America is far superior to that of Europe.

"And now, dearest Nancy, I am at the end of my paper. A thousand kisses for you and the children. May heaven's richest blessings rest upon you. Pray constantly for me, love, as I do for you. The Lord has preserved me hitherto, and I shall need His protection to the end. As soon as I can return, I will. Besides the charms of my own family, my own country has a thousand attractions for me. I candidly believe that America is the first nation on the globe ; and all through the continent of Europe, the American flag is honoured and respected. I am proud of my nation, and prouder still, after having seen others. May God bless you and keep you.

Believe me, as ever, your devoted husband,

J. H. THORNWELL."

The chart of travel here laid down does not appear to have been pursued; for, on the 3d of September, we find a letter, written in New York, announcing his arrival in his native land, and that a few days of railroad speed will place him once more in the bosom of his family. The patriotic fervour which glows in the closing sentence of the preceding letter was one of the deepest sentiments in Dr. Thornwell's heart; of which there will be occasion to speak more fully hereafter. Perhaps the most amusing,

as well as enthusiastic, exhibition of it, was given in connexion with this return.   In his land journey from Charlotte, North Carolina, to Lancaster, where his family then
was, it is related of him that, upon crossing the line
which separates the two Carolinas, he sprung suddenly
out of the carriage, prostrated himself upon the soil of his
native State, and kissed it reverently with his lips.   It
was but the sign of a devotion more conspicuously illustrated at a later date.   In truly earnest natures, what is
merely sentiment with others becomes a deep and consuming passion; and there was a depth in this man's soul,
which it took a mighty civil revolution to disclose.

CHAPTER XIV.

OLD AND NEW SCHOOL CONTROVERSY.

THE current of the narrative has borne us to a point at
which we must pause and retrace our course, in order
to place the subject of our story in the councils of the
Church, and to sketch the active part he bore in the religious controversies of his day. No part of his public
work was more important than that which he performed
as a polemic; and no man in the Southern Presbyterian
Church wielded so vast and so acknowledged an influence,
in moulding the legislation of the body to which he belonged. He was introduced into the ministry just as the
great controversy was culminating in the schism, which
rent the Presbyterian Church into two large rival communions; and the first General Assembly in which he sat
as a member was that of 1837, famous in our annals as
the Assembly in which the Reform measures were carried
through, which precipitated and effected the rupture. To
many readers of this book the story is familiar as a thrice-
told tale, for the actors in those stirring scenes have not
all passed away; and many who began their ministry
shortly after, were compelled to be conversant with all the

181

details of that painful struggle to maintain the ascendency of truth. But after the lapse of more than a generation, there must be large numbers to whom the story is known only in its general results; whilst readers outside the pale of the Presbyterian Church, into whose hands this book may fall, know nothing of the principles that were involved, nor of the agony of effort by which they were at length preserved.

The discussions, in which Dr. Thornwell took so lively an interest, were left over as a residuary bequest of this fierce controversy, and cannot be adequately comprehended without some acquaintance with that out of which they were born. It seems indispensable, therefore, to arrest the continuity of this biography, by a preliminary sketch of the original controversy, and of the schism in which it terminated; to which, accordingly, the present chapter will be devoted.

The cardinal issue, in the whole dispute, was that of a strict or a lax construction of the acknowledged standards; since all the deviation from sound doctrine claimed to be *salva fide*, and therefore within the limits of the Confession of Faith; and the authority of the Form of Government was held not to be infringed in the practical administration of Church affairs. The evidence, however, is cumulative, that, up to the beginning of the present century, through a period of nearly one hundred years, no subscription of the Westminster Confession was tolerated which did not accept it in its entirety. The ingenious artifice of receiving it only for "substance of doctrine," was the invention of a later and more degenerate age.

The first proof of this is found in the language of the Adopting Act, passed in 1728-29; showing a formal and judicial promulgation of these Standards to be necessary as a *test of orthodoxy*, and a barrier against erroneous opinions setting in from various quarters, especially from England and the north of Ireland. The pioneers, who first planted Presbyterianism upon this continent, had all subscribed these Standards at the time of their ordination; and though now living in a foreign country, they naturally regarded themselves as members of the mother Church at home. It was not until the Church of their own planting had expanded into fair proportions, that they recognized her distinct and independent existence. The omission, so natural at first, of not having adopted, "as a body politic, and by the conjunct act of their own representatives," a public Confession, was corrected just so soon as the necessity became apparent that doctrinal tests were needed to guard against the influx of error.

The second proof is, that, after the agitation produced by this proposed measure was calmed, and the opposing parties came, through discussion, to fuller acquaintance with each other's views, the Westminster Confession was adopted with entire unanimity, after excepting certain clauses in the twentieth and twenty-third chapters, which related to the jurisdiction of the civil magistrate in ecclesiastical matters; which could have no application in this country, and for resistance to which interference these men had been driven as martyrs from country and home. Now, *exclusio unius est expressio alterius:* the exception of these specified clauses was the adoption of all that remained; so that, as the historian remarks, "as these clauses are no longer in the Confession, there is not an article or expression in that formula to which these men did not assent. Such was the latitudinarianism of those days"! *

If doubt can linger upon any mind as to the strictness of this subscription, it will be removed by a subsequent declaration of the same body, when, in 1736, they explain certain ambiguities of expression in the original instrument, which had alarmed the jealousy of some: "The Synod doth declare that the Synod have adopted, and still do adhere to, the Westminister Confession, Catechisms, and Directory, without the least variation or alteration, and without any regard to said distinc-

* Dr. Hodge's History of the Presbyterian Church, vol. I, p. 183.

tions,"* alluding to certain expressions in the Adopting Act
by which these persons were stumbled. Earlier than this
in 1730, the Presbytery of New Castle, anticipating this
explanatory act of the Synod, "solemnly declared and
testified that they own and acknowledge the Westminster
Confession and Catechisms to be the confession of our
faith, being in all things agreeable to the Word of God,
so far as we are able to judge and discern, taking them
in the true, genuine, and obvious sense of the words."
The Presbytery of Donegal uses similar language, in the
formula of subscription which they drew up: "In all
things agreeable to the Word of God, taking them in the
plain and obvious meaning of the words."† The whole
body of the Church, and the several parts thereof, speak,
therefore, with the same explicitness on this point.

A third link in this chain of evidence is, the enforcement
of the same strict subscription upon all intrants into the
ministry, in the following Act, passed by the Synod in
1730: "Whereas, some persons have been dissatisfied at
the manner of wording our last year's agreement about
the Confession, etc., supposing some expressions not sufficiently obligatory upon intrants, the Synod do now declare that they understood these clauses, that respect the
admission of intrants or candidates, in such a sense as to
oblige them to receive and adopt the Confession and
Catechisms, at their admission, in the same manner, and
as fully, as the members of the Synod did that were then
present."‡ To render this act operative, inquisition was
made each year of the Presbyteries, as to their compliance
with it; so that "there is not the slightest evidence that
any of the Presbyteries ever admitted, during the period
under review, any minister who dissented from any of the
doctrinal articles of the Confession of Faith."§

* Records of the Presbyterian Church, p. 125.
† Dr. Hodge's History of the Presbyterian Church, vol. I, pp. 190, 194.
‡ Records of the Presbyterian Church, p. 96.
§ Dr. Hodge's History of the Presbyterian Church, vol. I, p. 197.

Fourthly, the marked contrast in the terms used in adopting the Form of Government, fixes the sense in which the purely doctrinal symbols were received. As to the former, we have the following Deliverance in 1729: "The Synod do unanimously acknowledge and declare, that they judge the Directory for Worship, Discipline, and Government of the Church, commonly annexed to the Westminster Confession, to be agreeable in substance to the Word of God, and founded thereupon; and therefore do earnestly recommend the same to all their members, to be by them observed as near as circumstances will allow, and Christian prudence direct."* Fifty-seven years later—that is to say, in 1786—we have the reason given for this precise language: "The Synod also receives the Directory for Public Worship and the Form of Church Government, recommended by the Westminster Assembly, as in substance agreeable to the institutions of the New Testament. This mode of adoption we use, because we believe the general platform of our Government to be agreeable to the Sacred Scriptures; but we do not believe that God has been pleased so to reveal and enjoin every minute circumstance of ecclesiastic government and discipline, as not to leave room for orthodox churches of Christ, in these minutiæ, to differ with charity from one another."† Here, then, for the first time in our ecclesiastical annals, we meet with the relaxed phrase, "*agreeable for substance;*" which a later period sought to carry over into the Confession of Faith, but which is employed by these fathers expressly to discriminate betwixt the two. In regard to the Confession, the subscription is explicit and particular. It is not received for substance, but in all its articles, with a single specified exception; whereas a latitude is allowed in the adoption of the Form of Government, it being comprehensively embraced only in its general principles; and even in these a clear dis-

* Records of the Presbyterian Church, p. 93.   † Ibid. p. 519.

tinction is recognized as to their relative importance, when compared with the doctrines of grace.

The fact is, the principles of Presbyterian Church government have never been as articulately wrought out, nor as fully expounded, as the doctrines of its faith. Unfriendly influences have warped them from the period of the Reformation, giving them a set which it has been impossible, even to the present day, wholly to overcome. It is well known that the famous Westminster Assembly itself was not exclusively a Presbyterian council. As at first constituted, it embraced Episcopalians and Independents as well; and though the former soon withdrew, the Independents remained through its entire sessions— few in number, perhaps, but powerful in influence. Sound Calvinists as they were, they harmonized perfectly with Presbyterians in the statement of Christian doctrine; but differences emerged as soon as the Constitution and Polity of the Church were touched. The Form of Government bears thus upon its face the traces of a compromise, especially in the exposition of the Eldership.* It was not such an instrument as strict Presbyterians would have prepared, as a full statement of their principles. We signalize this difference of terms in the adoption of the Form of Government, as showing that the fathers of the Church in this country were not so rigid in their views of order as of doctrine; and because, as we shall presently see, it was precisely through this breach in the walls the Trojan horse, with its belly full of armed Greeks, was introduced within the citadel of the Presbyterian Church. It gives the key to the Plan of Union in 1801, to many of the questions which occasioned the disruption in 1837,

---

* The Westminster Assembly, after a triangular conflict between the Presbyterians, Independents, and Erastians, did affirm the Divine Right of Presbytery. This, however, was disallowed by the Parliament; who softened its language into the following declaration: "That it is lawful, and agreeable to the Word of God, that the Church be governed by Congregational, Classical, and Synodical Assemblies." See Neal's History of the Puritans, Part 3d, Chap. 6.

and to all the discussions in which the subject of these
Memoirs, and others of like mind, were afterwards engaged.

Fifthly, if there had been a disposition to abate the
authority of the Confession, it would most naturally have
revealed itself during the memorable schism, in 1741, between what was then designated as "the Old and New
Side." But so far from this, both sections, immediately
upon their separation, renewed their subscription of the
Standards, in identical terms as at first;* and upon their
reunion, in 1758, the first article in the basis was a joint
declaration of their adherence to the same.† This chain
of proof runs down to the formation of the General Assembly in 1788; which, having purged the Confession of
the objectionable clauses relative to the civil magistrate,
declared it to be a part of the Constitution of the Church.
This is certainly emphatic; for, "whoever heard," says
Dr. Hodge, "of adopting a Constitution for substance?
Is the Constitution of the United States thus adopted or
interpreted? It is, on the contrary, the supreme law of
the land; and all who take office under it are bound to
observe it, in all its parts."‡

Sixthly, in addition to this documentary evidence, we
have also the testimony of contemporary writers to the
same fact; and a series of judicial decisions, extending
from 1763 to 1810, in which the Confession is rigidly
applied in the repression of error. A simple allusion to
this is sufficient; as the cases in detail may be found, by
those who desire it, in the records of those times.

This summary—necessarily imperfect, because so condensed—establishes the historic sense in which these
Standards were received by the Church, from the beginning. It is important, as justifying the measures by
which, after a temporary departure, she was reformed
back to her original orthodoxy; and because the attempt

* Records of the Presbyterian Church, pp. 157, 232.   † Ibid. p. 286.
‡ History of the Presbyterian Church, vol. 1, p. 218.

will be renewed from age to age to escape from the obligation of an extended creed, by an ambiguous subscription of its articles.

In an evil day the Presbyterian Church paused in the development of her distinctive principles, and formed an alliance with New England Congregationalism; which, in a third of one century, brought her to the brink of ruin. The controversies of this period have so revealed the essential differences of the two systems, that we now look back with wonder at the attempt to amalgamate them. But we should do great injustice to both the parties, if we fail to notice the influences which drew them together in relations that could not be established now. The first settlers in New England were largely Presbyterian in sentiment; carrying with them their symbols of faith, which were used for household instruction almost as familiarly, in that province, as in the districts where Presbyterianism gained the ascendency. It does not concern us now to consider the causes which in New England put the Congregational system in the advance, and repressed the development of pure Presbyterianism. It is sufficient to notice the general historical fact, that two systems, identical in doctrinal belief, and separated only by differences of external administration, are never found to prosper equally upon the same soil. The one almost of necessity absorbs the other; because the distinction appears too immaterial, to resist the tendency to union in points that are essential. Thus Presbytery has never been able to push its way in New England, pre-occupied, as it is, by a system so nearly co-ordinate with it; and Independency has never struck its roots into the soil already covered by Presbytery. The process of absorption, however, rarely leaves either system unaffected by the foreign ingredients that are incorporated. Thus it happened, that the early Congregationalism of New England was largely moulded in its form by the Presbyterian influence with which it was impregnated. Especially was this true in

Connecticut, where, at the close of the Seventeenth Century, the Presbyterians formed nearly half of the entire population. Thus, the Cambridge Platform, adopted in 1648, acknowledged the Westminster Confession " to be very holy, orthodox, and judicious, in all matters of faith; and we do, therefore, fully and freely, consent thereunto, for the substance thereof; only in those things which have respect to Church government and discipline, we refer ourselves to the platform of Church discipline agreed upon by this present Assembly."* It is astonishing how nearly, even in government, this platform approximates the two systems. It recognizes the Eldership, and distinguishes between the two classes of those who teach and those who only rule. It defines exactly the office of the deacon. It affirms that "Church government, or rule, is placed by Christ in the officers of the Church." It recognizes "Synods, orderly assembled, according to the pattern, Acts xv., as the ordinance of Christ;" whose decisions are binding, so far as consonant to the Word of God, not only because of that agreement, but " also for the power whereby they are made, as being an ordinance of God." In like manner, the Saybrook Platform, formed in Connecticut, in 1708, "provided that the elders of a particular church, with the consent of the brethren, have power, and ought to exercise discipline, in all cases within that church. The churches in each county form a Consociation. The council of this body consists of all the teaching and ruling elders of the churches; which are also at liberty to delegate lay messengers, who are entitled to deliberate and vote as members; provided, how-

---

* See the original authorities quoted in Dr. Samuel J. Baird's History of the New School, p. 143. We take this opportunity to acknowledge our indebtedness to this work, published by the author in 1868, for the remaining facts in this chapter, which are simply condensed from its pages. It is a book of great value, from the skill with which its materials are compiled, and from the documentary evidence with which its statements are substantiated. It brings the history of this great struggle within narrow compass, and is perfectly accessible to all.

ever, that no matter shall be determined without a majority of the elders."*

Still later, in 1799, we have the following statement from the old Hartford North Association, as to the constitution of the Connecticut churches: "This Association gives information to all whom it may concern, that the constitution of the churches in the State of Connecticut, founded on, etc., is not Congregational, but contains the essentials of the government of the Church of Scotland, or Presbyterian Church in America, particularly as it gives a decisive power to Ecclesiastical Councils; and a Consociation, consisting of ministers and messengers, or lay representatives from the churches, is possessed substantially of the same authority as a Presbytery. The judgments, decisions, and censures, in our churches, and in the Presbyterian, are mutually deemed valid. The churches, therefore, in Connecticut at large, and in our district in particular, are not now, and never were, from the earliest period of our settlement, Congregational churches, according to the ideas and forms of Church order contained in the book of discipline called the Cambridge Platform. There are, however, scattered over the State, perhaps ten or twelve churches (unconsociated), who are properly called Congregational, agreeably to the rules of Church discipline in the book above mentioned. Sometimes, indeed, the associated churches of Connecticut are loosely and vaguely, though improperly, termed Congregational. While our churches, in the State at large, are, in the most essential and important respects, the same as the Presbyterian; still, in minute and unimportant points of Church order and discipline, both we and the Presbyterian Church in America acknowledge a difference."†

It is not strange that the Presbyterian fathers—who, as we have seen, never took the highest ground as to the Divine authority of their system—should feel a cordial

---

* Baird's History of the New School, pp. 145–'6.   † Ibid. pp. 146–'7.

sympathy with Congregationalism of this modified type; nor that the pressure of mutual interests should bring the two into confidential relations. And it is a notable fact, that the intercourse always began with the churches of Connecticut, the most predisposed to Presbyterian views, and afterwards extended to those of the other eastern States. As early as 1723, hopes were entertained of union between the General Synod and the churches of Connecticut; which, however, was not then consummated. Again, in 1766, they drew together in prolonged conference, in joint resistance to the introduction of an American Episcopate; the objection being, not to the office itself, but to the authority of Parliament in appointing it; which, it was feared, would draw after it a Church Establishment, with its attendant dangers, of which they had had such sensible experience in Europe. The correspondence thus begun was suspended by the American Revolution, and was not resumed till 1791. The two parties each appointed delegates to attend the sessions of the other, with the right only to deliberate; which right was enlarged, in 1794, so as to include the privilege of a vote.

The way was thus gradually opened for what is known as "the Plan of Union," formed in 1801: a more enlarged and methodized convention between the two bodies, which, during the six and thirty years of its continuance, brought upon the Presbyterian Church an " Illiad of woes." History does not afford a better illustration of the evil wrought by good men, whenever, from motives of policy, they swerve from principle. Their virtue lends a sanction to their schemes, while it does not estop the fatal results. This agreement was not only established by good men, but it originated in the sweetest and most godly intentions. The tide of population setting in from the Atlantic coast into the interior of the country, bore upon its bosom a mixed material for the formation of churches. In the western portions of New York, and in Ohio, Presbyterians and Congregationalists found themselves side by side, both being too weak to enforce the Church organization which each preferred. What more Christian object could be proposed than to facilitate a union between these discordant elements? Unfortunately, this was not attempted by a process of natural fusion, each giving way and conforming to the other as circumstances might dictate; but by an artificial convention, making a composite of both. This Plan of Union, as it was termed, contained the following provisions: That Congregational and Presbyterian churches might select their pastor, each from the communion of the other, the church in each case conducting its discipline according to the principles of the body to which it belonged; that difficulties arising between the minister and his people should be referred to the Presbytery, or to the Association, just as he might happen to be a Presbyterian or Congregationalist; or, if both parties preferred, to a Council equally composed of both sides; that if the church was made up of both Presbyterians and Congregationalists, it might settle a minister of either persuasion, in which case the government should be in the hands of a Standing Committee, chosen by the church, from whose decisions an appeal might be taken by a Presbyterian to the Presbytery, or by a Congregationalist to the body of the communicants; and the members of these Standing Committees, if deputed, should have the same right to sit and act in Presbytery as ruling elders of the Presbyterian Church."*

It is scarcely necessary to point out the anomalies in this hybrid system, which was really less conformed to Presbyterianism than the very platforms which Congregationalists had constructed for their own government. Under these, indeed, a sufficient diversity had been exhibited in churches associated and churches dissociated; in churches governed by the brotherhood, governed by

* Assembly's Digest, Ed. 1856, p. 555.

elders, and governed by a mixture of both; in Con-
sociations to which laymen were admitted, and Associations from which they were excluded: but under this
arrangement, with its committee-men, who had given no
pledge of adherence to any symbols of faith, admitted to
all the functions of the eldership; with its complex ad-
justments between two distinct systems of discipline, and
with the constant overlapping of the two jurisdictions on
either side; we are presented with a conglomerate the
strangest that was ever conceived. Churches, Presbyteries, and finally Synods, were born of it; which, like
Jacob's cattle, were "ringstreaked, speckled, and grizzled"
—a motley assemblage, with every hue and colour of the
ecclesiastical prism. The new districts, in which the provisional scheme was intended to operate, soon filled up
with a teeming population. Under this altered condition
of things, the scheme itself should have been superseded
by an orderly separation of the two elements; which, as
distinct communions, might have lived side by side in
friendly relations. It was, however, continued in force,
after the necessity for its existence had ceased. We
condense the following facts to illustrate its practical operation: In 1808, the Middle Association was received into
the Synod of Albany, with its twenty-one churches, all
Congregational, and which "retained its own name and
usages in the administration of government." The year
after, it was sub-divided into two Presbyteries, "both of
which, in written constitutions, planted themselves on the
Plan of Union, and were Presbyterian only in name." In
1812, these, with the Presbytery of Geneva, were erected
into the Synod of Geneva; which was soon enlarged by
the addition of the Congregational Association of Onon-
daga. In 1821, the Synod of Genesee was erected out of
four Presbyteries detached from the Synod of Geneva;
in which, also, "the Plan of Union was recognized as paramount to the Constitution of the Presbyterian Church."
In 1826, the Presbytery of Chenango was organized, with

five ministers, and without a single church; but, placing itself upon "the Plan," drew into it the Union Congregational Association. In 1829, the Synod of Utica was erected, largely composed of Congregational material, having swallowed up the Oneida Association, besides the accession of other churches. Thus, within the space of twenty-eight years, in the State of New York alone, three Synods were constituted, to a large extent of elements absorbed from Congregational churches, and resting upon the Plan of Union for a basis. In Ohio, the Synod of Western Reserve was formed, in 1825, in precisely the same manner, and chiefly of the same materials. It was composed of the Presbytery of Grand River, organized in 1814, of Portage, in 1819, and of Huron, in 1824; which, by written constitutions, recognized the Plan of Union as their charter.* Four great Synods were thus created, which never assimilated with the Presbyterian body, of which they professed to be a part. This brief recapitulation will enable the reader better to understand the character of the Reform measures of 1837.

This gradual undermining of Presbyterian government was of itself sufficient to condemn this wild scheme of comprehension; but it was far from being its worst result. In the history of the Church, laxity in doctrine is always sure to accompany contempt of discipline and order. It is notorious that, during this period, New England was rife with dangerous theological speculations. The metaphysical writings of the elder Edwards had stimulated the naturally subtle New England mind to very bold invasions of the orthodox faith. The limits of this digressive chapter will not allow a detailed statement of these various aberrations from the sound doctrine of earlier times; nor of the swift progress from the ambiguities of the Hopkinsian School, to the scarcely disguised Pelagianism of the New Haven divines. Indeed, any private expo-

* These statements are all condensed from Dr. Baird's History of the New School, pp. 159 to 166.

sition of these issues would be open to the suspicion of prejudice, unless substantiated by large quotations, upon which the reader might rest an independent judgment. We prefer, therefore, to leap at once to an official document, the Testimony and Memorial adopted by the Assembly of 1837, in which there is a specification of errors widely disseminated in the Presbyterian Church, viz.:

"1. That God would have prevented the existence of sin in our world, but was not able, without destroying the moral agency of man ; or that, for aught that appears in the Bible to the contrary, sin is incidental to any wise moral system.

"2. That election to eternal life is founded on a foresight of faith and obedience.

"3. That we have no more to do with the first sin of Adam than with the sin of any other parent.

"4. That infants come into the world as free from moral defilement, as was Adam, when he was created.

"5. That infants sustain the same relation to the moral government of God, in this world, as brute animals; and that their sufferings and death are to be accounted for on the same principles as those of brutes, and not, by any means, to be considered as penal.

"6. That there is no other original sin than the fact, that all the posterity of Adam, though by nature innocent, or possessed of no moral character, will always begin to sin when they begin to exercise moral agency; that original sin does not include a sinful bias of the human mind, and a just exposure to penal suffering; and that there is no evidence in Scripture that infants, in order to salvation, do need redemption by the blood of Christ, and regeneration by the Holy Spirit.

"7. That the doctrine of imputation, whether of the guilt of Adam's sin, or of the righteousness of Christ, has no foundation in the Word of God, and is both unjust and absurd.

"8. That the sufferings and death of Christ were not truly vicarious and penal, but symbolical, governmental, and instructive only.

"9. That the impenitent sinner is, by nature, and independently of the renewing influence or almighty energy of the Holy Spirit, in full possession of all the ability necessary to a full compliance with all the commands of God.

"10. That Christ does not intercede for the elect until after regeneration.

"11. That saving faith is not an effect of the special operation of the Holy Spirit, but a mere rational belief of the truth, or assent to the Word of God.

"12. That regeneration is the act of the sinner himself, and that it consists in a change of his governing purpose, which he himself must produce, and which is the result, not of any direct influence of the

Holy Spirit on the heart, but chiefly of a persuasive exhibition of the truth, analogous to the influence which one man exerts over the mind of another; or that regeneration is not an instantaneous act, but a progressive work.

"13. That God has done all that *He can do* for the salvation of all men, and that man himself must do the rest.

"14. That God cannot exert such influence on the minds of men, as shall make it certain that they will choose and act in a particular manner, without impairing their moral agency.

"15. That the righteousness of Christ is not the sole ground of the sinner's acceptance with God ; and that in no sense does the righteousness of Christ become ours.

"16. That the reason why some differ from others in regard to their reception of the Gospel, is that they make themselves to differ."*

The close affiliation with Congregationalists, under the Plan of Union, opened wide the door to the influx of these errors; and they were especially prevalent in those districts which this Plan covered with its influence. Yet the men who, in the Presbyterian Church, embraced and taught these views, had subscribed the Confession of Faith, from which they deviated so widely. This course was reconciled with honesty only on the plea, that no subscription to any extended creed could be exacted, consistently with freedom of thought and the right of conscience, except it be restricted to the general system inculcated, and for "substance of doctrine" merely. This elastic and slippery phrase is scarcely susceptible of defi-

* Assembly's Digest, Edition of 1856, pp. 728-'9. A protest against this paper, signed by fifteen members of the Assembly, disclaiming these errors, and giving their exposition of the points involved, was presented and admitted to record. (See Assembly's Digest, Edition of 1856, pp. 730-'5.) This exposition, even if satisfactory, could do nothing more than purge the individual signers of suspicion in the premises. It did not touch the design of the paper itself ; which was to testify against errors widely diffused, and to show the necessity of a strict subscription of the standards, in order to protect the Church from being infected with the same. The Assembly made an unusual disposition of this protest, in sending it down to the Presbyteries of the signers, "calling attention to the developments of theological views contained in it," and ordering an "inquiry into the soundness of the faith of those who have ventured to make so strange avowals as some of these are." Digest, p. 735.

nition or limitation. By far the most exact expression of
its meaning, is that put forth by the New Haven Professors, in the attempt to reconcile their speculations with
the pledges they had given when inducted into office. It
is worthy of being preserved, as the nearest to a successful effort to imprison in words what is inconstant and
shifting as caprice itself. It is in these terms:

" It will be generally agreed, that the cardinal doctrines of the Reformation were the following: The entire depravity and ruin of man by
nature, as the result of tue sin of Adam ; justification by faith, through
the atonement of Christ, to the exclusion of all merit in the recipient;
the necessity of regeneration, by the special or distinguishing influences
of the Holy Spirit; the eternal and personal election of a part of our
race to holiness and salvation ; the final perseverance of all who are
thus chosen unto eternal life. These, taken in connexion with the doctrine of the Trinity, of the eternal punishment of the finally impenitent, and of the divine decrees, which is partly involved in that of election, constitute what may be called the Primary Doctrines of the Refor-
tion. In addition to these, we find, in the writings of some of the
Reformers and of the Puritan divines, another class of statements,
whose object was to reconcile the doctrines above enumerated with the
principles of right reason, and to reduce them to a harmonious system
of faith. These may be called the Secondary or Explanatory Doctrines.
As examples of these, we may mention, the imputation of Adam's sin
to all his descendants, in such a sense as to make them guilty, and pun-
ished, in the operation of strict justice, on account of his act ; the imputation of Christ's righteousness to the believer, as the ground of his
participating, on the same principle of strict justice, in the benefits of
His death ; the doctrine of particular redemption, or the limitation of
the atonement to the elect ; the doctrine of man's entire want of power
to any but sinful actions, as accounting for his dependence on God for
a change of heart, etc.
" Many of the old divines attached high importance to this latter class
of doctrines, though differently stated by different writers ; but they did
so only because they considered them essential to a defence of the primary doctrines enumerated above. In the progress of mental and moral
science, however, a great change of sentiment has taken place in this
respect. One after another of these secondary or explanatory doctrines
has been laid aside. Other modes have been adopted of harmonizing
the orthodox system of faith, and reconciling it to the principles of
right reason, more conformable, it is believed, to the simplicity of the
gospel; without diminishing, but rather increasing, the attachment felt
for the primary doctrines of the Reformation."*

* Dr. Baird's History of the New School, pp. 209, 210.

To receive a creed, then, "for substance of doctrine," means simply to get all the substance out of the doctrine, and to hold the shell, which is harmless from its emptiness. No one acquainted with the Calvinistic system would care to contend long for the primary doctrines, after the secondary were all of them eliminated; and the Confession of Faith may innocently be subscribed, when it has been eviscerated of all that renders its testimony of any value. Such is a brief account of the doctrinal issues that were involved in the schism of 1837–'8.

There is another branch of the controversy, which contributed an almost equal share in effecting the breach: it was the question whether the Church should do her own evangelistic work, or remit it to irresponsible agencies outside of her pale. In her early history, the duty was plainly recognized of doing, in her organic form, the work for which she was instituted. Itinerant missionaries were sent out to explore the waste places; and settled pastors were detached, for weeks and months, from their respective charges, to supply the destitute with the gospel. The Church courts were occupied, at every session, in devising means to spread the knowledge of Christianity into "the regions beyond." The work of training ministers was undertaken at the very outset; and in 1771, the General Synod, before the organization of the Assembly, entered upon a systematic plan for the support and education of her candidates. As early as 1751, a collection was ordered to be taken each year, in every church, to propagate the gospel among the heathen; and upon this fund Mr. Brainard was sustained among the Indians, until his death, in 1781. In 1802, the Synod of Pittsburgh resolved itself into a missionary society, with a regular constitution and officers. In the same year, the Synod of the Carolinas sent two missionaries to the Natches Indians, and one to the Catawbas; conducting the work through a commission, regularly appointed. At the same period, 1802, the General Assembly appointed a Standing

Committee of Missions, whose powers were gradually increased, until, at length, in 1816, it was erected into a Board.* Had the Church been allowed to pursue her course untrammelled, with her own expansion there would have been a corresponding enlargement of her efforts; and her history would have been, what the history of the Church ought ever to be, that of a great evangelistic society. But the fatal complication with Congregationalism, which so nearly corrupted her faith, almost brought her in bondage to the great national societies, which boldly attempted to usurp her functions.

Independency, from the incompleteness of its organization, is compelled to work through agencies outside of itself. Hence originated, in New England, three large corporations, known as the American Education and the American Home Mission Societies, and the American Board of Commissioners for Foreign Missions. The prefix, American, to each of these, sufficiently indicates the ambition of their aim. It was nothing less than to become, to the largest possible extent, national in their scope; by uniting the Congregationalists, the Presbyterians, the Dutch Reformed, and the Associate Reformed, in one phalanx, to carry out these several enterprises conjointly. Of course, this involved, on the part of the three last named, the abdication of their trust as distinct and separate churches, who must all become tributary to the first, as auxiliaries to the only agency which they could possibly construct. It was a splendid scheme of unification, similar to that which is dazzling the minds of so many at this day; and perhaps the careful reader will be struck with the parallel, in more than one particular, between the history of the Church in the first and last third of the present century. It is necessary to trace the conflict with each of these three associations.

The American Education Society was organized in 1815, in the city of Boston, "with admirable skill for

* For these facts, see Baird's History, pp. 271-282.

acquiring complete control over ministerial education
throughout the country." With its close corporation,
and independence of all supervision; with its large
receipts, and honorary memberships purchased with
money; and with its branch societies distributed over the
country; it was armed with power to beat down any
feeble competitors that might enter the field. But the
instinct of danger, which never wholly deserts a living
Church, took in at once the fatal consequences of yielding
to the supremacy of so ambitious an agency. In 1818,
measures were concerted which resulted in the organization of a Presbyterian Education Society, in Philadelphia, "which should be under the inspection of the
General Assembly, and a faithful representative of the
whole denomination." But the Church could not be a
unit. The foreign influences, which had been imported
into the body, set themselves at once to counteract the
policy thus indicated. A rival organization was instantly
created, under a similar name, which refused to acknowledge Assembly control, and soon went over bodily to the
American Education Society, and became its active instrument in promoting its ascendency within the entire
limits of the Presbyterian Church. Meanwhile, the Church
Board languished for years, by reason of this opposition,
its own restricted powers, and general inefficiency in its
management, until, in 1831, it was re-organized under the
auspices of the Rev. John Breckinridge, D. D., as its
Secretary; when it sprung into vigour, and held its own
against all rivalry, until the hour of complete deliverance
from all this thraldom was chimed in 1837.* So far, then,
the Church, though crippled and harassed, has refused to
subordinate herself to a foreign power.

The triumph, however, of the American Board of Commissioners for Foreign Missions was complete. We have
sketched the early efforts of Presbyterians to extend the
gospel among the heathen. Besides the organization of

* Dr. Baird's History, pp. 283-292.

the Synods of Pittsburgh and of the Carolinas to that
end, various local societies had sprung up, all subject to
the Church. But, in 1817, this great subject was brought
before the Assembly; and the result was the organization
of "the United Foreign Missionary Society," so called
because it was composed of members of the Presbyterian,
Reformed Dutch, and Associate Reformed Churches, and
received the sanction of these bodies respectively. It was,
however, from the nature of the case, a voluntary society,
and in its management independent of ecclesiastical control. It prosecuted its work with vigour, gradually absorbing the different local societies, and was able, within
eight years from its establishment, to make a favourable
comparative exhibit of its success with that of the American, or Congregational, Board, during its first eight years.
In 1824, the Synod of Pittsburgh transferred their missions to its care, under the impression that it was, and
would remain, distinctly Presbyterian in its character. At
the very moment, however, of this transfer, negotiations
were pending with the A. B. C. F. M.,* by which it was
soon absorbed. The only remaining missions of the Presbyterian Church were those conducted by the Synod of
the Carolinas, dating back to 1802. In 1818, these were
in turn transferred by treaty to the American Board,
which was thus sole master of the field.

This termination filled many with profound grief, and
measures were soon concerted for rallying the Church to
her appointed work. The proposal was to organize an
Assembly Board of Foreign Missions, which should not
be antagonistic, but co-operative with the American
Board. The lamented Dr. John H. Rice penned, from
his death-bed, the overture to the General Assembly of
1831, which appointed a committee of conference on the
subject; but, "to the proposition for a co-ordinate Board,
the reply was, without alternative, the American Board,

* The abbreviated title of the "American Board of Commissioners for
Foreign Missions."

and that only." Renewed defeat served but to arouse the Church the more. The next measure was to revive "the Western Foreign Missionary Society," at Pittsburgh, which had been sold out in 1824. It was accordingly organized, and presented itself for recognition before the Assembly of 1832, with its first missionaries chosen, and Africa as its field of operations. It was so prospered in its work, that, within three years, it represented twenty missionaries under its care, labouring in western Africa, northern India, and among several Indian tribes at home. In the Assembly of 1835, a committee was appointed to confer with the Synod of Pittsburgh, relative to the transfer of this Society to the General Assembly. In the following year, however, the Assembly, under the foreign influences which controlled it, receded from the proposals of its predecessor, and the Western Society was rejected as a recognized institution for the whole Church.* The consternation and alarm created by this decision contributed not a little to the revolution which, one year later, swept Moderatism, as it did heresy, out of the bosom of the Church.

The great battle, however, for the liberties of the Church, was fought upon the Home Mission field; where, by God's grace, a full victory was achieved. We have seen the Assembly Committee of 1802 expanding, in 1816, into a Board, with enlarged powers. Its efficiency was nevertheless crippled by the opposition of the "lib-

---

* Dr. Baird's History, pp. 298-308, 447-461, 490-496. The line of argument pursued, in the Assembly of 1836, against the Church's engaging in the work of Foreign Missions, illustrates the nature of the struggle, and fills the reader with equal astonishment and sorrow. It was denied that the Assembly had any authority to undertake this work ; that it had received no authorization from the Presbyteries ; that the command to evangelize the world was given to the Church universal, which is an unorganized body ; that the Assembly cannot delegate the power of creating missions to any Board ; that, if it does, this is to perpetuate itself after its own dissolution ; that the gospel is not sectarian, and should not be so exhibited to the heathen, etc. See Baird's History, p. 495.

eral" party in the Church; who set to work organizing local societies, in which some indulgence would be extended to theological aberrations.   These were, in 1822, consolidated into what was termed "The United Domestic Missionary Society;" which, in 1826, resolved itself into "The American Home Missionary Society," "planned in a meeting of delegates from the New England churches, held in Boston early in the same year."   Dr. Absalom Peters, the determined head of this institution, addressed himself to the task, which he unflinchingly pursued, of absorbing the Assembly Board, or at least of making it wholly tributary.   He accordingly, in 1828, communicated his views to the General Assembly.   The result, however, was the adopting, by that body, of a paper recognizing prerogatives in its own agent that had never been conferred before.   A correspondence was then begun between the two Boards, in which an elaborate argument was attempted to show that they could not co-exist in harmony, if independent.   Dr. Peters next visited Philadelphia, and succeeded in gaining over to his views Dr. Ely, the Secretary of the Assembly Board.   The two laboured together for the amalgamation of the agencies which they represented, upon the basis that fifty directors should be chosen from the different bodies that should embark in the scheme, distributed to each in proportion to the number of ministers upon its roll.   This bold proposition was promptly rejected by the Assembly Board, on the ground that it had no authority to entertain it, and also from a deep conviction that "the interests of the Presbyterian Church, and the sacred cause of missions, require that the character and powers of the Board should remain as they are."   In consequence of this resistance, the matter was not brought before the Assembly at all, and a new system of tactics was compelled.   This was to plant a branch of the American Society in the West, at Cincinnati, and to invite the Assembly to transact its operations in the West through this branch, as a common agency.   This project, however, failed to secure the approval of the Assembly. The design evidently was, either to drive the Presbyterian Church out of the West, as a field of operations, or so to control her movements that they should be wholly subordinate to the interests of Congregationalism.

In the Assembly of 1831, a long discussion ensued upon certain overtures relating to missions in the West; which resulted in a recommendation to all the Western Synods to correspond with each other, and to agree upon some plan which should be satisfactory to themselves, and report the same to the next Assembly. In pursuance of this advice, a general Convention of these Synods was held, in November of that year, at Cincinnati. After a week's session, in which various measures were discussed, the question at issue was definitely settled, in the following resolution, to the entire and final defeat of all the schemes of the American Society: "Resolved, that, under these circumstances, they deem it inexpedient to propose any change in the General Assembly's mode of conducting missions, as they fully approve of that now in such successful operation; and that the purity, peace, and prosperity of the Presbyterian Church materially depend on the active and efficient aid the Sessions and Presbyteries under its care may afford to the Assembly's Board."*

The vigour of the assault upon this particular arm of the Church will be understood at a glance. It was the precise spot in which a breach was to be effected in the Presbyterian Church, and the defences here were to be carried by storm. With the American Education Society to train a ministry in the lax theology, and with the American Home Missionary Society to distribute and support them in their field of labour, it was simply a question of time to trample the Confession of Faith in the dust, to lay prostrate the whole constitution and order of the Church, and to render the entire Presbyterian Church the bound vassal under New England theology and New

* Dr. Baird's History, pp. 310–326, 376–386.

England control. The instinct of life alone preserved her from surrendering, just where defeat would have been fatal.

Such were the issues, both in doctrine and polity, by which the Presbyterian Church was agitated; widening with the discussion of every passing year, and finding no solution but in open disruption. The doctrinal controversy was brought to a head, in the trial of Rev. Albert Barnes; which was accepted on both sides as a test case, and to which, therefore, an extraordinary interest was attached. Certain views announced by him as early as 1828, in a sermon, entitled, "The Way of Salvation," led to resistance, in the Presbytery of Philadelphia, to his settlement as a pastor within its bounds. The case went up through the Synod, and came, by reference, before the Assembly of 1831. It was disposed of by a minute, censuring the sermon of Mr. Barnes as "containing a number of unguarded and objectionable passages;" but accepting his own explanation of the same, and deciding that the Presbytery ought to suspend all further proceedings. Thus ended Mr. Barnes's first trial. In 1835, however, he was a second time prosecuted, by the Rev. Dr. George Junkin, upon charges based upon alleged errors in his " Commentary on Romans," recently issued from the press. By reason of various delays, it did not reach the Assembly till 1836, when Mr. Barnes appealed from the condemnatory sentence of the Synod, and was sustained in it by the decision of the Assembly. This decision, in a confessedly test case, was regarded as fixing the doctrinal complexion of the Church, and determined the orthodox upon vigorous measures of reform.

The utter disregard of constitutional principles which now exhibited itself in the highest court of the Church, led to another flagrant outrage; which was the creation of what was appropriately designated an " Elective Affinity Presbytery," in the Synod of Philadelphia, and against its remonstrances; which consisted of certain enumerated

ministers and churches thrown together because of their
doctrinal sympathies, and irrespective of geographical
boundaries. Still worse, in order to place this Presbytery
beyond the reach of Synodical action, it was erected,
with two others of like sentiments, into the Synod of Delaware. Thus was not only a secure asylum provided for
those who were unsound in the faith, but a fit instrument
was created for licensing candidates who would elsewhere
be rejected, and sending them forth with clean papers to
demand admission into every other Presbytery in the land.
Clearly, it was high time to act, for each year saw the
sound and evangelical portion of the Church drifting
under the power of a majority becoming larger and larger by means the most unscrupulous.

The nature of the steps necessary to recover the Church
from her deep declension had been foreshadowed as early
as 1831, in an overture from the Synod of Pittsburgh, to
the effect "that every Church Session and Presbytery be
required to keep a book, in which the following formula
shall be recorded, viz.: I, A. B., do sincerely receive and
adopt the Confession of Faith and Catechisms of the
Presbyterian Church, according to the plain and obvious
meaning of the words in which they are expressed," etc.;
and "that any Synod, Presbytery, minister, or elder, refusing to comply with the above conditions, shall be considered as renouncing the jurisdiction of the Presbyterian
Church, and consequently no longer to be considered in
connexion with that body." In July, 1833, a conference
was held of certain gentlemen in Ohio, which addressed
to the General Assembly of the following year, what is
known as "The Western Memorial," testifying against
nine specified doctrinal errors, and urging the repeal of
the Plan of Union, and of any special arrangement with
the Congregational churches. During the session of the
Assembly, in 1834, a conference was held, at which the
famous "Act and Testimony" was drawn up, of which
the Rev. Dr. R. J. Breckinridge was the author, who, as

an elder from Kentucky, had three years before signalized
himself as a champion of sound doctrine and constitutional order. This paper, after the enumeration of doctrinal errors, and suggesting measures for their repression,
closed with the recommendation of a convention, to be
held the next year, to "deliberate and consult on the
present state of the Church, and to adopt such measures
as may be best suited to restore her prostrated standards."
At this convention a careful memorial was prepared, identical with the "Act and Testimony," which received a
measure of consideration from the Assembly, and raised,
in some, the hope of ultimate reform. It was a hope excited only to be blasted. The Assembly of 1836 was the
most radical of all that had preceded; and, as we have
seen, the acquittal of Mr. Barnes dashed the expectations
of the most sanguine to the ground. In 1837, for the
first time in several consecutive years, the orthodox party
found itself in a small majority. The memorials and testimonies of preceding years had not been without effect
in arousing the supine, and in convincing those who had
heretofore been sceptical as to the extent of the danger
in which the Church stood. The business of reform was
brought before this body in an able "Testimony and
Memorial," from the pen of Dr. Breckinridge, making
sixteen specifications as to false doctrine, which have been
already transcribed in this chapter, and proposing the
immediate abrogation of the Plan of Union, the discoun-
tenancing of the American Education and Home Missionary Societies, and other measures likely to promote
discipline and sound government. Pending the discussion
upon this paper, committees were appointed from both
sides, to agree, if possible, upon an amicable separation;
which, having failed, the vote was taken upon the abrogation of the Plan of Union, which passed by a majority
of thirty-three. It was then carried, that, by this abrogation, the four Synods of Utica, Geneva, Genessee, and
Western Reserve, which were founded upon this platform,

"are, and are hereby declared to be, no longer a part of the Presbyterian Church in the United States of America." This action has been assailed as unconstitutional and severe, and as reaching, by one sweeping legislative decree, an evil that should have been redressed by judicial process. But if anything was clearly demonstrated, it was the utter futility, in the existing state of the Church, of bringing any party to public trial on charge of heresy. The cases of Barnes, Beecher, Duffield, Sturdevant, and Kirby, were all on record as warnings of this fact. Besides, the error to be reached was so diffused as almost to defy prosecution by its universality; and in the districts which were covered by the operation of the Plan of Union, the guilty were safe in the mutual protection of each other, and process could not be begun in the courts having immediate jurisdiction. If, too, the Plan of Union was established by a legislative act, it could *ex æquali* be legislatively declared null and void, as unconstitutionally created in the first instance.* Of course, as soon as the platform was stricken away upon which they rested, the Presbyteries and Synods that were erected upon it as a basis naturally and necessarily fell through.

The last struggle, however, remained which was to test the Assembly's power to enforce its own decree. In the following year, 1838, the commissioners from these "exscinded" Synods presented themselves with their credentials. No sooner had the opening prayer been offered than Dr. Patton arose, with certain resolutions in his hand. The Moderator, adhering closely to the rules, pronounced him out of order, since, until the roll was reported of those with regular commissions, there was no house to deliberate. Dr. Patton appealed from the chair to the house. The Moderator replied, there was no house to appeal to. The scheme was to intrude these excluded commissioners upon the house before the organ-

---

* See Assembly's Pastoral Letter, from the pen of Dr. Alexander: Digest, Ed. 1856, p. 745.

ization; and failing in this, to organize the minority as
the Assembly, and to supersede it.   Being defeated by
the tact and firmness of the Moderator, the only resource
was to organize in a tumultuous way, in the midst of the
business of the Assembly, by a loud call from Mr. Cleave-
land, in the body of the house, upon Dr. Beman to take
the chair.   This gentleman stepped into the aisle, where,
in the utmost confusion, the throng about him responded
to several questions, and the whole party retired to organize in another building.   The disruption was effected.
The Old and the New Schools were now distinctly apart;
and those who stood by the Constitution of the Church,
in a strict interpretation of her symbols of doctrine and
principles of government, rejoiced in a great deliverance.

CHAPTER XV.

POLEMIC CAREER BEGUN.

PROVIDENTIAL TRAINING FOR HIS FUTURE WORK.—MEMBER OF ASSEMBLY
IN 1837.—INSIDE VIEW OF THAT COUNCIL.—GRADUAL SIFTING OF THE
CHURCH.—TESTIMONY BEFORE THE SYNOD.—TRACT PUBLICATION.—
LETTER OF CONDOLENCE.—CALLED BACK TO THE COLLEGE.—HIS DE-
CISION ANNOUNCED.—PASTORAL RELATION DISSOLVED.—ASSUMES THE
CHAPLAINCY IN THE COLLEGE.

DR. THORNWELL was licensed in the fall of 1834,
and was ordained the following spring. His ministry
opened, therefore, just as the two parties in the Church
were marshalling their forces for the final struggle. His
was not the temperament to remain a listless spectator of
these movements. Endowed with all the natural characteristics of a leader, his place could not be other than in
the front. His intense love of truth, simply as truth,
made him regardless of considerations merely prudential.
As we have seen, too, his first religious impressions were
derived from a mother whose teachings were strongly
Calvinistic; and his determination to the Presbyterian
Church was through a casual introduction to the Westminster Confession, at the time his first serious investigations in religion were set on foot. His future work
was to be that of a reformer, in an age of great spiritual
declension; and Divine Providence chose to cast him, at
the outset, into the mould of those venerable symbols
which most accurately defined the faith of the universal
Church.

The distant South was fortunately too far removed
from New England to be easily manipulated; and the
Presbyterianism which existed there was of that sturdy
Scotch type, which had proved itself so competent around

Pittsburgh to enter the lists with error. His first appearance in this conflict was as a member of the famous Assembly of 1837, in whose proceedings, however, he took no conspicuous part. He did not appear in the body until the ninth day of its sessions, and therefore had no hand in the Convention which preceded it, nor in preparing the Memorial and Testimony that shaped its deliberations. The modesty of youth kept him in the background; especially since, as he afterwards expressed it to his friend Dr. Breckinridge, there were others in the lead who were doing the work bravely and well. The following extracts from letters, written at the time, reveal the deep interest he felt in the proceedings, and give also an inside view of the same:

"PHILADELPHIA, *May* 26, 1837.

"MY VERY DEAR WIFE: After many delays and unforeseen hindrances, I reached this city about four o'clock this afternoon. * * * * * I just reached here at the point of time for the agitating questions that will come up before us. Mr. Robert J. Breckinridge gave notice this evening, that he would introduce a motion to-morrow for the appointment of a committee, to consist of equal members of both parties, for the purpose of devising the most peaceable mode of dividing the Presbyterian Church. I have no doubt but that this Assembly will settle all the difficulties of the Church. We shall, in all probability, get rid of the New School men, and be enabled hereafter to preach and propagate the gospel without molestation or controversy. Men, who heretofore have been moderate, are now taking high ground. The importance of the questions at issue begins to be generally felt. * * * * * * The results of this Assembly may and will be felt to the end of time. The future history of the Presbyterian Church will depend, under God, upon the measures adopted now, by the highest of her judicatories. There should be much prayer, much study of the Scriptures, and much watchfulness over our words and thoughts. May the Lord preside in all our deliberations, and order all things so as to promote His glory, in the up-building of Zion and the spread of the truth. * * *
"Your affectionate husband,
J. H. THORNWELL."

In another letter, of date June 5th, he writes:

"The vote was taken to-day on excluding the Synods of Utica, Geneva, and Genessee, which, with the Synod of Western Reserve, will make four Synods that have been excluded from the Church. They never, constitutionally and regularly, formed a part of the Church, and therefore it was no hardship to say so. We shall probably dissolve the Third Presbytery of Philadelphia and the Presbytery of Wilmington, which were formed upon the Elective Affinity principle; and then cite to the bar of the next Assembly such other ecclesiastical bodies as are reported to be unsound. The work of reform seems to go on prosperously; the Lord has opened up an unexpected door of deliverance to His people. I know that you feel anxious about me, that you entertain fears about my temper and spirit. You may make yourself easy on these points. I have not opened my mouth in the Assembly or Convention, except to give a vote, and I do not expect to do so. I have sought constantly guidance and direction from the Lord; and though I am conscious of much sin and imperfection, yet I have endeavoured, in the strength of Divine grace, to discharge my duties faithfully. I have been deeply grieved and humbled at the spirit which has been too frequently manifested in this body; and in the midst of the excitement, and the mutual recrimination and personality, which have been too freely indulged, I have often wished myself at home, where I could enjoy the peace and comfort of my own family. The Lord has shown me, in the proceedings of this General Assembly, that there is no confidence to be placed in man; that the best of us are weak and erring mortals, who cannot see afar off. I rejoice, however, that the agitating subjects, on which we have heretofore been employed, are drawing to a close. We will soon be engaged in more peaceful and quiet business, unless the members who have been excluded should undertake to disturb our deliberations. The spectators who have attended our deliberations have behaved, in several instances, very uncourteously. We have been *hissed* from the galleries three or four times to-day. Our New School brethren, in too many instances, have made their speeches only to the galleries; in other words, their object seems to have been to produce a popular impression against the orthodox. They have treated the questions which came up before us with a great deal of unfairness; and one hour spent in the General Assembly would convince your mind that the two parties ought never to meet again in the same body. They have no confidence in one another; they are wide apart in spirit, principle, and doctrines; and nothing but confusion and disorder can result from their being united." * *

Such a schism, as described in the preceding chapter, could not but shake the Church, from its centre to its circumference. In all parts of the land were to be found many who were disaffected to those measures by which the rupture had been produced; some, perhaps, because themselves tainted with the prevalent unsoundness in doctrine, but many more influenced by mere sympathy with the excluded Synods, and who regarded the abrogation of the Plan of Union as the violation of a covenant, and as having been accomplished in an extra-constitutional, if not unconstitutional, way. The sifting of the two parties, throughout the whole country, could only be gradually secured. In some places, after the disruption and formation of two rival Assemblies, there was a disposition in Presbyteries and parts of Presbyteries to hang undecided between the two. It became necessary, therefore, to push the question, until the position of every one in the Church should be definitely ascertained. Accordingly, the Assembly of 1838 passed an Act, enjoining upon all Presbyteries in its connection to take order in the premises for the general reform and pacification of the Church, and to do so between the dissolution of that Assembly and the fall meetings of the Synods.

It so happened that, within the bounds of the Synods of South Carolina and Georgia, some dissatisfaction with these Reform measures did exist, though confined to but one locality in either State. When this Synod met, in the autumn, Mr. Thornwell presented the following paper, which was adopted by that body by a vote of forty-nine to eight:

"Whereas, disputes and contentions, which have existed among the members of the Presbyterian Church, have resulted in a division of our communion into two denominations, differing from each other, as we suppose, on topics of faith, involving essential elements of the Gospel plan; and whereas, it is the duty of all the courts of the Church to contend earnestly for the faith once delivered to the saints; we, as a Synod, feel called upon, in the present crisis of our ecclesiastical affairs, to bear this, our solemn testimony, for the truth as it is in Jesus, in opposition to the errors and heresies which are now abroad in the land.

"1. It is a fundamental article of the Christian faith, that the guilt of Adam's first sin is imputed to all his posterity, descended from him by ordinary generation, so that they are born in a state of condemnation and depravity; that this imputation is immediate and direct, having no reference to their subsequent concurrence in his sin by voluntary transgression, but founded solely upon the fact, that he was constituted, by the sovereign appointment of God, their federal head and representative.

"2. It is a fundamental doctrine of the Gospel, that Jesus Christ was actually the substitute of a chosen seed; that He assumed their legal responsibilities, and rendered a true and proper satisfaction to Divine justice on their behalf, by enduring the penalty of the law in their name and stead ; that the obedience and death of Christ constitute the alone ground of a sinner's acceptance before God, and that ' to all those for whom Christ purchased redemption, He doth certainly and effectually apply and communicate the same.'

"3. The inability of the sinner to comply with the demands of the Divine law, to believe the Gospel, or to exercise any holy affection, is absolute and entire ; so that regeneration is effected alone by the direct and immediate agency and power of God the Spirit ; the subject of this work of grace being passive, in respect to the vital operation of renewing the heart. We believe, moreover, that the saving grace of God is always efficacious and invincible, and its final triumph sure.

"4. We believe that the form of doctrine usually called Hopkinsianism, though a milder form of error than Taylorism, or Pelagianism, is inconsistent with the Presbyterian standards ; and if fully carried out in its consequences and results, is utterly destructive of the fundamental principles of the Gospel.

"5. This is our solemn testimony of the truths of the Gospel. And for the satisfaction of those brethren who have been perplexed with anxiety and doubt in regard to the theological instruction which is given in our Seminary, we, the members of this Synod, including the Professors of the Theological Seminary, do pledge ourselves, that no contrary doctrine shall be taught in the Seminary, or in our pulpits ; and that, as professors and ministers, we will endeavour to guard our pupils and hearers against all the heresies condemned in this testimony."

He was at this time not quite twenty-six years of age, and had been but a few months a Professor in the South Carolina College, when his influence began to be felt thus in the councils of the Church. In 1840, when, it will be remembered, he was settled as a pastor in the town of Columbia, his zeal for the spread of orthodox views was displayed in another direction. He conceived the project of publishing a series of tracts, chiefly the reproduction of the writings of the old divines, relying upon their sale to meet the expenses of publication. Such a scheme, however, requires an energetic agency for the purpose of distribution, for want of which this particular enterprise fell through, after issuing two of the series. The first was an extract from the writings of Traill; the other was a brochure from his own pen, on Election and Reprobation,

which will be found in the second volume of his works.
This scheme is brought to view in the following letter to
his friend and brother-in-law, Dr. J. J. Wardlaw, of Abbeville, S. C.:

"COLUMBIA, *February* 14, 1840.

"MY DEAR SIR: I write you at present for the purpose of enlisting
your interest in behalf of an enterprise in which I am warmly engaged,
and for which I feel a lively concern.   After much deliberation, I have
determined to publish a series of theological tracts on the fundamental
doctrines of the Gospel, selected from the writings of standard orthodox
divines, if the sale will cover the expenses.   The first of the series,
which is a letter of the Rev. Robert Traill, vindicating the doctrine of Justification from the unjust charge of Antinomianism, is now in the press,
and will be ready for delivery in a few days.   It is printed in octavo
form, and will consist of upwards of thirty pages, and will be sold at
twenty-five cents per copy.   If it should fail to pay for itself, the whole
project will be abandoned.   Now, I am anxious that you should see Dr.
Barr, and get him to interest himself in the matter.   He can do much,
if he can only be brought to take an active part in the matter.   He
knows that such things are desperately needed.   We have had a national
religion long enough.   We want something on the peculiar and distinguishing doctrines of the Gospel.   You can tell him that the tracts are
intended to be after the 'most straitest sect' of ancient Presbyterianism;
for they will be selected from the writings of the divines of the seventeenth and eighteenth centuries.   I wish all your ministers and people
in Abbeville District could be waked up, and made to take a lively interest in the spread of unadulterated truth.   I do not ask for contributions; I barely ask that they would *buy* the tracts and read them.

"We were very sorry to hear that your dear little son has had to fare so
uncomfortably.   You begin to know now something of the anxieties of
a father.   I pray that the Lord may give you grace to discharge faithfully
and acceptably the solemn and interesting duties of that relationship.
At such times, when such serious obligations are crowding upon us, we
should seek the special favour and assistance of God.   He only can
make us a blessing to our children, and them a blessing to us, and to
the world. *Satis verbum sapienti.* * * * Yours sincerely,
                                        J. H. THORNWELL."

The following letter is addressed to his friend and former patron, General James Gillespie, and reveals him as
a "son of consolation:"

"COLUMBIA, *October 2nd*, 1840.

"MY VERY DEAR GENERAL: The mournful event which has recently
occurred in your sister's family,* has produced a deep impression upon
                        * Death of the eldest son.

my mind. It is one of those riddles in the dispensation of Divine Providence which baffles the wisdom of the wisest, and brings the most careless to reflection. My heart has bled, as I thought of the blasted hopes
and disappointed expectations of a fond mother. I know that she had
looked upon him as, in some measure, the head of the family, and was
preparing to lean upon him as the prop of her declining years ; but in
a moment, the bright anticipations of a parent's heart are shrouded in
the darkness of cheerless despair. I could well conceive the agony of
that dreadful moment, when all the hopes of his recovery were found to
be delusive, and the awful certainty of death was irresistibly felt. It
was, indeed, a moment of fiery trial : and I am seriously apprehensive
that the shock has been too great for your sister's frame. But I rejoice
that she is in the hands of a merciful God, and most sincerely pray that
He may preserve her from all temptation to distrust His goodness, or
murmur at His ways. Though ' clouds and darkness are round about
Him, righteousness and truth are still the habitation of His throne.' It
should always be a sufficient argument to reconcile our minds to any
proceeding, however mysterious, that it is the Lord's doing ; and since He
is as merciful as He is wise, we may rest assured that He doth not willingly afflict, nor grieve the children of men. Our times of trial are
times of temptation ; and precious is that faith which loses nothing but
its dross in the heat of the furnace.

" I know that your own feelings have been deep and strong. I sympathize most heartily and unfeignedly with you ; and should much rejoice to see you, that I might walk with you through these deep waters
of affliction. Oh ! how it endears the Saviour, when the cords which
bind us to life are successively snapping asunder, and leaving nothing in
time but a dreary prospect of desolation ! Every day I am becoming
more and more convinced of the utter vanity of the creature. I feel
that God is the only adequate portion of the soul ; and I endeavour to
sit loose to all the things of earth. Every death reminds us that the
distance between time and eternity is very short, and that the Judge
stands ever at the door. Our highest wisdom is to be always ready.

" My church is growing ; the congregation has been almost doubled,
and the Lord has accompanied the truth in several instances with remarkable outpourings of the Spirit. My people are devoted to me. To
a man they will bitterly protest against the efforts of the Board to carry
me back to the College. In regard to that matter, I am in a perplexing
strait. I know not what to do ; but I have no doubt of being directed
by Him who has promised to give wisdom to those who ask. When first
solicited, I positively and unconditionally declined ; but when urgent
entreaties came from different individuals in different parts of the State,
I felt bound to pause and consider ; and there the matter rests.

          " Yours as ever,   J. H. THORNWELL."

His restoration to the College, alluded to above, was
the great turning-point in his career. Having occupied

the chair of Metaphysics, with great acceptance, during the year 1838 and 1839, he had been pressed in conscience to resign, in order that, as a minister of the gospel, he might preach the Word. For one year (1840) he filled the pastorate of the Columbia church, with the results detailed in the preceding letter. The election, however, of the Rev. Dr. Elliott, to the Episcopal Diocese of Georgia, left vacant the chaplaincy of the College, together with the professorship of Sacred Literature, to which it was united. All eyes, not only in the Board, but also in the State, were turned to Mr. Thornwell, as a most suitable successor. Amongst the loose papers which he left behind, is a carefully prepared "Statement of Reasons," for and against the proposed transfer; showing how anxiously he surveyed the whole ground, and with what conscientiousness a decision was finally reached. This decision was formally announced in a communication to the congregation, from which a single extract will suffice; which we give simply because it covers a principle which he had occasion to apply at other critical periods of his life, and upon which he always laid a peculiar emphasis: " The general principle upon which I acted—and I think that the principle will commend itself to your judgment— was this: that the dispensations of Providence are intended for our guidance and direction, whenever they do not come into collision with the express and implied precepts of the Word of God. In all other cases they are designed to try us, but in these to lead us, being unambiguous intimations of the Divine will. In the present instance you are familiar with the facts, and can apply the principle. * * * * Guided by this principle, and from a spirit, as I trust, of obedience to God, I consented, after a long and painful struggle, and after much earnest prayer, to accept the appointment which was unanimously tendered to me. I can truly say, with Paul, that ' I go bound in the Spirit,'" etc.

In January, 1841, the pastoral relation was accordingly

dissolved, and he entered upon his duties immediately as chaplain in the College, and a second time filling a Professor's chair within the same. It is a little curious, how often the station we are called to fill in life differs from that we would ourselves have chosen. A series of providential events, through a succession of years, shuts up a man to academic life, who, three years before, could write, upon the occasion of his first appointment, "I confess that it is not the situation of my choice. I had rather be the pastor of a church than to be the most distinguished Professor of whom the world could boast." The position, however, which he now filled, gave to him the cure of souls, in which the scruples of his conscience and the longings of his heart were alike satisfied. The interruption of his labours in his new calling, and the voyage to Europe for the recovery of health, have already been recited.

CHAPTER XVI.

THE BOARD QUESTION.

IT has been stated, in a preceding chapter, that most of the discussions in which Dr. Thornwell was engaged, were a sort of remainder from the original controversy by which the Church was rent, in 1837–'8. The first that emerged into view was the discussion about Boards. During the period when the Church was brought under a species of vassalage to Congregationalism, the great National Societies, which usurped her functions, conducted their operations by the agency of Boards. The Church had become familiar with that mode of action; and when the effectual blow was struck for her emancipation, this was supposed to be fully accomplished, when these national organizations were disowned. The great principle upon which the argument turned, that the Church, in her organized form, must do her own work, was supposed to be satisfied, when Boards exactly analagous were established by the Church herself, as the agents by whom her will was to be carried out. It could not be long, however, before it was perceived that the above-named cardinal principle must be extended further: that a Board, consisting of many members, distributed over a large territory, to whom her evangelistic functions were remitted, did not satisfy the idea of the Church acting in her own capacity, and under the rules which the Constitution prescribed for her guidance. Dr. Thornwell was one of those who planted themselves firmly against their continuance in the Church. It is not the business of the biographer to discuss his views, but only to afford him the opportunity of presenting them. It may be remarked, however, that he was not opposed to combined or united action on the part of the Church, but only insisted that the central agency should be simply executive: the mere instrument by which the Assembly acts, and not an agent standing in the place of the Assembly, and acting for it. The first occasion on which he publicly developed his views was at the meeting of the Synod of South Carolina and Georgia; where a stiff debate was held upon the principles involved, and in which the Rev. Thomas Smyth, D. D., of Charleston, S. C., was his chief antagonist. An incident is related of this debate, so characteristic of the man, that it deserves to be recorded. In the heat of the discussion, he suffered himself to be borne beyond the bounds of strict propriety. The old spirit of invective and sarcasm, which later years so perfectly subdued, manifested itself in expressions a little too scornful of his opponent, and the impression was not pleasant upon the house. It so happened that his speech closed exactly at the hour of recess at noon, and there was no opportunity for rejoinder. Immediately upon re-assembling, he arose and apologised in handsome terms for the discourtesy into which he had been betrayed, and declared his profound esteem for the learning, ability, and piety of his adversary. It was done so spontaneously, and with such evident sincerity, that criticism was completely disarmed; and there was a universal feeling of admiration for the magnanimity and courage which could so fully redeem a fault.

This discussion is thus referred to in the first of many letters it will be our pleasure to transcribe, addressed to Dr. R. J. Breckinridge, with whom he was thoroughly associated in the discussion of all these Church questions:

"COLUMBIA, *December* 17, 1840.

"REV. AND DEAR SIR : Above you have a draft on the Commercial Bank of Pennsylvania for seventy dollars. I endeavoured to procure one on some of the banks of Baltimore, but could not succeed. You will please apply the money to the Evangelical church at Lyons, and the Theological Seminary at Geneva. I read to my people the correspondence between your church and that of Lyons, and between yourself and J. H. Merle d'Aubigne; and without any other solicitation than what is contained in your Magazine, they made up among themselves the amount forwarded. It is but a pittance, but still it is a free-will offering. You may give half to the church and half to the Seminary.

You will probably hear exaggerated accounts of the discussion in our Synod on the subject of Boards and Agencies. For your February number, I intend to send you a document which I have carefully prepared upon this subject, and which has received the sanction of a very respectable minority among us. I would have sent it to you before; but affliction in my family, combined with other circumstances which it is useless to mention, prevented me from complying with the promise which I made in Philadelphia

"Your sincere friend and Christian brother,

J. H. THORNWELL."

This was followed, a month later, with a fuller exposition of his views on the same subject, in a letter addressed also to Dr. Breckinridge:

"COLUMBIA, *January* 27, 1841.

"REV. AND DEAR SIR: I have detained my manuscript in my hands much longer than I had any idea of doing, when I wrote to you before. My object in the delay has been to copy it; but day after day has passed over, and I have been so constantly occupied that I have had no time for the drudgery of re-writing it. I send it to you, therefore, with all the imperfections of a first draft. It was written before the meeting of our Synod, with the view of presenting it to that body, and in their name sending it as a memorial to the Assembly. This, however, was not done. I submitted the manuscript to a few members of Synod, who cordially concurred in its leading statements. My object in publishing it is not to gain a point, but to elicit discussion. I believe that the Boards will eventually prove our masters, unless they are crushed in their infancy. They are founded upon a radical misconception of the true nature and extent of ecclesiastical power; and they can only be defended, by running into the principle against which the Reformers protested, and for which the Oxford divines are now zealously contending. This view of the subject ought to have been enlarged on more fully than has been done in the article, because the

principle involved in it is of vital importance; but I thought it better
to reserve a full discussion of it for some subsequent article.

"There is a fact connected with the influence of the Boards that
speaks volumes against them. A few men in the Church have presumed
to question the wisdom of their organization. These men are met with
a universal cry of denunciation from all parts of the land. If, in their
infancy, they (the Boards) can thus brow-beat discussion, what may we
not expect from them in the maturity of manhood?

"It is not to be disguised, that our Church is becoming deplorably
secular. She has degenerated from a spiritual body into a mere petty
corporation. When we meet in our ecclesiastical courts, instead of attending to the spiritual interests of God's kingdom, we scarcely do anything more than examine and audit accounts, and devise ways and means
for raising money. We are for doing God's work by human wisdom and
human policy; and what renders the evil still more alarming, is that so
few are awake to the real state of the case. Your Magazine is the only
paper in the Church that can be called a faithful witness for the truth.
I do sincerely and heartily thank God for the large measure of grace
which He has bestowed upon *you*. I regard the principles which you
advocate of so much importance, that I could make any sacrifice of comfort or of means, consistent with other obligations, to aid and support
you.

"I rejoice that you remember me and my poor labours in your
prayers. My field of labour in the College is arduous and trying; but
God has given me the ascendency among the students. I have an interesting prayer-meeting and a Bible-class. My sermons on Sunday are
very seriously listened to; and I have succeeded in awaking a strong
interest in the evidences of our religion.

"I have formed the plan of publishing an edition of 'Butler's An
alogy,' with an analysis of each chapter, a general view of the whole
argument, and a special consideration of the glaring defects in the
statement of Christian doctrine, with which the book abounds. It is a
subject on which I have spent much patient thought, and on which I
feel somewhat prepared to write. What think you of the scheme? If
you should favour it, any suggestions from you would be gratefully received. At some future day—I shall not venture to fix the time—you
may expect an article from me on Natural Theology. I have been carefully collecting materials on the subject, and shall embody them in a review of 'Paley's Theology,' Bell and Brougham's edition.

"In regard to the article on Boards,* I give you leave to abridge,
amend, correct, wherever you deem it necessary. If you can conveniently do so, I would be glad to have you return the manuscript, as I
have no copy of it.

"Sincerely yours,   J. H. THORNWELL."

* This article appeared in the Baltimore *Literary and Religious Magazine*, in 1841. It will be found in the fourth volume of his collected
writings.

A little earlier than this, his opinions on this and kindred topics are given in a letter addressed to the Rev. John Douglas, one of his bosom friends through life:

" COLUMBIA, *August* 4, 1840.

" MY DEAR BROTHER: I received your letter of inquiry, warning, and rebuke, a few days ago; and was not a little amused at the apprehensions which you expressed in relation to the *rectitude* (I use the word in its primitive acceptation) of my course. If I were disposed at this time, I might break a lance with you on the great principle which you have assumed, as axiomatic in relation to the use of reason in matters of religious worship. I shall just refer you to the second question in the "Shorter Catechism," with its answer, for the *only* rule of *practice* as well as faith ; and the answers to the one hundred and eighth and the one hundred and ninth questions of the "Larger Catechism," for the true ground on which all the inventions of man, no matter how reasonable, are to be disapproved, detested, and opposed. And if I am singular, at the present day, in maintaining that the Bible is our *only* rule, and that where it is silent we have no right to speak, I have the consolation of knowing, that I stand on the same ground which was occupied by Calvin, Chillingworth, Owen, and the venerable Assembly of Divines at Westminster. I would particularly direct your attention to ' Calvin's Institutes,' Book IV, chapters 8th, 9th, 10th, and 11th.

" I am satisfied that there is a dangerous departure, in the present age of bustle, activity, and vain-glorious enterprise, from the simplicity of the institutions which Christ has established for the legitimate action of the Church. He has appointed one set of instrumentalities, and ordained one kind of agency in His kingdom; but we have made void His commandments, in order to establish our own inventions. I believe that the entire system of voluntary Societies and ecclesiastical Boards, for religious purposes, is fundamentally wrong. The Church, as organized by her Head, is competent to do all that He requires of her. He has furnished her with the necessary apparatus of means, officers, and institutions, in Sessions, Presbyteries, Elders, Pastors, and Evangelists. Let us take Presbyterianism as we have it described in our Form of Government, and let us carry it out in its true spirit, and we shall have no use for the sore evil of incorporated Boards, vested funds, and travelling agencies. If it is wrong to hold these principles, it was certainly wrong to lay down such a form for the goverment of the Church ; and if we do not intend to execute the form, let us cease requiring our ministers to assent to it. Such is a skeleton of my views. I should like to go into a full investigation of the subject with you, but a single letter would hardly give room for an introduction.

" In relation to Temperance Societies, I am accustomed to draw a distinction. I regard them as secular enterprises, for temporal good, having no connection whatever with the kingdom of Christ ; a mere embalming of the corpse to arrest the progress of putrefaction. In this light, I think it well that the potsherds of the earth should engage in them. They are of great service to society. Others regard them as really helps to the cause of Christ, instruments of building up His kingdom; that is, as a *means* of *grace*, for the kingdom of Christ on earth consists in grace. In this sense, I oppose them, because they are not appointed by Christ. Their true position is among the institutions of civil society. There I cordially recommend and encourage them.

"Remember us kindly to Mrs. D., and let us have a full chat before you set me down as an Antinomian.

"Your friend and brother,

J. H. THORNWELL."

The next contribution of his pen was destined to bring him more conspicuously before the public as a controversialist, and involved him in labours which he never anticipated. It was an article on the Apocrypha, written at Dr. Breckinridge's request, and published in his Magazine in 1841. Being subsequently reprinted in a local paper in South Carolina, it drew forth a reply from Dr. Lynch, subsequently a Bishop of the Roman Catholic church in Charleston. Dr. Thornwell's rejoinder expanded into a book, which was published in 1845, and entitled "Romanist Arguments Refuted." They may all be found in the third volume of Dr. Thornwell's "Collected Writings." With this preliminary statement, the reader will readily understand the allusions in the correspondence which follows, opening with a letter to the Rev. Dr. Breckinridge:

"SOUTH CAROLINA COLLEGE, *March* 3, 1841.

"MY DEAR BROTHER: According to your request, I send a short article on the Canonical Authority of the Apocrypha. As I write a free and open hand, and the sheets are small, I do not suppose that it will fill more than two columns of such a paper as the *Visitor*. I have written under some disadvantage. I presume that it was your desire that I should keep my eye upon the article of the Priests, in one of the papers sent me. This I endeavoured to do, but I had to rely exclusively upon my recollection of its contents, as one of my servants destroyed the paper soon after I received it. Whether my article notices all that was important in their's, I cannot say. I have noticed all that made sufficient impression upon my mind to be remembered. If what I have written meets your approbation, and will be of any sort of service to you in this controversy, it is at your disposal. I sincerely hope that God may bring great good out of this unexpected movement in Baltimore.

"The destruction of the paper is my excuse for not verifying the quotations of the Priests for you. If you are at any expense in sending the numbers of the *Visitor*, containing this controversy, I would thank you to put down my name as a subscriber for *the year*. By the first opportunity, I wish to send for your 'Papism in the Nineteenth Century in the United States.'

"Praying that God may guide you and bless you in all your ways, I remain,

"Your sincere friend and brother in Christ,

J. H. THORNWELL."

Upon his return from Europe, and resumption of his duties in the College, the discussion on the subject of the Boards was revived. This was occasioned by a reply to his first article, from the pen of Dr. Smyth. The history will be developed in the correspondence that follows:

"SOUTH CAROLINA COLLEGE, *October* 14, 1841.

"MY DEAR BROTHER: Having recently returned home, I have been able to accomplish nothing yet. In fact, I have been threatened with fever every day since my return. I sent you Paxton's tract, 'Reading no Preaching,' which I have had copied; how correctly, I cannot say. If you think it worth publishing, it is at your service. I presume that *Smyth* is the reviewer of my article on Boards. I shall soon notice his lucubrations. I have many things to say to you, but have not time now. May grace, mercy and peace be multiplied upon you.

"Your sincere friend,

J. H. T."

To this Dr. Breckinridge replies:

"BALTIMORE, *November* 12, 1841.

"DEAR THORNWELL: After a long and painful absence, I returned to this city the last of October; and found here your favour of October 14, with the tract inclosed. I will print it in our January number. If you can, let us have something about your European trip. We and the public will be glad; when, and as you please. Your reply on the Boards, (which should cover the whole ground, nearly all which is *given up* in the long review of your article,) should be in time for our spring Presbyteries. By the way, there is a deep and wide feeling growing up in our Church; and there must be, and will be, a change in our mode of conducting benevolent operations. The review rather confirms me in my former opinions. The writer seems to consider the *brief and annual meetings* of the Assembly conclusive against its doing its work

personally. But besides the clear distinction between a small, standing, and responsible Committee, and a large, permanent, ill-constituted,
and virtually irresponsible Board, what should forbid the Assembly itself, or a commission of it, to meet as often, by adjournment, as our
Boards do? none of which meet oftener than monthly; one, at least
(the Foreign one,) only yearly; and as fourteen commissioners, by our
constitution, make an Assembly, (and, in point of fact, not so many as
fourteen persons regularly attend our Boards,) the argument is for us,
and not for the reviewer. Excuse this. God bless you.

"In much haste and much esteem, yours ever,

R. J. BRECKINRIDGE."

Three letters from Dr. Thornwell follow in quick succession, on the same subject, and addressed to Dr. Breckinridge:

"SOUTH CAROLINA COLLEGE, *January* 17, 1842.

"MY DEAR BROTHER: I am sorry that my reply to Smyth's review
will not be ready for the next number of your Magazine. I shall commence writing it to-morrow, and shall easily finish it in a week; so that
you will receive it early next month. You may think me very slow in
my motions; but I have been waiting for some books which I purchased
in Europe, and which I have been expecting every day. They have not
yet arrived; and wind and tide are so uncertain, that I do not know
when they will arrive. Some passages in the review have filled me
with grief and amazement, and show but too plainly that the first principles of ecclesiastical polity are not clearly understood among us. The
fundamental fallacy of the whole production, and of the system which
it is designed to uphold, is that the Church, instead of being the *kingdom* of the Lord Jesus Christ, is really one of His counsellors and His
confidential agent. This rotten principle is the basis of the whole fabric
of discretionary power, and the multitude of inventions which have
sprung from human prudence. But I have no idea of troubling you
with an argument here, of which you will have enough in due time.
I am satisfied that what of all things we need most, is a revival of pure
religion in all our churches. The cause of Missions lags, and all our
interests decay, because the Spirit of Life, to a mournful extent, is withdrawn from our congregations. The Church has almost dwindled down
into a secular corporation; and the principles of this world, a mere carnal policy, which we have nick-named *prudence*, presides in our councils.
Until she becomes a spiritual body, and aims at spiritual ends by appointed means, and makes faith in God the impulsive cause of her
efforts, our Zion can never arise and shine, and become a joy and a
praise in the whole earth. It is my fervent prayer that God would bless
us, and that right early. I am satisfied that our Church has a noble destiny to accomplish. With all her defects, I believe her to be the purest
Church on earth; and as I am fully persuaded that our beloved country

must take the lead, and that at no distant period, in the civilization of the world, I would fain hope, that the purest Church in our land will be particularly prominent in sending forth the waters of salvation, to gladden and fertilize the earth. Hence, I am earnestly desirous that she should be furnished for the enterprise to which I believe her to be called. * * * * * *

"You ask me to give some account of my excursion abroad. You will laugh when I tell you, that the notes which I took have never been written out, nor reduced to any kind of order. These are mere *memoranda*, made for *my own satisfaction*, and not worth publishing. Still, I would cheerfully comply with your request, if I had the leisure to write them out; but in addition to two sermons every Sunday, I am preparing lectures on Natural Theology, and certain branches of Christian Evidences, and a series of discourses on the Inspiration of the Scriptures. These labours are as much as a feeble body can sustain. Your kind letters were of great service to me, particularly in Glasgow. I left there your reply to Wardlaw, and would have had it published, if Dr. Mitchel had not dissuaded me from it. In the hope, and with the earnest prayer, that God may be with you, and abundantly bless you, I am

"Your sincere friend,

J. H. THORNWELL."

"SOUTH CAROLINA COLLEGE, *February* 7, 1842.

"MY DEAR BROTHER: I send you my reply to Smyth. I am sorry that I have been obliged to confine myself to a mere reply to his argument. I should have liked to enter into a full and positive vindication of my own principles, but my article would have been too outrageously protracted. I hope I have said nothing offensive or unchristian. If I have, please strike it out. I have been obliged to write in mere scraps of time, and therefore have indulged in repetition, which would be corrected if I had time to copy. I wish you would take up Boards on the ground of experience, and show how little they have really accomplished. I have not the details which are necessary for an argument of this sort. The thought has occurred to me, that the next General Assembly ought to appoint a committee, to take the whole question of Boards into consideration, and report to the succeeding Assembly. Let the committee consist of men on both sides, and let two reports go up, bringing the whole matter fully before the body. Something must be done. I trust my article may be in time for the March number.

"In great haste, I am your sincere friend and brother,

J. H. THORNWELL."

"SOUTH CAROLINA COLLEGE, *February* 23, 1842.

"MY DEAR BROTHER: I received your letter this morning, acknowledging the receipt of my manuscript, and of the letter which succeeded it. In regard to a central agency, I have expressed no opinion, because my object has chiefly been to awaken our Presbyteries to a proper sense

of their own responsibilities. Whenever they shall undertake, in good
earnest, the work of the Lord, in conformity with the spirit of our system, the details of their plans will not be found, I apprehend, very hard
to settle. On the present plan, our churches are not reached; the whole
body is not, and cannot be engaged as one man; the principles of our
polity, by which we are bound together and united into one body, are set
aside; and we are evidently proceeding in a method suited only to the
lame and crippled constitution of the Independents. This clumsy method I wish to see abandoned; I want our distinctive principles clearly
brought out; and I am very indifferent as to the details by which this
may be done, so that it is effectually done. If a central agency can be
suggested, which shall give us a proper security against error and abuse,
and interfere with the regular operations of no part of our system, I
shall have not a word to say against it.

"I deplore bitterly that our ecclesiastical courts, to such a mournful
extent, have ceased to be spiritual bodies, and degenerated into hewers
of wood and drawers of water. Our business is, for the most part,
purely secular; and when we have nothing of this sort to engage our attention, we are apt to complain that we have no business; are impatient
to adjourn and return home; though a world is lying in wickedness, and
millions are perishing daily for lack of knowledge. Our courts must be
roused up to a just sense of their true relation to our dying race; they must
be brought to feel the spiritual nature of their vocation, and to appreciate the work which they are required to do in the vineyard of the
Lord. This deplorable state of things the Boards have a tendency to
engender and perpetuate. And on this account, apart from all other
considerations, I must regard them as an incubus upon the body. But
when you combine with their dangerous results their unsoundness of
principle, I cannot see how any true hearted Presbyterian can give them
his sanction. I must again urge you to expose, more fully than you
have done, their inefficiency. Do join issue with their advocates, upon
the plain matter of fact, and show that they have not accomplished what
they were established to do; that, in sober truth, they are an utter failure,
as agents of the Church. This you can do, and I cannot. I have not the
facts; and a method of reasoning like this would be ten-fold more effective
than all the abstract arguments that could be produced from now till
dooms-day. It would absolutely demolish them; for they stand only by
creating the impression that the Church can, by no manner of means,
get along without them.

"Your Magazine will soon become the favourite periodical of this
part of the Church. You have only to be as diligent, faithful, and un-
compromising as heretofore, and the Lord will richly and abundantly
bless you and your labours. I cannot better express to you my sense
of the value and importance of your labours, than by mentioning to you
a fact, which I do simply to encourage you. During my absence from
home, when tossed upon the ocean, and wandering in a foreign land, I
do not know that I ever bowed my knees to the God and Father of our

Lord Jesus Christ without specially remembering you. I sometimes had reason to think that I was very near the eternal world; and as I thought myself approaching the Church above, I felt a deeper interest in the Church below; and loved to pour out my heart before God in regard to its faithful and tried servants. The children of God, how widely soever separated, form but one family; their hearts and sympathies are one, their aims are one, and their home shall finally be the same.

"I am very busily engaged in preparing my course of lectures on Natural Theology. I remember that we had a conversation on Paley's argument, in Baltimore; but I am not sure that I am master of the process of reasoning by which you made him prove an indefinite number of gods. I should be glad that you should state it in your next letter. By the first private hand, I will send you an article, which comprises the substance of my first sermon here as chaplain. I think it suited to the design of your paper, and I hope it is calculated to do good. You need not be afraid that I intend to flood you with my lucubrations; I shall probably not trouble you in this way very often. I am very busily engaged, just now, upon my lectures. * * * *

"Your sincere friend and brother,

J. H. THORNWELL."

CHAPTER XVII.

HIS own experience of the benefit of a sea trip induced him, after his return from Europe, to urge the experiment upon Mr. Robbins, whose failing health gave tokens of the fatal disease which finally terminated his life. In terms of strong affection, begotten of the old relations when Mr. Robbins stood to him as a second father, he pleads with this gentleman to "flee for his life, not to the plains, but to the sea." The voyage was eventually undertaken; and in a letter addressed to him in Paris, dated the 27th August, 1842, this paragraph occurs, in which his views are expressed as to the political prospects of France:

"Your items of French news were quite interesting. There are evidently three parties in that beautiful but unsettled country, which God seems to have made a striking example of the weakness, ignorance, and folly of man; and which of these parties will ultimately prevail, it is hard to determine. The old Bourbon dynasty still has strong friends, the present royal family has its own alliances, and republicanism is still a golden vision to the minds of multitudes of the French people. Liberty and Protestantism are the only things, in my poor judgment, which can give dignity and stability to the French character."

It is curious to read these lines, written two and thirty years ago, and to record their exact application to the same terms which enter into the French problem after the lapse of an entire generation.

On the same day in which these words are mailed to Paris, a similar expression is directed to his correspondent at Baltimore:

"SOUTH CAROLINA COLLEGE, *August* 27, 1842.

"MY DEAR BROTHER: I had hoped to see you this summer, but have been prevented from going northward by the circumstances of my family. Mrs. Thornwell has recently lost her father, and she could not bear the thought of being left alone; neither could I reconcile it with my own feelings to be separated from her, when her spirit was bowed down with affliction.

"The two letters which you were kind enough to enclose to me, I read with great interest, and shall return them by the first safe opportunity. The condition of France at this time is particularly interesting. Liberty and Protestantism are the only things which can give dignity, stability, and real glory to the French people. As long as they continue to be cursed with Popery, their efforts to establish free institutions must be abortive. Protestantism would redeem them from their national infirmities, and make them truly great. They have the elements of a noble character; but their atheism, idolatry, and philosophy, prevent them from being developed. I know of no event more devoutly to be hoped for than the thorough evangelization of that beautiful portion of the globe. D'Aubigne's work, the 'History of the Reformation,' I do not possess in the original, but have sent for it. I have read it in the translation with great interest. It may be taken as a specimen of what the French mind is capable of achieving when properly directed. *   *

"I wish you would, at your leisure, suggest to me such thoughts as have occurred to your mind on the question of the "existence of God." I would like particularly to have your view of Clarke's argument. I call it Clarke's, not because it was original with him, (I have found it in the schoolmen,) but because he has most elaborately unfolded it. I know that you have reflected maturely upon it, and can suggest some valuable hints. This winter I shall write my Lectures (at least some of them) out, having collected most of my materials. You are right in supposing that a good book on the 'Being, etc., of God,' is needed; but one which is much more needed is a judicious and learned treatise on the Holy Spirit. The only works, in English, upon the subject, of any value, are those of Owen, Ridley, and Heber. Owen's style is bad, and his plan was not sufficiently extensive. The history of theological opinion upon the subject ought to have been given, together with the doctrine of Divine influences as held among the heathens. Heber's work I regard as mistaking the meaning of our Saviour's promise, and as entirely too low in its view of spiritual religion. Ridley's book I have not yet read. There ought to be a masterly work on the Spirit.

"Yours, etc.,   J. H. T."

The reader will demand no apology from us for putting side by side the letters of two such men as Drs. Breckinridge and Thornwell. Apart from the fact that they belong together, and that either would be incomplete without the other, it is rare that Providence throws two minds so richly gifted into close companionship. It is beautiful to see how they laboured together in the propagation of similar views, and that no spark of rivalry or jealousy was ever struck out by their contact with each other. They were both of them too pre-eminently great, in their respective spheres, to be affected by this infirmity of smaller minds. The two letters now to be given have an inexpressible tenderness and pathos in their tone, which will amply repay perusal. The first is from Dr. Breckinridge:

"BALTIMORE, *October* 17, 1842.

MY DEAR BROTHER : 'I find, on my return to this city, after an absence of six weeks, your letter of 27th August, which must have arrived soon after my departure. I have been to Kentucky, and rapidly through other portions of the West, and return to my post to take the harness and the *chain* again. My appropriate work, my duties as a minister of the gospel, are full of sweetness to my soul; but this everlasting wrangle, and correction of proof-sheets, and devouring trash, this is murderous to me. My life is hastening away without fruit. An inexpressible restlessness of mind and heart often takes possession of me; and I feel like one condemned, for having not only done nothing, but attempted nothing, worthy of my Master or my age. I am sure I am capable of better things; would to God I had the space and opportunity of trying. This much I can do; I can beseech those who are able to guide the mind of this age and the next, to nerve up themselves to the work. Our spirits are often gifted with intuitive knowledge of what other men are, and can do. My dear brother, you must do great things, or you must give a great account; and you must do it soon, for the blade is too sharp for the scabbard; and men like you rarely live to be old. Concentrate your powers, then, and produce a great work, a monument of our principles, our hopes, our struggles, our Church, our age. Your mind has been directed to a channel which few are able to explore : a work on the Godhead, the God of the Bible, that Jehovah who is Father, Son, and Holy Ghost. Write such a book; you alone are capable, of all the men I have known, of doing this, by God's help, as it should be done. I say this in profound conviction, and to make you feel how much it is your duty to do this thing; and I feel as if I should promote the cause of God, and human nature, more effectually, by urging you forward to such an undertaking, than by living almost a double life-time.

"If you can devote two or three days to the labour of throwing together the results of your thoughts and reading on geology for our pages, it will be a very great service done to the public, and a favour to me. You will find in one of my numbers, about three years ago, a very able philological article, by Horwitz, the Jew, on the questions arising upon the Mosaic cosmogony. My knowledge of the subject (of geology) is general, and by no means accurate; but my decided conviction is, that the whole matter is in an exceedingly crude state, and is receiving a decidedly wrong impression. * * * *

"It is of the last moment that the regular action of our system should be restored, and all the temporary contrivances into which we have fallen be laid aside; and with them all those irregular and dangerous influences which have grown up with them, and for the sake of which they are so stiffly defended. God is bringing all this about, steadily and surely. Let us take courage, and be patient. '*Cunctando restituit*,' was the motto of the Massini family, that has lived the longest and done the most of all the private families amongst men. God counts not slackness as some men count slackness; human wisdom and divine faith agree for once. Let me hear from you soon; and let me have an interest in your prayers.

"With true regard, ever and faithfully yours,

Ro. J. BRECKINRIDGE."

The reply to this letter is dated:

"SOUTH CAROLINA COLLEGE, *October* 25, 1842.

"MY DEAR BROTHER: I am sorry to learn that you suffer yourself to be dejected by occasional reflections, founded on what I conceive to be a great mistake. Your observation has taught you that, among the lights of our world, there are two classes of men, each eminently useful, and each largely entitled to the gratitude and benedictions of the race. One class embraces those whose lives are spent in retirement; who are unknown to their contemporaries; who exert no influence upon existing generations; but who are enabled, by God's blessing, to leave behind them a valuable legacy for those who come after them. These men live in the future; they are as dead, in their own day; and enjoy only that 'life beyond life, which is embalmed and treasured up in a good book.' Their books are all of themselves that the world knows or feels; they act upon mankind only through these precious representatives. There is another class, of those whose influence is felt in their own day; who shape the destiny of their age; who act through themselves, and impress their life, and spirit, and energy, upon the mass of their fellow-men. These are the lights, the guardians, and ornaments of their own times; they make the age what it is; and it is through their influence that posterity receives a glorious birthright. If they should

never pen a line to reach distant generations, their image is impressed
upon history; and the memory of their actions and living speeches, their
personal efforts and noble sacrifices, will always live, and secure them the
love, admiration, and gratitude of the truly great and good. They are
the most illustrious benefactors of their race; eminent instruments, in
the hand of God, of bestowing blessings on mankind. Now, I speak in
the deepest sincerity when I assert that, if every production of your pen
should perish, the influence which you have been able to exert upon
your age would still be written in such characters, that it could not fail to
be read and appreciated in coming generations. You have not produced, it may be, a standard work on divinity or morals; but you have
done something better and more glorious: you have moulded the character of the present times. Your name is identified with the progress
and prosperity of the cause of religion, humanity, and liberty. Your
noblest monument is the impression you have made upon your own
times. Why, then, should you despond? God has eminently blessed
you. He has enabled you to do what no man living has done, or can do.
The result of your labours will be felt and rejoiced in, when you are
slumbering in the tomb. The ball, which you have set in motion, will
continue to roll, long after the hand which first touched it shall be
withered in death. I am afraid, however, that I belong to neither of the
classes to which allusion has been made. I have done but little for the
present times, and there is but little prospect that I shall ever be known
to other generations. I have an aversion from writing, which makes it
an intolerable burden. I have formed many a fine scheme, but find it
almost impossible to overcome my mortal dislike to the pen. I can
hardly bear to read anything that I have written. It fills me with loath-
ing and disgust. I fall so immeasurably short of my own conceptions of
excellence, that I become disheartened and chagrined. It is an infirmity
which I lament, and from which I would be gladly delivered; but it
binds me in fetters of brass, and paralyzes all my efforts. I am afraid,
therefore, that I shall never produce anything beyond such occasional
lucubrations as involve no responsibility except to truth; which can be
thrown off at a dash, and abandoned, like the eggs of the ostrich, by the
parent that brought them forth. You may judge how deeply this feeling
has possession of my mind, when I assure you that I have not a single
copy of a single article I ever wrote, with one exception. I sometimes
feel that I *might produce* something that should live. But when I undertake to carry out any plan, I become sickened at my efforts. Still, I feel
bound to endeavour to mortify this sickly sensibility.

"I had many other things to say, but my paper is exhausted. Let me
hear from you soon.

"Your sincere friend and brother,
                                        J. H. THORNWELL."

The reader who is acquainted with the after history of
these two remarkable men, will doubtless smile at the sym-

pathy expressed in this letter to the one, and the confession which is made by the other. It pleased God, in His adorable providence, to place them in similar positions, as teachers of divinity to the rising ministry in the Church; and both, under the pressure of that position, were stimulated to produce "Standard Works on Divinity," which, with that wrought out in the Princeton school, and recently given to the world, are grand representatives of the theology of this age; and are, perhaps, as noble contributions to the science of theology as any age has been permitted to make.

We do not regret the necessity of interrupting this correspondence upon the Church questions of the day, by interposing a few letters of Christian condolence addressed to the children of sorrow. The first is written to Mrs. Ann B. Crawford, a "mother in Israel," of the Lancaster church, to whom he was warmly attached. It is not only full of tenderness, but rich in suggestions of scriptural truth:

"SOUTH CAROLINA COLLEGE, *September* 19, 1842.

"My DEAR AUNT ANN: I need not say that the sore and bitter bereavement, which you have recently sustained, has filled me with the profoundest sympathy. As I know that you are not a stranger to the throne of grace, nor to the pleasures which flow from communion with God, I cannot but hope, that this solemn visitation will be improved to increase your intimacy with that 'Friend who sticketh closer than a brother,' who alone can dry up the tears of sorrow, and give us 'beauty for ashes, the oil of joy for mourning, and the garment of praise for the spirit of heaviness.' The gospel of God is particularly designed for the broken-hearted and afflicted; and if you mark the footsteps of the flock, you will find that they all lead through much tribulation to the kingdom of heaven. The house of mourning has been the familiar resort of all the saints. The great Redeemer Himself was a 'man of sorrows, and acquainted with grief,' and bedewed His path to glory with tears, and sweat, and blood. Think not, therefore, that some strange thing has happened to you; the like sufferings have been accomplished in all your brethren before you, and must be accomplished in all who would reign with Christ for ever. Jacob wept for his beloved Rachel, and David mourned a rebellious son. How does your calamity compare with that of Aaron, who beheld his sons consumed with fire from the Lord, in th very act of audacious iniquity; and yet was forbidden to uncover his head, to rend his clothes, or give any visible sign of grief? 'Son of man,' says Jehovah to Ezekiel, 'behold, I take away from thee the desire of thine eyes with a stroke; yet neither shalt thou mourn nor weep, neither shall thy tears run down;' and at even his wife died, and he forebore to cry, and made no mourning for the dead. You are not alone, my sister, in the chamber of affliction. You are where Jesus was, where all His saints have been, where prophets, martyrs, and apostles have stood, and where, in the issue, you will find it a privilege to be. It is God that deals with you; stand still, and acknowledge His hand. He is your Father; and what He doeth, though you know not now, you shall know hereafter. Though clouds and darkness are around Him, His footsteps in the sea, and His paths in the great waters, righteousness and truth are the habitation of His throne, and He will finally speak peace to His children. He who reproved kings for their sakes will assuredly Himself do them no harm. Fear not, therefore; the flame shall purify, but not hurt. Jesus can more than make up all your earthly losses. He can turn them into mercies; and, therefore, though the fig tree shall not blossom, neither shall fruit be in the vine, yet, like the prophet, rejoice in the Lord, and joy in the God of your salvation. Only believe; and as He said to the weeping sisters of Lazarus, so He says to you, 'Thou shalt see the glory of the Lord.'

"Perhaps, my sister, your greatest distress arises from uncertainty concerning the salvation of your beloved son. You feel that you could be comforted, if you knew that he was safe; but that you can never know. The destinies of men are in the hands of God; and it is enough for us to know, that He is righteous in all His ways, and holy in all His works. When your mind shall be more enlarged, and your heart expanded in love, you would not choose to alter a single arrangement of the Lord. If you could see the end from the beginning, you would say all is right. Oh! then, trust God in the dark. All opposition to His government is sin, and 'every wish to alter the appointments of His wisdom is folly.' Your business, therefore, in this and every other dispensation, is to put your hand upon your mouth, and keep silence before Him. 'Be still,' is His language, 'and know that I am God.' Others have encountered more trying afflictions than yours. You are only uncertain; but Eli had no ground to hope that his sons were saved, but every ground to believe that they were lost; and yet the good man submitted: 'It is the Lord; let Him do what seemeth Him good.' Absalom was slain in the very act of atrocious rebellion; and Nadab and Abihu were consumed by the immediate vengeance of God. What ingredient of bitterness in your calamity can be found answerable to their's? And yet Eli, David, and Aaron were the special friends of God. Take courage, then, and be not like Rachel, weeping for your children, and refusing to be comforted, because they are not. Take courage, and do your duty to the living, and prepare to follow the dead. Trim your lamp, gird up your loins, and stand ready to welcome the midnight cry, Behold, the bridegroom cometh! Let the conviction of your own mortality settle upon your mind; look away from earth; look up to Heaven; deposit your treasures where neither moth nor rust can corrupt, nor thieves break through and steal. Here we have no continuing city. 'All ranks and conditions of men are but so many troops of pilgrims, in different garbs, toiling through the same vale of tears, distinguished only by different degrees of wretchedness.' The patriarchs and prophets all confessed that they were strangers on earth ; here they had no home ; but they sought a better country; they looked by faith to that building of God, that house not made with hands, eternal in the heavens, and there they expected to rest. Let us follow their faith and patience, and we shall receive the same glorious reward. 'But this, I say, brethren, the time is short; it remaineth that both they that have wives, be as though they had none ; and they that weep, as though they wept not; and they that rejoice, as though they rejoiced not; and they that buy, as though they possessed not; and they that use this world, as not abusing it; for the fashion of this world passeth away.' 'I am,' says David, 'a stranger with thee, and a sojourner, as all my fathers were.' Then, what our hands find to do, let us do it with our might; we shall soon go hence, never to return. A Christian is one who looks for the second coming of his Lord. He waits for it, and desires it, because then his sorrows shall be over, his days of mourning ended, and his soul at rest for ever. Then, my sister, be heavenly-minded ; live for God, for immortality, for eternity; and your light afflictions, which are but for a moment, shall work out for you a far more exceeding and eternal weight of glory.

"I would earnestly impress upon your mind, that the bitterest of all calamities is an *unsanctified* affliction. In His providences, God is teaching us; and it hardens the heart, and darkens the understanding, when His solemn instructions are unheeded. When, therefore, He lifts the rod, and takes away, with a stroke, the desire of our eyes, instead of dwelling upon the circumstances of our bereavement, and tearing open our wounds afresh, by calling to mind the endearing associations connected with the departed, we should at once look to the hand that smites, and inquire what lessons a merciful Father designs to convey. Our great anxiety should be *improvement.* God is speaking ; and our chief business should be, to open our ears, and hear. You will find yourself greatly tempted to think of your son, as you have seen him in infancy, in boyhood, in youth; to call to mind his proofs of affection, his interesting sayings, his promising actions, and all the endearments which silently, secretly, irresistibly bind a mother to her child; and every recollection will send a pang to your heart. These reminiscences, which we are so prone to cherish, are the cruel devices of a self-torturing heart. Turn away from them to God, and humbly ask your Father why He has smitten, and bow your head and worship. Receive His instructions with an humble spirit, and He will soon bind up your wounds, and send you away, though 'sorrowful, yet rejoicing.'

"If you have been conscious of any neglect of duty towards the departed, repent; but with that Godly sorrow which flows from a full conviction that God will freely pardon. Repair the mistake by greater diligence to the living; but let nothing keep you from the pure consolations of the gospel of Jesus. In your present situation, religion proposes to you her sweetest cordials. You can understand the gospel now. Affliction has revealed to you the vanity of man, the deceitfulness of life, the certainty of death, the instability of all sublunary good; and in striking contrast presents the unchanging perpetuity of an unchanging state, and the glories which await the child of faith. You can now almost advance by strides towards the heavenly kingdom. And if earth is rendered less pleasant, Jesus more charming, and heaven more desirable, by the dark providence which has called you to mourning, you will bless God through all eternity for His chastising rod.

"This melancholy event, let it be remembered, speaks not only to you, but to all your household. It says to each and every one of your family, whether bond or free, You, too, must die; prepare to meet your God! When you least expect it, when you are dreaming of many days, and pleasing your fancies with brilliant prospects, your hopes may at once be crushed, your sun go down at noon, and your golden visions wrapped in the funeral pall and shroud. Oh! that the warning may reach the hearts of the living. Oh! that they may be wise, understand this, and consider their latter end.

"I have thus, my much valued friend, endeavoured to direct your mind, now softened by grief, and capable of receiving permanent impressions, to such meditations as I thought would be most conducive to your good. It will be my greatest joy, if God should give you grace to adorn the gospel, as you walk in deep waters of sorrow. It is only in affliction that the *real greatness* of Christianity is seen. It imparts then a moral grandeur to the character, which philosophy cannot compass, and which the world never can understand. It sustains, elevates, ennobles the soul. It teaches it 'the heavenly science of gaining by losses, and rising by depressions.' The saints are a wonder in the earth, a wonder to angels, and a wonder to themselves. They are God's chosen portion, the lot of His inheritance; and this is enough to make them hold up their heads, though all their earthly comforts should be stripped from them. Their main portion—their Father in heaven, their glorious Redeemer—must remain for ever. Let this, my sister, be your consolation. Death has robbed you of nothing you shall want in eternity. Your real inheritance is safe. And now, that the God of all grace may sanctify you wholly, and do exceedingly abundantly for you above all that you are able to ask or think, is the sincere, fervent, and heartfelt prayer of

"Your friend and fellow Christian,

J. H. THORNWELL."

A similar bereavement, the loss of a son, called forth a like sympathy in a letter to Mr. Robbins:

"SOUTH CAROLINA COLLEGE, *November* 17, 1842.

"My Dear Sir: I need not express to you my profoundest sympathies in the accumulated afflictions which you 'have been called upon to endure. God is evidently showing that he sets a high value on the trial of your faith; and His grace will no doubt enable you to pass through the furnace, not only without harm, but with vast accessions to your spiritual stores. That your trust in God remained unshaken amid your severest tribulations, and that, in these dark hours, when nature was ready to faint, and to say 'all is lost,' you were able to cling to the mercy-seat, is to me a matter of most devout thanksgiving, and an evident token of the presence, power, and love of God's Holy Spirit. I should only mar the instructions of the blest Comforter within you, by suggesting consolatory thoughts. He knows your frame, and He will lead you to such truths as it is most important for you to ponder. Our great High Priest sympathizes with us in all our sufferings. He knows when and how to console us; and the methods of His grace will always be found to be methods of wisdom. You may be well assured that in all your afflictions I am afflicted; and my dear wife, particularly, feels the deepest interest in everything that concerns you and yours. It is a great comfort to me that she is so much delighted, as she is, with my two dearest earthly friends, yourself and the General. She loves you both, as much as if you were members of her own father's family.   *   *   *   *   *

"Yours most sincerely,

J. H. THORNWELL."

Other labours than those purely controversial, engaged Mr. Thornwell's thoughts. In a letter to Mr. Robbins, of date February 14, 1843, he thus writes:

"I am preparing a course of sermons, with a view to publication, on that great and glorious theme, *the Atonement.* I have already preached three of them. The theme is rich and extensive. Many points, which other writers have slurred over, I propose to bring out prominently; and difficulties, which have been rather evaded than removed, I propose to discuss throughly; at least, I shall attempt it. The age requires a good book on this subject; and if God shall enable me to produce one, I shall regard myself as singularly favoured. My heart is much set upon this enterprise. My greatest perplexity is that my own glory should form so large a part of the motives which induce me to engage in the undertaking, as I am often afraid that it does. Humility I find to be the hardest lesson in the Christian life. I experience no difficulty in despising riches, pomp, and splendour; but the love of fame is an instinct which was born with me, and which I cherished so long, that it gives me many a bitter pang, now that I perceive its folly and wickedness. I *wish* to live only for the glory of God; but self is a powerful idol.

"I am somewhat at a loss as to the form in which it would' be best to publish my work; whether to retain the form of sermons, or to arrange my materials in chapters and sections. There are advantages and disadvantages in both plans. A didactic treatise can preserve a more unbroken continuity of thought; but sermons can have more fire and more pungency of practical application. The characteristics of style in the form of sermons would be better adapted to the mass of readers; the prospect of permanent success would be greater in an unbroken treatise. So that I am in a strait."

In a later epistle, March 7th, 1843, to the same correspondent, he thus sketches the plan of his book:

"In regard to my contemplated work on the Atonement, I shall take your advice, and write it in the most enduring form. My plan will embrace, first, the *Nature* of *Atonement;* which will lead to an examination of Socinian, Pelagian, and Hopkinsian views. In the explanation of its nature, its necessity will be sufficiently exhibited without devoting a special head to that department of the subject. Under this head, the nature of God's moral government will be fully declared, so far forth as I shall be enabled to do it; and of course the origin and purpose of sacrifices. The next point will be the *Efficacy* of the Atonement. Here will be set forth the Person of Christ, the Eternal Covenant between the Father and the Son, the Incarnation, the Federal Headship, the Mystical Union, etc. The third general division will embrace the *Extent of the Atonement;* the last, its *Grand Results.* This is only a vague outline; a mere blazing of the trees, so that you may see the road. God grant that I may make the way of salvation plain to many a wanderer."

Had this work been executed, it would have gone far towards supplying a sequel to his "Lectures in Theology," which death arrested just at the point when he should have entered distinctively upon the doctrines of grace in the scheme of redemption. We shall discover presently how he was diverted from the execution of his purpose.

The next letter discloses his watchfulness of opportunities to bring the gospel personally to the unconverted. It is addressed to his kinsman by marriage, Dr. J. J. Wardlaw, at the time not a professor of religion:

"SOUTH CAROLINA COLLEGE, *February* 14, 1843."

"MY DEAR DOCTOR: I have been threatening to write to you for some time back, but procrastination has again and again nipped my good resolutions. I am truly sorry to learn that your venerable pastor is no more. He was a man whom I was anxious to know; and had promised to myself great satisfaction in his company next summer. But we know not what a day or an hour may bring forth. I sincerely trust that, though dead, he will long continue to speak to you all in the savour of his influence and example. It is a solemn thought, that you must meet him at the judgment bar, and give an account of the effect which his sermons, prayers, warnings, and expostulations have had upon you. May God grant that you and your dear wife may be prepared to give it with joy, and not with sorrow. Nothing would afford me a richer or purer satisfaction, than your conversion to God; and nothing, be assured, ought· to be more earnestly sought, or eagerly desired by you, than those true riches which neither moth nor rust can corrupt, nor thieves break through and steal. * * * * *

"Your sincere friend,

J. H. THORNWELL."

The correspondence with Dr. Breckinridge, of course, reopens Church questions; those which immediately follow, however, not so directly:

"BALTIMORE, March 18, 1843.

"DEAR BROTHER THORNWELL: Many cares, and sicknesses, and duties, have made me let slip the pleasant duty of writing to you, for a long time. Indeed, you are partly in fault; for I have been hoping all along to hear from you about that article on Geology, which, as you did not refuse, I allowed myself to hope you would prepare. If you can have it ready to send on by some of your Commissioners to the approaching Assembly, I shall be under a new obligation to you. Unless, indeed, you will be a member of that body yourself, and so bring it, instead of sending it; which I should rejoice at doubly; for, besides the pleasure of seeing your face once more, there are many and important questions which will come before the Assembly, in the decision of which I could heartily wish you had a voice. I believe our Church is by far the purest that exists; but alas! we are far from what we ought to be; and a very large portion of our leading men seem far from believing this. Unless I see you here, I know not that I shall see you more, till we meet together <i>at home</i>; for which my wasting strength admonishes me to be ever ready. If I were called away, it would be a joy to me to reflect that I left you behind to testify for the <i>true truth</i> of God. * * * * *

"I have been for a long time much exercised in mind in regard to the distinctive points which characterize the Millenarian controversy; and have come pretty fully to the belief, that the common opinion held of late years, and, indeed, since the publication of Whitby's views, are not sustained by the word of· God; and although I cannot call myself a Millenarian, either of the ancient or modern school, yet I suppose the bulk of men, who distinguish little, would call me so. Upon several points my convictions are clear; as, for example, that the millenium we expect will not be produced by the work of the Divine Spirit, as now operating; but by some new dispensation or manifestation of the '*Son of Man*,' which is the distinctive title and appropriated name of the Lord Jesus, the Word incarnate, and now glorified; which is the key to all consistent expositions of those scriptures which touch the subject, and is the question which draws after it all the rest; though this fact seems not be perceived, and therefore the contradiction and perplexity which men exhibit on the whole subject. I should be greatly gratified to know your mind on these matters.

"Farewell, dear brother. Remember me at our Father's throne of grace, and be assured of the sincerity with which

"I am ever and faithfully yours,

Ro. J. Breckinridge."

"South Carolina College, *March* 28, 1843.

"My Dear Brother : I received your truly welcome and affectionate letter last night, and shall give you the best demonstration of my esteem by proceeding to answer it at once. I am sorry that I did not know you were expecting from me an article on Geology. I should either have undeceived you, or gratified your wish. For reasons which I am about to name, it will be impracticable for me to do so now. I have more on my hands than, I am afraid, I shall be able to accomplish. I have got into a war with the Romanists. The article on the Apocrypha, which, you may remember, I wrote at your request, has been recently republished by Mr. Weir, in his newspaper here. Without informing me of his intention, until the proof-sheets had passed through the press, he appended my name to the piece. The consequence is, that a writer in the *United States Catholic Miscellany*, of Charleston, has commenced a series of articles, directed personally to me, which I feel bound to notice. He is a weak scribbler; and unless he has strong friends, concealed behind the curtains, he will not be difficult of conquest. There was much craft, however, in their seizing upon me as their object of assault. They, no doubt, supposed that my public position, as an officer of the State, would, in some measure, muzzle me; they presumed that I would feel a delicacy in exposing freely the enormities of any portion of the citizens, whose taxes go to my support; or that, if I did not act from these selfish considerations, they would raise a clamour against me in the community, which would compel me to retire from the College. These are my suspicions of their motives. I know their craft so well, that I do not consider it ungenerous to suspect them of any meanness. Why else the personal address? Was it not as easy simply to review the article, as a production of mine. My mind is made up. I shall accept the challenge. If a clamour is raised, I shall distinctly make the issue whether this is a Protestant institution or not? If there should be any disapprobation of my course among the Board of Trustees, I shall promptly resign. The war must go on. We need a controversy here. The Papists have almost taken possession of Charleston; and among the leading men in the State, the dreadful apathy on the subject of religion, which they too much manifest, turns all their sympathies in favour of the Papists. Controversy cannot make things worse, and may make them better. Trusting in God, and the power of His truth, I shall endeavour to vindicate Christianity, and expose the abominations of Popery to the light of day. Still, my brother, I am not ashamed to confess to you that I feel weak. I am badly prepared for this contest. In the first place, all Columbia does not furnish a library adequate to the exigencies of a full and complete controversy with Rome. In the second place, I have not studied this matter as accurately as I should have done. My attention has been turned more to doctrine, logical exposition of truth, to philosophy, and studies of an abstract nature, than to minuteness of historical details. Still, if I had the books, which I have not, I could say with Milton, in his apology for Sinectymnuus, that, 'if they provoke me, I will in three months be an expert councilist,' (sec. 12.) I shall endeavour, however, so to conduct the discussion as to make it turn on principles. Now, you must help me. You can give me hints, direct me to important sources of information which I might overlook, and occasionally give me an article, which you can re-publish in your Magazine, and thus make it a part of your editorial labour.

"To the Millenarian controversy, I have never minutely turned my attention. I have been so struck with the confusion, contradiction, and perplexity which have characterized the most of the expositions that I have consulted, as to be deterred from forming any opinion with my present degree of light. When I can give you an opinion worth recording, I will cheerfully do so. Uutil then, my crude speculations would be a waste of ink and paper, * * * * *

"Ever your sincere friend and brother,

J. H. THORNWELL."

The response to this is marked by that exhilaration which the war-worn veteran always feels at the sound of the bugle:

"BALTIMORE, *April* 3, 1843.

"MY DEAR BROTHER AND FRIEND: How many reasons have we to know that God's ways are not like ours? Who would have supposed my great confidence in your learning and abilities, and the pride and affection of Mr. Weir, were to be the means of obliging you to win honour; and what is so much better, greatly promote the truth, by becoming in the South the champion of the Reformation, and of the Bible? The Papists are surely mad. Not one of those who have done, or will do them most harm, would have been induced, probably, to give themselves seriously to this great and widespread controversy, if they had been let alone. The hand of God is in this thing. I need not, therefore, say, Arise, and in His might, do the work to which He calls you, for which He will surely reward you, and by which here or hereafter He will surely honour you. But so much I may say : no event could have made me feel more assuredly that God is on our side, than that He obliges you to take up arms in this quarrel. Anything it is possible for me to do, I will gladly do, both for the cause's sake and for yours ; so that you have only to command me, and to point out the particular service as occasion requires it.

"On one point, I will venture to caution you. Let not your high Southern blood drive you to any such step as you intimate. Don't think of resigning your Professorship. The old Huguenot and Scotch blood of Carolina only sleeps; it is not dead. Only give it a fair chance to manifest itself. If the worst comes, let the Trustees, or the Legislature, take the responsibility; and in that case, the worse the better. To make the community what it should be, it is just needful to know exactly what it is. This, I know, will be, if it arises, the worst part of the trial to *you*; that is, to your feelings; but it is all-important to meet it; for it may be the reason of the higher and more evident success of the truth; and let it fall out as it may, it will surely be for your own personal honour. I know how you feel, and how you will argue. But have I not been indicted like a felon ? Would I not rather have been burned at the stake ? But did not God turn all this to the confusion of His enemies and mine ? You are in many ways precisely the man, and precisely situated as you should be, to make a noble and imperishable defence, by deed and by word, for the glorious inheritance which is ready to be snatched from the world. May God, our Saviour, stand ever at your right hand.

"With great affection, ever your brother and friend,

RO. J. BRECKINRIDGE."

In the sketch of Mr. Robbins, given in the third chapter of this book, his death is mentioned as occurring on the 26th of March, 1843. It was the snapping of a very tender tie, and no tears were shed upon his grave more sincere than those of his former pupil and ward. The letter which follows, addressed to the widow, will better tell the story of his grief.

To Mrs. H. R. Robbins, Cheraw, S. C. :

"SOUTH CAROLINA COLLEGE, *April* 4, 1843.

'MY DEAR FRIEND : I had heard, the day before I received your letter, that the Lord had 'taken away your head.' My mind was prepared for this solemn event. Through the kindness of Brother Coit, I was kept informed of the precise condition of Mr. Robbins's health, and, therefore, was not surprised when, at length, it was announced that the last conflict was over, and the last enemy subdued. I was extremely anxious to be with you, and to mingle my tears with yours, at the grave of one whose memory I shall never cease to venerate, and whose works of faith and labour of love have followed him to his rich and blessed account. Nothing but the very serious sickness of my dear companion prevented me from hastening, at once, to the chamber of my dying friend. For a whole week I was kept in awful suspense, as to the probable result of a violent inflammation, which had seized upon Mrs. Thornwell's head. By the mercy of God, she has completely recovered. How often have I uttered Balaam's wish : ' Let me die the death of the righteous, and let my last end be like his,' since I heard of the triumphant departure of your sainted husband. Horses of fire, and chariots of fire, were round about him, to conduct him in safety and peace to the court of the King of kings. Death to him was not a calamity ; his soul marched in triumphal procession, in invisible, but glorious state, to its chosen home, the scene of its abiding rest.

"No, my sister, let us not weep for *him*, but weep for *ourselves*. We are the *sufferers*, we the *losers*. But his gain may also become our joy, if we follow the example of his faith and patience. The departure of our friends should be employed as a means to wean our affections from the vanities of earth, and to fix our regard upon that city which hath foundations, whose maker and builder is God. Under no circumstances, to the believer, is Heaven a land of strangers. He has walked with God upon earth, and has counted it his highest glory to know Him, and to be known of Him ; he has found Christ to be an affectionate Brother, and the Holy Spirit a precious Comforter. When brought into more intimate and endearing alliance with these august and blessed Persons, he will not feel lost; he will be *at home.* Is it presumption to add, that his familiarity with the place will be somewhat increased, by finding, among his companions, those with whom he had taken sweet counsel on earth ? Is not Heaven sometimes presented in a more attractive garb—is it not made more tangible, more capable of being embodied as a reality—when we reflect that it contains those whom we had loved here below ? They have gone before us ; and are we not greatly stimulated in our Christian course, by the prospect of meeting them at the end of our journey, and of being once more united, and that in the presence of the Lord ? Be this as it may, every opening grave, and every funeral bell, should forcibly remind us that here we have no continuing city ; that the time of our sojourning is short; and that our grand and paramount duty is to be found ready, with our loins girded, our lamps trimmed, and our lights burning, whenever the midnight cry shall be heard, ' Behold, the Bridegroom cometh ! ' Eternity is just at hand; for that we should prepare. Our tears can hardly dry up for the departed, before it shall be said, we too are gone. For myself, I expect soon to be with *your* husband and *my* friend. My wasting strength daily reminds me that my sands are running out, and that what I intend to do for God and for my race I must do quickly.

"You have many great and precious promises to sustain and support you in this affliction. Your dear little babes are the heritage of the Lord; and not a hair shall fall from their heads, without His special and controlling care. They will be loved for their father's sake. Fear not, therefore; the Lord, the Shepherd of Israel, who neither slumbers nor sleeps, will watch over them, and suffer no enemies to do them harm. I need not say that I shall be happy to be employed as an instrument, in God's hand, of rendering any service to you and your little ones. For yourself, I can only say, make the *Lord* your *husband.* He is never deaf to the cry of the widow. Follow that track of light which irradiates the path of your beloved husband: it will lead to glory and immortality. There are many mourners around his grave. It was a sore bereavement to my dear wife, for she loved the departed tenderly. Oh! how many of us, that now mourn together, shall hereafter rejoice together with him around the throne of God! My dear sister, I hope you enjoy that peace which flows from the sprinkling of the blood of Jesus. If not, give no rest to your eyes, nor slumber to your eyelids, until the Lord has revealed His Son to you, and in you, as the *hope of glory.* That God may be merciful unto you, and bless you, and cause His face to shine upon you, is the sincere and fervent prayer of one who shall always rejoice to be considered, and to be esteemed by you, as well for your own as for your husband's sake, what he now subscribes himself,

"Your true and faithful friend,

J. H. THORNWELL."

CHAPTER XVIII.

THE ELDER QUESTION.

Assembly Decision upon the Quorum of a Presbytery.—Upon the Imposition of Hands by Elders in the Ordination of Ministers.—Letters on these Topics.—Article Published.—Argument of Dr. Breckinridge, before Synod of Philadelphia, Reviewed.—Further Correspondence on the Eldership.—Letters of Sympathy.—The Intimations of God's Will from the Leadings of Providence.

THE General Assembly of 1843 is memorable for the decision it rendered upon what is technically known as "the Elder Question;" which divides itself on the two points of *jurisdiction* and *prerogative*. This subject had been brought before the preceding Assembly, and was passed over as unfinished business to the next. It could, therefore, be anticipated, and is accordingly hinted at, in the letters we have already given. The decision finally reached was embodied in two resolutions: First, "that any three ministers of a Presbytery, being regularly convened, are a quorum competent to the transaction of all business, agreeably to the provision contained in the Form of Government, chapter 10, section 7." Second, "that it is the judgment of this General Assembly, that neither the Constitution nor the practice of our Church authorizes ruling elders to impose hands in the ordination of ministers."*

The year following, the whole subject was again raised by overtures from different parts of the Church, and the above decision was confirmed by explanatory action of the Assembly, to wit: that in respect to the quorum of a Presbytery, "the decision is based upon the fact, that ministers are not only preachers of the gospel, and admin-

* Digest, Ed. 1856, p. 43.

251

istrators of sealing ordinances, but also ruling elders, in
the very nature of their office;" and in respect to the right
of ruling elders to impose hands in ordination, that, "as
the rite of ordination is simply a declaratory ministerial
act, the laying on of hands, as a part thereof, belongs
properly to ordained ministers; while to ruling elders is
left unimpaired, and unquestioned, the full and rightful
power of ordering the work of ordination, and of judging
in the discipline of ministers, in common with those presbyters who labour in word and doctrine, as in all other
cases."[*]

Under this adjudication, the question has remained from
that day to this, although large numbers in the Church
have never acquiesced in it, as either sound or true. A
moment's reflection will show that the principles involved
go down to the very core of our Presbyterian system;
and the discussion upon them was far more earnest and
long continued than that previously maintained on the
subject of Boards. That branch of the question which
relates to the quorum of a Presbytery, evidently touches
the whole relation which the ruling elder, as a distinct
officer, sustains to the courts, the constitution, and the
government of the Church; while the other branch of it
involves, besides this, the natural import of ordination:
whether in any degree sacramental in its character, the
sign and seal of an invisible grace, or merely an act of
government, setting apart to certain duties and functions,
and therefore one of *joint*, and not *several*, power. It is
not to be supposed that a decision, which so materially
involved the essence of Presbyterianism, would escape the
criticism of two such champions as Drs. Breckinridge and
Thornwell. We will, therefore, gather into this chapter
the entire correspondence relating to this matter, which
will reveal the extent and method of their opposition to
the Assembly's decree.

[*] Digest, Ed. 1856, p. 44.

Dr. Thornwell thus writes:

"ABBEVILLE C. H., *July* 8, 1843.

"MY DEAR BROTHER: * * * * * * * *
* * * * The point, however, about which I sat down to
write to you, concerns *your controversy*, not *mine*, except so far as it is
a matter which interests the whole Church. I have been chagrined and
mortified beyond measure, at the proceedings of the last Assembly, in
reference to questions which involved the distinctive principles of our
system of ecclesiastical polity. Unless light is thrown upon the peculiar
and characteristic features of Presbyterianism, the points in which it
differs from Congregationalism, on the one hand, and Prelacy, on the
other, we shall soon lose all that is discriminating, and be reduced to
an incoherent mass of discordant elements. I cannot understand how
our ministers and elders, who profess to have studied our system, should
give utterance to such sentiments as were avowed, more than once, in
the discussion upon a question, which never ought to have arisen in a
Presbyterian Assembly, touching the membership of ministers in the
Church. The decision, too, of the right of ruling elders to participate
in ordination, took me by surprise. This matter must be discussed before the churches. And if you do not disdain such feeble assistance as
mine, I propose to give you an article, showing that, in the *Primitive
Church*, the right was not only *conceded*, but freely exercised, and that
Prelacy was actually introduced by its gradual denial. I have looked
with some attention into this matter, and am persuaded that there is
something more in it than a mere question of usage. It involves a
principle which lies at the very foundation of our system. The truth
is, my dear brother, we have been so long accustomed to institutions
and organizations foreign to our polity, that we are rapidly losing sight
of our glorious constitution. Scores of our ministers, and thousands of
our people, do not understand the real strength, and consequently, do
not feel the beauty of our Church. Her walls, and towers, and magnificent bulwarks, have been fenced out of view; and we are content to
stand in an outer court, where we cannot behold the glories of the Temple. We must pull down these earthly contrivances, and reveal our Zion
in her true proportions, as the chosen heritage of God. In my tour
through the country, I have kept my eye steadily upon the prospect and
condition of our churches, and am completely satisfied that our coldness
and declension may be ultimately traced to ignorance or forgetfulness of
the *true vocation* of the *Church*. Our brethren are treating symptoms as
they are developed, one by one, without going to the root of the disease.
Their labour, consequently, fails of its purpose. * * * * *

"Your faithful friend, and fellow-servant in the Gospel,

J. H. THORNWELL."

To which this is a rejoinder:

"BALTIMORE, *July* 13, 1843.

"MY DEAR BROTHER: * * * * * * * * *
* * * * You will easily suppose that I was much distressed
and mortified at the result of the matter about ruling elders, in the last
Assembly. I knew the Church was not ready for the question; but I
had no conception of the extent of its ignorance and false principles.
I had no hand in bringing on the question there, none in bringing it
up; and desired its discussion put off. Last year, when I was in the
Assembly, they put it off, rather than hear me on it; this year they
would not hear of delay. The *Repertory*, the *Presbyterian*, the *Watchman of the South*, and a paper at Pittsburgh, and one in Ohio, by agreement, and perhaps concerted move, carried the matter by a *coup de main*.
I intend, if the Lord permits, to bring up the question in our Synod
this fall; and carry it to the Assembly, if it is decided against me, as I
am pretty sure it will be. I will also pretty soon write a notice of the
arguments on the other side, merely to expose them; and thus show
that they do not prove what they were used to prove. Except this, I will
write no more about the matter, till I bring it before the Assembly.
Would it not be well for you to bring up the matter before your Synod
also? or would it perhaps be better for you to leave that alone for a
third trial, and come up in the Assembly of 1845, if we are beat in that
of 1844, as we perhaps shall be? I thank God He has induced you to
examine this matter fully; and I beg that you will carry out your idea,
both of writing on it, and of being in the next Assembly. * * * *

"I would be really obliged by your thoughts on the other question,
about which you express yourself, so as to show that your opinion is decided, but not so as to enable me to determine what it is; I mean about
the membership of ministers in churches. My mind is not clear on the
matter. I concede, of course, that if ministers be members of particular churches, it is only in such form as to give them the rights of
membership, while the *responsibilities* thereof are to the Presbytery.
But except we make them members of the Church *general*, they must
be members of some particular church; otherwise they are not in the
visible Church at all. For, though *officers* of the Church, they are not
the Church, which were Popery. But is there any mode of being a
member of the *Presbyterian* Church *general*, except by being a member
of a *particular* church? If elders may lay on hands, it is because they
are Presbyters; but they are members of particular churches; why not
ministers? Indeed, as you are aware, in the early French Discipline,
the elders could, on occasion, discipline and silence their pastors; and
so could the Kirk Session, under the second Book of Scottish Discipline.
Indeed, for twenty years after the commencement of the Scottish Reformation, there was not, in all Scotland, any other Presbytery than an
Eldership, which was about what two or three of our Church Sessions
would be, if met. I incline, therefore, to think ministers are members.
I fear you think otherwise, and so I desire your views; and will not

commit myself till I hear from you, which is what I would not say to five men in the world.

"I seriously believe that the germ of High Churchism and Popery, is to be found in the ultimate principles, which lead our ministers to the cast of opinion which prevails around us. Their notions lead them to disesteem the Church Courts, to lower the office of elder, to sink the body of the people of God, to question the divine warrant for Church Order, to deny it for Presbyterial Church Order; and the germ of all seems to me to be a notion of *their own inherent exaltation*. A Board is as good as a Presbytery, if *they* are in it; a Presbytery is complete, if *they* are there; a man is ordained, if *they* put hands on him; membership is not for those who own the body. How otherwise shall we explain the varying opinions, which seem to agree only on this solitary point, that ministerial ordination is a mysterious, if not magical, thing, and carries with it a kind of *opus operatum!* May God ever bless and keep you, is the prayer of

"Your faithful friend,

Ro. J. Breckinridge."

From Dr. Thornwell:

"Yorkville, *August* 15, 1843.

"My Dear Brother: Your letter reached Abbeville after I had left, and was forwarded to me at Table Rock, in Pickens's District. The dilapidated state of your health is to me a matter of the profoundest grief; and I sincerely pray that God may restore you to your strength, prepared by affliction for still greater labours in the service of your Master. I know of no event that would fill my heart with greater heaviness, than your prostration from sickness, debility, or death. I have long felt that your principles were in advance of the age; but I am fully persuaded that they are destined, in another generation, to a complete and glorious triumph. They are the *true principles* of the Presbyterian Church; and there cannot be a stronger proof of the degeneracy of our times, than the slowness with which they are comprehended, and the coldness with which they are greeted. The Lord, however, has not wholly deserted us. I have met with men, here and there, in the Church, who have given a hearty response to them, and who are prepared to lend their aid, in bringing back our beloved Zion to a cordial acknowledgment of them.

"Touching the matter of ruling elders, the Assembly has shocked scores by the *second resolution*, who would not have been alarmed by the *first*. The decision, that a Presbytery can be constituted (a quorum) without ruling elders, has produced in this State a general dissatisfaction; in some cases, severe indignation. This oversight, for I can regard it in no other light, reveals the real bearing of their principles who supported the first resolution, and will arouse the Church to reflection and sober, patient investigation. God often overrules evil for good;

and men are frequently taught the truth, by being made sensible of the effects of error. I am satisfied that every *Presbytery* in *this State* (I cannot speak for Georgia) will solemnly remonstrate against the decision in question; and I think, too, that a large portion of our ministers and elders will be found in favour of the whole truth, upon the subject of the eldership. Upon consultation with several of our best men, I have determined to bring the matter before our Synod. Should the brethren from South Carolina be generally present, we will have a *very strong vote.* The Georgians, I do not know. Many of the ministers in that State are Northern men, and, I am afraid, too much under the influence of Princeton and the *Repertory.* I think that the Synod should respectfully memorialize the Assembly, and put that body in possession of the *real state of the argument.* I shall prepare such a document, move that a committee be appointed for the purpose, and thus be able to introduce my views fully and at large. If the majority be against me, the memorial will still exist, and be published and circulated as an argument. Many would unite with me in presenting it to the Assembly as an individual matter, and thus we could succeed in getting it before them. A similar memorial from a portion of your Synod, coupled with the resolution of the Synod of Kentucky, would show the Assembly that the question would have to be met upon other grounds than those of authority. The discussion will be productive of vast good, in unfolding the real nature, as well as the capabilities of our system. There is a profound ignorance upon this subject, and an ignorance which does not like to be disturbed. The treatment of your Bi-centenary Report shows the apathy, in regard to our Church Order, which has taken possession of the Church. We have so long been walking in the light of our own eyes, and rejoicing in our own contrivances, that we have quite forgotten that the Church, in its outward organization, as well as in its essential principles, is a *Divine institution.* The next step will be to deny any Scriptural authority— that is, any *specific* warrant from Scripture, for the office of ruling elder—at all. It will soon be put upon the ground of expediency, and then the next step will be to abolish the office altogether.

"In regard to the church-membership of ministers, I apprehend that there is no difference of opinion, when the terms are once defined. A minister is not *so* a member of *any particular* church as to be *subject* to its *Session;* this is granted. Again, he is *entitled* to privileges in *any particular church,* not by reason of his relations to any such church, but by virtue of his connection with *Presbytery.* Now, the Presbytery stands in the same relation to *all* the churches within its bounds, which the Session sustains to a particular church. Hence, a member of Presbytery is *ipso facto* a member of *every* church under its care. When a minister comes to us from Ireland or Scotland, he is received by the *Presbytery.* He does not apply to any *particular church* for admission, but to the *Presbytery.* When received by that body, he is entitled to ordinances *in all its* congregations. Under our constitution, the case is not the same with a *ruling elder;* because the court of which he is a

standing member has jurisdiction only over a single congregation.
Ruling elders are consequently dismissed from *congregation* to *congregation* Ministers would be in the same category with them, if our
Presbyteries, as in primitive times, embraced only the Session ; that is,
if the *Presbytery* of *every particular church* were the body which ordained. I have not time to write more, especially as I am writing with
a detestable pen. I hope, however, you can read it.

    "I am, as ever, your sincere friend and brother,

                        J. H. THORNWELL."

    In the fall of 1843, Dr. Breckinridge delivered, before
the Synod of Philadelphia, two elaborate arguments upon
both branches of this double question, on the composition
of the quorum of a Presbytery, and on the right of ruling
elders, when members of Presbytery, to impose hands in
the ordination of ministers of the Word. They were
subsequently published in a pamphlet, bearing the significant title, "Presbyterian Government not a Hier-
archy, but a Commonwealth; and Presbyterian Ordination not a Charm, but an Act of Government." It is,
perhaps, as fine a specimen of forensic reasoning and eloquence as the controversies of the Church in these times
afforded. They were fully and favourably reviewed by
Dr. Thornwell, in the pages of the *Southern Presbyterian
Review*,—a quarterly then, and since published at Columbia, South Carolina;—which, together with a prior
article, on "The Ruling Elder a Presbyter," published in
The Spirit of the Nineteenth Century, a magazine conducted by Dr. Breckinridge, in Baltimore; and a sermon
preached in 1856, at the ordination of certain elders in
the church at Columbia, are all the contributions made
by him to this discussion. They are all to be found in
the fourth volume of his "Collected Writings," to which
the reader is once for all referred. The letters which
follow relate to these matters. The first is from Dr.
Breckinridge:

                    "BALTIMORE, *November* 27, 1843.

    "MY DEAR BROTHER THORNWELL : I am in your debt a letter or two, and
also for your fine article, which will appear in my next—my last number.
My farewell address will so fully explain my views, that I will not trouble

you now. I have been very busy for the last two weeks, in all odd times, writing out my argument, delivered before our Synod, on the quorum of a Presbytery ; and am about to write out that on the question of ordination.   They will both appear in the *Presbyterian*, and a very large edition in pamphlet form.   I have written them out at the request of the largè majority of the ruling elders of this city.   I consider the whole question of Church order involved in the two propositions, and treat them accordingly : for if *jurisdiction* or *ordination* be in the hands of preachers, as preachers, there is an end of Presbyterianism.   I wish that you would get your article, that will appear in my next number, copied into the paper at Charleston ; it is short, clear, conclusive.   And now, you may rest assured that no effort will be left untried to defeat us. * * * *   I will look after it in the *Presbyterian ;* it will be fully attended to in Kentucky.   It remains to take care of it in the South, and at Pittsburgh.   At this latter point I will do what I can, if nothing better occurs.   It will devolve upon you, my dear brother, to uphold this cause at the South. * * *   This will not reach you, I presume, till your return from your Synod.   My heart and my prayers will be with you there.   If you can carry it, it puts our cause in the ascendant ; for, taking the votes of the Synods of Kentucky and Philadelphia, the matter is about tied.   You cannot tell how I feel strong, when I reflect that you are so deeply interested in this great question.   God has given you great abilities.   You have also facilities the most of us have not. Stir up your strength, then, my dear brother, and we shall see the truth cut its way. * * *

"Let me hear from you soon, and let me have an interest in your prayers.

"Faithfully, your friend and brother,

Ro. J. Breckinridge."

Several letters follow from Dr. Thornwell's pen, no replies to which are in our possession.   These, however, trace the general progress of the discussion :

"Columbia, *March* 1, 1844.

"My Dear Brother : You were *almost*, though not *exactly*, right as to the cause of my silence on the elder question.   My own health has been as good as usual, but I have had another protracted case of typhus fever in my family.   This is the thirty-eighth day since my brother-in-law was attacked by this horrible disease, and he is now just able to go upon his legs.   He was very seriously ill, and at one time his physicians manifested considerable anxiety about him.   My leisure time was, consequently, devoted to him.   I hope, however, by God's blessing, to be able to furnish something upon the question, next week.   Your speech,*

---

* The argument delivered before the Synod of Philadelphia, to which reference is made by us already.

however, has so completely exhausted the subject, that you have left
nothing to be gleaned after you; and if you should find that I avail
myself rather freely of your labours, you must attribute it, not to the
poverty of the subject, but to the richness of your argument. Within
the whole compass of my reading, I have never met with a clearer and
abler exposition of Presbyterial Regiment than your two speeches afford.
There are only one or two points which I wish you had contrived to incorporate in them, so as to have made them perfect. The first is the *expansive* character of Presbytery, enabling it to preserve the unity of every
possible condition of the Church, in regard to numbers and extent. A
single church may be Presbyterian, by being under the government of
a congregational Presbytery, or Session. Two or more churches have a
common Presbytery, in the classical Presbytery, and so on. This point
you have touched upon in your letter to ruling elders. Our courts of
appellate jurisdiction, as an expansion of the Presbytery, to meet the
growth of the Church, has always struck me as one of the most beautiful
features of our system. This matter I shall probably develope in my
argument.

"I have written in great haste, and in considerable pain of body. You
must excuse me, therefore, if I have sent you but a scrawl. One thing
you may depend on: the sincerity of my love, and the earnestness of my
prayers, for you and yours.

"Very truly, your brother,

J. H. THORNWELL."

"SOUTH CAROLINA COLLEGE, *April* 16, 1844.

"MY DEAR BROTHER: I have sent to Dr. Plumer* a long article on the
Elder question. I could easily make a book upon it. My essay contains
only *three* arguments: the first, drawn from the constitution of the
Church; the second, from the nature of ordination, as an act of government; and the third, from the prelatical tendencies of the opposite doctrine. This, you will perceive, is only a fraction of what might be said.
In developing the argument from the constitution of the Church, I have
laid down principles which, if the article should be thought worthy of
attention at all, will produce an intense agitation. I have spoken what
I believe to be the truth. The ultimate triumph of our cause is certain.
We are gaining ground every day. In this State, the leaven is gradually
working among our ministers and elders, though we have a tremendous
tide of prejudice to stem.

"Dr. Miller's sermon I have not seen, but I am satisfied that my main
positions are true. I have brought them out again, in my second article.
There is one point which I must shortly discuss, and that is the *distribution* of power among our Church Courts. This occasions a difficulty
to many minds, and prevents them from appreciating the *simplicity* of
the Presbyterial organization.

* At this time editing the *Watchman of the South*, at Richmond, Va.

"Let me hear from you *before* you leave Baltimore, and *while* at the Assembly. I wish we were so situated that we could often meet in the flesh. I know of no man on earth with whom I would more delight to hold frequent communion.

"Very truly, your friend and brother in Christ,

J. H. THORNWELL."

"SOUTH CAROLINA COLLEGE, *May* 1, 1844.

"MY DEAR BROTHER: I have just dispatched another article to the *Watchman of the South*, which will close my present contribution to this controversy. I wrote the thing to-day, and was compelled to do it in such great haste, having but a small portion of time to allot to it, that it presents no other attractions but those of naked truth. My object was to show that the charge of Independency, which has been so freely and so confidently urged against us, is utterly without foundation. I think that I have put this charge, the offspring of ignorance, engendered by malice, completely to rest. I have written calmly and dispassionately, though the egregious misrepresentations of Dr. Miller and McCalla were sufficient to provoke me. I have determined, however, to enter into a controversy with neither of them, unless it should be forced upon me in such a way that I could not honourably decline it. Since writing to you before, I have procured a copy of the Doctor's sermon. In the small portion devoted to my article, he falls into two singular mistakes. 1. He represents me as saying that Calvin, Owen, and others, endorse my views of the distinction of ministers and elders, as such; whereas, I simply referred to them as maintaining the ancient and Presbyterian exposition of the passage to which I appealed in Timothy. 2. He is wrong in saying that Owen did not hold, upon this subject, the same opinion as myself. I did not refer to him, in the article, as holding them; but still he does most stoutly and resolutely maintain them. To say nothing of his elaborate account of the difference in gifts which preachers and elders require, he is very particular to state, that the pastor combines *both* offices; and in consequence of his being an elder, and *in consequence of that fact alone*, he is entitled to rule in the Church. Take the following passage, which you will find in his works, (vol. 20, p. 486, London edition, 1826): 'Unto pastors and teachers, as such, there belongs no rule; although, by the institution of Christ, the right of rule be inseparable from their office. For all that are rightfully called thereunto are elders also, which gives them an interest in rule.' Can anything be more explicit and distinct? How, then, could Dr. Miller say that Owen held the doctrine of his sermon? This great man made the eldership *one*, and *every* elder, whether a teacher or not, so far as he was an elder, partook of the *same* office. Dr. Miller, however, makes two distinct sorts of elders. The eldership of which a minister partakes is, according to him, a *different kind* of eldership from that which is possessed by the ruling elder. I cannot understand how the Doctor could misrepresent Owen so egregiously, when he was professedly taking me to task for the same sin.

"Ministers without a charge, will think that a regular conspiracy has been formed against them; but I cannot see any method of evading the conclusion at which I arrive, in my first article for the *Watchman*. The same view was held by other bodies, besides the Burgher Synod, to which I referred. See Owen, Vol. 20, page 457.

"I have read the article in the *Biblical Repertory*. It has added nothing to the argument, and I am sorry Princeton is in such a temper. There is one fact, however, which I wish to see explained. You and the writer both quote the Belgic Confession, and yet neither of your quotations agree with the copy to be found in the *Corpus et Syntagma Confessionum Fidei*, which was published at Geneva in 1654. What edition did you use? The various readings are so striking, that I should like to know when, where, and how, the changes were made. The discrepancies between the reviewer's copy and mine, satisfied me that each of you might be right in his quotations, having followed different editions.

"Your third, in reply to Dr. McLean, is capital. You have taken what I conceive to be the only sensible view of a quorum, and effectually put down the ludicrous trifling into which the good Doctor had fallen. I feel much solicitude about your success before the next Assembly. I sincerely trust that God may give you grace to maintain your position, so as to glorify His name, even if you should be defeated in the object of your suit. Maintain, my brother, the spirit of Christ, and its contrast to the temper in which you have been assailed will speak volumes in your favour. I hope that the Master will be with you, to guide, direct, and sustain you. Do not forget to give me an occasional line, informing me how matters go with you. My interest will be intense, and I shall be able to get nothing from the papers, except through the *Presbyterian*.

"An organ of some sort we must have. Give us a paper, and we shall certainly win the day. I attached so much importance to this matter, that I had determined to write to you about it. I hope, therefore, that you may succeed in setting a paper on foot.

"I have been preparing a series of discourses on the Eternal Sonship of Christ. I have been so much interested in the subject, that, if I could overcome my mortal repugnance to the pen, I might be tempted to put them in a permanent form.

"May grace, mercy, &c.,

J. H. THORNWELL."

"SOUTH CAROLINA COLLEGE, *July* 12, 1844.

"MY DEAR BROTHER: Having been disappointed in my expected trip to the North, I drop you a hasty line, to let you know that I have determined to put my letters on the Apocrypha to the press at once. I have sent them to Leavitt, Trow & Co., with instructions to print one thousand copies. I have no hopes of being able to pay the expenses from the sale; but I concluded to try my fortunes with the public. I shall depend on you to give me a lift in getting them into circulation.

"I am about to come out in the *Charleston Observer*, in reply to 'Geneva.' I think I shall be able completely to demolish him. I have already written most of my reply, and would be happy to have you see it. How does your pulse beat since the adjournment of the Assembly? I have been looking for a letter from you.

"Very truly and affectionately,

J. H. THORNWELL."

"COLUMBIA, *August* 10, 1844.

"MY DEAR BROTHER: * * * * * * * It is very evident that our brethren of the majority are consoling themselves with the delusive hope that the war is ended on the subject of elders. I have written sixteen manuscript pages of my reply to 'Geneva,' and as soon as I finish the remainder, I shall send it to brother Gildersleeve. In the course of my argument I have attempted to show, that the words pastor and bishop are both generally employed, in profane and sacred authors, to denote those invested with authority, and not merely teachers or instructors. This fact will take them by surprise; as in all their discussions they have quietly assumed that a *bishop* must be a *preacher*. They have never thought of appealing to the Septuagint and to classical writers, for the *usage* of the word, which, if they had done, they would find that' there is *not* a *single instance* in which it is used in anything like the sense to which they would exclusively restrict it. I shall present them with some stubborn facts upon this point, that they will not find it very easy to digest. Another circumstance has been strangely overlooked. In the African Church they find Presbyter and Senior used, one in reference to ministers, the other to ruling elders. They infer that the words are not synonymous, because they are apparently applied to different officers. Why not, say they, call both Presbyters, or both Seniors? The question is obvious, they wanted distinct terms, and accordingly went to the *Latin Bible*, where they find the *same Greek* word in reference to the *same officer* sometimes rendered Presbyter and sometimes Senior. The more I reflect upon the subject, the more I am satisfied that the truth of the case is with us.

"I am glad to learn that brother Dunlap is in Baltimore; as I know that he will strengthen your hands, and aid you in every good word and work. Please make my kindest remembrances to him. You may tell him, moreover, that his last letter was duly submitted to a committee of clerks and printers; and after having been deliberately examined, *mark* by *mark*, was pronounced to be wholly *illegible*. Still, after divers and sundry efforts, as I had some general knowledge of what I suppose he intended to say, I succeeded in guessing out (for I cannot say that I spelt a word) the strange hieroglyphics, which were scrawled before me, like the tracks of snails on Southern ceilings.

"I see that you and Dr. Plumer and Mr. Rice have challenged all the bishops, archbishops, priests, and deacons in the United States, so they come not more than three at a time. They are too cunning to take you up. Let me hear from you soon, etc.,

"J. H. THORNWELL."

"SOUTH CAROLINA COLLEGE, *December* 27, 1844.

MY DEAR BROTHER: I have been resolving every day, for some weeks past, to write you a long letter, but have not been able to command sufficient time to say all that I wanted to say. Your sermon* is *exactly the thing*; it is, in every way, seasonable and to the point. All I fear is, that you have not given it a sufficiently wide circulation. I wish it were in the hands of every minister, and every candidate for the ministry, in the land.

"Our Synod has just adjourned. I had no opportunity of bringing up the resolutions which I had prepared on the elder question. The first business on which we entered, was that of division;† and the arranging of the details connected with the constitution and funds of the Seminary, took up our whole time. I was on the Board of Directors, and had to be a great deal engaged in committee. So that I could not have argued the matter, if any one else had brought it up. I was very sorry, as this was our last meeting in a united body. I think that, in the new Synod (to be erected) of South Carolina, we shall have a *very* strong minority. My impression is, that the State is almost equally divided; a majority of ministers being against us, a majority of elders in our favour. In Georgia, we have next to no strength at all. The question has come up in two Presbyteries in this State, South Carolina and Harmony; and the two parties were considered about equally balanced. I have to preach the opening sermon of our Presbytery, in Charleston, at its next meeting in April; and shall take occasion, in imitation of your example, to lift up my voice like a trumpet. It is my anxious desire to be a member of the next Assembly, and I want you to be one too. We must get the matter up again, in some shape or other; and I think I have a plan by which it can be done. If you should be a member of that body, supposing that my scheme should not succeed, it would be proper in *you* to agitate the question, as you were refused a hearing by last Assembly. It would be simply an act of justice to yourself, to hear the grounds on which you maintain your opinions.

"I am about to come out with another sermon, of which I will furnish you a copy as soon as it is published. The subject is, the *Necessity* of the *Atonement*.‡ The students have requested its publication, and I did not feel at liberty to refuse. It was preached on the Sunday before commencement; the day on which I usually preach a valedictory sermon to the graduating class.

---

* The reference is to a published sermon of Dr. Breckinridge, entitled, "The Christian Pastor one of the Ascension Gifts of Christ;" preached at the installation of the Rev. R. W. Dunlap, in Baltimore. A review of it by Dr. Thornwell, in 1847, in the *Southern Presbyterian Review*, will be found in Vol. IV, of his 'Collected Writings.'

† The Synod of South Carolina and Georgia was, at this meeting, divided into the two Synods of South Carolina, and of Georgia.

‡ Found in Vol. II, of the 'Collected Writings.'

" *Entre nous*, I have serious fears that my usefulness in College has reached its climax.   *   *   *   *   *   *   *   *   From what I can learn, I am the real nexus that binds the religious community to the College. This is a position of perilous responsibility, which I do not like to hold. I endeavour to preach the Gospel faithfully, and no man dares to interfere with me. I have the esteem and affection of the young men; but still, I feel solitary, and I do not like to waste my strength upon so few. If the providence of God should place before me a *pastoral charge* suited to my mind, and offering a reasonable prospect of usefulness, I should feel strongly tempted to accept it. These things are said to you, in the confidence of most unbounded Christian love, with the view of eliciting your opinion, to which I always, and on every subject, attach great value. I can assure you that you had my warmest sympathies in your recent affliction. I did not know how much I loved you, until I heard you were in deep waters. Still, I had no doubt but that a covenant-keeping God was passing you through the furnace, for your own good, and for His glory. For myself, I have been often desponding, since I saw you. I have been painfully impressed with a sense of worthlessness. I feel that, if I should die, I should sink into the grave like a stone into the water, unmissed, unlamented, unregarded. Pray for me, my brother, that God may give me grace suited to my day.

"As ever, yours,   J. H. THORNWELL."

A heavy affliction in the family of Dr. Breckinridge drew forth a brief letter of sympathy:

"SOUTH CAROLINA COLLEGE, *December* 28, 1844.

"MY VERY DEAR BROTHER: I have just this moment heard, from Colonel Preston, of the severe and awful calamity with which you have been visited. My heart is full, and I know not what to say. All that I can do is to pray that God may be with you, to comfort, support, and sanctify you. My beloved brother, when I think of your desolate fireside, and still more desolate affections; your motherless children, and the perilous responsibility that is now accumulated upon their only parent, my heart bleeds within me. I enter into your sorrows; I share your bereavement; I partake of your anxieties. But it is in affliction that the real greatness of Christianity is seen. You have a covenant God to whom you may flee, unbosom your sorrows, and make known your wants; and it is His prerogative to be a *very present* help in time of trouble. He careth for you; and can make this calamity, bitter as it is, conduce to your good. You know, you have tasted, His love; and it is His own word, that He doth not willingly afflict or grieve the children of men.

"I cannot but think that your thoughts are now much set upon the heavenly state. Another charm is now given to the place, since the dearest object of your affections is now gone to be for ever with the Lord. The separation betwixt you and her is only temporary. The Master will soon call for you also; and then sorrow and sighing will flee away for ever. In the meantime, your little ones may be safely entrusted to the Shepherd of Israel; who has promised to bless the seed of the righteous, and who loves them for their father's sake. I might, my brother, write you a long letter, suggesting the ordinary topics of Christian consolation; but I prefer to leave you in the hands of the blessed Spirit, who will teach you effectually, and administer comfort as He sees it to be good. To Him I commend you, begging you to accept my assurances of profound sympathy and of fervent prayer in your behalf.

"Very truly, your friend and brother,

J. H. THORNWELL."

The letter which follows forms a link in Dr. Thornwell's personal history; and is equally appropriate as the conclusion of this chapter, or as the introduction to the next:

"SOUTH CAROLINA COLLEGE, *March* 12, 1845.

"MY DEAR BROTHER: Since receiving your last kind and welcome letter, I have been confined to my chamber, for about ten days, with catarrhal fever. My whole family have suffered not a little with sorethroat. But through the good hand of the Lord upon us, we are all now restored to our usual health.

"The circumstances in which you are placed must be full of embarrassment and perplexity. Broken in health, wounded in spirit, with two calls before you to different and responsible stations, you must feel very sensibly your need of Divine guidance and direction in guiding your steps. I have but a single suggestion to make; and, though it may not be new, it deserves none the less to be seriously pondered, by those who would aim singly at God's glory. We are too often prone to misinterpret what are called the leadings of Providence, and to take those things as the *intimations of Divine will* which are, perhaps, designed to be *trials of our faith*. I am quite satisfied that no one can ever reach the will of God, in his own particular case, by judging merely from promising appearances. The measures of human probability—it is a lesson recorded on every page of the Bible—are not the standard of Divine wisdom. Every striking instance of faith commended in the Scriptures was *against* the conjectures of our narrow philosophy. Had Moses reasoned according to the prevailing principles of our day, he would not have refused to be called the son of Pharaoh's daughter. The prospect of extensive usefulness was so much greater in the court, the sphere of his influence would have been so much wider, he had so singularly been raised to that elevated station, and the hand of God was so visible in the whole affair, that, if he had reasoned, as multitudes do, from the leadings of Providence and probable appearances, he would have felt justified in accepting the glittering bribe which was offered him. In this, however, he would have followed the impulse of *human reason*, and been no example of *faith*.

"My friends sometimes charge me with a spice of fanaticism; but it is my deliberate conviction, that the only way of arriving at a knowledge of the Divine will, in regard to us, is by simplicity of purpose and earnest prayer. If we really desire, with an honest heart, to know our duty, and apply to God to be instructed by Him, He will impress upon the conscience a *sense of duty*, just in the direction in which He would have us to move, and which we shall feel it perilous to resist. This sense of duty may be produced by some principle of the word which we perceive to be applicable to the exigency, or by an immediate operation upon the mind, which we are unable to explain. This is my test; and I confess that, until after having sought from God, with simplicity and honesty, His divine direction, I feel such a sense of duty upon my conscience, such a 'woe is me' upon the heart, I should feel it unsafe to move. That you may have the counsels of your heavenly Father, and be guided by a wisdom better than yours or mine, is my sincere prayer. I am sure it is your purpose to glorify God, and I am equally sure that 'the meek He will guide in His way.'

"I am sorry to learn that brother Dunlap has been so seriously afflicted. This is indeed a vale of tears; and they whose robes are washed and made white in the blood of the Lamb, are they who have come out of great tribulation. Oh! how precious the thought, that there is a land of rest, where sorrow and tears are unknown for ever! and how anxious should we be that, through God's grace, our earthly afflictions may wean our hearts from sublunary things, and fix them on things above, where Christ sitteth at the right hand of God. It is in the house of mourning that the real greatness of Christianity is seen. As I have stood by the grave of departed friends, and looked at the prospect of a glorious resurrection, my feeelings have been almost insupportable. Worlds multiplied on worlds could not induce to me give up that precious text, 'Them that sleep in Jesus will God bring with Him.' No doubt, my brother, resurrection and the glory beyond have been much upon your thoughts, since the Lord removed from you the 'delight of your eyes.' Oh! how grand is the Christian's hope! The time is short; we shall soon lay aside the weapons of our warfare, and buckle on the panoply of light for ever. Please make known to brother D. my Christian sympathy, and assure him of an interest in my humble prayers.

"I sincerely wish that, in your projected tour for the recovery of your strength, you could be induced to visit your friends here. I should be delighted to see you, and hold converse with you, touching the things which pertain to Jesus Christ. I am sure that you have learned much in the house of mourning, and I should delight to have you recount the rich and precious consolations of God's grace. My own path is dark and uncertain; but I have endeavoured to commit my way unto the Lord. Let me hear from you soon; and I would like to hear your views in relation to my situation here, as developed in a recent letter to you.

"With warmest Christian affection, your friend and brother,

"J. H. THORNWELL."

CHAPTER XIX.

CALL TO BALTIMORE.

A HINT has already been given, in Dr. Thornwell's
correspondence, of his dissatisfaction in the College,
and of a disposition to enter upon some suitable pastoral
charge. At the close of 1841, the Hon. R. W. Barnwell
had been compelled, by ill health, to resign the presidency of the institution; and the present administration
had not proved to be either popular or successful. Dr.
Thornwell did not feel himself to be cordially supported
by the authorities, in his office as chaplain. He, therefore,
was meditating a change; when, by a singular coincidence,
movements were on foot, which resulted in the transfer of
the Rev. Dr. R. J. Breckinridge from the pulpit of the
Second Presbyterian Church, in the city of Baltimore, to
the presidency of Jefferson College, at Cannonsburgh,
Pennsylvania. Considering the intimate friendship between the two men, and the constant correspondence
maintained at this period, it was most natural that the
attention of the church in Baltimore should be turned to
Dr. Thornwell, as the successor of his friend. A call was
made out in due form, and was laid, by the commissioner
of that church, before the Presbytery of Charleston, on
the 6th of October, 1845. After mature deliberation, the
call was placed, by the Presbytery, in Dr. Thornwell's

267

hands, and was by him accepted. The proper testimonials were also ordered to be given him; and he was directed to repair to the Presbytery of Baltimore, by whom the proper steps would be taken for his regular settlement as the pastor of said church. It was a decision arrived at, with marked reluctance on the part of the Presbytery; one evidence of which was a written communication from the Second Presbyterian Church, of Charleston, of which the Rev. Dr. Thomas Smyth was the pastor, expressing "the hope and desire that Dr. Thornwell may still remain in his present ecclesiastical connexions, and may find a field of usefulness within our bounds." There was, however, no option left to the Presbytery, but to grant the petition of the church in Baltimore, since Dr. Thornwell was clear as to his duty in leaving the College, and this was the only providential opening which just then presented itself. A few days before the matter was matured in this form, the letter found below was addressed to Dr. Breckinridge:

"SOUTH CAROLINA COLLEGE, *October* 4, 1845.

"MY DEAR BROTHER: *   *   *   *   *   *
     *   *   *   So far as I am concerned, the matter is settled in relation to the Baltimore call. If the Presbytery puts it into my hands, which I have no doubt will be done, it is my fixed purpose to accept it. There is strong opposition to my leaving the State, as many of *my* friends, and the friends of the College, are bent upon raising me to a higher position than the one which I now occupy; but I have no ambition, and no desire, for the station to which they would promote me. In the present aspect of ecclesiastical affairs, I feel that it is my duty, not merely to preach the gospel, which I do here, but to preach the gospel under such circumstances as shall bring me closely into contact with the Church; which is not the case here. Had it been in my power to choose my own field of labour, I should never have thought of leaving South Carolina; but I bow to the will of a sovereign God, and acquiesce, without a murmur, in the plain intimations of His providence. I shall move to Baltimore as soon as I can get a release from the College; which in no event can be earlier than December, and may be as late as January.

"The distinction you have conferred upon me, I ascribe entirely to your personal partiality. I presume, when you announced the matter to your Board, there was a general look of astonishment, each asking the other, whence this man came; but such, no doubt, was the strength of their faith in *you*, that they acceded to your request, in the hope that if I *were* not, I *might* become eventually, worthy of the honour. All that I can promise you is, that I shall endeavour not to disgrace you. Last week I received a letter from Brother Sparrow, President of Hampden Sidney College, stating that his Board had also conferred the same degree upon me; so that D. D., in my case, may stand for 'Doubly Dubbed,' as well as Doctor of Divinity.

"I cannot express to you my gratification at receiving the engraving which you sent me. I shall have it elegantly framed, and transmit it as a legacy to my children. I wish very much you had come with McElderry. It would have afforded me great pleasure to have seen you on my own dung-hill, and interchanged thoughts with you about the present position of affairs in the Church. But I hope to see you often in coming days.

"There is a matter which has weighed much upon my mind, and upon which we have conversed a little together, and that is, the establishing of a paper, to represent and defend our views. I have no doubt but that we may get anything into the *Watchman* and *Observer*. But we, ourselves, would feel a sense of delicacy in making too many applications to it. But how a paper is to be set agoing I do not see. I have been in hopes some good man would undertake a quarterly in New York, and make large promises of contributions from distinguished scholars on points of Theology, Biblical Literature, and Church Government; which promises might be made in great sincerity, and, perhaps, a sufficient patronage might be secured to justify the undertaking. Fugitive articles are not what we want; but elaborate discussions, which we can leave as a testimony behind us. There are many matters of great interest which might be embodied in such a work, and many ways in which it might be commended to popular favour. But the rub is, to get an editor, supposing we can get patronage. I have more faith in the *abiding* and *ultimate* influence of a quarterly, than of a weekly newspaper; though the latter would be more rapid in its effects. I hope you will not forget to write a review of D'Aubigne for the *Southern Quarterly*. It will do great good. That periodical has a much more extensive circulation than I supposed it had when I was in Kentucky; and you will reach a class of minds that know very little about the real character of the Reformation.

"The result of the action of Presbytery shall be communicated to you, as soon as practicable; but I presume that there is no doubt of what it will be.

"Very truly, as ever,

J. H. THORNWELL."

The Doctorate alluded to above, as conferred by the authorities of Jefferson College, and duplicated by Hampden Sidney, in Virginia, was triplicated by Centre College, at Danville, Kentucky. These distinctions were showered upon his head by three institutions, within a few days of each other, in perfect ignorance, of course, that they were combining to do honour to one who was conspicuously able to bear the triple burden.

The transfer to Baltimore, was, however, unexpectedly arrested, by the action of the Trustees of the College, in enforcing what had been regarded as an obsolete law, which required a twelve months' notice of a resignation. It was, of course, only one of those measures of protection, intended to be used when great interests demanded its application. None of the parties, therefore, anticipated the embarrassment which its enforcement, in this instance, occasioned. In connection with this interdict, which, of course, could operate only for a year, a complete and most satisfactory change was made in the administration of the College. The Hon. W. C. Preston, distinguished in the history of South Carolina as an orator and a statesman, was, by the acclamation of the State, elected to the Presidency; and the College received a vigorous impulse from the change.

This movement, on the part of the Board of Trustees, drew forth the strictures from Dr. Breckinridge, which are found in the letter that follows:

"JEFFERSON COLLEGE, CANNONSBURGH, *December* 4, 1845.

"MY DEAR THORNWELL: I never closed my whole responsibility, and active interest and participation in any subject, more to my own satisfaction, than when I ascertained finally that you would come to Baltimore. Satisfied that the hand of God removed me from that field of labour; convinced, as far as my own short and dim vision can penetrate, that you were the man to occupy the post; rejoicing in the unanimous and cordial—and, I will add, spontaneous—conviction of the congregation to the same effect; I greatly rejoiced in God, and felt a great care taken off my hands, and a great mercy to be conferred even personally on me, when I found the matter settled, and your going there fixed. I am sure you will find a wide field; in some respects, not as desirable as the situation you have left; but, on the whole, and in its entire bearings and influence, of immense importance, and capable of being used with unspeakably more power and efficiency than it has yet been. My prayers are for your great happiness and usefulness; and I now see, with great clearness, if I ever doubted, that whatever God may have designed as to me, in removing me from Baltimore, He designed mercy to that city, and to the people of my old charge. Almost the last thing I said to them, on leaving them, was almost prophetic: 'Do you think that God will forget your goodness to the pastors He has sent you heretofore? Do you think He will send you a man inferior, in any way, to those you have rendered happy by your unfailing kindness, your constant reverence and love?' That is not our Master's way of rewarding His people; and what I so confidently felt, from what I knew of His dealings and His revealed will, He would do, verily He has done; and heartily do I rejoice, and thank Him. * * * * * * * *

"*December* 5.

"So far I had written yesterday, being interrupted. I have since received information in regard to the action of your Board of Trustees, appointing Colonel Preston to the Presidency, and refusing your application for leave to resign; and, what fills me with sorrow and alarm, your inclination to submit to this refusal. I have weighed the matter as fully as I could; and will now give you, with the freedom of a friend, my views of the case as thus presented. Consider: 1. This act of the Board of Trustees, if contrary to your wishes, is a fraud upon you, considering that they had virtually acquiesced in your informal notice of your intention to resign. 2. That, in any aspect of the case, the obligation upon you, under the circumstances, as regards that notice, was virtually complied with; so that the pretext of holding you bound is the merest idle technicality, destitute of all moral obligation. 3. The Trustees supposed they acted in accordance with your wishes, in refusing you leave to go; therefore, their act is no more a rule of duty, or a discharge of opposite obligations absolutely incurred, than a reluctance on your part to fulfil those obligations is a discharge from their binding force. 4. The mere supposition, much less the painful reality, that the Trustees believed it would be very disagreeable to you for them to refuse to let you go, even if they were in error in that belief, yet, seeing it to be the ground and motive of the act, this places you in a position which obliges you to refuse, under the circumstances, to obey their act. 5. This refusal of a civil corporation, acting contrary to the clear conclusion of God's Church, lawfully reached, in due course, upon full scriptural process and conclusions, is the idlest thing in the world, as *matter of authority*. Viewed in any other light than simply as authority, you owe it to yourself to repudiate it absolutely. 6. The people at Baltimore were under the full conviction that you *could* and *would* leave it, if you saw it to be your duty to accept theirs, or any pastoral call. 7. They have been to considerable expense, endured considerable privations, done all that was fair, generous, and right, in the complete reliance that this new aspect of the case was one out of the question, and, in fact, disposed of. It is, therefore, morally obligatory that, as to them, and their affairs and relations to you, it should be considered and treated as out of the question, utterly and absolutely. 8. That church will, in all probability, be irreparably injured, divided, and scattered, if you now refuse to go there; and as to them, all this injury is gratuitous, and from a quarter that was contemplated, plainly and clearly, as being already disposed of, in every part of the previous arrangements. So this matter looks to me. May our God and Saviour give you grace to resist this temptation ; for so it seems to me most clearly to be, taking the case in its present aspect. As to the real importance of the places, or their claims upon you abstractly, or your fitness for them, all these are questions not now to be discussed. They are solemnly, finally, religiously adjudicated ; and the whole question is, can anything, much less this new act, set aside the result actually reached, unless by the complete consent of the other party, the church? I say, No! as plainly and clearly as ever I saw any question whatever. I again say, May God strengthen you against this temptation.

"Believe me, my dear Thornwell, I fully enter into your difficulties in this case. Excuse me, if I have said too much. Two objects, very dear to me, seem at stake : the good of the church at Baltimore, and your good name; which is not a whit less dear to me. I am, perhaps, mistaken in my view of what the course of duty and propriety seems to me so plainly to indicate. If so, excuse what I have written, in all love. May God ever bless you.

"Your friend and brother,

RO. J. BRECKINRIDGE."

One can scarcely fail to trace, in the matter and style of this paper, the hand of the lawyer, working in a case for the interest of his client; and is a little curious to see how these specifications will be set aside. We have some misgivings lest these details may prove a little too minute and tedious. But besides that both letters are eminently characteristic of the writers, the case terminated so remarkably, that we prefer the reader should be in full possession of all the facts pertaining to it. The reply to these strictures is very long; but it is so frank and generous in its tone, reveals a sensibility to considerations of honour, and discloses principles upon which difficult questions of duty may be resolved, that we give it without abridgment :

"SOUTH CAROLINA COLLEGE, *December* 13, 1845.

"MY DEAR BROTHER : I received your letter a few evenings ago ; and, in the midst of the deep tribulation in which it found me, the very appearance of your handwriting was refreshing to my heart. This is now the sixteenth day since my poor wife took her bed, having been seriously indisposed for a week before. She was, at first, threatened with violent inflammation of the brain, then of the bowels, and finally her disease settled down into a continuous fever of the typhoid type, marked by two violent paroxysms in the twenty-four hours. My mind has alternated between hope and fear. I have had anxious days and sleepless nights; and, though I endeavour to cultivate a spirit of entire resignation to the will of God, it is my constant prayer that He may not afflict me above measure. The symptoms to-day, I am rejoiced to say, are more favourable than they have been; but I have been so often deceived by flattering appearances, I am almost afraid to indulge in hope.

"In connection with these distresses has been a severe and painful conflict, in reference to the action of the Board of Trustees of this institution; and as I value your opinion upon any subject upon which you will venture to pronounce one, more than that of any man living, I have been deeply grieved that your conclusions differ so widely from my own, as to the precise light in which that action should be viewed. I am persuaded, however, that your mind labours under some radical misapprehension of the facts of the case, and that your opinions have been formed from inadequate data. It is due to you, therefore, to give you a detailed account of the whole matter, and of the motives and ends which have governed all parties.

" There is, as you are probably aware, an express and positive law of the College, that no Professor shall resign his office without giving one year's previous notice to the Board of Trustees. This is a part of the stipulated condition on which he holds his place; and imposes on him a moral obligation, from which he cannot be released but by the consent of the Board. When that body met, in November last, I transmitted them a letter, in which I begged leave to resign my Professorship, the resignation to take effect immediately after Commencement, so that I might reach Baltimore by the middle of December; agreeing, at the same time, to remain until the 1st of January, if they thought it absolutely necessary. I deprecated, in that letter, the severity of holding me to the one year's notice, as altogether unprecedented; as unnecessary, in the present case, as the ends of that notice had been abundantly answered. I had no idea that any other action would be taken, than that of formally accepting my resignation, and dismissing me, at once, from the College. Just about one hour before the Board was to meet, the gentleman to whom I had entrusted my letter, in a casual interview, which did not last five minutes, observed to me : 'I have read your letter, and find that you will regard it as an act of ungenerous harshness to be held to the legal notice. I merely wish to say to you, that I shall use all my in·fluence to hold you to the law; and I am anxious that you should understand that I mean no unkindness to you personally, but am governed, as I trust, by the fear of God, and a solemn sense of public duty.' I replied to him, that I knew he was incapable of doing an intentional unkindness to any one, much less to me; and, in the present case, I could afford to be generous, since he would only lose his breath and his pains; and, in parting with him, ridiculed the futility, the utter idleness, of his project. So sanguine, indeed, was I, that the Board would at once dismiss me, that I had made most of my arrangements for leaving. I had sold a considerable part of my furniture, had disposed of my servants for the ensuing year, and settled such of my worldly business as required immediate adjustment. I never dreamed that any human being would think of detaining me; and the *only* intimation which I received was the one I have mentioned, given about an hour before the meeting of the Board. The argument, in my letter, against such a course, I considered as ample and complete. You may judge of the light in which I regarded the proposition, from the fact of my making it a matter of jest in the family, after the interview referred to.

"The Board met; and the next day I received a letter from the Secretary, stating that my resignation had been laid on the table. I found, upon inquiry, that many of the best men in the Board were disposed to hold me, on the legal technicality by which I was bound. The whole matter, then, struck me as a serious affair. I made it a matter of calm reflection and earnest prayer. The men who were principally moving in this business, were men of God, distinguished equally by generosity and piety. They had prayed over this thing, and were evidently governed by a solemn sense of public duty. The conclusion to which I came was this: I shall quietly leave the result to the Providence of God. If He permits these men to enforce upon me a legal claim, which creates a moral obligation in me to stay in the State, it is His will that I should not go to Baltimore; for He would never sanction my breach of an express stipulation. If, on the other hand, it is His will that I should go, He can turn their hearts, as the rivers of water are turned, and induce them to accede to my request. I therefore kept my letter before them and until their action was taken, I was *fully* persuaded that I would be released, though, I knew, not without strong opposition. I had no agency in the matter. I never expressed to them any desire, wish, or inclination, to stay; but just the opposite. I prosecuted the resignation in good faith; and submitted, in the end, to the extraordinary conclusion which was reached; because I believed that it was the language of God's Providence to me, forbidding me to go. In your letter you seem to have received the impression that the Board detained me because they thought I desired to stay. This is a mistake. No such desire, either directly or indirectly, was either expressed by me, or authorized to be expressed by any one else for me. All the correspondence which I had with the body was the very contrary. I have inquired into the representations which were made by the mover of the resolution on the subject, and it can be abundantly certified that he disclaimed acting in consultation with me. He said that he had avoided me, to keep me from hampering him in what he believed to be his duty, and whatever he said or did in the premises proceeded solely from himself. It was, therefore, wholly and exclusively, *their* act, and not *mine*. But, being done, my duty was decided. I was under a solemn obligation to remain. I had made a contract upon taking my chair, and it was not for me to dissolve it.

"Before proceeding further, I want to remove from your mind the conviction which you seem to feel, that the Trustees acted towards me in bad faith. If this were granted, however, I do not see that it annuls my obligation to act towards them in good faith; but still, I think a full review of all the circumstances will vindicate their honour from all suspicion. In the spring, I had drawn up a full communication, setting forth grievances under which I laboured in the Chapel, and suggesting various remedies; stating, at the same time that, as I would be absent from the State when the Board met, and could not be made acquainted with its action until it had adjourned; and as, moreover, I could not consent to retain my connection with the College, if such grievances were permitted to continue, I begged them to regard the communication as a notice of my intention to resign, at the end of the year, unless they could do something effective in the premises. This communication I handed to a friend to give to the Board, he being himself a member. He begged me to withhold it, as it would do mischief to have the report circulated that I proposed to leave the institution; and assured me that, as there had never been any difficulty in past cases, so there would probably be none in this; and so far as his influence went, there should be none in giving me leave to resign at the end of the year, if my difficulties were not removed. Such was the pledge. At that time I had no idea anything *would* be done, or *could* be done, to amend the law. I expected my suggestions to meet such opposition in the Board, or if adopted there, to be so feebly supported by the President, that I had deliberately come to the conclusion, that, under all the circumstances, I ought to leave. But the Board have met me here by enacting my suggestions into a law, and by giving a President to the College who can enforce the law. The Board, therefore, has exonerated itself from the implied pledge of one of its members. It has even gone farther, and voted an appropriation to render my place of preaching much more elegantly comfortable and inviting than it is now. All these things have been done mainly on *my* account. I have gone thus into detail, in order that you may not do injustice, even in your thoughts, to the best body of men in the State. That Board comprises some of our noblest citizens, and would instinctively shrink from doing an act of meanness. That I may have given you, in Baltimore, the idea that I meditated an *absolute* resignation, is very likely; for at that time such was the fact; that I may also have led you to believe there would be no difficulty in the way, is equally likely, for such I then also believed to be the fact. There never had been difficulty in any previous case; and the implied pledge to which I have alluded, showed that the gentleman who made it dreamed of no such difficulty. Upon reviewing all the circumstances, two things seem perfectly clear: 1. The Board had a *legal* right to detain me; and, 2. I was under a *moral* obligation, growing out of my own stipula-

tions, to stay, unless they were willing to let me go.   Such, as it strikes
my mind, is the aspect of the case between me and the church at Baltimore.

   " In the first place, that congregation knew of the existence of the law
in question ; and if they looked upon it as a dead letter, they did it for
the reasons that have been mentioned : the fact that it never had been
enforced in any previous case.   This rendered its future enforcement
improbable, but not *impossible*.   Previous lenity did not destroy the
right of the Board.   They called me, therefore, subject to an obligation
which was not *likely* to be enforced, but yet which *might* be enforced.
I mentioned the fact, that such a law existed, to every member of that
congregation who gave me the opportunity ; and in every instance stated
the other fact, that it had always lain dormant.   They knew, therefore,
just as much as I did, the real posture of affairs.   They attached no importance to the law.   Neither did I.   They acted upon the supposition that
I would be released on the first of January.   So did I.   Our conduct
was predicated on the same premises ; but our false conclusions did not
destroy the reality of the law, nor the corresponding right of the Board ;
and, therefore, my obligation to the church was strictly conditional.
My acceptance was predicated on its not conflicting with any other duties.
If the Board had met before the call was prosecuted in Presbytery, I
should have applied to it for a release before answering ; but as it could
not meet before the last of November, I answered upon the best light
I had.   That my answer was conditional, is shown from the fact, that I
expressly told the church that I could not go *until* released ; that the release would not take place until the meeting of the Board ; that it was
not likely to be granted to take effect before the first of January ; and
that they must wait until then, when I had no doubt of the issue.   This
whole process implied a *conditional* engagement ; and the anticipated
condition having failed, the obligation, of course, ceases.   This is the
light in which the thing strikes me.

   " But put the affair in a stronger point of view.   Suppose the church had
known nothing of the law, and that I had merely stated to it my convictions that I could go at the close of the year, without stating the grounds ;
even in that case, my obligation would have been conditional.   The reason is, that our Book of Discipline supposes that a call is open to reconsideration and review, at any time from the period of its prosecution, up
to its consummation in the installation of the pastor.   Hence the question is distinctly put, ' Are you *now* willing, &c.'   His *previous* states of
mind do not settle the duty of Presbytery, nor his own ; it is his present state of mind that fixes the thing.   He is bound, in other words,
to do what *seems* to be the will of God ; and if, after the acceptance of
a call, circumstances should arise to change his impressions of the leadings of Providence, he is bound to withdraw that acceptance.   The
whole matter is open for new light, until the pastoral relation has
been actually established.   When he accepts, he declares what he feels
to be his duty *then ;* but the Book evidently contemplates the possi-

bility of change or mistake, and hence does not impose an *absolute*, but a *qualified*, obligation.

"In conformity with these suggestions, if I had accepted the Baltimore call, under the full conviction that there was no let nor hindrance in the way, and afterwards found that there was, my previous acceptance would not have bound me. It was predicated *implicitly*, if not expressly, upon a condition, which is afterwards ascertained to be false in fact. A church, in calling a pastor, endeavours to obey the will of God; a pastor, in accepting, aims at the same rule. They both follow the indications of Providence, and their mutual acts are formal expressions of the light in which they regard those indications. Now, should anything transpire which marks this conclusion as evidently *repugnant* to the Divine will, the matter is ended; no obligation exists on either side, except to follow the clearest light. Apply these principles here. The people of Baltimore, in obedience to the will of God, as they suppose, call me to be the pastor. I believe that I ought to accept, and accordingly engage to do so. An event takes place, which shows that I cannot go to Baltimore without the breach of a moral obligation. This settles it, that it is not the *Divine will* that I should go. They then cease to be bound by the call, and I by the acceptance.

"Now, the light in which I regard the action of the Board, is the closing event in the series of Providences, by which my duty was to be finally ascertained. God had conducted both parties up to this point, by a way they knew not; and here He reveals the line of duty so plainly, that there could be no possibility of mistake. It is His hand that I contemplate in the matter, and not the authority of a civil corporation. And this suggests a difficulty in your mind, which I must endeavour to clear up. You insinuate that, in yielding to this action, I yield to civil, rather than ecclesiastical, authority, in a spiritual matter. The mistake is this: It is *my own promise*, *my own* solemn compact, that I respect, and not *authority*. I do not stay because the Board says, 'You must stay;' but because I myself had virtually promised to stay. It is my *contract*, and not their power, that I reverence in the matter. Again, you are mistaken in supposing that this affair, in any of its present aspects, was ever adjudicated in any Church court. The Presbytery of Charleston deliberated on the call two nights; the Second Presbyterian church of that city entered a solemn remonstrance upon the minutes of Presbytery against its prosecution; and the issue which the Presbytery decided was, that I had better go to Baltimore than to Charleston, where an effort was then making to get me. But the opinion of the Presbytery, so far as expressed, which was informally, and not judicially done, was, that I had better remain in the College than go to either place.

"I protested against staying in the College, then; because, under the President we had, and the laws that existed, I considered my labours as seriously hindered. No change in the College was proposed, but that of making me President; and my mind was immovably set against that. My purpose, therefore, was absolute, to leave if I could; and under that state of the case, the Presbytery said, go to Baltimore. When the Board had acted, there was a talk here of calling a *pro re nata* meeting of Presbytery, to express its approval of that course, and urge upon me to stay. The church in Carolina is delighted with the result, and clear, so far as I have heard, as to my duty. This is the aspect of the case, *ecclesiastically.*

"One word more about the Board. It acted from a solemn sense of duty. Under the existing administration, the affairs of the College had reached a crisis. Public sentiment was strongly against it. That sentiment was largely called out by my projected removal. The people would, perhaps, have submitted, if they could have kept me; but when it was found that I was going, the tide set in with greater fury. A change was made; but a new experiment required the co-operation of an experienced friend; and the Board felt that their high and paramount duty, as Trustees, required them to use every lawful means of preserving my influence, and attracting to the College the confidence which the people felt in me. They determined, therefore, if I went, to throw the whole responsibility of going upon me; and they were careful to remove all the difficulties which had originally excited my dissatisfaction. They, no doubt, largely overrated my importance; but what they did was the offspring of honourable motives, and in the due execution, as they believed, of a solemn trust. They had never enforced the law before; because they had never had such a case. To fill my place this year, was out of the question. It required a prudence and circumspection, the conditions of which were satisfied in no candidate that offered; and to leave the place vacant for a year was equally ruinous. They had only the alternative of enforcing the law, and thus keeping, or doing what was in their power to keep, a man with whom they were satisfied.

"I need not say that I have felt deeply for the condition of the Baltimore people. My heart had been much set upon that field of labour; and I never was more surprised, disappointed, confounded, than by the course which things have actually taken. But my conscience is clear. I regret the past, but I have no remorse. From first to last, I have acted in good faith; and, if I know my own heart, I have as humbly, patiently, and prayerfully endeavoured to ascertain the will of God, as I ever did anything in my life; and whatever may be the lamentations of my friends, or the censures and reproaches of my enemies, I feel that I have learned and obeyed the voice of my Heavenly Father in the final result. I cannot persuade myself that the church has been injured; it has been kept together by the prospect of my going; it has been able to save a portion of its income; and is, upon the whole, in no worse condition than if I had refused the call at first. Whatever divisions may take place *now*, are divisions that would probably have taken place *then*. It stands, as I conceive, about where it stood *before* the call was prosecuted. What I most regret, is the possible loss of their personal affections. They may be induced to view the matter as you have done, and attach to me a degree of blame which your charity does not allow you to pronounce. If the righteous smite me, however, I hope to take it as an excellent oil, that shall not break my head. I had hoped that you would understand the matter at once, and would aid me in relieving their minds of any unfavourable misapprehensions; and had, accordingly, intended to write to you upon the subject, as soon as my family afflictions would permit. But upon your aid, I am afraid, I cannot reckon. Let me beg you to review the whole thing, calmly and prayerfully. In fact, I know you will do it; and I know that, whatever you may think of the propriety of the course, in itself considered, you will do me the justice to believe that I have, at least, acted honestly, and humbly aimed to discharge my duty. You may condemn my judgment; but I am confident that you have seen too much of me to question my integrity. Thank God, my record in this matter is on high!

"The deep affliction of my family, which, under any decision, would have rendered a removal, at the projected time, impossible—and dangerous in any time of the winter—has struck me with great force. The action of the Board has been a mercy to my wife. Her physician told me, before he heard what was done, that I must not think of taking her to Baltimore this winter. The condition in which she is, coupled with the state in which the fever was likely to leave her, if she recovered, rendered the change hazardous in the extreme.

"I am rejoiced to learn that your institution flourishes under your auspices, and trust that God may impart rich and abundant consolation to your inner man.

"The Board of Trustees has informally requested me to prepare a work on Moral Philosophy; and I have a mind to undertake the task. Any suggestions that you may make, either in regard to defects in existing treatises, or as to what a treatise on the subject should be, will be very thankfully received. Let me hear from you often; the oftener, the better. I am always refreshed by a letter from you, even if it condemns; for its censures are proofs of love.

"May God be with you, and bless you.

"Your faithful friend,

J. H. THORNWELL."

The church in Baltimore felt no inclination to abandon its claim, and resolved to wait for his coming at the expiration of the year. The effect of this determination upon Dr. Thornwell's mind is thus stated by himself, in a letter to Dr. Breckinridge:

"SOUTH CAROLINA COLLEGE, *February* 17, 1846.

"MY DEAR BROTHER: I received your very kind letter a few weeks ago; and since that time, things have undergone a great and unexpected change. You have probably heard of the action of your old charge, in refusing to abandon their call; and, after the most prayerful and deliberate reflection, I feel myself shut up to the necessity of going to Baltimore. To me, the hand of God seems to be conspicuously displayed; and though I had supposed that the whole matter was settled, finally and definitely settled, in another way, and had begun to shape my arrangements accordingly, I am now clear, that, let the sacrifices be what they may, it is my imperative duty to accept the call of your old flock. I shall not attempt to unfold the reasons; suffice it to say, that I felt my honour implicated when the Providential hindrances, which I had regarded as an immovable bar, was not permitted to be a final obstruction by the church. I shall transfer my family to Baltimore on the first of July, spend the summer there, and then, if no other arrangement shall be made, return myself in October, and remain until Commencement. It will give me great pleasure to meet you there, and have you join with me in a series of labours to promote the spiritual interests of those who, on so many accounts, must be dear to you; and it would add to the pleasure, if I could get you to accompany me here, and attend our Commencement exercises, the *last*, perhaps, in which *I* shall ever be officially engaged, and the *first* in which Colonel Preston has been called to preside. You may feel some curiosity to know what I think of his prospects, and I can say with confidence, that I regard them as eminently promising. He possesses rare qualifications for the office he holds. His personal dignity inspires respect; the elevation of his character gives him security, and adds great authority to his counsels or reproofs; and the fire of his genius is communicated to his pupils, kindling a blaze of enthusiasm in their minds, and making the business of instruction delightful alike to the teacher and the taught. The students are wonderfully attached to him; and I am sure that, under his auspices, if God should spare his health, which, I am sorry to say, is still feeble, our institution will soon be attended by a larger number of students than its most sanguine friends ever dreamed it would possess. There is but one drawback, in my view, upon his eminent fitness for the station; and that is, the absence of personal religion. I do not mean to say that he is not, in a general sense, a *religious* man; but I have no reason to believe that he is what you and I would call a converted man.* His influence is in favour of religion, as far as it is possible that he who is not with Christ in heart can be with Him in act. What his religious sentiments precisely are, I do not know; but one thing is certain, his station requires him to attend the Chapel, and there I am sure he hears the gospel. There are many respects in which his connection with the College is likely to prove a permanent blessing to the State. He has a weight of character which will enable him to effect many salutary reforms, which feebler men would be incompetent to exercise; and he has a practical wisdom, from his enlarged acquaintance with the world, which saves him from all rash projects, and merely chimerical speculations. My impression is, that he is the *only* man in the State who could have filled the station just at this juncture; and I am heartily rejoiced that

---

* At a later period, he became a communicant in the Episcopal Church.

God sent him to us, and earnestly pray that he may be brought, through grace, to a saving knowledge of Jesus Christ.

"The prospect of the Presbyterian Church in this State, is to me a matter of intense and painful interest. Our large congregations in the country are becoming very much enfeebled, by emigration, and their reluctance to support the ministry is still more discouraging. There prevails a deplorably *low tone* of personal religion, and the idea of making anything like *sacrifices* to sustain the institutions of the gospel, seems to be foreign from their minds. Unless a radical change should take place, it seems to me that our churches must die out in many sections of the country. I contemplate the prospect with dismay. What is to be done? What are the means that we must couple with prayer, to stir up the slumbering piety of those who are God's children, and waken a deeper and more absorbing interest in the prosperity of His kingdom? We present the appearance of a spiritual waste; and my heart sickens, as I reflect upon what must be before us, unless God, in great mercy, should revive His work.

"Your sincere and faithful friend,

J. H. THORNWELL."

The removal to Baltimore was destined to be finally defeated. A short time before the meeting of the Presbytery, in the spring of 1846, the President of the College waited upon the writer of these pages; and the interview deserves to be recorded. as an evidence of the estimation in which the subject of this Memoir was held by the most gifted men in the State. "We cannot afford," said Colonel Preston, "to lose Dr. Thornwell from the College. In the first place, he is the representative there of the Presbyterian Church, which embraces the bone and sinew of the State, without whose support the institution cannot exist. In the second place, he has acquired that moral influence over the students, which is superior even to law; and his removal will take away the very buttresses on which the administration of the College rests. An arrest has been laid upon his movements, as you are aware; but at the end of the year, the authority of the Board ceases. There is no body that has jurisdiction over him, except the Church; and I have called to invoke her interposition, if there be any form in which her control may properly be exercised." To which appeal the writer replied by drawing a paper from his desk, saying, " There, Colonel Preston, is the draft of a paper, which I have prepared to submit to the Presbytery, at its approaching meeting. That body will be in full sympathy with the object which is intended to be accomplished; but I cannot tell whether it will agree with me as to the stretch of power which is there claimed. Dr. Thornwell expects nothing else than to go to Baltimore, to which he evidently feels himself shut up, by a sense of honour. I have not consulted him in relation to this paper ; and have rather avoided, in my intercourse with him, all allusion to his plans, that I might not be hampered in the course which I propose to pursue." The paper, above referred to, was submitted to the Presbytery on the 11th of April, 1846; and was amended, and finally adopted in this form:

" The Presbytery, learning through the public prints, that the arrangement proposed by the Second Presbyterian Church of Baltimore, and one of its Presbyters, the Rev. Dr. Thornwell, and which was suspended by the action of the Trustees of the South Carolina College, is, at the end of the year, to be consummated, think it their right and duty to inquire whether there has not intervened such a change of circumstances, as to require a reconsideration of their former action in the matter

" The question first arises, whether the Presbytery has not lost jurisdiction of the case, and whether the papers of dismission given to Dr. Thornwell do not bar all further consideration of his removal.   In relation to this, it must be observed that the Book of Discipline, chapter 10, section 2, distinctly affirms the jurisdiction of Presbytery over *dismissed members*, until such moment as they shall become, in act and in form, connected with a co-ordinate body. Of course, then, notwithstanding papers of dismission were given in October last, Dr. Thornwell still continues a member of this Presbytery ; which has entire ecclesiastical cognizance of his conduct, and may of right determine the propriety of his translation to another sphere of labour.

" It may be further observed, that a call is inchoate, until consummated by the actual connection of a church and pastor ; and is manifestly subject to the recision of any or all the parties, if, in the interim between the acceptance of the call and the act of installation, such changes occur as shall modify their views of duty. Now, there are three parties concerned in the settlement of a pastor : the church making the call, the Presbyter called, and the Presbytery of which he is a member; the consent of all of whom must be obtained in effecting the installation. If, then. a change in the condition and view of the first two parties may arrest a call, while it is in progress, the same will hold true *ex equali* of the third party; and if the call should providentially be suspended, for so long a time as to allow an entire change in those circumstances upon which that third party gave his concurrence, it may be their most imperative duty to review the whole case.

"It will be distinctly remembered, by those members of Presbytery who were present at the *pro-re-nata* meeting, held in October, that the consent of this body to the removal of Dr. Thornwell was predicated solely upon his fixed determination to leave the College; the only real question being, whether he should remove to Baltimore or elsewhere. As no other door of usefulness presented itself sufficiently open, the call was received, and placed in his hands. Since that time, however, important changes have taken place in Dr. Thornwell's personal relations to the College; which, if they had existed at the time, must have exercised a strong influence upon his determination; and his opinion of his own efficiency, in his present important position, may be modified by the developments of a year. In addition to this, within the present year, an important enterprise has been set on foot within the bounds of this Synod, of vast consequence to the Church; and it is the deliberate conviction of this Presbytery, that the complete establishment and further prosperity of the Theological Seminary will be greatly promoted by our brother's continued residence and labours within our own bounds, where he may exert a direct influence in favour of this institution.

"Be it, therefore, *Resolved:*

"1. That, in view of the changes which have occurred since last October—changes which would have affected materially the decision of this body as to his removal, had they taken place at the time—this Presbytery, in duty to themselves, and to the Christian public, are unwilling to consent to Dr. Thornwell's transfer to Baltimore.

"2. That the fields of labour now opening, in the providence of God, before our brother, in our own bounds, afford most ample scope for his ability and learning. And it is the most deliberate judgment of this body, in view of the necessities of the Church within this State, of the movements which are now on foot amongst us, and of the *status* which he has acquired in this portion of the Church, that he should not remove without the limits of this Synod.

"3. That a communication be addressed to the church at Baltimore, stating these views, and requesting their concurrence in them; desiring them to release Dr. Thornwell from his present obligation; or, if they are unwilling to do so, at least to show cause, either to this body, or to the Synod, at its next meeting, for their desire to continue to urge their call."*

---

* Minutes of the Presbytery of Charleston, pp. 403–406.

A silent acquiescence in this decision closed the negotiations with Baltimore; and Dr. Thornwell's connection
with the College was continued.   It is the strongest illustration of Presbyterial power of which the writer is aware.
Many instances occur, in which the Church courts have
exercised a veto, thereby disappointing the wishes both
of ministers and of churches; but it is usual only in cases
actually pending.   This action, however, cancelled a call
which had already been accepted, and revoked a dismission which had already been granted; and did not pass
without some criticism at the time.   The record is of
value, as showing that Presbyterianism is a government,
and the Church courts are something more than advisory
councils.

CHAPTER XX.

QUESTION OF ROMISH BAPTISM.

ASSEMBLY OF 1845.—DEBATE ON ROMISH BAPTISM.—IMPRESSIONS OF THE
WEST.—VIEWS ON ABOLITIONISM.—PATRIOTIC FEELING.—"BIBLICAL
REPERTORY" ON ROMISH BAPTISM.—ARTICLES IN REPLY.—CORRESPON-
DENCE ON THE SAME.—LETTER TO COLONEL PRESTON; ALSO TO HIS
CHILDREN.—PLANS IN RELATION TO THE COLUMBIA SEMINARY.—
"SOUTHERN PRESBYTERIAN REVIEW" PROJECTED.—ITS OBJECTS EX-
PLAINED.

IN the year 1845, Dr. Thornwell was returned a commissioner to the General Assembly, which met at Cincinnati, whose decision, on at least two important subjects,
he assisted largely to mould. The first was that of
slavery; upon which this Assembly made a deliverance so
temperate and well guarded, that it put to rest, to a considerable degree, the hurtful agitation of that subject,
and formed the basis upon which the Church continued
to stand until the disruption occasioned by the late civil
war. Dr. Thornwell, though not a member of the Committee charged with this matter, was, nevertheless, pri-
vately consulted; and his views were largely embodied
in the Report, which was finally presented and adopted.*

The second subject related to the validity of Romish
baptism; which was ably discussed, and was the leading
topic that engaged the attention of the body. Dr.
Thornwell's elaborate argument not only enhanced his
own reputation as one of the first debaters in the Church,
but was admitted by all parties as having determined the
overwhelming vote of one hundred and seventy-three to
eight,† against the recognition of such baptism.

---

* See Assembly's Digest, Edition 1856, pp. 812, 813.

† Assembly's Digest, Edition 1856, pp. 77–79; where may be found a
summary of reasons for the decision.

These matters are opened in a letter, written at the time, to Mrs. Thornwell:

"CINCINNATI, *May* 19, 1845.

MY DEAREST WIFE: * * * * My mind is in a state of constant and intense excitement connected with the business of the Assembly. Everything thus far has been nobly done. The spirit which pervades the Assembly seems to be the spirit of Christ and the Gospel; and I sincerely trust that God is with us, guiding and directing us in all our deliberations. For two days and a half, we have been discussing the question, whether Roman Catholic baptism is valid or not? I made a speech to-day, *two hours long*; which was listened to with breathless attention, and, from what I can gather, is likely to settle the question. I have a host of applications to write out my speech, and print it, which I have no notion of doing. It has made me the subject of a great many undeserved attentions, which I would not otherwise, perhaps, have received.

"The question of slavery has been before the house, and referred to a special committee of seven. Though not a member of the committee, I have been consulted on the subject, and have drawn up a paper, which I think the committee and the Assembly will substantially adopt; and if they do, abolitionism will be killed in the Presbyterian Church, at least for the present. I have no doubts but that the Assembly, by a very large majority, will declare slavery not to be sinful, will assert that it is sanctioned by the word of God, that it is purely a civil relation, with which the Church, as such, has no right to interfere, and that abolitionism is essentially wicked, disorganizing, and ruinous. I feel perfectly satisfied that this is the stand which the Assembly will take. The Southern members have invited discussion, and they will triumphantly gain the day. It will be a great matter to put the agitations on slavery at rest, and to save the Church from dismemberment and schism; and particularly to do it here, in the stronghold of abolitionism.

"The marriage question will come up to-morrow. The result will be, that the Assembly will maintain its former ground, and enjoin upon the Church courts to discipline, in every case, in which a man marries his wife's sister. Whether the Elder question will come up, in all its bearings, before us, I cannot say; but we have so much to do, that I think it will not. * * *

"I have had a delightful time among all the brethren, from all sections of the Church. It would do you good to see the harmony, courtesy, and Christian feeling, which characterize the Assembly. God grant that it may not be disturbed during the whole course of our business. May God bless you and keep you. Kiss the children for me.

"As ever, your devoted husband,

J. H. THORNWELL."

"P. S.—Since writing the above, I received your sweet letter from Abbeville, and devoutly thank God that you are all getting on so well. The vote on Popish baptism has passed by a tremendous majority, only six members, out of one hundred and eighty, voting against it. The committee did not adopt my report fully on slavery, but will bring in one that takes nearly the same position; one which vindicates the South, and will put the question at rest. * * * My speech has made me the object of general attention and curiosity. I have had compliments, which God grant may not injure my humility. Let me hear from you soon, and often."

The letter given below is interesting, not only as conveying his impressions of the West, but as disclosing his intense love for the whole country, and the ambitious dreams he indulged of its expansion and glory. It is addressed to his wife, from Wheeling, Va., and is dated the 14th June, 1845:

"I took my departure from Cincinnati, for Baltimore, on Thursday, at 11 o'clock; and, as the river is too low for boats, I had to resort to the stage coach. I have been travelling now two nights and two days, without intermission, except for meals, in crowded coaches, and am now fairly tired out. I got to this place this morning, and shall stay here until Monday; when I shall have to take a stage coach again, for one hundred and thirty miles, to Cumberland, across the mountains; there I shall take the railroad to Baltimore, where I shall spend the remainder of the week. * * * * *

"Tiresome as it has been, I do not regret that I had to travel from Cincinnati to this place by land. It has given me an opportunity for seeing the country; and I would not have missed seeing what I have seen, and hearing what I have heard, for a great deal. My impressions of the West had been greatly erroneous, in many important respects; and my convictions of its importance are greatly increased. The more I reflect upon the subject, the more I am satisfied that the mission of our Republic will not be accomplished, until we embrace in our Union the whole of this North American continent. If the New England people are disposed to kick up a dust about the annexation of Texas, I am prepared to take the ground that it would be better for this country, and for the interests of the human race, to give up New England, than to abandon any new territory which we may be able to acquire. I go for Texas; I should like also to have California; we must hold on to Oregon, if we have to do it at the point of the bayonet; and I would be glad even to get Mexico itself. You see that I am grasping at territory. There must be a grand imperial Republic on this continent, and God will bring it about, and accomplish great purposes through it. As to disunion, we have nothing serious to apprehend. If the Yankees feel disposed to leave us, let them go; but the West and the South can never be separated. There is at work, in this land, a Yankee spirit, and an American spirit; and the latter must triumph. But enough of politics. I will only add that abolitionism is a humbug. A prudent course, on the part of the South, will kill it entirely. We have done the North and West injustice on this subject. Take out the Yankees, and the overwhelming force of public opinion is with the South. I have kept my eye on this matter, and know what I say."

It could hardly be expected that the Assembly's decision upon the invalidity of Romish baptism would pass without challenge. The Princeton *Journal,* in its annual review of the Assembly, pronounced with great emphasis against the doctrine of that decree. The guantlet was not thrown down in vain. On the 4th of October, Dr. Thornwell thus writes to Dr. Breckinridge:

"It seems that Princeton has fairly turned out to be an apologist for Rome. I read with much interest a series of articles in the *Herald of Kentucky,* reviewing the *Repertory,* which I attributed to you. I would have written something myself before this, ; but I have been in an unsettled state of life, moving about from pillar to post, until last week, when I returned home. As soon as I can command leisure enough, I shall try my hand. This is one instance in which the fathers and brethren have reckoned without their host. The Church, as a body, is dead against them. I have not seen a single minister who does not condemn the strictures of Hodge, and sustain the Assembly. I think it can be clearly shown that there is no principle on which Popish baptism can be sustained, that will not apply with equal force to *any* baptisms, regular in form, administered by *any* body to *any* body. Just let Tom, Dick, and Harry apply water, in the name of the Trinity, to the first person either shall meet on the street, and intend it to be Christian baptism; and Christian baptism, according to Princeton, it is and must be. I have examined this whole subject pretty throughly, and shall soon begin to write in the *Watchman and Observer.* Perhaps Engles may copy the article into the *Presbyterian.*"

Again, on the 17th of February, 1846, he writes:

"I have screwed up my courage at last to begin my projected reply to Princeton, on the subject of Romish Baptism. My article will appear in the *Observer and Watchman* under the signature of 'Henley,' which is my middle name. I have treated the brethren there with the respect that is due to age and station. Perhaps—for the heart is deceitful—there may be something of policy in it. My object, however, has been to give *strong* arguments and *soft* words. My first number does not enter into the marrow of the subject; but the succeeding ones, unless I am greatly deceived, will not be so easy to answer."

A series of articles was accordingly begun, in fulfilment of the above promise, on the 5th of March, which were afterwards gathered into three articles for the *Southern Presbyterian Review*, and may be found by the reader in the third volume of Dr. Thornwell's published works. They go down into all the principles which discriminate the Romish system as an apostasy from the truth, and are valuable for the exposition they give of the great doctrines of grace. As the reply was directed against the gentlemen at Princeton, the discussion was characterized with all the courtesy that was due to their station and influence, which drew from his friend, Dr. Breckinridge, a rather splenetic note, to which the letter which follows is the rejoinder:

"SOUTH CAROLINA COLLEGE, *March* 24, 1846.

"MY DEAR BROTHER : You will, perhaps, be astonished at my moderation, when I tell you that, though deeply wounded, I was not offended at the bitter, and, as I conceive, unmerited censure of your last letter. The truth is, it will take something more than momentary expressions, thrown off in a fit of spleen or excitement, to alienate my affections from one whose life has been distinguished by arduous services and painful sacrifices, in the cause of our common Master. You may grievously misunderstand me, and rank my name in a catagory to which it does not properly belong. This is the bitterest evil of life, to be misapprehended and censured by those whose good opinion we most desire, and in regard to matters in which we most deserve it. What you call my 'Eulogy on Princeton,' is a conciliatory introduction to a series of articles, in which Princeton is destined to figure with no enviable distinction. The expressions are, with a single exception, so framed as to refer to the *personal* qualities of the Fathers there, Drs. Miller and Alexander. I thought it advisable to let them see that they were held responsible, as well as Dr. Hodge, for the sentiments of the *Review*; and to intimate that the profound veneration which was felt for them personally, instead of commending their apology for Rome to the reception of the Church, had only inspired, and was only calculated to inspire, pity for themselves. The whole tenor of the exordium exonerates me from the charge of personal *pique*, which I had reason to believe would be attributed to me. I speak of the article as written with *evident ability*, and an ability not of learning, not of eloquence, not of argument, but of sophistry. The expression is limited to the 'ingenuity and skill,' with which the writer managed his materials, the best that could be had. That I intended to strengthen the influence of Princeton, is just the reverse of my real object in the whole thing. While I gave its Professors credit for piety, learning, and every Christian quality; while, in other words, I commended them as men, the whole tenor of my articles is against the *doctrines* they sustain; and I think, in the result, you will find that they have produced an effect anything but favourable to the Princeton ascendency. My aim is to break the charm, which I think as dangerous as you do; and I have so managed my attack as to reach the very persons whom we ought to reach, the admirers of Princeton. They will see that this is not a *personal war;* that we have nothing to say against the Fathers and brethren, as private men and Christians; that, as followers of Jesus, we love them; as in error, we pity them; but that, in the influence which they, as a body, exert, we see perils which must be resisted and averted. Whether, in this respect, I have judged wisely, the event will prove; and if you can so overcome your disgust as to read the articles to the end of the discussion, you will probably change your first opinion, and be fully satisfied that I have transferred, as skilfully as it should be done, the associations against Popery, to men high in station, who keep it in countenance. It was a little odd that, at the very time you were charging me with bolstering up Princeton, I was pushing ahead an enterprize which I was induced to undertake, from a deep conviction that Princeton must be checked. The very qualities which my article attributes to the men are, in my view, the qualities which make their errors dangerous. And as I believed that Princeton had pursued a disastrous course on the Elder question, on the Romish question, and in regard to national Societies, and ought to be checked, I could devise, at present, no better plan of curtailing her influence than that of strengthening the hands of other Seminaries. Hence, I set on foot the scheme of organizing our own institution more perfectly. The thing was first broached to me, after repeated interviews with brethren, who thought as I do upon these points. You yourself know that I am no great advocate of Theological Seminaries; but as the Church is wedded to them, I am willing, as the next best thing that can be done, to make them checks upon each other. But enough of this matter. Your labours, where you are, must be retrenched, or your health will be ruined. You do the work of at least three men. Could you be induced to come South? The third Professorship in our Seminary here will be fully endowed this spring; and we shall have to elect a Professor of History and Church Government in the fall. My attention has been turned to yourself. The place, in many respects, will be pleasant; and it will be a fine field for you, until Providence shall open a wider. My fixed purpose, in regard to you, is to exert what influence I possess—should I be alive at the time, and you in a condition of health—to transfer you to the same department in Princeton. I have looked upon it as unlikely that you would ever again become a pastor; and a position of this sort is the next most useful, and is one eminently adapted to your talents.

"Very truly, as ever,

J. H. THORNWELL."

The hint here thrown out, of placing Dr. Breckinridge in the Theological Seminary at Columbia, was doubtless suggested by the fact that his health was inadequate to the labours of his position at Cannonsburgh. It was not, perhaps, very seriously entertained by either party; though it is referred to a second time, in a subsequent letter, dated July 24, 1846:

"I have been much distressed to learn, from various sources, that your health is still precarious. God grant that you may be long spared to labour for the glory of His name and the prosperity of His Church. This is no time, according to the estimate of human probability, in which we can dispense with your services, and those of men like-minded with yourself. The discussion in the last Assembly, on the subject of inter-communion with the New School party, has filled me with sadness. I was not prepared to see, so soon, a disposition, so openly manifested, to forsake our former testimony. That there were many who cherished loose sentiments in their hearts, I had no doubt; but that the time had come to avow them in the highest court of the Church, I did not believe. I am seriously afraid that the foolish liberality of the age will speedily plunge us into the same disasters from which we have just escaped. Our whole system of operations gives an undue influence to money. Where money is the great *want*, *numbers* must be sought; and where an ambition for numbers prevails, doctrinal purity must be sacrificed. The root of the evil is in the *secular* spirit of all our ecclesiastical institutions. What we want is a *spiritual* body; a Church whose power lies in the truth, and the presence of the Holy Ghost. To *unsecularize* the Church should be the unceasing aim of all who are anxious that the ways of Zion should flourish. I need not say that my heart was fully with you in your noble testimony in the last Assembly.

"We have completed the endowment of the third Professorship in this Seminary. Can you not send us some students? I think that you would not regret it; for whatever may be the sentiments of some of the Professors on some points, a stronger power is brought to bear upon the students *out* of the Seminary, than is exerted *in* it. Most of them leave the place much *sounder* than they came. Should it be so that your health is inadequate to the discharge of your duties in your present situation, *will you come here*, for two or three years, or as long as you please? You would have a delightful climate, easy labours, exemption from preaching, and fine society. We must elect a Professor in the fall; and, if you will agree to come, my mind is made up as to the man. This field is, of course, not to be compared with the one you at present occupy; but it is better than absolute idleness, and I suggest it to you only upon the supposition that you are too feeble for any other work."

It is pleasant to interrupt this correspondence, generally so polemic in its cast, by transcribing a letter as entirely spiritual. It is addressed to his colleague, the Hon. W. C. Preston, the President of the College. It is a beautiful commingling of personal sympathy under sorrow, with faithfulness of effort to win the soul to Christ:

"SOUTH CAROLINA COLLEGE, *August* 4, 1846.

To HON. WILLIAM C. PRESTON:

MY VERY DEAR SIR: I see from the papers, that you have again been called, in the providence of God, to taste the bitterness of grief. Though, in ordinary cases, the affliction with which you have been visited is one which takes us less by surprise than any other form of ordinary bereavement, yet in your case, the event, I learn, has been wholly unexpected; so that the severity of the stroke has been greatly augmented by the suddenness of the shock. Your feelings under such circumstances I can readily conceive, and nothing but profound veneration for the sacredness of your grief has prevented me from disturbing the solitude which such sorrows always court, and expressing in person what, in the freshness of your calamity, it would, perhaps, have been no relief to receive, my sympathy and condolence. Be assured, my dear sir, that my *heart* has been with you, and my prayers and my tears both freely accompanied you, when I saw you descend into the house of mourning. Your tenderest associations are dearly linked to the grave, or rather they are tied to Heaven. A sainted sister, a cherished daughter, and now she who nursed your infancy, are there before you. Death is no unfamiliar subject, and the hopes of a future life I trust no strange theme.

"The *remainder of our flesh*," is the forcible and beautiful language in which the Hebrew writers are accustomed to designate our kindred and relatives. It is an expression true to nature. We feel them to be a portion of ourselves. Our hearts pursue them in the grave; the sod which conceals their bodies cannot interrupt our communion with their spirits; they live in our memories, they revive in our hopes. I know, from your own affectionate nature, and from the tender relations which they bore to you, that those whom God has taken from you will be felt to be, in a pre-eminent sense, part and parcel of your being; they were, indeed, the '*remainder of your flesh.*' And does not this consideration, my dear sir, suggest a new incentive for cherishing a strong attachment to Heaven, and for giving all diligence to acquire that love to the Saviour

which will secure reunion with your friends? If Jesus possess not the
same attractions for you that He does for His saints, so that you desire
to be absent from the body in order to be present with the Lord; if His
presence and glory be not sufficient to wean your heart from all sublunary good, and commend his rest to your affections; yet, as nature yearns
to be joined again to the departed, you must feel impelled to turn your
eyes to Him as 'the way, the truth, and the life." The loved ones of
your soul beckon you to Him, and through Him to their own society,
and to everlasting blessedness. The providence of God is designed to
give emphasis to the calls of His grace; and afflictions fail of their end
which do not conduct us to Him who bore our sickness and carried our
sorrows.

"If you will pardon the liberty which I take, for I can assure you
that what I shall say is dictated by the sincerest friendship, and accompanied by the warmest prayers, I will frankly state my apprehension,
that you are prone, from the very nature of your mind, and the character of your past pursuits, to fortify your heart rather with the lessons of
philosophy than the promises of God. But if it is the purpose of your
Heavenly Father to lead you to Himself, if He has taken '*the remainder
of your flesh*' as an earnest of the mercy in reserve, is it not as ungrateful
as it is rebellious, to seek consolation in bereavement from the topics of
this world's wisdom, while the exhaustless treasures of Divine love are
before you? Who would be content with heathen *fortitude*, when the
jewel of Christan *patience* may be won? The discipline of philosophy
may engender a dogged submission to calamity, but can never give the
victory that overcomes the world. It is the distinguishing glory of the
gospel to brace the soul against the pressure of ill, to subdue sorrow, to
conquer death, to rejoice in tribulation. He alone whose heart is fixed,
trusting in the Lord, 'shall not be afraid of evil tidings,' since he knows
that all things must work together for good to them that love God. You
may rely upon it, dear sir, that there *is* comfort, pure and sweet, in the
love of the Father, the grace of the Son, and the communion of the
blessed Spirit. There are consolations rich and abundant in the promises of the new and everlasting Covenant, a joy unspeakable and full of
glory, even in the midst of fiery trials, to those who believe in the Saviour. This joy I am anxious for you to feel. In the eye of your
Christian friends there is but one thing you lack, and that one thing
would impart a new grace to your splendid abilities, give new power to
your eloquence, and shed a Divine lustre upon the commanding station
which you occupy. The whole dispensation under which we are placed is
a dispensation of mercy, and the tendency of all its arrangements is to
conduct to Jesus as the only Saviour of men. Prosperity and adversity,
blessings and afflictions, all speak the same language: '*believe and be
saved.*' In your case, I cannot but feel that this language has been most
solemn and emphatic. The prejudices which a mind like yours would
be likely to entertain against evangelical religion, have been signally
forestalled by the testimony of those whom you loved most, and all men

were bound to respect. You have seen its reality, you have witnessed its power. You know that there is such a thing as a change of heart, such a blessing as justification by free grace ; for you have the personal assurance of those whose faith God commanded you to follow. I trust that you will obey His voice. He has called you to prosperity, enabling you to achieve for yourself 'a name which posterity will not willingly let die ;' all venerate you, multitudes love you, and God commands you to give the glory to Him. He has once and again called you by afflictions, and all your afflictions point you directly to Heaven. Oh! that He may now call you affectionately by His grace, and make you partaker of His Son! To this blessed Spirit I commend you, and wherever you go, my affections and my prayers shall go with you ; and if it should be the will of God that we meet no more on earth, (for thousands have run a shorter course than ours,) let us endeavour to meet on the great day, at the right hand of the Judge, where all tears shall be wiped away, and sorrow and sighing are no more known.

'With the sincerest Christian sympathy and love, most truly yours,

J. H. THORNWELL."

It will form, perhaps, an agreeable contrast, to set over against this letter, addressed to a distinguished and cultivated man of the world, a brief note, written at the same date, to his children, left in Columbia at school, whilst he and their mother were enjoying a little recreation with relatives at Abbeville. Nothing brings out a man's heart so completely as the intercourse he holds with his own children. Dr. Thornwell was a most affectionate father; and amongst his loose papers are many short letters to them, in which he never fails to impress on their young minds the importance of early piety. Let us see how the great orator and profound debater will condescend to babes :

"ABBEVILLE, *August* 17, 1846.

"MY DEAR CHILDREN : Your mother and myself, with your little brothers and sisters, reached your uncle Wardlaw's on Friday evening, in health and safety. We desire to thank God for having taken care of us, and we want you to thank Him too. He saved us from all accident by the road; He provided us with every necessary comfort; and, through His goodness, we are now among dear and valued friends.

"Your little cousins have inquired a great deal about you, and are very sorry that you did not come up with us. Aunt Mary and Uncle Joe also expressed great desire to see you. Your father and mother would be happy to have you with them, but they know it to be better for you to be at school with aunt Peck. Father wants you to be good children, to give Mrs. Peck no trouble, and to learn to read good, so that you may be able to read God's Word for yourselves. You must pray to God every night when you go to bed, and every morning when you get up. You must ask Him, for the sake of Jesus Christ, to give you His Spirit. The Spirit will make you feel that you are sinners, that you need a Saviour; and will enable you to believe in Jesus Christ. You must begin early to fear God. Jesus Christ saves children, as well as grown people. You must also pray for father and mother, and your little brothers and sisters, and for each other. When Aunt Peck takes you to church, you must be good children, behave prettily, and listen to what Mr. Palmer says. Your father and mother think of you every day, and pray for you, and send a thousand kisses to you.

"Very affectionately, your father,

J. H. THORNWELL."

Among the reasons assigned by the Presbytery for retaining Dr. Thornwell in South Carolina, allusion was made to certain enterprises which had been set on foot, which his influence was needed to foster and sustain. One of these was a more complete endowment and equipment of the Theological Seminary at Columbia. This was soon carried out by adding a third Professorship, and, at a later period, a fourth; to which, eventually, the munificence of Judge Perkins, of Mississippi, added a fifth; so that, prior to the late war, it was one of the best endowed and most throughly furnished institutions of the kind in the whole land.

A second enterprise was the establishment of a religious quarterly, at Columbia; to which, by anticipation, we have had occasion already to refer. The measures for this last were perfected during the year 1846; and in the month of June, in the year following, the first number was issued of the *Southern Presbyterian Review*, under the conduct of "an association of Presbyterian ministers, in the town of Columbia;" and which has continued its existence to the present hour. In both of these schemes Dr. Thornwell was deeply interested; and the complete success achieved in both, fully justifies the wisdom of the Presbytery in retaining the services which so powerfully contributed to the same. Many of the most valuable

articles in the *Review* were from his pen; which, in all
probability, would never have been written, but for the
editorial responsibility which pressed upon him.   To that
extent, the Church at large is a debtor to this enterprise;
as will be acknowledged by all who discover how large a
portion of the four volumes, already published, is made
up of monographs culled from the pages of this *Review*.

A few extracts, from letters relating to this undertaking,
will conclude the present chapter.   To Dr. Breckinridge,
in a letter bearing date September 25, 1846 :

> " I have just returned from a long and painful visit to a region full of
> sickness and affliction.   My absence accounts for my not having sent
> you a prospectus before.   I have no idea that we can get *subscribers* in
> your region, but I hope that we can get *articles*.   *You* must write.   We
> will give you a fair and full field on the Elder question.   Can you not
> get Drs. Green and McGill to write ?"

On the 6th of November, he writes to the same, with
a little more fulness :

> " I am rejoiced to learn that you will become a constant contributor
> to our proposed *Review*.   You must be under no sort of apprehension
> that you will write too often, or too much.   We have not yet received
> sufficient encouragement, in the way of patronage, to feel that the en-
> terprise is safe.   At Synod, which meets in Charleston on Thursday
> next, returns will probably be made to us, from which we can judge
> whether it will be advisable to put to press, or not.   We shall start if
> we can get five hundred subscribers.   We have four hundred now.
>
> " The editors of the concern are Dr. Howe, brother Palmer, and my-
> self.   We intend to make it a free journal on the subject of Eldership,
> Boards, Agencies, *et id omne genus*.   We shall not, like Princeton, put
> an extinguisher upon any candle that emits any light.   My own impres-
> sion is, that, except in cases where a writer may particularly desire the
> contrary, the names of the contributors should be given.   No man ought
> to write who is not willing to be responsible for what he says.   There
> may be considerations of delicacy which, in some instances, might ren-
> der it improper to give the author of an article ; and in such cases, the
> name might be suppressed.   But, as a general rule, I do not like strictly
> anonymous publications.   The *Review* has been coldly received in some
> quarters, having been prejudiced and condemned as likely to be a vio-
> lent and acrimonious advocate of extreme opinions.   I hope that it will
> be free from bitterness ; but if God gives me health and strength, I am
> determined that it shall contain some things which will require some-
> thing more than appeal to custom to refute."

CHAPTER XXI.

ASSEMBLIES OF 1847 *AND* 1848.

DR. THORNWELL had been a member of three Assemblies: those of 1837, of 1840, and of 1845; becoming more conspicuous in each, until, in that of 1847,
which convened in the city of Richmond, Virginia, the
highest ecclasiastical honour was conferred, in elevating
him to the Moderator's chair. He was, we believe, the
youngest who had ever filled that distinguished position,
being only in the thirty-fifth year of his age. Upon being
conducted to his seat, in a neat salutatory, he reminded the
Assembly of the importance of Parliamentary rules, and
of a punctilious observance of them, in order to the despatch of business; and of the still greater importance, in
a spiritual court, of the presence of Christ, in the power
of His Spirit, and of singleness of purpose to promote
the glory of God. Delivered with the tone of sincere
conviction which marked all his utterances, it made a
sweet impression upon the body, and gave a pledge of
that dignity and courtesy, that impartiality and efficiency
in the discharge of his official duties, which, at the close
of the sessions, brought upon him the encomiums of all
who witnessed the proceedings of each day. This much

may be allowed to be said for him, since he could not say it for himself. As to all the rest, he shall speak directly to the reader, in the confidential letters addressed to her, who shared with him his innermost thoughts:

"RICHMOND, *May* 20, 1847.

"The Assembly has just closed its morning session. Dr. Hodge preached a very able sermon, from 1 Cor. ix. 14. The subject was, the duty of the Church, as a united, collective body, to support the gospel ministry. Some of his views were very striking and impressive, though in some things there seemed to me to be a confusion of ideas. He read it slavishly, and without any animation; and the congregation, I thought, were not much interested. I presume it will be published. After the sermon, the Assembly was constituted; and, though some Presbyteries are not yet represented, the delegation is very large, and the body is truly imposing.

"I was elected Moderator, which, I have no doubt, will surprise you and my Columbia friends very much. The Assembly is to meet every morning at nine o'clock, and adjourn at one; then meet again at four, and adjourn at half-past six. The adoption of this rule, and the election of officers, are all that was done this morning. I have no idea what sort of a time we shall have; but I trust that the Lord will be merciful to us, and grant us His Holy Spirit. I do wish very much that you were here. You could not fail to be interested and delighted. You would meet with so many old friends, and extend your acquaintance among so many kind and hospitable people, that you would feel it to be a treat.

"Father McIver, from North Carolina, is here, to prosecute a complaint against Fayetteville Presbytery and the Synod of North Carolina, for restoring McQueen to the ministry. The old man is full of the subject. He seems to think that all will come to desolation, if men are allowed to marry their wives' sisters. He is a good man, and his zeal and earnestness on this subject are truly amusing. I do not know yet in what shape the question will come before us; but my speech is killed by being put in the Moderator's chair."

To the same, dated May 27, 1847:

"This is the eighth day of the sessions of the Assembly. Everything has gone on quite smoothly and harmoniously. We came very near having a breeze on the question of reading or not reading the letters from the General Assembly of the Church in Ireland, and the General Assembly of the Free Church in Scotland; but the letters were finally read, and the whole affair passed off very pleasantly. They were very strongly against slavery, but produced no ferment. Our Assembly returned a very firm, calm, and dignified answer to both. The McQueen case is not yet decided; but I am inclined to think that the decision of the Fayetteville Presbytery, restoring him to the ministry, will be sustained. If it could come up on its merits, this would probably not be the case; but it comes up hampered with a decision of the Assembly of 1845, which rather shuts us up, in the opinion of many, to the adoption of this course.

"I preached my sermon on Popery last night, to a very large congregation. The weather was very bad; it rained the whole evening, and I expected but few hearers. To my surprise, the house was crowded to overflowing. I had to omit a great deal of it, which I was sorry to do. This morning the Assembly voted me their thanks for it, and ordered it to be published. It seems to have taken remarkably well.

"Dr. Hodge preached a sermon to-night on parochial schools. He is not an interesting preacher, although he is a clear and able writer. He wants animation and fire. As a man, he is exceedingly popular in the Assembly, and has great weight. He is very mild and gentle and affectionate in his temper. Next Sunday we are to celebrate, as an Assembly, the Lord's Supper. The action sermon will be preached by Dr. Hoge, of Columbus.

"I have been so much occupied with the business of the Assembly, that I have been able to accept only two invitations to dine out. As my sermon on Popery is now off my hands, I shall have more time at my command; and shall endeavour to accept, in future, some of the invitations which have been kindly extended to me. I have promised Dr. Green and Peck to visit them in Baltimore upon the rising of the Assembly, and I have been strongly urged to go to Philadelphia. My movements, however, are not yet arranged. You shall know them in due time. It is now twelve o'clock at night. May the Lord be to you a sun and a shield."

The sermon on Popery was preached under an appointment of the Assembly of 1845; which, from providential hindrances, was not fulfilled the following year, and was continued till the next. The topic discussed in it was the doctrine of the Mass; and was delivered from full notes, without being written in connected form. It is a little singular, considering the call for its publication, and the deep interest which the speaker felt in all parts of this Romish controversy, that it was never given to the press. It remains in the same crude shape, too incomplete and disconnected to be inserted in his "Collected Writings." It was declared by one of our most learned divines, who listened to it when pronounced, to be a masterly exhibition of truth, and showing a thorough acquaintance with the

learning of the subject.*   The Mass was discussed under
its two forms, as a sacrament and as a sacrifice.   It was
shown to be the central doctrine in the Romish system;
and the arguments in its defence were articulately considered, whether drawn from tradition, from reason, or
from Scripture.   One peruses it in the rude outline, with
profound regret that it was never wrought up in the finished style which would have rendered it a valuable and
permanent contribution to the controversial literature of
the Church.

The following letter, written about this time, to Dr.
Breckinridge, discloses the habitual feelings with which
he regarded his work in the College.   The view presented
as to the particular form in which his usefulness was most
conspicuous, will be endorsed by all who are familiar with
those times; though eternity alone will reveal in how
many souls he planted "the incorruptible seed," which,
in later years, brought forth fruit unto holiness:

"SOUTH CAROLINA COLLEGE, *March* 12, 1847.

"MY DEAR BROTHER: With your feelings in reference to your position
in College, I can most heartily sympathize; and if I had yielded to my
own impulses more, and less to the convictions of others, I should not
have been here to-day.   From long experience, I am satisfied that the
possibilities of usefulness in such a situation are largely overrated.   The
influence which a good man can exert is rather negative than positive;
it consists more in preventing evil, than in directly doing good.   This
negative sort of usefulness has never been enough to fill up my desires.
But Providence seems to have cast my lot where my labour is drudgery,
and my reward is disappointment.   My time is so frittered away by the
constant intervention of external duties, that I can pursue no consecutive
plans of study; and what little writing I am able to perform, and it is
little enough, must be done at the expense of sleep or recreation.   But

* In addition to this testimony, we find the following from Dr. J. W.
Alexander, in the memorial of him entitled "Forty Years' Familiar Letters:" "Dr. Thornwell is the great man of the South, and I do not think
his learning or powers of mind overrated. His speech, on taking the chair,
was a *chef d'œuvre*. His sermon was ill delivered, but nevertheless a model
of what is rare, viz.: burning hot argument, logic in ignition, and glowing more and more to the end: it was *memoriter*, and with terrific *con-
tentio laterum*."

here I am, mysteriously shut up to a position which is not the object of my choice, discouraged, mortified, distressed at the fruitlessness of my efforts, toiling day after day without hope, worn down by a constant pressure of responsibility, and unsustained, for the most part, by sympathy, co-operation, or approval, on the part of those around me. If there are any who envy me my chair, they would gladly relinquish to me all its honours after six months' experience of its cares. My conscience testifies that I have faithfully preached the gospel here; I have preached it through good report, and through evil report; I have preached it when I stood almost absolutely alone; but what has been the result? In only one aspect of the case, do I feel that I have done a valuable work; and that is, in breaking down the spirit of infidelity, which had largely taken possession of the State. Under God's blessing, I have succeeded beyond what I could hope, in changing the whole current of association upon the speculative question of the truth of Christianity. This is something, but it is not *salvation*; and the salvation of souls is the object of my toil.

'Very truly, as ever,

J. H. THORNWELL."

In a later epistle to the same, October 20, 1847, he writes:

"There is another matter which I would also commend to your notice. It strikes me that D'Aubigne has not done justice to the character of Zuingle. That great and good man ought to be set in a fairer light. Now, history is familiar to you as household words; and I should be delighted to receive from you an article on this point.

"Our Synod has just closed its sessions. A large committee was appointed, of which I am chairman, to draw up a paper, to be presented to the next Synod, on the subject of slavery, defining the true position of our Church, and suggesting means for rectifying some of the abuses and evils incidental to the institution. We shall probably recommend a petition to the Legislature, praying that a law may be enacted, to protect the family relations of the slave; and that the disgraceful statute, which prohibits them from learning to read, may be repealed. I shall take great pains in the preparation of the document, and would be glad to receive any suggestions."

As the retiring Moderator, Dr. Thornwell opened the Assembly of 1848, with a sermon from Acts xvii. 32, "And when they heard of the resurrection of the dead, some mocked; and others said, we will hear thee again of this matter." According to usage, he filled the important position of Chairman of the Committee on Bills and Overtures. He had the opportunity of broaching his opinion on two important subjects, foreshadowing what, at a later date, in the revision of the Book of Discipline, he sought to incorporate into the Constitution of the Church.

An overture was presented, asking whether Church Sessions have the right to allow members to withdraw from the communion of the Church, who are not guilty of any immoral conduct, but feel that they have never been made the subjects of renewing grace. This question it was proposed to answer in the affirmative. In the debate which followed, Dr. Thornwell is reported as saying:

"The point of the overture is entirely misapprehended. It is asked whether persons may withdraw from the Church who have been received unadvisedly, and are now satisfied that they are not converted persons, yet are regular in all their private and public duties. It is the custom of the Church, when members absent themselves from the communion, to visit them by committee. Suppose a member gives as a reason for staying away, 'I am satisfied that I am not a member of Christ; and when the pastor charged all those to retire who had not knowledge to discern the Lord's body, I was constrained in conscience to obey the command.' What is to be done? Will you discipline him? For what? For doing the very thing which you require him to do, and which, if our principles are true, he was solemnly bound to do. What is the object of a trial? Is it not to ascertain whether a man is, or is not, a member of Christ's body? But if he confesses that he is not, it is the best evidence that can be given, and the Session may declare the fact to the Church. It was the doctrine of Erastus, that the Church was the channel of grace, and had no right to excommunicate members for any cause. But this is not the doctrine of any Christian Church, at the present day. Now, we hold that union with Christ is the basis of union with the Church, and a credible profession simply declares the fact. Will any Church Session undertake to affirm that a man is, and shall be, a member of the Church, when he tells them that he is not a member of Christ? Certainly not. It is now proposed that, in such a case, the Session shall place him in the same position with the baptized children of the Church, and not make him a heathen and publican.

"Another point: The Protestant Church knows no man, unless he is voluntarily subject to her authority; and the vow of subjection is binding no longer than he feels that he has a right to submit to them. The Roman Catholic view is, that a man is everywhere bound by his vow to the Church: that once a virgin, bound by a vow, always a virgin; once a monk, always a monk   But, with us, the vow is not to the Church, but to God; and He will be the judge.   We propose no innovation, but the assertion of a right that is inherent in our Church, and ought to be distinctly set forth.   Thus we shall separate the chaff from the wheat, purify the Church, and publish the fact to the world.   The Church has been spoken of as a voluntary society; but there was this obvious feature: a voluntary society prescribes its own rule, but the Church has its laws from its Head; they are not to be altered or amended."*

These arguments did not, however, carry the Assembly; and the recommendation was rejected.

Upon the other subject, Dr. Thornwell was more successful, securing the unanimous consent of the body to his views.   It was the relation which the Church should sustain to temperance, and other moral reform societies. Without quoting the minute † at large which he submitted, it is sufficient here to state that it set forth, with great clearness, the nature and functions of the Church as a spiritual body, the kingdom of Jesus Christ, governed by His laws, and having for its aim the gathering and perfecting of the saints, to the end of the world.   It cannot, therefore, league itself to any secular institutions for moral ends, nor be subsidiary to associations founded upon human policy.   It is a matter of Christian liberty whether connection shall be had with these or not; a liberty which the Church does not infringe, either by enjoining or interdicting them, as long as false principles are not promulgated, and wrong practices are not indulged.   And in pressing these distinctions, Dr. Thornwell only urged the doctrine which he uniformly taught through life, as to the province of the Church, and her immediate and entire subjection under the authority of her Lord and Head.

The only letter extant, written during the sessions of this Assembly, is the following to his wife, from which we make one or two extracts.   It is dated,

* See Biblical Repertory for 1848, pp. 409–410.
† It will be found in the Assembly's Digest, Ed. 1856, pp. 797–'8.

"BALTIMORE, *May* 20, 1848.

" My DEAREST WIFE :   *   *   *   The Assembly was opened on Thursday, by a sermon from myself, which occupied an hour and a half in the delivery.   Dr. McGill, of Pittsburgh, was elected Moderator.   I have been made Chairman of the Committee on Bills and Overtures, which is the most laborious and important committee of the house.   It is the channel through which most of the business enters the house.   You perceive, therefore, that my hands are full.   We have had, thus far, a very pleasant time.   All our Southern members are delighted with the hospitality of Baltimore.   It is indeed a delightful city.   *   *   *   Mr. Spreckelson sent me yesterday a small box of very costly cigars, which, I am afraid, will so corrupt my taste that I will find it hard to come down, when I return home.

" The great Democratic Convention meets here, next Monday.   The object is to nominate the candidate of the Democratic party for the Presidency of the United States.   We shall have all the great men of the Union here.   Congress has adjourned until it is through, so that all the leading members of Congress will be present.   I am proposing to myself a good deal of interest, in occasionally witnessing its deliberations and proceedings.

" We have some interesting questions to come before the Assembly next week.   The Marriage question will be up again, in several forms : 1, As a judicial case ; and 2, The abstract doctrine.   It will, in all probability, be fully discussed ; and I hope that it will be so settled as to put an end to every future agitation of the subject.*   The Elder question will not come up ; at least there is no prospect of it at present.

" We had yesterday rather a scene in the house, from the conduct of a lady, who seems to be partially deranged.   She brought a case before the Assembly, complaining against the Synod of New York.   Her papers were reported to be irregular by the Chairman of the Judicial Committee ; and a motion was made to dismiss the case.   She was in the house at the time, and became so excited, that she rose to make a speech in her own defence.   We succeeded, however, in getting her quiet, without permitting her to produce much confusion.   She was directed to wait on the Judicial Committee, and make her statements to it.   She accordingly did so.   I was in the adjoining room, presiding over another committee, and heard her inflict a terrible belabouring upon the Judicial Committee, which afforded me no little amusement.   She is said to be a woman of education, of good family, and of good circumstances ; but she is crazy on the subject of prophecy, and thinks the time has come to cleanse the Sanctuary.   Hence, she has impeached all the ministers

* The judicial case was the complaint of Rev. Colin McIver against the restoration of Mr. McQueen, which was dismissed, as having been concluded by the preceding Assembly.   The proposition to submit the question to the Presbyteries, of striking out the law on this subject, was not concurred in.

of New York; and is grievously offended that the Assembly will not help
her to purify the sons of Levi. The nature of her complaints I do not
exactly understand. I believe that she charges some of the New York
ministers with making mouths at her; others, with treating her rudely,
in ordering her out of the house; and some with turning her over to
the police. The whole affair is equally strange and ridiculous; but the
poor woman is certainly to be pitied. * * *

" Your devoted husband,

J. H. THORNWELL."

Upon his return from the Assembly, he spent a day in
Washington, D. C., from which place he writes, on the
5th of June:

"I came here this morning, from Baltimore; and being too late for
the boat, have spent the day here, which gave me an opportunity of seeing Congress in session. The Assembly was dissolved on Saturday
evening, and I preached yesterday in the First Presbyterian Church, of
Baltimore. A great many members of the Assembly came over to see
the great guns at Washington. Mr. Calhoun and Colonel Burt were very
polite to me; and I have an engagement to spend the evening with
them. Mrs. Burt is here, keeping house for them; it will give me great
pleasure to see her, and discuss old times. I have seen nearly all the
South Carolina members. There is very little doing now, as the Whig
Convention meets to-morrow in Philadelphia, to nominate a Whig candidate for the Presidency of the United States."

This letter is introduced for the purpose of recalling
the fact, that Dr. Thornwell's acquaintance with Mr. Calhoun did not begin at this date. During the summer of
1843, he called upon Mr. Calhoun at his residence, in
Pendleton, and spent a morning with him. The conversation took a wide range over the subjects of education,
metaphysics, and politics. Dr. Thornwell possessed rare
powers of conversation, and rejoiced in letting them out,
when it took this particular form of a dialogue between
two. When thrown in contact with men of great abilities, his ambition put him upon his mettle; his mind was
roused to as much activity, and he drew upon his stores
of learning with as much fervour, as when addressing a
large assembly. The writer remembers the account, given
by himself, of this particular interview, and the terms of

strong satisfaction in which he dwelt upon the rehearsal
of it. Mr. Calhoun is also represented to have expressed
his own delight, to the gentleman who had brought them
together; saying that Dr. Thornwell was the only divine
he had ever met, whom he thought comparable with his
old preceptor, Dr. Dwight, the former President of Yale
College. He further stated, "I expected to find Dr.
Thornwell perfectly posted upon his own department of
study; but when he came over into mine, I was not prepared for the thorough acquaintance he exhibited with
all the topics that are generally familiar only to statesmen." The mystery is not really so great as it appears;
for an accomplished theologian is compelled to master
the great principles which underlie all government and
law. But Dr. Thornwell, in addition to this, was remarkably conversant with history, and had mastered the science of Political Economy. He was, therefore, entirely
competent to range with Mr. Calhoun over all the topics
which lay in the bounds of that profession which either
pursued.

The following letter to Dr. Breckinridge, contains his
last reference to the Assembly of 1848. Some sentences
in it will afford the reader some idea of the playful
humour in which he so often indulged in personal intercourse.

"SOUTH CAROLINA COLLEGE, *July* 18, 1848.

"MY DEAR BROTHER: I received your last letter some months ago,
and can hardly frame any decent apology for having neglected to answer
it so long. The truth is, I have a great aversion to the use of the pen;
and I do not know if I ever should write to my friends, if it were not for
my anxiety to hear from them. From *you*, particularly, a letter is always
thrice welcome; and it is more to draw something from you, than to
communicate anything of my own, that I now undertake to bring you in
debt to me. You have probably heard from Berryman, and gathered
from the papers a better account than I could give you of the last Assembly. I am satisfied that a gradual reaction is generally taking place
in the Church, which, in a few years, with proper efforts, will put it in
the position we would like to see it occupy. Something effectual might
have been done in Baltimore, if the Assembly had not been so completely
worn out by the mass of judicial business to which it was called to attend.

There was no possibility of a full discussion of any great question. But straws show how the wind blows; and I saw enough to make me bless God and take courage. The people of Baltimore manifested a princely hospitality, and they will long be remembered in the prayers, affection, and gratitude of the ministers and elders, who never expect to see them again in the flesh. No one left the city without regret. Our good friend McElderry kept an inn, as usual; and if he chanced, on any day, to have no more than his table could accommodate, he seemed to be afraid that he had not done his duty. I charged him with standing at the corner of the streets, and pressing every man he met to come and partake of the fat things he had prepared. At his house I met with your friend S——, who occupied, for several nights, the same room with myself. He left the city in self-defence, protesting that a few more nights with me would kill him; and pitying my wife, who, from year to year, had to endure the plague of a man who neither slept nor waked, according to the laws which govern civilized human beings. It was amusing to see him, poor fellow, denude himself, about ten o'clock, of his wearing apparel, slip into his long shirt, and stretch himself upon his couch, to woo the embraces of kind 'nature's sweet restorer, balmy sleep,' and then permit himself to become so absorbed in conversation as to forget his position, jump up, fumble about his breeches' pocket for a quid of tobacco, or sponge on me for a good cigar; and thus, lying, sitting, walking, all in a shirt of prodigious length, forget the hours, until signs of day began to appear. He is a noble fellow, and I found his society a treat. I think a brief campaign with me would completely cure him of the infirmity of feeling sleepy at night. ᵀ endeavoured to impress upon him that the noblest beasts, sucu as the lion, take the nights for their feats of activity and valour. To work in the day, when every one can see you, savours too much of ostentation for a generous and modest spirit; anu to be eating by eight o'clock in the morning, indicates a ravenous propensity for the things of earth. * * * * *

"Are you writing anything for us? We shall be more than glad to hear from you. How comes on your Commentary on Acts? Have you seen Lord's 'Theological Journal?' It promises to be a valuable contribution towards the interpretation of the prophetic Scriptures. His review of Stuart on the Apocalypse is well done. Have you seen Nevin's reply to Hodge? I have been much amused in reading his article, and have had some curious questions suggested to me concerning the influence of language on thought. Let me hear from you soon.

"Very truly, as ever,

J. H. THORNWELL."

The two letters which are annexed, are letters of private friendship, and reveal the affectionateness of his nature. The first is addressed to Mr. A. H. Pegues, one of the companions of his childhood:

"SOUTH CAROLINA COLLEGE, *June* 27, 1848.

"MY DEAR FRIEND : I do not know when I have been more gratified than I was, a few days ago, at the reception of your letter of the 2d instant. It was like good news from a distant land, or cold water to a thirsty soul. Reminiscences, which never can fade from my mind, were called up with the freshness of the original events; and for a time I gave myself up to the power of the past. I was particularly delighted to find that the vicissitudes of your Western life had wrought no change in your early affections, and that you still turned with pleasure to one whose love to you is as strong and fresh as when we pored together over the delicious lines,

"'——— The native wood-notes wild,
Of sweetest Shakespeare, fancy's child,'

Or nerved our minds to higher efforts over the exquisite pages of Locke, Stewart, or Reid. Those *days* are gone, but their *impressions* remain; and nothing on earth would afford me more pleasure than to meet you in person, and review face to face the numberless events which have bound my heart to yours.

"In regard to the subject of your letter, you will permit me to say, that, while I am touched with your kindness and partiality, I must yet decline being presented as a candidate for the place in question. The position which I occupy here I cannot relinquish; it opens a wide and increasing field of usefulness, and is, in many respects, the most desirable in the Southern country. I would be glad, however, if you could exert your good offices in favour of my old friend and classmate, Rev. Mr. Gladney. He is an excellent man, of sterling integrity, of much more than ordinary talents, and a good scholar. He has the decision and firmness which are absolutely essential to the President of a College. I would also bespeak your aid in behalf of my young friend, Gamewell, (a son of our old Methodist preacher,) who will appear as a candidate for the chair of Mathematics. He is a prodigy of genius, having, in my opinion, no superior in the State.

"I hope that your enterprise will be eminently successful; but you must not be too sanguine. The erection of a College is the work of years; and no organization can give it an efficiency beyond the demands of the actual condition of society. I do not altogether like the distribution of your departments of instruction. More prominence should be given to the Moral Sciences. It is too much to assign them all to one Professor. I think, too, that the combination of Modern and Ancient Languages will have the effect of preventing an adequate attention from being paid to either. I am afraid that your course of study has not been sufficiently digested; and I am sure that experience will not only suggest, but demand, material alterations in the details of your system. It will give me great pleasure to hear from you often. Let our old correspondence be renewed.

"As ever, most truly yours,

J. H. THORNWELL."

A second of these letters is addressed to Professor Matthew J. Williams, who had been elected in December, 1846, to the chair of Mathematics in the South Carolina College. The friendship between the two was recent, but very strong and sincere, and continued throughout life. Professor Williams was a member of the Methodist Church, a man of liberal and catholic views, gentle and loving in disposition; in every respect deserving the expressions of esteem lavished upon him in this letter:

"SOUTH CAROLINA COLLEGE, *July* 17, 1848.

"MY DEAR MAJOR: I received your kind and interesting letter last week, and would be glad to have a similar infliction every week of my life. We had often spoken of you in the family, and promised ourselves much gratification, in the expectation of hearing from you; and when the desired document arrived, we were far from being disappointed. I count it one of the happy circumstances of my life, that I have been brought into such nearness of contact, and such intimacy of communication, with one who daily grows upon my esteem, and to whose character I often appeal, as illustrating some of the loveliest graces of the gospel. I speak with the utmost candour, when I assure you that the impression which you have made upon me is no stronger than that which you have made upon other members of the Faculty, particularly upon the President and Mr. Pelham. These things I say, not to flatter you, but to shame you out of all thoughts of ever relinquishing your post here. You occupy a field of extended usefulness, a position suited to your talents and acquirements. You are (what, I take it, was never *adequately* the case with you before) appreciated; and while this should contribute to your happiness, it increases your obligation to remain, and devote yourself, in this field, to the glory of God. I hope, therefore, that you will listen to no persuasions from any quarter, either to retire to your farm, or to take an office which will bring you more directly into the society of your brethren. God has put you *here*, and you should wait till He removes you. I will say no more on this point, though I have felt very deeply on account of the occasional hints which have dropped from you, touching the subject of a removal.

"The campus is a scene of quiet, amounting to desolation. Nothing disturbs the dreary stillness, but the occasional sound of the hammer, from the buildings which are in the process of erection. The President and Pelham are all that remain of our force, and how long they will stay I am unable to tell you. We had a meeting to-day of such members of the Faculty as are in town, and such members of the Board of Trustees

as could be induced to attend, and elected a bursar, to go into office on
the 1st October, and to remain in office until the meeting of the Board
of Trustees. Colonel Gladden, who has just returned from Mexico with
his laurels green upon him, was the unanimous choice of the meeting.
I trust that he will prove an acquisition to the College; and that arrangements may be made, under his administration, to relieve the Professors
of the grievous penance of attending at commons.

"My mode of life here is all that I could desire, as to physical comfort. I sit up all night, reading, musing, and smoking; and just before
the sun, with its orient beams, dispels ghosts, goblins, and infernal
spirits to their respective jails, I stretch my limbs upon an ample couch,
continue my cogitations till my soul is locked in the silent embrace of
slumber sweet; and I abide in the land of dreams until it becomes a
man to refresh nature in a more active way. Ham, coffee, and biscuits
completely restore me to this world again; and after a proper pause, I
proceed to commit depredations upon watermelons, which would be
appalling to one who measured the danger by the bulk that was consumed. Sometimes, after these vigorous onsets, I give no dubious
promise of attaining a judge-like condition of corpulency; but soon the
increased enlargement disappears, and I am like a dropsical patient just
tapped. The truth is, I have no hopes of growing fat; I am lean, lean,
hopelessly lean. But it is a comfort, that *all* of my friends cannot laugh
at me.

"I was very much gratified at your commendation of my long article
on the Elder question. With whatever feebleness they are stated, it is
certain to my mind that it contains principles of the highest importance,
in their application both to Church and State. I am afraid that the tendency of things in this country, is to corrupt a *representative* into a *democratic* government; and to make the State the mere creature of popular
caprice. The question of civil liberty is one of the nicest and most
interesting in the whole circle of political inquiry; and more mistakes
exist in regard to it, than upon any other point of political philosophy.
France is now blundering, and I am afraid will continue to blunder,
until her redemption becomes hopeless. A ball has been set in motion
upon the relations of capital and labour, whose progress it will be extremely difficult to arrest; but the Lord reigns.

"The present posture of the nations baffles the speculations of philosophers and statesmen. I turn from all carnal calculations to the sure
word of prophecy; and as I believe that the only safe guide is to be
found in the prophetic Scriptures, I have begun with increased zeal the
study of a book, which has heretofore been to me, as it has been to the
great majority of Christians, a sealed volume: the Apocalypse of John.
That sublime document contains the history of the world, from Christ
to the end of time; and though its figures are mystic, they are not
hopelessly obscure. There is a key which can unlock its secrets, and
make its hieroglyphics speak the language of common life. We are

upon the eve of great events; and watchfulness and prayer are the posture in which we should be found. God is riding on the whirlwind, and directing the storm; and out of the chaos and tumult of the nations, He will surely evolve His own grand purposes, and make the angry passions of men subservient to the scheme of His glorious providence.   *   *   *

"Very sincerely, your friend and brother,

J. H. THORNWELL."

CHAPTER XXII.

PERSONAL FRIENDSHIPS.

DURING his brief pastoral connexion with the church at Columbia, in 1840, Dr. Thornwell was made the instrument, under God, of the conversion of a young man, the son of a widow, "a mother in Israel," who still survives, in a green old age, to bless that church with the influence and example of her fervent piety. Of course, this laid the foundation for a friendship of no ordinary kind, with the young disciple, who henceforth sat at his feet, preparing to preach the unsearchable riches of that grace, whose power was first felt under the exposition that fell from his lips. It was the old, sweet relation which subsisted between Paul and his son Timothy, whom he had "begotten in the gospel." It must have been with emotions of devout gratitude to God that Dr. Thornwell watched the career of his young protegé, from his early and successful ministry in the city of Baltimore, until his transfer to the Theological Seminary at Prince Edward, Virginia, as a teacher of those who should fill the pulpits of the land; a man whose convictions of truth are not a whit less intense than those of the master from whom he first imbibed them; and whose superior attainments are veiled beneath a humility so deep, that it may possibly conceal what should be more conspicuously revealed. The singular modesty of the Rev. Dr. Thomas E. Peck will

313

recoil, we fear, from this measure of publicity; yet his ardent affection for one to whom he is so largely indebted, will allow his name to be woven thus into the chaplet that is thrown around the memory of his friend. This personal reference is necessary, as an introduction to some precious letters, which were surrendered to us, with this statement from the recipient: "One of these letters I value very highly, not only as a memorial of his kindness to me, but as an evidence of his single-hearted devotion to our common Lord. It was of infinite service to me at the time it was received; and, I think, might be of great service to any young minister, discouraged in his work, and weary of the conflict with sin in his own heart, with the contradiction of sinners, and with the devil." We suspect the letter here referred to, is that which immediately follows.

To the Rev. Thomas E. Peck:

"SOUTH CAROLINA COLLEGE, *August* 4, 1848.

"MY DEAR THOMAS: I received your kind and welcome letter this evening; and proceed to give you the strongest possible proof of the value which I attach to your correspondence, by answering your favour in a few hours after the reception of it. You are the frequent theme of conversation in my family, and we all feel towards you as we would feel if our own blood coursed through your veins. We rejoice to hear of your prosperity, share with you in your sorrows, and lament the hours of darkness which so frequently come upon you. I am glad to learn that your prospects are brightening before you, though I have never entertained a doubt that you were the Lord's instrument, to accomplish the Lord's work, in the sphere of your labours. When the first stone of the edifice in which you minister was laid, there was not a man, of all who engaged in the enterprise, who even knew you by name. It was God who sent you to Baltimore, when the building was ready for a preacher. He put it into the hearts of the people to elect you. He disposed your mind to accept the call; and He will protect, guide, and defend you, until you shall have done the business for which this whole train of providential dispensation was ordered and adjusted. Have faith in God; aim singly at His glory; and the crooked shall be made straight, and the rough places plain. Be not impatient of success; for the purposes of Him with whom the measures of time are unmeaning—one day being as a thousand years, and a thousand years as one day,—are generally as slow in their development as they are majestic in their nature. Wait on the

Lord; be of good courage, and He will strengthen thine heart. Wait, I say, on the Lord. The discipline of patience is one of those precious trials of our faith, which at once attest its reality, and measure its degree. I am preaching to you the same lessons which, in my own position, I have constantly to preach to myself; and no one can be more sensible than I am, how little mere preaching avails to impress them on the heart. My difficulty lies, (and I presume it is also the case with you,) not with the abstract propositions, but with their practical relations to myself. If I could only be assured that I was in the way of duty, labouring *where* the Almighty would have me to labour, and *as* He would have me to labour; if I were not conscious that so much is mingled with my services, my purposes and plans, which He cannot approve; it seems to me that I could easily in patience possess my soul. But the suggestion often arises, that perhaps I have run where I was not sent; that I am more zealous for my own name than the Lord's glory; and that my want of success is, after all, a righteous judgment for my sins. These are the thoughts which cast down my soul, and cause it to be disquieted within me; these are the difficulties in the way of patient waiting on the Lord; these are things which make me constantly feel that I have more concern with repentance than with resignation; more to fear than to hope. How precious is the reflection, that the blood of Christ cleanses from *all* sin, even from the uncleanness and foulness of those who bear the vessels of the Lord! Of all sins, those of a minister would seem to be the most aggravated; and of all men, preachers must cherish the deepest consciousness of the necessity of atonement. I bless God for the gift of His Son. But while we are conscious of unworthiness, and deeply bewail our sins and iniquities, we should not forget to magnify our office, and implore the assistance of the Holy Spirit, that we may address ourselves to its duties with faithfulness and zeal. It is a great matter to understand what it is to be a preacher, and how preaching should be done. Effective sermons are the offspring of study, of discipline, of prayer, and especially of the unction of the Holy Ghost. They ought to combine the characteristic excellencies of every other species of composition intended for delivery; and ought to be pronounced, not merely with the earnestness of faith, but the constraining influence of heaven-born charity. They should be seen to come from the heart, and from the heart as filled with the love of Christ, and the love of souls. Depend upon it, that there is but little preaching in the world; and it is a mystery of grace and of Divine power that God's cause is not ruined in the world, when we consider the qualifications of many of its professed ministers to preach it. My own performances in this way fill me with disgust. I never have *made*, much less *preached*, a SERMON in my life; and I am beginning to despair of ever being able to do it. May the Lord give *you* more knowledge and grace, and singleness of purpose!

"I am glad that you were pleased with my article on the Elder question. Palmer has sent you, by Morse, a few copies of it for gratuitous distribution. The sentence which perplexes you does not seem to me to be fairly liable to the interpretation you put upon it. I do not say that all ministers, who have been lawfully called and ordained, have a right to *sit in Presbytery* ; but that they are Presbyters. At their ordination they become so, and, according to our book, the Elder's office is perpetual. They may cease *to act* as Presbyters ; but they can never cease, save by deposition, to *be* Presbyters. Whether *all* Presbyters are entitled, without regard to circumstances, to deliberate and vote in the councils of the Church, is a very different proposition. I agree with you, that the Session is the radical court in our Church ; but then, it is equally true that *all* our courts are essentially the same ; and I am not prepared to say that a seat in some existing Session is indispensable to the rightful possession of a seat in a higher judicatory. You concede the point in the case of evangelists. To say that they are *extraordinary* officers, is only to say that they belong not to the order of a settled and organized congregation, and, therefore, cannot be members of a Session ; but they can sit and preside in Presbyteries, as we know from the Acts of the Apostles and the Epistles of Paul. Hence the proposition cannot be true, that *all* ministers must be members of Presbytery in order to act as Presbyters anywhere else. A lawful ordination accomplishes two results : it makes a man a minister and elder, both in relation to the particular church which calls him, and to the *whole* Church of Christ at large. He cannot be made a minister and elder without a special designation ; but as this special designation involves a general relation, that does not cease because the other may have ceased. He may still act as a minister and elder, though not a member of any Session. But when a man is absolutely without charge, when he is neither a pastor nor evangelist, nor filling an office to which he is elected by the Church, then he refuses to *act* as a minister or elder, and ought not to be allowed to sit in Presbytery. A man, however, who has never been ordained upon a call, or as a true evangelist, is not, so far as I can see, a Presbyter at all ; and such men can sit in no court. But I have not room to enlarge. Tell McElderry that I am looking anxiously for a letter from him. Remember me very kindly to Mrs. S., and to her excellent husband, when you write to him ; as also to Boggs and his family. I want you to write something for our *Review.* It will do *you* good as well as us. Smyth completed in the coming number his dissertation upon the call to the ministry. I was much amused at his confounding my notions with the doctrine of the Quakers. Logic is evidently not his forte. Mrs. Thornwell and James Anderson send their kindest remembrances to you. As you are in the weekly receipt of your mother's newspapers, it would be presumption in me to send you a budget of news. I am glad to be exempt from the responsibility ; for, like the needy knife-grinder's story, I have none to tell, sir. I was disappointed in going to Athens. I regretted it very much ; but the condition of my family was such that I could not leave home. Palmer has the blues ; thinks he can't preach ; but he has no reason to be dissatisfied. Write soon.

"Very truly, as ever, your friend and brother,

J. H. THORNWELL."

Dr. Thornwell's warm sympathy with young men brought him into easy relations with many of this interesting class; and he embraced every fitting occasion to press upon them the claims of personal religion. The following letter affords an illustration of his method in such cases. It is addressed to Mr. Martin P. Crawford, of Lancaster District, a young relative of Mrs. Thornwell, to whom he was greatly attached, and who, while a student in College, was an inmate of his house. This young man died in April, 1862, in the hospital at Richmond, a victim of the late war; which event, though occurring but a short time before his own death, Dr. Thornwell took to heart as a sharp and personal sorrow:

"SOUTH CAROLINA COLLEGE, *April* 27, 1848.

"MY DEAR MART: You may be surprised at receiving a letter from me; but I can assure you that you are often remembered, and are the frequent subject of interest and conversation in my family circle. The favourable impression which you made upon me, while a member of my household, apart from the considerations which will readily suggest themselves to you, has caused me to feel the deepest solicitude in reference to your welfare. And when I speak of your welfare, I hope you will not understand me as alluding to your temporal prosperity, or the success of your efforts in the world. In relation to this, I have never had the least degree of concern. Your exemption from bad habits, your general manliness and independence of character, and the abundant means with which God has blessed you, are sufficient to remove all anxiety from the minds of your friends, in regard to your prospects in the present life. My solicitude extends to your future, your eternal interests; and I hope you will excuse me for suggesting a few friendly hints on a subject which your own good sense must assure you is of the highest importance. 'What is a man profited, if he should gain the whole world, and lose his own soul?' I know that you cannot be wholly unconcerned about death, judgment, and eternity. Your previous education, and the providences of God towards you, have forced these topics, to some extent, upon your mind. You are not now, for the first time, to learn that you are a sinner against God, and that the soul that sinneth, it shall die. But, my dear friend, there may be a general, a formal, and vague admission of your guilt, without any adequate conviction of the nature, the extent, or the malignity of your disease. It is not possible that a finite understanding can fully comprehend the exceeding sinfulness of sin. It pervades the whole mind, darkens the understanding, pollutes the affections, perverts the will, and enslaves the soul to the lusts of the flesh and the dominion of

the world. It is born with us; grows with our growth, and strengthens
with our strength; and so utterly alienates the heart from God, that we
can never be fit for his service, without experiencing a new and spiritual
birth. I hope that you will pray to God to impart to you His Spirit, in
order that you may be led to see and to feel something of the horrors of
your true condition as a sinner against Him. The whole revelation you
could not bear; but I do not wish you to be satisfied with vague and
general admissions. I wish you to be persuaded of the real extent and
loathesomeness of the abominations that fill the chambers of imagery in
that most hateful object, a natural heart. The core of the evil is to be
found in its *ungodliness*. God is not in all its thoughts. The sinner
lives just as he would live if there were no God at all. He feels not his
obligation to serve and to glorify that Being, in whom he lives, and
moves, and has his being. This is enough to make all God's creatures
conspire against him. Now, my dear Mart, you may be free from vice;
you may be moral, and honourable, and consistent in your deportment;
you may be an affectionate son, a faithful friend, and an upright citizen;
but still, with all these virtues, which none more cheerfully and gladly
concedes to you than I do, you are, by nature, a sinner against God; or,
as the Apostle expresses it, without God, without Christ, without hope,
in the world. This is your case, the case of every unconverted man;
and it is a case of unspeakable danger. God will by no means clear the
guilty. His wrath is revealed from heaven against all ungodliness and
unrighteousness of men; and no impenitent transgressor shall be permitted to escape.

" These solemn and momentous truths I hope you will seriously and
prayerfully ponder. They will lead you, under the blessing of the
Holy Ghost, to apprehend your need of a Saviour. They will not *fit* you
for the Saviour, but they will convince you how urgent is your case.
They will not of themselves make you any better; they cannot change
your heart; but they may be the means of conducting you to Him who
can abundantly pardon, and cleanse you from all unrighteousness. Jesus
Christ is our only hope. We must trust in Him, or perish. God reveals and proclaims Him to you, and to all men, as a Saviour; and He
has made it your duty to entrust your soul into His hands. The blood
of Jesus can purge the guiltiest conscience, and the spirit of Jesus can
change the hardest heart. He is not only able to save; He is as willing
as He is able. He is our brother in the flesh. He has a heart to sympathize with us in our troubles and distresses. We can go to Him in all
our guilt and filthiness, with our hearts as millstones, and our minds as
dark as night; and He will cheerfully receive us, give us beauty for
ashes, the oil of joy for sorrow, and the garment of praise for the spirit
of heaviness. But you may complain that you *would*, but *cannot*, believe.
It is true, faith is not in the power of nature; but it is your duty to
·pray God to bestow it upon you, to enlighten your mind, so that you may
see the glory of Christ, and to renew your heart, so that you may feel
His unspeakable preciousness. You may complain of the hardness of

your heart, and lament that you cannot repent of sin ; that you cannot feel as you desire. It is true, the natural heart *is* hard as the nether millstone ; but Christ does not require you to come with a soft heart. He *gives* you repentance. You are to go to Him simply as a *sinner*, and cast yourself upon God's mercy through Him. That is your only plea. You may be tempted to delay until you have made yourself better, but this is a suggestion of the devil.

"Let me urge upon you to be much engaged in the prayerful study of the Scriptures. Be not ashamed to *ask* God, and to depend upon God to enable you to understand them. It would be well, too, to read books on experimental religion, such as 'Boston's Fourfold State,' 'Halyburton's Great Concern,' and 'Doddridge's Rise and Progress.' Be very careful not to resist any light that you may have. Grieve not the Spirit. Guard against the spirit of procrastination and delay. Seek the Lord with your whole heart, and seek Him diligently. These few hints I have hastily and rapidly thrown out, from a sincere desire to promote the best and the highest interest of one whom I have long regarded as a devoted friend. I shall not cease to pray for your salvation ; and if, when I see you again, you shall have been enabled to make your calling and election sure, it will be a matter of unspeakable joy to me. I shall always be more than glad to hear from you.

"As ever, your sincere friend,

J. H. THORNWELL."

It forms a happy sequel to this letter, to mention that the subject of so much religious solicitude not only became a member of the visible Church, but filled the office of a ruler ; adding the graces of the Spirit to natural qualities as generous and noble as ever formed the character of a virtuous man.

Whilst recording these instances of private friendship, it will be appropriate to state, that Dr. Thornwell amply repaid to others the benefits which, in his own youth, had been lavished upon himself. Throughout his connexion with the College, he was rarely without a beneficiary on his hands, whom he graciously assisted in obtaining a liberal education. Naturally this charity was extended to those of his own blood ; and in the different branches of his family circle, there were those, more or less related to him, whose necessities justified this call upon his liberality. We are not disposed to lift the veil over these. It was not, however, confined to them. We may be permitted, at least, to record his kindness to one, the younger brother of his intimate friend, the Rev. Pierpont E. Bishop, whom he partially sustained, whilst laying in College the foundation of that scholarship which he purposed to use to God's glory, in the ministry of His Son. It was the Divine pleasure to call him to a higher service, in the kingdom which is above. In his senior year, within a month of graduation, when the highest honours of his class had been already decreed to him, he was removed by death. During a tedious and wasting illness from typhus fever, he was tenderly nursed, as though he had been a brother, in Dr. Thornwell's house; and after death, honourable mention of his virtues was made, in an elegant Latin epitaph upon his tomb, erected by his fellow students, in the Presbyterian grave-yard, at Columbia.

The letters which follow will introduce to the reader another, whose grateful heart looks up to Dr. Thornwell as a spiritual father; who, under the stimulus of his favour, broke off from mercantile life, in order to devote himself to the ministry of reconciliation. Many years of faithful labour have separated him from the time, when he first entered upon the severe novitiate which was necessary, to prepare him for the work he still lives to pursue; but during all those years of patient study, he was aided by the counsel and friendship which breathe themselves into these lines:

"SOUTH CAROLINA COLLEGE, *February* 2, 1847.

"MY DEAR MORSE: Though you may think that I ought to begin my letter with apologies and excuses, yet I shall just throw myself upon your generosity at once, presuming that your knowledge of me will suggest to your own mind the true reason of my not having written before.

"We have just had a sad visitation in the death of M——, whom you may know to have been one of the most promising members of the Senior Class. He died of typhus fever. The event came unexpectedly upon us. We all thought that he was getting well, when his disease took a sudden turn, and carried him off in a few hours. I am unable to speak with any confidence of his religious condition. His mind had been seriously turned to the contemplation of the one thing needful, and there were some things about his case that were encouraging. It is enough to know that he is in the hands of God.

"The thing which presses upon me, is the condition of those he has left behind, his class-mates and companions. It is my earnest and constant prayer, that God may sanctify this visitation to the spiritual good of the College. I hope that you do not cease to pray for us. We need the prayers of all God's children. My anxiety in regard to the religious condition of the College has, for some time back, been a heavy burden to my spirits. All things externally are going on well. I have never known such admirable order, quiet, and regularity. Our large Sophomore Class is unusually promising and well-behaved; but in the midst of our numbers, few are professedly pious. The thought that so many young men of promise should be without God in the world is almost too much for me. Oh! that God would pour out His Spirit upon us! I have had a sort of secret hope that the death of M—— may be designed, in the good providence of God, to prove a spiritual blessing. I have been in hopes that He meant it for good; and, though I cannot state my reasons, the impression exists, and has somewhat strengthened my hands. I shall preach a sermon in reference to this matter, next Sunday.

"Dr. F—— is also lying very low. There is *little*, if *any*, hope of his recovery. He himself expects to die. I trust that he is prepared. His religious exercises have been very strong and marked. My conversations with him have been refreshing to my own soul. His family is most sadly distressed; and his death, if it should take place, will be seriously felt.

"Ah me! what is life? Take away the hopes of a blessed immortality, and what wise man would desire to live? My dear friend, live for eternity. It is a matter of very little consequence whether you spend your time here in rags or a palace. We shall soon be gone; then comes our DESTINY, and for that we should strive to be prepared. May God give you grace to be supremely devoted to His cause; for that is the only wisdom. My chief regrets, in looking upon the past, are occasioned by the feebleness, the sinfulness, the slothfulness of my spiritual labours. You cannot learn too soon, nor too well. Oh! that I knew the lesson better, that *self-denial*, amounting to the crucifixion of the flesh, is indispensable to the enjoyment of religious peace and comfort! Deny thyself, and take thy cross; this is our vocation. What have we to do with worldly ease and carnal indulgences, when heaven is before us, and Christ is waiting to receive us? What signify crosses and privations, when we are looking for a far more exceeding and eternal weight of glory? I want you to read McCheyne's Life, published by our Board. I cannot tell you how much use that little book has been of to me. Read it, and pray over it; and may God bless it to your soul, as, I hope, He has done to mine. Let me hear from you soon.

"Very truly, as ever,

J. H. THORNWELL."

To the same:

"SOUTH CAROLINA COLLEGE, *April* 6, 1848.

"MY DEAR MORSE: If I have not written to you before, it has not been from any want of interest in your affairs. But the incurable habit of procrastination, and my violent repugnance to the use of the pen, compel me to draw largely on the patience and forbearance of my friends. I have again and again resolved to write to you, and again and again been diverted from my purpose.

"I do not know that I can give you any material assistance in the direction of your studies. Witsius is a standard work. It would be well to read, in connection with him, Boston on the Covenants; though the two books are not to be compared in point of learning, scholarship, and general ability. But Boston was eminently imbued with the spirit of the gospel. On Church government, there are few valuable works defending our views that are accessible. On many accounts, it would be well to read the great work of Hooker, on Ecclesiastical Polity; it contains the best defence of Episcopacy that has been written. Owen's works on Church government are also truly valuable. But I consider nothing necessary to licensure, in this department, but the principles embodied in our standards. The extended study of the Congregational and Prelatical schemes will be the work of future years. In Church history, Milner and Mosheim will be sufficient for the present. But I would earnestly inculcate the systematic study of the Bible. Take up book by book, and endeavour to master it, to digest its contents into order, and to have a general scheme of it in your mind. Study the age of each writer, his peculiarities; and in this way you will make satisfactory progress in Biblical criticism. Gray's Key to the Old Testament will be a great help. Horne's Introduction will also assist you. But much depends upon yourself.

"You must exercise your own judgment, in prayerful dependence upon God, in the interpretation of the Scriptures. I hardly know what general commentary to recommend. *All* will aid you, and *none* can be fully trusted. 'Poole's Synopsis' has some advantages, as presenting the views of a multitude of critics, which Scott, Henry, Whitby, Lowth, etc., do not possess; but you can hardly get access to it in the country. Real progress, however, can be made without a multitude of books. Compare the Bible with itself; and you will be surprised to find how one part throws light upon another. I trust that the author of the Bible may be your great teacher.

"You will find it interesting, to study the Confessions and Apologies of the Reformed Churches. This will show you the substantial unity of faith that has prevailed among God's people; and these Confessions are, besides, most valuable compends of theology. The 'Corpus et Syntagma,' etc., and 'Niemeyer's Collectio,' will be sufficient for your purpose. But I will not trouble you with any further hints. Your studies must depend much upon your opportunities.

"My family are as usual. Patty has begun to go to school, and is perfectly delighted. The General* would like to go, but we think him too small. He has a bright notion of shaving, and getting him a wife. James Henley is flourishing; though he and his mother, just now, are on cross-questions touching the matter of his waking up after midnight and eating a big supper. She wishes to break him of the habit; but he demurs against her purpose, as a cruel proceeding. The baby promises to be a man, but he continues to be anonymous. Write to me soon.

"Very truly, as ever,

J. H. THORNWELL."

To the same:

"SOUTH CAROLINA COLLEGE, *February* 22, 1849.

"MY DEAR MORSE: Don't be scared at this small paper; it is very nearly as large as yours, and I can put more in it than you did in yours. I hope—indeed, I have no doubt—that you will pass your trials successfully; and then you will feel as you never felt before. Responsibility contemplated at a distance, is very different from the sense of it actually pressing on the soul. You will often be compelled to exclaim, Who is sufficient for these things? and in your ignorance, dulness, coldness, and incompetency, you will find no retreat but a throne of grace, and the promises of an all-sufficient God. That you may be eminently useful, is my fervent prayer. I can give you no aid in regard to a field of labour. The churches mentioned by Brother Bishop are very feeble; and I can say nothing of the extent of the field they will open to you. You must go and see for yourself.

"The affairs of the College are getting on as usual. The new Professor has arrived, and is giving entire satisfaction. I have seen but little of him yet, but my impression is favourable. Preston is in a very precarious state. His friends entertain doubts as to the possibility of his entire recovery. He may be restored to such an extent as to perform the physical conditions of life; but it is apprehended that he will never be himself again. I hope that these forebodings may not prove true, but I cannot say how well or ill-founded they are. I trust that his affliction may be truly sanctified; and that he may be made a partaker of what is better than intellect, eloquence, or fame.

"The next number of the *Review* will contain some of my cogitations, which, as usual, do not amount to much, always excepting the article on the Elder question. What do you think? I actually went to hear Wilson sing his Scotch songs. I attended his concerts two nights, and would probably have gone the third, if it had not been Saturday, and funds rather low. It was, indeed, a treat; and I begin to think that, after all, I really have some music in my soul. The Major was still more delighted than myself. He even ventured out on Saturday night, and I am afraid thought about it on Sunday. * * *

"You must come and see us upon your journey to or from Presbytery.

"Very truly, as ever,

J. H. THORNWELL."

* A little boy of four years of age, named after General Gillespie.

CHAPTER XXIII.

STATE EDUCATION.

DR. THORNWELL'S connection with the South Carolina College almost compelled him to become the advocate of State education. We do not mean, of course, that
his opinions were determined by that fact, for no man ever
lived whose convictions were founded less upon accidental associations of any sort; but simply that the subject
had a deeper interest to him in that position, and that a
degree of necessity was put upon him to stand forth as a
champion on this side of the controversy, then pending in
the country. He unquestionably took a wide view of the
prerogatives and responsibility of the State; and, perhaps,
fully coincided with his favourite, Aristotle, in the aphor-
ism, πόλις γινόμενη μέν τοῦ ζῆν ἕνεκεν, οὖσα δέ τοῦ εὖ ζῆν.
Among the highest obligations of the State he reckoned
this, of providing for the education of her sons.

His sentiments, too, in relation to the Church, forbade
his subscribing to the opposite doctrine, which places
secular education among the positive duties she is called
to fulfil. On the contrary, all the controversies in which
he had been engaged turned upon the assertion, that she
was a purely spiritual body, instituted for exclusively
spiritual ends, and limited in her authority by the express
law of her King and Head, which she might not transcend in a singular particular. According to his strict

construction of her charter, her duty terminates with the religious training of mankind. The sanctuary is her class-room; the pulpit her chair; and the gospel of Jesus, her discipline. It is not the historian's province to arbitrate in such a controversy; but only to set forth the opinions held by the subject of his story. He found able critics upon either hand: those who upheld, in this matter, the prerogative of the Church; and those who as stoutly denied his postulate touching the duty of the State.

The impression has been created in some quarters that upon this, as well as upon some other ecclesiastical questions, Dr. Thornwell's opinions were somewhat modified in the later years of his life. A highly-esteemed minister has expressed a hint of this sort to the writer of these pages, adding, with a tone of regret: "And yet I consider his defence of the position, that the Church is simply and nakedly a witness for the truth of God, as revealed in His Word, as the most important service rendered by him to the Church, in the department of ecclesiasticism."

We more than suspect this misapprehension to have its origin in two sources. Dr. Thornwell was never factious in his opposition to views prevalent in the Church. Intense and clear as his own convictions to the contrary might be, this very confidence in the truth he maintained, enabled him to bide God's time, and to wait for their recognition and acknowledgment in the future. Above all men whom it has been our privilege to know, Dr. Thornwell possessed a sublime faith in the majesty and power of truth; assured that, though buried for a time, it will rise again, and assert its own supremacy in the world. Hence, after a fair effort to win the Church over to the adoption of his views, if defeated, he submitted, with meekness and grace, to what he yet sadly deplored. He did not surrender his own convictions; but wisely abstained from a hurtful and useless agitation, until the time should arrive for promulgating them anew. Thus, after a full discussion on the subject of Boards, he was silent for many years, until it was brought up anew, in the Assembly of 1860, at Rochester. And it is remark- able, that the last great debate in which he participated in the old Assembly, should have been the first in which he fleshed his sword after the disruption in 1837. The reader will have occasion, too, to see that one of the closing acts of his public life, was to ingraft his views on this question upon the policy of the Southern Presby- terian Church, in her first General Assembly, in 1861. This, then, could not have been one of the subjects upon which his mind had changed. In regard to the Elder- ship, this question went down so completely into the heart and essence of the Presbyterian system, that no one who knew the man could believe that he changed his views upon it, without a square and open retraction of his pre- vious error.

Another feature of Dr. Thornwell's character, out of which this suspicion may have sprung, was his passionate attachment to his friends; which led him to yield, as far as was possible consistently with a good conscience, active opposition to their cherished plans. And this complai- sance, which was only the sign of a gentle and loving nature, may have been construed, at times, as an assent of his judgment.

But whatever be the origin of the charge, we have not the least evidence of its truth; and upon the topic now before us, the writer is able to set it aside by his personal testimony; at least, if Dr. Thornwell's opinions were al- tered upon the relation of the Church to secular education, the change must have occurred during the last six months of his life. Dr. Thornwell died in the month of August, 1862. The writer's last personal intercourse with him was in December, 1861, at the organization, and during the sessions, of the first General Assembly of the South- ern Presbyterian Church, at Augusta, Georgia. The pro- ject of establishing a great University, which should be

common to Presbyterians throughout what was then
known as "the Confederate States," had been lying in
the minds of some. A public meeting was held, entirely
outside of and distinct from the Assembly, to discuss the
desirableness and feasibility of this project. This meeting
was addressed by Dr. Thornwell, amongst others, in advocacy of the proposed measure. At this stage, nothing
was under discussion, but the general idea of an institution
which should be worthy of, and should command, Presbyterian patronage throughout the country. The details
of its management and control had not yet been reached,
and, through the pressure of the civil war, then in progress, were never reached. In private conversation, when
solicited by the writer to lend his countenance and assistance to the scheme, Dr. Thornwell replied, that he would
do so cordially, provided it were not made a Church institution, organized and controlled by the Church, through
her courts. He thought a University might be created
by the Presbyterian people of the land, which should be
penetrated by their influence and piety, without contra-
vening the principle, for which he had always contended,
that the Church, as such, should not embark in the business of general education. At that time he had not re-
siled from his original position on this subject; but, on the
contrary, he explicitly re-affirmed it, not considering the
principle on which it was based as open to any question.
Indeed, his opinions, on all public and disputed topics,
were formed with singular caution, and were never pronounced without antecedent investigation. They were
not prejudices, but convictions; and, being slowly matured, were not subject to fluctuation and change. The
reader will discover marks of this caution in the letter
that follows, written as early as 1846, to his friend, Dr.
R. J. Breckinridge:

"My mind has been much turned of late to the subject of State
schools and State colleges. From some remarks of yours, in the General Assembly, I perceive that you have been reflecting upon the same

subject. The difficulty is, to introduce into them the principles of evangelical religion. There are two questions: 1. Whether it is the business of a school to teach religion; or whether that duty devolves upon the parent, catechist, or pastor. If schools are merely *secular* institutions, intended to communicate *secular* knowledge, the problem about the introduction of religion is easily solved. 2. Supposing, however, that schools have a higher object, the formation of character, as well as the discipline and cultivation of mind, religion must enter as an element. But by what *authority* does the *State* introduce it? Is not the State an institution founded essentially upon the relations of justice betwixt man and man? No doubt, if it has a right to introduce religion at all, it is bound to introduce the *true* religion; but the opinions of the magistrate are a poor security for the permanent introduction of an evangelical faith. My mind, however, labours on the question of *right*. Religion may be introduced as a matter of *science*, a thing that ought to be *known;* but as a living power, a system of Divine grace, what has the State, as such, to do with it? I know that you have reflected much on these things, and I should like to have your matured opinions. The complexion of the age must be largely determined by the part which our Church shall take in regard to these questions. What we do, should, therefore, be done with great prudence, deliberation, and caution. My mind has rather leaned to the side of State education, but I have difficulties. Let me hear from you soon; and do not omit to say distinctly, whether, in case of the failure of your health, you will consent to become a South Carolinian. The Lord bless you and keep you.

"Your sincere friend and brother,

J. H. THORNWELL."

A little later, his scruples appear to have been resolved, and his opposition to Church schools becomes more pronounced; as will be seen from the letter below, also addressed to Dr. Breckinridge:

"SOUTH CAROLINA COLLEGE, *February* 24, 1849.

"MY DEAR BROTHER: One good turn deserves another. Your article, in the last number of the *Southern Presbyterian Review,* has done us so much credit, that I am constrained to apply to you again. There is one subject particularly, on which I want you to put out your strength; and now is the time, or never. That subject is, the System of Denominational Education, which the Assembly is endeavouring to set agoing. We shall have a disputation from Dr. Smyth, on Parochial Schools, in our next issue. I objected to its insertion; but finally consented, upon condition of entering a protest against it. But the ceaseless declamation which is poured upon the Church, from all quarters, will have its effect, unless some competent man will take the subject up, and discuss it on its merits. Now, *you* are the man to do it. An article from you on this topic, at this juncture, will be read with profound interest, and will do great good. Your studies and inquiries have recently been exactly of the character which fit you for the task; and I think you owe it to the Church to give her the matured result of your reflections and experience, when so many are dosing her with speculations, conjectures, and visionary schemes. I sincerely hope, therefore, that you will not say 'Nay' to this request.

"Have you seen the *New England Puritan?* It evidently winces under your article in our last number.

"Brownson has at last fulfilled his promise, to review my book on the Apocrypha. He has devoted three articles to my benefit, in the April, July, and October numbers of his *Quarterly.* His pieces I regard as very feeble; but am not resolved in my own mind as to the best course to be pursued. My disposition is to answer him; but if I notice every reviewer who may take me in hand, I may make business enough for myself to occupy my whole time. If I do not answer him, the Papists may crow, and pretend that they have gained a triumph. It would, no doubt, be more seemly for some other person besides myself to take up Brownson. But I know of no one who can do it, but you; and it is a task which I could not expect from you, in the midst of more important and pressing engagements. Then, again, any reply would be addressed to readers, for the most part, who never saw or read the *Review.* The only point gained, would be stopping their mouths, who might represent silence on my part as a confession of defeat. What do you think I ought to do?

"Our College is quite flourishing as to numbers. We have two hun- and thirty students. Preston's name has been a word to conjure with. The institution has risen, as if by magic, under his influence and exertions. But I am very much afraid the charm is soon, too soon, to be broken. He has been, for six or eight weeks, in a precarious condition; and his physicians seem to think that, if he ever recovers at all, it will be a work of time, and of great care; and the utmost he can recover, will be some portion of his physical strength. He can never, under any circumstances, be himself again. I do not know exactly how to describe his disease. He was taken first with influenza, which at the time was prevailing here as an epidemic. It brought him to a state very closely approximating paralysis. His brain became affected, his mind very much enfeebled, and his speech became thick and indistinct, his pulse was as low as thirty beats a minute. His tongue was as black as tar, and his nervous system seemed to be exhausted. He was kept up by strong and oft-repeated stimulants. As soon as he could ride, he went, by slow stages, to Charleston, where he is at present; and I learn, from a letter received here last night, that the physicians there think very gloomily of his case. It is a mournful visitation of Providence; it has caused me many sad reflections. Learning, genius, and eloquence are feeble things to depend on. Without a Saviour, what shadows we are, and what shadows we pursue. I trust that he has been brought to feel and see the importance of an interest in Christ. His mind, I know, has been very seriously turned to the subject. If he should be compelled to leave the College, I shall have but little inducement to stay here. I have endured the bondage long enough already; and if the society be taken from me, which alone has rendered it tolerable, I shall be strongly tempted to seek a field for the exercise of my ministry, less exhausting, and more congenial with my feelings.

"Let me hear from you soon, very soon; and be sure to send me an article on Parochial Schools, or Denominational Education.

"Very sincerely, as ever,

J. H. T."

The book on the Apocrapha, to which reference is made in this letter, was the re-publication, in a more permanent form, of the articles written in the controversy with Dr. Lynch, of Charleston. The volume was brought out in 1845, and elicited from the *Edinburgh Review* the high eulogium that it was worthy of a comparison with Chillingworth. Dr. Breckinridge's reply gave the promise of a review of Brownson's attack upon it, as well as of an article on Denominational Education. It reads thus:

"LEXINGTON, KY., *March* 16, 1849.

"MY DEAR THORNWELL: Your letter of 24th ult. was long on the way. It has only been received within a few days. I will endeavour to comply with your request in regard to the article on Denominational Education. If I am not mistaken, your periodical appears this month. If you prefer the matter for the June number, and will let me know the fact by immediate reply—I believe I had better promise it at once, lest, by delay, my mind pass away from the subject, and other things engross me. At any rate, I believe I will just write out my thoughts, and send them to you at once.

"As to the other matter, the review of Brownson's article on your work, if you will trust that matter to me, I will undertake it with pleasure. But you must do several things: 1. Send his articles; I have never seen them. 2. Send me, from your pen, such matter, the more the better, as you would like worked into the review of him. 3. Send me such criticisms, or denials of his quotations, and references to authority, and such quotations and references to support your own, as may be needful; for my own library is still in boxes.

"I will be extremely obliged, if you will send by some one to the General Assembly, a bundle of your articles on the Elder and Ordination questions. I never had more reason to thank any friend than you, for those articles, on every account, public and private.

I have been very much of an invalid for some months past, and in a peculiar and very distressing way. For a long time I have occasionally suffered greatly, after preaching too much; but how or why, seemed uncertain; that is, everything but the suffering was obscure. For many months past, the malady became gradually more concentrated, in a sort of spasm of the whole contents of the chest, or some of the more vital of them, after violent speaking; and these attacks, increasing in frequency and violence, are beginning to assume a very serious aspect. I await calmly the indications of Providence; in the meantime, doing the best I can, and confidently committing all to God. May God bless and keep you, is the prayer of

"Your attached friend,

Ro. J. Breckinridge."

The promised contribution to the *Southern Presbyterian Review*, on the subject of Church schools, was duly made, and published in the July number of 1849. It is thus acknowledged:

"South Carolina College, *May* 18, 1849.

"My Dear Brother: Your very able and satisfactory article on Denominational Education has been received, and will appear as the leader, in our next number. The printer has tormented us very much in regard to our last number; so much so that we have taken the work out of his hands, and have made a contract with another man, which, we think, will insure punctuality. I have communicated to Preston the substance of your article; and he not only cordially approves of it, but is very much gratified that such views are about to be printed. He takes great interest in the whole subject; and as your opinions are the ones entertained by the leading men of this State, their publication, at this time, will be productive of much good. Such discussions as those which we have already had, can settle nothing. They either prove too much, and, therefore, prove nothing, or they are directed to a wrong point. No one doubts the importance of religion as an element in education, and no one doubts that the Church is a witness to God's truth. But that her commission to teach the gospel includes a commission to teach reading, writing, and ciphering, is not so plain. In other words, that a commission to teach *one* thing is a commission to teach *every* thing, is, to say the least of it, not self-evident. And yet, this is about the substance of the arguments of Drs. Junkin and Smyth. It never seems to have struck them, that their method of reasoning might be just as successfully employed to divest the Church of all power of rule, as it has been to divest the State of all right to teach. They say, for example, that a commission granted to the Church to teach at all, includes every department of instruction, and excludes the State from any participation. Upon the same principle, a commission to the State to rule at all, includes every kind of government, and excludes the Church from the possession of any kind of authority. I shall append to our next number a critical notice of Dr. Junkin's inaugural oration, which, together with your article, will put before the Churches the precise position of those who are not prepared to swallow down the scheme of the Board of Education.

"As soon as I can procure them, I shall send you Brownson's articles in review of my book; and then leave it to your judgment whether they should be answered or not. They require no learning; it is simply moral reasoning, the application of logic, and that alone. He has exposed himself to serious attacks on the whole subject of the relation of Church to State; and to expose the tendencies of Romanism on this head, has been my strongest inducement for thinking he ought to be noticed at all. His articles, in my judgment, are deplorably feeble. But if you take him in hand, he will furnish you a text for disclosures which, if our country will heed them, will save our children much trouble.

" I sent you, by our commissioner, one hundred copies of my article on the Elder question. We have still a large number, which we would cheerfully mail to any addresses you might recommend. I have never had a firmer confidence in the ultimate triumph of any cause, than in the final success of the doctrines which it is the object of that article to maintain. Even Princeton is beginning to discover that a Presbyter, *as such*, is a ruler.

"Preston's health is still very feeble. The Board of Trustees have given him a dispensation from all his duties until the 1st October. He leaves early next week, for Glenn Springs, in this State, and will spend the time in travelling about from place to place. I am seriously apprehensive that he never will be himself again. The only hope is the absolute relaxation which he has resolved to try. I do not think that he has been made aware of the precise opinion of his physicians in regard to his case;, but Mrs. Preston informs me, that they have given her very little reason to hope that he can ever be restored. Her mind is greatly distressed, though she endeavours to conceal her anxiety from him. He looks well, possesses apparent physical vigour, and, for a short time, enters into conversation with spirit; but he soon becomes utterly exhausted in mind and body. His whole system is toneless. It is a painful spectacle to see such a man a mere wreck. He was much gratified with your letter. I have been strongly and tenderly attached to him, and have done all in my power to soothe and comfort him in this deep affliction.

"I cannot close this letter without expressing to you my warmest thanks for the promptness with which you have offered to assist me in the case of Brownson. Your expressions of kindness touched me very deeply; and I had rather see him in your hands than the hands of any other man in the Union. His articles are *nothing;* but the subject is important. And my mind is so utterly undetermined as to the course that ought to be pursued, that I must leave the matter entirely to *you;*

pledging myself, if a general war should ensue, to stand by you to the last. May God bless you and keep you, is the sincere prayer of
         " Your devoted friend,
                       J. H. THORNWELL."

The reader who desires to peruse at length Dr. Thornwell's opinions on this important subject of education, as controlled by the Church, will find them presented in a published letter to Governor Manning, of South Carolina, written in 1853, whilst he was President of the College. The topic, it is true, is only incidentally introduced, as a branch of the general argument that the State is properly charged with the higher education of its citizens, and to repel the assumption that religious instruction cannot be adequately conveyed in institutions which are supported from the public treasury. This elaborate paper will be found in the fifth volume of his "Collected Writings." But, as it may not fall into the hands of all who read these pages, and since this subject is interwoven with his whole personal history, we append a few extracts, for the purpose of defining his position in his own language:

" The true and only question is, Does education belong to the Church or State? Into the hands of one or the other it must fall, or perish. This, too, is the great practical question among us. The most formidable war against the College will be that waged on the principle of its existence. I respect the feeling out of which the jealousy of State institutions has grown. A godless education is worse than none; and I rejoice that the sentiment is well nigh universal in this country, that a system which excludes the highest and most commanding, the eternal interests of man, must be radically defective, whether reference be had to the culture of the individual, or to his prosperity and influence in life. Man is essentially a religious being; and to make no provision for this noblest element of his nature, to ignore and preclude it from any distinct consideration, is to leave him but half educated. The ancients were accustomed to regard theology as the first philosophy; and there is not a people under the sun whose religion has not been the chief inspiration of their literature. Take away the influence which this subject has exerted upon the human mind, destroy its contributions to the cause of letters, the impulse it has given to the speculations of philosophy,—and what will be left, after these subtractions, will be comparatively small in quantity, and feeble in life and spirit. We must have religion, if we would reach the highest forms of education. This is the atmosphere which must surround the mind and permeate all its activities, in order that its development may be free, healthful, and vigorous. Science languishes, letters pine, refinement is lost, wherever and whenever the genius of religion is excluded. Experience has demonstrated that, in some form or other, it must enter into every College, and pervade every department of instruction. No institution has been able to live without it. But what right, it is asked, has the State to introduce it? What right, we might ask in return, has the State to exclude it? The difficulty lies in confounding the dogmatic peculiarities of sects with the spirit of religion. The State as such, knows nothing of sects, but to protect them; but it does not follow that the State must be necessarily godless. And so a College knows nothing of denominations, except as a feature in the history of the human race; but it does not follow that a College must be necessarily atheistic or unchristian. What is wanted is the pervading influence of religion as a life; the habitual sense of responsibility to God, and of the true worth and destiny of the soul; which shall give tone to the character, and regulate all the pursuits of the place. The example, temper, and habitual deportment of the teachers, co-operating with the dogmatic instructions which have been received at the fireside and in the church, and coupled with the obligatory observance (except in cases of conscientious scruple) of the peculiar duties of the Lord's day, will be found to do more in maintaining the power of religion, than the constant recitation of the Catechism, or the ceaseless inculcation of sectarian peculiarities. The difficulty of introducing religion is, indeed, rather speculative than practical. When we propose to teach religion as a science, and undertake, by precise boundaries and exact statutory provisions, to define what shall, and what shall not, be taught; when, by written schemes, we endeavour to avoid all the peculiarities of sect, without sacrificing the essential interests of religion; the task is impossible. The *residuum*, after our nice distinctions, is zero. But why introduce religion *as a science?* Let it come in the character of the Professors; let it come in the stated worship of the sanctuary; and let it come in the vindication of those immortal records which constitute the basis of our faith.

"Leave Creeds and Confessions to the fireside and the church, the home and the pulpit. Have godly teachers, and you will have comparatively a godly College. But what security have we that a State College will pay any attention to the religious character of its teachers? The security of public opinion, which, in proportion as the various religious denominations do their duty in their own spheres, will become absolutely irresistible. Let all the sects combine to support the State College, and they can soon create a sentiment which, with the terrible certainty of fate, shall tolerate nothing unholy or unclean within its walls. They can make it religious, without being sectarian. The true power of the Church over these institutions is not that of direct work upon the hearts and consciences of all the members of the community. Is it alleged

that experience presents us with mournful examples of State institutions
degenerating into hot-beds of atheism and impiety? It may be promptly
replied, that the same experience presents us with equally mournful examples of Church institutions degenerating into hot-beds of the vilest
heresy and infidelity. And, what is more to the point, a sound public
opinion has never failed to bring these State institutions back to their
proper moorings, while the Church institutions have not unfrequently
carried their sects with them, and rendered reform impossible. In the
case of State institutions, the security for religion lies in the public
opinion of the whole community; in the case of Church institutions,
in the public opinion of a single denomination. And as the smaller
body can more easily become corrupt than a larger; as there is a constant play of antagonism, which preserves the health, in the one case,
while they are wanting in the other; it seems clear, that a State College,
upon the whole, and in the long run, must be safer than any sectarian
institution. As long as people preserve their respect for religion, the
College can be kept free from danger.

"The principle, too, on which the argument for Church supervision
is founded, proves too much. It is assumed that, wherever a religious
influence becomes a matter of primary importance, there the Church has
legitimate jurisdiction. 'This,' it has been well said, 'puts an end to
society itself, and makes the Church the only power that can exist; since
all that is necessary is, for any officer, or any power, to be capable of
moral effects or influences, in order to put it under the dominion of the
Church. The moral influence of governors, judges, presidents—nay,
even sheriffs, coroners, or constables—is as real, and may be far more
extensive, than that of schoolmasters. The moral influence of wealth is
immense; that of domestic habits, nay, even personal habits, often decisive.'* The truth is, this species of argument would reduce every
interest under the sun to the control of the Church. It is just the principle on which the authority of the Pope over kings and states has been
assumed and defended. The argument, moreover, is one which can very
easily be retorted. If, because education has a religious element, it must
fall within the jurisdiction of the Church; a fortiori, because it has multiplied secular elements, it must fall within the jurisdiction of the State.
The Church is a distinct corporation, with distinct rights and authority.
She has direct control over nothing that is not spiritual in its matter, and
connected with our relations to Jesus Christ. She is His kingdom; and
her functions are limited to His work, as the Mediator of the Covenant,
and the Saviour of the lost. And if education, in its secular aspects, is
not a function of grace, but nature; if it belongs to man, not as a Christian, but simply as a man; then it no more falls within the jurisdiction
of the Church than any other secular work. * * * *

"Apart from the principle involved, I have other objections to sec-

* Dr. Breckinridge, in *Southern Presbyterian Review*, vol. 3, p. 6.

tarian education. I say, sectarian education; for the Church, as catholic and one, in the present condition of things, is not visible and corporate. What she does, can only be done through the agency of one or more of the various fragments into which she has been suffered to split. In the first place, it is evident, from the feebleness of the sects, that these colleges cannot be very largely endowed. In the next place, they are likely to be numerous. From these causes will result a strenuous competition for patronage; and, from this, two effects may be expected to follow: first, the depression of the general standard of education, so as to allure students to their halls; and next, the preference of what is ostentatious and attractive in education, to what is solid and substantial. It is true, that there can be no lofty flight, as Bacon has suggested, 'without some feathers of ostentation;' but it is equally true, that there can be no flight at all, where there are not bone, muscle, and sinew, to sustain the feathers.

"It is also a serious evil that the State should be habitually denounced as profane and infidel. To think and speak of it in that light, is the sure way to make it so; and yet this is the uniform representation of the advocates of Church education. They will not permit the State to touch the subject, because its fingers are unclean. Can there be a more certain method to uproot the sentiments of patriotism, and to make us feel that the government of the country is an enormous evil, to which we are to submit, not out of love, but for conscience sake? Will not something like this be the inevitable effect of the declamation and invective, which bigots and zealots feel authorized to vent against the Commonwealth that protects them, in order that they may succeed in their narrow schemes? Instead of clinging around the State, as they would cling to the bosom of a beloved parent, and concentrating upon her the highest and holiest influences which they are capable of exerting; instead of teaching their children to love her, as the ordinance of God for good, to bless her for her manifold benefits, and to obey her with even a religious veneration; they repel her to a cold and cheerless distance, and brand her with the stigma of Divine reprobation. The result must be bad. "The fanaticism which despises the State, and the infidelity which contemns the Church, are both alike the product of ignorance and folly. God has established both the State and the Church. It is as clearly our duty to be loyal and enlightened citizens, as to be faithful and earnest Christians."

I think, too, that the tendency of sectarian Colleges, to perpetuate the strife of sects, to fix whatever is heterogeneous in the elements of national character, and to alienate the citizens from each other, is a consideration not to be overlooked. There ought surely to be some common ground on which the members of the same State may meet together, and feel that they are brethren; some common ground on which their children may mingle without confusion or discord, and bury every narrow and selfish interest in the sublime sentiment, that they belong to the same family. Nothing is so powerful as a common education, and the thousand sweet associations which spring from it, and cluster around it, to cherish the holy brotherhood of men. Those who have walked together in the same paths of science, and taken sweet counsel in the same halls of learning ; who went arm in arm in that hallowed season of life when the foundations of all excellence are laid; who have wept with the same sorrows, or laughed with the same joys; who have been fired with the same ambition, lured with the same hopes, and grieved at the same disappointments : these are not the men, in after years, to stir up animosities or foment intestine feuds. Their college life is a bond of union which nothing can break; a divine poetry of existence, which nothing is allowed to profane. * * * * All these advantages must be lost if the sectarian scheme prevails. South Carolina will no longer be a unit, nor her citizens brothers. We shall have sect against sect, school against school, and college against college ; and he knows but little of the past, who has not observed, that the most formidable dangers to any State are those which spring from division in its own bosom, and that these divisions are terrible in proportion to the degree in which the religious element enters into them."

CHAPTER XXIV.

CALL TO CHARLESTON.

OCCASIONAL DISSATISFACTION WITH ACADEMIC LIFE.—CAUSES OF IT.—
RURAL PURSUITS IN VACATION.—HIS FARM.—CARE OF HIS SLAVES.—
PRIVATE CORRESPONDENCE.—CALL TO CHURCH IN CHARLESTON, SOUTH
CAROLINA.—RESIGNATION OF HIS PROFESSORSHIP.—RELEASE FROM THE
COLLEGE.—REMOVAL TO CHARLESTON.—BRIEF LABOURS IN THAT CITY.—
CORRESPONDENCE.—ELECTED TO PRESIDENCY OF THE COLLEGE.—MEN-
TAL CONFLICT.—ACTION OF THE CHURCH.

THROUGH the whole period of his connection with
the College, there were seasons of restlessness, when
Dr. Thornwell seemed to chafe under the restrictions of
his position, and to sigh for other fields of labour. Those,
however, mistook the case, who assigned this to fickle-
ness and love of change. Perhaps none but ministers of
the gospel can fully appreciate the conflicts which earnest
and faithful men of their class often experience. No one
is able to stand outside of himself sufficiently to estimate
the efficiency of his own labours. He is conscious of the
force that goes out from him, but he is not able to measure fully its influence upon others. There often appears
to be a vast disproportion between the amount of the
toil, and the result that accrues; the disproportion is
greater still between the desires which are cherished, and
the fruit that is actually gathered. Moments of deep
dejection occur to all, when they are prompted to adopt
the remonstrance of the ancient prophet: "O Lord,
Thou hast deceived me, and I was deceived; then I said,
I will not make mention of Him, nor speak any more in
His name." But it always ends as it did with the faithful
Jeremiah: "His word was in my heart as a burning fire
shut up in my bones, and I was weary with forbearing,

339

and I could not stay." Such seasons of gloom, it could
not be supposed Dr. Thornwell would wholly escape;
and whilst all about him, in the Church and in the State,
recognized his work as grand and blessed beyond what
common men could hope to achieve, it was not strange
if he sometimes sighed over opportunities that seemed to
be slipping away without fruit. Of course, this was only
occasional. In the main, he was cheered by the assurance,
that he had been made the instrument of working a stupendous change in the religious sentiment of the College,
and, indeed, of the State, in the complete overthrow of
that blatant infidelity, which previously had seated itself
upon the high places of intelligence and power. He was,
too, not without precious seals of his ministry in the conversion of sinners, who broke down under the majesty of
his appeals, and were led by him to the feet of the Saviour.
But it was not possible for him to know what multitudes
he established in the faith of the gospel; nor in how
many young hearts he planted " the incorruptible seed,"
which, though it lay dormant for a time, sprang up in
after years, and bore rich fruit to the glory of God.

Another cause contributed to this occasional dissatisfaction with the College. Dr. Thornwell, notwithstanding his early preference for scholastic life, which his
intellectual tastes fitted him pre-eminently to enjoy, was
constituted for action rather than repose. He possessed
that peculiar power of magnetizing those with whom he
came in contact, which is the first quality in a great leader.
His convictions were too intense to be locked up in his
own breast; they must have expression, or he must die.
He could not be a man given to speculation merely. His
beliefs wrought themselves into his whole being, and were,
almost without a figure, as a burning fire shut up in his
bones. He could not but be conscious, also, of his immense power in speech to sway the passions, and control
the actions of men. The instinct of the orator was in
him, always craving an audience; a theatre upon which

its practical efficiency may be displayed. He craved an audience, not of youth just crystalizing in their character, and shut in, like himself, to speculation and theory; but an audience of men in the sap and vigour of life, plunged into all the activities of the world's great battle, whom he might stir to deeds of renown in the kingdom of his Master. A temperament so ardent, inspired with all that is lofty in truth, and conscious of a living energy which can impress itself upon others, could not always be resigned,

> "——— Through the loop-holes of retreat
> To peep at such a world, and see the stir
> Of the great Babel, and not feel the crowd."

Traces of this will be discovered in the correspondence of this period, and in a temporary withdrawal from the College, which continued, however, only for a few months. The first two letters are addressed to Professor Matthew J. Williams:

"DRYBURGH ABBEY, *July* 17, 1850.

"MY DEAR MAJOR: You will perceive that I am now fairly rusticated. We reached Lancaster Courthouse the day after we left Columbia, spent the Fourth of July in the village, and on the Monday following we came out to our plantation, where we have been settled ever since. The change is prodigious, from the intense heat of Columbia by day, and its musquitoes by night, to the refreshing breezes and invigorating atmosphere of the up-country. My wife is delighted; and unless she should become tired before the summer is out, it will be hard to get her back to the College campus. There is one consideration, however, which, in our circumstances, will not be without force. The prospect here of making any available amount of the '*ready*,' is very slim. Drought, drought, drought, is all the cry. The corn is stunted and withering; and a few more dry, windy days, will make the likelihood of making bread very slender. There is no chance of reaping twenty-five hundred dollars from these red hills. With seven children to educate, and a host of backs to cover, we need some other dependence than Dryburgh Abbey affords us. So we shall be constrained, with as good a grace as possible, to go back to Columbia. But the situation here is delightful. Our residence is on a high hill, in a deeply shaded grove, and commands a rich and extensive prospect on all sides. We are never without a breeze, and the sound of a musquito is never heard. I enjoy the change very much for the present; and if I were to consult my feelings, instead of yielding to my convictions of duty, I should be tempted to settle down in rural life.

"I suppose you have seen the account of the death of the President of the United States.* What it means, it is difficult to conjecture. But it seems God is giving us warning after warning, line upon line, and precept upon precept. Every good man should be found constantly wrestling at the throne of grace for our bleeding and distracted country. I am satisfied that nothing but repentance on our part, and wonderful mercy on the part of God, can save us from the just consequences of our national sins. We have forgotten God, and have been sacrificing to our own drag; and unless His rebukes should bring us to acknowledge Him, we may be left to 'eat the fruit of our own ways, and to be filled with our own devices.' The subject is constantly in my thoughts and in my prayers; and there is nothing that I would not cheerfully do, or suffer, to promote the peace of our beloved country. I have hope that God does not mean to destroy; that His purpose is to inflict judgment after judgment, until His chastisements shall have been effectual; and then He will return, and have mercy on us. If He meant to root us up and destroy us, He would probably withhold the rod, saying, 'Ephraim is joined to his idols; let him alone.'

"I am engaged in preaching every Sunday. We have several big meetings projected here, in which I am to take part. It is an omen of good, that, in several places in the State, the Lord has visited His people. I sincerely trust that the outpouring of the Spirit may be universal. Write to me soon. Next to the pleasure of seeing you, is that of hearing from you.

"Most truly yours,

J. H. THORNWELL."

In explanation of the foregoing letter, it is proper to say that Dr. Thornwell acquired, by marriage, a small estate in Lancaster District, to which he was accustomed to repair with his family during the vacation in the College. To this place he appears to have transferred the name of one of the most romantic spots which he visited while in Europe; and of which, in one of the letters we have already transcribed, he speaks in terms of great enthusiasm. His interest in the spot is marked in naming his cozy retreat "Dryburgh Abbey." His plantation was never of much pecuniary benefit to him. He was an easy and indulgent master; and it is doubtful if his slaves made

* General Zachary Taylor, the twelfth President of the United States, died in Washington, D. C., on the 9th of July, 1850.

their own support; certainly, they never accomplished much more; and were often a tax upon him, rather than a source of revenue. He was exceedingly conscientious in securing to them every religious privilege, and contributed regularly to a minister, who made it a part of his duty to visit the place, to catechize and to preach. Arrangements of this kind were common throughout the Southern country, under the old regime, which has now passed away. Besides being at perfect liberty to attend the sanctuary on the Sabbath, the gospel was brought to the slave at his own door, by the special labours of ministers, who performed the duty with constancy, and by system. When present at the place, Dr. Thornwell was assiduous in the same work, as a catechist and preacher.

"DRYBURGH ABBEY, *August* 26, 1850.

"MY DEAR MAJOR: Your delightful letter has been lying by me for two weeks unanswered. Although my heart has prompted me every day to subdue my reluctance to take the pen, every day I have succeeded in flattering myself that it would be easier to write to-morrow. The truth is, I have been attending several protracted meetings, and have returned from each pretty throughly broken down. My labours, at the first, left me in a state of prostration from which I apprehended serious results; but, through the mercy of God, my system has recovered its usual tone. For two days I was occasionally spitting blood; my chest was very sore, and my voice very feeble. But I have not only recovered my health, but have received gratifying tokens that the labours which exhausted me have been a blessing to others. One can afford to be broken down, when his decay is the life of others.

"My family has enjoyed usual health, and my wife and children are delighted with the freedom of a country life. We have had fruit and melons in abundance, and ample space to expand our limbs and lungs. Our friends have been very kind; and, in the plenitude of their charity, they have never permitted us to be wanting in either good cheer or good company. We look with reluctance to the period—alas! too rapidly approaching—when we must go back to the walls of our prison. College is to me like a dungeon; and I go to its duties like a slave whipped to his burden. Nothing keeps me there but the fact that God's providence has put me there, and I am afraid to leave without some marked intimation of the Divine will. Perhaps a day of greater usefulness may come; or perhaps the Almighty may open a way for my escape. But I have so often expressed to you my feelings upon this subject, that it is useless to say more upon it now.

"The article upon Morell* which you sent me, follows very closely in the wake of the article in the *North British Review*, upon the same subject. The discriminations were just; and I suppose the *Advocate* copied the piece as some atonement for its own extravagant panegyric of the book when it first appeared. I am sorry to see, however, that rationalism is making such progress in this country; and, if God spares my life, I intend to deal some harder blows than I have yet done. It is insidious and deceitful, and is specially suited to captivate the young and vain. The man who has pondered, and is prepared to answer aright, the question, *What can we know?* is the only man who is competently furnished against the temptations of this seductive and shallow philosophy. He sees precisely where it stumbles. That all knowledge begins with the incomprehensible, and is bounded by the incomprehensible, is a truth which the arrogant disputers of this world are slow to apprehend. The longer I live, and the more I think, the more profound is my conviction of human ignorance. I can say, too, that I have a growing attachment to the great truths of Christianity. I feel that I am rooted and grounded in the gospel; that its doctrines are incorporated into my whole life, and are the necessary food of my soul. I have looked at the matter on all sides; and I can say, from the heart, that I desire to glory in nothing but the cross of the Lord Jesus Christ. The distinction of being a Christian is the highest honour I would court; and the shallow metaphysics that would take from me the promises of God's Word, I do most heartily despise.

"Upon the subject of the inspiration of the Scriptures and the authority of the Bible, we shall have some desperate battles to fight with false brethren, before the enemy is subdued. The world will be on their side. They will make the impression that they are very learned and very profound; and that their opponents are equally ignorant and shallow, mistaking the spirit of bigotry for the spirit of religion. Reproaches of this sort, which will turn the multitude against us, we must bear patiently. They are part of the cross which attaches to discipleship in our day.

"I was much gratified that you approved my article on slavery. No one besides has expressed to me an opinion upon it, and I have seen hardly a notice of it in any of the papers. * * * In regard to the article on the Bible Society, it strikes me that the question there discussed involves a matter of no little moment. Is the Bible Society a *religious* institution, or is it only a secular corporation? If it be a *religious* institution, upon what principle is prayer excluded? How can persons be united in religious duties, when they do not worship the same God? The Socinian and Trinitarian cannot pray together; they cannot be members of the same church; how, then, can they unite in any other religious institution? If the Society is only a *secular* corporation, then it is only a contrivance to get up a cheap book store; and

---

* The Philosophy of Religion. By J. D. Morell, A. M., author of "The History of Modern Philosophy."

every variety of motive may animate its members. The *principle* of these national societies never has been clear to my mind. Their platforms, so broad as to admit everybody that will contribute, no matter who or from what motive, I have never been able to understand. At least, the subject is not free from embarrassment. I never read the article in the *Review* until after its appearance; but I thought it calculated to awaken inquiry.

"I have long been anxious that you should write something for us connected with your favourite pursuit. It is a duty to employ our talents for God's glory, and the good of our fellow men; and as the Almighty has furnished you with eminent gifts in regard to a particular department of human knowledge, you should not conceal your light under a bushel. There are many subjects which you might discuss, and which I know you *can* discuss with signal ability; and you know not what good you might do.

"The time is rolling on when we must put on the harness once more. One consideration relieves the gloominess of the prospect: it is that I shall meet some whom I sincerely love, and who fully reciprocate my affection. How glad I would be to see you here! I know not what efforts I should not put forth to show you how much I esteem you But I hope to meet you in Columbia. In the meantime, let me hear from you again. Your letters are delightfully refreshing; they are like cold water to a thirsty soul.

"Most truly and sincerely, your friend,

J. H. THORNWELL."

To his old friend, General James Gillespie, he writes, under date of June 17th, 1850:

* * * * "I have just finished a long article on slavery,* for our *Review*, which is now in press. I endeavoured to grapple with the philosophical argument of Dr. Channing and Professor Whewell. It is the substance of a sermon which I recently preached in Charleston; and which, I learn, gave great satisfaction. At the earnest entreaty of men whose judgment I respect, I have agreed to publish it; and selected the present form as the most durable and useful. As soon as it is out I will send you a copy.

* This article, referred to also in the preceding letter, will be found in the fourth volume of Dr. Thornwell's "Collected Writings"; together with another important paper on the same subject: a Report submitted to the Synod of South Carolina, adopted by that body in 1851, and ordered by them to be published. These documents give the prevailing opinions held by Christian people at the South on a subject which is now purely historic, and are still valuable as a clear statement of the principles which were involved in it.

"What an unexpected calamity was the death of Elmore! What a lesson in regard to the vanity of man, and the emptiness of human honours! His funeral was the most solemn and impressive scene that I ever witnessed in my life; and was about as profitable to me as any circumstance that has recently happened. I never felt more powerfully than on that occasion, the transcendent value of Christian hope; it is indeed an anchor to the soul, both sure and steadfast. His corpse arrived just about nightfall, and he was buried by the light of a few stars above, and a few lanterns below. The body was in such a condition that it could not be kept until morning. His wife fainted at the grave; his eldest daughter knelt down and prayed; and everything around us was still and solemn as eternity. The scene impressed me so much, that all sleep was taken from my eyes. I gave myself up to my thoughts; and was able to pour forth my feelings next day in a sermon, which, I trust, will not be lost upon the young men. My text was, ' Be ye, therefore, also ready.' Mr. Barnwell has, I hear, accepted the appointment to the vacancy. The Governor could not have selected a better man ; and I sincerely trust that our difficulties at Washington may be satisfactorily adjusted."

We interpose here a portion of a letter to his brother-in-law, the Rev. A. J. Witherspoon, who had long been an inmate of his house as a student in College, and for whom he cherished the strongest affection:

"SOUTH CAROLINA COLLEGE, *December* 10, 1850.

"MY DEAR JACK: I received your letter, written from Greensborough, last night, giving us the not unexpected intelligence, that you are soon to be married. Nothing, I assure you, would afford me more pleasure than to be present on the occasion, and to pronounce the words which would for ever bind you, in sacred and mysterious union, with the object of your choice. But this happiness I am compelled to forego. My duties in the College, and the condition of my family, render it impossible for me to leave home at present. But, although my person must be absent, my heart shall be with you. My prayers shall be mingled with yours, that the blessing of Almighty God may descend upon you, and that you and your love may live habitually as heirs of the grace of life. You are entirely too dear to me, on many grounds, to permit me to be indifferent in regard to an event of so much importance. I congratulate you upon your prospects; for if anything can be inferred from the name,* you have every omen of prosperity and happiness. My experience has taught me that it is noble blood to flow in the veins of a wife. I bid you a cordial God-speed; and trust that every returning

* The bride was a Miss Witherspoon, from a branch of the same family with that of Mrs. Thornwell.

anniversary of the event may be an Ebenezer in your history, in which you shall delight to recount the manifold memorials of Divine goodness.

"Your sister, I need not say, is highly gratified at your prospects; and if it were within the compass of possibility, she would not fail to be present, to grace your nuptials with a sister's smile, and a mother's blessing. All the children greet you; for there is not a soul about my house, whether young or old, bond or free, that does not love Uncle Jack, nor a heart that does not leap at the mention of his name. Your boy* knows that *something* is about to happen, but he cannot precisely comprehend its import. * * *

"Give our kindest remembrances to all of Dr. Witherspoon's family; and may the blessing of our covenant God rest upon you and yours, now and ever, is the sincere prayer of your sincere friend,

J. H. THORNWELL."

The year of 1850 was a turbulent one in the history of the College. The Lord of Misrule, who so often delights to break up the peace of our Colleges, asserted now his supremacy. For some trivial reason, the whole Junior class rose in rebellion against the authorities, and and were suspended, making a fearful chasm by their removal. Other causes, of a more private and personal nature, conspired to render Dr. Thornwell uncomfortable in his position, and predisposed him to listen to overtures from abroad. In the month of March, 1851, the Glebe Street Church, in Charleston, South Carolina, made out a call for his pastoral services, which he accepted. This church had been organized, under the Rev. Abner A. Porter, D. D., as an off-shoot from the Second Presbyterian church of that city. It was then in the feebleness of its infancy. Dr. Thornwell's resignation was accepted by the Board of Trustees, and he entered upon his duties in the month of May. His own letters will give the best account of his brief connection with that church. On the 7th of May, he thus writes to the Rev. A. J. Witherspoon:

"DEAR JACK: I have received your kind letter. The Board of Trustees is now in session, and I shall keep this letter open to inform you,

_____

* One of Dr. Thornwell's little sons, who was named in honour of Mr. Witherspoon.

in a postscript, of the result of my application.   My impression is that,
under all the circumstances of the case, I shall be released.   I have put
it on the ground of a personal favour, after thirteen years' hard labour.
Besides arguing the matter very ingeniously in a letter, I have gone
round among the members of the Board, and fairly begged off.   They
were very much disposed to kick, in the hope of detaining me finally,
and breaking up the Charleston movement altogether.   But when I
assured them my honour was pledged, and this result was altogether
hopeless, they seemed disposed to accommodate me.   I think, therefore,
that matters are in a fair way.   Should I get off, I will probably be in
Charleston on Sunday, the 18th.   *   *   *

"Most affectionately yours,

J. H. THORNWELL."

P. S.—The Board has adjourned.   *I am released.*   The Church, therefore, may look for me on the 18th.

"CHARLESTON, *May* 24, 1851.

"MY DEAREST WIFE: Upon my return this evening from Sullivan's
Island, I found your delightful letter, written partly in Columbia, and
partly in Camden.   I had heard from one of the students, who was down
here on leave of absence, that Gillespie had fallen from a wall.   He also
assured me that the doctor had said that he was not hurt; and to relieve
me of all anxiety, said further, that he had seen him, as usual, playing
in the campus, the afternoon of the accident.   But what gave me most
comfort was, that I received no telegraphic dispatch from you; which
I was sure that I would have received, if the child had been seriously
hurt.   I am very thankful that the Lord has been so kind to us, in preserving him in the midst of danger.   I sincerely trust that He will yet
make him the means of saving multitudes from the awful dangers of
sin.   Let us endeavour to consecrate him, and all our children, to God's
service, and to train them up for God's glory.   *   *   *

"I have just returned from a second excursion to Sullivan's Island.
It is certainly the most delightful summer retreat that I have ever visited.
I met with Mr. Adger's family there, and they took me out to ride.   We
rode about five miles on the sea-shore, with the water roaring near us,
and the cool breezes blowing fresh upon us; and I could hardly keep
from shedding tears, that you were not there to enjoy the scene.   I
thought of you, plodding your way, through clay and dust, up to Lancaster; annoyed by children, ill served by servants, and in feeble health.
How I wished you were here.   *   *   *

"I have visited eight or ten families in the congregation, and have
been very much pleased with them.   They are all plain people, but very
spiritual.   I have been agreeably surprised at the tone of piety and
prayerfulness, which seems to prevail amongst them.   This circumstance
has encouraged me more than anything else.   They are people that I
know you will like, and will feel at home amongst them at once.   Mr.
Caldwell and his family have been very kind to me.   They have treated

me with the most cordial and whole-souled hospitality. I sometimes insinuate that my toes begin to ache already with incipient gout. They know what good living is, and yet everything is utterly unpretending. Their hearts are entirely in the cause of Christ, and especially in the Glebe Street Church.

"You will see, from my account of myself, that I am leading a deplorably idle life. I have read hardly anything but the Bible since I came here. I wander about, and take exercise, and bathe. I sleep when and as I please. All study I have carefully avoided; and every one congratulates me upon looking so well. I have certainly improved; the sea air is just the thing for me. * * *

"May the Lord keep you as the apple of the eye.

"Most devotedly, your husband,

J. H. THORNWELL."

To the same:

"CHARLESTON, *May* 26, 1851.

"MY DEAREST WIFE: * * * * I preached twice yesterday, as usual. The congregation was good in the morning, but crowded almost to suffocation at night. The pews are to be rented this week; and we shall, perhaps, be able to make some guess as to how we are likely to succeed. The time is not most favourable now, as many are away, others preparing to go away, and many unsettled. But it was very fortunate, or providential, for the church, that I came down at once. I am anxious to have an eye single to God's glory. If it were my purpose to *please* the people, I could soon gather a large congregation; but I want to build up a *spiritual church*, and that cannot be done without the special agency of the Holy Ghost. I could soon draw around me those who have itching ears; but I wish to attract people, not to myself, but to the cross of my Divine Redeemer. Such a work requires patience, watchfulness, and prayer.

* * * "I am getting very impatient for you to come down. The amplest arrangements are made for your accommodation. As soon as you come, you will go over to Sullivan's Island, and enjoy the fresh air, and the delightful walks and rides upon the beach; and, if you will risk it, the bathing in the sea. Take the best care of yourself; and be sure to come down at the time appointed.

"Most devotedly, your husband,

J. H. THORNWELL."

To the Rev. A. J. Witherspoon:

"SULLIVAN'S ISLAND, *June* 17, 1851.

"MY DEAR JACK: I was truly rejoiced to hear from you this evening, though extremely sorry to learn that your health has been so feeble. You must not overtask yourself; a righteous man is merciful to his beast.

You have no right to commit suicide. The ministry of the gospel is a
noble calling; but, like every other pursuit, we must engage in it according to our strength, and not beyond it. I have some experience in
the matter, and am fully satisfied that, in reference to it, as well as every
other enterprise, the old maxim, *festina lente,* is a wise one. You will
be able to accomplish more in the long run, by not overtasking yourself
at the beginning. He that has a long race before him, sets off at a
moderate pace. The thing to be guarded against is, sparing ourselves
from indolence, or the love of ease; that is sinful. But when a man
really aims at God's glory, and husbands his resources for larger and
more effective service, he is no more to be condemned than the thrifty
economist who guards against a prodigality which his means do not
authorize him to indulge in. I have nothing to say in regard to the
Louisiana scheme, but to urge you to do, what I know you will not be
backward to do, to commit the whole matter to the Lord, and to ask
counsel from him. If He does not call you, He will make it plain to you
in some way or other, if you humbly and honestly seek His guidance.
All that I would say is, the Lord's will be done.

"Your sister reached Charleston on Saturday. I was deplorably lone-
some without her, occasionally very blue; but her presence has acted
like a charm, and cheered me amazingly. The church here is getting
along as well as could be expected. The congregations are very good in
the morning, and at night we have a perfect jam. So many people have
had to be turned off from inability to get into the house, that I am afraid
they will be discouraged from coming. I have been preaching some very
close and searching sermons. My impression is that, in the course of
the winter, I shall be able to gather a very respectable permanent congregation. The prospect, at least, is a very encouraging one; and I am
not sanguine about such things. * * * * The Lord bless you and
and keep you, and guide you into all truth and duty.

"Most truly yours,

J. H. THORNWELL."

The following is addressed to his little son, not yet
seven years of age. It reveals him as a Christian father,
in his intercourse with his little ones:

"SULLIVAN'S ISLAND, *June* 17, 1851.

"MY DEAR GILLESPIE: Your mother is now with me, and we often
think and talk and pray about our dear little boy in Sumter District. We
know that you are in the hands of kind friends, who will take the best
care of you. But we are very anxious that you should try and be a good
boy yourself. You must mind everything that cousin Sarah Ann, or Mr.
Knox, says to you. Learn all the lessons they give you; use no bad
words; answer your questions every Sunday; and pray to God every
morning and night. It would do your father a great deal of good to see

you fond of reading the Bible, and other books. I hope that God may yet make you a preacher. There is nothing that would please me so much as to see you a good man, and in the pulpit. You must not think it smart to be rude and boisterous, and cruel to poor animals, that cannot help themselves. You must not curse or swear, for anything in the world; and no matter what you do, never tell a story; always speak out the truth, whatever may be the consequences.

"I wish you could be here to see the great sights that are to be seen. Your mother goes down every day into the big waters, and lies down in them until they cover her up. It is good for her health. She has already improved a great deal since she came down. We often walk on the sea shore; and she picks up a whole parcel of pretty little shells, which she intends to carry home, and give them to you children. We see a great many ships, and steamboats, and little boats, sailing about every day. You would enjoy it very much. But I know you are happy among the tall pines of Sumter. You get so many good things to eat, I am afraid you will not be willing to come home again. I want you to be happy, and to enjoy yourself; but at the same time, I want you to be good. May the Lord bless you, my son, and take care of you; and make you, some day, a useful preacher.

"Your affectionate father,

J. H. THORNWELL."

To the Rev. Thomas E. Peck:

"SULLIVAN'S ISLAND, *July* 1, 1851.

"MY DEAR THOMAS: I received your welcome letter on Saturday, all the more welcome for being gratuitous. As to your mental depression, I can hardly prescribe a cure. If it arises from dyspepsia, nervous irritation, indigestion, or costiveness, the best thing you can do will probably be to take a blue pill. If it arises from a sense of sin, of guilt, unworthiness, and misery, there is a fountain open for such disorders; and the way of access you know better than I can tell you. If your gloom is occasioned by a feeling of unprofitableness as a minister, by doubts as to the propriety of your occupying your present position, your true place is to remain cheerfully and comfortably where you are, until God, in His providence, calls you to another sphere. An honest desire to know God's will is the best security against mistake. He will not permit those who humbly seek His direction, to wander in forbidden paths. You may not have the success that you want; but if your labour is accepted of God, that is enough. Wait upon Him, and He will guide you with His eye.

"I have been here now for seven weeks, and have spent most of the time upon the sea shore. The atmosphere has been balmy and refreshing; and the entire exemption from all labour, except that of preaching on Sundays, has been very grateful to my body. The prospect of success, in my new charge, is not without encouragement. There are some circumstances, however, which are calculated to operate against us. The church itself is not a comfortable building. It is not only small in its proportions, but jammed and crowded in its pews. The location, also, is very obscure; and, in addition to all this, the idea of a pauper missionary enterprise seems to have been associated with it. None of these considerations have any weight with me, but the first. I wish the house were larger and more comfortable. I do not wish a *fine* church; I have no idea of drawing people to Christ by bricks and mortar; but I want it like a gentleman's dress, free from criticism. We shall either have to build another, or to remodel the present. Our congregations at night are very large; our morning, which is *our* congregation, seems to be steadily increasing. But I can form no definite opinion as to the result of my removal, until next winter. We shall then see whether there is much demand for our pews. My great wish is to organize a congregation whose bond of union shall be the gospel in its life and power.

"Pungent and searching evangelical preaching is much needed in this city. Fine houses, splendid organs, fashionable congregations,— these seem to be the rage. It is not asked, *what* a man preaches; but *where* he preaches, and to *whom*. If he has an imposing building, adorned with sofas for the rich to lounge on, where they are lulled into repose by an equally imposing orchestra, that is the place for a gentleman; and to go there twice on Sunday, is to worship God. This state of feeling I am anxious to see thoroughly undermined, and broken up. It insinuates itself under the most artful and seducing pleas; and we often find ourselves the victims of its influence, when we supposed that we were only zealous for the diffusion of religion. I am afraid that, throughout the country, our Presbyterian population is too much giving way to it. We cannot wield such weapons; they belong to Prelacy and Popery. And if, in a silent, secret, imperceptible way, I can do anything here to arrest it, I shall feel that I have accomplished a noble work. If I can make *what* is preached the standard of judgment, in regard to a minister or church, I shall feel that I have done much.

"I am glad that Dr. Breckinridge is about to discuss the subject of instrumental music. It is getting to be a very great evil. Every church here, I think, has an instrument of some kind, but mine and the Methodists. At any rate, there is a decided taste for them.

"Do you still eat sheep? If so, this is the place for you. The Charleston market abounds with *lambs*, from a month to a year old; but I have not touched them. Let me hear from you soon.

"Most truly yours,

J. H. THORNWELL."

The foregoing letters give the account of Dr. Thornwell's very brief connection with the Glebe Street church, in the city of Charleston, which was destined to be very suddenly broken. It is remarkable that every effort made by him to escape from the duties of academic life, was instantly arrested. Indeed, his whole career shows how often Divine providence holds a man to a given station, even against his own wishes in the case, until his work in it is fully done. This was the third attempt to leave the College for a pastoral charge, since 1837, when he first entered its service. On the 2d of December, 1851, Dr. Thornwell was elected President of the South Carolina College, in the place of the Hon. W. C. Preston, whom increasing ill health compelled to resign. The letter which follows discloses the conflict through which he passed, before this position was accepted:

"CHARLESTON, *December* 12, 1851.

"MY DEAREST WIFE: I am surprised at your looking for me home, as you must remember that I told you I had a speech to make before the Charleston College to-night. It was for that reason that I have spent the week here. I made my speech to-night; and, so far as I know, it took very well. It was delivered in the chapel of the Charleston College. The auditory was small, but select; and the speech amazingly dry and metaphysical. * * *

"I have passed a week of severe and bitter conflict. It has been my earnest desire to know and to do the Lord's will. I have endeavoured to suppress every other feeling, but a simple eye to the glory of God. But I had no idea of the strength of attachment that is felt here for me. The people cannot speak upon the subject without bursting into tears. The prospect of usefulness is more promising than it has ever been before; and the congregation has endeavoured to meet the thing in the right spirit. They had a special prayer-meeting last night; and every member of the church, that was not providentially hindered, was there. and the scene was a truly melting one. They say that Martin prayed like a man inspired. These things have moved me very deeply. I know the people respected and esteemed very highly; but I had no idea of the *love*, the real love, that they had for me, as a minister of the gospel. It makes the trial very severe and painful to me. The Session had a meeting last night; and we have determined to lay the matter before the congregation on Monday. I feel that, after all the prayer which has been offered in the case, the decision of the congregation will be for the glory of God. They will approach the subject in the right spirit; and I am persuaded that God will direct them. Whatever they decide, I shall feel bound in honour to abide by. If you could have been with me this week, you would have been satisfied that it is a most serious step to give up so delightful a charge for the martyrdom of College. My impression is, that the congregation will hold on to me. I think their existence, in a measure, depends upon it; and if they do, they will cling more closely to me than they would otherwise have done. I am reconciled to whatever Providence may order, as I have honestly sought to know my duty. Under this state of the case, you may have the comfort of knowing that our suspense will soon be over. On Monday the question will be settled; and I sincerely trust that your mind may be reconciled to any issue. As a matter of *feeling*, of comfort, of happiness, of usefulness to my family, I prefer the Church. In some other respects, the College may have the advantage; though even here my mind is not clear. The thing that most distresses me is, that you may not be satisfied to leave Columbia; and to do a thing that would grieve you, would almost take my life. But the Lord reigns. Let us both submit the matter to Him, and endeavour to acquiesce in His will. The Lord bless you. Kiss all the children; and pray for me in this strait.

"Your most devoted husband,

J. H. THORNWELL."

By the resolution adopted by the Glebe Street congregation, in the spirit of a noble self-sacrifice, he was left free to obey the dictates of his own conscience, under the guidance of Divine providence.

CHAPTER XXV.

PRESIDENCY OF THE COLLEGE.

DR. THORNWELL entered upon his duties, as President of the South Carolina College, in the month of January, 1852. He brought to this responsible position a large experience as a Professor in this very school, and was fully acquainted with its excellencies and its defects. His views upon the whole subject of education were also fully matured. He properly considered its first object to be the *discipline* of the mind, to elicit its dormant powers, and to train these for vigorous self-action; whilst the mere acquisition of knowledge he regarded as secondary in importance. His favourite idea was to restrict undergraduates to studies by which the mind may be systematically developed; and at the close of a prescribed and compulsory curriculum, to engraft upon the College the main features of the University system, with its large and varied apparatus for the fuller communication of knowledge. He has been accused of disparaging the natural sciences as a part of liberal education; in which there is undoubtedly a misapprehension of his true position. He certainly did not estimate them highly as instruments of mental discipline; and thus assigned them a small place in that scheme of education which is intended to train the mind. But he would give them ample scope in that broader

355

scheme, which takes the disciplined mind and adorns it with various knowledge. He simply shifted their position from the gymnasium to the University; and would rejoice in their cultivation as the furniture, rather than as the diet of the mind.

He was a zealous advocate of common school education among the masses; but firmly held to the opinion, that knowledge, after all, is diffused by its own law of descent from above, below—percolating through society from the surface to the lowest bed beneath. Hence, he laboured to promote the highest education among the few, as the surest way to quicken and enlighten the less favoured masses. It is hard to swim against the current of the age. His grand ideal of an institution, which should unite the thorough training of the gymnasium with the large culture of the University, was never realized; and he has left the great problem of education yet to be solved: how to adjust the wide diffusion of knowledge with that depth and accuracy of learning which it was the object of his life to secure.

A few extracts from his celebrated letter to Governor Manning will present his views on these points authoritatively to the reader. He thus speaks of the design which the College has in view:

"Devoted to the interests of general, in contradistinction from professional, education, its design is to cultivate the mind without reference to any ulterior pursuits. 'The student is considered an end to himself; his perfection as a man simply, being the aim of his education.' The culture of the mind, however, for itself, contributes to its perfection as an instrument; so that general education, while it directly prepares and qualifies for no special distinction, indirectly trains for every vocation in which success is dependent upon intellectual exertion. It has taught the mind the use of its powers, and imparted those habits without which those powers would be useless. It makes *men*, and consequently promotes every enterprise in which *men* are to act. General education being the design of a College, the fundamental principles of its organization are easily deduced:

"1. The selection of studies must be made, not with reference to the comparative importance of their matter, or the practical value of the knowledge, but with reference to their influence in unfolding and strengthening the powers of the mind. As the end is to improve mind, the fitness for the end is the prime consideration. * * * Hence, the introduction of studies upon the ground of their practical utility is, *pro tanto*, subversive of the College. It is not its office to make planters, mechanics, lawyers, physicians, or divines. It has nothing directly to do with the uses of knowledge. Its business is with minds, and it employs science only as an instrument for the improvement and perfection of mind. With it the habit of sound thinking is more than a thousand thoughts. When, therefore, the question is asked, as it often is asked, by ignorance and empiricism, what is the use of certain departments of the College curriculum? the answer should turn, not upon the benefits which in after life may be reaped from these pursuits, but upon their immediate subjective influence upon the cultivation of the human faculties. They are selected in preference to others, because they better train the mind. It cannot be too earnestly inculcated, that knowledge is not the principal end of College instruction, but habits. The acquisition of knowledge is the necessary result of these exercises, which terminate in habits, and the maturity of the habit is measured by the degree and accuracy of the knowledge; but still, the habits are the main thing

"2. In the next place, it is equally important that the whole course of studies be rigidly exacted of every student. Their value, as a discipline, depends altogether upon their *being* studied; and every College is defective in its arrangements which fails to secure, as far as legislation can secure it, this indispensable condition of success. * * * The curriculum must be compulsory, or the majority of students will neglect it. All must be subjected to catechetical examinations in the lecture-room, and all must undergo the regular examinations of their classes, as the condition of their residence in College. The moment they are exempted from the stringency of this rule, all other means lose their power upon the mass of pupils. * * * * * *

"3. Another cardinal principle in the organization of the College, is the independence of its teachers. They should be raised above all temptation of catering for popularity, of degrading the standard of education for the sake of the loaves and fishes. They should be prepared to officiate as priests in the temple of learning, in pure vestments, and with hands unstained with a bribe. * * * The true security for the ability of the professional corps, is not to be sought in starving them, or in making them scramble for a livelihood; but in the competency, zeal, and integrity of the body that appoints them, and in the strict responsibility to which they are held." * * * *

He then proceeds to refute the objection, that the higher education benefits only the privileged few who can avail themselves of it:

"It is great weakness to suppose that nothing can contribute to the general good, the immediate ends of which are not realized in the case of every individual. * * * The educated men, in every community, are the real elements of steady and consistent progress. They are gen erally in advance of their generation; light descends from them to their inferiors; and by a gradual and imperceptible influence, emanating from the solitary speculations, it may be, of their secret hours, the whole texture of society is modified, a wider scope is given to its views, and a loftier end to its measures. They are the men who sustain and carry forward the complicated movements of a refined civilization; the real authors of the changes which constitute epochs in the social elevation of the race. Pitt could not understand, and Fox refused to read, the masterly speculations of Adam Smith upon the Wealth of Nations. He was ahead of his age. The truth gradually worked its way, however, into minds of statesmen and legislators; and now, no one is held to be fit for any public employment who is not imbued with the principles of political economy. * * * The solitary scholar wields a lever which raises the whole mass of society. It is a high general education which shapes the mind, and controls the opinions of the guiding spirit of the age; it is this which keeps up the general tone of society; it is at once conservative and progressive. * * * *

"In the next place, it should not be omitted that general education is the true source of the elevation of the masses, and of the demand for popular instruction. Every educated man is a centre of light; and his example and influence create the consciousness of ignorance and the sense of need, from which elementary schools have sprung. Defective culture is never conscious of itself, until it is brought in contact with superior power. There may be a conviction of ignorance, in reference to special things, and a desire of knowledge, as the means of accomplishing particular ends; but the need of intellectual improvement, on its own account, never is awakened spontaneously. * * * * Hence, it is knowledge which creates the demand for knowledge, which causes igno- rance to be felt as an evil; and hence it is the education, in the first instance, of the few, which has awakened the strong desire for the illumi- nation of the many. Let knowledge, however, become stagnant; let no provision be made for the constant activity of the highest order of minds, in the highest spheres of speculation; and the torpor would be commu- nicated downwards, until the whole community was benumbed. * * * Scholars are, therefore, the real benefactors of the people; and he does more for popular education who founds a University, than he who in- stitutes a complete and adequate machinery of common schools. The reason is obvious: the most potent element of public opinion is wanting, where only a low form of culture obtains; the common schools, having no example of anything higher before them, would soon degenerate, and impart only a mechanical culture—if they did not, which I am in- clined to think would be the case, from their want of life—if they did not permit the people to relapse into barbarism. Colleges, on the other hand, will create the demand for lower culture ; and private enterprise, under the stimulus imparted, would not be backward in providing it."

With these views as to the importance of the higher education, and of the discipline necessary to its attainment, Dr. Thornwell entered upon the administration of the College. He evinced his zeal in the discharge of his new trust, by devoting the first vacation to a visit northward, that he might inspect the methods which obtained in the older and more celebrated institutions of Cambridge and Yale. His impressions will be best communicated in the letters which he wrote during that tour. The first is addressed to the Rev. A. J. Witherspoon ; which we introduce, partly because it opens his plan of visitation, but chiefly because it reveals a severe bereavement in the death of a little daughter, his youngest, at the age of eighteen months.

"COLUMBIA, *June* 28, 1852.

"MY DEAR JACK: It has been a long time since I heard from you, and though I have been extremely anxious about you, I have been living in hopes that every day would find you on your return to your dear native State. I am just from the Waxhaws, whither I had gone on a melancholy errand, the burial of my sweet babe, Mary Elizabeth. She died on the 20th inst., and I took her to the last resting place of her little sister, who had preceded her to heaven by many years. It was a sad office, but I trust God has sanctified it to my good. I feel that my child has blessed me in her death, though it was denied her to bless me by her life. But it moves many a painful thought, that such was my ingratitude, such my guilty distance from God, that it cost the life of my little one to bring me to a sound mind. * * * * *

"Our vacation has begun. I shall leave the last of this week for Charleston, and from there I shall go to the North. I propose to visit several of the northern Colleges, Harvard, Yale, Dartmouth, &c., at their commencements, in order to collect such hints as may be useful to me in the conduct of this institution. I have endeavoured to persuade your sister to go with me, but she is very reluctant to leave the children.

"The wife of Wade Hampton, Jr., Colonel Preston's sister, died suddenly yesterday. She will be buried this afternoon. Such is life ! In health one day, in the grave the next ! Her husband had completed a magnificent mansion ; it was splendidly furnished ; all things were ready to begin to live; and, lo! in an instant, vanity is written upon all these hopes and preparations.   *   *   *

"Most truly, as ever,

J. H. THORNWELL."

"BALTIMORE, *July* 12, 1852.

"MY VERY DEAR WIFE: I arrived at this city about six o'clock on Saturday afternoon, and am lodging with Mr. Coulson, a member of Peck's congregation. I preached only once yesterday, and that was for Peck. * *

"I had a very pleasant time in Washington. I could have spent a week longer with interest. Mr. De Saussure was very kind and attentive. We called on the President together, but failed to see him, as he was very much engaged at the hour of our call. I spent an evening with General Hamilton, in company with Mr. De Saussure and Colonel Burt. Hamilton gave me letters to the very first men in Boston—to Everett and Sparks. Burt also gave me a letter to Mr. Winthrop, the former Speaker of the House of Representatives, a man of very high standing. By means of these letters, I shall be enabled to accomplish very pleasantly all that I have in view at Cambridge. I had many other invitations from gentlemen at Washington, which, for want of time, I was compelled to decline. Butler returned while I was there, and was extremely courteous. He hunted me up, as soon as he came, and offered his services in any enterprise which I might wish to prosecute. I saw none of the clergymen in Washington or Georgetown. * * * * As to my health, I think that I am improving. The pain in my hip troubles me less than it did, though I still feel it occasionally. In every other respect I am as well as usual. But I have a good deal of anxiety about you and the children. You must not expose yourself during this intensely warm weather. You must keep your mind free from care and anxiety. Abjure the *needle*. Give yourself up to light employments and recreation. It would be a source of great satisfaction if I had you with me. But at this particular time, a man can do nothing but keep to the house and eat ice cream.

"May the Lord watch over us both, and keep us in perfect safety; and bring us together again, in health of body, mind, and soul. Kiss all the children.

"Your devoted husband,

J. H. THORNWELL."

"CAMBRIDGE, *July* 21, 1852.

"MY CHARMING, DARLING WIFE: I had not thought to write to you until to-morrow night, as we are now in the midst of the Cambridge festivities; but I was so delighted to-night upon receiving two letters from you, that I must drop you a line, even before the exercises are all over. This has been Commencement day. The crowd that attended was numerous. The exercises were held in a large church, and it was

literally jammed and crammed. We had thirty *speeches ;* just think of
that. We commenced at ten o'clock, and came out at three. I was
assigned a conspicuous place on the stage, next to ex-Presidents Quincy
and Edward Everett. After the speeches, I joined the Faculty and
Overseers in the College dinner. It was a very interesting affair, well
served up, and we had good appetites for it. They concluded the dinner
by singing the seventy-eighth Psalm. This has been an old custom,
handed down from the Puritan fathers. It was really an imposing ceremony; and I should have enjoyed it very much, if I had not remembered
that they were all Unitarians, witnessing, in this very service, to their
own condemnation. The exercises of the young men were not equal to
those we have in our own College.

"This evening I spent with Professor Walker, one of the ablest men
connected with the faculty of this ancient University. We had a great
deal of pleasant talk about College discipline and College studies. To-
morrow is to be another great day. Mr. Winthrop, late Speaker of the
House of Representatives at Washington, is to deliver the annual oration
before the Alumni of the University, after which they all repair to a
splendid dinner. I am invited as a guest. I am told that it will be a
splendid affair; all their best men will make speeches at the table. Mr.
Everett is to preside. He has been very polite and attentive to me, and
is certainly one of the most accomplished men that I ever saw in my
life. As soon as I arrived and sent my card, he despatched a very
handsome note to me, inviting me to attend the dinner, and called upon
me this morning before I was up. We sat together upon the stage
to-day, and had a good deal of pleasant, desultory talk. He is what you
would call a *finished man.* We have no other such man in America.
Yesterday evening, Dr. Sparks, the present President, called upon me,
and made a very favourable impression. They have not been content
with mere courtesies. They have also given me some work to do. I
have been appointed by Sparks upon a committee to sit in judgment upon
the exercises of a number of students to-morrow morning, who will
speak for a prize. I accepted the appointment, because I wanted to see
and learn as much as I could about the working of this ancient and
venerable institution.

"You cannot imagine how attractive this place is to me. There is but
one draw-back, and that is the *religion ;* it makes me sad to see such men,
so accomplished, so elegant, at once such finished gentlemen and such
admirable scholars, sunk into so vile a faith. I have really had scruples
about associating with them as I have done. But it must be confessed
that Boston is a great city. There are things about it that make you
proud of it as an American city. It is the most elegant city in the
Union. Here you have the noblest specimens of the Yankee character.
The people here remind you very much of England. There is none of
the littleness that you meet with in other parts of New England.

"Tell Nanny I am much obliged to her for her letter, and will buy
her the breast-pin. Harvey I must excuse, and take the will for the deed.

Bless all the children, and kiss them for me. The Lord preserve you all. As ever,

"Your devoted husband,

J. H. THORNWELL."

"BOSTON, *July* 24, 1852.

"MY PRECIOUS, CHARMING WIFE: Though I have written to you so recently, yet I know you will not take it amiss that I write to you again, as it gives me great pleasure to commune with you in spirit, when I am absent from you in the body. Last night I attended a very pleasant and agreeable party at President Spark's. This morning he called on me quite early, and we had a great deal of conversation about Colleges, and so on.

"This morning I came into Boston, and spent the forenoon with Mr. Everett, in his library. I was invited to dine there, but declined, as I wanted to hunt up the Harts. After dinner I set out upon that errand. I could find no such hospital anywhere. I inquired at all the leading hotels, and no one there had ever heard of such an institution. I looked at all the Directories, and could get no clue to it. I inquired of gentlemen in book stores, and they could tell me nothing. I remembered that Colonel John Preston told me he thought the institution was at Roxbury. So I jumped into an omnibus, and went over to Roxbury. I inquired at the principal hotel there; no one had ever heard of such an institution there. I was at the end of my row, and thought I should have to return to Boston with my finger in my mouth. But I persevered. I went into a store, and asked a shop-keeper. He knew nothing of it; but said if there was such a thing any where in that region, I could find out by calling on a physician that lived near. So I plucked up courage, went to the doctor's house, rung the bell, a servant appeared. I asked if Dr. Cotten was at home. 'Yes, sir.' 'Will you please ask him if he will step to the door? A stranger wishes to speak with him a moment.' The servant withdrew, and Dr. Cotten soon appeared. 'Excuse me,' I said, 'for intruding upon you, sir; but am a stranger from South Carolina, and wish to obtain directions for finding the hospital for spinal patients.' 'Did I not see *you*, sir, the other day at Cambridge?' he replied; 'and did I not hear you speak? Are you not Dr. Thornwell, of the South Carolina College?' I told him I was. He then very politely asked me into his drawing-room, gave me a book to read, saying that he had to despatch some patients, who were waiting on him, and would instantly join me. He soon re-appeared, and told me that there was no such hospital; but added, 'I know the place you want to find; it is a private establishment, where a Dr. Barre attends to cases of that sort.' He then got a map of the town, and showed me exactly where it was. I told him that I was very much obliged to him, and would instantly order a cab. 'No, sir,' said he; 'I will take you myself.' With that, he ordered his chaise, or buggy, drove me to the place, where I found the Harts; and would wait for me until I got through my call. He then made me get in again, and drove me for two hours among all the villages and fine scenery for six miles around Boston, explaining everything to me as we went. Now, can South Carolina beat that? My heart was deeply touched at the unostentatious kindness which was thus heaped upon a stranger. I found the Harts enjoying themselves. They were in good spirits; and thought that the child was decidedly improving. They were very much gratified at my call. I told them that I would not have persevered so long in trying to find them, if I had not been afraid to go home without seeing them; that it would be one of the first questions you would ask, whether I had seen them; and that I should be obliged to tell a lie, which would hurt my conscience, or get a terrible rasping. So, for the sake of peace at home, I was determined to find them out.

"Though I have received nothing but kindess and courtesy in Boston and Cambridge, I sigh for home. I am sick of knocking about; it is a sort of life that does not suit me. I sometimes get very blue, deplorably low-spirited, and think myself an utter blank in the world. My health is about as usual, except a cold that I caught at Cambridge, in consequence of a sudden change in the temperature. It is not at all serious, but it helps to depress me, and make me wish that I was at home again. This eternal bustle in cities, steamboats, omnibuses, and railroad cars, is no rest; and it is so horridly distasteful to me, that it keeps me moody. Tell Nannie I shall not forget her pin; let each say what he or she wants, and I will try to get it. So, good-night, love; pleasant dreams to you, and a speedy meeting with

"Your devoted husband, J. H. T."

"P. S.—As I did not get your letter to the office last night, I add a postscript, to let you know that I went to church twice to-day; in the morning, at the Old South Congregational church; to-night I heard Dr. Fuller, of South Carolina. He produced a deep effect. He is, in some respects, a very striking preacher. I think I have profited by both sermons that I heard; but my Christian comforts are low."

The next letter bears the same date, and touches upon the same incidents; but it is addressed to his colleague, Prof. Matthew J. Williams, and exhibits the affection he had for his confidential friend.

"BOSTON, *May* 24, 1852.

"DEARLY BELOVED MAJOR: I received your letter yesterday afternoon; and to show you how much I prize your correspondence, I reply to it at once. This is Saturday, and I have been in this vicinity ever since Monday. The festivities at Cambridge occupied Wednesday and Thursday. I have been through them all; and may say of them, *quorum pars parva fui*. Wednesday was Commencement day. There were forty-one appointments, as *we* would call them; they call them *parts* here; and of these forty-one, thirty actually spoke. Only think of patience on a monument, and listening to thirty speeches from so many College boys! Well, they are no better than you and I are used to at home. We then repaired to a grand College dinner, and the ceremonies there were exceedingly interesting. Of course, after the siege we had had, we set to work *con amore;* we talked some, but ate more. The dinner was prefaced by a prayer that would not have seemed so long, if we had not been so hungry. At the conclusion of the dinner, the whole company—and an immense one it was—united in singing the seventy-eighth Psalm. This has been a custom ever since the institution was founded, and is a living witness of its Puritan origin and aims. That evening I took tea with a Professor of Cambridge, and we had a great deal of metaphysical talk; and I was very near coming to the conclusion that I knew as much he. So passed Wednesday. Thursday was, however, the great day of the feast. It was a day for the meeting of the Alumni from all quarters of the land. Great pains had been taken to secure a general attendance; and there was, accordingly, a multitude there, from the veteran of eighty to the boy that graduated yesterday. Hon. R. C. Winthrop delivered the oration; it was two hours long, but it was a splendid production. I was actually carried away with it. After the speech, we repaired to the Alumni dinner; and I assure you it was an imposing spectacle. Edward Everett presided, and opened with a beautiful speech. We had several other speeches, among which was a very short, and a very poor one, by your humble servant, and a very capital one by John S. Preston, whom I had introduced to Mr. Everett. At the conclusion of Preston's speech, there were three hearty cheers given to South Carolina. They made the very welkin ring in shouting "hurrah" for our State. The whole thing passed off delightfully. In my speech, I alluded in very flattering terms to W. C. Preston, as a specimen of what our college had accomplished for the country. I praised his eloquence and genius, etc., and took occasion to state that his brother was by my side. When they heard that a brother of Col. Preston was there, they soon called him out; and he made one of the most beautiful and appropriate efforts that I ever heard. Mr. Everett afterwards spoke of its appropriateness to me in flattering terms.

"Friday, I spent the morning in Boston, and returned in the afternoon to Cambridge, and spent the evening most delightfully with President Sparks; and this morning he was at my lodgings before I was up; but I soon came down, and, though he professed to be in a great hurry, he did not leave me for two mortal hours. As soon as he left, I came into Boston, and spent the morning with Mr. Everett, in his library. * * * On Monday I leave for New Haven, where I propose to spend a week; and then what I shall do remains to be determined. I have met with nothing to offend me; but, Major, notwithstanding all, I have not been myself. I was not myself at Cambridge. I am low-spirited, and withal grievously home-sick. But still, I am glad that I came. I have learned much. My interviews with Everett and Sparks have confirmed my opinions upon some matters of the last importance to our College. I shall have a learned report for the next Board.

"But my sheet is full. Remember me kindly to Mrs. W., Henry, and Fanny; and believe me, as ever, dear Major,

"Your faithful friend,

"J. H. THORNWELL."

We next find our friend enjoying "the feast of reason and the flow of soul," at New Haven, Connecticut. Of this visit no memorial remains but the following letter to his wife:

"NEW HAVEN, *July* 30, 1852.

"MY MOST PRECIOUS WIFE: I have been here ever since Monday, and this is Friday, and you cannot imagine how anxious I am to get a letter from you. I found one here upon my arrival, dated the 20th, and have received none since. What can be the matter? I have had a thousand imaginations; but have finally tried to comfort myself with the thought that 'no news is good news.' I am staying at Dr. Wells'.* He and his family have been extremely kind. They live in the finest part of New Haven, and in one of the finest houses in the city, and are surrounded with every luxury. They have really set themselves to enjoy life.

"I never was more kindly treated than I have been here. I have been invited to several parties, and have become acquainted with most of the literary men of the place. The festivities connected with Yale College Commencement terminated last night; and the first leisure I have had has been to-day. On Wednesday there was a meeting of the Alumni, at which I was invited to be present, and where I made a speech that, I believe, was remarkably well received. Yesterday was Commencement. The exercises were very tedious; but I sat them out. * * *

"I shall remain here over Sunday. I am to preach for Dr. Bacon, and I shall give his people the truth. I have had an amusing interview with Dr. Taylor, the father of New Schoolism. He has been very attentive to me. My health is about the same as when I last wrote. By Dr. Wells's advice, I keep my hip blistered with croton oil. That pain has almost entirely disappeared; but I feel that my system wants tone and strength. I do not feel that I am perfectly myself. Dr. Wells proposes to take a tour of two or three weeks with me, to various points; to go into Vermont, or to go to Niagara Falls. It will all depend upon hearing from home. My heart is with you and the little ones; kiss them all for me. May God bless you all, and keep you. Direct your letters to New York, until otherwise informed.

"Your devoted husband,

J. H. THORNWELL."

* A warm personal friend, who formerly resided in Columbia, South Carolina, and for many years a distinguished physician of that place.

We cannot more appropriately close this chapter than by transcribing the speech made by him at the Alumni dinner of Yale College, from the rough draft found amongst his papers:

"It is with unfeigned diffidence that I rise to respond to the sentiment which has just been drunk in behalf of the South Carolina College. I rejoice that in letters, as in religion, there is neither North nor South, East nor West. There should be no local jealousies, no sectional distinctions. The prosperity of one is the prosperity of all, as it indicates the partial attainment of the end for which all are instituted. I assure you, therefore, that in beholding this scene—a scene which touchingly and beautifully illustrates the past achievements and the present renown of your ancient and venerable institution, though I am a Carolinian by birth, by education, and love my native State, and my own *Alma Mater*, with a love passing the love of woman, yet I share with you—nay, more, I enter with full sympathy into the pride and generous exultation with which you must contemplate these trophies of Yale. Here are the fruits of her labours. These scholars, these educated men from every walk of life, from every liberal profession—physicians, lawyers, divines, and men more exclusively devoted to the pursuit of letters—these are the witnesses of her parental beneficence; and I can cheerfully unite with them, as they come from all quarters of our wide-spread country, to bring their votive offering, the tribute of their gratitude and the token of their affection, to her venerable feet. Sir, I cannot describe to you the feelings which, on an occasion like this, agitate my breast. It is not quite a week since I was invited to participate in similar festivities at that mother of American colleges, at Cambridge. It was the first time in my life that I had ever sat down with such a multitude of men, whose sole bond of union was letters. I looked around me: on the one hand, was the hoary veteran of four-score years; on the other, the boy who had graduated yesterday; and between them, all the stages of human life. There were all classes of opinion, all kinds of occupations; but all their differences were melted down; their hearts were fused into a common mass; they were all pervaded by the genius of the place, and that genius was the love of letters. By a similar courtesy, I witness a similar scene to-day; and with unfeigned sincerity, I open to you a brother's heart, and extend to you a brother's hand. These things remind us, sir, that 'the schoolmaster is abroad in the land.' The hope of our country is in the combined influence of letters and religion. Our colleges and schools are bulwarks and fortresses, stronger and mightier than weapons of brass or munitions of rock. A pure religion and a sound literature, these are our safety, and should be our highest glory. Education is the cheap defence of nations.

"I rejoice to say to you, sir, that the institution with which I have the honour to be connected, and where I learned the little that I know, is a sister whose kindred the noblest institution of New England need not blush to own. The South Carolina College is organized upon the same principles, conducted in the same general way, and devoted to the same ends, with the institutions of your own section of the country. She has made, too, the same mistake ; she has aimed to do too much. I am satisfied, sir, that our American Colleges have conceded too much to the utilitarian spirit of the age; and, in obedience to it, have aimed at something more than that intellectual discipline which should be the object. They have undertaken, not simply to teach men *how* to think, but *what* to think. They have undertaken, not merely to *educate*, that is, to bring out, and polish, and perfect, what is *in* man ; but they have also undertaken, over and above this, to put *into* him what the exigencies of life may require. This, sir, is too much. It is enough for them to fashion and sharpen the instrument, not to give the materials upon which it is to operate. We have all erred in this respect; but I am proud to say that South Carolina has not sinned so grievously as some of her sisters. But still, sir, she has sinned enough. Our course, as projected, looks to much more than a simple education, or effective discipline. It is largely scientific ; and though we do not turn out men ready fashioned as lawyers and doctors, we help them amazingly to the no less mysterious art of rearing a crop, or calculating the changes of the weather. We have enough of the practical to show that we belong to the nineteenth century.

"It will certainly be conceded to us, Mr. President, that we have made our mark upon the country. As I boasted—in no vain spirit, however—at Cambridge, so I boast here, that we have produced at least one scholar, of which any College and any country might well be proud. No name in this country stands higher than that of HUGH S. LEGARE. His article in the *New York Review* upon Demosthenes is enough to immortalize him ; but that was only the earnest of his strength. In the walks of public life, though we are not yet fifty years old, and of course never saw Abraham, we have sent men to the councils of the nation, with whom it was perilous for the boldest and best from other quarters to enter the lists in intellectual strife. Need I tell you of McDUFFIE ; not the politician, not the statesman, but McDuffie the orator. He was one of the few men that could still to silence, and chain in the profoundest attention, that most tumultuous, most disorderly, most ungovernable of all public bodies, the House of Representatives of the United States. It hung with breathless interest on his lips. Like Pericles—for it was of Pericles, and not Demosthenes, that Aristophanes wrote the sentence—he wielded at will that fierce democratic. Need I tell you of another, in some respects still more accomplished ; a more graceful, if not so vigorous; more attractive, if not so resistless ; one who could charm as well as persuade. I have listened for hours, sir, to the gifted PRESTON, and have forgotten, under the fascination of his eloquence, that there was such a thing as time. He ruled, like a wizard, the world of the heart ; and we point to him with pride, as one of the jewels of our beloved institution. Sir, if in less than half a century we had done nothing but help to make these men, our time and efforts and money would not have been ill-spent. This thought suggests to me an anecdote. Ours, you know, is a State institution. We have no funds, no endowment, and but one scholarship, the munificent donation of a wealthy, noble, high-minded citizen, now in the vigour of his faculties. We are dependent upon an annual vote of the Legislature for all our means. When the College was first established, there was a good deal of prejudice in certain quarters against it; and some districts sent representatives to the Legislature, who were not favourable to its continuance. On one occasion, while Mr. McDuffie was a member of the Legislature, after he had made one of his splendid speeches, the question of the College came up. The venerable Judge Huger, then a member of the House, rose and said, in his peculiarly slow and emphatic style: "Mr. Speaker, if the South Carolina College had done nothing, sir, but produce that man, she would have amply repaid the State for every dollar that the State has ever expended, or ever will expend, upon her." The appeal was irresistible; opposition was disarmed; and every year, sir, we receive nearly twenty-five thousand dollars from a small State, and from a poor people.

"But, sir, enough of ourselves. I cannot sit down, sir, without expressing to Yale our debt of gratitude for the part she took in fashioning a man, of whom South Carolina will be proud as long as her people can appreciate genius, patriotism, integrity, and disinterested zeal in the service of his country. Sir, you number among your Alumni a name which cannot be pronounced in Carolina without the profoundest emotion; and may I not say it, it is rather a glory to you than to him, that his name is found on your catalogue. You took him, sir, when we had no place for him to go to. You honoured him; you understood his worth; and you sent him out to gladden and bless the land. Sir, we thank you for it; we cannot cease to love you for it; and as that dear and cherished name is one in which we have a common interest, permit me, without any reference to any type of political opinions, permit me, on this occasion, to give as a sentiment:

"THE MEMORY OF JOHN C. CALHOUN."

CHAPTER XXVI.

RESIDENCY CONTINUED.

WHILE the subject of these Memoirs is occupied with the routine of College discipline, we will employ the leisure in tracing his private life, as opened in the correspondence of the period. The first letter is dated a little back, and is addressed to his friend, Dr. R. J. Breckinridge, in which he criticises the action of the Assembly of 1852, that met in the city of Charleston:

"SOUTH CAROLINA COLLEGE, *June* 28, 1852.

"MY DEAR BROTHER: It has been in my heart to write to you, ever since the meeting of the Assembly ; but cares and afflictions have combined to prevent me so long, that I am now almost ashamed to take up my pen. I have just committed to the grave a lovely babe, nearly seventeen months old. It was snatched away most unexpectedly : and though I trust that I am fully resigned to the Divine will, my heart has bled at this sudden and unlooked for bereavement. It was our youngest child, and a sweeter babe never delighted a father's heart. I am happy to say that the rest of my family are well; but when I see them gathered around me, I cannot describe the peculiar sadness which comes over me as I contemplate the breach in our little circle. Seven children yet remain to me ; two are gathered into the bosom of the great Shepherd.

"You have probably heard that I did not attend the Assembly. One of our Professors was absent at the time, and another sick ; so that a mass of extra work was thrown on me, which rendered it imprudent that I should leave the College. There were parts of its proceedings which were very unfortunate. The Synod of South Carolina, at its last session, disapproved as irregular, without pronouncing invalid, a *pro re nata* meeting of the Presbytery of Charleston, at which no ruling elders were present. The terms of the resolution are as follows :

"'*Resolved,* That, in the judgment of this Synod, the *pro re nata* meeting of the Presbytery of Charleston, at Charleston, on September

369

9th, 1851, was irregular; inasmuch as it constituted and proceeded to business without a ruling elder. The Synod, however, admit the validity of what they did.' (Printed Minutes of the Synod of South Carolina, p. 19.)

"This resolution was especially excepted by the Assembly, in approving the Records of the Synod. (See the session of the eighth day, Friday, May 28th.) What makes this bad matter still worse, I have seen no one yet who seems to have understood what he was voting about. The thing was hurried through the house without explanation or discussion, and a heavy blow struck at the constitution of the Church in sheer blindness. It was a wretched piece of work, view it in what light you will. Wretched as it was, however, it is outdone by the resolution in the case of the Charleston Union Presbytery. That resolution quietly ignores all the great principles which were involved in the whole New School controversy. In the first place, the Charleston Union Presbytery is a *mixed* body. It was originally formed by a union of Presbyterians and Congregationalists. Hence its name. The Assembly, therefore, in admitting it *as a Presbytery*, constituted as it is, has virtually endorsed the old doctrine of the Plan of Union. This is *one* step backwards. * * * * * *

"But further, the Assembly has, out and out, endorsed the principle of elective affinity. It has made arrangements upon *two* Presbyteries upon precisely the *same* territory. The Charleston Presbytery, and the Charleston Union Presbytery, are to occupy the same ground.* All this mischief was done upon an ex-parte statement of the Charleston Union Presbytery, which statement was *never read* in the Assembly at all, but referred to a committee, and that committee reported by *naked resolution*. The facts of the case were not before the House. The committee reports its *judgment* upon the facts, and that judgment is all that the Assembly had regularly before it. Was there ever such a monstrous perversion of justice? The 'statement' was printed, but not circulated, until *after* the committee reported. So, at least, I have been informed. There

---

* This exception is well taken, looking only at the terms of the resolution adopted by the Assembly, which was all, at the time, before the writer of this letter. The resolution read thus: "*Resolved*, That if the Charleston Union Presbytery shall make known to the Stated Clerk of the General Assembly their adhesion to this General Assembly, and its doctrinal standards, prior to the next annual meeting of the Synod of South Carolina, it shall be the duty of the Stated Clerk to communicate the same, without delay, to said Synod; and the Synod shall thereupon enrol them as a regular Presbytery in connexion with this body."

It is proper to add, that the Synod, in obeying the injunction of the Assembly, at once amalgamated the two Presbyteries, which, doubtless, it was expected they would do. But so far as the action of the Assembly is concerned, no guard was thrown against the re-enactment of the exploded elective affinity principle.

were the strongest local reasons why the Assembly should not have touched this business. The Charleston Presbytery had adopted, and was systematically pursuing a line of policy which, in a few years, would have extinguished Independency in the low-country. We were gradually absorbing all its churches. New Schoolism was dead. All we wanted was to be let alone. But now things are put back where they were twenty years ago. * * * * *

"My dear brother, I am sick at heart. Here have I been working and toiling for the past twelve years to bring things into their present posture; and when everything was moving on beautifully and promisingly, it is hard to see the result of so many labours frustrated by rashness and inconsiderate haste. I am depressed and cast down. The Church is going backwards. She has forgotten her past testimonies.

"The suppression of the Popery sermon was significant of the spirit and temper of the men who compose the body. But I have said enough, perhaps too much.

"Our vacation has begun. I shall leave in a few days for the north. I shall be at the Harvard and Yale commencements. It would do me a great good to see you again in the flesh. Can you not meet me somewhere in the course of the summer?

"The Lord be with you and bless you.

"Most truly, as ever,

"J. H. THORNWELL."

To Dr. Wardlaw, of Abbeville:

"SOUTH CAROLINA COLLEGE, *December* 13, 1852.

"MY DEAR DOCTOR: I write to impress you with a deep sense of my gratitude for the favour you have conferred upon me in the exquisite cigars. They have but a single fault, and that modesty forbids me to mention. Still, I may be permitted to regret, for the sake of those generous souls that are disposed to remember their friends, that it is becoming at all fashionable to put up *such* cigars in such *small* boxes. I would have you to understand that there is no virtue that I admire more than I do gratitude; the ancients prized it very much, and Walpole has defined it to be "*the expectation of future favours.*" The cigars will not certainly last for ever; and even if they should, it should not be forgotten that hog-killing comes only once in a year, and *sausages* are always welcome. We love our friends so much, that we rejoice in everything which gives them an opportunity of showing how much they deserve to be loved. As Mary delights in the commendations of her housewifery, and as there is no one who is fonder of bestowing well-merited praises than myself, I should not at all be disposed to decline the trying of any articles of her preparation, just for the purpose of praising her skill. You have no idea of what eloquent eulogiums I would pronounce, as I discussed her sausages, her turkeys, her hams, her cakes, or any other knick-knack that she might wish to submit to my criticism.   I love to accommodate my friends.   And if *you* should come across another box of cigars, and should be doubtful whether they are better than the ones sent or not, you need not scruple about sending them to me for my judgment, as I assure you it will put me to no sort of inconvenience, and I will take great pleasure in resolving your doubts.

"I am sorry that you and Mary were not with us this winter.   There is no person that I like to see better than yourselves.   If the railroad were not out of joint, I should be tempted to run up and take Christmas dinner with you.   One meal at your house would do me for almost a year.

"Most truly, yours as ever,

J. H. THORNWELL."

To the Rev. (now Dr.) Thomas E. Peck:

"SOUTH CAROLINA COLLEGE, *April* 15, 1853.

"MY DEAR THOMAS: I was delighted a few weeks ago at receiving a letter in your well-known, familiar hand-writing.   My wife and myself came very near having a scramble to determine who should read it first; but we settled the matter by my agreeing, with all humility, to read it aloud.   It was curious to watch the workings of her countenance, as I passed leisurely over your protracted introduction, in which, according to the rules of art, you conciliate attention and propitiate favour.   You were perfectly successful.   After your preamble of compliments, if we had had a thousand ears you should have had them all.   It was literally '*erectis auribus,*' that we passed on to the next head of your discourse. I could notice that, as you proceeded from topic to topic, there was an air of impatience, and of eager expectation, on the part of the fair auditor, which I was unable to explain.   I could not understand what disturbed her interest in as sweet a missive as I have had discharged upon me for many a day.   When I reached the peroration, however, the mystery was solved.   A long letter, and not a word about his wife!   'Well, well, I am done with Tom Peck!'   I endeavoured to apologize; but all in vain. Perhaps, said I, it is not a pleasant subject, and you would not have him vent his misfortunes on his friends.   Or, perhaps it is so pleasant that he is afraid to trust himself with it, lest he should be charged with extravagance or insolence; or perhaps he has not yet vanquished the shyness incident to his new relation, and feels a little ashamed when he talks of '*my wife*' or '*my dear.*'   I reminded her that all newly married folks felt a little sneaking at first.   They had to get used to it, before the thing sat easily.   I cannot say that my oratory has been very successful.   She cannot yet comprehend the mystery, that a man should be able to exclude his wife from his mind long enough to write a whole letter.   But you will perceive that my efforts have been very laudable to save your reputation.

"I have just returned from Presbytery.   It was a bitter pill to be 'hail fellow, well met,' with a parcel of men who have done all that they could, within the last ten years, to break down Presbyterianism in South Carolina. So far as churches are concerned, there is a present addition to the strength of the body. But, in the long run, I am afraid that we shall lose rather than gain. Some of us are determined to set our faces against the introduction of any more Congregational ministers. This will inevitably produce disturbance. The next pastor of the Circular Church, and of all the little Island churches will, of course, expect to be received on the same footing with their predecessors. The opposition which will be made will lead to controversy, and perhaps to schism. On the score of doctrine, I apprehend but little mischief. I think, some of them are disposed to learn. At any rate, they will have so little sympathy, if, after all their professions, they should venture on anything unsound, that there will be no difficulty in managing them. Upon the whole, my impression is that the union has put back the cause of Presbyterianism in the low country about a quarter of a century. My comfort is that the Lord rules, and that He can bring good out of evil.

"We installed Dr. Kirkpatrick, pastor of the Glebe Street Church. I never saw him until Presbytery. He preached once, and his sermon was very sound and evangelical, and had, besides, a good deal of unction. I trust that he may prove a real acquisition.

"We have sent Adger and Dr. Smyth to the General Assembly. Adger is one of the truest men I know; a man after God's own heart. It is a great pity that his eyes incapacitate him for regular and steady labour.

"I see that Robinson has raised a breeze in Baltimore. I cannot say that I am disappointed in the result. There must have been some who were longing for the truth, or they surely would never have called him; and it was quite natural that these should cling to him, when his faithfulness was driving others from him. The schism, in my judgment, is an event not to be deplored.

"I have recently read Bunsen's Hippolytus, and rose from its perusal with a feeling of the deepest sadness. It is an elaborate effort to prove that the Christianity of the early Church was moulded in the type of Schelling's philosophy. Under the pretext of zeal for the cause of evangelical religion, it annihilates every distinctive doctrine of the Reformed Church. It is in the same vein with ———. They have drunk from the same fountains, and if possible, it is still more superficial. Where will this thing end?

"There ought to be some thorough-going exposure of the vanity and folly of the whole school of the transcendental philosophy. There is the root of the evil; and until the axe is laid there, nothing effective can be done. I am meditating an article on the subject; but it will require time and patience. I have been studying that philosophy afresh, and am taking it at its fountains. I am now reading Kant carefully and critically in the original. I have sent for the works of all his prominent successors. In the mean time, I am going thoroughly into ancient philosophy; and by such a course I hope to be able to beard the lion in his

den. I have really been a close student this winter, and as the result of
it feel that I know less than I ever did before.   The sense of ignorance
daily grows upon me, and frequently disheartens me.   And what is still
more distressing, my anxiety for knowledge I find to be too much an
anxiety for glory.   What a pity that a man must be kept a fool, in order
to keep him humble.

"The College is getting along very smoothly.   We have never had a
more quiet and orderly time.   What, above all things, we want, is an
outpouring of the Divine Spirit.   I have prayed for it, and waited for it,
but I see no signs of it.   I rejoice to hear that the Lord has blessed your
labours, and I trust that you may yet see abundant fruit of your faith
and patience.   The death of Mr. Spreckleson was a great loss.   I felt
deeply for you when I heard of it.   Let me hear from you soon again;
it always refreshes me to receive a letter from you.   My kindest regards
to your good lady.

"Most truly, your friend,

J. H. THORNWELL."

To the same:

"SOUTH CAROLINA COLLEGE, *August* 24, 1853.

"MY DEAR THOMAS: I received your letter last Friday, and together
with it, your *thank-offering*, which, in your humility and poverty, you
have represented as a *dove.*   It is well that, like the painter in the fable,
you have been considerate enough to write the name under your picture,
as otherwise there might have been some difficulty in detecting the dove-
like properties of the animal in question.   It has something so much like
talons and claws, and manifests so marked a propensity to bite, tear, and
devour, that, in the absence of positive and authentic information to the
contrary, one might have been tempted to mistake it for a vulture or a
hawk, a species of animal that was never offered in sacrifice.   But dove,
vulture, or hawk, be it what it may, I am glad to receive it; and if such
contributions are to mark the birth of every child, I could wish that the
usual period of the event were shortened in your case, and that you might
have new claims to be considered as a father every three months, especially
if the ardour of your gratitude should keep pace with the frequency of
the blessing.   There is nothing like writing to make a man exact.   In
all seriousness, I would advise you often to use the pen in rendering an
account to yourself of the attainments you have made.   It has been the
mistake of my life that I have written so little.   Learn from *my* experience.

"The passage in Sir William Hamilton, I presume, perplexed you
only on account of the introduction of the terms *encentric* and *eccentric*.
The figure is this: consciousness is compared to a circle; whatever is
given in consciousness, is *within* the circle, encentric; whatever is not
given, is *without* the circle, *eccentric*.   Now, those who hold that the
absolute is a *positive* element of thought, maintain either that it is *known*,
a thing given in consciousness, and therefore has objective reality; or
that it is merely a notion, represented in thought, without objective

reality. The first make it an intuition, an immediate manifestation *within* the *circle* of consciousness of the objective reality. This is an *encentric intuition.* The other make it merely a notion, necessitated by the laws of mind; in other words, a law of thought. These are still *within* the circle of consciousness, but not of intuition. There is no *matter* given, which is necessary to intuition. There is merely the thought. This was the position of Kant. Others maintain, that the absolute can neither be *known* nor *thought;* that it lies wholly *beyond* or *without* the circle of consciousness; that it is *vox et prœterea nihil.* These make it an eccentric generalization. Now, the opinion that it is thinkable, is intermediate between the doctrines that it is knowable, and that it is not conceivable. It agrees with the first, in saying that it is something positive in the human mind; it agrees with the last, in saying that no matter corresponds to it. Kant brought the absolute within the circle of consciousness, but not of intuition. Fichte brought it within the circle of both. Hamilton excluded it from both. I do not know that I have made myself intelligible. If not, it may necessitate another letter from you.

"You ask my opinion of Sir William's doctrine of cause and effect. I must say that, with all my respect for his learning, and admiration of his genius, he appears to me to have tripped here. His doctrine concerning the integrity of being, and the impossibility of increasing or diminishing it, is really a new form of the absolute; and involves, as it seems to me, that species of pantheism into which Schliermacher fell in regard to the relation of the universe to God. Creation is either a substantive addition to being, or it is only a manifestation of what previously existed substantially in God. If the latter, it is a *part* of God in a new form; if the former, the fundamental postulate of Sir William's doctrine of cause and effect falls to the ground. I am chary of all opinions which conflict with the *individuality* of God. He must be kept separate from His works. He is a Person, and acts from will and choice; and anything of causation which approximates the idea of a development or a derivation from Him, is revolting to my mind. I tremble at anything that has a tendency to make God a principle, or a law. He is a free agent, and does as He pleases. The universe is to be considered as an arbitrary product of will. It might have been different; it might not have been at all; it was all a matter resting with the choice of an individual, a personality. Hence, to know the universe, *a priori*, is to know God.

"But a truce to metaphysics. * * * I am at present alone. My wife is on a visit to Abbeville, to nurse her sister, Mrs. Wardlaw, who is very ill. I saw your mother a day or two ago, in the street, who was very much shocked at the simplicity of my dress. She had just been buying some finery, and I suppose her judgment was perverted.

"Let me hear from you soon. Love to all.

"Most truly, your friend,

J. H. Thornwell."

To the Rev. John Douglas:

"SOUTH CAROLINA COLLEGE, *July* 5, 1854.

"DEARLY BELOVED BROTHER: I was sitting down entertaining company—and a stranger, too, from a distance—when your note was put into my hands, announcing the mission of the watermelons. I forgot all the restraints of decency and custom, and gave expression to my joy according to the spontaneous dictates of the moment. My exclamation soon collected all the household, to see what was the matter. I pointed to the letter; they read, and were delighted too. How much happiness one generous action produces! He is blessed himself, and blesses others, in whom there is much of '*the milk of human kindness.*'* What made the watermelons particularly acceptable was, that I had just been delivering a cold water speech in a cold water (Baptist) church; and although it was the Fourth of July, I did not feel at liberty to venture in my festivities beyond the region of cold water.

"I was glad you reached home without melting. We have had fine rains since you left, but the weather still continues deplorably warm. I am afraid to poke my nose out. The family, however, all continue to enjoy good health. I cannot promise to visit you; I have too much to do. Mrs. T. joins me in kindest regards to Mrs. D. and yourself.

"Yours, most truly,

J. H. THORNWELL."

The temperance address to which allusion is made above, was delivered at the request of the Central Committee of the State Temperance Convention, which was then moving in an effort to secure proper legislation for the suppression of drunkenness. This general policy Dr. Thornwell advocated, though he did not commit himself to any particular measure. Indeed, the movement was only in its incipiency, and no détails were as yet fixed upon. In this address, he contended that the whole subject came properly under the jurisdiction of law. Law is founded on the *rights* of men; and whatever interferes with these rights, with the peace and prosperity of the community at large, falls within the province of legis-

---

* Dr. Thornwell never missed an opportunity of quizzing his friends. A poor creature, whom he sent off to Mr. Douglas, after getting tired of taking care of him, was fond of praising his new-found friend as a man "full of the milk of human kindness." It became afterwards a standing joke against Mr. Douglas.

lation. Drunkenness, he argued, *is in the single act a crime*. It is a sin against the whole man, and against the whole law. It makes a man worse than a beast; for the impulses of a beast are his law, whilst ours are blind, and need a law. It would be a great advance if public sentiment could be brought to brand it with disgrace, and not simply to regard it as a misfortune. Again, drunkenness, in *its principle, is a conspiracy against the law of a refined civilization*. It is marked by the predominance of the animal over the rational; and society is therefore called upon, for its own protection, to strike at an enemy that threatens the very citadel of refinement. Further, he argued that it operates like a *disease*. In the act, it is a momentary derangement; in the habit, it is a general incapacity. In both forms it affects the rights of others; and the law should interpose, and deal with the drunkard as it deals with the minor, or with the maniac. But all legislation, he concludes, should be founded on the *moral convictions* of the community, which alone enables a State to execute its penal code; and a law, properly framed, would serve to educate public opinion, and mark the moral progress of a people.

The following *jeu d'esprit* is addressed to the Rev. Dr. J. B. Adger :

"SOUTH CAROLINA COLLEGE, *September* 15, 1854.

"DEAR BELOVED ADGER : I received your note, two or three days ago, upon my return from the up country, and could not but notice how much easier it is to ask questions than to answer them. That is decidedly the opinion of the students; and facts seem to confirm it. Business, however, of a carnal kind, is not always embarrassing, and therefore I shall begin with something of that sort.

"Be it known to you, then, that my wheat seed is run out, and I want to renew it with a fresh kind. Your reputation as a planter has reached these parts, and I know of no one who is so likely to be able to gratify my wishes. Besides, as dogs will not eat dogs, one Presbyterian preacher will hardly cheat another in a trade.

"Without further ceremony, I want you to send me twelve bushels of your best wheat. I want it of the early kind, and without beards. If you have not got so much yourself, you must try Maxwell, or some one that can supply me. I am going to take a fresh start in wheat sowing, and must have *good seed.* I have already the *good ground ;* and my past failures are owing, beyond doubt, to the *seed.* It may be well to inform you, too, that I have to buy all my flour the present year. A hint is enough to the wise. Now, the supply of the wheat I make a condition to my answering any hard questions. I must see a reasonable prospect of having something to eat, before I condescend to minister to any man's curiosity.

"I have received another long letter from Breckinridge. He speaks in the kindest terms of you ; and is so marked in his rapturous admiration of the feminine portion of your household, that I think it well for the peace and safety of you both that so many miles lie between you. I am sure that Mrs. Adger never treated him, as she did me, to ice cream flavoured with spirits of turpentine. She must have had on a magic cap ; and as she has marvellously succeeded in getting her name up, I advise her to follow my example in all such cases : to be very reserved, and let 'distance lend enchantment to the view.' I have a great horror, when once my milk pail is full, of kicking it over.

"I see Palmer every whip-stitch ; he is really beginning to look down-right *well.* On the 22d—that is, this day week—I shall be in Abbeville. Can you not meet me there ? I should like very much to see you, and talk matters over with you. I think I could give you a wrinkle or two. Be sure to meet me. My family is well. I have been helping to dig some potatoes, and my hand is so tremulous, in consequence, that I can hardly write. My kindest regards to Mrs. A. *Don't forget the wheat.*

"Very truly, as ever,

J. H. THORNWELL."

To the same :

"SOUTH CAROLINA COLLEGE, *September* 20, 1854.

"MY DEAR BROTHER : I have just received your *scratch,* and reply in a decent and gentlemanly hand, by return mail. It will be impossible for me to visit you. I wish I could do so, but I am engaged in printing a little book, which requires my constant attention. I begrudge the time I shall spend at Abbeville. But that engagement is of long standing. I shall remain there till next Tuesday. You do not know how much I want to see you. I wish very much that you would come down. My best compliments to Mrs. A.

"Most truly yours,

J. H. THORNWELL."

This unimportant note is introduced, only because of its reference to a little volume, entitled "Discourses on Truth," published, in 1855, by Robert Carter and Brothers, New York, and which will be found republished in the second volume of his "Collected Writings." The Discourses were originally delivered in the chapel of the South Carolina College, in his regular ministrations to the students, as their Chaplain. A single sentence in the preface states the true character of the work: "The structure of the sermons may be explained by the circumstance, that the author sustains the double office in the College of a preacher of the gospel and a teacher of Moral Philosophy. It is his custom to make the pulpit and the lecture room subservient to each other." The reader will not, therefore, be disappointed in finding in them an authoritative exposition of Moral Science from the teachings of the Bible. No higher testimony to their merit can be given than the following expression, which they drew from Sir William Hamilton, in a note addressed to the author:

"EDINBURGH, *July* 23, 1855.

"SIR: I beg leave to return my warmest acknowledgments for your *Discourses on Truth.* I have read them with great interest, and no less admiration. I was particularly pleased with the justice with which, it seems to me, you have spoken of the comparative merits of Aristotle, as a moralist, and cordially coincide with your judgment upon Paley and other modern ethical writers. I need hardly say that I feel much flattered by the way in which you have been pleased to make reference to myself; and I remain, Sir,

"Your most obedient servant,

W. HAMILTON."

CHAPTER XXVII.

CLOSE OF HIS PRESIDENCY.

Movement to Transfer Him from the College to the Theological Seminary.—Reasons for it.—Action of the Synod of South Carolina and of Georgia.—Relative Importance of the Two Positions Discussed, in Correspondence, with Dr. Breckinridge.—Resignation of the Presidency.—Arrested for a Twelve Month.—Letters.—Assembly of 1855.—Debate on the Board Question.—Termination of His Connexion with the College.—Review of His Vast Influence over the Students.—Elements of Character that Explain it.—Illustrations of it.

DURING the third year of Dr. Thornwell's presidency, a movement was begun which resulted in terminating finally his connexion with the College, and transferring him to the chair of Theology, in the Divinity School at Columbia, South Carolina. The change involved many and great sacrifices, the largest of which was the loss of influence, which the Presbyterian Church exerted, through him, over the College and the State. In the light of worldly policy, this was an unwise surrender; but it was justified by weighty considerations, on the other side. In the first place, honourable as was the station which he filled, it necessitated a devotion to the duties of mere police, which, with a man so richly gifted, was felt by many to be a great waste of power. The anxiety and care, too, which were wrapped up in this work of simple administration, were evidently consuming his physical strength; and it was only too apparent that a constitution, feeble at best, could not for a great while endure these exertions. A strong desire also existed in the Church, that he, who was regarded with so much pride as pre-eminently a representative man, should leave be-

381

hind him some work, which would be an enduring memorial of his genius and of his fame.   He had already
given two smaller books to the world; and had contributed to the *Review* many valuable monographs upon most
important subjects.   But these were accepted only as an
earnest of what more abundant leisure would enable him to
achieve.   The Church, it was argued, which had so long
lent him to the State, should now reclaim him to her immediate service; and the controlling motive with those
who advocated his translation to the Theological Seminary, was that, in the prosecution of its sacred studies,
he might pour out upon the Church, and upon the world,
the treasures of knowledge stored up through years of
patient acquisition.   Alas! that the wish, so ardently
cherished, should have been only half realized!   The
reader will not close the perusal of his Theological Lectures, in the first volume of his " Collected Writings,"
without a sigh that the Church did not have the wisdom
to effect the change in his position at least five years
earlier.   As Dr. Breckinridge says, in one of the letters
we have given, " The blade was too sharp for the scabbard."   Too much study, and too much care, had already
done their fearful execution upon a feeble frame; and
death came in with his sad arrest, before the great work
which the Church desired was half executed.   In addition to these considerations, there was a general advance,
at this period, in the matter of theological education.
Princeton, Prince Edward, and Alleghany Seminaries,
were all recruited by the addition of superior talent to
their Faculties; and Danville Seminary had been created
only the year before, with the greatest intellectual force
that could be commanded in the West.   The institution
at Columbia could not be expected to hold her place in
this honourable competition, unless she was lifted out of
the crippled condition in which she had existed from the
beginning, and equipped with a full corps of instructors.
The scheme was, of course, slowly matured in a few

minds, and was discussed at first only in private circles. At length it took shape, in definite resolutions, adopted the last of June, or first of July, 1854, by the Board of Directors of the Columbia Seminary. These resolutions contemplated the appointment of Dr. Thornwell to the chair of Theology, and of the writer of these pages to the chair of Church History and Government, which he had been provisionally occupying for some time, in connexion with his pastorship of the Columbia church. At the annual meeting of the Synod of South Carolina and Georgia, the whole subject was fully debated; and the well digested plans of the Board of Directors were carried through. In accordance with this intimation of the will of the Church, Dr. Thornwell tendered his resignation of the Presidency of the College, on the 29th of November, 1854; but was met, as once before, with the enforcement of the law, which required a year's notice before the resignation could take effect. He was not, therefore, actually released until December, 1855, which forms the date of his entrance upon the duties of his Professorship in the Theological Seminary. This brief rehearsal will give the key to allusions found in the correspondence that follows:

To the Rev. Dr. Breckinridge:

"SOUTH CAROLINA COLLEGE, *July* 18, 1854.

"MY DEAR BROTHER: Your kind and welcome letter, received from Buffalo, has remained unanswered, because I have been indulging the delusive hope of saying to you in person much more than I can impart on paper. I had thought of making a tour, in the course of the summer, to terminate at Danville. But my plans have been defeated; and I must resort to pen and ink for what the tongue could have done much better.

"I am glad to see that Adger left Buffalo with so warm an attachment to yourself. It is an additional bond of sympathy between us. I am apt to measure a man's claims to respect by the estimate he forms of you and oᶠ your services; and as I have a very high opinion of Adger, I was gratified to find that he gave this proof of deserving it. He is indeed a noble Roman, or rather an Israelite in whom there is no guile.

"You have probably seen the resolutions adopted by the Board of

Directors of this Seminary in their last meeting. Things had reached a crisis, and something vigorous was to be done, or the Seminary virtually abandoned. It was ascertained that, if things remained another year as they were, the next session would, in all likelihood, open with the merest handful of students, not more than six or eight. The Board determined to propose a measure which, it was thought, would remove these grounds of complaint. They nominated me for the chair of Theology, and Palmer for that of History. This procedure has, of course, been a very embarrassing one to me. The station which I now occupy is not lightly to be resigned. The field of influence is wide; and the indications are, that my labours are not without success. On the other hand, it was a grave responsibility to say that this Seminary should be closed. The work in it is most important, and a work for which I have some qualifications that are not universal. The proposition was most unexpectedly made to me, and was accompanied by so many strange coincidences, that I was afraid peremptorily to decline it, lest I should be found fighting against God. I resolved, therefore, to throw the whole matter upon the two Synods, requiring them, not to pronounce directly upon the question whether they would like to have me in the Seminary, but upon the question whether I ought to leave the College for that situation. The question, consequently, as it will go before the two Synods, is as to the comparative importance of the two posts; and in this aspect of the matter, the decision is extremely doubtful. Trifles have their weight; and one little thing, which, if all men were magnanimous, would hardly have suggested itself to me, has really had a very considerable influence. In going to the Seminary, I shall have to make an annual sacrifice of fifteen hundred or two thousand dollars; and I want it to be clear to all men that, if I am retained here, I have not been retained because I was unwilling to encounter loss in the service of God.

Now, I want you to give me your frank opinion upon this whole subject. You are able to compare the situation I now fill, with that which I am asked to fill. I am sure that I cannot be unanimously elected; too many members of this Synod are interested in this College for that; and if there should be a respectable minority against the change, the question will have to be decided by myself, upon the best view I can take of its merits. A unanimous vote I should look upon as a clear call of God, precluding all debate on my part; a divided vote, as I distinctly announced to the Board, I should feel under no obligations to treat with any further respect than to consider the question it raised. Now, in case of a divided vote, which I confidently expect, what, in your judgment, are the principles which should immediately control my decision? I really want your counsels and your prayers.

"It has given me great pleasure to hear of the prosperity of Danville. Your policy is a lofty magnanimity, and in your hands, I am sure it is a policy which will be pursued.

"I have nothing of special interest to communicate. I work hard, but accomplish little. Let me hear from you soon, very soon. I hope to see you in Columbia next winter. We are to have a celebration in commemoration of the fiftieth anniversary of the College. It will be quite an occasion, and you will be invited to attend. Turn the thing in your mind, and be sure to come.

"Most truly yours, as ever,

J. H. THORNWELL."

From the Rev. Dr. Breckinridge:

"*July* 28, 1854.

MY DEAR THORNWELL: Your letter of the 18th inst. has been delayed in reaching me, by reason of having been directed to Danville. I have, as yet, not been able to make such arrangements as to remove my family to that place, though eight months of the year are spent there by me; the remainder being spent mainly at this place, the spot dearest to me, and where the first years of my early manhood were passed, with my young family. In truth, of all my changes, this one to Danville has been attended with the greatest personal and domestic inconvenience and sacrifice; and by far the most cruelty and unkindness on the part of other persons. It is only the strongest sense of duty that has induced me to embark in the work, or that sustains me under its toils and responsibilities. At every step I have appeared to have no alternative, except the one embraced; and at every step, while everything has been every time put to risk, thus far every step has been attended with success. And that is still our condition. Similar favour from God will carry us, far and soon, on our way; but one false movement may ruin everything much faster than it has been built up. At present, all seems promising.

"At Buffalo, I was made acquainted, confidentially, with the scheme which the immediate and enlightened friends of the Seminary at Columbia were meditating; and which has since then been made known to the public, and partly carried to maturity. As to the proposed changes in that Seminary, the proposed addition of yourself and Palmer to its professors, there can be but one opinion. No Seminary in this country can compare with that, if these arrangements can be perfected. And, frankly, after what has occurred within the last few months, I hardly see any great need of our Danville Seminary at all. McGill is a great addition to Princeton, in some important respects; B. M. Smith and Dr. Dabney are both decided gain to Prince Edwards, in many things of great importance; Plumer will make an era in Western Pennsylvania; and if you and Palmer enter Columbia, that Seminary must immediately occupy the very first rank. I cannot help feeling, and I rejoice to be allowed to think, that our movement in Kentucky has not been without an important bearing, in stimulating others to these new exertions; so that, if we do nothing more, our efforts will not have been unfruitful; and if we can live amidst the noble competition thus created, it is better a hundred fold than to have swallowed up the poor things our Seminaries were fast becoming. Thanks to God for all good, every way!

"As to yourself, I would not hesitate to give the advice you ask, if I had sufficient information to render it proper for me to do so. But you need not feel any apprehension. The Lord will direct you plainly what you should do. On either hand, you have a great work; and if neither work were within your reach, many others would be offered to you, equal to either of them. And if none were offered, you have only to use, any way and any where, the gifts and graces God has bestowed on you, to accomplish what few others could accomplish at all. There is really less, after all, in particular positions, than men persuade themselves there is; and in our day, less than formerly; and less and less hereafter. Still, I am able to see that, in the Seminary at Columbia, you could render a service to our own ministry, and eventually to the cause of our Master, which it would be impossible to estimate; while, at the same time, I rather suppose that Seminary would not be the most favourable position for such a work as you could do, except so far as your connexion with it would most materially overrule many unfavourable peculiarities of its position. Whether the additional good you could hardly fail to do to the Church, would compensate for the evil done to your State, and society at large, by your change; and whether, even admitting this, the additional good is adequate, besides, to require the very serious personal sacrifices required of you; whether, on the whole, the deliberate conviction of the Church itself in your two Synods, especially your own Synod, is clear for this charge on your part: these, and similar questions, which enter largely into the case, I cannot determine. This much I may say: that, in the presence of the Assembly of 1853, I publicly said, if I supposed there was the remotest possibility of your listening to such a proposition, you were, of all men, the one we would select for any chair you would agree to fill in our Danville Seminary. Therefore, there is every reason why I should say, if fitness is the *only* question, by all means accept; but also every reason why I should say that, all questions considered, I, who despaired of moving you in 1853, am unable to say now, in 1854, that I can advise you to accept a similar, and certainly not more important, place. Still, I must confess that, if such were the will of God, I should feel glad for you to accept the position offered to you under such peculiar circumstances, and for so needful a work to our Church. May God bless and direct you, is the prayer of

Your faithful friend,

Ro. J. BRECKINRIDGE."

To the Rev. (now Dr.) Thomas E. Peck:

"SOUTH CAROLINA COLLEGE, *February* 23, 1855.

"DEAR THOMAS: Upon receiving the first number of the *Presbyterial Critic*, I began a letter to you; but not being in the right vein, I had to discontinue it, and wait for a freer inspiration. That inspiration has not yet come; but in consequence of the recent fire at the College, I have been compelled to worship with the Presbyterian people in town, and am subject to a ceaseless catechism from certain mothers in Israel, which a regard for my own peace requires that I should put to rest by writing you what may pass for a letter. Direct assaults I might, perhaps, be able to resist, at least to parry; but if you could see the numberless ways in which I am invaded—the oblique hint, the sly inuendo, the caustic inference, the leering suspicion—you would perceive at once that there was no use in holding out; that I had better set to work, and do what I can. Excuse me, therefore, as necessity is laid upon me. My small paper is to be taken as no presumption against my good faith; as from the closeness and compactness of my handwriting, I put more upon a sheet of this size, than most folks do upon foolscap or quarto. If you will only take the trouble to count the letters, you will be surprised at the quantity of matter, the *multum in parvo*, of my unpretending little document.

"The appearance of your Magazine has reminded me very much of Hamlet's ghost, at least, in its first effect upon the public mind. 'Thou com'st in such a *questionable* shape, that I will speak to thee.' The *Presbyterian, Watchman,* and *Observer,* and other similar papers, seem to be in a great strait as to your real character; whether 'a spirit of health, or goblin damned;' whether thou 'bring with thee airs from heaven, or blasts from hell;' whether 'thy intents are wicked, or charitable.' I hope, however, that you will prove an 'honest ghost,' and teach us, in the long run, that there are 'more things in heaven and earth than are dreamed of in our philosophy;' in other words, that all the wisdom of the Presbyterian Church is not locked up in one or two places. But to be serious: I think that such an organ as you propose to give us is greatly needed. The only mischief to be apprehended is, that you may run too fast. *Festina lente;* let that be your motto, and you cannot fail to accomplish great good. With the tone and temper of the articles I was entirely satisfied; except that, in one of them, there were foreshadowings of principles which I am not prepared to endorse. I allude to the queries in "Hints for the Times," in relation to the press. So, also, on the subject of theological education; I am not sure that I understand the nature of the change which has been introduced at Danville, and which, it is insinuated, is an indication of progress. The unity of a subject is not destroyed by synthetical teaching; and synthesis has always been regarded as the true method of instruction. The other method I do not comprehend. If a subject has parts, let the parts be mastered and put together, and you have the whole. How you can get the whole in any other way, is more than I can divine.

"These things have nothing to do with the general principle and aims of your work; and it is perhaps well that they should be thrown out as problems, to elicit thought. You need not be assured of my cordial concurrence in your views of Doctrine and Polity; and of my cordial wishes, that your labours may be crowned with complete success.

"Permit me to return you my thanks for your kind notice of my little book. I do not know that it has attracted any attention at the North. It has sold remarkably well here. My prayer is, that God may make it an instrument of good to the young.

"Let me hear from you often. It always refreshes me to get a letter from you. Send your *Critic* regularly. I shall always look for it with interest. The Lord bless you and yours.

"Most sincerely your friend,

J. H. THORNWELL."

To the same:

"SOUTH CAROLINA COLLEGE, *October* 27, 1855.

"DEAR THOMAS: You have, no doubt, discovered by this time that I am a poor correspondent, and not much better in any other respect. One thing, however, I can say, and that is, I am not blind to my transgressions; they are, indeed, ever before my eyes. But some how or other, the great American figure of speech has become a part of my nature; so much so, that the only use which I make of the present, is to live in the future. I am *always going to do*. The review of Dr. Hodge is still *in posse*. I am ashamed to say that I have never yet finished reading the document. I had to take it in broken doses, and the last has not been reached yet. But, by the way, I am inclined to forgive Dr. Hodge for all his sins against Presbyterianism, on account of the able and satisfactory review of Sir William Hamilton, in the last *Repertory*. Upon internal grounds, I should be inclined to ascribe the article to Tyler, of Frederick City; but I have heard nothing as to its authorship. No matter who wrote it, it is well done.

"Your *Critic* has been excellently sustained. It is the best paper in the Church; more manly and independent than any other. I must try and write something for you *in the future*. The same notion has flitted before my mind in regard to our *Review*, which has become so poor, that I am ashamed to see it. I wish somebody would invent an instrument for daguerreotyping thought, without the trouble of writing. If your ideas could be instantly transferred from your mind to the paper, without any effort on your part, what a blessed consummation it would be!

"The time is drawing near for my removal; and in anticipation of the event, as the merchants say, I have been taking stock. But to my infinite horror, I found the shelves either all empty, or filled with nothing but old rat-eaten articles, that are not worth transporting. I understand your mother is in Paradise. She has just got where she can hear something that is fit to be called preaching. All I have to say is, that if she never heard a sermon until she went to Baltimore, she ought to hear very rare ones now, to make up for lost time. I hope she does with you what she never could do with me, *remember the text*. Give our kindest remembrances to her. We all want to see her. Excuse this hasty note; and believe me,

"As ever, most faithfully,

J. H. THORNWELL."

The authorship of the article on Sir William Hamilton, above referred to, was soon definitely ascertained in a pleasant note, which is without date, and which we transcribe, as showing the esteem in which one great thinker is able to hold another:

"MY DEAR SIR: Please accept, as a token of my respect for you as a thinker, the copy—which is sent with this note—of an article on Sir W. Hamilton and his Philosophy, which I contributed to the *Princeton Review* for this month.

"You are one of the few who are competent to appreciate these higher speculations. I prepared the article in the midst of the most arduous labours on Law-reform, as well as in my profession. I therefore crave your indulgence.

"Sincerely yours,

SAMUEL TYLER."

Dr. Thornwell was a member of the Assembly of 1855, which met in the city of Nashville, Tennessee. It was memorable only for a debate on the subject of Boards, in which Dr. Thornwell was conspicuous as their opponent, and the Rev. Drs. Boardman and Plumer as their advocates. This discussion arose upon the proposition to separate the work of Church extension, or the erection of houses of worship, from the Board of Domestic Missions, and to place it under independent management. The alternative was to appoint a separate committee, or to erect another Board for this purpose. The opportunity, of course, could not be missed of attacking the principle upon which all these Boards were constructed, even though the opposition amounted to nothing in the result, but to record a protest against the established policy of the Church. This necessity cannot always be avoided in our ecclesiastical courts; but it is always unfortunate when questions of fundamental principle cannot be dis-

cussed *simpliciter*, with the view of determining abstractly
the modes in which the Church shall display her activity
and life. In this case, the proposition which was submitted to debate assumed the policy of the Church to be
settled, and only asked for its extension in a new direction. The discussion of that policy itself could only be
incidentally introduced, and a satisfactory vote, which
should clearly ascertain the mind of the Church in reference to this, could not possibly be reached. The result
would doubtless have been much the same, even though
the abstract issue had alone been made ; for the opponents
of the Boards were doubtless in the minority in the
Church at large. But consistency and truth required the
opposition, although it was unavailing. In the course of
the argument, some reflections were indulged which drew
from Dr. Thornwell a beautiful tribute to his friend, Dr.
Breckinridge : " He would never regard, otherwise than
with reverence and respect, the man who had been the
author of the Act and Testimony, and who had, under
God, been the means of our deliverance." He had occasion also to render a delicate vindication of himself. One
of the speakers had associated him with the great Calhoun, in a connexion to disparage his influence as a
dreamer and a theorist : "I listened," said Dr. Boardman, "to his speech, which was a chain polished and
bright, as to the beautiful and ingenious speculations of
the great statesman of South Carolina." In rejoinder,
Dr. Thornwell indulged in a lofty panegyric upon the
dead statesman ; but proceeded to say that, in all his great
political views, he had been constrained to differ from him.
"As to one thing, however, I am glad : I am glad to be
called an abstractionist. The abstractionist stands upon
principle ; and it was one of the most eloquent passages of
that great man's life, worthy of a great statesman, worthy
of Calhoun himself, when he defended himself as an abstractionist. I cannot be frightened by epithets. I have
but one single rule, which is to preserve a conscience void

of offence towards God and towards man, and to abide
strictly by the principles of the Word of God."

It is not proper to close Dr. Thornwell's connexion with
the South Carolina College, without bringing into prominence the wonderful ascendency which he had acquired
over the students.   Ten years before, the Hon. W. C.
Preston volunteered the testimony to the writer, that his
moral power in the College was superior even to the authority of the law; and the only criticism ever ventured
upon him, as a disciplinarian, was precisely this substi-
tution of a personal influence, instead of the pressure of
mere legal obligation.   Yet, how could it be helped, if, by
the force of personal character, he moulded the opinions
and shaped the conduct of the students, so that they had
no need to consider the stern authority with which the
laws of the College invested him?   Certainly it was never
true that he failed to uphold their supremacy; but his unfailing method was so to impress convictions of duty upon
the conscience, as to render the obedience spontaneous,
rather than enforced.   With each generation, as it passed
under his hands, there was a quiet formation of character,
and honourable principles were adopted which were a law
of themselves, and spared the necessity of hard collision
with mere external authority.   Surely, this is the perfection of discipline, when, under "the law of liberty,"
obedience is rendered from a sense of right; and the control under which the student is held becomes an element
in his moral education, the matrix in which the permanent
character is moulded.

Dr. Thornwell possessed a great advantage, in the vast
reputation he enjoyed as a man of genius.   The only
aristocracy in College is that of mind.   It is, perhaps, the
only community on earth in which the artificial distinctions in life entirely disappear.   Brought together for the
single purpose of acquiring knowledge, the sole measure
by which all are tried is talent.   Next to those instincts
which constitute the gentleman, comes the degree of in-

tellect which may be possessed; and the instances are not rare, both with professors and with students, that men, otherwise unpopular, are sustained through the reputation for learning and genius which has been acquired. In the case before us, the fact was indisputable. All men throughout the State conceded to Dr. Thornwell this rare endowment; and to the students he was a crown of glory; they rejoiced in him as the ornament and pride of the institution, and felt as though a portion of his honour was reflected upon each of them. His reputation was a pedestal upon which he stood as an idol before their eyes.

The office which he held as a preacher of the gospel, was also of inestimable service in securing to him this paramount influence over the students. In the class-room he expounded the principles of moral philosophy, and then ascended the pulpit to enforce the sanctions of the Divine law. And perhaps the combined positions were never used with greater efficiency in dealing with the human conscience. In the one case, he laid bare the grounds of moral obligation, as these are implicitly contained in the nature of man; in the other, he stood outside of that nature, as the representative of the Divine authority, before whose supremacy the conscience of the creature is compelled instinctively to bow. It requires the skill of a master to wield the two in their harmonious co-operation; but, with him, the eloquence—which has been defined to be "logic on fire"—enforced the deductions of philosophy with all the terrors of the final judgment, and gave to him that control which belongs only to one who has made himself master of the consciences of men.

Dr. Thornwell, moreover, commanded the love of young men by the fulness of his sympathy in their struggles with temptations and defeats, in their aspirations, their hopes, their joys. His disposition was thoroughly genial and affectionate. He never wrapped himself in the artificial dignity which repels approach by exacting an homage scarcely consistent with another's self-respect. The perfect simplicity of his character was reflected in the easiness of his carriage; and the generosity of the youthful heart gave to him an exuberance of respect, the more sincere because it was unchallenged and free.

But the great secret of his marvellous power, as a College officer, lay in the strong conviction he produced of his own honesty and fairness.   It seems a small thing to say of any man, that he is truthful; but no attribute begets such confidence as this, when it is recognized as a pre-eminent trait in the character.   No one ever accused Dr. Thornwell of duplicity in any of the relations of life. He never resorted to indirections to accomplish his purposes.   If he could not achieve success by fair and open argument, he submitted to defeat.   He inspired the young students with unbounded confidence in his honesty; and the most reckless among them, when brought into straits by their indiscretions, would lay their case in his hands with a perfect assurance that nothing would be allowed but what was proper and right.   They knew him to be incapable of favouritism or double-dealing; and that his moral perceptions were so clear, that he could not easily be deceived.   With College students—who, when wrong, are generally the victims of their own sophistries—he was regarded as an umpire; and his decision, supported by the reasons he was always able to advance, were generally accepted as final upon all questions of propriety.   Coupled with this high moral attribute, Dr. Thornwell's mind worked with amazing rapidity through the perplexities of a case, and seized at once the real issue upon which it should turn.   This was due to the logical structure of his mind, and to the habit he had cultivated of carrying that logic into all the practical duties of life.   It rendered him invaluable as a counsellor, and equally efficient as a disciplinarian.

Three instances will be given of these qualities in actual exercise, which will serve also to illustrate the nature and extent of the moral power which he wielded.   The first rests upon the authority of the gentleman who acted as secretary of the meeting; the second, upon the writer's own recollections of the incident, when it occurred; and the third, upon the testimony of one who was a participator in the scene.

Two young gentlemen, upon their application to enter College, were found deficient in one or two departments of study; but were admitted conditionally, upon the promise to make these up within a specified time. Upon reexamination, they were found even more delinquent than at first. The Professor in these studies was naturally indignant, and insisted at a meeting of the Faculty upon their immediate dismission. A warm discussion ensued, in which there was a general concurrence in the opinion that some punishment, at least suspension for a month, should be meted out to the culprits. Dr. Thornwell, meanwhile, was walking around the room, looking abstractedly at the books upon the shelves, with no apparent interest in the matter. At last, his opinion was challenged by the presiding officer, when he came forward with a simple syllogism, and cut the problem in two: "These young gentlemen were admitted on a certain condition; this condition has not been fulfilled; consequently they are not members of the College. You cannot expel or suspend them, without recognizing them as members. As a matter of grace, I propose that we give them another month; at which time, if the deficiency is not made up, they may be told they are not admitted." It is only one instance out of many, in which, while others were talking round and round a subject until it was in a perfect tangle, he would, in his incisive way, cut down to the point which all had missed, and settle the case almost with a word.

Upon one occasion, some strolling minstrels had an exhibition in the town, during which some indecorum among the audience drew forth a sharp rebuke from the performers. It was unfortunately levelled at some students, who claimed to be innocent of the offence. The result was a row, in which the meeting was broken up in great disorder. In the progress of the affair, the students became arrayed against the young men of the town, and very soon a serious riot was threatened in the public streets. The students rallied to a man, like an old Scotch clan in the times of border warfare, and could not be persuaded to disperse by those who harangued the tempestuous assembly. Dr. Thornwell appeared late upon the ground, and when the storm was at its height. Without wasting breath upon men who were delirious with passion, he sought out the parties originally aggrieved; ascended into the hall with them, confronted the other party from whom the alleged grievance came; heard both sides of the story, and made up his mind quickly upon the merits of the case. He satisfied the minstrels that they had been mistaken as to the real authors of the outrage, and exacted of them a promise to repair the error by coming the next day into the College Chapel, with a formal retraction of the charge. He then descended to the street, and simply informed the infuriated students that the case was amicably settled, and would be reported to them on the morrow. This simple affirmation from one in whose honour they implicity confided, appeased the storm, and in a few moments the street was as quiet as a church yard. On the next day, the public apology was made in the College Chapel, and the affair was ended. The reader does not need to have pointed out to him the tact displayed in the management of this case, nor the absolute repose of the students upon his veracity and innate sense of honour.

The case, however, now to be recorded was a far more superb illustration of the majesty of his sway over the students of the College. It occurred in the year 1856, after his relations to them were terminated. One or two of the young men, in a night frolic, came into collision with the town police, one being finally arrested and incarcerated. This, of course, brought the whole College to the rescue, who succeeded in liberating their companion. The next day two of the students resolved to avenge the insult by an open attack upon the offending policeman, and in a short time the town was in commotion. The students rushed to the scene of conflict, with such arms as they could extemporize. The alarm-bell was rung, and the militia called out to oppose them. The two parties were drawn up in array, as in regular battle; and a single pistol shot would have been the signal for a massacre, that would have carried mourning into the best families of the State, and stained the soil of Columbia with the blood of the proudest sons of the Commonwealth. Gentlemen of the highest character stood and walked between the combatants, vainly entreating the students to retire from the conflict. In the exigency, a runner was despatched for Dr. Thornwell, who was at the moment lecturing to his class in the Theological Seminary. Moving rapidly between the contending ranks, he addressed the students in substance thus: "I know nothing of the origin of this trouble, and this is no place to make the inquiry. Come back with me to the campus; and if I find you are in the right, and there be no redress but in fighting, I will lead you myself, and die in the midst of you." Turning upon his heel, and shouting, "College! College!" he walked in the direction of the campus, followed by the entire body. After getting them in the chapel, he addressed them at length, representing the impropriety of such riotous demonstrations; and appealing to their magnanimity not to bring a stain upon the escutcheon of the College, which would make the State blush that she had created it. The aroused passions were by these appeals finally calmed down, and peace was fully restored. It is not at all unsafe to say, that he was the only man in South Carolina who could have achieved that thing. The cry throughout the town was for days afterwards, "Wonderful man! But for him, our town would have been stained with a crime which would have made it the horror of the State."

CHAPTER XXVIII.

EDITORSHIP OF "SOUTHERN QUARTERLY REVIEW."

THE election of Professor C. F. McCay, on the fourth of December, 1855, as his successor, released Dr. Thornwell from the Presidency of the College; and he entered at once upon his duties as Professor of Didactic and Polemic Theology, in the Theological Seminary at Columbia, South Carolina. In connexion with this great work, he assumed new and heavy responsibilities by undertaking the editorial supervision of the *Southern Quarterly Review.* This valuable journal had, in former days, under the conduct of such men as Legare, Harper, Elliott, and others, taken the first rank among the periodicals of the country. Through insufficient patronage, it preserved an intermittent existence, sometimes suspended, and then revived; until now, sanguine hopes were cherished that, under the prestige of his name, it would rise speedily to its ancient renown, and command a more honourable support. He entered upon the task with energy and enthusiasm. Letters from such men as the Hon. Edward Everett, George Bancroft, Samuel Tyler, of Maryland; George F. Holmes, of the Virginia University; Bishop Elliott, of Georgia, President F. A. P. Barnard, of the Mississippi University, and many others, attest the kind of talent he sought to secure to the enterprise. The promise of co-operation from most of these, warranted expectations of success, which were doomed to be blasted by the indifference of the public, who suffered it, after a brilliant career of less than two years, to perish, from the want of means to sustain it.

Dr. Thornwell's connexion with it during that period enables us to enrich these pages with a correspondence, which the reader cannot fail to peruse with delight. It opens with the following note, which unfolds his plan:

"COLUMBIA, January 8, 1856.

"GEORGE F. HOLMES, ESQ.:

"DEAR SIR: A publishing house in this city proposes to purchase the *Southern Quarterly Review*, provided I will undertake the editorial supervision of it. Two conditions I have insisted on as indispensable. The first is, that I shall be put in a condition to *pay promptly*, at not less than three dollars a page, for every article furnished and accepted. The second is, that I can obtain the promise of men whom I know to be able to write well, to become regular contributors. My design in addressing this note to you is simply to inquire whether I may rely upon your co-operation in case the proposed arrangement should be made. If the *Review* cannot be made a first rate journal, we had better let it linger out and die. But there are talents and learning enough in the country to make it equal to any other periodical in the Union. If our means should justify it, I will give *five* dollars a page; but for the present, I cannot promise more than *three*. Let me hear from you at once, as my answer will depend upon the answers given by those to whom I have applied.

"Very respectfully,
J. H. THORNWELL."

To the same:

"COLUMBIA, June 17, 1856.

"MY DEAR SIR: I owe you an apology for not having written to you sooner, but I have been very much engrossed by a severe and protracted case of fever in my family.   *   *   *   I am happy to say that your article on 'Slavery and Freedom' has given great satisfaction; and you will draw on E. H. Britton for ninety-seven and a half dollars, which, I assure you, I consider a poor compensation for such an essay. Your other article, 'Greek in the Middle Ages,' is in press. I gave it to the printer without reading it, as your name was a sufficient security for its quality. I wish I could say the same of all my contributors. I have a drawer full of essays, which the kindness of friends has sent to me, but which no blindness of friendship can induce me to accept. The necessity of giving pain to others, and to persons whom I highly esteem, is itself a great pain to me: ἀμφοῖν γὰρ φίλοιν ὄντοιν ὅσιον προτιμᾶν τὴν ἀλήθειαν.

"I see that your friends are pressing your claims upon the Virginia University; and I was glad to find that the Presbyterians have espoused your cause so warmly. The article in the *Central Presbyterian* must have been gratifying to you. If I can serve you in any way, do not hesitate to command my efforts. * * * *

" With high esteem, your obedient servant,

J. H. THORNWELL."

To the same:

"THEOLOGICAL SEMINARY, *July* 30, 1856.

"DEAR SIR: I received your kind letter a week or two ago; and am happy to say that my little boy, who was ill for so long a time, has quite recovered. The *Review* will be out in a week; we have only thirty or forty pages to print. My absence at the General Assembly, and the condition of my family, on my return, prevented me from preparing an article on 'Ferrier's Institutes of Metaphysics,' which I had been meditating, and had partially executed. I have written, however, an elaborate essay on Miracles, in opposition to the prevailing tone of speculation imported from Germany on that whole subject. The article wants finish; but the doctrine is sound, and, I think, seasonable. The contents are more miscellaneous than in the last number. * * * *

" Can you select any one to whom I can entrust the task of reviewing Motley's 'Rise of the Dutch Republic?' Bating a few eccentricities of language, it has struck me as one of the noblest works that has issued from the American press. It is conceived in the true American spirit, and executed with great artistic skill. If you will either write yourself, or procure from one who is able to do justice to the subject, a suitable article, you will do what I am sure the country will regard as a good work. * * *

" Very truly yours,

J. H. THORNWELL."

From Mr. Holmes to Dr. Thornwell:

"BURK'S GARDEN, TAZEWELL COUNTY, VA., *August* 8, 1856.

"DEAR SIR: By yesterday's mail I wrote to you, and sent an article on 'Speculation and Trade.' My messenger brought back your obliging letter of July 30th, which requires an immediate acknowledgment. I ordered from New York the twelfth volume of Grote, and thus learnt that it had not been re-published. I will finish my article without it, by the 1st of September. Is there any sufficient assurance that the twelfth volume is, or will be, the last? 'Speculation and Trade' may wait patiently for once.

"Your Essay on Ferrier's Institutes would have been very welcome. For my own encouragement, I trust your judgment is against it. I find in the book the appearance, without the substance, of demonstration; neoterisms in expression, rather than novelty of idea; and an irresistible tendency to a low grade of Pantheism, or its opposite and twin extreme, Panhumanism. I am no admirer of the rebels in Scotland against Sir William Hamilton.

"I learned accidently from Mr. Tyler, that an essay on this last and late philosopher might be expected in your *Review*. I infer, and hope, that it will be from your own pen. I should be anxious to see the keen scrutiny of your logic applied to his doctrine. I have been asked to write an essay on the subject for the *New York Methodist Quarterly*. Your letter and its indications are full of interest. Your exposition of the question of miracles will be very acceptable at this time, as a confirmation of the understanding of believers, as an illumination of unsettled minds, and as a refutation of the premises of current infidelity. I recently examined this important dogma with much care and solicitude.

"Thank you for the information in regard to the criticism of ———, and the course you thought proper to adopt. There should certainly be concord, if not absolute harmony, in the pages of the *Review*. I have no fear for the validity of my conclusions. I believe in political economy as the restricted theory of aggregate wealth; I do not accept it as the complete science of society. In this pretension, I regard it as the Muses of Plocheirus regarded the worldly-wise man:

$$ ^{"}\varOmega\ X\rho\upsilon\sigma o\lambda\acute{\alpha}\tau\rho\alpha,\ \pi\epsilon\pi\lambda\alpha\nu\eta\mu\acute{\epsilon}\nu o\varsigma\ \mu\acute{\epsilon}\nu\epsilon\iota\varsigma, $$
$$ \tau\eta\varsigma\ \delta^{'}\ \dot{\alpha}\rho\epsilon\tau\tilde{\eta}\varsigma\ \tau\grave{\eta}\nu\ \delta\acute{o}\xi\alpha\nu\ o\dot{\upsilon}\delta^{'}\ \ddot{o}\lambda\omega\varsigma\ \varphi\iota\lambda\epsilon\tilde{\iota}\varsigma\cdot $$
$$ \varphi\iota\lambda\epsilon\tilde{\iota}\varsigma\ \mu\epsilon\theta\acute{\upsilon}\sigma\alpha\iota\ \tau\grave{\eta}\nu\ \pi o\lambda\acute{\upsilon}\chi\rho o\sigma o\nu\ \mu\acute{\epsilon}\theta\eta\nu. $$

"Sincerely yours,

GEORGE FREDK. HOLMES."

From the same:

"BURK'S GARDEN, TAZEWELL COUNTY, VA., *August* 25, 1856.

"DEAR SIR: Last mail brought me the August number of the *Southern Quarterly*. I have had time to read over only one of the articles, that on Miracles. By it I have been equally instructed and delighted. The general argument is irresistible, and establishes, with a rigid logical coherence, the important fact that miracles cannot be discredited, without destroying the sufficiency of all testimony, and the validity of all knowledge.

"On one or two points I venture to dissent from you, even after carefully studying your essay. The dissent, however, I am aware is more

apparent than real.   I cannot regard a miracle as a violation of the laws
of nature, but only as a violation of the customary laws; or, more
properly, a suspension of the ordinary and familiar laws, by the intervention of superior laws, or of the supreme Fountain of all law.   This pro-
vides for real miracles of two sorts, by direct action, and delegated
power; and relative miracles of two kinds, produced by super-human
knowledge, and superior human knowledge.   I hold to the position of
S. Augustine, quoted by S. Thomas Aquinas, in continuation of your
extract from Summa I. Qu. CV, Art. VI: "Deus contra solitum cursum
naturæ facit ; sed contra summam legem nullo modo facit, quia contra
seipsum non facit." Though S. Thomas Aquinas is as indistinct on the
subject of miracles as on election and predestination, this appears to be
his own conclusion, from his quotation from S. Augustine, and from the
conclusion of his reply to the first objection alleged in this article of his
treatise : "Cum igitur naturæ ordo sit a Deo rebus inditus, si quid præter
hunc ordinem faciat, non est contra naturam.   Unde Augustinus dicit,
loc cit, quod id est cuilibet naturale quod ille fecerit a quo est omnis mo-
dus, numerus et ordo naturæ." This doctrine is also corroborated by the
language and illustration employed in Summa I, Qu. XXII, Art. I.

"My apparent dissent from you on this point turns, as the tenor of
your remarks show that you perceive, on the latitude assigned to the
meaning of 'nature.' You consider it unwarrantable to extend its signifi-
cation beyond its ordinary employment. Do you remember the chapter
of Aristotle's Metaphysics on the ambiguities of this term, and the commentary of Alexander Aphrodisiensis on that chapter? Under the term,
'nature,' may be included, I think, the whole economy of the created
universe, or any complete sub-division of that total.   Only a portion of
this economy is apprehensible, and a much smaller portion ordinarily
apprehended by men.   To this limited part the designation of nature is,
by a convenient restriction, usually applied.   But it implies the larger
sense, which seems the more correct, because logically the more complete
and precise, if only one significance is to be received.

"Pardon me for hazarding these remarks.   I acquiesce cordially in
the aim, and I believe in the general purport of your argument; and
venture to call your attention to this topic, because I deem the recognition of a miracle, as a violation of nature, an important concession to
the polemics of Hume. I say nothing of other differences, which are
trivial, and would probably disappear on comparison of the precise
views entertained.   They do not impair my cordial agreement with your
happily-timed, conclusive, and most serviceable argument, which is
directed against the centre of modern rationalism, and offers the sole
chance of a solid reputation of Strauss.

"You have assigned a most honourable position to my essay on
'Greek in the Middle Ages,' which it did not deserve, in company with
yours on 'Miracles.'   I wish mine had been on a more popular subject,
or cast in a more popular form.* * * * *   I ascribe to you the article
on Plato's Phœdon, in consequence of the partiality avowed for Aris-

totle. You are the only peripatetic known to me in this country. I incline, rather than pretend to belong, to that school.

"With high respect and regard,

"Yours sincerely,

GEO. FREDK. HOLMES."

Reply from Dr. Thornwell:

"COLUMBIA, *September* 8, 1856.

"MY DEAR SIR: I returned from the up-country about three weeks ago, and have since been engaged, night and day, in waiting upon my mother, who appeared to be approaching her end. Her disease has, however, taken a favourable turn, and I have resumed my studies and my ordinary cares. Your letters have given me great satisfaction; and I am especially obliged to you for your friendly and ingenious criticisms of my article on 'Miracles.' I am sorry that I did not elaborate the point in relation to nature a little more. The argument would have gained in clearness, and, I think, you would have found that your objection was obviated. The word is used in none of the senses signalized by Aristotle; but as a compendious expression for the whole created universe, considered as a definite constitution, as made up of properties and powers which operate in a fixed and regular manner. The domain of nature is, accordingly, the domain of law. Now, my notion is, that from no properties and laws of the existing order of things, could the miracle ever result. It is an order of events of a different character; it belongs to a distinct sphere, though bearing upon the same ultimate moral end. In nature, the power of God is always *mediately* exerted; in the miracle, *immediately*. In nature, the agents—that is, the direct agents—are the properties and powers of substances, or the creatures that God has made; in the miracle, He is the sole agent Himself. If nature, however, should be taken to mean God's plan, or the Divine idea of the universe in all phenomena and events, then the miracle is natural, in the sense that it is necessarily included in the plan. It is a part of the original scheme of things. Now, it is only in this sense, I think, that Aquinas admits a miracle to be no violation of nature. It is no departure from the Divine plan. It is not an after-thought, suggested by an emergency. It was always contemplated as one of the elements of the Divine government. These hints will be sufficient to indicate how I would have presented the point; and I am not sure but that I shall not develope it a little more fully. In return for your kindness, let me refer you to 'Saurez Disputat. Metaphys. Disput. XV. Sect. XI, 4, for an acute stricture upon the senses signalized by Aristotle.

"I do not know in what terms to express my sense of the value of the article on 'Speculation and Trade.' I have made it the leader in my next number, which will be really a very fine one. I have already

a collection of choice articles.   *   *   *   I am now studying Brandis'
Aristotle, having not had the opportunity of seeing it until last week.
"With much esteem,

J. H. THORNWELL."

From Mr. Holmes to Dr. Thornwell:

"BURK'S GARDEN, TAZEWELL CO., VA., *September* 16, 1856.

"REV. AND DEAR SIR: By last mail I received your most kind and
obliging letter, for which I offer you my most cordial thanks.   I am
truly indebted to you for the very handsome testimonial enclosed in it.
I hope in some future day to merit it better than I can now suppose
myself to do.   Notwithstanding the previous manifestations of your
favourable opinion, I have been surprised, gratified, and, I may add,
alarmed, at such an announcement of it.   Your testimonial arrives in
excellent time for the election to the Professorship of History, which
will take place on the 2d of January.   This is to me much the more desirable position, comporting directly, as it does, with the contemplated
course of my future studies; and there seems to be an entire unanimity
amongst my friends and the public in designating me by preference for
that position.

"I hear, with sympathizing pleasure, of the restoration of your mother's health.   It is with difficulty I realize the fact that we met only
once.   I knew the acquaintance to be very limited; but you have been
so long familiar to my thoughts, so long the object of my sincere respect
and admiration, and you were so often the subject of conversation with
common friends, during my residence in South Carolina, that it had almost escaped my recollection that we had only met and parted like
ships on the sea.   I trust, for my own sake, that we are not bound for
different ports.   *   *   *   *

"The explanation afforded by you of your views of nature, in your
essay on Miracles, accords with what I deemed to be very probably
your meaning; and enables me to agree freely with your main argument.   The ground of disagreement seems to me the same as that which
divided Clarke and Leibnitz on the subject, in their celebrated correspondence; and that appears to me to have been occasioned by the
equivocation of terms, and the absence of an admitted definition.   I
find myself able to assent substantially to the views of both, except so
far as the doctrine of the pre-established harmony is involved.   I agree
with Leibnitz and yourself: ' Quand Dieu fait des miracles, que ce n'est
pas pour soutenir les besoins de la nature, mais pour ceux de la grâce;'
and that, in one sense, ' le surnaturel surpasse toutes les forces des creatures.'   I hold with Clarke, (and with S. Thomas Aquinas, and your
explanation of him,) ' il est certain que le naturel et le surnaturel ne
different en rien (I would strike out en rien) l'un de l'autre par rapport
a Dieu: ce ne sont que des distinctions selon notre manière de conce-

voir les choses. Donner un mouvement reglé au soleil ou à la terre, c'est une chose que nous appelons naturelle; arrêter ce mouvement pendant un jour, c'est une chose surnaturelle selon nos idée. Mais la dernière de ces deux choses n'est pas l'effet d'une plus grande puissance que l'autre; et par rapport a Dieu, elles sout toutes deux également (strike out également) naturelles ou surnaturelles.' To this part of the discussion, as to that relative to different orders of miracles, is applicable what Leibnitz remarks relative to the latter topic: 'On pourra dire que les anges font des miracles, mais moins proprement dits, ou d'un ordre inférieur. Disputer la-dessus serait une question de nom.' My objection to 'en rien' and 'également' are, that, in ordinary parlance, consonant with the view *ex parte humana*, there is a wide distinction between the natural and the supernatural; and that this distinction ought not to be obliterated in attempting to contemplate the subject *ex parte Dei;* because the ordinary and extraordinary procedures of God are logically and metaphysically distinct, although they may be termed, according to the purpose designed, natural or supernatural, or both, or neither.

"This explanation will, I trust, prove my virtual agreement with your entire argument. If I remember rightly, the allusion made by me to the diversity of meaning involved in the term 'nature,' as signalized by Aristotle, was introduced without reference to the mode in which you had employed the term, and simply as a compendious illustration of its numerous ambiguities. Suarez I know only by reputation. He has always been inaccessible to me; but I think I have seen his criticisms on the diverse senses assigned to nature by Aristotle. You speak of studying Brandis' Aristotle. Do you mean the edition of the Berlin Academy, edited by Bekker and Brandis, in four volumes, 4to.? or the separate edition of the Metaphysics and their scholia, by Brandis alone? If the former, can you tell me whether the fifth volume, containing the preface and remaining scholia, has ever been published? If the latter, are the scholia more complete than in the entire works of Bekker and Brandis? These have been my companions for more than fifteen years. The more I study Aristotle, the less necessity do I discover for any other philosophy than modernized and Christianized Peripateticism Aristotle is still, as in the thirteenth century, '*il maestro di che chi sanno.*'

"I am happy to find you dissenting from the positions of the article on the Infinite. I think the writer has been misled, like Calderwood, into an *ignoratio elenchi*, a misapprehension of the real issue. No one denies the conception, or the actual existence, of the Infinite, except the most narrow-minded enthusiast of the narrowest materialism. The question is simply as to the apprehensible significance of the Infinite, the character of our conception of it. In words, it is incapable of anything but a negative verbal definition; is it capable of a positive mental definition? That is the sole question. St. Thomas Aquinas and Leibnitz accord with Sir William Hamilton; and it is to Leibnitz that we owe the definition employed by President McCay.

"It is to be anxiously hoped that you will execute your design of re-curring to the subject of miracles. If you would permit me to suggest for your reflections a topic that would embrace it, and which you would handle in such a manner as to render extensive service, and much in-struction and gratification to many others besides myself, I would indi-cate, as a thesis, the Divine Economy of the Universe, or the conciliation of the realms of nature and of grace. Without, in any respect, imitating or following Butler, Leibnitz, or McCosh, you could weave a stronger argument, by rising to higher, more abstract, and more general con-siderations. * * *

"Excuse the tedious length of this letter. With sincere respect and esteem,   Yours, etc.,

GEO. FREDK. HOLMES."

Dr. Thornwell to Mr. Holmes:

"THEOLOGICAL SEMINARY, *October* 9, 1856.

"MY DEAR SIR : * * * * I had heard that you were not a can-didate for the chair of Greek in the University, and therefore made no effort for you in reference to that department. My own impression, too, was very clear, that History was precisely the chair you ought to fill; and I sincerely hope that Providence will allot you to the station in which you seem pre-eminently qualified to be useful.

"Your article on Grote is a noble production ; and if you had never written another line but that, it ought to be enough to elect you. * * * I was much amused at the mistake into which I led you in relation to Brandis's Aristotle. It was not the Scholia to Bekker's edition to which I referred, but a far less formidable undertaking. It was the little trea-tise, '*Aristoteles, seine Akademischen Zeitgenossen und nachsten Nach-folger,*' of which I have only the first half, published in Berlin in 1853. If the second volume of the Scholia has ever been published, I have not heard of it. We have only the first in our library. I have myself only the Oxford reprint of Bekker's text, with the Sylburgian Indices, without the Scholia or the Latin translations.

"The prospects of the country fill me with sadness. The future is very dark. The North seems to be mad, and the South blind. I have been anxious to get a good article on the subject, written in the spirit and temper of Legare's noble article on the American system, in the sixth volume of the old *Southern Review.* It has occurred to me, from the tone of their speeches in Congress, that Mason or Hunter would do the thing well. I have no personal acquaintance with them, and am, there-fore, reluctant to approach them. Could you sound them for me? The *Review* must have something political ; but I shall for ever exclude the topic, unless it is treated in a manly, patriotic, statesman-like, philo-sophical style. But I have perhaps wearied you with my gossip. At any rate, advancing dawn reminds me that it is time to go to bed.

"Very sincerely, your friend,

J. H. THORNWELL."

To the same:

"THEOLOGICAL SEMINARY, *November* 20, 1856.

"MY DEAR SIR: You will need no excuse for my long silence, when you come to know the circumstances in which I have been placed. For more than two months my house was a hospital. My mother was first seized, appeared to be recovering, then relapsed, and after a series of dreadful sufferings, expired on the 18th of last month. A daughter, nearly grown, took her bed about two weeks before the death of my mother, and lingered in such a way as to fill us with dismal apprehensions, until, about two weeks ago, she manifested decided symptoms of conval-escence, and is now, I am happy to say, quite restored. My mother's corpse was carried to her own home; and while I was absent at her fu-neral, a lovely little boy followed her to the unseen world. I found him a corpse when I returned. These sad visitations, in such rapid succes-sion, weighed down my spirits. I had no heart for my everyday work. But although I have suffered, and suffered keenly, and suffered, as I hope, never to suffer again, yet I can truly say that I was not conscious of the first emotion of rebellion against the Providence of God. I could trust Him in the deepest darkness which surrounded me. The gospel which I have long believed, and preached because I believe, was a very present help in time of trouble. I felt its truth, and was strengthened by its grace. But I shall not trouble you with my private griefs any further than is necessary to vindicate myself from the imputation of neglect.

* * * I am anxious for an able review of Motley, which shall present the relations of the Dutch movement to the great principles of constitu-tional freedom. The state papers of William of Orange strike me as containing the germs of every great doctrine of English and American liberty. It is in this aspect that the subject is so profoundly interest-ing, and I know of none better qualified to do it justice than yourself.
* * * * *

"Very truly, your friend,

J. H. THORNWELL."

Mr. Holmes to Dr. Thornwell:

"BURK'S GARDEN, TAZEWELL CO., VA., *December* 1, 1856.

"MY DEAR SIR: The narration of your severe domestic afflictions enlists my cordial sympathies in your great and irreparable distress. There is no agony which can befall a good man on earth greater than that you have recently experienced; there is no consolation which heaven affords for the mitigation of human calamities, more cheering and acceptable than the resignation which an earnest Christian faith blessed you with in the hour of trial. I feel deeply the crushing blow which has fallen upon you, and spread clouds over this life, but compensated the gloom by exhibiting a brighter radiance and a more permanent satisfaction in the eternal world. With what yearning anxiety the heart turns to God, as it follows the departing spirits of the good and the innocent of our own blood! * * * *

"I will use my best endeavours to procure a suitable essay on 'The State of the Country,' and to procure it promptly. There is no indication of authorship to the articles in the November number. The last is by Mr. Tyler, of Maryland. I ascribe to you that on Maimonides, and the exquisite notice of 'Cicero de Officiis.' I read the appeal on the fourth page of the cover with equal regret and shame. I trust it may be successful. * * * The *Review* ought to be sustained. It has been an honour and a bulwark to the South; it has been a crown of glory to South Carolina, and that State could well afford to lose one-half of her cotton crop rather than to let her *Southern Review* go down.

"Yours truly,

GEO. FREDK. HOLMES."

From the same :

"BURK'S GARDEN, TAZEWELL CO., VA., *December* 30, 1856.

"REV. AND DEAR SIR : Dr. Moore, of Richmond, has very kindly sent me the number of the *Central Presbyterian*, containing your generous communication relative to the Chair of History in the University of Virginia. If I could only feel conscious of meriting, in any degree, the praise you have so graciously bestowed, I should feel much better satisfied with myself, but could not be more grateful for your gratuitous commendations. You have, however, set before me an ideal, which I must endeavour to approach, though without hope of reaching it.

"I shall finish to-day an essay on the 'Philosophy of Sir William Hamilton,' for the New York *Methodist Quarterly*. I am not satisfied with it; but when published, shall take the liberty of sending it to you, with the hope of receiving your frank *castigation* of its views. * * * I know no one in the country so competent as yourself to indicate its blunders, and expose its weak points. And as I have been anxiously seeking a philosophy capable of furnishing a complete conciliation of reason and faith, there is no severity of judgment which will not be acceptable.

"I am ready to take up Motley; but I cannot do justice to him; my library is too scant. I admire both the spirit and execution of his work ; but I miss with regret any suitable inquiry into the social condition and commercial progress of the Low Countries; and he has failed to avail himself of the illustration of the intrigues, treacheries, and jealousies of the nobles, and the hostility of parties furnished by the family connexions and hereditary traditions of the members of the Netherland aristocracy. The Duke of Aerschot was a sovereign prince of the Holy Roman Empire, as well as the Prince of Orange. But this, and other points like this, are not mentioned by Mr. Motley.

"I have in hand for you an essay on 'the Relations of Paganism and Christianity, during the first three or four centuries.' My collections on the subject are extensive, but deficient in regard to the patristic evidence. The topic is an interesting and instructive one; and I think I can treat it in such a manner as to exhibit some novel aspects.

"Yours sincerely,

GEO. FREDK. HOLMES."

From the same:

"BURK'S GARDEN, TAZEWELL CO., VA., *January* 17, 1857.

"REV. AND DEAR SIR: Your obliging note of the 9th inst. has just reached me. I had nearly finished the rough draft of a notice of Motley, and commenced transcribing it to-day. I will dispatch it in the course of the coming week. This is not the first time that I have experienced the wisdom of the old rule: if you desire information on any subject, write upon it. Facts, recollections, suggestions, have started up from obscure hiding-places in the crannies of the brain; and though, when I commenced the paper, I thought I was entirely ignorant of the age, I have been unexpectedly oppressed with the redundance of my matter. You will find traces in my article of 'many a curious volume of forgotten lore;' but no quotations except from Motley, and those brief. I feel confident that it will meet your approbation; it is infinitely better than the notice of Grote. * * * *

"It is with deep concern I am informed by you of the unpromising aspect of the fortunes of the *Southern Quarterly*, and of the possibility of your retiring from its superintendence. Either would be a great calamity to the South, and to its literature. * * * *

"Believe me, with grateful regard and esteem,

"Yours truly,

GEO. FREDK. HOLMES."

Dr. Thornwell to Mr. Holmes:

"THEOLOGICAL SEMINARY, *February* 28, 1857.

"MY DEAR SIR: It gives me great pleasure to congratulate you upon the manner, even more than the fact, of your election to the chair of History in the University of Virginia. It was honourable to you, and honourable to the Board. Our young men will be encouraged to devote themselves to letters, when they find that real excellence is not destined to pass without reward. Though it is true that Mammon is not the inspiration of genius, and that philosophy should be sought for itself, and not for the dowry, yet the native glow of inspiration requires a sun to warm it, and disinterested love must have favourable circumstances to expand it. As well might we expect the eagle to soar in void space, without a supporting atmosphere, as the most gifted mind to unfold its powers without opportunities. I rejoice that you have found a field suited to your talents and your taste. God grant that you may long live to occupy and adorn it!

"There are two portions of modern history which, in my judgment, have not received the attention they deserve. The first is the reign of Henry IV, of France, and the other is the period intervening, until the commencement of the French Revolution. It might be called the Rise and Growth of Absolutism in France. A life of Henry, and a general philosophical history of the subsequent period, would fill a chasm which I know of no work of any signal ability that supplies. What think you of either, or both, parts of this great enterprise? Whoever should execute it well, might adopt the language of Thucydides, and call it a work for all time.

"In relation to the *Review*, I am sadly discouraged. The February number I have kept back, of purpose, hoping to stimulate a greater degree of interest. I do not see that much has been accomplished. The work has been warmly praised; but praises pay neither printer, editor, nor contributors. A project is on foot to make it the property of a joint stock company, with a sufficient capital to sustain it adequately. One hundred stockholders, at one hundred dollars apiece, would put it on a firm foundation. I trust that, if kept up, you will not remit your interest in its prosperity.

"Let me express the hope that you may find occasion to revisit South Carolina; and, in that case, let my claims upon your person, as a captive or a guest, be regarded supreme.

"Very truly, your friend,

J. H. THORNWELL."

From Mr. Holmes:

"BURK'S GARDEN, TAZEWELL CO., VA., *March* 7, 1857.

"REV. AND DEAR SIR: * * * * * Thank you for your valuable suggestion in regard to the reign of Henry IV, and the succeeding times in France. I agree with you in your estimate of those ages, and their long disregarded importance. They attracted my attention at one time, but I discontinued my researches, from the difficulty and expense of procuring the requisite documents. Since that period, my mind has been gradually forced backward to the consideration of the phenomena of decay in the society of the Roman Empire, and the equally interesting characteristics of the reconstruction of society, and the germination of modern civilization in the remoter period of the Middle Ages. My collections on this subject are already extensive. * * *

"You afford a gleam of hope for the perpetuation of the *Review*. If the scheme be carried out, I may be able to aid in giving it some assistance when I reach the University. My interest in the existence and honour of the *Review* cannot fail. It exercised and promulgated my earliest speculations; it gave me my first reputation; it has been instrumental in securing my present appointment; and your kindness has finally linked my name with its fortunes and honours." * * *

"May 30, 1857.

* * * "I had hoped to have heard your judgment of the criticism of Sir William Hamilton, which I directed to be sent to you in the numbers of the New York Methodist *Quarterly,* when it was published. I am solicitous for this, as the points discussed are, in my estimation, of great importance; and there are few, if any, who can as readily detect their importance and bearing, and estimate their validity or invalidity.

* * * "Believe me, very respectfully and sincerely yours,

GEO. FREDK. HOLMES."

Dr. Thornwell to Mr. Holmes:

"THEOLOGICAL SEMINARY, *July* 7, 1857.

"MY DEAR SIR: Your articles on Hamilton were read by me with great interest; and it may gratify you to know that I put them into the hands of my class in the Seminary, to whom I was delivering, at the time, some side lectures on Kant. Sir William's changes in logic—the exclusion of the categories and all material considerations, the thoroughgoing quantification of the predicate, the consequent extension of propositional forms, and the simplification of the whole doctrine of conversion—have always appeared to me specimens of a keen, but perverse, ingenuity. I cannot see their importance; and I am sure, and he even admits, that language is not constructed with reference to them. And yet, are not the laws of language the laws of thought? Then, again, the unfigured syllogism, I am quite certain, can be reduced to shape. Propositions, in which the terms are not related as subjects and predicates, seem to me harder to understand than the doctrines of St. Paul.

"The philosophical reason you suggest for not recognizing the quantification of the predicate in affirmative propositions, was quite new to me; and, I am disposed to think, is not without more significance than you have attached to it. That the very forms in which we embody our positive knowledge, should contain intimations that there remains much more to be known; that all science should be a confession of ignorance, is in exact accordance with the spirit of Sir William Hamilton's philosophy, and the real state of the case.

"Upon the point in dispute between Sir William and Cousin, I have always thought that the victory was with Sir William. And yet I am not clear that the Infinite and Absolute are species of the same genus, exhaustive of the whole sphere of the Unconditioned; still less can I admit that all positive thought is mediated between two extremes, neither of which is cogitable; but one of which—and, as far as the statement goes, no matter which—must be admitted. The Infinite and the Absolute appear to me as different aspects of one and the same thing: different phases under which it is contemplated by the mind. It is the Infinite, when considered in itself; the boundless sphere of being, the substratum or ground of all existence. It is the Absolute, when considered as determining being, as conditioning and regulating the finite and limited. The Infinite One is the Essence in itself; the Absolute, that Essence as entering into, and giving force to all dependent existence. The Infinite is the negation of the finite; the Absolute involves its affirmation. These seem to me the senses in which these terms are employed by the Absolute philosophers.

"There is only one thing in your articles to which I must demur; and that is your low estimate of my old friend, Dugald Stewart. His work was the first to inspire me with any love for philosophical pursuits, and I confess that I prize his writings very highly. His candour, his love of truth, his modesty in stating his opinions, his scrupulous precision in the use of language, are beyond all praise. The man who inspired into his pupils the enthusiasm kindled by Stewart, must have had more than ordinary merit. His sketch of modern philosophy is an exquisite morceau. His speculations upon the real nature of mathematical reasoning, his remarks upon axioms, and the proper place of first truths, strike me as all indicating no mean talents for philosophy. As an expounder of Reid's system, he has been very successful in eliminating its radical principles, and in guarding them from abuse. Take out his silly speculations upon language, especially the Sanscrit, and a few other blemishes, and I know of no other books that can be read with more interest, profit and delight, than the speculations of Dugald Stewart. From the influence of early associations, I love him as Tam O'Shanter loved his drouthy crony. I love him 'as a very brither.' But I am, perhaps, tedious. I have written these hasty lines without your articles before me, and without having seen them for more than two months. I lent them to some of my pupils; and it may be that I have written unadvisedly. Wishing you every prosperity, I am,

"As ever, your sincere friend,

J. H. THORNWELL."

"P. S.—The article on the 'Disuse of the Latin Language,' I had retained for the next number of the *Review*. What shall I do with it? Shall I return it to you? or shall I send it to any other journal?

This postscript is the last note of the bell, as the foundering ship went down beneath the flood. The *Southern Quarterly* was no more! In a second postscript to the above letter, Dr. Thornwell says: "I will re-peruse your article on Hamilton, and give you my opinion more in detail." In reference to which promise, Mr. Holmes writes: "The more detailed views of Hamilton's Philosophy were never sent. The decease of the *Southern Quarterly Review*, and the occupations of us both, soon terminated the correspondence." We find, however, among the loose papers in our possession, a fragment, which was evidently intended as the fulfilment of his pledge; and though it bears upon its face evidence of being only the commencement of an extended criticism, the two points signalized in it are so important, as the expression of his philosophical views, that it would be criminal to withhold it. The reader cannot but be gratified to learn, from his own pen, the precise estimate in which he held the contribution made by Sir William Hamilton to philosophy:

"My Dear Sir: In one respect I rejoice, in another I am sorry, that I promised to give you a more detailed review of your admirable article on Sir William Hamilton's philosophy. I rejoice, because the reading and re-reading, and reading of them again, which it rendered necessary, have been to me a source of the purest satisfaction. Your essays have not only confirmed my impressions of your learning, but given me an insight into qualities of mind which, I frankly confess, I was not prepared to attribute to you, in anything like the degree in which you have shown yourself to possess them. You will not be surprised, therefore, that I regret having made the promise, as the execution of it is likely to be of as little profit to you as credit to myself. One revenge, however, I shall inflict on you for the loss of my time and pains—that of passing over in silence, or with a mere allusion, those parts of your essay in which I can find nothing to censure, and dwelling upon those in which there seems to be a chance of picking holes. I could not justly claim to be a critic, if I found no fault.

"1. I am glad to see that you appreciate so justly the subordination of philosophy to faith. For myself, I have long looked upon the Scriptures as containing the key to the true solution of the problem of existence; and I have been struck, in several instances, with the remarkable fact, that the speculations of Aristotle break down just where a higher light was needed to guide him. He has tracked truth through the court and sanctuary to the mystic veil, which he was not permitted to lift. One hint from revelation would have perfected his theory of happiness; a single line of Moses would have saved a world of perplexity, touching the relations of matter and form. Any system of philosophy must be fundamentally false which does not lay a foundation for the possibility of revelation; and to do this, the notions of a personal God, and a strict and proper creation, must be vindicated. In all this we agree; but I have been unable to determine to what class of philosophers you refer (p. 24), as being inclined 'to look upon the created universe as an episodical digression.' The predominant vice of modern philosophy, it seems to me, is just the opposite; it is to look upon nature as *the all.* Whatever form of the Absolute you take, it quietly proceeds upon the category of the *immanent,* assumes the doctrine of *substantial identity,* and recognizes no principle but that of necessary development, or inevitable self-manifestation. The consequence is, that a personal God, with all free causation, is excluded. Where there is no design, there can be no episodes; and where all is necessary, nothing can be incidental.

"2. Your estimate of the Scotch school is so different from my own, that I am constrained to believe that either you or I have misapprehended its characteristics. In my judgment, your articles breathe the very spirit of the Scottish philosophy; and every exception you have taken to the tenor and bearing of Sir William's speculations is only in instances in which he has diverged from the track of Reid and Stewart, and the scope of your criticism is to bring him back. His great merit is that he has explained, purified, vindicated, and enlarged the doctrines of his masters. He has supplied deficiencies, corrected errors, suggested amendments; but his whole effort has been to bring the system into harmony with itself. His philosophy is only that of Reid and Stewart, perfected by an instrument—a sound logic—which they did not possess. I cannot agree, therefore, that he has introduced 'something like system, substance, order, and coherence into their vague experimental psychology, *by a sweeping and revolutionary legislation,* (p. 27.) Apart from a more thorough exposition of the criteria of our fundamental beliefs and primitive cognitions—two things, by the way, which Sir William Hamilton does not, and Stewart does, distinguish—apart from a consistent and logical account of the conditions indispensable to the possibility and validity of the philosophy of common sense; these contributions, and the distinctions and explanations which the theory of realism supposes, such as those in relation to presentative and representative knowledge, and the real nature of consciousness, I know of nothing that Sir William has contributed to philosophy; and these are all in accordance with the system of Reid and Stewart, except the effort to define more precisely the limits of human knowledge in the Philosophy of the Conditioned. That, as far as it is sound, is out and out Scottish; as far as it is unsound, it departs from the characteristics of the school. The estimate which I have expressed of Sir William's relations to the Scotch school, is precisely that of Cousin. In that beautiful and exquisite letter which he wrote to Professor Pillans, when Sir William was a candidate for the chair of Logic and Metaphysics, he represented him as the very impersonation of the Scottish philosophy; and the question before the electors was the question of giving a *successor* to *Reid* and *Stewart.* You will find the whole letter, (and a reference to it would have graced your article) in 'Peipi's Fragments de Philosophie.'

CHAPTER XXIX.

SEMINARY LIFE.

INTIMATION has been given, in a preceding letter, of
the bereavement he sustained in 1856. His mother,
left a widow in 1820, contracted a second marriage, on
the 26th of February, 1829, with Mr. Ananias Graham,
a plain man, but of excellent character and good position.
This relation continued unbroken until her own death, on
the 18th of October, 1856. It must have been to her a
great privilege to fall asleep, as she did, in the arms of
her distinguished son. It was so ordered, by a kind
Providence, that she was on a visit to him, when she was
taken down with typhoid fever; and after lingering many
weeks, during which he nursed her with the utmost tenderness, she fell asleep in Jesus. He accompanied her
remains to Bennettsville, South Carolina, which was her
home, and returned immediately to Columbia, to encounter, if possible, a heavier sorrow. Two of his children were lying ill, of the same disease, when he left.
Upon entering the house, the family met him at the door,
with countenances veiled with peculiar sadness. "Tell
me the worst," he exclaimed; "tell me if my dear
daughter is dead." She was thought, at the time of his
departure, to be the sicker of the two. "No," was the

reply; "but Witherspoon is; he died about half an hour
ago." He was completely overcome by the tidings, and
had to be assisted to his room; but, adds the gentle nar-
rator, " He had the sweet assurance that his darling boy
was with Jesus; he had given every evidence of a change
of heart before he was sick."

This little boy, who was taken away when a little over
nine years of age, had been, in some respects, a remarkable child from his birth. He was distinguished, not
only by a singular sweetness of disposition, but by an uncommon development of religious feeling. This was
indicated, not so much by the usual childish curiosity
about religious subjects, as by the prayerful exercises in
which he secretly engaged. It was not an uncommon
thing to find him alone, in some unfrequented place, upon
his knees; in one instance, just before his illness, concealed behind the wood-pile, in the yard. Some weeks
after his death, the writer asked of his father, what was
his opinion as to the salvation of children who died at the
dubious age of his own son, when it was so difficult to fix
the boundaries of personal accountability? After stating,
in reply, the more special grounds of hope afforded in
this case, Dr. Thornwell added: Independently of all this,
however, I believe the covenant which God has made with
His people, and which is sealed to their faith in the baptism of their offspring, to be a real and a precious thing;
and where Christian parents have, in faith, laid hold upon
this covenant, and have pleaded its promises on behalf of
their seed, they may, when dying in these early years of
childish immaturity, be laid, without a particle of apprehension or distrust, upon the bosom of that promise, " I
will be a God to thee, and to thy seed." We do not embrace this statement in quotation marks, simply because
we cannot reproduce the exact language, after the lapse
of so many years. But an experience of our own, in a
similar bereavement, had made that view of the baptismal
covenant exceedingly precious; and this confirmation of

it, by one whose opinions were so carefully formed, made an impression too distinct to allow any mistake of his meaning.

Dr. Thornwell was a member of the General Assembly, which met in New York city, in 1856. In reference to him, however, there is nothing worthy of special mention but the delivery of the sermon on Foreign Missions, by appointment of the preceding Assembly. It was published, by order of the Assembly, and may be found in the second volume of his "Collected Writings." Its theme was, "The Sacrifice ot Christ the type and model of missionary effort." Dr. Addison Alexander, himself a wonderful example of pulpit eloquence, heard it delivered, and pronounced it "as fine a specimen of Demosthenian eloquence as he had ever heard from the pulpit, and that it realized his idea of what preaching should be :" a noble testimony from a source which no one can afford to disparage, and honourable to the frank and generous heart from which it sprang. They are both in heaven: can one conceive the fellowship between the two, before the Throne, rising together, from the learning and philosophy of earth, to the higher scholarship known only to the immortals ?

The following letter is transcribed with a melancholy interest. It is the only one that can be identified, with certainty, as addressed to his eldest daughter, Nannie, of whom there will be a touching memorial in the sequel :

"COLUMBIA, *June* 7, 1856.

"MY DEAR DAUGHTER: We have just received your letter, and were becoming very anxious on account of what appeared to us as your protracted silence. There must have been some irregularity in the mail which brought it, or some detention of it in your own hands after you had written it, or it could not have been so long on the way. We were gratified to learn that your health was preserved, and not astonished to find you complaining of a feeling of lonesomeness. This will wear off, as your mind becomes interested in the objects around you. I want you to improve the opportunities you enjoy, and to evince, when you return, the benefits of your trip.

"The first thing, my dear child, that I would impress upon you is the care of your own soul. That, after all, is the business of life. I do not mean merely that you are to read your Bible with regularity and attention, and observe your hours of private devotion. This, I am sure, you will not neglect. But I am anxious to see you really interested in the great salvation. Nothing would delight me so much as to hear that you felt yourself by nature a lost and miserable sinner, and that you were trusting in Jesus for the pardon of your guilt. Do not be easy until you have a good hope that your sins are forgiven, and that your heart is renewed. Try to profit by the sermons you hear. Apply them to yourself; pray over them, and beg the Lord to make them contribute to your good. True religion will be the greatest accomplishment you can possibly require. Seek it until you find it.

"In the next place, be attentive to your studies. Endeavour to store your mind with useful and elegant knowledge. You may abandon the study of Latin, but give yourself closely to the acquisition of French. I want to see you so perfectly master of that language, as to write and speak it with fluency and ease. Give attention also to English composition. Now is the time to form your taste. If you have an opportunity, and I have no doubt they are frequent in New York, you would do well to take lessons from a writing-master, so as to improve your hand. You see that I do not wish you to be idle, and I do not wish you to be diverted from solid pursuits by company or visiting. There is one exercise which I must exact from you, and you must be sure to perform it punctually; and that is, to write me every Monday an account of the sermons you heard on Sunday, particularly the morning sermon. This will be profitable to you, and very interesting to me.

"We found Charlie very ill upon our return, and for several days I despaired of his life. But he is now much better, and I feel encouraged to hope that he will recover from the attack. He is a mere skeleton, but his spirits are good, and he frequently talks about Nannie. He made us read your letter aloud to him, and was as much interested as any of the family. The little fellow has been a model of patience and self-denial, and I sincerely trust that God is sparing him for some valuable end. * * * * All keep well but Charlie. You must write to us twice a week, and do not forget the sermons on Monday. It is Saturday night, and I must get ready for to-morrow. So farewell for the present.

"Your affectionate father,

J. H. THORNWELL."

This allusion to preparation for the Sabbath, renders it proper to state, that the Columbia church being at that time vacant, he was invited to fill the pulpit, by a people who gratefully remembered his ministrations to them fifteen years before. In consequence of this arrangement, Dr. Thornwell, in adition to his duties as a

Theological Professor, and as the editor of a leading quarterly, found himself in the service of one of the most important churches in the South.

We insert here a letter to a near kinsman, upon the death of his young wife. It is full of valuable counsel to such as are temporarily thrown off their balance by sorrow; and exhibits a proof of that friendship which does not hesitate to wound in order to heal.

"THEOLOGICAL SEMINARY, *September* 4, 1856.

"DEAR DONNOM: I regret very much that I did not have the opportunity of seeing more of you, during your short visit to Columbia. Your case has excited an intense interest in my mind, not only in the way of sympathy for your sore and terrible affliction, but in the way of apprehension for the use you are likely to make of it. You must excuse me for speaking plainly; my anxiety on your behalf will not allow me to hold my peace, or to speak what your feelings would prompt you to ask. Your situation is critical, much more critical than you and your friends may possibly suspect. You are in danger of pursuing a course that may terminate in serious and lasting injury to your character and prospects.

"In the first place, Donnom, let me say to you frankly, that the want of fortitude which you seem to feel it no reproach to exhibit, is inconsistent alike with the dignity which becomes a man, and the submission which belongs to a Christian. To bear with firmness what cannot be avoided, is the dictate of philosophy; to bear with resignation what God appoints, is the dictate of religion. To be unnerved by calamities, to nurse our sorrows, to foster our grief, and make it our whole business to mourn, is a spirit of rebellion and insubordination, which not only cannot be justified, but cannot even be excused. It has no parallel but in the case of children, who pine over their losses in stubborn fretfulness, and refuse all the kindness and condescension of their parents to soothe their petulance. The language of such a course to the Almighty, when rightly interpreted, is a language of defiance, which a creature should shudder to use. It is a virtual declaration that because God has crossed you in your schemes and hopes, you are resolved to enjoy no more of His gifts, and to discharge no longer the duties He has imposed upon you. It is the language of sullen resentment. I do not object to the pungency of your grief: it is right to feel afflictions, and to feel them keenly. Religion does not convert us into stones. But while, like Jesus, we may weep at the tomb of our friends, we should never permit our nerves to be unstrung, nor our loins ungirded, for the duties and responsibilities which still rest upon us. We are still *men*, and still sustain the relations of *men*. With subdued and

chastened spirits we should return from the grave to the earnest calls of
life.   There should be a dignity in our bearing, a majesty in our woe, that
should command the respect and awe the sympathy of all who take
knowledge of us.   This is the deportment that I want to see you adopt.
I have been distressed to see you moping about, and arming yourself
with industrious patience, against the invasion of every thought that
would divert you from your loss, as if your sole business now was
simply to fan the flame of your sorrow.   You seem to have forgotten
that you are a son, a brother, a master, a man.   You are resolved to extinguish every relation of life in the disruption of the tie which bound
you as a husband.   It is a serious, and may prove in the end, unless
you summon your energies to correct it, a fatal mistake.   You must
resist this weakness.   Pardon me for saying that I was shocked when
you told me that you intended to sell your property and return to
Alabama, for the purpose of being constantly associated with those who
could nurse your sorrows, and keep the sore everlastingly running.
Donnom, this must not be.   I say to you in all earnestness, as you prize
your best and highest interests, do not think of making, in the present
condition of your mind, any permanent change in your arrangements
for life.   You are not qualified to form an impartial judgment, and the
spirit and end of the proposed scheme are such as to promise nothing
but disaster.   Wait till reason and reflection have resumed their ascendency, before you venture to disturb the existing state of your
affairs.   Do nothing without the advice of your father.   He is cool and
collected, and is competent to counsel you with discretion.

"But, Donnom, my worst fear in relation to you is, that this affliction
is likely to pass off without any profit.   If it is not sanctified to your
spiritual good, it will do you incalculable harm.   As I told you, in the
brief conversation I had with you, your mind was turned to none of
those Christian aspects in which, as a visitation of God, your bereavement should be contemplated, but was wholly absorbed in the selfish
considerations of your own personal loss.   You have obstinately refused
to see the hand of God; you fix upon nothing but the happiness which has
fled from your grasp.   Now, the effect of this perverseness cannot fail to
be disastrous.   However improbable it may now sound to you, time will do
its work; other associations will eventually take possession of the mind;
the intensity of your anguish will pass away; and unless your human
nature is different from that of all other men, the reaction will be as
violent to the other extreme; and you may be the victim of a levity as
unbecoming as your present unmanly grief.   If selfishness is to rule
the hour, this must be the effect.   It will keep you for a while in your
present state of mind, making morbid luxury of tears; but the same
law which produces this result will, after the satiety of grief is over,
seek a different species of luxury in other channels.   Mark my words.
I have studied that mystery of inconsistencies and contradictions, the
human heart, and I know what I am saying.   The effect of such a reaction will be fatal to all seriousness of character.   If you permit this

season to pass without having the selfishness of your nature eradicated or subdued, it will become the predominant principle of your life; and, though it may not assume offensive forms, it will be as deadly in its hostility to religion as if it wore the hateful and disgusting shapes which provoke the reprobation of the world. Your character is now passing through a crisis. Self is uppermost; God has called you to a dreadful sacrifice of that principle. He has taken what is dearest to self: and now self shows its power by refusing to be comforted, or even to submit, because its pride has been wounded. Let this spirit continue to regulate your feelings, and you become a confirmed votary to self, and an incorrigible rebel against God. Your afflictions will turn out to be a curse, instead of being improved as a blessing. It is, therefore, of the last importance that you should begin to consider your case in a new light; to look upon it as a dispensation of God, designed to answer salutary ends; and to seek, by prayer and devout meditation, to have its lessons impressed upon your mind.

"The first thing which the pungency of your grief should teach you, is the bitterness of sin. I do not say that your affliction is any judgment upon you; we have no right so to interpret the events of Providence. The estimate of personal character is not to be measured by outward circumstances. But all pain is ultimately due to sin; and the degree of pain which exists in the world may give us some notion of the extent to which God hates sin.

"Now, you know how much you have suffered by this bereavement. From the intensity of your anguish, learn the intensity of that poison which has infused all this bitterness into your cup. If, in this world, sin can produce so much sorrow, what are we to expect from it in a world of righteous retribution, where it is to receive according to its nature and deserts. It has occasioned you an awful loss here, the loss of a wife; it will occasion you hereafter, if not renounced and forsaken, the still more awful loss of your soul and God; and you will be made to feel these losses there with a weight of sorrow compared to which your present agony is joy. In all your distresses, see *sin* as the cause; from what it has cost you, learn to hate it, and to flee from it. Unless this lesson is mastered, the rod has been in vain.

"In the next place, you should learn that man's portion is not here below. This is neither our home nor our rest. How forcibly has this been impressed upon you! You had a pet lamb; you loved it, and nursed it, and watched it; you garnered your affections upon it, and rejoiced in the consciousness that this beautiful and lovely creature you could call your own. God took it at the very height of your self-satisfaction; and all to teach you that you were to have no pet lamb of your own, but that you must regard supremely His own Lamb, the Lamb of God, which taketh away the sin of the world. You were making yourself warm in your nest, and God has stirred it up, and driven you from it. He has been teaching you the great truth, that life is a pilgrimage; that we are strangers and sojourners here, and that we must seek a city

which hath foundations, whose builder and maker is God. If you can
only now be disgusted with sin, and allured to thoughts of the heavenly
city, you can have no difficulty in the way of life, which is none other
than the Lord Jesus Christ; and this consideration suggests the last
thought which I wish now to commend to your attention. It is the
importance of a personal communion with Jesus. He was a man of
sorrows; he knew what affliction and distress meant. Your cup is
sweetness compared to His; and all, that He might be a merciful and
faithful High Priest. He is the Friend of sinners. Go to Him; He
will receive you kindly and tenderly; He will enter into your griefs;
He will soothe your woe; and give you the oil of grace for the spirit of
heaviness. You need just such a friend. Look away from men, and
fix your eye and your heart steadily upon Jesus; and you will find one
who is more than father, or mother, or wife, or sister; who sticketh
closer than a brother. Do this, and your soul shall live.

"I have written to you, Donnom, these hurried lines, from a sincere
desire to minister to your profit. I have always loved you, and have often
prayed for you; but I love you more, and pray for you more tenderly,
now, since the Lord's hand is upon you. It may be that my plain dealing may offend you. If so, I shall regret it; there is nothing farther
from my heart than to give you pain. Your sorrow is sacred in my
eyes; but I have seen your danger and your snare, and I have endeavoured faithfully to put you on your guard. I would have preferred
talking with you, but your brief stay precluded that. May the Lord
bless you, and guide you, and keep you, and make all things work to
your good and His own glory.

"Most sincerely, your friend,

J. H. THORNWELL."

The following letter, to the Rev. Dr. Adger, discloses
his views upon a grave public question, at that time somewhat agitated in political circles:

"THEOLOGICAL SEMINARY, *December* 10, 1856.

"MY DEAR BROTHER: Send your article by the first of January. My
judgment and my feelings are decidedly opposed to the slave trade, in
every respect in which the subject can be viewed, and I am sorry that it
has been agitated at all. In the first place, it would change the whole
character of the institution, as it exists amongst us. It is now domestic
and patriarchal; the slave has all the family associations, and family
pride, and sympathies of the master. He is born in the house, and
bred with the children. The sentiments which spring from this circumstance, in the master and the slave, soften all the asperities of the relation, and secure obedience as a sort of filial respect. This humanizing
element would be lost, the moment we cease to rear our slaves, and rely
upon a foreign market. In the next place, it would render the institu-

tion positively dangerous. Lawless savages imported from Africa, many of whom have been accustomed to command, to war and to cruelty, and none of whom have been accustomed to work, would be about the surest instruments of insubordination and rebellion that could be desired. We should have to resort to a standing army, as they do in the West Indies, to keep our plantations in order. In the third place, the whole thing proceeds on a blunder. Capital and labour with us are not distinct. The slave is as really capital, as he is a labourer. To reduce his value, therefore, is not simply to cheapen labour, it is to reduce the amount of capital. The country will be no richer by the foreign importations. In the fourth place, it will operate as a constant cause of wars and seditions in Africa, and will involve largely the additional crime of man-stealing. These are mere hints, but they show my way of thinking. I have expressed my opinions freely to the Governor himself, whom I highly esteem. The sentiments of the State will revolt at the thing; it cannot go.

"In relation to yourself, the difficulties which are gathering, or have gathered around you, only render your duty the more manifest. Your external call* was clear and unambiguous; it was indeed very remarkable. The internal one must be equally obvious, if you will only reflect upon the state of your own mind beforehand. You wanted the door open, and you professed a willingness to make any sacrifice to enter it. God has opened it, and put you to the trial. He has thought you worth trying, and therefore father, and brother, and sister are permitted to rise up against you, to give you the opportunity of showing that His voice is louder in your ears than theirs. The case to me is very plain, and I shall really tremble for you, if you decline. Your mouth must be shut against any prayer hereafter for a field of ministerial labour. God may say, 'I called, and ye refused.'

"Most devotedly, your friend,

J. H. THORNWELL."

On being returned to the Assembly of 1857, at Lexington, Kentucky, Dr. Thornwell made a tour of more than two months through parts of Alabama, Mississippi, and Tennessee, in behalf of the Seminary at Columbia. His object was to awaken a more general interest in its welfare, and to complete its endowment, which had been successfully initiated by other parties visiting the southwest. His preaching was attended with great power wherever he went; and in the freedom of epistolary inter-

---

* His election to the chair of Church History and Government in the Theological Seminary, recently vacant by the writer's removal to his present field of labour.

course he refers, with humble gratitude, to the universal acceptance of his labours.   A warm friend of his in earlier days thus speaks of his visit to him in Mississippi : " I was enthusiastic in my love and admiration for him. After my removal from South Carolina to Mississippi I often told my friends here of his powers.   At length, one gentleman, an eminent lawyer, and a particular friend, told me that he thought my enthusiasm led me to exaggerate.   A few days after this conversation, I received a letter from Dr. Thornwell, informing me that he would pay me a visit on his way to the General Assembly at Lexington.   I called on my friend, and told him that he would soon see and hear for himself.   He came according to promise, and preached twice each of two Sabbaths, and twice through the week.   The community was held entranced by his pulpit discourses ; and after he left, my friend voluntarily said to me, " you did not tell the fourth part."

His letters, written home during this absence, are addressed often to his children, and adapted in their style to their different ages.   We present brief extracts, only for the purpose of bringing him more distinctly before the reader in his family relations.

The first is to his son, Gillespie, twelve years old.

"TUSCUMBIA, ALA., *May* 4, 1857.

"MY DEAR BOY: If you will take a map, and look upon that part of the State of Alabama which lies upon the Tennessee river, and is near to the States of Mississippi and Tennessee, you will see where your father is. The river is a noble stream. Steamboats run up it for nearly five hundred miles. In some places, it lies between banks of mountains of limestone, and you see tall mountains lying on both sides of it in the distance. It abounds in fish. I have seen whole wagon loads caught in it in a short time ; and you would enjoy yourself very much here with a hook and line. Between Tuscumbia and Florence the river is nearly a mile wide, and we have to cross it in a little steamboat. The whole region is full of limestone, and abounds in bold springs. There is a spring here which runs almost like a river; boats come to its very head, and it will often swim a horse. The water is clear as crystal, and gushes from a solid bed of rock. This spring supplies the whole town of Tuscumbia with water. In wet weather the country is very muddy; and the lime makes the mud stick more than it sticks in Lancaster. But it keeps the soil from washing away. They have no large gullies in the fields, like we have in the Waxhaws. It is a beautiful region.

I spent night before last with Dr. ——, and I was delighted to find that his oldest boy was a professor of religion. I thought what a comfort it would be to me to have my oldest boy, as indeed all my children, children of God. Begin now, my son, to fear and love and serve the God of your father. Do nothing which your Bible condemns. Pray from the heart; and earnestly seek that you may have a heart that loves to pray. * * * The Lord bless you, and make you a blessing to your fellow men.

"Your affectionate father,

J. H. THORNWELL."

The next is to one of his daughters:

"HOLLY SPRINGS, MISS., *May* 14, 1857.

"MY DEAR PATTIE: I received your welcome letter to-day; and though I wrote to Jennie this morning, I cannot refrain from dropping you a line to-night. Your letter was a great comfort to me; and I was particularly delighted at your saying that you wanted to be a Christian, and that you hoped to be one soon. Nothing would do me so much good as to see my dear little daughter converted to God. The Lord has promised His grace to those who seek Him early. You cannot begin too soon. For, lovely as you are in my eyes, you are a sinner in the sight of God; and your first care should be to obtain pardon through the Lord Jesus Christ, and to get a new heart. Pray to God, for Christ's sake, to give you the Holy Spirit. He will be willing to hear the prayers of a child. Study your Bible, and try to trust in the Saviour. Give yourself to Him; and beg Him to save you, and make you a true child of God. * *

"I love to read your letters. I did not know that you could write so well. And now, my dear child, may God bless you and keep you, and lead you in the way everlasting. I sincerely pray that I may find you a Christian when I come back home.

"Your affectionate father,

J. H. THORNWELL."

To Mrs. Thornwell:

"MEMPHIS, TENN., *May* 18, 1857.

"MY DEAREST WIFE: I reached here on Friday night, and spent Saturday in looking around this young and flourishing city, which, within a quarter of a century, has sprung up like magic, and is daily increasing in an astonishing ratio. To have an idea of the real progress of our country, one must come to the West. He will see the reason why we are compared to a young giant. On Saturday morning I saw the Mississippi river for the first time. It was in its glory; almost to high water mark; and well deserves the name of the Father of Waters. Memphis contains about eighteen thousand inhabitants, and is as well supplied with churches as most of our older cities. It has the appearance of great activity and enterprise; everything is full of life and bustle.

"The scale on which they make cotton in Louisiana, Mississippi, and Arkansas, reduces us in South Carolina to mere pigmies. A man who does not make a thousand bales, weighing five hundred pounds apiece, is a small planter. Some make upwards of three thousand bags. Their trades are on an equal scale. They talk of a hundred thousand dollars as we talk of a thousand; and they think no more of a draft of fifty thousand dollars, than a prosperous planter in South Carolina would think of five thousand. * * *

"I preached yesterday to a large and attentive congregation. Both the Presbyterian churches here are strong and influential bodies. My trip to the West has impressed me more than ever with the importance of our Seminary. The gospel must keep pace with the tide of population; the hope of our country depends upon its being pervaded with the spirit and institutions of Christianity. And I think I have a clear notion of what sort of preachers we want. I feel that we have a great work to do; and I am resolved, in God's strength, to gird up my loins and set about it. I have made several acquaintances here. The Lord has raised me up friends wherever I have gone. He has truly sent His angel before me, to keep me in the way, and to bring me from place to place. Every day adds some new memorial of His goodness. I leave this afternoon for Kentucky; and I sincerely trust that the same goodness, which has followed me hitherto, will conduct me still.

"I presume that this letter will find you at home; but you may be in Sumter. My heart is with you, wherever you go. I earnestly pray that your health may be preserved, and that your soul may prosper. I cannot tell you how often and how tenderly you are in my thoughts and my prayers. The Lord has greatly blessed me in my family, and I feel myself utterly unworthy of His kindness. My journey has been sanctified to me, in bringing me much into communion with my own heart, and revealing to me my spiritual wants and defects. I am resolved, by God's grace, to live a holier and more devoted life. I want to be entirely consecrated to God, weaned from self, from pride and vanity, and knowing nothing but Christ and Him crucified. Pray for me, my dearest love, for I need much prayer. God bless you, and comfort you and keep you.

"Your devoted husband,

J. H. THORNWELL."

To the same:

"GENERAL ASSEMBLY, LEXINGTON, *May* 26, 1857.

"MY DEAREST LOVE: I seize a moment amid the business of the Assembly, and while a member is making a long-winded speech, to hold communion with the being who is dearest to me of all other beings on earth. Your letter from Sumter has been received, and you have a thousand thanks for its precious contents. I trust that I am unfeignedly thankful to God for all His mercies to me; and especially in the restoration and preservation of your health, and for the health of all my children and servants, since I left home. I have a very pleasant time here; meeting many acquaintances, and receiving a thousand marks of kindness and esteem. The Lord has enabled me to preach with great acceptance.

"We had a fine day yesterday. It was devoted entirely to the subject of Foreign Missions. I made a speech, which I hope the Lord blessed to the good of us all. I go next Sunday to Cincinnati, and preach there. I have so many solicitations to preach at different places, that it humbles me to think how much God honours me when I am so unworthy. The only setting down that I have had in the way of compliment was the question which was asked, if I did not wear a wig. But I am thought to be much younger looking than was expected. Everybody inquires after you. There is a great curiosity to see you, as it is thought you must be a very remarkable woman. I tell the people that I have the greatest wife in the world, and they all believe it. Much love to all the children; kiss them all, and remember me to the servants.

"Your devoted husband,

J. H. THORNWELL."

To the same:

"STEAMER 'EMPRESS,' OHIO RIVER, *June* 5, 1857.

"MY DEAREST LOVE: I was so beset and occupied with calls the day that I left Lexington, that I had not time to write to you what my heart prompted me to say. We had a most delightful meeting of the Assembly. The Lord gave me special favour in the eyes of the people; and I sincerely trust that every sermon which I preached was accompanied with His blessing. I preached one night to the students of Transylvania University; and as I was leaving Lexington, I received a letter from them, at the hands of a committee, beautifully and touchingly written, begging me to accept a splendid silver pitcher, which I had work to get into my trunk. I have said nothing about it, as I do not like to make a blowing-horn of such things; but I know it will be gratifying to you to learn that the Lord has prospered my way.

"We are now on the river; and the weather for two days has been so cold that we have found fires necessary to our comfort. I am afraid that we shall not be able to get beyond Memphis for Sunday. * * * I dread the trip which I have to make; but the interests of the Seminary will be greatly promoted by it. I have done much good already. Kiss all the children for me, from Nannie down. God grant that they may all be children of His grace! Tell the boys that I am particularly anxious to hear good reports from them. They must not pass a day without reading their Bibles, and calling upon God in prayer. Remember me also to the servants. And now, dearest, may the Lord be with you, and keep you, and bless you, and lead you in the way everlasting!

"Your devoted husband,

J. H. THORNWELL."

The only part of the proceedings of the Assembly of 1857 with which these Memoirs are concerned, was the appointment of a Committee to revise the Book of Discipline, with Dr. Thornwell as its Chairman. The subject came up before the Assembly through two overtures, one from Dr. R. J. Breckinridge, proposing a change from Presbyterial to Synodical representation, and a limitation of the General Assembly to fifty ministers and fifty ruling elders, each; the other from the Presbytery of Philadelphia, proposing a form of judicial proceedings. The first suggestion was, to commit these topics to suitable men for consideration, who should report to the next Assembly. This was enlarged so as to require an examination and revision of the whole Book of Discipline. The Rev. Dr. Hoge, of Ohio, proposed to add the Form of Government also as a subject for revision, which was resisted by Dr. Thornwell, on the ground that the Church was not yet prepared for this. This measure was therefore dropped, and the Book of Discipline was put for revision into the hands of a committee, consisting of Rev. Drs. Thornwell, Breckinridge, Hodge, Hoge, McGill, Swift, and Judges Sharswood, Allen, and Leavitt. It may be added, that the subject continued to be under discussion until the breaking out of the war,·and the separation of the Southern Church from the Northern. It was taken up in the Southern Assembly after its organization, under a committee of its own, which reported a revised code for adoption. The Presbyteries not being sufficiently agreed, the work was laid by; and thus the matter at present rests. The reader will be interested in the following letter from the lamented Dr. Van Rensselaer, the Moderator by whom the appointment of the original committee was made. It is addressed to Dr. Thornwell:

"PHILADELPHIA, *August* 10, 1857.

"MY DEAR BROTHER: I feel some solicitude about the results of the action of the committee, appointed by the last Assembly, to revise our Book of Discipline. I say *solicitude*, chiefly because I had the responsibility of the appointment of the committee, as Moderator. On reviewing the whole matter frequently, I have always come to the conclusion that I could not have done better. I firmly believe that it is in your power to bring in a report satisfactory to the great body of our people. The reasons why I named you as chairman were, first, your conservative views on the subject of altering our Book; second, your influence in carrying the question in the Assembly; third, the great confidence and love of the Church towards you, and the respect entertained of your mental endowments; fourth, I wished to avoid the appearance of giving too much predominance to this section of the Church; fifth, I was strongly drawn towards you that night, by an influence which seemed to me more like a special Divine influence than anything I remember to have experienced during my whole life. My mind was led to you, and to none but you.

"Under these circumstances, I have a strong desire to see the work done, and done by you; and I believe that, under God, *you can do it*. Alterations in the book are unquestionably called for; and if they are made with judgment and decision, and are not too numerous, the Presbyteries will adopt them."

Here follow some matters of detail, as to the meeting of the committee. The letter concludes:

"Praying that you may fulfil the best hopes of the Church in the important work committed to your care, I am,

"Yours respectfully and fraternally,

C. VAN RENSSELAER."

Although Dr. Thornwell had occupied the chair of Didactic and Polemic Theology in the Seminary, from the beginning of 1856, his inauguration, as a matter of form, did not take place till near the close of the second year of his incumbency. On the 13th of October, 1857, in the presence of the Board of Directors, and of many of the members of the Synod of South Carolina, he delivered his Inaugural Discourse, in the Presbyterian church, Columbia, South Carolina. The services were solemn and imposing throughout. A felicitous charge was first given,

by the Rev. Dr. Smyth, of Charleston, to the Professor
elect; who then publicly subscribed the formula prescribed
in the Seminary constitution, binding him to teach nothing
contrary to the standards of the Presbyterian Church.
The discourse then pronounced had been written at a
single sitting the preceding night, but, as he said, "with
his mind at a white heat;" and though occupying but ten
pages in the first volume of his "Collected Writings," in
the expanded form in which it was delivered, without
notes, one hour and a half were consumed, without weariness to his delighted auditors.   The subject was as comprehensive as it was appropriate: "The Scope of Theology: its claims to be considered as a science, and the
principle which should regulate the arrangement of the
parts, and their combination into a complete and harmonious whole."   The subject, the occasion, and the
speaker, were alike worthy of each other, and the scene
one never to be forgotten by those who were privileged
to witness it.

It is proper to state that, about this date, during the
summer or autumn of 1857, the additional title of Doctor
of Laws was conferred upon him, we believe, by Ogle-
thorpe University, of Georgia.   There being nothing in
the papers we have in our hands to fix either the date or
the source of this academic distinction, we are forced to
rely upon the impressions of his friends as to the latter,
and upon a comparison of dates for the former.

CHAPTER XXX.

SEMINARY LIFE CONTINUED.

VISITS THE SOUTHWEST ON BEHALF OF THE SEMINARY.—IMPRESSIONS
OF NEW ORLEANS.—EFFECT OF HIS PREACHING.—DEATH OF HIS
FRIEND, REV. MR. BISHOP.—LETTER TO HIS WIDOW.—ASSEMBLY OF
1859.—HIS REPORT ON REVISION.—REMARKABLE SPEECH IN THE AS-
SEMBLY.—LETTERS FROM INDIANAPOLIS.—RETURN HOME.—DEATH OF
HIS OLDEST DAUGHTER.—AFFECTING CIRCUMSTANCES ATTENDING IT.
HIS AFFLICTION AND RESIGNATION.—LETTER DETAILING HER SICKNESS
AND DEATH.—ANXIETY FOR THE CONVERSION OF HIS CHILDREN.—LET-
TER OF SYMPATHY.—ASSEMBLY OF 1860.—HIS DEBATE WITH DR. HODGE
ON THE QUESTION OF BOARDS.

IN the early part of the year 1858, Dr. Thornwell
visited the city of New Orleans, in the interest of the
Seminary at Columbia. It had always been the design
of this institution to extend its influence over the entire
Southwest, which seemed to be the territory from which
its patronage should largely be drawn. As early as
1855, a deputation had been sent to the churches in this
region, to draw more closely the bonds of sympathy and
union. Dr. Thornwell's mission was, however, to the
Synod of Mississippi, which met, later than usual, at New
Orleans. It was the author's unspeakable pleasure to
receive the friend whom he loved into his home as a
guest, and to hear his voice proclaiming the gospel of the
grace of God, as in former years, from his own pulpit.
The few discourses which his strength enabled him to
deliver, are held in sweet remembrance by many at this
day; and are mentioned still as the standard—the highest
they had ever known—of what pulpit eloquence should
be. The brief letters of this date will convey his own
impressions of what he heard and saw; mutilated, as
these letters must be, of all personal reference to him by
whose hand they are here transcribed:

431

"New Orleans, *January* 12, 1858.

"My Dearest Wife: The Synod of Mississippi adjourned last night
about eleven o'clock. My meeting with the brethren has been very
pleasant, and my mission for the Seminary far more successful than I
had any right to expect. Our proposition was not accepted, to have
this Synod adopt the Seminary, as Alabama had done; but resolutions
were unanimously passed, expressing confidence in us, commending us
to the churches, and declaring that 'it was never the purpose of the Synod to tie itself to Danville. We have gained more than might have
been expected, when the efforts of Danville for several years are considered, and the resolutions of two other meetings of Synod in favour
of Danville are taken into the account. If I had not come, we should
have been apt to lose Mississippi entirely. As it is, the country is now
pretty safe.

"I had a meeting yesterday evening of the leading gentlemen connected with Dr. Palmer's church, and laid the claims of the Seminary
before them. They were very cordial, even warm and zealous in our
favour. They advised me to remain another Sunday, and to make the
same statement to the public which I made to them. They thought
that the impression would be very happy, and that I would prepare
the way for a handsome donation, as soon as the present pressure was
in some degree relieved. My aim is to get New Orleans to shoulder the
debt for Dr. Smyth's library; that is, to guarantee to us fifteen thousand dollars principal, and the interest until it is all paid. I think
they will do it; and if they do, I shall feel that I have been enabled, by
the blesing of God, to accomplish a most important work here. My
next effort will be at Mobile. I intended to be there next Sunday, but
this new arrangement will throw me back a week later. Anxious as I
am to be at home, I feel that, while I am out, it is my duty to explore
the field, and do what I can. My own fireside is all the world to me.
Still I am glad that I have made so many interesting acquaintances. It
has enlarged my sphere of usefulness. * * *

"Your devoted husband,

"J. H. Thornwell."

To the same:

"New Orleans, *January* 15, 1858.

"My Dearest Wife: It seems to me almost a year since I left you and
the little ones at home. * * But I am reconciled to my long and dreary
absence by reflecting that I am on the Lord's business, and that I am
promoting the interests and glory of His kingdom. My visit here has
been of signal benefit to the Seminary. The people here have received
me with open arms; and my only regret is, that I have not been able to
labour more efficiently among them. I have suffered very much from a
bad cold; and the weather has been so wet and warm, that I can make
very little headway in recovering. The climate here is like spring,

flowers are blooming, trees budding; English peas, lettuce, and spring vegetables, are abundant. So far from needing fire, most of the day we have to leave the windows open. It is, no doubt, unusually warm; but the climate is far milder than ours. But the moisture is very great. The ground is saturated with water; and, where they are not paved, the streets are intolerably muddy and nasty. * * *

"I shall leave here on Monday or Tuesday, for Mobile. How long I shall remain there, I cannot say, until I feel the pulse of the people. Kiss the children for me, and accept any quantity of love for yourself: and believe me,

"Your devoted husband,

J. H. THORNWELL."

The next letter is addressed to one of his daughters:

"MOBILE, *January* 20, 1858.

"MY DEAR DAUGHTER: I received your welcome and affectionate letter yesterday, just as I was leaving New Orleans; and was rejoiced to hear that you were well, and were gratified with your visit to Abbeville. I was particularly delighted that you prized so highly the privilege of the Lord's Supper. It is indeed a feast to those who love the Lord Jesus Christ in sincerity and truth. He is the food of our souls. To His precious blood we look for pardon; to His righteousness, for favour; and to His Spirit, for holiness. He is as willing, as He is able, to bless us; and it is a glorious thing when we can resign ourselves into His hands, feeling that we are nothing, and that He is everything. Endeavour, my dear child, to live close to Him, and to seek His guidance and His favour in everything. Confide in Him as a friend, and trust Him with all your cares. Lean upon Him, as you would lean upon your father, and He will keep you in all your ways. Never forget to pray, and to study the Holy Scriptures, and ask for light to understand them.

"I left New Orleans yesterday, after a pleasant stay of two weeks. My mission was quite successful. The people have determined to raise there fifteen thousand dollars for the Seminary, certainly, and perhaps more. They were very cordial to me, and seemed highly edified with my preaching. It is a great place, and one of the widest fields of usefulness on our continent. * * *

"The Lord be with you all, and bless and keep you.

"Your affectionate father,

J. H. THORNWELL."

The death of the Rev. Pierpont Bishop drew forth a letter to his bereaved widow, in which are expressed his feelings of veneration and love for one whose depth of piety and religious zeal never failed to impress those to whom he was known:

"THEOLOGICAL SEMINARY, *March* 9, 1859.

"MY DEAR MRS. BISHOP: I have just this moment received the painful intelligence of your husband's death. Little did I dream, when I left him on Thursday morning, and when he so confidently expected to visit us in May, that my eyes should never more behold his venerated form. Still less did I dream, when I received, two weeks ago, a letter of condolence and of sympathy from him, that I should so soon be called upon to administer consolation to his beloved family. I need not say to you how deeply I sympathize with you in your sad bereavement. You have reason to weep. You have lost one who has left few equals on earth. He was a man of God; a man whose heart was in heaven, while his body freely mingled among the sons of men. He was a man of prayer, full of the Holy Ghost, full of zeal in his Master's cause, and full of charity to his fellow men. None knew him without loving him; and the more they knew, the more they loved him. I always esteemed his intimacy and friendship as among the richest blessings of my life. Your loss is great. But in the midst of your sorrow you have much to be thankful for. You should be thankful for the many years you were privileged to enjoy the society, guidance, confidence, and love, of such a man. It was a rich boon, and a boon conferred upon very few of your sex. You should be thankful for the precious memories which you are permitted to cherish of his conversation, his charities, and his zeal. You should bless God for the noble legacy he has left you and your children, in a pure example, a treasury of prayers, and a hearty consecration of you all to God. Depend upon it, you have been highly favoured; and you must not forget that, if your affliction is unusually severe, it is only because your blessings have been pre-eminently great. You know, too, that you shall see him again. Those who sleep in Jesus will God bring with Him. He is not dead, but sleepeth; and the Saviour, at the proper time will assuredly wake him; and you shall then see that his death, at this precise juncture, was for the glory of God. In the meanwhile you are not a widow; for the Lord Jehovah promises to be your husband. Trust in Him, make His promises your portion, and, above all things, murmur not against His will. His ways may be in the dark; but infinite wisdom, and goodness, and love, regulate all the dispensations of His providence to His children. What He does, you may not know now, but you shall know hereafter; and when you come to understand it, you will cordially approve it. Trust, therefore, in Him, and commit yourself and your children into His hands. Could your husband speak to you from the skies, this is what he would say to you.

"My whole family deeply sympathize with you. Every child in my household loved the very name of Bishop. God grant that we may all imitate his example, and follow him as he followed Christ.

"I have written in great haste, upon the very instant of receiving the sad news. I almost regret that I had not remained to pay the last tribute of respect to his remains; and yet I do not know how I could have borne the sad spectacle. I apprehended no danger. The Lord bless

you and keep you, and be the Guardian, Friend, and everlasting portion
of you and yours.

"Most truly your friend,

J. H. THORNWELL."

Dr. Thornwell was a member of the Assembly of 1859,
which met at Indianapolis; and there, as chairman of the
Committee on the Revision of the Book of Discipline,
submitted his first report.   The subject, after full discussion, was recommitted; and remained in the hands
of the Committee until the war, and the division of the
Church, which that necessitated, in 1861.   Those who
desire to be minutely informed of the changes which
were proposed in the revised code, are referred to the
full exposition and defence of them by the chairman, as
found in the fourth volume of his "Collected Writings."
They were intended to simplify the book; to remove ambiguities; to state more accurately what are "offences,"
in the view of our standards; to adjust the relations of
the lower and the higher courts, in cases of appeal; to
define with greater exactness the sense in which the baptized and non-communicating members of the Church are
under its discipline, and the like.   The intense conserva-
tism of the Presbyterian Church has hitherto resisted all
efforts to remove even the acknowledged defects and
anomalies of the existing book; and that, too, in the face
of a very general admission that most of the changes,
which have been suggested in these various revisions, are
a manifest improvement.   The writer frankly acknowledges himself to be of that class, who would hail with
delight a more articulate and a more pronounced exposition of our principles of Church Order and Government,
as these have been elucidated in the discussions and controversies of the last thirty years.   Both in Europe and
America, the Presbyterian Church has been, to a greater
or less extent, embarrassed by complications, which have
hindered the fullest expression of all her principles; and,
in the struggle to emancipate herself, has been plunged

into controversies which have brought these out more and more distinctly into view. In the Southern branch of the Church, a degree of unanimity prevails upon all essential points, most favourable to an authoritative exposition of them, but for the restraint imposed by a simple dread of the spirit of restlessness and change. The Church, indeed, is safe under a proper and strict interpretation of her law, as it stands; but it would be an immense gain if that interpretation itself were fixed for ever by the removal of ambiguities from the code by which she is governed.

Near the close of the session of this Assembly, Dr. Thornwell delivered a short speech, far less elaborate than many we have heard from his lips, but which was an admirable specimen of his forensic power, in sometimes sweeping an audience away with a burst of impassioned feeling. A paper had been introduced commending the African colonization scheme. Dr. Thornwell was seated on one of the front benches, at the side of the rostrum, in a listless and inattentive mood. The writer touched his hand, and said, in a whisper, " Now is your time; this is an unembarrassed issue in which to urge your views as to the spiritual functions of the Church." He sprang instantly to his feet, and, without a moment for the arrangement of his thoughts, proceeded to argue, that "the Church is exclusively a *spiritual* organization, and possesses only a *spiritual* power. Her business was the salvation of men; and she had no mission to care for the things, or to become entangled with the kingdoms and policy, of this world. To this view," he said, "the Church has been steadily coming up; and in consequence, what a spectacle does she present to the country and the world! And why does our beloved Zion stand thus 'the beauty of the land?' It is because the only voice she utters is the Word of God; because no voice is heard in her councils but His. He gloried in the position of this Church. He was once attended by a young gentleman, a

native of Great Britain, through the Tower of London;
and we passed through the long apartments and corri-
dors in which were deposited the trophies which England's prowess had won in her many wars. As my
companion pointed with becoming patriotic pride to
these trophies," said Dr. Thornwell, "I raised myself to
the fullest height my stature would permit, and replied,
'Your country has carried on two wars with mine; but I
see no trophies won from American valour.' Let our
Church," he continued, "lend herself, in the name of the
Lord, and in her own proper sphere, to her own mission,
and her enemies will never rejoice over trophies won
from her. The salt that is to save this country is the
Church of Christ, a Church that does not mix up with
any political party, or any issue aside from her direct
mission."

The generous patriotism that breathed in these closing
sentences, a patriotism which gloried in the American
name, sent an electric thrill through the house; and it is
the only occasion on which the writer has ever known
the gravity and decorum of an ecclesiastical court disturbed by an involuntary, though subdued, applause,
which was instantly repressed by the Moderator's gavel.
The whole passage has a melancholy interest to those
who reflect how completely, and in how short a time, this
glowing picture of a Church, true only to her own mission, was reversed and turned to the wall. We pass,
however, to the letters of this period:

"INDIANAPOLIS, *May* 19, 1859.

"MY DARLING WIFE: I have waited till night to write to you, that I
might give you some account of the organization of the Assembly. As
Dr. Scott, the last Moderator, was not present, Dr. Rice opened the
Assembly with a sermon, which gave very general satisfaction. After
the sermon, the Assembly adjourned until four o'clock in the afternoon.
We then met, and elected a Moderator, Dr. W. L. Breckinridge, who
was unanimously chosen, all other nominations being withdrawn.

"I have met a great many old acquaintances, and they all seem glad to
see me; a number that served with me at Nashville, New York, Lexing-

ton, and Cincinnati. What the course of business will be, and what the temper in which the business will be conducted, I cannot yet conjecture. Much will depend on the committees to be reported to-morrow. But I sincerely trust that the Spirit of God will be poured out upon us, and that we may be guided in all our deliberations by Divine wisdom." * * *

Again, under date of May 30th, 1859:

"MY BELOVED WIFE: This is Monday morning; and before the Assembly opens, I seize a moment to drop you a line. I preached yesterday morning in one of the churches, to a very large congregation. The house was jammed, and many had to go away. The sermon seems to have produced some impression, though I did not preach to my own satisfaction. We held communion yesterday afternoon. It was a very pleasant and refreshing season; and my affections and prayers were earnestly engaged in behalf of the dear ones at home.

"My speech on the Revision question was well received, and produced a decided effect. The body still continues very harmonious, and a fine spirit prevails. It is feared that the disappointed party, after the election shall have been made for Professors in the North Western Seminary, will try and make trouble; but I hope that there is no foundation for the fear. The Assembly will probably not adjourn until the second or third day in June. I shall then have to spend a day or so in Kentucky. I am very reluctant to go, but I feel it to be my duty; and all Dr. Breckinridge's friends think it very important that I should see him.* If so, I may not be at home before the 10th of June. * * * * Love to all. To God I commit you. Abide under the shadow of His wings.   Your devoted husband,

                                     J. H. THORNWELL."

It was during this meeting that Dr. Thornwell preached a sermon from the text, "Simon, son of Jonas, lovest thou Me?" which is said to have melted the whole audience into tears. The statement does not surprise those who are familiar with the marvellous unction with which he would often expound Divine themes, when he seemed borne out of himself by a secret and resistless impulse, and was only less than inspired. He himself afterwards said of this sermon, that he had prepared it but a short time before, in his ministrations in his own pulpit, and never anticipated the great impression produced by it on this occasion. The fact is, the grandest illustrations of his power were not to be found in his elaborate and set

* Dr. Breckinridge had recently lost his wife.

discourses, which were sometimes overweighted; but in his ordinary preparation, on occasions when the Divine afflatus was upon him, and he would appear more like one of the old Hebrew prophets, upon whom rested some "burden of the Lord," forcing its utterance from the lips.

Dr. Thornwell returned home from Indianapolis to encounter a great sorrow. His eldest daughter, Nannie Witherspoon, just twenty years of age, had been taken ill two days before his return, and within a week was laid in the tomb. He was accustomed to say of her that, of all his children, she was most like himself in the order and structure of her mind; and, perhaps on this account, he felt in her a peculiar joy and pride. She was the idol of his heart. His first meeting with her, upon his return, was affecting in the extreme; but, as it is simply said in the account from which we draw, it was "too sacred for any eye save of those bound to him by ties of blood." In the progress of her disease, he wrestled with his grief, and could not easily give her up. When it became apparent that she must die, he took his wife into the adjoining room, and there the two knelt and prayed for help and for submission. At intervals, he read and prayed with the departing one; and she, in the triumph of her faith, became his comforter, and sought with tender words to reconcile him to the inevitable separation. It was a beautiful scene: this reversal of positions between the dying child and the strong father, writhing in the crucifixion of his affections. But, like David, when the blow fell, his prayer for help was answered, and he bowed himself, and said, "It is the Lord!" The peculiar circumstances of this bereavement threw around it an inexpressible tenderness. The young lady was on the eve of her marriage, with one for whom she knew it would be a joy to live. The father had hastened back to bestow his parental blessing upon the union that seemed to be so auspicious. The invitations to the wedding had already been issued. So violent had been the illness, and so

sudden its termination, that such as were sent to a dis
tance could not be recalled. The bridal dress became the
shroud; and just a little after the day when she should
have plighted her vows before the altar, the very attendants who, in a different scene, should have "rejoiced,
hearing the bridegroom's voice," with their white gloves
lifted the bier, and bore it to the grave. In the peaceful
Elmwood Cemetery, at Columbia, a marble slab bears the
simple inscription of her name and age, with these appro-
words beneath:

"PREPARED AS A BRIDE ADORNED FOR HER HUSBAND."

It was a sorrow from which the stricken father never
fully recovered. From this time his health became feebler,
a tinge of sadness rested upon his countenance, the Christian graces became sweeter and softer every day, and it
was evident to all that he was himself mellowing rapidly,
to be gathered above with her who had gone.

The letter which follows was addressed to Mr. Robert
Carter,* of New York, presenting some details of this

* We cannot refrain from subjoining the note of Mr. Robert Carter,
accompanying a copy of this letter, when sent to the writer. It is so
honourable to him, and bears such a cheerful testimony to the worth of
our common friend. What shocks Christian affection has power to survive! The differences of earth may cause it to tremble like the magnet,
but cannot throw it from its delicate poise:

"NEW YORK, *August* 29, 1874.

"Your letter, dear sir, calls up many pleasing and many painful recollections. Dr. Thornwell was one of my dearest friends. We were thrown
together in London, in 1841, and sailed together, in the 'Britannia,'
home. I had the opportunity of meeting him at many of our Assemblies. We spent a delightful day at Chattanooga, on Lookout mountain,
on our way to Nashville; and he spent the last days he was North at my
house, when the dark cloud was thickening which shrouded his latter
days. My heart bleeds when I think of one whom I loved so dearly,
and whom I shall see no more on earth. I consider him one of the most
eloquent preachers I ever heard. As a friend, I can scarcely speak of
him. He was so confiding, so winning, so witty, and, in his graver moments, so tender and spiritual, that I look around in vain for one to take
his place.	Yours fraternally,

ROBERT CARTER."

sweet young Christian, which we have reserved to be given in the father's own words:

*"THEOLOGICAL SEMINARY, *June* 27, 1859.

"MY DEAR FRIEND: I have just received your kind and cordial letter of Christian sympathy; and as the subject is one upon which I take a melancholy pleasure in dwelling, I proceed at once to answer your tender and affectionate inquiries. You may remember that I told you of her approaching wedding. She was to have been married, on the 15th instant, to a young man eminently worthy of any heart or any hand.† I reached home on the morning of the 9th, and found her in bed with a raging fever. She had then been sick two days. Her symptoms appeared to me unfavourable, and I called in two other physicians. The next day I became alarmed, and on Friday gave her to understand that her case was critical. She was not at all disconcerted. She assured me that her peace was made with God; that, though she had many earthly ties, and some of them very tender, there was nothing that she loved in comparison with the Lord Jesus Christ, and nothing that she was not ready to sacrifice at His call. She called all the family to her bed side, united in prayer with them, and gave to each a parting benediction. The scene was sublime beyond description. To see a young girl, elegant, accomplished, and highly esteemed, with the most flattering prospects in life, just upon the eve of her marriage with one whom she devotedly loved, resign all earthly hopes and schemes and joys with perfect composure, and welcome death as the voice of one supremely loved, was a spectacle that none who witnessed can ever forget. It was grand; it was even awful. It impressed some who were in the room in a way they were never impressed before; and I felt more like adoring God for that wondrous triumph of His grace, than weeping for my own loss.

"After this scene she rallied; and the next day, the physicians thought that there was a fair prospect for her recovery. When it was announced to her that she might yet get well, she said that she wished to have no choice in the matter. All that she desired was that God might be glorified, whether by her life or her death. For the sake of others, she might desire to live; but upon the whole she would prefer, if it was the Lord's will, to depart and be with Jesus. She spent the whole day in listening to the Scriptures, and conversing with me about the condition of the soul after death. She was perfectly calm and collected; and what she said was the deliberate utterance of faith, not the language of excitement.

"Before the last hour came, she had a momentary conflict; but gained a glorious victory, and her joy was irrepressible. She threw her arms around my neck, and told me that her happiness was beyond expression. She felt the presence of Jesus, and rejoiced in Him with joy inexpress-

† The Rev. (now Dr.) T. Dwight Witherspoon.

ible, and full of glory. It was a glorious death, a triumphal procession. What makes the whole matter more consoling is, that there had been for months a marked and rapid progress in Divine things. She had been much in prayer · and as a proof of her intense spirituality, she has left behind her a paper, containing her reflection§ and feelings and purposes in the prospect of her marriage, and all bespeak the condition of one whose eye was single to the glory of God. It is a precious document, absolutely amazing for her years. Two days before she was taken sick, she had been on a visit to a friend in Sumter; and upon her return, spoke to her mother of the delightful communion she had enjoyed with God in prayer. The Master was evidently maturing her for heaven. The family has been amazingly sustained. The truth is, we dare not murmur. The grace has been so transcendent, that it would be monstrous to repine. I feel my loss, for I loved her very tenderly. But I bless God for what my eyes have seen, and my ears heard. We have been afraid to grieve, the triumph was so illustrious. My second daughter is a professor of religion, and, I think, a true child of God. My boys are still out of the ark. Pray for us, my dear friend; especially pray that I may have no unconverted child. The event has been greatly sanctified to me and my wife. God grant that we may never grow faint. I never relax my hold upon the covenant. Jesus has been more precious to me than I have felt Him for a long time, and the gospel more glorious. Henceforth I am bound, I trust, for eternity. I want to live only for the glory of God. Pray for me and mine. The Lord bless you, and reward you for your kind and Christian sympathies.

"As ever, yours,

J. H. THORNWELL."

His anxiety for the salvation of his children is expressed in almost every letter, and is never omitted in those written directly to them. We give extracts from two, addressed to his eldest son, Gillespie, than a boy of fifteen. The first is dated—

"RICHMOND, *August* 4, 1859.

"MY DEAR BOY: * * * * * I have endeavoured to commit you all to God; and there is nothing on which my heart is so much set as to see you all enlisted in the service of the Lord Jesus Christ. My cup of earthly happiness would be full, if you, and Jimmie, and Charlie, were only true Christians. You would then be safe for time and for eternity. Depend upon it, my dear son, you will never repent of it, if you should now give your heart unto the Lord. Let me beg you to seek, this summer, the salvation of your soul. You will have time to think, and read, and pray. Write to me that you are not neglecting the one thing needful. Be all that you know you ought to be. I think of you all the time, and never cease to pray for you. * * * *

The second letter is addressed to him at Oxford, Mississippi, where he was pursuing his studies with the Rev. T. Dwight Witherspoon, who had shared so deeply in the late great sorrow. It is more various in its counsels, and is given because it brings out the affection which marked his intercourse with all his children:

"THEOLOGICAL SEMINARY, *November* 6, 1859.

"MY DEAR BOY: I received your welcome letter the first of the week, and in consequence of the pressure of my public engagements, have deferred answering it until to-day. I need not say to you how much I am delighted at your purpose to study resolutely and continuously. Be on your guard against passing over things too rapidly. There must be a certain degree of dwelling upon any matter, in order that it may stick in the memory. * * * I am glad to hear that you are getting fonder of Greek. It is a great language, and I want to see you thoroughly master of it. Now is the time to lay the foundation broad and deep. Make yourself perfect in the Grammar, and the difficulties are all surmounted. I would like for you to read something besides your lessons. Plutarch's Lives, Bancroft's History, Hume's History, Irving's Life of Washington, or any books of the sort, will be of immense benefit to you. Try and get a love for reading; make notes of what you read; and often run over what you have read in your mind; so as to fix it in the memory. I want you also to commit a great deal to memory; it is one of the best exercises in the world. A good memory is indispensable to a man of letters. It is useless to have a thing, if you have no place to put it.

"The accounts which I have had of you are very gratifying. They have done me good. If you hold out as you have begun, you will make a man of yourself. But, above all things, keep constantly in view your dependence on God. I never bow my knees without thinking of you and Dwight. I look upon both of you as my boys, and I feel that both of you are safe only in the hands of God. Make it your great business to grow in grace. Watch the whole frame of your mind. Live close to the Lord Jesus Christ. Let nothing induce you to neglect prayer, or the reading of the Scriptures, and try to understand what you read. * * * *

"You may drop Virgil, if you are tired of it; but you ought to read the whole of it at some time. You must learn to scan all the Odes of Horace; make yourself master of them. I would advise you to take pains in trying to write a good hand. Imitate Dwight's; he writes beautifully. If you hold out as you have begun, and please me in all things, I shall be very happy to make you a present of my fine blooded mare, when you return home. The pups have grown finely. Jimmy and Charley attend to them every day. Much love to Dwight.

"Your devoted father,

J. H. THORNWELL."

About this time he paid a second visit to the Southwest, to strengthen the interest he had awakened the preceding year in the Theological Seminary. He did not, however, get beyond Mobile, being compelled, by indisposition, to return home from that point. He thus writes to his brother-in-law, the Rev. A. J. Witherspoon:

"THEOLOGICAL SEMINARY, *December* 28, 1859.

"MY DEAR JACK: You have probably heard before this of my indisposition in Mobile, which prevented me from going to New Orleans, and from attending the Synod of Mississippi. The whole thing was ordered in wisdom and love. It caused me to return home at once, where I found a letter requiring immediate attention, in relation to the business of my widowed sister. Had I executed my original purpose, she would have been left in great distress, without an adviser and without a friend in whom she could repose implicit confidence. During my absence, too, one of my little negroes, a very promising child of Norah's, died suddenly and unexpectedly. I sincerely trust that she was prepared for the change.

"I am very intent on raising the fifty thousand dollars in the Synod of Alabama, by finding fifty men who will become responsible for a thousand dollars apiece The scheme must not fail. We must put the Institution upon a footing worthy of the South. The Lord is smiling upon us, and it becomes us to take courage, and do more than we have ever done before. I want you to exert yourself, and find men who will come into the arrangement. Last night one of our seminary students fell asleep in Jesus. He was the victim of a rapid, hereditary consumption. My own family are all in usual health, and all join in much love to you and yours.

As ever, your devoted friend,

J. H. THORNWELL.

The great comfort he experienced in the triumphant death of his own daughter, brought him into close sympathy with one who was partaker of the like sorrow and like consolation. The following, addressed to the Rev. John F. Lanneau, of Salem, Va., may be read as a commentary upon the Apostle's declaration, "We glory in tribulation also."

"THEOLOGICAL SEMINARY, *January* 30, 1860.

"MY DEAR BROTHER: I have just seen the account of the death of your darling 'Jimmie,' and must beg the privilege of being permitted to rejoice with you in this wonderful triumph of Divine grace. It would be monstrous ingratitude to talk of grief in a case like this. There may be, and there must be, the pang of separation; there may and there must be those tears of nature, which testify to a father's interest, and a father's love; but anything that deserves to be called grief, must not enter where God and Christ are so gloriously present, and where the chamber of death is irradiated with the light, and joy, and blessedness of the eternal city. God has honoured you, and your proper attitude before Him is that of profound and intense thanksgiving. I want to join with you in your song of praise. I write to you now, not to comfort you, but to congratulate you that God has done such great things for you. How delightful to think that your dear boy is now safely housed for ever, and that his young faculties are destined to expand and mature amid scenes in which there shall be nothing to disturb, distract, or obscure. Gone to heaven to be educated! what an honour!

"I have just finished Calvin's Commentary on Genesis, and cannot tell you how much spiritual refreshment and comfort I have derived from the light which his own experience and grace enabled him to throw upon the dealings of God with the ancient patriarchs. Every day enlarges my views, and deepens my convictions of the infinite riches of Divine wisdom and goodness. We serve no hard master. Our religion is no cold and lifeless homage to an unsympathizing superior. We have a Saviour that loves us, that enters into all our joys and sorrows, that permits us to converse familiarly with Him, and that shows, in the confidence of friendship, the secret of His covenant. 'Our light afflictions, which are but for a moment, work out for us a far more exceeding and eternal weight of glory.' 'It doth not yet appear what we shall be, but we know this, that when He shall appear we shall be like Him,' and shall be everlastingly participants of His glory. Rejoice, my brother, that you are a child of God; rejoice, again, that you are permitted to be father of sons and daugthers of the Lord Almighty; and rejoice above all things, that after a few more changes and vicissitudes, you and yours shall be for ever gathered to the Lord.

"Excuse these hasty lines, coming from a sympathizing heart. I could not forbear to speak; and yet I have almost felt it an intrusion to say anything where God is so conspicuously present. My whole family have expressed the profoundest interest in your case. We know how you feel. The Lord be with you, and bless you, and keep you in the way of holiness and peace.

"Very truly, as ever,

J. H. THORNWELL."

The Assembly at Rochester, New York, was the tenth and last General Assembly of the united Church in which Dr. Thornwell sat as a member. It is no slight proof of the estimation in which he was held as a presbyter, that he should have been returned to this supreme council of the Church at two-fifths of its annual sessions, from the year 1836, when his ministry began, to the year 1860. During almost this entire period, moreover, he was connected with the same Presbytery, and that Presbytery rather remarkable for the number of distinguished and representative men upon its roll.

The Assembly at Rochester is chiefly memorable for the earnest and able debate which was held on the subject of Church Boards. It was hardly possible that the two sides of this question could have been better represented than by Drs. Thornwell and Hodge; and as both were giants, the whole strength of the argument, on the one side and on the other, was brought out. In the fourth volume of Dr. Thornwell's "Collected Writings," the entire debate has been reproduced, with impartial fairness, by the editors. Not only the speeches delivered on the floor of the Assembly may be found, but the essays in the Princeton and in the Columbia *Reviews*, in which the arguments of both parties are more fully expanded. We cannot, of course, in these pages, re-state this controversy; but, in justice to him whose career we are undertaking to sketch, it is proper to set forth the estimate he had of its importance. In his judgment, "the whole question is but an offshoot from another question, which is *the organization of the Church itself*. One party holds that Christ has given the materials and principles of Church government, and has left us to shape them pretty much as we please; the other party holds that He has given us a *Church*, a constitution, laws, Presbyteries, Assemblies, presbyters, and all the functionaries necessary to a complete organization." Proceeding from this view, he argued "that the Boards were an *organism*, and not an *organ;* that they are the *vicars* of the Assembly, and appointed in *its place;* and that the principles of action by which they are governed were unfavourable to the development of the life and zeal of the Church." His speech did not carry the Assembly, though it **was** deeply moved by it. In the conclusion, when he summoned the whole host of God's elect to come up to the great work of giving the gospel to a lost world, the whole audience was held in breathless attention, their hearts vibrating as the heart of one man, to the fervent "Amen, and amen" with which he closed.

A single brief letter is all that gives his own impression of this Assembly, and of the part he took in its proceedings:

"ROCHESTER, *May* 28, 1860.

"MY DARLING WIFE: The Assembly is still in session, and likely to continue so for two days longer. The debate on the Boards has ended, and the other side carried the day by a large majority: but I think we had the best of the argument. Their victory will not do them much good.

"We had an address from Father Chiniquy to-night, and it was the most interesting and touching thing I ever listened to. He is evidently a true man, and the work among his people is a wonderful work of God. I never had my heart more stirred than in listening to his simple story of the dealings of God with him.

"I have preached twice here, and, I have reason to think, with great acceptance. The people have been very kind and hospitable. I am so occupied, day and night, that I cannot steal the time to write as often as I desire; and I pray God that you may constantly experience a sense of His love, and confidence in His protecting care. As the time approaches for me to sail, I am strongly tempted to draw back. The thought of not seeing you all, for so long a time, is a heavy burden. I shall probably not write again until I get to New York, and make all my arrangements. I will inform you of my plans, and how to address letters. Kiss the children; and may the good Lord bless you all.

"Your devoted husband,

J. H. THORNWELL."

CHAPTER XXXI.

SECOND TRIP TO EUROPE.

UPON the rising of the Assembly, Dr. Thornwell went immediately to New York, to embark for Europe. His constitution was visibly impaired, though neither he nor his friends perceived that it was irrecoverably broken. Nineteen years before, a sea-voyage had restored him, when threatened with a serious decline; and large hopes were cherished that he would again be toned up by a second trial of the sea, and the recreation of foreign travel. The Church in Columbia had recently associated with him, as co-pastor, the Rev. F. P. Mullally, then just out of the Seminary; so that he was relieved of all public care in making the trip. He was more fortunate than when he first crossed the Atlantic, in being now accompanied by congenial friends. His own suite consisted of his second daughter, a young bride, with her husband, the Rev. Robert B. Anderson; his nephew, John A. Witherspoon, a student of Divinity, and the Rev. P. H. Thompson, a recent graduate from the Seminary; these, with his intimate friend, Rev. John Douglas, wife, and niece, made up a party of eight; most of whom were young, and buoyant with life and hope. His letters, therefore, are more cheerful, and less filled with expressions of loneliness and home sickness, than those he formerly penned from Europe.

On the second of June, 1860, they sailed from New York, in the steamship Adriatic, and landed at Southampton, England, on the twelfth. The reader will remember the reflections which Dr. Thornwell indulged, on the wearisome monotony of the ocean. His friends describe him on this voyage as evincing little admiration for the wide expanse of waters, and as rarely coming upon deck, except for a few moments between supper and dark; giving occasion for the jocose remark that he was like a racoon, never leaving his den so long as he could see his own shadow. He preached but once during the voyage, which terminated without any of the incidents which are noted in his journal before. The day following his arrival in England was spent in a delightful excursion on the Isle of Wight, the beauty and cultivation of which formed an exquisite contrast with the confinement and monotony of the vessel. Dr. Thornwell had great enjoyment in scenes rich with historical associations, and the Isle of Wight abounded in these. He explored the ruins of Carisbrook Castle, where Charles the First was imprisoned before his execution; and said that he was greatly assisted in bringing before his imagination the civil convulsion that resulted in the execution of Charles, and the elevation of Cromwell.

But the story of his impressions will be told best in the language of his own letters, which are indeed the only chronicle from which we are able to draw:

"LONDON, *June* 18, 1860.

"MY DEAREST WIFE: I reached London last Friday, having made beforehand a pleasant excursion to the Isle of Wight. We visited Carisbrook Castle, and spent the night at Portsmouth, where we had most wretched accommodations. We have been very much annoyed in trying to get comfortable quarters in London. We squeezed in, the first night, at a hotel in Westminster, and were most outrageously gouged. We spent a day in seeking private quarters, and have found a place in the northern part of the city, in which we are constantly annoyed by the want of servants. It has disgusted the whole party with London, and they are anxious to get away. We have visited St. Paul's, the Tower, and

Thames Tunnel. Jennie has enjoyed herself very much. Her health has improved steadily; she eats heartily, sleeps soundly, and is always in a good humour. She and I did not go to church yesterday, on account of rain. The rest of the party went in the morning to hear Dr. Hamilton, and in the afternoon to hear Dr. Cumming. Jennie and I remained at home, and read our Bibles, and talked, and thought, and prayed about the dear ones in America. You cannot imagine how much I long to see you all; and if it were not for the comfort and consolation of prayer and faith, I would not be able to endure the pangs of separation. But the Lord has been very merciful to us since we left home, and it would be most ungrateful not to trust Him still for the continuance of His grace. I thought of you all yesterday, in your public worship. I could see you getting ready for the house of God. I could see you, as you set out from home; and I could fancy Mullally in the pulpit. You had my earnest prayers for the blessing of God upon you.

"This is the gay season in London. The city is crowded with the nobility and with strangers. Parliament is in session, and parties and balls are given every night by some attendants of the court. Of course, the Queen has not heard of our arrival, and we have received no invitations to the great Vanity Fairs!

"You may be surprised to hear that I have kept away from the bookstores. I do not intend to enter into temptation. I want to keep money enough to bring me home. I even keep my old hat, and it is a perfect curiosity here; the English all wear the high, stiff beaver. I intended to get a new hat, but was gouged so badly at the Brunswick hotel, that I have got into an economical fit, and will not spare the money. They charged us, at that hotel, for one day, about ten dollars apiece. We are now living at about two dollars a day, all expenses included. We have rented a house for a week, furnished; and the landlady is to supply us with everything. But her husband has been opposed to the operation, and the servants have been hindered, by the cross-firing between the parties, from giving us proper attention. We are in a very retired and quiet part of the city, and in a very pretty situation; but not as comfortable as we might be in Westminster.

"The weather has been very cold. We have fires every day, and sleep under two blankets and a counterpane every night. It is said that the oldest Englishman has no recollection of so cold a spell in June. But the climate is very bracing. My own health seems to be as good as it ever was. I can walk ten miles a day without fatigue, and sleep well for me. I have, as yet, made no acquaintances. I have not called on the American minister. I want to go to Oxford and Cambridge this week; next week we shall visit Edinburgh, then run over to Ireland, and then set out for the continent. * * * * * *

"Kiss all the children; remember me to the servants. The Lord be with you all, and bless you a thousand fold.

"Your devoted husband,

J. H. THORNWELL."

His next letter is addressed to his daughter :

" LONDON, *June* 19, 1860.

" MY DEAR PATTIE : Though I have recently written to your mother, yet, as the weather prevents me from going out to-day, I cannot spend the time more pleasantly than in conversing with the dear ones at home. Your mother and the children are never out of my mind. I think of you by day, and dream of you by night ; and would suffer much from home-sickness, were it not that the company around me is all so merry and full of frolic. * * * * * *

" I called on Mr. Dallas, the American Minister, yesterday. He was very polite and kind. I had a letter to him from Mr. Bancroft. We went yesterday to Westminster Abbey, to the two Houses of Parliament, and to Westminster Hall. We saw the courts in session, and were much amused with the white wigs. We heard a case partially argued before the Lord Chancellor, in the House of Lords. We went into another court, where there were three judges on the bench in their wigs ; and they were quietly eating a lunch, while a barrister was pleading, with great earnestness, before them. We rode round St. James' Park, and took a view of Buckingham Palace and St. James' Palace.

I have an invitation to-night to a sort of conference at Stafford House, where the Earl of Shaftesbury is to preside. Stafford House is the finest Ducal residence in the city. It belongs to the Duke of Sutherland. If you take down my Guide Book for London, you will find a full description of it. I intend to go, as it may be the means of introducing me into society. I expect to find an interesting party there. Mr. Dallas has promised me a letter to Professor Mansell, of Oxford. The Commencement is still going on there. I intend to go there, either this week or next. I propose also to visit Cambridge, on my way to Edinburgh. About the middle of July we shall go to Paris. For myself, I am tired of sight-seeing ; when one makes a business of it, the thing becomes very laborious. I much prefer meeting with educated men, and conversing with them.

" I leave it to Jennie to tell you all the sights ; she is full of them, and enjoys them very much. The party has a great deal of fun every night in writing up journals. I write nothing at all, except what I scribble home. I hope Gillespie will study hard, and get ready for College. I intend to bring him a handsome gold watch, with hunting case. Tell Jimmie and Charlie that they will get some fine presents from Europe, if they study to be good boys. I want them to attend very closely to their books. But, above all, exhort them to seek the favour of God. The great thing is true religion. There is nothing I desire so much as to see all my children walking in the fear of the Lord. I have consecrated them all to God, and sincerely pray that they may consecrate themselves. My efforts cannot save them. They must pray for themselves ; they must repent and believe in Christ for themselves. They must seek the salvation of their own souls. Let me beg you all to attend earnestly to this great matter.

"I hope Mullally is getting on well in the church. I never cease to pray for him, and the people of our common charge. Remember me kindly to all friends. Kiss all the children, and remember me to the servants. The Lord bless you all, and keep you.
"Your affectionate father,
J. H. Thornwell."

Three days later, he writes to his son, Gillespie; from which the following extract will suffice:

"Yesterday we went to Windsor Castle, built by William the Conqueror, more than eight hundred years ago, and refitted by George the Fourth. We were admitted into the State rooms, and some of the private apartments of the Queen. The paintings, I suppose, are very fine, as they were executed by the best masters; but I am no judge of excellence in that department of art. The grounds embrace a circuit of many miles. We rode about fifteen. Here is the forest which is the scene of Shakspeare's play of "The Merry Wives of Windsor." About a mile from Windsor, on the other side of the Thames, is Eton College, to which Gray devoted a beautiful ode. Its chapel is a fine Gothic structure. The College was founded by Henry the Sixth, and some of the noblest scholars of England have been educated at it. The education it gives is only preparatory to the Universities of Oxford and Cambridge. * *
"The great Commencement took place at Oxford yesterday. I missed it by not knowing the day; but I have had a full account of it from eye witnesses. It was a grand occasion. We shall be here nearly a week longer. There is still much for the young folks to see. The Queen has a great military review on Saturday, and they all expect to go. There is also to be a grand concert at the Crystal Palace, on Monday or Tuesday, and they expect to be there. A thousand loves to all the family. The Lord bless you all, and keep you.
"Your affectionate father,
J. H. Thornwell."

The trip to Ireland and to Scotland was a hurried one, and is thus glanced at in a letter to his old friend, General James Gillespie:

"London, *July* 21, 1860.
"My Dear General: I arrived in England about six weeks ago, after a smooth passage of ten days from New York to Southampton. After spending ten or twelve days in London, I set out for Oxford, Warwick, Wales, and Ireland. I spent only a week in the Emerald Isle, and chiefly in Belfast, where I met a great many Presbyterian preachers, the General Assembly being in session at the time. I was treated with great courtesy, and repeatedly pressed to preach, which I declined to do. The great revival has left its impress very strongly marked upon the

country. It was certainly a very wonderful work of grace. The recitals made in the General Assembly, and the accounts which I received from individuals, were profoundly interesting. I procured a history of the work, prepared by the Professor of Moral Philosophy in the Belfast College, with whom I formed a very pleasant acquaintance.

"From Belfast I crossed the Channel to Glasgow, and then proceeded to Edinburgh, where I lingered for more than a week. The society there was truly refreshing. I was a great deal with the Principal of the New College, the Rev. Dr. Cunningham, an able and learned theologian; and spent part of a day very happily with Professor Fraser, the successor of Sir William Hamilton in the University of Edinburgh. I was gratified to find that I was not wholly unknown to the clergy of Scotland. Several of my articles in the *Southern Presbyterian Review* had been re-published in the *British and Foreign Evangelical Review*, and some of them had been complimented very highly. I went to Melrose, Dryburgh, and Berwick-on-Tweed; thence to York, where I had the opportunity of attending a Cathedral service; and from York to London, where I am at present. On Monday I embark for the Continent. At York I went into the Court. A most exciting case was on trial, the impeachment of a member of Parliament for bribery. The result speaks well for British justice. The man was convicted, and fined fifty thousand dollars; or, in default of payment, sentenced to ten year's imprisonment. My health has been greatly improved. The climate here is bracing; but I have never seen the like for rain; six times a day in London is a modest allowance. While my body is here, my heart is in America. I remember you all with intense interest, and never cease to pray for you. I shall write to you again from Switzerland.

"As ever,

J. H. THORNWELL."

Before taking a final leave of England, it may be well to record the testimony of one of his party: "Dr. Thornwell, like Dr. Samuel Johnson, had a great partiality for London. He admired the great solidity of everything about it; and loved to dwell upon the interesting associations that clustered around the grand old city, as she stood, a huge monument of the past. Her ancient history was our history; her people were of our race and lineage, and possessed our language and literature. He loved to linger in Westminster Abbey, and stroll slowly through its long nave, and numerous passages; to pause at the dust of the illustrious dead, from the tombs of the earliest monarchs, statesmen, warriors, and poets, to the new-

made grave of Lord Macaulay. A favourite spot with
him was the Tower of London, with its rich depository
of relics, memorials of the reign of every monarch, and
its countless trophies of war.

"Still more did he love the British Museum; he never
grew tired of inspecting its wonderful curiosities, and
looking in silent admiration upon its mammoth library
of six hundred thousand volumes.

"Paternoster Row, (a street made up mostly of bookstores,) was a place of great attraction to the doctor. He
loved to explore those immense second-hand bookstores,
where rare books of great value could be bought for a
few shillings. He did not preach in London, on this visit
to the city, though earnestly pressed to do so by Dr.
Hamilton and others. He admired the spirituality of
Hamilton's religion, and the gospel unction that imbued
his sermons. He heard Baptist Noel, and Dr. Cumming;
the simple gospel preaching of the former pleased him
very much; the latter, he never admired. Melville was
sick, and Spurgeon was taking a trip to the continent;
though most of the party heard him more than once, later
in the season. Mr. Dallas, who was then the American
Minister at the Court of St. James, presented Dr. Thornwell with tickets of admission, for himself and friends,
to the Parliamentary debates. They were present at an
animated discussion, participated in by Gladstone, Palmerston, Lord John Russell, and others. It was the unanimous opinion of the party that Gladstone was incom-
parably the first man amongst them, the balance were
poor debaters, except Palmerston, who was a good second-
class speaker."

His next letter, written from Paris, on the 8th of August, possesses no general interest, and we pass on to
another, which is dated—

"BASLE, *August* 15, 1860.

"MY DEAREST WIFE: Here we are in Switzerland, in the city of
Erasmus, where one of the first copies of the Bible was printed. Here,

too, three hundred and twenty-four years ago, when persecution was raging in France against the Protestants, Calvin published the first edition of his immortal Institutes, and dedicated it to Francis the First, in defence of the principles and faith of his suffering brethren. Here, too, a council was held in 1431, which elected the Duke of Savoy as Pope. The city is divided into two unequal parts by the river Rhine, which flows through it. The view from the river is quite striking. Our hotel is immediately on the river; and our rooms look out upon it, and give us a noble and refreshing prospect. Last night we spent at Baden-Baden, where Napoleon lately held his conference with the Princes of Germany. It is a fine watering place, romantically situated in the midst of mountains, and reminds you very much of the Virginia Springs. This place is particularly celebrated for its magnificent arrangements for gambling. There is a large house, with splendid saloons, elegantly furnished, for the purpose of carrying on this nefarious business; and the first families in Germany crowd around these tables, and patronize the business. There is one immense hall, in which the tables are, and the other saloons are for promenading, lounging, eating, and what not, by way of attraction. From morning till midnight the work goes on; and you find ladies as freely as gentlemen, Princes, Dukes, and Duchesses, all mingling in the scene. Of course, I did not go in; but —— and —— slipped off at night, taking care to leave their money, and reported what they saw.

"The day before coming to Baden, we spent at Heidelberg. This city is situated in a narrow valley, on the banks of the Neckar, between two ranges of mountains. On one of the mountains is one of the finest ruins in Europe. It is an old castle, which, in its day, was a city within itself. The views from the towers are as commanding as those from the highest point of the Warm Spring mountain, in Virginia. The city takes name from the huckleberries that grow upon the mountains. Heidelberg means 'the mountain of huckleberries.' Here I found Underwood, who spent two years under me at Columbia. As soon as he saw me, he threw his arms around my neck, and hugged me for very joy. He came on to Baden with us, and spent with us our whole time there. You may well guess that I was delighted to see him. At Cologne, where I spent the first night after leaving Brussels, I bought a few bottles of the pure water for you and Pattie. They sell it higher than you can get it in Columbia. From Cologne I went to Bonn, the seat of a flourishing University; and there I found some South Carolina students. Since leaving Brussels, besides Cologne, Bonn, and Heidelberg, we have passed through the beautiful towns which lie between Bonn and Heidelberg—Coblentz, Mayence, and Darmstadt; and also Carlsruhe, the capital of Baden, which lies between Heidelberg and Baden-Baden. The finest city between Baden and this place is Freibourg. It has a noble situation, in a spacious valley on the Rhine, between extensive ranges of mountains on every side. The whole country on the banks of the Rhine is enchanting. The river is skirted by mountains, and on both sides is dotted with towns and villages; while the ruined battlements of antiquated castles frown upon you every four or five miles. The valleys are luxuriant with the vine, with corn and to-bacco; and the people seem cheerful, contented, and happy. Through the fields, and all along the road-side, crucifixes are erected of wood, some of them very large, to secure blessings upon the country, and to attract the devotion of the traveller. They always excited my pity. I could not but lament that they had substituted dead images of wood and stone for the living Saviour. To-morrow we go to Geneva, the city of the great Calvin, where we propose to make our headquarters for a week or ten days, and where I expect to receive letters from you.

"It seems to me incredible how much I have accomplished since the 12th of June, the day that I landed at Southampton. In two months and four days I have traversed England, Ireland, and Scotland. I have run over France, Belgium, and a considerable portion of Germany; and am now in Switzerland. I have seen so much, that I can hardly retain a distinct recollection of the different places and the different scenes. It appears to me like a dream; and at times I am almost tempted to doubt that it can be true, that I am five thousand miles from home, and in a foreign land. If I had you and the dear little ones with me, I should be delighted to spend the winter at some of the German Uni-versities, and give myself to unbroken study. But the Lord has other work for me to do, and I am content. One great benefit of travelling, is to make us prize our own country. After all, there is no land like our own. In all that makes a people great and powerful, we are de-cidedly in advance of Europe. There is no such population on the globe as our own; and if we can have the grace to deal justly and hon-ourably with one another, and to hold together as a people, the time is at hand when the distinction of being an American citizen will be as proud and glorious as it ever was to be a citizen of Rome. On the continent of Europe we are every where respected. The very conductors on the railways show us marked civilities. Our example is looked up to with deference; and the great mass of thinking men sigh in their hearts for American institutions. We are felt to be a model people. What a shame it will be to forfeit, by our follies and our sins, the noble inheri-tance to which Providence has called us! I am happy to say that the Church in America is very far ahead, in spirituality and power, of any Church in Europe. I have kept my eye closely upon this point, and I am sure that I am not mistaken. The tone of piety is higher; the liberality to religious institutions, in proportion to wealth, is greater; and the efficiency of the pulpit superior beyond comparison. Our church edifices are better, far better, in their adaptation to the uses of religious worship. In technical learning, we are still behind; in power of pure thought, ahead. Our scholars are inferior; our men, greater. But I forget. I am not writing an essay; I am writing to my wife. You must excuse me that I permit myself to think aloud in your de-lightful presence. * * * * * * *

"I have written to Liverpool to secure my passage on the 22d of September. If so, I shall leave Geneva in eight or ten days, and return to Paris by Constance, Augsburgh, Munich, Dresden, Berlin, Hanover, and Brunswick. After you receive this letter you need write no more, as I shall probably be on the ocean when your letters would reach Liverpool. The party have all continued well. Jennie was a little outdone by the fatigue of travel for the first few days after leaving Paris, but is quite recruited again. I think it likely that none of the party will attempt to get to Rome, though J. and T. have their hearts mightily set upon it. I have no notion of hazarding the trip myself. My thoughts are on Berlin, the metropolis of modern learning.

"It is now late at night. The river is roaring at my feet, just as it sounded in the ears of Cæsar nearly two thousand years ago. His thoughts were those of ambition and of conquest; mine are of wife, children, and friends. Rome was the centre of his affections; a little town, in the remote, and then unknown, province of America, is mine. How gladly would I bridge the Rhine, if that could bring me home!

"Kiss all the children for me. Remember me to the servants. Tell all the congregation that I remember them all, and trust that they remember me. May grace, mercy, and peace be multiplied upon them all.

"Your devoted husband,

J. H. THORNWELL."

To the same:

"GENEVA, *August* 20, 1860.

"MY PRECIOUS WIFE: Here I am in Geneva, the city of Calvin, of Beza, of Farel, of Viret, of Turretin, and of Pictet. I have stood under the same canopy which covered the head of Calvin three hundred years ago, when he preached the gospel in the dawn of the Reformation. The pulpit has been destroyed, but the canopy still remains. The church has been somewhat remodelled, but all its essential features are unchanged. I visited also his grave. There is no monument to mark the spot. He gave orders in his will against all ostentation. There is nothing but a little stone, with the letters 'J. C.' marked upon it; but I felt the inspiration of his genius, of his learning, and of his piety, as I stood over the earth which contained his mortal remains. I visited to-day the Public Library, where many of his letters, and volumes of his manuscript sermons, are preserved. It contains, also, portraits of all the illustrious men of Europe during the sixteenth and seventeenth centuries. I could have lingered there for days. The site of Geneva is most enchanting: on a beautiful lake, just at the point from which the Rhone emerges, surrounded on all sides by majestic mountains. It is a fit place for heroes and poets. The city itself is not striking. The ancient part is made up of tall, unseemly buildings, and pervaded with very dark, narrow streets; but the suburbs are romantic and picturesque beyond anything that I have seen in Europe. I had also the satisfaction of meeting here Professor Mansell, of Oxford, whom I missed seeing in England. He and his family are here on an excursion of pleasure. I found him very simple and unassuming. I should never have taken him, from his appearance, for the great man that he is. We had at dinner to-day quite a learned table. Beside Mansell of Oxford, there were Tazewell of Rhode Island, Professor Pierce of Cambridge, near Boston, Dr. Adams of New York, and several others, whom I cannot take time to name. This is a great place to see the world; everybody comes here. Yesterday we attended preaching in the English chapel, and heard a very evangelical sermon. At night we had a meeting of the Americans in Dr. Adams' room. The room was crowded, and we had representatives from no less than eight States. I led the meeting. You may well imagine that it was very refreshing.

"To-morrow we make an excursion to Chamouni, to see the glaciers and the sea of ice. We have already had a distant view of them, and we want to see them closer at hand. When we return, we shall set our faces homeward. I have almost given up my expedition to Berlin, It is so far, and I am getting tired of travelling. We are all satiated with sight-seeing, and are anxious once more to be in our native land. I count the days until the time of going on board the Arabia, and then I shall count them until I reach America. The Lord be with you, and bless you, and keep you.

"Your devoted husband,
J. H. THORNWELL."

To the same:

"GENEVA, August 25, 1860.

"MY DARLING WIFE: Since I wrote to you before, we have made an excursion to Chamouni, in Savoy, where we enjoyed the grandest scenery that adorns the continent of Europe. The distance from Geneva is fifty-four miles. We set off in a heavy rain, but before we had travelled far, the clouds dispersed, the sun appeared in his strength, and the mountains rose before us in all the grandeur of their eternal repose. It is perfectly idle to attempt a description of the wild and majestic scenes through which we passed. Our road lay in the valley of the Arve; and at times we seemed to be entirely surrounded by beetling crags, to which it almost made us dizzy to look up. The summits were capped with snow, transparent streams were rattling down the sides, and occasionally a bold waterfall varied the magnificent prospect. As we ascended the mountain on the other side of Pont Pelessier, Mount Blanc broke upon us from his throne of rocks, in his diadem of snow; and the prospect was so overwhelmingly grand, that the first impulse was to fall prostrate to the earth, and adore the majesty of God. We were on a plain, four thousand feet above the level of the sea; we were surrounded by mountains on all sides, from five to six thousand feet above the level of the plain, and in full view before us, towered Mount Blanc, the old monarch of mountains, nine thousand feet above the tallest cliff around us. The clouds girdled its sides, the sun shone splendidly on its summit, and the snow reflected his beams in rays of living glory. Oh! how I wished that you had been with us, to enjoy the sight. My imagination had never conceived of ought that approximated the sublime reality. The mountains of our country are rich, and beautiful, and picturesque; but the Alps are awful. It is tame, to call them sublime; their grandeur is absolutely awful. They make you hold your breath, and pause before them in deep and solemn veneration. That one view has repaid me for all the fatigue and anxieties of the journey. At Chamouni, we climbed Montauvert, and went to the famous sea of ice, one of the most wonderful glaciers in the Alps. It is upwards of six miles long, and more than a mile wide; and in parts, the ice is nearly one hundred feet thick. It is a marvel of this marvellous region, which I am wholly incompetent to explain. Anderson and Johnnie went over it; none of the rest of us had the courage to risk it. Just a few days before, three young Englishmen had perished by falling into one of the crevices.

"After an absence of three days, we returned to Geneva, and here our party divided. Mr. Douglas left this morning for Italy. We—that is, Anderson, Jennie, Johnnie, Thompson, and myself—remained behind. We shall spend Sunday here, and then we divide. Johnnie and myself, and, perhaps, Thompson, will go, on Monday, through Zurich, Linden, Munich, Augsburgh, and Nuremberg, to Berlin; Anderson and Jennie will go through Lyons and Marseilles to Paris, and wait for us there. I shall remain in Berlin several days, and then return to Paris; and after making a few purchases there, set out for Liverpool.

"Jennie enjoyed Chamouni very much. She walked down Montauvert, a descent of about five miles, and suffered no inconvenience from it. We ascended it on mules; and in places the path was so narrow, and the precipices so steep, that I had to shut my eyes to keep my head steady. Every now and then my mule would stop and look over the precipice, as if he proposed to tantalize me, or try the strength of my nerves. I think I must have walked eight or ten miles in the course of one day's excursion. If you were only with me, my enjoyment would be perfect. The glorious scenes cannot drive away home-sickness. I think of you in the Alps, as well as in the busy hum of the city, or on the lone highway of the sea. It is strange to me that the inhabitants of these Alpine passes are so miserable and degraded in their physical appearance. Their throats are horribly disfigured with goitre; their heads are large and flat; and many of them are hardly above the level of an idiot. Where nature is grandest, man is meanest. The mountains endure no rivals. But one thing can be great at a time; and the soul dwindles where rocks tower in majesty.

"Yesterday evening Thompson and I walked about four miles on the edge of Lake Leman. The moon was shining in her beauty, the sky was perfectly clear, the waters of the lake as smooth as a mirror. We passed terrace after terrace, beautifully adorned, and surmounted by elegant chateaux. Among others, we strolled by the house which Byron occupied when he sojourned in Geneva. It was a fit place for a poet; and I could not but think of his beautiful description of the lake in ' Childe Harold.' The scene was romantic; and ever and anon we broke its spell, by contrasting with its calm beauties the warmer attractions of home. When I returned, I found your sweet letter of the 31st of July, enclosing another from Charlie, and my cup was full. I poured out my heart in gratitude to God that He had preserved you all; and I prayed most fervently that we might soon meet again, to talk over, in gratitude and praise, the things we had witnessed.

" There was a little incident on our journey to Chamouni, which I had almost forgotten to mention. As we passed through one of the little villages that line the road, we encountered a bridal party, rigged out in all the pride and bravery of a rustic wedding. The bride was gorgeously adorned with flowers and ribands for a Savoy peasant's daughter; the bridegroom was in his best attire; and the party of rude friends were as lively as a gala day could make them. As we moved slowly along, one of the party hailed our carriages, and regaled us with an account of the festive scene. A dashing maiden posted herself near the carriage, drew a pistol, levelled it at us, and fired it in our faces, to the infinite amusement of the whole crowd. We shouted and hurrahed with the rest, and all seemed to be happy together. It was all a good-natured frolic; and I never saw fun so sincerely enjoyed in my life. Nature was acted out. McM. could have written a poem on the occasion. The village was on the side of the mountain, which commanded a noble view of Mount Blanc; and the contrast was refreshing betwixt the gayety below, and the awful, frowning, sullen majesty above us.

" I am afraid that you will think that I am losing my senses, in dwelling upon these frivolities; but they relieve the monotony of travel, and if they amuse you, I shall be content. I am greatly delighted to hear that things are going on so well in the church, and I bless God that He has given me such a colleague as Mullally. I anticipate a happy time in cultivating with him the vineyard which God has entrusted to our joint care. The work among the negroes is one in which I feel a special interest, and I do sincerely pray that Charles* may be led to the knowledge of true religion. For his faithfulness in my absence, I intend to bring him a handsome present. * * * * *

" My passage is taken in the Arabia for Boston, on the 22d of September. That is as soon as I can leave, in justice to the friends who have sent me abroad. By staying until then, I traverse nearly the whole continent of Europe. On Monday I leave for Berlin. It will take me three days to get there, but I pass through historic places and scenes.

"Again, dearest, may the Lord bless you. Jennie and Anderson send much love; for everybody loves you, and I more than all.

" Your devoted husband,
J. H. THORNWELL."

* His body servant, in whom he resposed great confidence.

It was in the ascent of the Alps described in the foregoing letter the incident occurred which we have recorded in the eleventh chapter, when the veil of mist was suddenly lifted, and the entire glory of the mountain scenery burst upon his sight at once, and filled his heart with adoring wonder. Though broken from its proper connection, for a special purpose, in the place we have chosen to put it, the reader will perceive how precisely it tallies with the expression of more than poetic admiration which fell from his own pen in this, as well as in the letter that follows.

To General James Gillespie:

"GENEVA, *August* 25, 1860.

"MY DEAR GENERAL: In this distant land I cannot describe to you how my mind reverts to the friends of my childhood and youth. I tread amid the monuments of the buried past, or gaze upon nature in her grandest forms; but the heart finds its home, the centre of its earthly attractions, far beyond the swelling mountains, or the the majestic deep. If there be a region on earth fitted to kindle in the soul the inspiration of great thoughts, that region is the one in which I am now sojourning for a brief season. Here, more than three hundred years ago, a youthful fugitive from France was arrested in his flight, and induced to take up his permanent abode. The world has felt the influence of his genius, his piety, and his learning. I have seen the spot where stood the house in which John Calvin resided. I have stood beneath the canopy under which he preached. I have gazed upon the tombs which met his eye as he ascended the throne of his power, the pulpit of St. Pierre; and have paused, in grateful meditations, over the humble grave, without a stone or monument, which covers his mortal remains. I bless God for the labours and sufferings of His honoured servant. Indeed, for the last six weeks, every inch of the ground beneath my feet has been hallowed ground. At Brussels, my soul swelled with the thought that there was the cradle of modern constitutional liberty. There, William of Orange conceived that glorious scheme of patriotism, which resulted in the independence of Holland, and formed an asylum for the martyrs and confessors of England and France. I went into the very hall in which Charles the Fifth, leaning upon the arm of the young Dutchman, who was afterwards to shake his throne, resigned his sovereignty in favour of his worthless son. I gazed upon the palace of the Duchess of Parma, the atrocious Alva, and the silly Don John. I saw the very spot on which Horn and Egmont were executed; and I mused along the very squares in which the beggars were accustomed to meet. The past came visibly before me. And then a few miles from the city was Waterloo, that place of skulls, with its enormous mound, and its endless historic interest.

"From Brussels I proceeded to the Rhine, the stream on which Cæsar gazed two thousand years before I was born; and as I traced the faded monuments of mediæval chivalry, and of mediæval superstition, ruined castles and convents and nunneries, I felt that I was in a new world, and for a while belonged to another age. I went up the Rhine from Cologne to Bonn; from Bonn to Mayence, Heidelberg, and Baden; from Baden to Basle; and from Basle to Geneva. Here Rousseau was born; here Voltaire sported his wit; here Byron sojourned for a season; and here, too, Maria Louise took up her summer residence when her husband was in exile. Here, too, flourished Calvin and Farel, and Viret and Beza, and, in later times, the Turretins and Pictets. Here, too, slumbers Sir Humphrey Davy. Here lie the ill-starred Neckar and his illustrious wife. But the grand attraction of this region of country is the Alps. I have just returned from an excursion to Chamouni. and to my dying day I can never forget the impression of the august scenes which my eyes have beheld. The road lay through the valley of the Arve. On both sides of the river, mountain after mountain rises in awful grandeur; and the path of the traveller is under frowning crags and beetling precipices, to which it makes him dizzy to look up. As we ascended the mountain beyond Pont Pelessier, Mount Blanc rose upon us, from his throne of rocks, in such awful sublimity that the first impulse was to fall down and worship the terrible majesty of God. [Here follows a similar description of details as in the preceding letter.] My imagination had never conceived such a spectacle. I gazed, and gazed, and gazed, and felt that I could never gaze enough. * * * *

"I could keep you up night after night with the wonders I have seen. But my native land is dearer than ever. America, after all, is the country for me; it is the country in which man is himself. May the Lord bless you. Most devotedly,

J. H. THORNWELL."

The following closes this series of letters written from Europe:

"ZURICH, *August* 29, 1860.

"MY DARLING WIFE: We are lodged to-night in a hotel which overlooks the beautiful lake of Zurich, just at the point where the Limmat emerges from it. The prospect by moonlight is as calm and tranquil as the repose of a peaceful conscience. The mountains in the distance furnish a striking background; and the memory of the illustrious Zuingle—who was second only to Calvin in the strength of his genius and the perspicacity of his views, and who was simultaneous with Luther in the promulgation of the gospel—gives a hallowed association to the place; which loses nothing of its softness from the history of the illustrious Lavater, the great physiognomist, who was born and murdered in this city. The gardens upon the lake are tastefully arranged, and the promenades which they afford are most enchanting. The waters are so clear that you see the fish sporting themselves below, and children amuse themselves by throwing out crumbs of bread, for which the finny tribe strive as manfully as the occupants of a farm-yard for a grain of wheat.

"We spent last night at Fribourg, a most picturesque spot; and I was fool enough to go to the Cathedral, and hear the celebrated organ, which is said to be the finest in the world. It was no doubt very grand. Everybody pronounced it unrivalled; but I was so green that I could hardly keep from going to sleep. We came to Berne for breakfast. That is the capital of the Swiss Confederation. Apart from the view which it affords of the Alps in the distance, and its attractive promenades, I cannot say that there is anything about it of special interest. The whole country of Switzerland is charming. The valleys are as lovely as the mountains are grand; and away from the Alps, the people seem healthful, industrious, and robust. The women all work, like negroes, in the field. They plough, spade, mow, and carry burdens on their shoulders. They are, like oxen, strong to labour. The hotels of Switzerland are about the best in Europe. The enormous amount of travel makes inn-keeping a very lucrative business. The summer climate is lovely, soft, and balmy, regaled alike by breezes from the lake and mountains. It is just the country that would take your eye.

"In the library of this city are whole volumes, in manuscript, of the correspondence of the Reformers; and what is particularly interesting, are three letters, in a neat, fair hand, of Lady Jane Grey, to Henry Bullinger. They are in Latin. I have not yet seen them. * * * * Our party is now small. Douglas and his party have gone into Italy; Thompson went back from Geneva to Paris. Anderson and Jennie and Johnnie are now my only companions. The air of Switzerland has agreed finely with Jennie; she has been better than at any time, except when we were in England. It has also been very propitious to me. I have been able to take a great deal of exercise without fatigue; and we are all always ready whenever meals, particularly dinner, are announced. But I am tired of travelling; I sigh for the quiet and repose of home. Sometimes I am tempted to break away, and come home without completing my circuit. Had it not been for those with me, I think I should have given out three weeks ago. But I sincerely pray that the Lord may soon bring us together again, no more to part. He has been amazingly good; and I do hope, when I return, to serve Him better than I have ever done before. Let us trust Him at all times. I am as ever,

"Yours devotedly,

J. H. THORNWELL."

The party of eight re-assembled at Paris, and there divided again on their route homeward. A portion sailed from Havre, while Dr. Thornwell and his suite embarked from Liverpool. The only incident that varied the return voyage was a severe storm. The great object for which the trip was undertaken seemed, however, to be accomplished, in the improvement of his health, and the ability to resume his public labours.

CHAPTER XXXII.

THE LATE WAR.

DR. THORNWELL returned from Europe to find the country already circling within the eddies of a mighty revolution. He landed upon his native shores in the month of September, 1860. On the 20th of the following December, South Carolina passed her Ordinance of Secession from the Federal Union; and by the first of February, 1861, her example had been followed by the States of Mississippi, Florida, Alabama, Georgia, Louisiana, and Texas. A Provisional Government for the seceding States was organized on the 4th of February, a Constitution was adopted on the 8th, and on the 9th, the administration was set on foot by the election of Mr. Jefferson Davis, as President of the new Confederacy. On the 15th of April, 1861, Mr. Lincoln issued his proclamation, calling for 75,000 troops, to suppress the so-called insurrection; the immediate effect of which was to add Virginia, Arkansas, North Carolina, and Tennessee to the roll of States which must be conquered.

Into this movement Dr. Thornwell threw himself, from the beginning, with all the ardour of his nature; and to the day of his death, laboured and prayed, with patriotic fervour, for the success of the Confederate cause. He was, in this, an eminent type of the great body of the Southern people; who relinquished with unspeakable pain their traditional attachment to the Union, from a stern conviction that they could no longer live under it with safety or with honour. For this reason we desire the more to trace his political career throughout, in ordei that through this, as a representative case, posterity at least may pronounce upon the supreme necessity which compelled the erection of another government, as the ark in which constitutional liberty might be preserved. A future generation will read these events by a better light than the present; for nothing is more certain than that principles will work themselves out, and reveal their true nature, in the results which they produce; and no men ever committed themselves to the vindication of history with greater confidence, than those who embarked in this struggle for independence. Such men as Dr. Thornwell were accustomed to take broad views of life, and were not in subjection to their passions. Indeed, in his case, all the sentiment and the prejudice were enlisted upon the other side of the question from that which he espoused.

His letters which have been already reproduced—written only for the eye of his family, and written at long intervals and under different surroundings, sometimes while traversing the great West, and sometimes visiting foreign lands across the sea—all breathe a fervent love for the country as a whole. He gloried in the American name. He rejoiced, almost in the spirit of covetousness, in the acquisition of territory, as extending the area of civil freedom, and adding to the splendour and triumph of republican principles. His imagination was dazzled with the vision of an entire continent covered with a net work of free States, and bound together in a harmonious confederation. Although, in one of his letters, he cannot but detect the tendency to slide from a Representative Republic into a turbulent and lawless Democracy, with singular hopefulness he counts upon the intelligence and virtue of the people to resist the danger, and to preserve the spirit as well as the form of our free institutions. It is impossible to read these passages in his correspondence, without being impressed with the breadth, as well as the fervour, of his patriotism. It gushes so freely and so warmly from his heart, as to burst through all the barriers of section and of party, and take up the whole country into its passionate embrace.

In addition to this general evidence, which lies sufficiently before the reader, we may recur to two periods in his history, when, as a pronounced Union man, he took open ground against the declared policy of his native State. Indeed, as a mere politician, he could never have risen to high position in South Carolina, the current of his views being in opposition to the prevailing sentiment on most of the great questions of his day. The first of these two periods was during the Nullification struggle in 1832. "South Carolina, as well as a number of the other States, held that the power to levy duties on imports, not with a view to revenue, but to protect and aid particular classes, was not delegated to Congress." An odious, because discriminating, tariff had been borne so long as it was necessary to provide for the existing public debt; but when this was cancelled, and a large surplus was accumulating in the national treasury, she demanded that this tariff should be conformed to a revenue standard. Failing to secure this modifiation by Congressional legislation, she interposed her prerogative as a sovereign State to judge, in the last resort, in all questions affecting her own rights, restraining the general government from collecting this revenue within her limits. We have no concern, in this connexion, with this measure, except as a simple fact of history; only adding that Congress soon afterwards passed what is commonly known as the "Force Bill," clothing the President with the power necessary to enforce the collection, and for this purpose putting at his disposal all the land

and naval forces. Collision was imminent between the
State and Federal authorities, which was averted by the
famous Compromise Act of Mr. Clay, yielding the principle of protection, and providing "a gradual reduction
of duties, until, at the expiration of ten years, twenty per
cent. *ad valorem* should be established as the uniform
rate."

Against this policy of Nullification, Mr. Thornwell,
then a young man just graduated from College, conspicuously planted himself, in a series of articles through
the public press. These early fugitive essays we have
not been able to recover and identify, and cannot state
the precise grounds of his opposition. He may not have
regarded the issue as sufficiently important to justify so
imperative an assertion of State sovereignty, which, abstractly, he always admitted; or he may have thought
it illogical for a State to remain in the Union, and yet
resist the legislation of a common Congress. For there
were many in that day who affirmed the right of secession, and did not recognize nullification as the proper
remedy against the abuse of power. Nothing, however,
is important to the purpose of this narative beyond the
fact itself, that, in this particular conflict, he withstood
the pressure of public opinion in his State, and was en-
rolled in the number of those who were designated under
the party name of " Union men."

The second period was in 1850, when the South stood
upon the brink of secession; which was at that time
averted only through the patriotic interposition of Mr.
Webster and Mr. Clay. It will be necessary to trace
briefly the steps which led up to that crisis. The agitation against slavery commenced at the North as early
as 1790, within two years after the adoption of the Federal Constitution, and within twelve months after Washington was inaugurated as President. "A petition,
headed by Dr. Franklin, was sent to Congress, invoking
the Federal authorities to take jurisdiction of this subject,

with a view to the ultimate abolition of this institution in the States respectively." To which it was replied, in the resolution adopted, "that Congress have no authority to interfere in the emancipation of slaves, or in the treatment of them, in any of the States; it remaining with the several States alone to provide any regulations therein, which humanity and true policy may require." This deserves to be noted, as showing how, from the beginning, the question as to the powers of the general government was interwoven with the slavery agitation, the former being the true pivot on which the controversy turned; the latter, simply the medium through which the aggressions of the central power were constantly pressed. No proper understanding can be had of the causes of the late war, without bearing in mind the interpenetration of these two questions, the convolution of the one within the other.

The struggle, once begun, was destined more and more to force its way into American politics. In 1803, France ceded to the United States, in the Louisiana purchase, a vast territory, extending from the Gulf of Mexico to the extreme north, on parallel 49° of north latitude, far up the Mississippi river, to Iowa and Minnesota; including Kansas and Nebraska, if not Oregon, and of course Missouri and Arkansas; and stretching westward to the Rocky mountains. In the treaty by which this immense domain was acquired, it was stipulated that "the inhabitants of the ceded territory shall be incorporated in the Union of the United States, and admitted as soon as possible, according to the principles of the Federal Constitution, to the enjoyment of all the rights, advantages, and immunities of citizens of the United States; and in the mean time they shall be maintained and protected in the free enjoyment of their liberty, property, and the religion which they profess." Under the double obligation, therefore, of constitutional law and of treaty stipulations, the States carved out of this territory were to be admitted

upon *the same footing* with the States already in the
Union. When, however, in 1818, Missouri knocked at
the door of Congress for admission upon these terms, the
attempt was made to fasten upon her the restriction of
slavery, in the provision "that the further introduction of
slavery, or of involuntary servitude, be prohibited, except
for the punishment of crimes, whereof the party shall have
been fully convicted; and that all children born within
the said State, after the admission thereof into the Union,
shall be free at the age of twenty-five years." The discussion which ensued shook the country to its centre,
during the two years in which it was protracted. But,
as the character of the speeches in Congress clearly shows,
the issue was simply as to the power of the Federal government to impose the restriction; and upon this issue
the debate exclusively turned: speakers, North and South,
insisting, without any regard to the morality or the policy
of slavery, that Congress had no power to interfere with
it.   The strife was, for the time, composed by the adoption of the well-known Missouri Compromise, running a
geographical line along the latitude of thirty-six degrees
and thirty minutes, above which slavery was for ever prohibited, and below which it should be allowed. This compromise was not a Southern measure. Its real author was
a Senator from Illinois; and it was reluctantly accepted
by the South, upon the principle of a division of the
public domain between those who were joint partners in
its acquisition : a division, however, by which she acquired
only about 232,000 square miles, against nearly 668,000
acquired by the North. This geographical line, too,
seemed to be the natural boundary of slavery under the
law of climate, fixing the habitat of the negro; so that to
have refused it might appear to be a contest for a pure
abstraction, whilst to accept it promised to put to rest
this vexatious assault upon her institutions and rights.
Unfortunately, it conceded the principle which lay at the
bottom of the struggle; which none was quicker to per-

ceive than the sage of Monticello, when, lifting himself
up in his retirement, he penned these memorable words:

"I had for a long time ceased to read newspapers, or pay any attention
to public affairs, confident they were in good hands, and content to be a
passenger in our bark to the shore from which I am not distant. But
this momentous question, like a fire-bell in the night, awakened me, and
filled me with terror. I considered it at once as the knell of the Union.
It is hushed, indeed, for the moment; but this is a reprieve only, not a
final sentence. A geographical line, coinciding with a marked principle,
moral and political, once conceived and held up to the angry passions of
men, will never be obliterated; and every new irritation will mark it
deeper and deeper. * * * I regret that I am now to die in the belief,
that the useless sacrifice of themselves by the generation of 1776, to
acquire self-government and happiness to their country, is to be thrown
away by the unwise and unworthy passions of their sons; and that my
only consolation is to be, that I live not to weep over it."

How solemn are the words of prophecy, when read in
the light of their fulfilment! And what a comment upon
the vanity of human glory, that the hand which penned
the immortal Declaration of Independence, should be the
hand to write this melancholy epitaph upon the institutions of his country!

The Missouri Compromise was never accepted as a
finality by the growing Abolition party at the North.
In the admission of Arkansas, in 1836, Mr. John Quincy
Adams moved an amendment to the bill, that "nothing
in this act shall be construed as an assent of Congress
to the article in the Constitution of the said State,
in relation to slavery, or the emancipation of slaves."
The same struggle was renewed in 1845, upon the admission of Texas; although both States lay south of the line
of division. The South, in both cases, asked for nothing
more, even upon this conceded territory, than that "the
people of the new States might regulate their domestic
affairs in this particular, and all others, as they might in
sovereign conventions determine for themselves, without
any dictation or control from Congress, one way or the
other." This makes it apparent that the principle which

lay in the heart of this whole controversy, was the constitutional incompetency of the general government to interfere in what concerned the internal polity of the State alone.

In 1846 the Mexican War occurred. In the anticipation of the new territory likely to be acquired, the celebrated Wilmot Proviso was introduced, for the exclusion of slavery from all the public domain, and ignoring entirely the compact of 1820. The issue was staved off for a time, until, in 1848, it became necessary to organize a territorial government for Oregon. Mr. Stephen A. Douglas made a manly effort to apply the principle of the Missouri Compromise, and succeeded in carrying the Senate. The House of Representatives, however, proved obstinate; until at length a bill passed both branches of the national Legislature with an unconditional restriction upon slavery: "that there shall be neither slavery nor involuntary servitude in any territory which shall hereafter be acquired, or be annexed to the United States, otherwise than in the punishment of crimes," etc. Thus, on the 12th of August, 1848, the Missouri Compromise, which had been proposed and accepted as a final settlement of all these issues, in the language of Mr. Stephens, "fell and was buried in the Senate, where it had originated twenty-eight years before."

We are upon the threshold now of the great crisis of 1850. The treaty of peace negotiated with Mexico had secured to the United States an immense domain of several hundred thousand square miles, in the acquisition of which the South had poured out blood and treasure equally with the North. The new territory of California, Utah, and New Mexico, must be disposed of in some way. The principle of a division of the public estate between the two sections having been repudiated, the alternative before the South was quiet submission to a perpetual exclusion from the common territory, or resistance in some form more effective than in the past.

The first was not to be entertained for a moment. It involved the abandonment of constitutional rights, and, therefore, dishonour. They would cease to be equal in the Union. Difference of opinion obtained as to the remedy. Many believed the only solution to be found in a separation between the States; others, more sanguine, hoped the Union might still be preserved by "the re organization of parties, to bring the administration of the government back to its original principles."

The agitation was profound throughout the Southern States; and the Thirty-first Congress met in December, 1849, under circumstances of the deepest responsibility. The debate turned upon the admission of California as a State, with an anti-slavery Constitution adopted by herself. To this feature the Southern Representatives did not object; but they steadfastly resisted her admission, until the whole territorial question should be satisfactorily adjusted. Their demand was simple: "that there should be no Congressional exclusion of slavery from the public domain; but that, in organizing territorial governments, the people under each should be distinctly empowered so to legislate as to allow the introduction of slaves, and to frame their Constitution, in respect to African slavery, as they pleased; and when admitted as States into the Union, should be received without any Congressional restriction upon the subject." After a long struggle in both Houses, what is known as the Compromise of 1850 was adopted; sweeping away all former restrictions, and providing that, "when a territory, or any portion of the same, shall be admitted as a State, it shall be received into the Union with or without slavery, as their constitution may prescribe at the time of their admission."*

* The statement of political events, contained in this chapter, is simply condensed from the Hon. A. H. Stephen's great work, "The War between the States;" and, to ensure accuracy, it has been couched, as far as possible, in his own language. Aside from the guarantees furnished in the reputation of the author, and the known moderation of his political views, he has been careful to substantiate every statement by

It was while these issues were yet pending, and with the public mind excited almost to exasperation, that Dr. Thornwell opposed the idea of secession, to which South Carolina was even then strongly inclined. He could not yet despair of the Republic. Not until the last expedient was exhausted to preserve the equality of the States, would he abandon the hope of preserving the Union, which he so sincerely loved. In a brief article from his pen, of about eight pages, in the *Southern Presbyterian Review*, of January, 1851, and which is marked No. I, in the Appendix to this volume, he sets forth his views with distinctness and power. He insists that the South demanded only justice; that it remained with the North to determine whether the Union shall be preserved; that the plea of conscience, and "a higher law," cannot be allowed to override the plain provisions of the Constitution; that the alternative, in that case, would be to withdraw from a compact they can no longer fulfil; and points out the fallacy upon which these conscientious scruples are based. On the other hand, he pleads with his own section to consider well the consequences flowing from a separation; and in glowing terms depicts the glory of that mission which this country is called to fulfil. The whole essay, brief as it is, is replete with noble thoughts; and glows with an ardour all the more intense from the effort to restrain it within language as calm as Christian philosophy can suggest. We would quote from it, but for the difficulty of separating any portion from its connexion, without, in some degree, misrepresenting his position upon the subject as a whole. It would not be difficult to construct from it his whole political creed, if this were not sufficiently revealed by subsequent events.

reference to the original authorities. Those, however, who distrust any book on this subject which is of Southern origin, are referred for similar statements to a work entitled "The Origin of the War," by George Lunt, of Boston, and identified, we believe, with its press.

It is proper, however, to give the substance of two letters, written at this period, revealing the intensity of his feelings in the matter. He writes in the following nervous strain to his friend, Dr. R. J. Breckinridge, under date of March 28th, 1851:

"MY DEAR BROTHER: I received your kind and welcome letter night before last. The approbation which you expressed of my short and hasty notice of a few sermons upon the great subject of the day, was very cheering to my heart. The state of feeling here is really appalling, and such sentiments as those which I have ventured to express are anything but popular. I have been gloomy and depressed at the prospect before us; but I see nothing that can be done here but to commit the matter to our sovereign God. When I trace the successive steps of our national history, I behold at every point the finger of the Lord. I cannot persuade myself that we are now to be abandoned to our follies, and permitted to make shipwreck of our glorious inheritance. I still hope that the arm which has been so often stretched out in our behalf, will be interposed again. South Carolina, however, seems bent upon secession. The excitement is prodigious. Men, from whom one would have expected better things, are fanning the flame, and urging the people on to the most desperate measures. From the beginning I have opposed, according as I had opportunity, all revolutionary measures. But I am sorry to say that many of our clergy are as rash and violent as the rashest of their hearers. Sometimes I seem to myself to perceive that the tide is beginning to ebb; and it is possible that time may bring with it discretion. But I can assure you that things look gloomy enough. You cannot imagine how the matter preys upon my spirits. It is the unceasing burden of my prayers.

"Did you receive a copy of my sermon on the death of Mr. Calhoun? I sent you one, but have never heard whether you received it or not. * * * * *

As ever,

J. H. THORNWELL."

The second letter is addressed, a year earlier, to the Rev. Dr. Hooper, of North Carolina, a former colleague of his in the College faculty. It bears date, March 8th, 1850; from which we extract the portion that relates to the state of the country:

"I can well and heartily sympathize with you in your despondency in regard to the condition of the country. The times are indeed portentous. The prospect of disunion is one which I cannot contemplate without absolute horror. A peaceful dissolution is utterly impossible. There are so many sources of discord and controversy: the division of the army, the navy, the territories; so that, however disposed we might be to an amicable separation, the settlement of these points would inevitably, and that very soon, engender a war. And a war between the States of this confederacy would, in my opinion, be the bloodiest, most ferocious, and cruel, in the annals of history. Then, again, the attempt to construct other governments, the formation of new constitutions, in this age of tumults, agitation, and excitement, when socialism, communism, and a rabid mobocracy seem everywhere to be in the ascendant, will lead to the most dangerous experiments, the most disastrous schemes. I have hardly been able to sleep in consequence of the deep conviction with which I am oppressed of the evils that threaten us; and my unceasing prayer is, that God would interfere for our relief. Vain, in this crisis, is the help of man. I agree with you, that every believer in Jesus Christ is most solemnly warned, by the signs of the times, to wrestle with the Angel of the Covenant in behalf of our bleeding country. The interests of the Saviour's kingdom are too intimately connected with the permanence and prosperity of this great confederacy, to allow any disciple to be a calm spectator of passing scenes. In the destruction of our government, the civil wars that shall follow, the agitation of socialist and atheistic principles, the upheaving of society from its very foundations, the anarchy and chaos that shall brood upon the land, where are to be the schemes of the different churches for the conversion of the world? I cannot dwell upon the subject. May the Lord mercifully turn the tide, and send peace and prosperity, at least in our days."

The following letter, addressed to Mr. A. H. Pegues, of Oxford, Mississippi, discloses his predilection for what was known as the American, or, more popularly still, as the "Know-Nothing" party. His attachment to the Federal Union was yet so strong that he gave his adhesion to almost any organization that held out the least promise of preserving it. At any rate, the letter is a record of his opinion upon one phase of the politics of the day:

"SOUTH CAROLINA COLLEGE, *July* 26, 1855.

"DEAR SANDY: I received your welcome and long-looked-for letter just on the eve of a short excursion into Georgia, and delayed answering it until after my return. You certainly did promise to write to me upon your arrival at home, and I have been seriously at a loss to account for your silence. As you were in some terror of the yellow fever when you left me, I did not know but you might have quietly departed this life, without letting any of your friends know what had become of you. The papers did not record your death, and I heard nothing from your family. So I still lived in hopes that you might yet come to light.

"Well, I am glad that you are alive and kicking. I could wish, however, that you would kick against something more worthy to be kicked
against than the American party. You know that I always was perverse
in politics. I was not a Nullifier in South Carolina, and I could not
have been a Repudiator in Mississippi. My heresies in these respects
might have prepared you for finding me in the ranks of the only organization which, in my judgment, can save the country from impending
ruin. There is not a principle of the American party, so far as its principles are known, which does not command my most cordial approbation. Its appearance and success is the most remarkable phenomenon
of these remarkable times; and if it fails, our last hope for the Union
is gone. But I shall not argue politics with you, though I cannot but
hope that we may yet see eye to eye on this subject. I am intensely
anxious that the whole South should come up as one man to the American ranks. We shall soon hear from Tennessee; then comes North
Carolina; then your State; and if they lead off properly, the rest of the
South will follow, and the Republic may be saved. * * *

"I set out to-morrow for the old Pee Dee. Do you not wish that you
could be with me? How it would delight us to revisit our old haunts,
and talk of ancient days! I do not think I could go to General Gillespie's mill without tears; I have not been there since you and I were
there together.

"As ever, most truly,

J. H. THORNWELL."

With these prepossessions in favour of the national
Union interwoven with every fibre of his being, and
strengthened by the very effort to retain them against
a surrounding pressure, how are we to account for his
attitude in 1860, when, abandoning his old traditions, he
flung himself into the struggle to establish a separate government, with a zeal second to that of no other man in
the Southern Confederacy? The change is immensely
significant, as showing how the thousands of thoughtful,
conscientious, patriotic, and Christian men in the South
felt constrained at last to rise up together, and strike for
independence. A few sentences will fill the gap in the
political history of these times. The adjustment, effected
with so much difficulty, and which placed the government back upon its original foundations, was not permitted to stand. The Compromise of 1850, if the term be
not a misnomer when applied to the mere assertion of a

principle, was doomed to fall, like its predecessor of 1820.
This brought despair to hearts which before had glowed
with hope. The agitation was renewed in 1854, when it
became necessary to frame territorial governments for
Kansas and Nebraska. The doctrine of Federal intervention was again broached; and the fanatical party,
which had always trampled upon the Missouri Compromise, now proclaimed it a sacred and binding compact.
This was clearly but a parliamentary device, under cover
of which the prerogative of Congressional interference
might be again resumed. But the South had recovered
the principle which, in 1820, had been yielded; and,
taught by the experience of the past, she refused to compromise it a second time. The Kansas-Nebraska bill,
framed in conformity with the measures of 1850, was
passed, it is true; but the whole subject had been re-
opened, exposed to all the fluctuations of popular opinion.
Distrust and suspicion were sown throughout the South; a
great impulse had been given to fanaticism in the North;
uneasiness, and a sense of insecurity, everywhere prevailed. The raid of John Brown at length occurred; the
accomplices in his crime were sheltered, not only by
public approval, but by official protection; the rendition
of fugitive slaves continued to be refused, in the face of
constitutional provisions and Congressional enactments,
until the "irrepressible conflict" was openly declared; the
doctrine of "a higher law" was proclaimed subversive of
all compacts and pledges; and, as the climax, the canvass
of 1860 resulted in the election of a sectional candidate,
by a sectional vote, who, by the force of his position, was
only the president of a party, and was pledged to carry
out the political theories of the section which had advanced him to power. In short, the precise issue upon
which the long legislative battle had been fought upon
the floor of Congress, was concluded against the rights of
the South, in the foregone and fore-announced interdic-

tion of slavery in the territories.* In this event, the South, in all her utterances, stood committed to a separation; and nothing remained but the execution of her purpose in actual secession. Under what forms this was achieved in eleven States, how these were confederated under a union and constitution of their own, and how they were overthrown in a long and disastrous war—these are facts of history, which need no recital here.

This altered attitude of the North wrought the change in Dr. Thornwell's course which we shall have occasion presently to exhibit. He had loved the Union with a passion almost rising to idolatry; but it was the Union which the Constitution had created. When the necessity came to elect between the two, it could not be doubtful upon which the choice would rest. The same principles which had led him to cling to the national ensign, so long as hope remained of preserving its symbolic significance, carried him away from it when that hope had fled. The same patriotism which gloried in the principles of American constitutional liberty, transferred his affections to that which gave some promise of their perpetuation. The change was not in him. He was the same man, with the same principles, affections, and desires. But the object of his hope was different: he turned slowly and sadly from

* That the South did not misinterpret the import of Mr. Lincoln's election, is proved by the speech of Mr. Chase, afterwards Mr. Lincoln's Secretary of Treasury, in the Peace Congress, on the 6th of February, 1861, after the secession of seven States had been accomplished. In this speech he frankly declares, "this election must be regarded as a triumph of principles, cherished in the hearts of the people of the Free States." "Chief among these principles is the restriction of slavery within State limits : fixed opposition to its extension beyond them. Mr. Lincoln was the candidate of the people opposed to the extension of slavery. We have elected him. After many years of earnest advocacy and of severe trial, we have achieved the triumph of that great principle. Do you think we, who represent this majority, will throw it away?" He declares, also, that the North never will consent to the reclamation of fugitive slaves, and that the constitutional provision requiring it must be a dead letter, (see it quoted in Mr. Stephen's "War between the States," Vol. 2, pp. 46–49.)

the old, which had disappointed him, to the new, in which
all that he hoped and wished were now enshrined. It
will not do to say, that he was swept away by a current
he found himself incapable of resisting. He was a man
that had been stemming currents all his life; and, in the
sphere of politics, had shown a tenacity of convictions
that was amazing. Not a solitary instance can be produced from his entire record, in which he ever surrendered
his own convictions of truth or duty. He often yielded
where opposition was useless, for he was not factious;
but he never supported a measure which did not command
his own approval. Nor is it sufficient to allege that, in
recognizing the doctrine of State sovereignty, he simply
bowed to the decision of South Carolina, and accepted her
fortunes as his own. This would explain acquiescence,
but not the enthusiasm with which he laid her cause upon
his heart, nor the devotion with which he sacrificed all
that was dear to its success, nor the attrition of care and
grief which helped to wear out his feeble life so much the
sooner. Far less than either from the truth is the stale
charge, that the tremendous hazard was incurred in the
interest and for the preservation of slavery. Indeed, this
never was more than the *occasion* of the war, either North
or South. It was the mere rallying cry on both sides, to
marshal the hosts into ranks, a concrete and tangible
issue upon which to concentrate the masses. The *cause*
lay deeper, in the irreconcilable theories maintained as
to the nature of the government; in comparison with
which all the interest and property vested in " the peculiar institution" were as dust in the balance. In relation
to this, however, it may be incumbent on the writer to
mention here a fact connected with the subject of these
Memoirs, which perhaps is known only to himself. Dr.
Thornwell said to him, in 1861, that whilst in Europe he
had made up his mind to move, immediately upon his return, for the gradual emancipation of the negro, as the
only measure that would give peace to the country, by

taking away, at least, the external cause of irritation. "But," added he, "when I got home, I found it was too late; the die was cast." So far was he willing to go in the spirit of sacrifice, to preserve the integrity of that Union which he so reluctantly abandoned. How useless the sacrifice would have been, is apparent to those who have studied this conflict as to the true theory of the government, from the convention of 1787 to the present hour.

An incidental expression occurs in one of Dr. Thornwell's previous letters, which gives the key to his whole course. In it he speaks of "an American spirit" in this country; and, in antagonism to it, what he terms "a Yankee spirit," which must be put down and controlled by the former. Just so long as the government was administered in the American or national spirit—nay, just so long as there was hope of bringing it back to the same, from temporary aberrations—so long he clung to the Union with almost religious devotion. When the sectional spirit finally triumphed, and the entire Federal authority was to be employed in enforcing its narrow and proscriptive policy, any peril seemed a refuge from its ascendency. In this, he undoubtedly represented the views and feelings of all his people. And to-day, if the country will but learn from the bitter experience it has encountered, the South will forget her sufferings, and displace her resentments, and will rise as one man to meet the North in placing the government upon its old basis. Not hankering after slavery, which she has abandoned for ever, she will be content if the government only be administered in "the American spirit." But if not, she will calmly float upon the current of events, without any sense of humiliation before men, in the quiet consciousness of her integrity; perfectly assured that a nation which resiles from its own principles, however great may be its material prosperity, only dances for a little while as a bubble upon the wave, and dances but to burst for ever.

CHAPTER XXXIII.

HIS COURSE IN THE WAR.

ENDORSEMENT OF SECESSION.—LETTERS.—PREVALENCE OF ORDER IN THE STATE.—OBJECT OF ATTACK ON FORT SUMTER.—ARTICLE ON THE STATE OF THE COUNTRY.—ANALYSIS OF IT.—COMPROMISE IMPOSSIBLE.—DESIRE FOR A PEACEFUL SEPARATION.—IMPAIRED HEALTH.—SUMMER EXCURSION.—LETTERS.—HIS VIEW AS TO A CONVENTION OF THE PRESBYTERIES.—NECESSITY OF ECCLESIASTICAL SEPARATION FROM THE NORTH.—EPISTOLARY JEU D'ESPRIT.—RESUMES HIS PROFESSORSHIP.—RESIGNATION OF PASTORAL CHARGE.—ANXIETY ABOUT THE COUNTRY.—ITS INFLUENCE UPON HIS HEALTH.

WE drift now into the natural channel of Dr. Thornwell's life, taking up events in the order in which they occur. The following letter, addressed to the Rev. Mr. Douglas, with its playful introduction, is chiefly interesting as containing his first endorsement of the secession movement. It was written, it will be perceived, just eleven days after South Carolina had set the ball in motion, by her famous Ordinance:

"THEOLOGICAL SEMINARY, *December* 31, 1860.

"DEARLY BELOVED BROTHER JOHN: I am astonished that a man so celebrated for 'the milk of human kindness' should be found making himself merry over the sorrows and misfortunes of his brethren. Friend Sanderson might change his opinion of the benevolence of your nature, if he could see how you exult over my crazy back and my tottering understanding. But let me tell you that it is all a libel about the tight boots. That part of the story was made up, and I have never been able to trace it to its author. * * * * * * * In relation to elders, I do not require the Session actually to impose hands, but I prefer that they should do it. The minister, acting in the name, and as Moderator of the Session, is enough. But the members of the Session ought to be present, and ought to give the right hand of fellowship.

"I have concluded my reply to Dr. Hodge.* To me it seems per-

* An article, entitled "Church Boards and Presbyterianism," growing out of the debate in the Assembly at Rochester, which may be found in the fourth volume of the "Collected Writings."

fectly conclusive. I think I have cornered him on every point that he
has made; and I have some curiosity to see how he will get out of the
scrape. * * * *

"Our affairs of State look threatening; but I believe that we have done
right. I do not see any other course that was left to us. I am heart
and hand with the State in her move. But it is a time for the people
of God to abound in prayer. The Lord alone can guide us to a haven
of safety. He can bring light out of darkness, and good out of evil.
* * * *

As ever,

J. H. THORNWELL."

The fragment which follows appears never to have
been finished, and does not bear upon its face for whom
it was intended. We are satisfied, however, from internal
evidence, that it was addressed to the Rev. Dr. J. Leigh-
ton Wilson, before his connexion as Secretary was severed with the Assembly's Board of Foreign Missions, in
New York. Its value is to be found in the testimony
given upon the prevalence of order throughout the State,
even in its troubled condition, and upon the motives
which led to the attack upon Fort Sumter:

"THEOLOGICAL SEMINARY, January 7, 1861.

"MY DEAR BROTHER: Your two letters have both been received; and
I was delighted to find what, of course, I was prepared to expect, that
your heart and your sympathies are fully with the people of your native
State. Every day convinces me more and more that we acted at the
right time and in the right way. Georgia will be out of the Union to-
morrow, or the next day. Louisiana, Arkansas, and Texas will speedily
follow; and we shall soon have a consolidated South. The rumours about
mob law in this State are totally and meanly false. The internal condition of our society never was sounder and healthier. The law never
was so perfectly supreme. Every right and interest of the citizen is
completely protected; and our people are bound together in ties of
mutual confidence, so strong that even private feuds are forgotten and
buried. The whole State is like a family, in which the members vie with
each other in their zeal to promote the common good. There is even
little appearance of excitement. All is calm and steady determination.
It is really a blessing to live here now, to see how thoroughly law and
order reign in the midst of an intense and radical revolution. You need
not fear that our people will do anything rash. They will simply stand
on the defensive. They will permit no reinforcements to be sent to
Charleston; and if Fort Sumter is not soon delivered up to them, they
will take it. In a few days we shall be able to storm it successfully. We

shall take the Fort, not as an act of war, but in righteous self-defence. We do not want war. We prefer peace. But we shall not decline the appeal to arms, if the North forces it upon us.

"I have just concluded a defence of the secession of the Southern States, which will soon be out in the *Southern Presbyterian Review*. It is the last article, and is already advanced in printing. I shall have a large edition in pamphlet form struck off. To me it appears to be conclusive; you can judge for yourself, when you see it. Dr. Hodge's article has been received with universal indignation. * * *

"The contributions to Foreign Missions among us will certainly fall off. We shall not be in a condition to contribute as we have done."

Here the fragment abrubtly terminates. Allusion is made in this letter to what Dr. Thornwell styles "a defence of the secession of the Southern States." It was an article published January, 1861, in the *Southern Presbyterian Review*, under the heading "The State of the Country," and will be found in the Appendix to this volume, marked No. II. As to the ability with which the subject is handled, it is sufficient to quote the testimony of one of the Chancellors* upon the South Carolina bench, distinguished amongst his compeers for the subtlety of his mind and the sharpness of his discrimination, who said to the writer of these pages: "I took up the article of Dr. Thornwell with great trepidation, fearing that a divine would make a muddle of the question; but I found it a model State paper." In this essay, the author first repels the charge that secession originated in "vain dreams of glory in a separate confederacy, or in a desire to re-open the African slave-trade; but in the profound conviction that the Constitution, in its relations to slavery, had been virtually repealed." He undertakes to prove that "the constitutional attitude of the government is one of ABSOLUTE INDIFFERENCE OR NEUTRALITY, with respect to all questions connected with the moral and political aspect of the subject." He overthrows the only two propositions upon which Federal jurisdiction over the case can be justified; to wit, that "the right of property in slaves is the creature of positive statute;" and

---

* Chancellor Job Johnston, of Newberry, South Carolina.

that it is "a right not recognized by the Constitution of the United States." Both assumptions are shown to be false in fact, and the deductions drawn from them utterly untenable. He then proceeds to prove that, under the change of public sentiment, the Government is made to assume an attitude of hostility to the South; that "it is made to take the type of Northern sentiment; it is animated, in its relations to slavery, by the Northern mind; and the South, henceforward, is no longer *of* the Government, but only *under* the Government;" "the North becomes the United States, and the South a subject province." This, he contends, "makes a new government; it proposes new and extraordinary terms of union." "The old Government is as completely abolished, as if the people of the United States had met in convention, and repealed the Constitution." "Mr. Lincoln has been chosen, not to administer, but to revolutionize the Government." "The oath which makes him President, makes a new Union." "The import of secession is simply the refusal, on the part of the South, to be parties to any such Union." "No people on earth, without judicial infatuation, can organize a government to destroy themselves. It is too much to ask a man to sign his own death warrant."

We give this analysis of a portion of this elaborate essay; and, as the reader will perceive from the marks of quotation, in the very language of the instrument, in order that Dr. Thornwell may define his own position, and be judged by others upon his own statements. It was the ground upon which the entire South stood, contending for the principle which gave vitality to the whole American Constitution; and her consolation is, in all her present suffering, that it has been incurred in an honest effort to preserve this in its integrity; and that, if she be slain, it is by the hand of another, and not her own. An unerring Judge will fix the responsibility of this conflict just where it belongs.

It has been exceedingly interesting to us, in preparing this biography, to find, among the loose papers of this period, little scraps, often the backs of old letters, written all over with fragmentary thoughts; seized, apparently, just as they arose in his mind, and thrown in this loose way upon paper, doubtless with a view to their being worked over at leisure. Perhaps they were all given, at different times, to the public, in the fugitive articles he was in the habit of contributing to the newspaper press. But in the fragmentary form in which they are preserved to us, they are precious as relics of the man, and as memorials how constantly the subject was in his thoughts. We transcribe one of these, evidently belonging to the early stage of the struggle, and before the gage of battle was actually thrown down. It is of consequence as rebutting the charge that he was seditious and bitter in his feelings, and as showing how earnestly the South deprecated the appeal to arms. It reads thus:

"How the duty of the Christian, to study the things that make for peace can be best discharged, in the present condition of the country, is a practical inquiry of the utmost moment. It is possible to embitter strife by the very efforts to extinguish it. The measures proposed must be judicious; and to be judicious, they must be adapted to the difficulties which they are designed to heal. It is not enough that they spring from a good motive. The motive does not determine the result. They must be adjusted to the nature of the case.

"Tried by this standard, that whole class of expedients, which aim to promote peace by a compromise of the difficulties betwixt the North and the South, and the perpetuation of the present Union, must be condemned as fostering only strife. The nature of the differences is such that there can be no compromise. There must be complete surrender, on one side or the other. It is a case of excluded middle. The North have said distinctly, that freedom is national, slavery sectional. In other words, they, and they alone, represent the real spirit and tendencies of the country; and the government must be entrusted exclusively to their hands. They must determine the social type of the territories; they must determine the complexion of all our laws; the whole life of the country is in them. The South is an appendage to the body, but no organic part of it. In such a controversy, there is no room for compromise. The positions are contradictory, and one or the other must be abandoned. But suppose the North yields, will that promote peace?

It depends upon what is meant by yielding. If to yield is only to suspend hostilities, while the sentiment of the people remain unchanged, it is evident that the causes of strife remain in all their power. The only measure which can promote peace is, that the parties should separate. The combatants must be parted.

"As it is clear that they must part, the next thing is to make the separation a peaceable one. To this point our Christian efforts should now be unceasingly directed. We should endeavour to prevent violence, and the acrimony and bitterness which must spring from an appeal to arms. If force is resorted to, it must fail. The Union can hold no States by conquest. A forced Union is an anomaly. Free consent, and that alone, should hold us together. If it fails to conquer the seceding States, much blood will have been shed in vain. It is idle, therefore, to resort to it. If the Union can be dissolved by the same free consent which created it, the most friendly relations might be instituted between the two sections; and the prosperity of both be almost as much promoted as by a Federal Union. Let Christian men, North and South, labour to have us part in peace."

Dr. Thornwell's health was not by any means restored. The temporary improvement resulting from his European trip the preceding summer, disappeared under the resumption of his labours, and the pressure of solicitude for the country. About the middle of January, while his pen was busy with the essays above presented, he was prostrated upon a bed of sickness, from which he did not recover until the spring. A relapse followed upon this, and the entire summer was devoted to a vain chase after health. Indeed, the short remainder of his life was spent in a useless conflict with the disease, beneath which he was destined to succumb.

In the month of June he resorted, with his third daughter, as companion and nurse, to Glenn Springs, in South Carolina, somewhat noted for the value of its waters in certain types of disease. From this place he writes:

"GLENN SPRINGS, *June* 17, 1861.

"MY DEAREST WIFE: As I know that you will be anxious to hear how we are getting along, I write to you again this morning. Yesterday was a very warm day, but we had a good western breeze. I walked in the morning to the spring, and back. We have a fine shade the whole way. There was preaching at a little Episcopal Church, built by McCullough, but none of us went. The Church is a very neat little building, just over the branch from the spring. The rector is a Mr. Jones; I know nothing of him. Late in the afternoon yesterday, I took another stroll, and found it delightful. The shades are so fine about here, that one is perfectly protected from the rays of the sun. I was very cautious in the use of the water. Last night I slept well. This morning I rose a little after seven o'clock, ate breakfast at eight, took a long walk, have drunk two glassfuls of water, and feel very comfortable. The air to-day is fine ; it is cool in the temperature, and made more so by a constant breeze. My strength seems to increase, and I am encouraged to believe that the place will agree with me. * * * *

"You cannot imagine how I enjoy these up-country forests. They are more interesting than they ever were before. I can gaze on the fine trees from morning till night; and at night, now that the moon is shining, it is most delightful to look out upon the starry heavens above, and the thick groves below. I find myself almost entranced by the influence of scenes around me and above me. You would enjoy the place very much.

"I am trying to get water sent to you, but it is impossible to procure a vessel of any kind, even a bottle. Strange to say, I am fond of it. Pat drinks it freely, and says it has given her an enormous appetite. She watches me closely, and will not let me eat what she thinks will not agree with me. The other evening I was about to take a piece of lamb-cutlet; but Pat sung out at the table, that she thought I ought not to eat meat at night; so I obeyed her, and let it alone. I have now emptied my budget of gossip. Love to all. May the Lord keep us all in health and safety. God bless you, dearest.

"Yours, most devotedly,

J. H. T.

Two days later he addresses the following to his eldest son, which could scarcely have been more faithful in its appeal, had he known how soon they would both be together in eternity:

"GLENN SPRINGS, *June* 19, 1861.

"MY DEAR GILLESPIE: It has been on my heart for some time back to have a serious and solemn conversation with you, touching the great interests of the soul. During all my sickness, nothing has pressed upon my mind more than the condition and prospects of my boys, in relation to the salvation of the gospel. I have dedicated you and your brothers to God. I have prayed that He would call you all into His kingdom ; and I once ventured to hope that I might see you all ministers of the gospel. There is nothing worth living for but the glory of God ; and I do most devoutly wish that your eyes may be opened to see the transcendent importance of eternal things. You have but one soul; and if you lose that, all is gone ; and once lost, it is lost for ever.

"You may say that you acknowledge the truth of all this, but you do not feel it. My son, you must strive to feel it. You must think upon the matter seriously and earnestly; you must pray over it; you must confess and deplore your hardness of heart, and seek from the Lord a clean heart and a right spirit. Resolve never to give over, until you find that you are interested, and warmly interested, in the great salvation. You cannot imagine what a comfort it would be to me in my declining days to see you humbly and sincerely following the Lord Jesus Christ. And why not do it? Can you gain anything by carelessness and remissness? Are you happier when you do not know but that, at any moment, you may be summoned before God altogether unprepared? Is not the fear of the Lord the beginning of wisdom? and do they not exhibit the soundest understanding who keep God's commandments? My son, you know not how much I love you, and cannot know how much I feel for your immortal interests. Do me, your father, the favour to give your mind to the matter at once, and decidedly. Seek to be a thorough-going, devoted Christian. Seek the Lord with your whole heart. Renounce all sin, and renounce it for ever; and betake yourself to the blood of Christ for pardon and acceptance. Do more; have an eye to the eternal good of your younger brothers. They look up to you; they respect you; they try to do as you do. Set them a good example. Go before them in the way of eternal life.

"Religion cannot be maintained without regular prayer, and regular reading of the Scriptures, and regular attendance upon the ordinances. Never omit your morning and evening devotions, and try to be interested in them; think over what you pray for; think before you pray. When you read the Bible, read in order to get knowledge. Meditate on what you read; and beg God to seal it on your heart by the Holy Ghost. At church, try to be profited. Apply to yourself what you hear. Look upon preaching as God's appointment, and expect His blessing in attending upon it. My dear boy, reflect upon what I have said to you; and gladden my heart, when I see you again, by your interest in all that concerns the glory of God, and the salvation of the soul. Pray over this letter; look upon it as your father's legacy; and for his sake, as well as your own, awake to the importance of these high themes.

"As to my health, I cannot say that there is any marked change yet. I think, upon the whole, I am improving. The atmosphere here at present is very cool and delightful. Our nights are charming; and I enjoy the magnificent forests about here very much. I can never gaze on these enough. And now, my boy, may God bless you. Be true to Him, and He will be faithful to you

"Your affectionate father,

J. H. THORNWELL."

The next letter shows a change of place, and is written to his colleague in the pastoral charge of the Columbia church, the Rev. F. P. Mullally:

"SPARTANBURG, *July* 10, 1861.

"MY DEAR MULLALLY: It has been on my mind to write to you for some time; but as I had nothing definite to say to my lord, I concluded to put it off until I could get a few more ideas. I find, however, that if I wait until I get something worth saying, I shall wait for ever. You must, therefore, take things as they come; and if my letter has no sense, be satisfied to reflect that it is full of love, and of the sincerest wishes for your well-being and well-doing. It makes me sad at times to think of the burden that has fallen on your shoulders through my infirmities; but I trust that the Lord will abundantly reward you for your generous and disinterested labours. It would delight my heart to be able to join you in your ministry. The people in Columbia are very dear to me; and their spiritual interests are the burden of many a prayer. I cannot tell you how much I am attached to the congregation; and if I could serve them as in former days, it would be the joy and rejoicing of my heart.

"I was glad to hear that you had a little holiday, and killed two birds with one stone by running up to Pendleton. I can well imagine what sort of a time you had there. How I should have rejoiced to be with you.

"You must not overwork yourself during the summer. A righteous man is merciful to his beast; and you must spare yours, or you may bring yourself to the pass that I am at. As to my condition, I have to speak with caution. Last week I considered myself nearly well. My uncomfortable symptoms had largely disappeared. I was as strong as usual; could ride eight miles on horse-back without fatigue; rode every day sixteen miles in a carriage; attended two night-parties; had a fine appetite, and was becoming quite cheerful. There came on a spell of rainy weather. I took cold, which settled on my bowels; and for thirty-six hours I suffered as much as I had ever suffered in that time before. I became depressed. The thing was so sudden and so unexpected; and I could attribute it to no imprudence of mine. But I am on the mend again. To-day I am nearly myself again, only a little weaker than before. My lung has greatly improved; the upper part is performing finely; the lower is still dull, though much better than when I left home. The Cherokee water has been of great service to my stomach and kidneys. The Glenn Spring water I could not stand at all. I am satisfied that it did me serious injury.

"I wish you would have a *pro re nata* meeting of our Presbytery called, to appoint delegates to attend a convention at Greensborough, on the 15th of August. You may put my name to the circular requesting the Moderator to call the meeting. It is very important to take initiative steps, while the Presbyteries are all harmonious, and before different schemes have got in agitation. If the Presbytery should appoint me as a delegate, I shall endeavour to attend. I can work in private, though I cannot make public speeches. Do have the matter attended to; let no time be lost.

"On the 16th instant, I leave Spartanburg for Wilson's Springs. I

shall remain there about ten days, if the waters suit me ; then go to
the mountains, holding myself in readiness to attend the convention,
when I see that it has been called. The climate here is very grateful.
I am delightfully situated, and enjoy every comfort and luxury. All
right *outside;* but *inwardly*, I am sorry to say, that I cannot make so
fair a report. Give my love to —— and ——, and all the long-faced
tribe. I love them all. My wife is the only Presbyterian I have seen
for so long a time, that I have almost forgotten how that sour race looks.
But I hope soon to see you all again ; and to see you in the full enjoy
ment of the comforts and consolations of the gospel.

"As ever,

J. H. THORNWELL."

At this point comes in properly the draft of a letter,
without date, to the Rev. Dr. Abner A. Porter, then
editor of the *Southern Presbyterian*, at Columbia. It
indicates the policy he thought the Southern churches
and Presbyteries should pursue, after the passage of the
"Spring Resolutions," in the Assembly of 1861, at Philadelphia. In the main, these measures were carried out
in reintegrating into the General Assembly of the Presbyterian Church in the Confederate States, which was
afterwards done at Augusta, Georgia:

"DEAR PORTER : I am glad to see that a call has been made for a Convention of the churches in the Confederate States, to determine their
future relations. The Presbyteries should lose no time in calling *pro
re nata* meetings, and electing their delegates. The number of delegates which each Presbytery should send ought to be the same as the
number of commissioners to which it is entitled in the General Assembly. The Convention should, first of all, settle the question of separation from the churches in the United States. And, in the next place, if
it determines to separate, it should prepare a constitution, to be submitted to the autumn Presbyteries ; and, until the constitution is finally
adopted, make arrangements for a Provisional Government. I would
have preferred that the Convention had been called to meet in Greensborough, North Carolina. Richmond, in July, will be very crowded,
and it will be hard for the members to find accommodations. I think
even yet the call should be changed from Richmond to Greensborough,
or Raleigh. I prefer Greensborough, because it is situated in a most
beautiful, healthful, and delightful region of country. Then, again, it
is more conveniently accessible than Richmond. It is nearer to the
Southwestern brethren; and a few days spent in breathing its atmosphere and drinking its water, will prepare the delegates from the

swampy region of the Gulf for hard service, when they return to their gnats and musquitoes.

"There should be no time lost in the permanent organization of the Confederate Church. She should be getting ready for embarking fully in the work of her Master. She should have, as speedily as possible, her Committees of Missons, Foreign and Domestic, of Education, and, if need be, of Publication and Church Extension. A great work is before her. Let her gird up her loins, and set resolutely about it. I hope, therefore, that every Presbytery in the Confederate States will send delegates to a convention, to be held at Greensborough, N. C., entrusted with full power to determine the future posture of the Church, subject to the review of the Presbyteries in the autumn."

He writes, a little later, to one of his younger sons, revealing his parental anxiety for their usefulness in this world, and their salvation in the next.

"SPARTANBURG, *July* 23, 1861.

"MY DEAR BOY: Your affectionate letter was duly received, and I am glad to see that you are so mindful of your father in his absence. Your father thinks and prays a great deal about you. He wants to see you a useful man in the world, if the Lord should spare your life. He would delight, above all things, to see you a faithful and able preacher of the gospel. Your first concern, my dear child, should be to be a Christian; and then your next, to enquire how you can most glorify God. You can never be useful without study and prayer. Master your books. Give your mind to your lessons, and always determine that you will get them; that you will not be outdone. Now is the time to lay the foundation, and you must not fool it away with indolence. I hope you will know your Latin grammar well, and be able to read when I see you. I want you to be a good scholar, and I do hope that you will begin to love your books. But enough on this point.

"We are still in Spartanburg. The weather has been too bad for us to leave. There have been rains every day. We shall leave the first good day, perhaps to-morrow. We shall spend a while in Shelby, and then meet you all in Lincoln, at Mr. Anderson's. Charles must keep my horses in splendid order, and things in fine trim on the lot when you leave. He must try himself to see how well he can manage. My health is something better. I would improve faster if the weather would allow me to get out, but the rains confine me to the house. Dr. Shipp's family is excessively kind. I do not know how I can ever repay them. His children are all fond of their books. He has no trouble in getting them to study. I have no news. I hope Gillespie was preserved in the battle on Sunday.* We must all pray for him, and for our country. The Lord alone can keep us in safety.

Very affectionately, your father,   J. H. THORNWELL."

* The first battle of Manassas.

The seriousness of these letters will be relieved by the following playful effusion, so characteristic of him in his bantering moods. It was in reply to a very serious appeal against his favourite habit.

"THEOLOGICAL SEMINARY, *September* 24, 1861.

"DEARLY BELOVED SISTER ADGER: My sympathies have been greatly moved by the piteous accounts I have received of your keen and manifold sufferings, in that most important of all organs to a woman, 'the human face divine.' I know how to feel for the sufferer, especially for such a sufferer as the wife of a friend who has no rival in my heart. My own experience has led me to recognize the fact, that one effect of our afflictions is to disarm us of capricious and idle prejudices, and to reconcile us to what we once abhorred. In my own case, this principle has been most signally illustrated. At one time in my life, sheep, blackberries, and tea were my utter abominations; and I marvelled how any human being could reconcile himself to the use of such monstrous articles of diet. But I was brought low. I had either to starve, or to feed on sheep with the voracity of an ancient patriarch or Jew; and I finally came to believe that even a Christian man might make dainties of the fruit of briers, the offspring of the fold, and the leaf from China. My prejudices are all gone; and I sit down to these abominations with as much composure as I would encounter ham, plum pudding, or roast beef. After giving up my prejudices, I began to mend.

"Now, it has occurred to me, that there is a proud place in your heart, which requires to be humbled. You have some unaccountable prejudices, from which it behooves you to be delivered; and my interest in your carnal comfort prompts me to deal very freely with you on this most delicate subject. I have no doubt that if you would open your mind to liberal views of that most delectable of all weeds, the tobacco plant, your sufferings might be greatly relieved, and greatly modified. Just reflect upon it as a balm which nature has kindly provided for aching teeth or agonized jaws. Let me advise you, as you prize your comfort, to provide yourself with a clean pipe and a short stem, and set to work upon the goodly process of inhaling the exquisite fragrance. There is no sight more truly venerable than that of a mother in Israel, in the chimney corner, with her children about her, refreshing their senses with gales of incense as sweet and cheering as the tones which proceed from her mouth. It is the very picture of dignified repose. The very idea of neuralgia to such a matron would be a contradiction in terms. Only try it. I never have tooth-ache, jaw-ache, or any other face ache. The reason, perhaps, is that I have had no absurd prejudices against 'kind nature's sweet restorer,' a genuine article of tobacco. How delightful it would be, if you could overcome your antipathies, to visit sister Adger, of a moonlight night, at her hospitable mansion, and join with her in the calm, quiet, dignified composure which the blended fumes of the pipe and cigar would so freely and completely signalize! My dear, suffering sister, smoke, *smoke*, and again I say, *smoke*. It will do you good. Once begin, and you will need no arguments to persevere. The odour of a good conversation and the odour of tobacco sweetly harmonize, and form an exquisite incense. But enough. We all want to see you very much. I think your husband needs looking after; and the worse feature in his case is, that he does not want you to come home. Lizzie, I suspect, is doing pretty much what the boy shot at. The truth is, your presence, provided your face is smooth, would work marvels. But my paper is out. Be sure to *smoke*, and let us hear no more of neuralgia.   As ever,

J. H. THORNWELL."

Dr. Thornwell returned in the fall to his duties in the Seminary, but his health was so shattered that he was called to sever his connection with the church in Columbia, the sole pastorship of which being devolved upon his young and estimable colleague, the Rev. Mr. Mullally. One letter more will close this chapter. It is addressed to General James Gillespie, near Cheraw, and gives a connected view of his sickness; enabling us to see, what neither he nor his friends apprehended fully at the time, that his disease had fixed itself in his constitution, and must soon finish its work:

"THEOLOGICAL SEMINARY, *November* 19, 1861.

" MY DEAR GENERAL : I received your message from Mr. Pelham, and lose no time in complying with your request. You have probably been apprised of my general condition during the past ten months. On the 15th of January I took my bed, from which I hardly arose until about the 1st of April. My system was utterly broken down ; and broken down, as the doctor said, in consequence of excessive work. About the 1st of April I began to amend; and had the folly to go down to Charleston, where I took an affection of the bowels, that kept me prostrate during the whole summer. I had no energy for anything, except to pray for my country and the Church. I went to Wilson's Springs in August, and there I began to recover strength a second time. I spent the remainder of the summer in Lincoln county, North Carolina, at the residence of my son-in-law, and, by the blessing of God, still continued to improve. At the opening of the Seminary, about the middle of September, I returned home, and have been able to discharge all my duties as a Professor. But I felt it my duty to give up the church. I am now free from the cares and labours of a pastor. I am still improving, but my right lung is still feeble, and my bowels in a great measure toneless. In other respects I am myself again. During the summer I spent a month with Mary Jane and Dr. Shipp, and a pleasanter month I have never spent anywhere. They are both noble people. Mary Jane is a true Gillespie, and Shipp is exactly the man that she ought to have married. Their family is a model household. I love every one of them, from the youngest to the oldest, as I love my own children. I was really delighted to find that Mary Jane had married so well.

One thing that has helped to break me down, is the profound interest which I have taken in public affairs. My heart has been distressed for my country. While abroad, I saw that secession was inevitable; and when I returned, I did everything in my power to promote it. I gave up the Union with great pain, but I saw no alternative. Black Republicanism had rendered it impossible to remain in it with honour. I always thought that war would be the consequence; but I preferred war to ignominious submission. The war has come, but I am not disheartened. Under God, I believe that the final result is certain. The hopes of liberty on this continent are centred in our success. We may have to suffer much, and to suffer long; but liberty is worth it all. You have heard of the disaster at Port Royal. I suppose it could not be prevented. But the enemy, after all, has gained but little. Mr. Barnwell's family is now at my house, all except himself. They fled from the invasion. Columbia is full of refugees from Beaufort and from Charleston. I do not think, however, that the enemy can take Charleston, and I doubt whether they will try it.　　　　As ever,

J. H. THORNWELL."

"P. S. Gillespie has been in this war from the very commencement, and is a true patriot. You have no reason to be ashamed of him; he has genuine pluck. There is no bacon in this part of the country; we have to live on sheep and cows. How fares the matter with you? We have been supplementing our small stock of coffee with rye, but we shall soon have to come down to sassafras."

CHAPTER XXXIV.

ORGANIZATION OF THE SOUTHERN ASSEMBLY.

A LLUSION has been made to a rupture in the Church as well as in the State, some account of which falls of necessity within the scope of this narrative. Immediately after his inauguration as President of the Confederate States, and in pursuance of a resolution of the Confederate Congress, Mr. Davis sent three commissioners to Washington, for the purpose of negotiating friendly relations between the two governments. As soon as possible after the organization of Mr. Lincoln's cabinet, these commissioners addressed a communication to the newly appointed Secretary of State, mentioning the object of their diplomatic mission, and assuring him that the President, Congress, and people whom they represented, earnestly desired a peaceful solution of these great questions. An *informal* an-

499

swer was returned, to the effect that Mr. Seward's " strong
disposition was in *favour of peace*, but that he wished to
avoid making a reply to the commissioners *at that time*."
An intimation was further given that Fort Sumter would
be evacuated within ten days.   At as late a date as the 7th
of April, Mr. Seward made reply to a note of inquiry,
" Faith as to Sumter fully kept; wait and see."   When
these words were penned, the relief squadron had already
left New York, and was approaching the harbour of
Charleston, to "provision and reinforce Fort Sumter,—
peacefully, if permitted—otherwise, by force."   The Confederate Commissioners, after being held at bay for the
space of three and twenty days, and amused with the prospect of peace, found themselves deceived and betrayed;
and, on the 9th of April, addressed a note to the Federal
authorities, to the effect that this act of aggression could
not be construed except "as a declaration of war against
the Confederate States."   In the language of Mr. Stephens,
whom we continue to quote, "It was more than a mere
declaration of war; it was an act of war itself."   It was
under these circumstances of urgent necessity that the
bombardment of Fort Sumter was begun, on the 12th of
April.   It is not our business to explain the duplicity of
this proceeding.   But whether it was a fraud from the
beginning, or whether the policy of the Federal administration was suddenly changed, under the influence of the
seven Northern governors who rushed to Washington at
the pinch of the crisis, history will be obliged to hold as
the aggressor, the party which made the first movement
to battle, and not those who first struck the defensive
blow.   The fall of Sumter was used with consummate
skill, to arouse the passion of the Northern masses, and to
inflame their resentment against the insult represented
as being given to the national flag.   The whole country
was in a blaze, and the four years' dismal and bloody
strife was begun.

It was during the outburst of this storm that the General Assembly of the Presbyterian Church met, in the month of May, in the city of Philadelphia. The ecclesiastical bonds between North and South were not yet broken. A partial representation from the Southern Presbyteries sat in this council, as in former years; determined that, in the severing of churchly ties, the aggression should come from the same quarter which had wrought the rupture in the State. Perhaps many indulged the vain hope of the writer, that the splendid opportunity would be embraced of demonstrating the purely spiritual character of the Church, as the "kingdom which is not of this world." It would have been a superb triumph of Christianity, if the Church could have stretched her arms across the chasm of a great war, preserving the integrity of her ranks unbroken. The golden vision was not to be realized. In defiance of the express statute in our code, which inhibits "Synods and councils from handling or concluding anything but that which is ecclesiastical, and from intermeddling with civil affairs, which concern the Commonwealth," the famous "Spring Resolutions"—so named from their venerable author, the Rev. Dr. Gardiner Spring, of New York—were adopted, by a vote of one hundred and fifty-four to sixty-six. It reads thus:

" *Resolved,* That this General Assembly, in the spirit of that Christian patriotism which the Scriptures enjoin, and which has always characterized this Church, do hereby acknowledge and declare our obligation to promote and perpetuate, so far as in us lies, the integrity of these United States, and to strengthen, uphold, and encourage the Federal government in the exercise of all its functions, under our noble Constitution; and to this Constitution, in all its provisions, requirements, and principles, we profess our unabated loyalty. And to avoid all misconception, the Assembly declares that, by the term 'Federal government,' as here used, is not meant any particular administration, or the peculiar opinions of any particular party, but that central administration which, being at any time appointed and inaugurated according to the forms prescribed in the Constitution of the United States, is the visible representative of our national existence."

This paper, from its very terms, was simply a writ of ejectment of all that portion of the Church within the bounds of eleven States, which had already withdrawn from the Federal Union, and established a government of their own. A pledge was made on their behalf by the Assembly, which it was not possible for them to redeem; so that, in the language of Dr. Hodge's own protest, they were driven "to choose between allegiance to their State and allegiance to the Church." 'This was not all. The utterance was exclusively and intensely political. It touched, as with the point of a needle, the precise issue upon which the war turned. The problem, in relation to which the most eminent statesmen, North and South, had been divided for seventy-five years, was to determine where sovereignty—the *jus summi imperii*—resided; whether in the people, as they are merged into the mass, one undivided whole; or in the people, as they were originally formed into colonies, and afterwards into States, combining together for purposes set forth in declarative instruments of union. This question, lying wholly within the domain of politics, the General Assembly assumed the right to determine; so that, even if not ejected by what was equivalent to an act of expulsion, the Southern Presbyteries were compelled to separate themselves, in order to preserve the crown rights of the Redeemer, and the spiritual independence of His kingdom, the Church.

During the summer and autumn of 1861, forty-seven Presbyteries, each for itself, dissolved their connection with the General Assembly of the Presbyterian Church in the United States of America; the ten Synods, to which they belonged, sealing the decison by a corresponding vote of their own. This separation was based, in every case, upon the unconstitutional character of the Assembly's legislation. We give the language employed by a single Presbytery, as showing the common ground upon which they all stood: "*Resolved*, That in view of the unconstitutional, Erastian, tyrannical, and *virtually exscinding act*, of the late General Assembly, sitting at Philadelphia, in May last, we do hereby, with a solemn

protest against this act, declare, in the fear of God, our
connection with the General Assembly of the Presbyterian Church in the United States to be dissolved." It
was to secure unanimity in this important measure, as well
as to prevent the evils which might arise from a temporary
disorganization, that Dr. Thornwell and others thought a
convention of the Presbyteries to be so important. In
reality, there was little danger of confusion, except from
diversity of opinion as to the time, and place, and mode
of coming together. The Presbyteries were of one mind
as to the necessity of separating from the Northern branch
of the Church, and not less so as to the importance of combining again in an Assembly of their own. During the
interval, the Presbyteries and Synods were completely
organized under a common constitution and polity; and
the only feature of the system that was lacking, was the
highest court, which should give expression to their visible
unity and fellowship. The proposed convention was held
in the month of August, at Atlanta, Georgia; and was
useful in directing various matters of detail, which were
indispensable to concert of action.

As the result of these deliberations, the General Assembly of the Presbyterian Church in the Confederate
States was organized on the 4th of December, 1861, in
the city of Augusta, Georgia; and its first act, after fixing
upon its name and title, was the formal and explicit adoption of the Westminster Standards as its constitution :
" *Resolved*, That this Assembly declare, in conformity
with the unanimous decision of our Presbyteries, that the
Confession of Faith, the Larger and Shorter Catechisms,
the Form of Government, the Book of Discipline, and
the Directory of Worship, which together make up the
constitution of the Presbyterian Church in the United
States of America, are the Constitution of the Presbyterian Church in the Confederate States of America, only
substituting the term " Confederate States" for " United
States." It was a body not large in size—a little less

than one hundred members—but august in character. It was composed of men who fitly represented the ability, the learning, and the piety of the whole Church, not only as to the ministers, but the ruling elders, who contributed so largely to shape the conclusions which were reached. Dr. Thornwell was, of course, one of its guiding spirits; and the papers which gave the largest character to this Assembly emanated from his pen, and were marked with the ability of his very best productions. We may be allowed to instance "The Address to all the Churches of Jesus Christ throughout the Earth," containing the clearest statement of the principles which had brought about the separation from the Northern Church; involving, as this did, a beautiful exposition of the nature and functions of the Church of God. It will stand as one of those documents to which the Church will ever appeal, as a testimony for the truth, in times of darkness and trial, when the witnesses for it were thought worthy only of being slain. It was not only expressed with that precision of thought and of language which was characteristic of the illustrious author, but it was pervadad with a sacramental fervour, which stamped upon it the impression of a sacred and binding covenant. The scene which was enacted at the moment of its subscription will be forgotten by none who witnessed it. Read, and read again, amid the solemn stillness of an audience whose emotions are hushed with awe, it was finally adopted and laid upon the Moderator's table; when, one by one, the members came silently forward and signed the instrument with their names. We were carried back to those stirring times in Scottish story, when the Solemn League and Covenant was spread upon the grave stone in the Grey Friar's church-yard, and Christian heroes pricked their veins, that with the red blood they might sign their allegiance to the kingdom and crown of Jesus Christ, their Lord and Head.

There were other scenes in that venerable court of only less interest than the foregoing. On the seventh day of the session, the Committee on a Charter made their report, submitting the draft of a bill to incorporate the Trustees of the General Assembly. The peculiar feature of this instrument was, that it made " all the committees, agencies, or boards, which the Assembly might establish for carrying on the general work of the Church, branches of this incorporation;" " any gift, conveyance, or transfer of estate in any wise, any devise or bequest made to the Trustees for either of these agencies, to be transferred to them in as full and as perfect a manner as if they had been especially incorporated to take and to hold the same." The object of this measure was to secure the complete subordination of all these agencies to the Assembly itself, so that they should never have the power to assert an independent authority, and " being kept together in one family, and under one family name, to exhibit the appearance of uniformity, sympathy, harmony, and a delightful Christian brotherhood."   The Assembly listened to the reading of the report with undivided attention, when the accomplished chairman, Judge Shepherd, was subjected to a sharp and critical interrogation from all parts of the house, which he sustained with admirable dignity, composure and courtesy. It was terminated at length by an observation of Chancellor Johnston, of South Carolina : " I think the Judge has passed a good examination, and I hope he will be allowed to retire."   To this, Dr. Thornwell added, with a glow of animation suffusing his pallid face, " To me this is a most delightful paper ; I can find nothing in it to be objected to, and I move, therefore, that it be received, so that the lawyers may have a chance at it."   Altogether, it was a scene of dramatic interest, the exact parallel with which we never before had witnessed in any Church court.

The great business of the body, however, was to equip the Church for the great work to which she is ordained by her Divine Head.   Executive agencies were appointed to superintend both Foreign and Domestic Missionary operations, as well as those of Education and Publication, with definite principles and rules laid down for their guidance. The cumbrous and useless machinery of Boards, interposed as a screen between the Assembly and its different agencies, was discarded without a dissenting voice. Simple committees were substituted in their place, composed of members residing in one locality, with merely executive functions, and immediately responsible to the Assembly, by whom they are annually appointed. The cordial unanimity with which all this was done, showed a remarkable advance in the recognition of a sound and pure Presbyterianism. Every one breathed freely, in a free Church, which could at length work out its own great principles, without the incubus of foreign influences and institutions. The time-honoured standards of the Presbyterian Church had been explicitly adopted, without any equivocation or reservation as to their interpretation; the watchmen in Zion seeing eye to eye, and all being of one mind, to rise and build up her broken walls. It was a sublime spectacle of faith : this Church, hedged in by a cordon of armies, looking out upon the whole world as its field, and quietly preparing herself for labours in the future; while stone was laid upon stone in the solid masonry of her organization, without the sound of hammer or chisel being heard in all her courts. It was when "the King of Babylon's army beseiged Jerusalem, and Jeremiah, the prophet, was shut up in the court of the prison which was in the king of Judah's house," that the word of the Lord came unto him, saying, " buy the field that is in Anathoth, for the right of redemption is thine to buy it." God's way, in calling His people to the exercise of faith, has been in all ages to load that faith down with all that it can bear; and here stood a Church doing a work in gloom and darkness, which was simply prophetic of the future, and a pledge of faithfulness to the principles which she had received grace to see and to glorify.

Two measures were proposed in this Assembly which

did not pass. One of these was brought up in the form of an overture, and thus an incidental mention of it is made upon the Minutes. The other came up in the form of simple resolution, and was withdrawn, and finds no record. They are both of interest, as illustrating the spirit and temper of the body, and form a part of its unwritten history. They are introduced here from their connection with the subject of these Memoirs, and reflect his views and his feelings. The first was a memorial which, it was overtured, should be sent to the Confederate Congress, for the incorporation of an article in the constitution distinctly recognizing the Christian religion. This proposition originated with Dr. Thornwell; but the overture not being reached on the calendar until the eighth day of the session, and being vigorously opposed by some who doubted the wisdom and propriety of the measure, it was withdrawn by the author, on the ground that there was not time for its discussion. He further felt that it should not be pressed, unless it could be adopted with cordiality and unanimity. The fact of its presentation, however, discloses his view upon a public question of no little importance, and merits a record in a detailed account of his own life.

The other question related to the sending of a letter to the Northern Assembly, announcing the organization of a co-ordinate body with itself, and setting forth the reasons for this action. Dr. Thornwell was not the mover of the resolution, but he favoured its passage. The discussion developed some feeling, which disinclined many against any act of courtesy towards a body whose course had been so unjust, and who were probably in no temper to appreciate it. As an evidence of Dr. Thornwell's mellowness of spirit, and the entire absence of anything approaching to bitterness, we quote his language in this debate: "Mr. Moderator, let us grant that the brethren of the Old Assembly have injured us, I can say honestly and conscientiously before God, that I forgive them for everything they have ever done to me or my Church. I have no resentment against them; and my only regret is that they have allowed themselves to commit this act of infatuation; and I do earnestly want to be able to have it said of this Church, that it was not influenced by passion or resentment; that they have not left in a pet, or through revenge; but that we have come calmly and dispassionately, in a spirit of peace and charity, to our present position. I do not desire that we should go before that Assembly to make representations of innocence, but to stand up before them as their equals, and, at the same time, as fellow Christians. They have erred, but they are men—'*humanum est errare*'—and does it become us to scorn one another? But it is a matter of self-respect to this body, that the world may know that it has not been influenced by low passions or undue anger."

The strength of the opposition induced the mover to withdraw his resolution, so that the sense of the Assembly was never taken. But if the reader is curious to know what would have been the tone of such a communication as Dr. Thornwell would have sanctioned, he will be gratified in perusing the following draft of a paper, which he had evidently prepared with a view to some such action being taken as would authorize its use. It is styled,

"*Farewell Letter to the General Assembly of the Presbyterian Church in the United States.*

" The General Assembly of the Presbyterian Church in the Confederate States of America, to the General Assembly of the Presbyterian Church in the United States of America, greeting.

" Be it known to you, brethren, that the Presbyteries and Synods in these Confederate States, which were formerly in connection with you, have withdrawn from your jurisdiction, and organized a General Assembly for themselves. They are now a separate and independent Church. We think it due to you in comity, that we should set forth a brief statement of the reasons which have impelled us to take this step, in order that you may see that we have not been influenced by the spirit of anger, resentment, or schism. We have no grudge to gratify; and whatever wrong may have been done us in your recent legislation, we freely and cheerfully forgive.

"We have withdrawn, first, because we are persuaded that, if we remain together, our harmony is likely to be disturbed by the introduction of our political differences into our Church courts.   We have taken warning from the example of your late meeting at Philadelphia.   Your proceedings there have been sanctioned by the general sentiment of your Presbyteries, and leave us no alternative but a choice betwixt useless strife, or a quiet and peaceable separation.

"In the next place, we are convinced that, as a general rule, Church organizations should be bounded by national lines.   A division of this sort is a division for convenience and efficiency.   It argues no breach of charity, and therefore implies no schism.   In the circumstances of the Confederate and United States, it seems to be peculiarly desirable that the Churches should be as independent as the Government.

"To this may be added, in the third place, that the efficiency of the Southern Church, in its efforts to evangelize the slave population, would be greatly impeded, in the present condition of affairs, by a Northern alliance.   We deem it unnecessary to expand these reasons.   They have appeared to us decisive of our duty; and in the fear of God, for the glory of His name, and for the honour and prosperity of His Church, we have, with perfect unanimity, dissolved our old ties, and assumed a position of equality with yourselves.   Your faith and order are ours.   Your noble testimony for the truth, in by-gone days, is still ours.   All that is precious in the past is still ours.   And we sincerely pray that the two Churches may hereafter have no other rivalry but that of love to the Master, and of holy zeal in His cause.   We bid you farewell."

It must be distinctly remembered that this is strictly a private paper, though moulded into the form of a public document.   It was never presented to the consideration of the Assembly; and is engrossed in this volume only as an illustration of the charity and Christian spirit of a man whose memory is precious.

Somewhat earlier than the events recorded, during the month of November, 1861, the Synod of South Carolina held its annual session, in the town of Abbeville.   Advantage was taken of the presence of gentlemen from different parts of the State to make a declaration upon public affairs.   Dr. Thornwell offered the following resolutions, which were adopted unanimously by the meeting:

"*Resolved*, 1. By the ministers and elders composing this Synod, not in their ecclesiastical capacity as a court of Jesus Christ, but in their private capacity, as a convention of Christian gentlemen, that our allegiance is due, through the sovereign State to which we belong, and shall be rendered, to the Government of the Confederate States, as long as South Carolina remains in the number.

"*Resolved*, 2. That the war which the United States are now waging against us, is unjust, cruel, and tyrannical, and in contravention of every principle of freedom, which their fathers and ours bled to establish.

"*Resolved*, 3. That we are firmly persuaded, that the only hope of constitutional liberty, on this continent, is in the success of the Confederate cause; and that we pledge ourselves, and we think we can safely say, the Presbyterian people of these States, to uphold and support the Government, in every lawful measure, to maintain our rights and our honour.

"*Resolved*, 4. That we heartily approve of the appointment, by our President, of next Friday, as a day of fasting, humiliation and prayer."

By a singular clerical error, in the shifting of hands through which the minute was passed, these resolutions were engrossed upon the Records of the Synod. Exception was entered against the entry by the Assembly of 1862, in their review of the Records; and immediately under the exception, by leave of the court, an explanatory note was appended, showing how this mistake occurred. The incident is of no great importance, except as proving the care with which the Southern Church kept herself clear of all political complications. In the first place, these gentlemen, though brought together as members of the Synod, are careful to say that they organize, not as a Church court, but as private citizens, in a voluntary convention. Their action was not ecclesiastical, but purely civil in its character. In the second place, when, by accident, their proceedings were entered upon the Records of a Church judicatory, it was disallowed, and censured by the superior court, and the error was both acknowledged and explained. The memoirs of these times are destined, by and by, to a sifting examination; every action will be subjected to rigorous cross-examination, and the facts will be all the clearer by the light of contrast in which they will be made to stand.

In further illustration of the caution with which, during these troubled times, politics were excluded from religious services, we append a prayer offered by Dr. Thornwell at the opening of the South Carolina Legislature.   To those who are sometimes called to officiate in this delicate service, it may be acceptable as a model, showing a proper reserve in alluding to the public exigencies, and maintaining the attitude and spirit of real prayer, when the temptation is so strong to obtrude our advice upon the Almighty, as to the administration of His providence.   The fact that it is found amongst his manuscripts proves that it was carefully premeditated.   But though, in consequence, more measured in its language than the public prayers usually offered at this period, it is still an exemplification of the restraint which ministers at the South imposed upon themselves in the devotions of the sanctuary:

"PRAYER.

"Almighty and everlasting God, the Father, the Son, and the Holy Ghost, the Creator of the heavens and the earth, we adore Thee as the only living and true God.   Thou only art the Lord.   Thou rulest over all, doing Thy pleasure among the armies of heaven and the inhabitants of earth; and none can stay Thy hand, or say unto Thee, what doest Thou.   Thy kingdom is an everlasting kingdom, and Thy dominion endureth throughout all generations.   Thou deservest to reign ; for Thou only art wise, and good, and holy.   Thou also art merciful and gracious. Especially do we thank Thee for Thine unspeakable love in the redemption of sinners by our Lord Jesus Christ.   In His name we present ourselves before Thee now, and for His sake we humbly implore Thy favour and blessing.   We confess ourselves unworthy to receive the least of Thy mercies ; for we have sinned, and sinned grievously, against Thee. O God, enter not into judgment with us, but grant us true repentance. Give us grace to seek Thee with our whole hearts, and keep us in the way of Thy commandments.

"We adore Thee as the King of nations.   We acknowledge the supreme authority of Thy law; and we beseech Thee to be our God, and the God of our children, throughout all generations.   Especially, O God, do we supplicate the guidance of Thy wisdom in all the deliberations of of this legislative Assembly.   Vain is the help of man.   We would entrust ourselves, and the interest of our country, into Thy hands ; and we beseech Thee to impart to this Assembly the inspiration of the Holy Ghost, giving to each member a sound understanding, pure motives, and a clear perception of what is right and fit to be done.   Save us from error, from pride, from unholy passions.   Clothe us with true humility.   Teach us Thy will, and give us strength to perform it.

"O God, if consistent with Thy will, rebuke the troubled elements; speak peace to the tumults of the people; restore truth, justice, and brotherly love.   Bind the States of this Confederacy together in the ties of righteousness and peace.   But whatever may be the issue, grant peace and prosperity to this Commonwealth, and to all the States which have a common interest with us.   Unite them together in harmony and love, and give them a name and an honourable place among the nations of the earth.   Oh! grant that we may own Thee as our God, and protect us from the power of every adversary.   Into Thy hands we commend our cause ; and all we ask is Thy fatherly guidance and blessing."

CHAPTER XXXV.

HIS DEATH.

DURING the winter of 1861–'2, Dr. Thornwell, in frequent communications to the daily press, sought to animate the people to maintain the struggle in which they were embarked.   These were far from being inflammatory appeals to their prejudices and passions, but well considered, though energetic, addresses to the reason and to the conscience.   He published, also, a tract of twelve pages, which was extensively circulated in the army, and amongst the people at home.   It was entitled, "Our Danger and Our Duty."   Under the first head, he depicted with fearful distinctness the results of our defeat, both as to the South and the North; under the second, he presented the spirit which should prompt every citizen of the Commonwealth, and without which the victory could never be won.   The reader will find in the Appendix, marked No. III, this elegant brochure, replete with classical references and allusions, which are introduced, not simply for their rhetorical effect, but as enforcing the argument, or exhortation, which they elucidate. We cite a paragraph, showing the revolution which would be accomplished in the character of the government, by the triumph of the Federal arms.   The reader can judge for himself how far the prediction has been pushed forward to its fulfilment, in the events that have happened

since the close of the war. Its republication may prove
one of those notes of warning which may yet waken the
nation from its fatal apathy :

"But the consequences of success on our part will be very different
from the consequences of success on the part of the North. If *they* prevail, the whole character of the Government will be changed, and, instead
of a federal republic, the common agent of sovereign and independent
States, we shall have a central despotism, with the notion of States for
ever abolished, deriving its powers from the will, and shaping its policy
according to the wishes, of a numerical majority of the people; we shall
have, in other words, a supreme, irresponsible democracy. The will of
the North will stand for law. The Government does not now recognize
itself as an ordinance of God; and, when all the checks and balances of
the Constitution are gone, we may easily figure to ourselves the career
and the destiny of this godless monster of democratic absolutism. The
progress of regulated liberty on this continent will be arrested, anarchy
will soon succeed, and the end will be a military despotism, which preserves order by the sacrifice of the last vestige of liberty. We are fully
persuaded that the triumph of the North in the present conflict will be
as disastrous to the hopes of mankind as to our own fortunes. They are
now fighting the battle of despotism. They have put their Constitution
under their feet; they have annulled its most sacred provisions; and, in
defiance of its solemn guaranties, they are now engaged, in the halls of
Congress, in discussing and maturing bills which make Northern notions
of necessity the paramount laws of the land. The avowed end of the
present war is, to make the Government a government of force."

In urging the question of duty, he eloquently dissuades
from apathy and insensibility to the magnitude of the
issue; from the spirit of avarice and speculation, which
would fatten upon the public distress; from the spirit of
faction, which is equally selfish, and still more divisive
and distracting; from indolence and love of ease; from
fastidious notions of etiquette, especially in military circles; from presumptuous self-confidence and pride; from
despondency under reverses of fortune; and concludes
with an appeal which rung out upon the land with the
sharp tone of the clarion : " We occupy a sublime position.
The eyes of the world are upon us; we are a spectacle to
God, to angels, and to men. Can our hearts grow faint,
or our hands feeble, in a cause like this? The spirits of

our fathers call to us from their graves. The heroes of other ages and other countries are beckoning us on to glory. Let us seize the opportunity, and make to ourselves an immortal name, while we redeem a land from bondage, and a continent from ruin."

The sorrows of the war were destined to touch him in his home. This will be best introduced in the letter which follows, addressed to General Gillespie:

"COLUMBIA, *May* 8, 1862.

"MY DEAR GENERAL : I have just received a telegram from Richmond, that my dear boy was wounded at the battle of Williamsburg, on Monday. I received the dispatch late this afternoon ; his mother and myself set out in the morning to go to him. The wound was a sabre thrust. It is represented as slight, but he is to be removed to Richmond. Of course, I feel very uneasy. He is represented as having acted very bravely. That I knew he would do ; he is all pluck. His heart is in the cause ; and he is, I assure you, a noble boy. Though under age, he has enlisted for the war, with my full consent. I knew you would like to hear about him, and have seized a moment to drop you this hasty line.

"The times are dark, but the Lord reigns. I feel an abiding confidence that we shall yet win the day. Our people are beginning at last to wake up ; they are rising in the right spirit all over the land. What we have now to fear is the spirit of faction. That must be rebuked ; we must silence the fault-finders and croakers. The President is mercilessly abused by some of the papers ; and if we are not ruined, it will not be because these spirits have not tried to destroy our confidence in our leaders. We must stand by Davis through thick and thin. We are all in the same ship ; and I am sure, moreover, that he deserves our confidence. Time will prove that he was the man for the crisis. The Lord be with you all, and bless you ; my heart is full.

As ever,

J. H. THORNWELL.

Upon arriving at Richmond on this melancholy errand, Dr. and Mrs. Thornwell found their son, Gillespie, kindly sheltered in the house of the Rev. Dr. T. V. Moore. His wound was within a hair's breadth of being fatal, but not so severe as to prevent his return, on furlough, with his parents. We find Dr. Thornwell at home, in Columbia, on the 26th of May, 1862 ; at which date he thus writes to the Rev. Joseph M. Atkinson, of Raleigh, N. C.:

"My Dear Brother: It will be many a day before I forget the delightful episode which I experienced at your house, in a dreary history. I cannot tell you how much I enjoyed it. My wife and myself constantly speak of it, and I am afraid that its effect will be, that hereafter I cannot pass Raleigh without remaining for a night to *bore* the good friends at the parsonage. Walpole described gratitude ' as the expectation of future favours.' Have a care lest I seek, in your case, to realize the definition.

"I was sorry to hear that poor Law. could not be moved. It was a kind Providence that put him in such good hands; but I cannot help feeling some degree of concern, that I was the occasion of taxing your family with a good deal of care and trouble. I know that you feel it to be anything but irksome to relieve the distressed; but still, more or less anxiety will be connected with such a charge.

"My own son continues to improve. He stood the journey remarkably well, better even than I did. For I had to go to bed upon reaching home, and have not been worth a chew of tobacco since my arrival. If I had not felt so good for nothing, I would have written to you before.

"You see that the gun-boat expedition failed against Richmond. I am now quite confident that the Lord means to defend the city. McClellan has fairly confessed that Johnson has outwitted him. He was verily persuaded that Johnson's retreat from Yorktown and Williamsburg was an honest flight, and that he would soon be able to drive him to the wall. He suddenly discovers that our numbers are too great to be pressed on, and that he must fall back on his old plan of ditching and trenching. I hope a period will soon be put to his operations. The sooner the better for the Confederate cause.

"Did you ever see anything more atrocious than the general order of Butler, in relation to the ladies at New Orleans? Can the civilized world stand that? Has the North lost all moral sensibility? It really seems to me to be on the verge of judicial abandonment. Upon the battle of Richmond, and that at Corinth, great interests are suspended. It is important for us that they be speedy, and that they be decisive. We should be earnest in prayer that God would interpose for us.

"When will you be in these parts? You cannot imagine how much pleasure it would give us to see you. We have a little hog and hominy left, and we can give you greens on the same dish with the ham, *a la Virginie*. Grace be with you.

Most truly,

J. H. Thornwell."

The Seminary vacation invited to repose and to travel; for it was only by incessant patching, his feeble constitution could resist the inroads of that disease by which it was secretly undermined. In the month of June he left for Wilson's Springs, in North Carolina; and after a short stay, found his way to the home of his son-in-law, the Rev. Robert B. Anderson, in Lincoln county, of the same State. From this place his next letter is addressed:

"ELDERSLIE, *June* 26, 1862.

"MY DARLING WIFE: I sent Gillespie to Charlotte yesterday with a letter, to be mailed from there to you. His wound was not well enough to authorize him to return to service; so I directed him to go home, and when he returned, to bring you with him as far as Charlotte. I want you to have some recreation from care and anxiety. But, more than that, I want to see you very much indeed. I think about you night and day; and every time I see the little grand-son, I think how much pleasure it would give you to see his monkey motions.

"I did not go with Gillespie to Charlotte, as I was reluctant to expose myself in the sun. I have begun to improve, and I was afraid of losing all that I had gained. I rub every night with the liniment of spirits of turpentine. I have also been taking some pills of turpentine. My appetite is good, and my strength is now nearly as great as ever. But my bowels are not exactly in tone. The diarrhœa has pretty well ceased, and all symptoms of dysentery have disappeared. I am as well now as before I went to Richmond. I drink the mineral water here all the time, and think it is as good for me as Wilson's. But next week I think of going to Wilson's, and seeing how the land lies. * * * * * * I am very particular about my diet. I eat no vegetables at all, but potatoes. The only meat I use is ham or dried beef. We have no fresh meats at all, not even chickens. I have not been out any where. The sun has been so hot, that I have been afraid to expose myself in it. The wheat in this neighbourhood is a great failure. The prospect of the corn crop is very promising, but the trying time is to come. Our interests are in the hands of God. He knows what is best for us. He may sorely chastise, and afterwards bind up and heal. Oh! that we could all but put our trust only in Him! Kiss the children. Love to all. The choicest blessings of heaven upon your own head. Grant that we may soon meet again. I long to be at home with my loved ones.

"As ever, your devoted husband,

J. H. THORNWELL."

Two days later he writes thus:

"ELDERSLIE, *June* 28, 1862.

"MY DARLING WIFE: I suppose that Gillespie has reached home by this time. He wrote to me a very satisfactory letter from Charlotte. I want him to see Dr. Fair, and have his wound properly dressed. From the slowness with which it has been healing, I am afraid that the mode of treatment with the court-plaster was not the best. He must not think of returning to Richmond until he is entirely well. I will arrange the matter with the Government so as to save him from all trouble.

"I think I am improving. The climate here is so refreshing, and the water of the mineral spring so grateful, that I cannot but hope, in a few days more, to be something like myself again. I have been able to keep down diarrhœa, but it is by the use of opiates. I am now trying to leave it off, and hope soon to be able to dispense with everything. * * * * * I have tried to keep my mind free from all care; but I cannot help thinking about you and your life of labour and anxiety. I reflect upon myself, that I am here, free from the bustle of the family, and you at home, working like a slave to keep up the family. My heart and my sympathies are with you. I share your burdens, though you know it not; and I pray for you night and day, that the Lord may give you strength suited to your day. Try and be cheerful. I wish that you could so arrange matters as to come up with Gillespie on his way to Richmond. I would meet you at Charlotte. If you can come, you can bring little Charlie with you. If you cannot come, I must be thinking about getting home. I cannot consent that you should have all the trouble on your shoulders.

"I suppose the great battle at Richmond has been joined, and is now going on. God grant that the victory may be ours. But it makes one sad to think of the fearful cost at which victory must be purchased. Thousands must fall; thousands more maimed for life; and scores of families must be hung in mourning. How earnest should we be in prayer that God would temper judgment with mercy! If we fail, the consequences to us will be the most gloomy. I dread to think of them. But we must not dream of giving up the fight. We must keep the field as long as there is a man who can bear arms.

"The family here are all well. Pattie reads and amuses herself with the baby. The boy is very interesting. He cannot yet talk, but he is beginning to try. He feels the want of language, and labours hard to express himself. All send much love to you and the children. Tell Gillespie I shall write to him on Monday. The Lord be with you all, and bless you, and keep you.

"As ever, your devoted husband,

J. H. THORNWELL."

Our hand trembles under the sorrow of a great bereavement, which, though twelve years have rolled away, is as fresh and keen to-day as when it was first encountered. It pauses over the subjoined letter with a lingering reluctance to transcribe the last relic of a dear and cherished friend. Within three weeks after it was penned, he had entered into the *Rest* to which he so touchingly alludes:

"ELDERSLIE, *July* 6, 1862.

"MY DARLING WIFE: I wish you would write to me, and let me know precisely what day Gillespie will be in Charlotte. I shall try to meet him there, if I should not be at Wilson's. I have written to Dr. Miller about having me good quarters there. If I cannot get them, I shall return home pretty soon. If I can get a good room, I shall spend two weeks there, and then return. I am desperately home-sick. I want to see you all very much indeed. Nothing but a sense of duty could reconcile me to the idle, worthless life I am leading here. I do nothing but lounge, eat, drink mineral water, and sleep. My thoughts are all the time with the dear ones in Columbia, particularly with my wife. I have long known that I have the best wife in the world ; and it is a great grief to me that I cannot do more to free her from care, anxiety, and sorrow. I want to see you happy. Particularly I am anxious to have servants that you can depend on ; and that will, of themselves, take trouble off your hands. But our true rest must be sought in another world. May the Lord prepare us for it. * * * *

"I preached for Dr. Morrison yesterday. McDonald is now here. He came up to help Anderson at his communion, at Dallas. I would have gone, but it is too far ; and I am now very careful about exposing myself in the sun.

"We have not yet heard the finále of the battle at Richmond ; but we have reason to hope that the Lord has given us a complete victory. Glory to His name! Oh! that we may have grace to use it wisely! * * * The Lord bless you, dearest.

"As ever,

J. H. T."

The arrangement indicated in these letters was carried out. Gillespie Thornwell, in company with his mother, came to Charlotte about the middle of July, where he was met by his father. After spending one day together, the young soldier, with his wound as yet imperfectly healed, returned to active service in Virginia. In parting here with this gallant youth, the reader will more than pardon a digression, which tracks him through a brief career, to the hour of his death.

GILLESPIE ROBBINS THORNWELL was but sixteen years and a few months old, when the bugle was first heard in Carolina, summoning her sons to the field. He was one of the earliest to obey the signal, and was in the ranks on the coast when Fort Sumpter was reduced. As soon as troops began to be massed in Virginia, he enlisted for the war in the cavalry service, and was, at the time of his death, in the Fifth South Carolina Regiment, belonging to General Wade Hampton's legion. Born, like most

Southern boys, on horseback, he rode like a Comanche Indian. Mounted on a fine steed, with that recklessness of bravery which characterizes youth, he did not hesitate to charge against heavy odds. It was thus he received the sabre wound, of which mention has been made. Generosity is always a twin virtue with courage. We will give two illustrations of it. On his journey from the battlefield to Richmond, a kind lady had provided him a mattrass; but seeing on the train a brother soldier worse wounded than himself, he surrendered its use; and as he sat upright in his seat, displayed such power of will in the endurance of pain, as to attract the attention of others, and elicit their praise. The other instance was of a still nobler type. He was offered the lieutenancy of his company, but another was anxious to obtain it, in whose favour he declined, saying, "He is an only son, and his mother is a widow, who will be comforted by his promotion." Truly, this exhibition of a noble nature entitled him to his father's praise, that "he was a noble boy," and showed that his father's blood flowed in his veins.

Exactly one year after receiving his first wound, he encountered a second, on the 3d of May, 1863, which was fatal. The account will be best given in the words of General Hampton, in communicating the sad intelligence of his death: "His wound was received in an attack on a regiment of Yankee cavalry, in which thirty of my men, together with seventy of Major Moseby's, routed and captured the whole regiment. But whilst they were bringing off the prisoners, another regiment charged them, and succeeded in rescuing the captured Yankees." This occurred in a skirmish near Warrenton, Va., and the wound was made by a rifle ball, in the abdomen, a little above the hip. He fell, of course, into the hands of the enemy, by whom he was kindly cared for, and sent to their hospital at Alexandria. Here he arrived at eleven o'clock at night, and died at six o'clock the next morning. His body was obtained by friends in the place, deposited in a private vault, and after the close of the war, in 1866, was brought home and interred in his native soil. In his whole career he was distinguished for his courage. His commanding officer, General Hampton, in a message of sympathy to his widowed mother, bears this ample testimony: " Her son was a noble and gallant soldier; and whilst she cannot but mourn, as only a parent can mourn for a child, she can well draw consolation from the knowledge, that he has fallen whilst sustaining nobly the sacred cause for which his father plead, and to which he had dedicated himself." Thus, when but eighteen and a half years old, did this brave youth seal with his life the cause he had two years before espoused; and thus, within the space of nine months, did the father above the stars greet the son who had been the burden of his prayers. He met death, not only with firmness, but with perfect resignation and composure. Although under circumstances which cut him off from the friends to whom he might have unbosomed himself, the hospital nurse says that " he talked beautifully" to him, saying he "did not fear to die, and was perfectly willing to go, only that he could have wished to see his mother and the dear ones at home once more." They rest in the sweet assurance that, through faith in his Redeemer's blood, he was ready for the change.

But we must return to a more peaceful scene, one of surpassing solemnity, but one the sadness of which is chased away by the light of Christian triumph and joy. On the very day when father and son parted in Charlotte, Dr. Thornwell took his bed, from which he was lifted only to be borne to his burial. From the beginning of the attack, he was impressed with the conviction that it was his last. The Rev. John Douglas, a tried friend of his from early College life, came to him at the first stage. As he entered the room, he said: "You have just come in time to see me die." As we have narrated, by what seemed an accidental circumstance, his beloved wife was at his

side. To her he mentioned the pleasing fact that, at
Wilson's Springs, from which he had just come in order
to meet his son, though in some respects uncomfortable, he
had had a time of great spiritual enjoyment. He seemed
to have been taken there, away from all whom he loved,
that in solitude and prayer he might be prepared for the
coming of his Lord. For nearly two weeks he lingered,
being tenderly nursed at the house of Mr. William E.
White, of Charlotte, by loving friends, who would cheerfully have saved his life by the surrender of their own;
until, on the first day of August, 1862, he gently fell
asleep. It was only this; there was not a struggle, nor a
groan. He threw himself back upon his pillow; lifted his
right arm and hand; it quivered spasmodically for a few
seconds, and then dropped; his eye became fixed; and
with a few short breaths his spirit passed away.

The nature of his malady prevented him from speaking
much. He had been threatened all his life with consumption, which perhaps settled upon a different organ
from the lungs. A chronic dysentery had slowly undermined his strength, and the toneless system had not power
to resist the final assault. The lethargy to which this
form of disease predisposes, made him quiet for the most
part; though he was easily aroused, and always with the
full recognition of those around his bed. Being asked if
he had any word to leave to his boys, he replied: "Oh!
they are the burden of my soul; if they were only children
of God, I would ask no more." Being further pressed to
know if he had any directions to give concerning them,
he added: "The same Jesus who has watched over me,
can take care of them." On being asked again, if there
was anything he wished done, when he was gone, the
triumphant word of faith came back, "The Judge of all
the earth will do right."

He lay much with his hands folded across his breast,
with lips moving as if in prayer. Then, at other times,
there would fall upon the ear troubled and incoherent

utterances, which, when caught, would reveal his mental
habits.   Lifting his finger, as if addressing an imaginary
class, he would say, "Well, you have stated your position,
now prove it."   Again, as if musing upon some metaphysical theme, he would articulate: "The attributes—
first the moral, then the intellectual, and thirdly, the religious or spiritual;" reminding one of the good Neander,
who, in a like condition, would lift himself on his dying
couch, and say, "To-morrow, young gentlemen, we will
resume our exercitations upon the sixth chapter of John."
It is our loss that there are not more last sayings to record
of such a master; for

> "The tongues of dying men
> Enforce attention, like deep harmony:
> The setting sun, and music at the close,
> As the last taste of sweets, is sweetest last,
> Writ in remembrance more than things long past."

Yet they are not needed.   Our brother's whole life was
a continued chant; and memory will preserve its music,
returning upon us with ceaseless echoes, till we, too, sleep.
The last time but one it was the writer's privilege to hear
him in the pulpit, in one of those outbursts of emotion so
characteristic of his eloquence, he exclaimed: "I am often
very weary.   Weary with work, as the feeble body reels
beneath its accumulated toils; weary in struggling with
my own distrustful and unbelieving heart; weary with the
wickedness of men, and with the effort to put a bridle
upon human passions; and I often sigh to be at rest."
Brother, thou hast entered into rest; and we are the more
weary for loss of thee!

The Holy Spirit placed his seal upon that pallid brow.
The partition is very thin between the two worlds, when
we come to stand upon the borders of both; and the beautiful light streams through the curtain which separates
them, and throws a strange radiance upon the dying believer, the prophecy of a glorious transfiguration.   Says
Dr. Adger, who came in at the last hour, just in time to

catch the last look of recognition and love: "Delightful smiles played over his countenance, as, on a summer evening, the harmless lightning plays, with incessant flashes, upon the bosom of a cloud." The last work of the Holy Ghost was being done, in completing the saint's likeness to his Lord; and that Lord was speaking with His servant face to face, as He did with Moses out of the cloud. The last broken words, upon which the departing soul was borne into the bosom of God, were ejaculations of wonder and praise: "Wonderful! beautiful! Nothing but Space! Expanse! Expanse! Expanse!" And so he passed upward, and stood before the Throne.

> "How glorious now, with vision purified
> At the Essential Truth, entirely free
> From error, he, investigating still,
> From world to world at pleasure roves, on wing
> Of golden ray upborne; or, at the feet
> Of Heaven's most ancient sages sitting, hears
> New wonders of the wondrous works of God."

His remains were conveyed to Columbia, in a car specially set apart by the kindness of the President of the railroad. The funeral services were conducted, on a Sabbath afternoon, in the Presbyterian church where he had so long proclaimed the gospel of his Lord, in the presence of an immense multitude, who had assembled to pay the last homage to greatness and to goodness. The Rev. Dr. John B. Adger, with difficult utterance, took, as the text of his discourse, the watchword of his departed friend, "Shall not the Judge of all the earth do right?" The Rev. Dr. George Howe, his colleague in the Seminary, and the Rev. F. P. Mullally, who had been co-pastor with him in the church, assisted in the impressive service. As the long procession moved through the streets of that beautiful town, to the resting-place of the dead, the city bell tolled its solemn and plaintive notes, expressive of the public and the common grief. In the family enclosure in Elmwood cemetery, the precious dust was committed to the earth, by the side of the loved daughter, who, but three years before, was laid to rest. There, in a quiet and beautiful spot, by the banks of a soft murmuring stream, the stranger will find a solid block of pure white Italian marble, upon whose face he will read only this inscription, in bold relief,

"JAMES HENLEY THORNWELL."

CHAPTER XXXVI.

GENERAL REVIEW.

His Death Lamented.—Review of His Public Relations.—As an EDUCATOR: His Qualifications; His Methods; Mastery over His Knowledge; Command of Language; Professor of Theology; Text Books; Lectures; Examinations. — As a PHILOSOPHER and THEOLOGIAN: Extent and Accuracy of His Learning, Caution and Independence in Speculation; His Place in Philosophy; Valuable Paper on this Point; His Theology Calvinistic; Scriptural; Symmetry of His Views.—As a PREACHER: His Power in Argument and Appeal; Exposition; Logic and Emotion Combined; His Diction; Preaching on Special Occasions; Extemporaneous; Views on the Whole Subject in a Conversation; His Criticism of His own Performances.—As a PRESBYTER: Practical Wisdom; Influence in Church Courts; Reasons for it; Principles Fixed; His Caution; His Penetration; His Positiveness; His Honesty; Knowledge of Church Principles and History.—As a CHRISTIAN and a MAN: Type of His Religious Experience; Growth in Piety; Testimony to His Character; His Personal Appearance; His Social and Moral Qualities; His General Bearing; His Playfulness and Love of Badinage; Warmth of His Affections; Attachment of His Friends.

DR THORNWELL'S sun went down at noon. He lacked but four months and eight days of completing his fiftieth year. His mental faculties were in the fulness of their vigour. The stores of knowledge, accumulated through a life of severe study, were ready to be poured forth in systematic form, already auspiciously begun in a series of lectures, intended to cover the whole range of theology. His Christian character, too, had become so mellow under the discipline of grace, as to impart singular unction to his writings. They were not cold and abstract discussions of truth, but discussions animated with the life of a most fervent piety. The influence, which can only be acquired through long years of trial and of

527

trust, was his to wield without resistance or dispute. He
was at the climax of his usefulness, and could ill be
spared at a period of almost pure construction in Church
and State. Upon the circle of admiring friends, which,
indeed, embraced the country, the intelligence of his
death fell with overwhelming suddenness. The thought
of his removal had, no doubt, often recurred to those who
loved him; but they put it aside with that cold shudder-
ing which one feels when the shadow of anticipated bereavement falls upon the soul. As he lived on from year
to year, and his frail body manifested a recuperative
power that was unusual, they had come to feel that, by
constant patching and repairing, it might yet survive to
a good old age. He seemed, also, so necessary to his
times; and his work, as others had mapped it out, was
apparently so unfinished, that perhaps the presumptuous
thought was hid away in the heart, that he *must* not,
could not, die. And when he fell, they drew the mantle
over the head, and mourned with a grief which had no
words.

> "Their size of sorrow,
> Proportioned to its cause, must be as great
> As that which makes it."

The thread is broken which has conducted us from the
cradle to the grave. How it was gathered up by unseen
hands, and woven into a broader and brighter web above
the skies, it is not for us yet to know. It has been a
privilege full of sweetness to trace a life which, to us,
seems as beautiful as a dream. But the task is not finished until we place the moving form again in all the
offices and relations which he sustained, and point out
the combination of qualities which made him, like Aga-
memnon, a king amongst men.

THE TEACHER.

We present him first as an EDUCATOR, in which relation
he stood so prominently before the public. His unrivalled

excellence in this sphere depended mainly upon two
things : the perfect command over his own knowledge,
and a definite conception of the end to be accomplished.
The latter determined his method, which was the Socratic;
the former enabled him to conduct it with success. The
object of education, in his view, was the development of
the intellectual faculties, and the discipline of these to
habits of thought. His first care was to study the mind
of the pupil, to take its guage, and to note its characteristics. Thus he was guided in the process of development ; checking those faculties which were more obtrusive, stimulating such as were more dormant; and bringing them all up together in due proportion. He advocated strongly the use of a text-book; which, however,
in his hands was little more than the connecting rod between his own mind, as a charged battery, and the mind
of the pupil, to be aroused by the electric shock. His
method was that of a critical examination upon the
author's text, so shaping his interrogations as to evolve
the truth from the mind of the student itself. Recitation by rote was an impossibility ; the repetition of the
text did not meet the requisitions of the class-room. Interrogation was poured upon the student's head like a
shower of hail, until he was driven back through all the
steps of a rigorous analysis. Then he must frame a precise statement of the truth in hand ; whilst a critical logic
stood by, to cut and pare, until it stood before the eye
with the utmost sharpness of profile. Finally, the student
was put upon his defence against every form of assault to
which the champion of truth might be exposed. If the
line of defence was unskilful, the pupil found himself in
the toils of an adversary, who wound tightly about him the
meshes in which he was involved. Not till then came
the hour of extrication. But at last there would follow
lucid exposition, searching analysis, resistless logic, disen-
tangling the web, and probing every difficulty to the core.
The class-room was thus a gymnasium, where the living

mind was taught to unfold itself according to its own law
of development, and work itself out in the consciousness
of knowledge, which is yet a part of its own texture. He
is a benefactor who communicates to me one new and
grand thought; but he is twice a benefactor, who helps
me to think that thought myself. Dr. Thornwell was not
satisfied with simply communicating knowledge, to be
passively received by the pupil, as a mere impression. In
the language of another, he trained his students to "think
in the light of other men's thoughts;" to take the suggestions, and work them over in the laboratory of their
own minds, to reproduce them again with the stamp of
their own coinage, and to systematize them into form by
a logic of their own. By question and answer, he led
them down beneath the surface of words, and even of
facts, searching for the principles which lay beneath the
whole; and stimulated and aided in the work of recon-
structing these again into harmonious systems of philosophy and science. He experienced the most intense delight in witnessing these early efforts of half-fledged minds,
and was patient with their embarrassments and failures;
just as the eagle watches the eaglets when thrust out from
the eyrie, and stoops beneath them, and bears them on
her wing, as they first try their weak powers in the element in which they will at length so proudly soar.

But this method demands complete mastery of one's
knowledge. In this Dr. Thornwell could not be excelled.
The accuracy of his knowledge was even more remarkable
than its extent. His learning was indeed immense, for
his reading was discursive and large; and such was his
power of concentration, that he seemed to take up knowledge by absorption. His mind was under such control
that, when closeted with an author, the door was locked
against all intrusive thoughts, and he digested all that he
devoured. His retentive memory held every acquisition
firmly in its grasp. It was by this assimilation that his
knowledge became so peculiarly his own; it entered into

the flesh and blood and bone of his own thinking, part and parcel of his own mental substance. It could therefore be reproduced at will, fresh and flowing from a living fountain. This enabled him to present truth under any form level to the student's apprehension. It was not locked up in stereotyped plates, which must always give one unvarying impression; but his thoughts were free to be cast into a hundred different moulds, suited to a hundred different minds. Hence his great facility of explanation. If one statement of truth failed to strike, it was instantly cast aside for another more clear and incisive. He studied subjects, moreover, as subjects, and knew them as such. It was of little consequence, so far as he was concerned, what text-book he employed, whether the masterly Analogy of Bishop Butler, or the defective Philosophy of Archdeacon Paley: his own acquaintance with the entire subject could string upon either what the compass of its literature would supply. A College student, who himself stood at the head of his class, once said to the writer: "Dr. Thornwell is the only teacher for whose recitation I can never say I am fully prepared. I study Butler until I can repeat every word, and fancy that I can answer every possible question, and in three minutes I stand before him a perfect fool, and feel that I know nothing at all. He has the happiest knack of bringing out of Butler what was never there, except as he put it in." The teacher knew, the pupil did not, how deep those simple and suggestive sentences of the author actually drew. Only an equal mind could take the soundings of such a book. The constant necessity upon him, as a teacher, to reproduce his knowledge, to think his own thoughts aloud, gave him increasing command over both, and of course greater facility and precision in the statement of truth. For true it is, in the words of the poet,

"No man is the lord of anything,
   Though in and of him there be much consisting,
   Till he communicate his part to others;

Nor doth he of himself know them for aught,
Till he behold them formed in the applause
Where they 're extended; which, like an arch, reverberates
The voice again; or, like a gate of steel,
Fronting the sun, receives and renders back
His figure and his heat."

As Professor of Theology in the Divinity School at
Columbia, his methods of instruction were naturally
somewhat modified. His pupils here were at a more advanced age, and had generally passed through the preparatory drill of a College course. The object with them
was not simply mental discipline, but intellectual furniture, fitting them for a professional career. His effort,
however, was still to compel the student to master what
he acquired, and to systematize it as knowledge, by fusing
it all over again in the mould of his own thought. His
selection of a text-book was typical of the man : it was the
" Institutes" of John Calvin. Wonderful association of
names ! drawn together by an affinity so close, that, with
the men transposed, the Calvin three centuries back might
have been the Thornwell of to-day, and the Thornwell of
yesterday might equally have been the Calvin of the Reformation. The same profound learning, free from the
pedantry of display; the same logical acumen, resolving
the most intricate problems ; the same massive intellect,
striking out thoughts capable of endless exposition; the
same " honesty of reason " in the investigation of truth,
and the same passionate love, which made both wor-
shippers at her shrine; the same Herculean industry,
which sported with labour, and found refreshment in toils
by which others were exhausted; the same practical judgment, whose foresight was almost akin to prophecy; the
same simplicity of character, which preserved the freshness of youth in the maturity of age; the same fearlessness
of soul, which shrank neither from reproach nor peril in
the pursuit of right; the same guileless sincerity, which
never understood *finesse*, nor worked by indirection: all

these, and other traits, run the parallel so close between the two, that, standing three centuries apart, they seem born twins. Nay, the resemblance is preserved in things we would call accidental. The same early maturity of mind, which enabled the one, at the age of twenty-five, to dedicate his "Institutes" to the French King, and placed the other, at the same age, in the Chair of Philosophy; the possession by both of a frail body, which scarcely contained the indwelling spirit, beating against its sides with every movement of its own activity, and threatening to batter down the walls of its feeble prison; and finally, the coincidence of their death at nearly the same age, closing a long life while it was yet high noon with both: these are points of resemblance which, however casual, one is prompted to observe.

Nor is it strange that the theologian of the nineteenth century should go back to the theologian of the sixteenth, to find a master for his pupils. He who had dug the truth for himself from the quarry of the Scriptures, and from the symbols of the Church, would naturally carry his pupils up the stream of theological tradition, to the very spot where it broke out afresh from the earth. Like the fabled river of Africa, systematic theology had, for ages, buried its channel beneath the superstitions and errors of Popery; and, as at the foot of a great mountain, it emerged anew at the period of the Reformation. Precisely here the waters would be found the purest, except as he might carry them higher still, to the original fountain, and cause them to drink from the oracles of God; but as a human aid in constructing an articulate system of doctrine, he found no master equal to the great theologian of the Reformation. John Calvin stands in the same relation to Protestant theology, as Francis Bacon to modern philosophy. Each was a constructor in his own sphere, and each put the stamp of his own thought upon the science of after times. Dr. Thornwell admired Calvin for his clearness and precision, for the compactness and order of his arrangement, and, above all, for his superior wisdom in founding his opinions upon the express declarations of Scripture, rather than upon the shifting speculations of human philosophy. He always kindled with enthusiasm,·whilst dwelling upon the merits of this great thinker of the past. One of his pupils speaks thus of his introductory lecture to the Institutes, when the class was entering upon its study: "I remember well the account he gave of his visit to Calvin's grave, and of his musings upon the moulding influence of the mighty Reformer upon theological thought; and the statement of his conviction, that the emergencies of the conflict with Rationalistic infidelity were now forcing the whole Church more and more to occupy Calvin's ground. His pale face alternated with flushes of red and white, as he was speaking, and his eye dilated until it seemed almost supernaturally large and luminous. Deeply moved myself, and fired with an enthusiasm for Calvin, which I hope never to lose, I turned a moment's glance to find the class spell-bound by the burst of eloquence and feeling."

The description is appropriate just here of his course of proceeding, furnished by another pupil: "When a class was about to begin a new study, he would introduce it with a general lecture, clearing away the ground, distinctly indicating the end to be attained, and directing to all available sources of information; after which, all must go to work, under the guidance and supervision of the great master. Each student had to descend into the quarry, and select, dig out, hew, cut, carve, and polish his own stones; and then each had to lay his own foundations, and build his own edifice. Over the work of all, Dr. Thornwell presided as the chief architect, trying every man's work with the plummet and square of his own logic, approving the materials which were good and true, and condemning the faulty and imperfect. Then he would erect his own structure, rising in the symmetry of its proportions, and in the strength of its logical compactness, like a magnificent Gothic temple, full of order and beauty." After the text of the author was mastered, he gave out "a series of written questions, which were made the basis of a subsequent examination. Each recitation opened with a resumé of the last; every step was taken in the way of development, from facts and principles already settled; and thus the whole grew into the beauty, and was consolidated into the strength of a logical system." Such was his mode, whether the text-book was the Institutes of Calvin or the Confession of Faith, which was critically studied chapter by chapter, or his own lectures, elaborately prepared and carefully pronounced. In all these severe interrogations he was yet genial and winning to the last degree. Tolerant of the opinions of others, he encouraged the freest and freshest utterances of his pupils, "drawing them out, until, detecting the tangle in their thoughts, he would put in his finger and extricate the thread." Such is the language in which he is uniformly described by his students in the classroom. In private, he was singularly accessible; laying down his own studies to listen to their perplexities; disrobing himself of all magisterial authority, and addressing them as his brethren, he won them by his grace and condescension, as much as he impressed them with his wisdom and genius. No instructor was ever more highly reverenced, or more truly beloved; and that, too, exactly in proportion to the student's own ability to appreciate his merit, and to profit by his methods.

The Philosopher and Theologian.

We shall be pardoned for combining next the Philosopher and the Theologian; not only because of the natural affinity between the two, but because of their actual conjunction in the history and labours of Dr. Thornwell. In them we have the ripest fruits of his genius; and upon these two pillars the whole of his future fame must rest. As we have seen, his mind was early biased towards philosophy. It probably would have been determined in this direction by its inherent proclivity. "His passion," says another, "was for speculation. He revelled in abstract thought, and soared with delight even to the utmost verge of the knowable and thinkable in the world of mind. His spirit craved communion with the Infinite, and

> " 'Rode sublime
> Upon the seraph's wings of ecstasy,
> The secrets of the abyss to spy.' "

One was, first of all, amazed at the *extent* of his philosophical learning. His references to the Greek philosophers, both in his writings and in familiar conversation, indicated a minute acquaintance with them in their original sources; not only in the critics and historians whom he diligently consulted, but in their own productions in their own language. Particularly was this the case with Plato and Aristotle, whom, after Sir William Hamilton, he was accustomed to describe as "the opposite poles of human thought, between which speculation has continued ever since to oscillate." The best editions of their works, handsomely bound, were among the most prized treasures of his library; and the group of scholars who sometimes pored with him over the pages of the Phædo, knew not which most to admire, the exquisite finish of his translation, or his philosophic commentary upon the text. As an illustration of the accuracy of his knowledge in this department, and of the readiness with which he employed it, we mention an incident too pleasant to be omitted. At a dinner-party given him in New York, at which were present Mr. Bancroft, the historian, and other gentlemen of literary distinction, the conversation turned upon some principle maintained by Aristotle. Dr. Thornwell contended that all the commentators had misunderstood his meaning. Issue was taken on this point, and an animated discussion ensued, which resulted in his bringing the entire party over to his construction of the case. The interview was signalized by his receiving, soon after his return home, from the hands of Mr. Bancroft, a splendid copy of Aristotle, with a Latin inscription on the fly-leaf, in the handwriting of the giver, indicating it as "a testimonial of regard to the Rev. Dr. J. H. Thornwell, the most learned of the learned."

With the mediæval scholastics his familiarity was equally great. Thomas Aquinas was frequently quoted, and even the ponderous tomes of Suarez had been keenly scrutinized. Says one of his pupils, "I remember coming upon him once, when the floor of his study was covered with the volumes of Saurez, as he was following the Jesuit's subtle reasoning upon some point in morals." The modern philosophy had, of course, passed under review in its original sources. The chief masters, Bacon, Des Cartes, Locke, Leibnitz, the Scottish School at home and in France, Kant and his disciples, Fichté, Schelling, and Hegal, were his daily companions. With the department of Logic he was particularly at home. Indeed, his familiarity with its formulas tempted him, perhaps, too often to employ them, for the sake of precision, in his popular writings, and rendered them sometimes a trifle too technical for the ordinary reader. His collection of treatises on Logic certainly justified his playful allusions, in the discussion with Dr. Hodge, on the floor of the Assembly at Rochester, to the treasures which his library contained in the literature of this topic.

In confirmation of these statements, as to his thorough mastery of philosophy, in its literature as well as in its principles, we may narrate an incident. The writer happened one day to be in his study; and taking up casually a volume of Cousin, lying upon the table, read from it a passage, which opened the way to a discussion upon some point in philosophy. Dr. Thornwell had just come in from a recitation with his class, and his mind was finely strung. Commencing with the rise of philosophy in the

seven sages of Greece, he traced its history through to
the present hour; distinguishing betwixt the different
Greek schools, and showing the principle by which each
was characterized, he passed regularly on through the
middle ages. Beginning again with modern philosophy,
he took up all the schools into which it is divided, and
pointed out every shade of opinion which had been advanced in each. The discourse moved on with an equable
flow for two hours, interrupted only by the whiffs of a fra-
grant Havanna, abounding in the sharpest discrimination,
illuminated often with beautiful illustrations, sometimes
rising into eloquence, and couched, from beginning to end,
in diction the most eloquent and sustained. His solitary
hearer sat listening to this extemporaneous harangue,
wondering all the while whether, if it had been an elaborate essay prepared for a congress of savans, it could be
exceeded in the fulness of its detail, the precision and
subtlety of its distinctions, or in the beauty and force of
its delivery. It was a wonderful proof, not only of his
complete possession of the subject, but also of the extent
to which his inspiration was derived from the theme itself, and not from the occasion which might draw him
out. For, however he might be stimulated by the presence of a fit audience—and, like a true orator, no man
ever felt this influence more—he soon fell back upon the
topic of his discourse, and drew his enthusiasm thence.

The traits which specially characterized his own speculations were *modesty* and *independence*. His first effort
was to mark the boundaries of reason, within whose limits
he thought with all the vigour and self-reliance of a mind
conscious of its own powers, but beyond which he never
permitted himself to pass. He was thus protected from
that presumptuous rationalism which so much disfigures
the thinking of modern Germany; and uttered his frequent
protest against "the rampant ontologists who attempt to
unfold the grounds of universal being from the principles
of pure reason." His mind was too positive in its tone

to rest on theories, however splendid, **without** a solid
basis on which to build them.   It was not content with
beating the air with its wings, however high it might
soar; nor did he ever mistake the fantastic scenery of the
clouds for the mountain landscape of which he was in
search. Taking his departure from the English and Scotch
schools, that all our knowledge begins in experience, he
concurred with them in the doctrine of fundamental beliefs as necessary to it, and by which alone it is made
available.   He thus struck a middle course between the
doctrine which makes the mind simply a passive recipient
of impressions, and the antagonistic view, which finds in
the mind itself the data of all knowledge, "of which universal and all-comprehensive principles the reason is held
to be the complement." He was able thus to steer betwixt
the Scylla and Charybdis of philosophy; between the Atheistic Materialism of the French Encyclopædists on the one
hand, and the Pantheistic audacity of the German Rationalists on the other.   His consistent and intelligible doctrine was that, while knowledge begins in experience, yet
"experience must include conditions in the subject which
make it capable of intelligence."   "There must be," he
says, "a *constitution* of mind adapted to that specific
activity by which it believes and judges."   The mind is
therefore "subjected to laws of belief under which it
must necessarily act"—"certain primary truths involved
in its very structure." As, "undeveloped in experience,
these do not exist in the form of propositions or general
conceptions, but irresistible *tendencies* to certain manners
of belief, when the proper occasions shall be afforded."
But when "developed in experience, and generalized into
abstract statements, they are original and elementary cognitions, the foundation and criterion of all knowledge."
While, however, "the laws of belief qualify the subject to
know, they cannot give the things to be known.   These
are furnished in experience; which thus not only affords
the occasions on which our primitive cognitions are de-

veloped, but also the objects about which our faculties
are conversant." Starting from these principles, which
we have given in his own language, it is easy to see that
the same reform is carried into mental philosophy, which
long since has been achieved in the natural or physical.
The knowledge acquired is real knowledge, because it is
confined to attributes and properties level to our apprehension, capable of being gathered by observation, and of
being generalized by induction. The mind, instead of
being lost in speculations which transcend its limits, settles with confidence upon truths which it is able constantly to verify. Feeling the ground beneath his feet
at every step, Dr. Thornwell speculated safely. With
fixed principles for his guidance, he wrought within this
broad field of observation and induction, in the language
of one who has described him, with "an acuteness of
mind that was marvellous, with a quickness of apprehension and rapidity of thought never surpassed, and
with a power of analysis which, as if by the touch of the
magician, resolved the most complex objects into its
simple elements."

As a thinker he was as independent as he was cautious.
He bound himself to no school, and became the partisan
of no master. Nor was he simply an eclectic, ranging
through all schools, gathering up shreds of doctrine, and
piecing them together as a parti-coloured robe. He exercised his own judgment upon the greatest questions;
availing himself freely of other men's thoughts, but only
to stimulate and direct his own, and pushing forward
himself nearer to the ultimate goal. As expressed by a
friend, who writes of him : "The furnace heat of his own
mind subjected everything, without fear or favour, to its
own crucible." "Alas!" writes another, "that death
should have taken him away just at the productive period! The Aqua Regia had dissolved the golden treasures of speculative theology and philosophy; but the
crystals seemed to separate painfully and slowly from the

powerful reactions that kept the mass in constant agitation. The world will never know what he was by what survives from the grave!"

We append here a valuable paper, prepared, at the writer's request, by the Rev. Dr. John L. Girardeau, of Charleston, South Carolina, which indicates, with great clearness and ability, the place which Dr. Thornwell occupied in philosophy:

"You insist that I shall give you my conception of the place which Dr. Thornwell occupied in philosophy.

"1. It is not difficult to fix his *general* position. He emphatically belonged to that class of thinkers who advocate what is known as the Philosophy of Common Sense, in contradistinction from the class whom he designates as Sensationalists. As both these classes hold that the materials of knowledge are in part derived from contact with the external world through sensation, they are distinguished from each other by the affirmation or denial of the existence of certain primary intuitions, or fundamental laws of belief, implicitly contained in the constitution of the mind, which, brought into contact with the materials derived from the external world, enable us to know. These the Sensationalists denied, the other class affirm. As Dr. Thornwell steadily contended for them, he must, of course, be assigned a place among the advocates of the Philosophy of Common Sense, as discriminated from either the pure, or the moderate, Sensationalists. So far as the origin of knowledge is concerned, he was no more a disciple of Locke, moderate as he was, than of Condillac and the French Encyclopædists, who pushed the principles of Locke to an extreme which he would have disavowed. He had a profound respect for the great English philosopher, and followed him up to the point at which the principles of the Common Sense Philosophy compelled a departure from him. At that point he ceased to be a disciple, and became an antagonist.

"2. In so far as Dr. Thornwell maintained the principles of the Common Sense Philosophy, in opposition to the Sensationalists, he is in alliance with the Absolute Ontologists of Germany and France. How is he to be distinguished from them? He himself answers the question. He divides the class of Common Sense Philosophers into two schools: that of the Rationalists, who not only make the fundamental laws of belief independent of experience for existence, but also for development; and that of those philosophers who, admitting that these primary principles are independent of experience for their existence, ground their development in experience alone. This latter school he designates as the School of Experience. He definitely claimed to belong to this school. He utterly repudiates the view of the Rationalists, who evolved from these fundamental laws of belief a Philosophy of the

Absolute and Unconditioned. He maintained that these laws would lie dormant and inoperative, were they not developed by the occasions which are furnished in experience. But Kant, who, in his advocacy of the ideas of pure reason, so far made common cause with the Rationalists in their opposition to Sensationalism, utterly opposed their ontological speculations. Dr. Thornwell, however, was not a disciple of Kant in reference to the office discharged by the fundamental laws of belief. Kant was a pure subjectivist. The certainty of existence for which he contended was altogether subjective. The Scottish school, on the other hand, found in the fundamental laws of belief vouchers and guarantees for the real existence of the external world; they grounded the objective certainty of knowledge in the subjective necessity of believing. This was Dr. Thornwell's position. You are correct, therefore, in assigning him, in the main, to the Scotch School of Philosophy. He must be regarded as belonging to that section oi the great School of Experience, which was represented by the Scotch metaphysicians, especially as it was expounded and corrected by the profound analysis of Sir William Hamilton. There are several considerations which will vindicate this assignment of Dr. Thornwell's place:

"1. That he thoroughly agreed with the Scotch School, in their doctrine as to the office of the fundamental beliefs and original concepts which lie imbedded in our mental constitution, is evident from the whole analogy of his expressed opinions, and from the special approbation which he pronounces upon 'Dugald Stewart's account of the relation of our primary beliefs to human knowledge.'

" 2. He definitely accepted the doctrine of the immediacy of our perception of the external world, the enouncement of which, it is conceded, was first clearly made by Reid, and imparted to him and the philosophers who followed him their undisputed title to be considered an original and distinctive school of philosophical thought. He not only sympathized with this school in the explicit rejection of both the extremes—pure materialism and pure idealism,—but also in the abandonment of the hypothesis which had so long been held by the great majority of philosophers, that in external perception, a representative image—a vicarious mental modification—mediates between the external object and the percipient mind. He was, therefore, not even a hypothetical realist or (as that class of thinkers is sometimes termed) cosmothetic idealist. But

" 3. He was, like the great masters of the Scottish School, very clearly a natural realist. Whatever may be thought as to the question, whether Reid was one or not—and those who best knew his system decide that he was—it is certain that Sir W. Hamilton, who was a pronounced advocate of natural realism, assigned the maintenance of it to the school of Reid. And Dr. Thornwell was at one with it and Sir W. Hamilton, in holding that, in the same concrete act of consciousness, there is an affirmation alike of the real existence of the Ego, and the real existence of the external world—different, and yet inseparably related.

"4. He was thoroughly in sympathy with Hamilton in vindicating the great distinction between presentative and representative knowledge. He seems to agree with Hamilton in rejecting the doctrine of Reid, that while we are immediately percipient of the external world, we are not, in external perception, conscious of it. He held, with Hamilton, that, in cases of immediate knowledge, we are conscious of the object known, as well as of the act of knowing And so he appears to agree with the same philosopher in maintaining that, in cases of mediate knowledge, we are conscious only of the mediating image which is immediately given, and not of the distant object, or past event, which is mediately given. To these special views he was probably led by his sympathy with Hamilton, and his opposition to Reid, touching the nature of consciousness. Reid held that it is a special faculty, co-ordinate with the other particular faculties. With Hamilton, Dr. Thornwell regarded consciousness as the generic condition of the exercise of all the faculties, the fundamental form of all knowledge. In this agreement with Hamilton, he differed from Reid, Dugald Stewart, and Royer-Collard.

" 5. He was very strenuous in maintaining, with Hamilton, the doctrine that all human knowledge is phenomenal and relative. He held, with him, that substance is, in itself, unknowable; that what we know is the phenomenal manifestation—the attribute or properties of substance; but that, at the same time, knowing these, we are impelled by a necessary law of our mental constitution to affirm the existence of the substance in which they inhere, and of which they are the manifestation. It must be confessed that sometimes, in his lectures on theology, Dr. Thornwell appears to deviate from this position. He rejects the absolute incognoscibility of the Infinite, which he attributes to Hamilton. What Hamilton held was, that we cannot *conceive* the Infinite by an act of the *thinking* faculty—we cannot *cognize* it ; but we are impelled to *believe* it, by an act of immediate inference. We do not know it because we conceive it; we know it because we believe it. At times Dr. Thornwell seems to affirm the Infinite as a positive datum of thought. But when his language is sifted, he appears to hold at bottom that a fundamental belief is the guarantee of our knowledge of the Infinite. Dr. Thornwell does not deny Hamilton's faith as the *ground* of our knowledge of the Infinite; Hamilton does not deny Dr. Thornwell's immediate inference by intelligence from that primary belief that the Infinite exists. That in which they seemed most to differ was the *mode* in which this inference is necessitated. Hamilton found it in the impotence of the mind to think an absolute commencement; Thornwell, in a positive necessity of the mind to think a First Cause, self-existent and necessary. [I am disposed to think that in the last analysis their difference is more apparent than real.]

" 6. Dr. Thornwell held with the Scotch School, in their great postulate that metaphysical inquiry be limited to the facts of consciousness, and that these should be rigidly investigated according to the demands of the Inductive Philosophy. So far he was in accord with them ; he rejected utterly the methods of the transcendental Rationalists.   But given the facts of consciousness, he was prepared to evolve from them all that could be legitimately inferred.   He was therefore a moderate Ontologist, with Hamilton and Mansell; and intimated his dislike of the restrictive psychological method by which some of the earlier Scotch metaphysicians excluded the consideration of all ontological questions.   While closely adhering to the maxims of the School of Experience, he allowed himself liberty, when the fundamental laws of belief are elicited into formal cognitions, to assume them as data upon which to ground legitimate speculation in regard to our relation to the universe of God; always, however, checking the progress of speculation by the admitted principle of the phenomenality and relativity of human knowledge.

"7. With Hamilton, he rejected the distribution of the Kantians, who distinguished between the understanding and the pure reason, and make the latter the seat of transcendental ideas.   The primary truths, fundamental beliefs, for which the school to which he belonged contended, he assigned, with Hamilton, to the understanding.   Reason and the understanding they regarded as the same faculty, while they may have admitted that the terms may sometimes be employed to emphasize distinctive special operations of the same general faculty.   At the same time, with Hamilton, he admits the Kantian doctrine that space and time are native conceptions of the mind, and, as such, conditions of all thinking, as to the space and time properties of matter, and not generalization from experience.

"The point in which Dr. Thornwell seemed most seriously to differ with Hamilton, was that at which philosophy and theology sit together to investigate the question of Divine providence.   Hamilton affirmed that there is no conceivable medium between fatalism and chance; Dr. Thornwell denied.   The latter enumerates three hypotheses: 'That of the Casualist, who asserts an absolute commencement; that of the Fatalist, who asserts an infinite series of relative commencements; that of the Theist, who asserts a finite series of relative commencements, carried up in the ascending scale to a necessary Being, at once Creator and Preserver.'   He held that the extremes of casualism and fatalism are not only inconceivable, but that they are self-contradictatory, and, therefore, false.   The hypothesis of theism he conceded to be also inconceivable, but he maintained that it is not self-contradictory, and that, upon the principle of excluded middle, it must be true.

"It is obvious, from what has been adduced of his views, that Dr. Thornwell affiliated more closely with Sir William Hamilton than with any other representative philosopher.   At the same time, he was not a partisan, who felt bound to fight for Hamilton's views, as he was not altogether a debtor, who felt bound to acknowledge to his teachings his obligations for his philosophical doctrines.   There were certain great distinctions which were signalized by Hamilton, which Dr. Thornwell expressly, though modestly, claims to have thought out for himself, before he ever saw the speculations in regard to them of the illustrious Scotsman. So, in reference to conscience, he mentions that the 'Divine government' of Dr. McCosh had brought out views which he had before held, and had it in mind to publish. Perhaps, to Dr. Thornwell is due the first explicit enouncement of the great formula: the fundamental laws of rectitude, implicitly contained in the conscience, sustain to it the same relation which the fundamental laws of belief, implicitly contained in the understanding, sustain to it.

"He belonged to the same school with Hamilton. Along with him he differed, in some points, from that school; and in the exercise of the same spirit of independent thought, he differed, in other points, with the greatest of the Scottish philosophers himself: a man whom he had likened to Aristotle in depth and acuteness, to Leibnitz in amplitude of learning, and to Bacon in comprehensiveness of thought."

Dr. Thornwell's studies in philosophy were not lost upon him as a THEOLOGIAN. If he sought to ascertain the bounds of reason in the one, he was not likely to transcend them in the other. Penetrated with the conviction that God can be known only so far as He has been pleased to reveal Himself, he bowed with perfect docility before the dogmatic authority of the Scriptures. The writer has heard him say a dozen times, "I have been cogitating upon such and such a subject, and can see no flaw in my reasoning, but I am gravelled with one verse in the Bible;" and then he would add, with inexpressible simplicity, "You know, P., that if there is but one passage of Scripture against us, our speculations must go to the winds." In this were signalized at once the modesty of the philosopher and the humility of the Christian. He brought all his conclusions to this touch-stone; and wherever he found a "thus saith the Lord," he ceased to reason, and began to worship. He first sought, by careful exegesis, to ascertain the meaning of God's word; then to collate and classify, until he built up a systematic theology. As the inductive philosopher ranges through nature, collects his facts, and builds up his science, so the theologian ranges up and down the inspired record, collects its doctrines as they are strewn in magnificent profusion through the histories, poems, epistles and prophecies of the Bible; and in the same spirit of caution,

constructs his scheme of divinity. The system deduced
by our brother from this authoritative testimony was precisely that articulately set forth in the Westminster standards. It was, in his view, the only complete system which
a thorough and candid exposition could extract from the
Bible. By many, doubtless, he was regarded as extreme
in some of his theological views; a prejudice resulting,
perhaps, from the positive tone with which his convictions, like those of all earnest men, were announced, and
the fervid zeal with which they were cherished and defended. Never was a prejudice more unfounded. His
examination was too cautious, and his knowledge was too
exact, to allow extravagance in any direction. His theology was uncommonly symmetrical in its proportions.
He knew the limitations upon any single doctrine, and
the relations of all in a common system, by which they
are checked and qualified. There could be no overlapping; for every part was so sharply cut and defined,
and the articulations were so close, that, to a mind severely logical, they must all stand or fall together. We
think it doubtful if a single instance can be produced in
all his writings, or even his extemporaneous addresses,
of that extravagance in language which shocks a pious
ear, and by which the forcible-feeble so often attempt
to make the truth intense. Always earnest, indeed, he
was remarkably exact in his statements of doctrine; cautious not to go beyond the clear testimony of the written
Word, and careful never to disturb the harmony between
the truths themselves, as constituent members of one system; and relying upon the simple majesty of the truth
to carry conviction to a loyal understanding. His discussions were exhaustive, bringing all the light of philosophy
to elucidate the principles of religion, which, as to their
substance, could only be derived by direct revelation
from Jehovah Himself.

The Preacher.

We next turn to view Dr. Thornwell in THE PULPIT: the ambassador of God to sinful men. From all that has been said of his logical proclivity and scholastic training, it may be rightly inferred that his preaching was addressed predominantly, though not exclusively, to the understanding. Looking upon man as a being of intelligence, and upon the truth as the instrument of sanctification, he caused that truth to knock at the door of the understanding until she was admitted and entertained. He had a sublime faith in God's ordained method of reaching the affections through the roclamation of His Word. Eschewing all effort to work upon the superficial emotions, or to play upon natural sympathies, he addressed himself in earnest to present the whole truth of God, and to discuss its fundamental principles before men. His analytic power was fully displayed in the pulpit. The clear statement of a case is often one-half of the argument. Stripping his subject of all that was adventitious, he laid bare to the eye the single principle upon which it turned; so single and so bare, that the most untrained were compelled to see precisely what was to be elucidated. Then followed a course of argument, close, logical, clear, profound, bending forward to one conclusion, towards which the hearer was carried, with his will or against it, led captive in chains of logic that could nowhere be broken. When the truth had won its way, and the mind was brought into a state of complete submission, the argument was gathered up in its weighty and practical conclusions, and hurled upon the conscience, compelling either the confession of guilt upon the one hand, or a complete stultification of reason upon the other. These appeals to the heart were often fearful in their solemnity; all the more because based upon the previous assent of the understanding. They were not mere exhortation, but a judicial finding in the court of the hearer's own conscience. The preacher stood there as an attorney from heaven, to indict and prosecute the sinner. The pleading has been heard; the argument for his conviction has been concluded; and the sinner only hears the sentence of condemnation from its throne of judgment, echoing through all the chambers of the soul. It was upon this plan most of the discourses of this matchless preacher were formed. It mattered little whether the exposition was of law or grace; there was the same enforcement of eternal and immutable principles, and the same judicial finding of guilt and shame, whether the offence was against the one or the other. But though argumentative, he was not polemic. Indeed, the current of his thought was too rapid and vehement to pause and deal with impugners and their objections. It was like the Nile, swollen with its mountain tributaries, and bursting through the sedge which impedes its flow. He rightly judged, that to build up truth in its positive form was the better way to remove difficulties, which, in its light, soon appear as mere impertinences.

But he was not thus exclusively argumentative. He excelled in the exposition of Scripture; and had he not been the first of logicians, he might have been the first of commentators. His analytical talent had room here for all its play. It dealt little in dry, verbal criticism; but after a sufficient elucidation of the text, it seized the great truths involved, and marshalled them in their due subordination: a form of exposition particularly useful, as presenting the Scriptures in their logical connexion before the mind. His relations, too, as preacher to young men, led him into much practical discourse upon the common duties of life; with the same exhibition of final principles, which, either as determining the nature of morality, or as affording specific rules for the conduct, revealed the strong thinker and the practical moralist.

The feature most remarkable in this prince of pulpit orators, was the rare union of rigorous logic with strong emotion. He reasoned always, but never coldly. He did not present truth in what Bacon calls "the dry light of the understanding;" clear, indeed, but without the heat which warms and fructifies. Dr. Thornwell wove his argument in fire. His mind warmed with the friction of its own thoughts, and glowed with the rapidity of its own motion; and the speaker was borne along in what seemed to others a chariot of flame. One must have listened to him to form an adequate conception of what we mean. Filled with the sublimity of his theme, and feeling in the depths of his soul its transcendent importance, he could not preach the gospel of the grace of God with the coldness of a philosopher. As the flood of his discourse set in, one could perceive the ground swell from beneath, the heaving tide of passionate emotion which rolled it on. Kindling with a secret inspiration, his manner lost its slight constraint; all angularity of gesture and awkwardness of posture suddenly disappeared; the spasmodic shaking of the head entirely ceased; his slender form dilated; his deep black eye lost its drooping expression; the soul came and looked forth, lighting it up with a strange brilliancy; his frail body rocked and trembled as under a divine afflatus, as though the impatient spirit would rend its tabernacle, and fly forth to God and heaven upon the wings of his impassioned words; until his fiery eloquence, rising with the greatness of his conceptions, burst upon the hearer in some grand climax, overwhelming in its majesty, and resistless in its effect. In all this there was no declamation, no "histrionic mummery," no straining for effect, nothing approaching to rant. All was natural, the simple product of thought and feeling wonderfully combined. One saw the whirlwind, as it rose and gathered up the waters of the sea; saw it in its headlong course, and in the bursting of its power. However vehement his passion, it was justified by the thoughts which engendered it; and in all the storm of his eloquence, the genius of logic could be seen presiding over its elements, and guiding its course. The hearer had just that sense of power, which power gives when seen under a measure of restraint. The speaker's fulness was not exhausted; language only failed to convey what was left behind.

But this picture will be incomplete, if we fail to notice the magnificent diction which formed the vesture of his noble thoughts. "It is," says one, "the plumage of the royal bird that bears him upward to the sun;" and Dr. Thornwell was far from being insensible to the power of language. In his early life it had been an affectionate study; and in later years, it was his habit, before any great public effort, to tone his style by reading a few pages from some master in composition. Sometimes it was a passage from Robert Hall, sometimes from Edward Gibbon, sometimes of Edmund Burke, sometimes of glorious old Milton; but oftener yet, he drank from that old well of eloquence, Demosthenes for the Crown. His spoken style was, however, unquestionably the result of his life's study. His habits of close thinking exacted a choice of words. We think in language, however unconscious of the process. It is the only embodiment of thought, without which we cannot represent it to ourselves. Style, therefore, is not so much cut and fitted to the thought by artificial and secondary labour, as it is woven by the thought in the course of its own development. Hence the precision which uniformly characterized Dr. Thornwell's style. He was, above other men, a close thinker; a thinker, who had daily to think his thoughts aloud in the hearing of his pupils. The utmost exactness in language was required, moreover, in the studies of his department. The subtle spirit of philosophy could only be held as it was caught and imprisoned in the precise word which fitted it; and thus his whole career as a teacher was a training for himself as a master in style. In addition to all, his copious reading opened to him the entire vocabulary of his native tongue. "Reading," says Lord Bacon, "makes a full man; writing, an exact man;

and speaking, a ready man." Dr. Thornwell was all three, habitually and through a long life. He read abundantly, and in all directions; and acquired insensibly that copiousness which formed one of the attributes of his style. But it was the union of precision with fulness which distinguished his utterances. In the most rapid flow of his speech, his diction was beyond impeachment. It was always the right word for the thought, and the whole vocabulary would not have furnished a substitute; while in the amplification of his thought, his mind, like a kaleidescope, presented an endless variety of images, and the same combination never palled by repetition. To this precision and copiousness was added a certain richness of expression, a courtliness of style, which can only be explained by the majesty of the thought, that disdained to appear in the dress of a clown.

To understand Dr. Thornwell's power, these several elements must be combined :* his powerful logic, his passionate emotion, his majestic style, of which it may be said, as of Lord Brougham, that "he wielded the club of Hercules entwined with roses." This generation will never look upon his like again; a single century cannot afford to produce his equal. It may listen to much lucid exposition, much close and powerful reasoning, much tender and earnest appeal, much beautiful and varied imagery; but never from the lips of one man can it be stirred by vigour of argument fused by a seraph's glow, and pouring itself forth in strains which linger in the memory like the chant of angels. The regret has been expressed that his unwritten sermons had not been preserved through the labours of a reporter. It is well the

* Rev. Nathaniel Hewitt, D. D., of Bridgeport, Connecticut, thus speaks of him, founding his eulogium upon a sermon, published as early as 1843: "Howe, Owen, and Robert Hall, re-appear in him. The philosophical acumen of Howe, the gospel unction of Owen, and the rhetoric of Hall, unite in this discourse; and, in my humble opinion, no sermon has been produced in our country, in my day, in any pulpit, equal to it."

attempt was never made.   What invented symbols could convey that kindling eye, those trembling and varied tones, the expressive attitude, the foreshadowing and typical gesture, the whole quivering frame, which made up in him the complement of the finished orator!   The lightning's flash, the fleecy clouds embroidered on the sky, and the white crest of the ocean wave, surpass the painter's skill.   The orator must live through tradition; and to make this tradition, we have described one, of whom it may be said, as once of Ebenezer Erskine, "He that never heard him, never heard the gospel in its majesty."

On special occasions, Dr. Thornwell sometimes committed the mistake of projecting his discourse on too large a scale.   The consequent necessity of slurring over some parts, and of omitting others, gave an air of incompleteness, and diminished the effect.   His anxiety to seize these opportunities for impressing broad views of truth led him to dwell upon generic principles, which involved discussion more or less abstract; and this, with his agonistic fervour, imparted an appearance of labour, in the judgment of those who were unable to discriminate.   We remember a criticism of this sort, from an eminent lawyer, after listening to one of his Commencement sermons: "He is, no doubt, a great man; but he seems to me to labour in his thinking, as though the effort was oppressive."   We ventured the foregoing explanation; and suggested, as delicately as possible, that the labour might be in the hearer's effort to follow the course of thought, which was insensibly transferred to the speaker.   The suggestion was accepted, with a smile, as the true solution of the case.   But, doubtless, the habits of his mind tended to this error.   One of his fondest admirers writes: "My own opinion has ever been, that the great preacher's only blemish, for a popular audience, was that his somewhat long chains of reasoning, couched in phraseology somewhat too condensed and technical—though natural to him from long habit—overshot very often the weaker ones." Still it is astonishing how, even in these cases, the impassioned fervour of his address bore the audience along in sympathy with his emotions, if not with his thoughts. To us Dr. Thornwell was always greatest in his ordinary ministrations; when, under a purely spiritual influence, he would often rise with his theme, and pour forth utterances that seemed only less than inspired.

As Dr. Thornwell never appeared in the pulpit with a manuscript, nor with the smallest brief, it may be interesting to some to know by what discipline he trained himself to such consummate excellence. This will be furnished in the sketch of a conversation with one of his Seminary pupils. He writes: "It was my privilege once to have Dr. Thornwell as a travelling companion from Columbia to Charlotte, and we had a talk of some two or three hours; some points of which I jotted down that night on paper. We first talked of extemporaneous preaching. The Doctor said that, as for the effect on the audience, the manuscript bears no comparison; the very presence of the paper is a barrier between the speaker and the audience, which prevents full sympathy between the two. It would be ridiculous for a man to rise with a manuscript in the British House of Commons, or before any audience where the object was to *move*. The style ought to be earnest and natural. Figures introduced for their beauty, and not for the assistance they render, are contemptible. But whilst a man speaks thus, he ought to write, as a general rule. Some few men may be excepted. It was by writing, by re-writing, and by polishing many of the finest passages, that Sheridan, Burke, Lord Chatham, and others, made themselves. It is astonishing what labour they bestowed upon their productions. An anecdote is told of Lord Brougham, that, when passing through the country, a dinner was suddenly gotten up, at which he delivered a powerful speech. When asked how he could produce such a speech on so short a notice, he replied: 'I had it all prepared some time ago, not knowing when just such an occasion would demand it.' So it was with Mr. Calhoun, who bestowed intense study, vast labour, upon his productions.

"Dr. Thornwell did not think, with some, that a man ought to keep a blank book, which he is regularly filling with compositions. It is a species of writing not suited to improve one. It is better to elaborate the finer passages of a particular address, which will tell upon the writer with much greater effect. There is something remarkable n the facility with which one man will catch another's man's mode of thinking. If, for example, we undertake to imitate any one in his awkwardness, to mimic his tones of voice and peculiar manner, we will soon find that we are moulding our *thoughts* into a likeness with his. So, a man brought up in good society will catch the ease and bearing of a gentleman, without trying to do it. The best thing, therefore, for a speaker, is to take a few of the best authors and master them—to read, think, criticize, analyze them; and he cannot help pitching his thoughts upon an elevation with theirs. If he were the teacher of sacred rhetoric, he would first cause his pupils to master the principles of rhetoric—in Campbell, for instance; and then he would spend the time in analyzing such works as those of Milton, Shakespeare, Lord Bacon, and Robert Hall. The man who does this is obliged to rise in the pitch of his thoughts. Some men, by reading thus, and then by walking the floor, turning their sentences over and over again, eliminating, reversing the order, and polishing, can at last have them entirely accurate and finished, *according to the man's ability;* and they will be so fixed in the memory that they can be produced whenever the occasion demands. These men can get along without writing, because, when the sentence is ready for the paper, it is at the fingers' ends, and there is no necessity for writing it out. Such a man I believe myself to be. But my experience teaches me, that care must be taken not to hammer out all the life of a production, so that, when you come to speak it, you will have no animation. This can be avoided by not allowing yourself too much time to do this thinking. Take, for example, two days for a sermon, knowing that it must go up in that time; and you will concentrate your powers of thought, so as to complete the address before it is worn out. Or it may be avoided thus: Make a sermon, then lay it by for a month or two, and take it up with a few hours' study. The man who makes himself the slave of the manuscript has to spend his spare time in the manual labour of writing, and has no leisure to spend with these authors. He compares himself only with himself, and never improves.

"Dr. Thornwell said, he himself scarcely ever writes, for two reasons: first, when he has a thing ready for the paper, he is master of it. In his Lectures on Theology—written out because he may some day publish them—no corrections are made on the paper. And, secondly, because, when anything goes down on paper, it so disgusts him that he cannot endure it; on the other hand, if it be extempore, when spoken it is gone. He never goes into the pulpit without knowing *every point*. The introductory sentences and the exposition are prepared to a word; after that, he only prepares *thoroughly* the divisions, sub-divisions, illustrations, and points. The exact language is not premeditated, unless it be on a point where great accuracy is required, or in the *finer* passages of the sermon. He does not now pay *less* attention to minutiæ, because of his experience. The above was his plan from the beginning.

"As to the increased facility in making sermons gained by practice, it is only this: that, if you are a thinker, you will have materials cut and dried. Dr. Thornwell frequently does what some folks call making a sermon in an hour, or in fifteen minutes; but it is only selecting and

arranging, for present use, materials long since thought
out and laid aside. So that, when he is asked how long
it takes him to make a sermon, he replies that he has
been making every sermon which he preaches all his life.
In regard to making an *apology* for a sermon, he never
did it in his life; though he has often felt that one was
needed. Some one has said that 'an apology always
stinks;' it does savour very strongly of human pride. He
frequently feels miserable after a sermon, considering it
a failure, even when the congregation does not agree with
him in the estimate. Several years ago, he was travelling
near Yorkville; came to a sacramental meeting, and
preached a sermon, than which he never preached a
meaner in his life; got on his horse, and sneaked away,
that he might see nobody. Two years afterward, he was
passing over the same ground; came to the same place at
another sacramental meeting; when two persons came
forward to unite with the church, who traced their convictions to that 'abominable sermon,' which, he still
thought, was the poorest of his life.

"Upon the question, whether a *town* or *country charge*
was the best for study, he remarked that, if a man had
the love for study which would lead him to redeem the
time, the country church was best. But there are few
men who will study except under pressure. Rubbing
against people keeps one alive; less time is required for
pastoral visiting in town, and when a visitor calls, you can
excuse yourself; whereas, in the country, you have to sit
with him and eat your thumbs a whole day, even if bored
to death. Hence the town church is best."

However true these remarks may be, as applied to
preaching generally, the Church has reason to mourn the
loss of much that she would have prized, from the ability
which Dr. Thornwell possessed of carrying his thoughts
locked up in his own mind; and still more from that
hyper-criticism which censured, with such morbid severity, what he did write. As an illustration, we recite what

is told by one of his most distinguished pupils: "I remember calling upon him for the manuscript of a lecture
on the Evidences; which, as a summary of the argument
for Christianity, based upon man's necessities on the one
hand, and upon God's personality and character, suggested by the analogue of human parentage, on the other,
surpassed all that I have ever met with outside of Butler.
It was a masterly discussion of the anti-supernatural position of the Oxford Essays, upon the model of 'Pascal's
Thoughts,' as he told us. When I asked for the manuscript,
he playfully replied: 'Why, B., I am astonished at you;
you really do not wish to have any more of that stuff! I
put it into the grate as soon as I got home, and was
ashamed to have kept the class listening for an hour and
a half to it.' In the perfect freedom which his gentleness
inspired, I responded earnestly: 'Then, Dr. Thornwell,
you have done very wrong; for you will die one of these
days, and deprive us of help which we know by experience
does us great service.' I then glanced uneasily at his
face, fearing that perhaps I had spoken too pertly. But
the quizzical smile had faded away, the spirit of banter
had given place to serious reflection. He remained silent;
and I have since thought that the impulsive words of a
mere stripling had revealed, for a moment, more clearly
than usual, the most developed weakness of his mind."
To the same morbid sensitiveness we owe the loss of
several of his written discourses, destroyed by his own
hand. One, for example, upon the Flood, and another
upon the Final Judgment, executed with such fearful
power of description, that they were never delivered
without moving the audience to the depths of the soul.

THE PRESBYTER.

We transfer Dr. Thornwell next to the CHURCH COURTS,
and view him as the ECCLESIASTICAL STATESMAN. It may
seem paradoxical to present this man of the closet as the
wisest of practical counsellors. Yet the combination is

not unexampled. Paul, the writer and logician among
the apostles, was, above them all, the man of action. He
had upon him the care of all the churches, and was not
inferior to the practical James in executive direction.
Calvin, the great theologian and expositor of the Reformation, bore upon his shoulders the whole weight of the
Genevan State. So solid was his judgment, that all portions of the Reformed Church turned to him for advice;
and the burden of his correspondence alone would have
overwhelmed any ordinary man. Thus it was with him
to whose memory these pages are consecrated. In every
sphere in which he moved, whether as Professor in the
College Faculty, or as Trustee in its Board of Administration, or in the broader area of an ecclesiastical council, he
was remarked for his practical good sense, and became a
leader among equals.

One secret of this is found in the fact, that his principles of action were all settled. They were not left to be
gathered up in the hurry of an emergency, amid the dust
and strife of debate. They were antecedently determined,
and no temptation could induce him to swerve from their
maintenance. No man was ever less under the guidance
of mere expediency than he, whether the question related
to the private intercourse of man with man, or ranged
upon a higher scale in matters of public policy. None
saw more clearly that so shifting a rule as that of expediency could never prescribe an even or consistent course.
He fixed therefore for himself, finally and for ever, the
great principles of private and public morality, and these
were his guides through every labyrinth of doubt. In
this is found the capital distinction between the statesman and the politician: the one starts out with catholic
and fundamental principles, which determine his entire
course; the other floats upon the current of events, is
borne off into every eddy, and reflects little else but
the changefulness of popular opinion. The former may
sometimes err in the application of his canons to partic-

ular cases; but he has the means of correcting his own aberrations, and will preserve a manly consistency through all the changes of a public career.

Another element of Dr. Thornwell's influence in council lay in the caution with which all his particular judgments were formed; waiting for a full rendering of all the facts, and suspending his opinion until the case had been considered on every side. Even in the intimacy of private life, this cautiousness was preserved. An innate sense of justice, and rare integrity of heart, served to check a premature expression. Thus, he was seldom obliged to retract his judgments. He was kept both from the weakness of vacillation, and from the criminal obstinacy of adhering to opinions which ought to be yielded. Public confidence was challenged by this prudence, which had its spring alike in the dictates of wisdom and propriety. He found an advantage, too, in the rapidity of his mental operations, sweeping him on to his conclusions in advance of others. His wonderful power of analysis resolved complexities in which others were entangled; and whilst they were searching for the clue by which to extricate themselves, he had already seized the ultimate principle which unravelled all difficulties, and settled every doubt. Nor should we omit, in this enumeration, a certain positiveness of mind, which lifted him above the danger of indecision, and, by a sort of internal necessity, compelled a judgment upon every issue. It is the infirmity of some minds to be always trembling upon the balance, incapable of deciding whether to descend upon this side or upon that, of every question. These are the unfortunate incapables who swell the list of *non-liquets* on the records of our Church courts; or who, in their desperation, leap blindly upon a vote, as a man leaps from a railway train, not knowing whether he will land upon a bed of sand, or upon a brake of thorns. On the contrary, every deliberative body reveals examples of men who, by their greater positiveness of mind

and character, lead those superior to them in ability and
general attainments: men in whom strength of will
stands in the stead of intellectual power. In a body of
counsellors, the ready always lead the unready. From
this imbecility Dr. Thornwell was perfectly free. In
every situation he could but think; if difficulties embarrassed the case, he thought with the more intensity; but
he always thought to a conclusion. If he was cautious
in framing his judgment, his convictions were nevertheless matured; and so he always led.

A notable illustration of this penetrative quality of
mind, and of the command it gave him at times over a
deliberative body, is mentioned by one who sat with him
in the Assembly of 1856. A judicial case came up,
wrapped in technicalities. The Assembly got into a
perfect tangle over it. No ten members agreed in any
one view. Motions, amendments, and substitutes were
piled upon each other in beautiful disorder. The rulings
of the chair were objected to and appealed from, and
chaos reigned supreme. After consuming three daily
sessions, the house must dispose of it. "What is the
question?" was asked by a dozen voices. It was stated
by the Chair. Then a dozen voices inquired as to the
effect of this motion, and of that. All was at sea again.
Through the whole of this, Dr. Thornwell sat half-hidden
under the gallery of the church, with his feet drawn up
on the seat, apparently unconcerned and unconscious of
the hubbrb around him. At length, in the moment of
extremity, he stepped forth into the aisle, and in ten minutes went through the case, unravelling the whole tangle;
and concluded by offering an amendment covering his
views, which was instantly accepted, and unanimously
carried. The vexed question was disposed of to the satisfaction of the house, and there was a great calm. It
was but one of many instances of the clearness of his logical processes applied to practical life.

But the moral quality which more than all contributed

to his vast influence, was the transparent honesty of his heart. He was no intriguer; had no by-ends to accomplish; never worked by indirection. His heart was in his hand, and every man could read it. When he rose in debate, his very tone seemed to say, "I believed, therefore I have spoken." None doubted his sincerity, or suspected a trap to catch the unwary. Straightforward himself, he dealt honestly with his colleagues; and if he could not cary his point by fair argument, he was content to fail. Winning confidence thus by his manly and truthful bearing, his reasoning met with little resistance, either of resentment or prejudice, and seldom succumbed under defeat.

For all the duties of a churchman, Dr. Thornwell was perfectly equipped. He had sifted the controversies which, through eighteen centuries, have been waged, touching the organization of the Church, and understood the principles which are fundamental to her existence. He had studied with care the constitution of his own Church, from those great truths which underlie her whole polity, down to the rules of order for her internal management; and no man ever surpassed him as an expounder of her laws. Believing firmly in the *jus divinum* of Presbyterianism, he was yet no bigot—in no sense of the word a sectary. The last sermon he was permitted to preach was delivered in a Methodist church; and the last prayer-meeting in which he took a part, was a united prayer-meeting on behalf of the country. He was also versed in those Parliamentary rules by which deliberative assemblies are usually governed; and was thus fitted, on every hand, to be a guide in ecclesiastical councils. Over the entire Church he wielded the influence, though not clothed with the authority, of an acknowledged primate. The Church signalized her appreciation of his abilities, not only by conferring upon him her highest honour,—that of presiding over her supreme court,—but still more by calling him to the most responsible and difficult duties in all her Assemblies. Before the rupture of our ecclesiastical bonds, the delicate task of revising her Code of Discipline was placed chiefly in his hands. And in his death, the Church was called, not only to mourn the loss of her greatest theologian and preacher, but the removal from her councils of her wisest statesman.

The Christian and the Man.

Our survey will be complete when we shall have viewed him as a Christian and a Man. As to the former, it will suffice to say, that the type of his theology was the type of his experience. He was not the man to divorce the understanding from the heart. He concurred with the Reformers in their definition of true faith, which, as Calvin says, "is not formed by the addition of pious affection as an accessory to assent, but the assent itself consists in pious affection." Those, therefore, misconceived him, who construed his religion as one of stern principle, separate from the affections. His life illustrated the union of both, in "the faith which worketh by love." The same strong views which the theologian held upon the nature of sin, bowed the Christian in penitential grief before the Redeemer's cross; the same clear exposition given by the one of man's helplessness and ruin. cast the other upon the infinite power and riches of Divine grace; the same discovery of the sufficiency of the atonement, that made this the centre from which the preacher's discourses all radiate, led the believer to throw the arms of his affection around the Saviour with rapturous delight; the same conviction of the necessity of a Divine revelation, which led the apologist to defend its inspiration, bowed also his reason into the docility of a child before its teachings; the same recognition of God's rightful supremacy, which, in the class-room, placed the crown of dominion upon "the King of kings," sustained the afflicted saint in the hour of bereavement, and filled him with awe as he passed beneath the rod; the same intelligence which owned the majesty of the divine law, brought the will into subjection to its commands; the same view of the resistless operations of the Holy Spirit, invoked His aid in the work of personal sanctification; and the same sense of the nature and functions of the Church of God, engaged him with his whole heart in her sublime efforts to evangelize the world. In short, an exquisite harmony obtained between his secret exercises and his public utterances. There was no conflict between his preaching and his prayers. It was not one man in the class-room with his pupils, and another man in the closet with his God; but a beautiful consistency ran through his character, both as a teacher and a Christian.

We only state the great law of the Christian life, when we speak of growth: first the blade, and then the full corn in the ear. Dr. Thornwell ripened in holiness to the hour of his translation. His humility became more profound, his faith more abiding, his love more glowing, his will chastened into deeper submission. He did not escape the discipline of sorrow, by which the Lord refines His people. The cup of bereavement, with its bitterest ingredients, was once and again put to his lips. A delightful softness was diffused over his Christian character. The sharper and sterner features were worn down into more perfect symmetry and grace. He became more gentle in his censures, more catholic in his love. His views of the Divine holiness, and of the Redeemer's glory, were always grand; they now became more adoring. He rose above the speculations of reason, into the region of pure and spiritual worship. But we suspend here our own description, and give place to a touching tribute to his memory, from one who had the privilege of being associated with him, first as a student, and then for a short time as a co-pastor, the Rev. Francis P. Mullally. He writes:

"My first impression of Dr. Thornwell was not pleasant. Even in the pulpit, his voice, gesticulation, and whole bearing, were at first repulsive to me. But as I learned to follow his glowing logic, and to appreciate his mighty thoughts, I came so to admire him, in every respect, that, when I began to preach, I found it hard to guard against an unconscious imitation of his manner.

"Although no other man ever so impressed me with the sense of his greatness, yet I never felt cowed or depressed by his presence. On the contrary, his instruction, and preaching, and conversation, were wont to inspire me with a courage, and energy, and vigour not my own. This is the more remarkable, because the effect of the great superiority of other men has ever been the opposite in my case. But even when preaching before him, so sure was I of his sympathy, that his eye conveyed strength into my soul.

"Dr. Thornwell's influence over me exceeds what I would have believed to be possible on the part of any merely human being, had I not actually come under it. I have never made a mental effort since I entered the ministry, without being consciously indebted to him; never analyzed a chapter, without recalling his instruction; never made an important judgment, without applying some principle taught by him. He seems to live as vividly, distinctly, and potently, in my soul, at every moment, as if we had parted but an hour before. My memory's photograph of the home of my childhood is not more minute in detail than are its pictures of the scenes and events of my life connected with Dr. Thornwell.

"As a philosopher, he was greater in conversation than on paper. I believe it was impossible to surprise him on any subject of thought connected with man's political, social, and spiritual interests. Within this wide domain, he seemed not only to have read, but digested and sifted, everything ever written, from the origin of literature to his own day. Yet, though indebted to all philosophers, he followed none. His intuitive convictions, moral and logical, were strong. He made speculative opinion a matter of conscience. He was pre-eminently single-minded. He loved the truth, as no miser ever loved gold—loved it for its own sake. Hence the result of his reading was not a mere acquaintance with what men had thought and said, but increased power in his own conscience, and in all the faculties of his soul; also the formation of opinions for himself, the completion of distinct and settled judgments by his own mind, in view of all that had been said on the particular subject. His utterances often indicated the range of his reading, but not by any slavish adoption of other men's thoughts. His use of books, whether he expressly quoted from them or not, showed that, while he read in the spirit of humble inquiry, he read also as a master of the art of thinking, and as an expert in the exchequer of truth. But the spring of his greatness as a philosopher was the strength of the intuitive convictions of his soul. To this, more than to genius or study, he owed his power as a teacher of philosophy and religion. My knowledge of him would suffice to convince me that a true heart is necessary to the development and growth of mental greatness.

"Among the things by which Dr. Thornwell was distinguished, to me, his respect for his fellow men was not the least remarkable. He honoured all men; respected man as man; reverenced mind, in whatever form or stage of progress it appeared. I never knew him to interrupt a student while endeavouring, or even pretending, to answer a question. The response might be no matter how far from the point, or blundering; might evidently invite interruption as a means of escape from painful exposure; yet would it have his unrippled attention till it came to a close. Once, in giving an analysis of Calvin's chapters on the Mediatorial Person, I made a mistake in a point at the very outset. Another would have stopped me right there; but he, giving no indication of my mishap, heard me through, with a charming expression of interest in his face; and then, kindly showing his gratification at my success, took me back to the one misapprehended point. This way of dealing with young men was of manifold benefit in its effects. It encouraged independent thinking, gave opportunity for the play of generous emulation and love of praise, rebuked pretense, and exposed idleness.

"In our co-pastorate he manifested the same trait very fully. He always made me feel that he gave any views presented by me as much attention as if they had been urged in person by the most distinguished and experienced Presbyter in the land. Probably the best exemplification of this was his yielding to me, in reference to a form for the admission of converts into the Church which he had prepared, to the extent of erasing more than half the questions it originally contained. What made this the more remarkable was, that he had undertaken to defend the propriety of asking such questions, and that he gave way after we had debated the matter. Though he had the strength of a giant, he did not use it as a giant.

"Dr. Thornwell did not despise the verdict of public opinion. He felt that the decisions of the human mind, formed apart from selfishness and prejudice, were apt to be in accordance with the views of God. He even held that, generally, the students were the best judges of the ability of the professor, and the congregation of the qualifications of the preacher. Hence he was far from being indifferent to the judgment upon himself. On the contrary, he desired to know what impression he had made, and derived pleasure from the approbation and gratitude of his hearers. Indeed, he was too humble to disregard what others said of him. On the other hand, no man yielded less to the fear of opinions growing out of enmity to God, love of sin, prejudice, or self-seeking. If he ever manifested any harshness, it was when brought in contact with states of mind thus originated.

"Probably the controlling element of his religious character was reverence for God. It was under the influence of this sentiment that he uttered the most thrilling denunciations of sin; that the cross inspired his noblest strains of eloquence; that his soul was wrapt in wonder at the love, humiliation, and condescension of the Trinity, in the purpose, execution, and application of redemption ; and it was this that gave the promises of the gospel their highest preciousness to his heart. He was emphatically a worshipper; not an admirer merely, but a worshipper of God in the fullest sense of the word. To him happiness lay in communion with God, and in working for God. Of the two great departments of human work, the receptive and the distributive, it is hard to say in which he took the most delight, or was the most successful. He received eagerly, that he might give largely; and in giving, he seemed to open inestimable treasures of truth in the fathomless depths of his soul. Unwearied as he was in investigating, faithful and judicious in appropriating, original and vigorous in creating, he was as disinterested and cordial in distributing the results of his individual efforts, made precious by the impress of his own nature, and by being set off with gems taken from the abyss of his own mighty mind. Dr. Thornwell was great as a receiver, great as a giver, and great in his profound humility before God.

"The only discovery he made in the pulpit of his wonderful attainments in metaphysics and logic, was by the superior force and clearness with which he expounded the Scriptures, and presented gospel truth. His subjects, and his treatment of them, were always evangelical and Pauline. No man ever more fully placed the cross between himself and the audience than he. In my intercourse with him, as a student and a co-pastor, his treatment of me was always that of a most affectionate father, with one exception: this was a continued protest against my consideration of his greatness, in the division of labour and responsibility. Only by a stubborn refusal on my part to have it otherwise, was he compelled to occupy the pulpit every Sabbath morning. It was a sad, sad day to me, when, with words of kind commendation, he left me alone in charge of a church which had been most highly privileged. Scarcely could I feel the burden of grief to be heavier in the day I heard that Dr. Thornwell was dead."

In personal appearance, Dr. Thornwell was of medium stature, of spare habit, with a forehead well developed, but not ample; the features of his face small, and with a carriage of the body rather marked by negligence than grace. His presence could not be described as commanding; yet he would have been singled out from a convention of men, even by a careless observer. His soft black hair, falling smoothly over his brow; his redeeming eye, deep-set and black, and capable of the utmost intensity of expression; and a certain air of abstraction upon his countenance; all denoted a man who was to be separated from others. When in repose, there

was a drooping of the eye-lids that lent a dreamy aspect
to his face; but even then the eye would peer forth from
the overhanging eaves with a witchery that strangely
fascinated. But when in full mental action, rising to a
climax in his discourse, his lithe form expanded and
quivered, the eye sparkled with a gleam such as the soul
alone can give, which riveted the gaze, until, through its
liquid depths, you seemed to go down into the cavern of
his spirit, from which the unearthly fire came that lit it
up as an orb before you. In manner, he was quiet and
unassuming, with none of that artificial dignity which
needs a page behind it to hold up its trail, but artless
and free as childhood itself in his intercourse with men.

The retirement of scholastic life, and the boundless resources he had within himself, withdrew him, in large
measure, from general intercourse with society. His
official relations sometimes forced him from this seclusion, and his valuable counsels were sought by many;
yet he did not ordinarily put himself forth to seek communion with the bustling world around him. Though
by no means an ascetic, and with warm sympathies, taking hold upon life on every side, he was singularly unobtrusive, and waited for the occasion which should draw
him out. Whoever desired, might freely approach him,
sure of never being repelled from his presence. To
strangers he was always reserved, unless known to him
by reputation, or endorsed by the commendation of mutual friends. This, however, was only to allow the
opportunity of taking their measure, and ascertaining
whether they would be congenial or otherwise. If the
impression was favourable, the coldness of mere politeness kindled into the warmth of friendship, and his heart
went out with his hand. He was never influenced by the
artificial distinctions of society. A man was a man to
him, whatever his station in life might be. He looked
beneath the stamp of the guinea, to the metal of which
it was made. Modesty, humility, sincerity, were quali-

ties that always attracted, whilst pretension and self-conceit instantly repelled. He enjoyed the encomiums of his friends, in whose sincerity he confided; but the slightest approach to flattery or sycophancy filled him with disgust. He was, therefore, tolerant of other men's opinions. His own independence of thought, and sincere love of truth, caused him to respect the rights of others in this regard; and though exceedingly pronounced in the statement of his own convictions, no man was freer from dogmatism, in the offensive sense of that term. Of course, one so intense as he could not be wholly independent of his prejudices; and some allowance had to be made, on this account, as to his judgments of men. Upon abstract questions of truth and duty, he could be safely relied on; but he was so far swayed by his affections, that he was prone to overestimate those whom he loved; and perhaps, in a corresponding degree, to depreciate those whom he did not fancy. But he was incapable of any intentional injustice, even in his thought.

In general society, for which he had a confessed aversion, he was thoughtful and silent, rather than communicative. But in the circle of his friends, and in the bosom of his family, he revealed his whole nature. Endowed with rare conversational powers, he emptied his stores of learning, and discussed his favourite topics in philosophy; or dived into the mysteries of religion, and uttered the experiences of his own heart; or else, descending from these graver themes, he sported in banter and jest, abounded in repartee, and diffused the glow of his genial humour. Full of anecdote, and fond of badinage, his lighter conversation sparkled with wit, pushed, sometimes, to excess, unless it were recognized as the recreation of a mind that needed to unbend itself, and which found refreshment only in the easier play of its own powers. He was an inveterate tease, but only of those whom he loved. It was with him an unfailing mark of confiding friendship. Those whom he disliked, he treated with distant politeness, but those honoured with his esteem were bound to enter the lists with him in many a fencing match. Sometimes he was not understood; sometimes the jest was carried too far. But if feelings were ever wounded, the amende honourable was always so cordial as to restore good fellowship at once. A little incident will serve to illustrate both traits. Having referred in a lecture to "Kant's Critique of Pure Reason," a member of the class immediately purchased a translation of the book. After puzzling over it for a night, and finding that it spake nothing to him, he sold it at a discount to another student; and thus it passed in quick succession to several owners, finally at less than half the cost. Dr. Thornwell enjoyed the story hugely. Meeting the first purchaser he accosted him: "Well, Brother ———, it took me weeks of hard study to master Kant, but I understand you got through with him in a single night." Stumbling then upon the last purchaser, he exclaimed, "Well, Brother ———, I suppose the next thing we shall hear of Kant, will be that you have sold him to old man Jack," (the bell-ringer.) This was a little too hard. He did not pause to think that the raillery had now put on the biting edge of satire. But as soon as informed of the pain he had inflicted, he went instantly and plucked out the sting by the assurance that it was only meant as a piece of good-humoured pleasantry.

Dr. Thornwell's affections were warm and endearing. Lifted by his own greatness above the temptation to jealousy, he rejoiced in the promotion of others. Generous in all his instincts, there was no sacrifice he would not make for his friends. Indulgent to his own household, he sought to make life's path less rugged to their feet by smoothing over every disappointment, not permitting them to be corroded by the anxieties of earth. Cherishing in his own soul the utmost loyalty to truth, and certain of her ultimate triumph, he was not soured when thwarted in his plans. In this way, the dew of his youth

was never exhaled. He remained elastic and fresh to
the last, no generous sentiment or instinct of his nature
being withered by age. , With such attributes, he had
the power of all truly great men, of magnetizing those
brought under his influence; and it must have been a
very strong, or a very feeble nature, that did not yield to
his attraction.   He bound his friends to him by cords of
love, which death itself has been unequal to break.

> "He was one,
> The truest mannered : such a holy witch,
> That he enchants societies unto him;
> Half all men's hearts were his."

Such was the man whom the Church of God has not
yet ceased to mourn; such a man as Mr. Carlyle describes, " a great thinker, who taught other men *his* way
of thought, and spread the shadow of his own likeness
over sections of the world's history."   One so brave, so
generous, so true, that admiration for his genius was lost
in affection for the man.   Alas! that death should have
power to crush out such a life!   Should an epitaph be
needed for his tomb, it might be inscribed in the lines
of Æschylus:

> Οὐ γὰρ δοκεῖν ἄριστος, ἀλλ 'εἶναι θέλει.
> Βαθεῖαν ἄλοκα διὰ φρενὸς καρπούμενος,
> Ἐξ ἧς τα κεδνὰ βλαστάνει βουλεύματα.

APPENDIX.

APPENDIX.

No. I.

CRITICAL NOTICE.

EVILS OF DISUNION: A Discourse, delivered on Thanksgiving Day, December 12, 1850. By ROBERT DAVIDSON, D. D., Pastor of the First Presbyterian Church, New Brunswick, N. J. J. Terhune & Son; 1850; pp. 15.

THE AMERICAN UNION: A Discourse, delivered on Thursday, December 12, 1850, the Day of the Annual Thanksgiving in Pennsylvania; and repeated on Sunday, December 15, in the Tenth Presbyterian Church, Philadelphia. By HENRY A. BOARDMAN, D. D. Third thousand. Philadelphia: Lippincott, Grambo & Co., successors to Grigg, Elliott & Co.; 1851; pp. 56.

THE AMERICAN CITIZEN: A Discourse on the Nature and Extent of our Religious Subjection to the Government under which we live; including an Inquiry into the Scriptural Authority of that Provision of the Constitution of the United States which requires the Surrender of Fugitive Slaves. Delivered in the Rutgers Street Presbyterian Church, in the city of New York, on Thanksgiving Day, December 12, 1850; and afterwards, at their request, as a Lecture before the Young Men's Associations of Albany and Waterford, N. Y., on January 14 and 15, 1851. By JOHN M. KREBS, D. D. New York: Charles Scribner, 145 Nassau Street, and 36 Park Row; 1851; pp. 40.

"THE HIGHER LAW," IN ITS APPLICATION TO THE FUGITIVE SLAVE BILL: A Sermon on the Duties Men owe to God and to Governments. Delivered at the Central Presbyterian Church, on Thanksgiving Day. By JOHN C. LORD, D. D., (Pastor of said Church,) author of Lectures on Government and Civilization. Buffalo: George H. Derby & Co.; 1851; pp. 32.

A SERMON ON THE DUTY OF CITIZENS, WITH RESPECT TO THE FUGITIVE SLAVE LAW. By G. F. KITTELL, of the Methodist Episcopal Society, Poughkeepsie. White Plains, N. Y.: Eastern State Journal print; 1851; pp. 20.

IT is not our design to criticise the sermons enumerated above. They are all able, bold, and manly; and though some of them contain sentiments to which we cannot subscribe, yet the general spirit of all of them meets our most cordial approbation. We sympathize with our brethren at the North in their laudable and Christian efforts to arrest an agitation which aims alike at the destruction of the Government and the subversion of religion. At the present crisis, a perilous responsibility rests upon the non-slaveholding States of this Union. It is for them to say whether the conditions of our Federal compact shall be faithfully observed, and the Union preserved in its integrity, or whether the Southern States shall be driven, in vindication of their rights, their honour, and their safety, to organize a distinct Government for themselves. We believe it to be in the power of the North to save the country. The South demands nothing but justice. She simply insists that the Federal Government shall not take sides on the question of slavery. It must not attempt either to repress or to spread it. The Constitution is a solemn compact between the States, and the powers delegated in it to the general Government cannot, without the grossest ill faith, be prostituted to the injury or destruction of the peculiar institutions of any of the parties. The Constitution knows no difference betwixt slaveholding and non-slaveholding States; and neither Congress nor the Executive possesses a shadow of right to take any steps that shall have the effect of determining whether new territories, the common property of all the States, shall or shall not exclude slavery, when they are prepared to be admitted into the Union. What their relation to this subject shall be, is a question that must be left to the providence of God. The soil should be kept open to any emigrants from any section of the Confederacy. The constitutional provisions in reference to the admission of new States should be carefully observed; and when they are complied with, it must be left to the people of the territories to frame their constitution for themselves. If these principles had been adhered to in the past legislation of Congress, there would have been no agitation now in the Southern States of the Union. What they complain of is, that the influence of the Government is turned against them; that, instead of preserving the absolute neutrality which it is bound in good faith to maintain, it takes sides with one section of the Union to the injury of the other, and perverts its trust to cripple and circumscribe the institution of slavery. The North pleads its conscientious convictions that slavery is wrong, and ought to be curtailed and abolished. Free-soilism falls back upon conscience, and protests that it cannot, without sinning against God, leave it an open question, whether this prodigious evil shall be extended or not. We cheerfully concede that there is a higher law than the law of man, and that, when human legislation contravenes the authority of God, it should not be permitted to bind the conscience. If slavery is necessarily a sin, no statutes or ordinances of earth can make it right, and no human enactments can make it obligatory to sanction or sustain it. But then it would be the duty of the Northern States, entertaining this opinion, to dissolve the Union themselves. They are criminal in remaining parties to a contract which, in their judgment, is a snare to their consciences. If they cannot, consistently with their convictions of duty, maintain the neutrality which the Federal Constitution requires; if they cannot, in other words, observe the conditions which they have voluntarily agreed to observe; they ought, in all frankness and candour, to withdraw from the contract, and openly proclaim that it is at an end with them. They are certainly entitled to their opinions upon this or any other subject. But they are not at liberty to make a treaty which they believe to be sinful, and to enjoy its advantages without complying with the stipulated terms. We are glad that a movement has been made at the North to exhibit, in its true light, the relation of the general Government to slavery. Fanaticism may be relentless, but the body of the people, we trust, will be brought to see and feel that good faith requires them, either to withdraw from the Union themselves, or to observe the provisions of the Constitution. Sober reflection must convince them that, whether slavery be right or wrong, they are not responsible for its diffusion through the territories. These territories accrue to us under the Union and the Constitution. The North possesses no power over them as the North, as non-slaveholding States, but only as members of the Confederacy; and if the terms of the Confederacy are such as to deny to them the power of interfering with this subject, their consciences should not be pressed for not doing what they have no right to do. They must also see that there is really no guilt in making a contract, which, at the utmost, only leaves them stripped of a power, of which it found them destitute. If they had *surrendered* the right to exclude slavery from these regions, their minds might be troubled. But they never had it; and the Constitution simply leaves them as they were. The North, therefore, should not feel itself burdened in the slightest degree with the guilt of this sin. Much less should it undertake to wield an influence which it has acquired under, and by virtue of, the Constitution to subvert the purposes of the Constitution itself. We would affectionately urge, therefore, upon our Northern brethren, the necessity and duty of allaying this agitation. If they love the Union, let them cherish the Constitution of our fathers. They deplore the dangers which threaten it; let them see to it, that, so far as they are concerned, these dangers are averted. Let the abolitionists and free-soilers be rebuked, and peace and harmony will be restored to the country.

For ourselves, we confess that we cannot calmly contemplate the probability of such an event as the dissolution of this great confederacy. That it can be broken up without strong convulsions, without dangers and disasters on all sides, we do not believe to be possible. The contentions of brothers are like the bars of a castle: when once the elements begin to dissolve, no human calculation can determine where the process shall stop. There is no natural reason why there should be only two confederations, a Northern and Southern, any more than three or a dozen. Let the South draw off; why not the West, also? Why not the States in the valley of the Mississippi form a separate confederacy, and California still another ? It may be easy in our closets to speculate upon the policy which the interests involved would dictate; but when masses are set in motion, and innovations are begun, all experience shows that passion, not reason, rules the day. The destruction of a settled order, of old and tried institutions, is like the upheaving of an earthquake. The forces at work are tremendous; but no one can predict their course or results until their fury has subsided. We have always associated the idea of a high and glorious vocation with the planting of this Republic. We have thought that we could trace the finger of God in every stage of its history. We have looked upon it as destined to be a blessing to mankind. Placed between Europe and Asia, in the very centre of the earth, with the two great oceans of the globe acknowledging its dominion; entering upon its career at the very period of the history of the world, most eminently adapted to accelerate its progress, and to diffuse its influence, it seems to us to be commissioned from the skies as the apostle of civilization, liberty, and Christianity to all the race of man. We cannot relinquish the idea of this lofty mission; we HAVE BEEN called to it; and if, in our folly and wickedness, we refuse to walk worthily of it, we may righteously expect, in addition to the ordinary disasters of revolution, the extraordinary retributions of God. Ours will be no common punishment, as it will be no common sin, if, instead of obeying the command which requires us to be a blessing to the world, we exhaust our resources, and waste our advantages, in biting and devouring each other. We cannot sympathize with the light and flippant tone in which the question of the value of the Union is too often approached, as if it were a mere question of ordinary politics. To our minds it is the most serious, solemn, and momentous that can be asked in connection with the earthly interests of man. To dissolve this Union is to jeopard all that our fathers gained, and to cover in midnight darkness the prospects and destiny of our own posterity. We tremble at the thought, and if it must perish, we freely confess that our tears shall bedew its grave; and our hopes for liberty and man be buried with it.

But the Union is the creature of the Constitution. The destruction of one is, and must be, sooner or later, the destruction of the other. The guilt of dissolving it must rest upon those who trample the Constitution in the dust.

There are two quarters from which the Confederacy is at present threatened, but threatened on very different grounds. The first is from those who are opposed to slavery, and would prostitute the powers of the general Government to their own fanatical ends. They repudiate the Constitution as conniving at sin; and their exasperation has risen to the height of actual rebellion, in consequence of the law passed at the last session of Congress, for the recovery of fugitive slaves. These men are confessed conspirators against the Government; they strike at that which gives it its very life, the Constitution of the land. The other party consists of those who believe that the Constitution has been systematically violated by the non-slaveholding States; that the contract which made the

Union has been broken; and that there is not only no obligation any longer to adhere to it, but that the danger of further aggressions is so great, that it is a duty to withdraw from it.

In reference to the opposition from these quarters, we have a few remarks to make. We would say first to the North, that she owes it to mankind to see that all just ground of complaint, as far as she is concerned, is removed. If she has thrown obstructions in the way of faithfully carrying out the provisions of the Constitution; if she has, in any degree, broken her faith, posterity will not acquit her of undervaluing the Union, however loudly she may vociferate its praise. To love the Union is to love the Constitution. Let her see to it, that no stipulations of the charter are disregarded by her; or if they have been heretofore, let her be prompt to retrace her steps. This would be manly, noble, heroic. It would be a patriotism for which she would never suffer. Let her not poise herself upon her power; good faith is a surer safeguard.

We would say to the South, that her first movement should be to restore the Constitution to its supremacy. We do not think that it is wisdom suddenly to destroy a government, because it has been perverted. If good in itself, if the evils are abuses and essential elements of the system, the effort to rectify and cure is worthy of an experiment. What surgeon would amputate a limb until he was convinced that it was the last resort? To our minds the dissolution of the Union is the last desperate remedy for the disorders of the government. Until all other probable expedients have failed, we cannot be justified in the eyes of God or of the race, in demolishing a fabric which Providence contributed so conspicuously to rear, which is hallowed by a thousand associations, cemented by illustrious blood, a temple of liberty in which our fathers worshipped, and which all nations have honoured. Let us never pull it down, until it has become utterly unclean, and freedom is driven from its sanctuary. The pollutions of the money-changers and traders can be cleansed; we may be able to upset their tables and to drive them out; and may still make the edifice what it was originally designed to be. Patience and effort in restoring the Government to what it should be, is not *submission* to wrong; it is *resistance*, the resistance which wisdom justifies and conscience will approve. The attempt to heal a disease is not acquiescence in its progress. If the Union of the Constitution is, indeed, glorious—as all confess that it is—it is not slavish timidity, it is the real love of liberty, which prompts us to labour for its preservation, until our labours shall be found to be hopeless. When we are driven to despair of the Republic, and not till then, shall we be justified in withdrawing. As to the charge of pusillanimous tameness to which such a policy may subject us, we can only reply, in the words of Thucydides:

"As for that slowness and dilatoriness with which you have heard yourselves upbraided, they flow from those institutions of our ancestors, which teach us, in public as in private life, to be modest, prudent, and just."

From this same noble speech, which this prince of historians puts in the mouth of Archidamus, we would commend to the young and impetuous, who are naturally much more inclined to follow the counsel of Sthenelaidus, the following salutary caution:

"If any spur us on by panegyric to perilous adventures, disapproved by our judgment, we are little moved with their flattery; nor if any one were to stimulate us by reproach, would indignation be at all more likely to make us alter our determination. By this orderly sedateness we are both brave in combat, and prudent in counsel."

But while we would make every effort which wisdom and partiotism would demand to save the Constitution and the Union, we are free to confess that, when the issue is forced upon us, of submitting to a government hopelessly perverted from its ends, and aiming at the destruction of our own interests, it will be our duty, as it is our right, to provide for ourselves. The continual agitation of the slavery question must, sooner or later, bring matters to this issue. The Southern States will not abandon their institutions. This is certain as fate. Their patience is now almost exhausted, and unless their constitutional rights are respected, they will set up for themselves. This Union must fall, and they will lift up their hands to heaven, and declare that they are clear of its blood. The guilt of the long train of untold evils that must follow the catastrophe, they will honestly believe rests not upon them. God grant that our country may be saved; that the North and the South may be brought to meet in harmony and peace, upon the common ground of our glorious Constitution; that a common ancestry, a common history, a common language, a common religion, may do their office in cementing them together, and binding them in the indissoluble bonds of truth, justice, and fraternal love.

We have but a single word further to add, and that is a protest against the policy which our own beloved State seems intent upon pursuing. Single-handed secession, which is understood to be the aim of the measures now in progress, however it might be justified in a crisis in which the Federal Government had become openly pledged to the extinction of slavery, under the present circumstances of our country, is recommended by not a single consideration that we are able to discover, of wisdom, patriotism, or honour. No master mind among those who are driving us to this issue has yet arisen, to throw a particle of light upon the thick darkness which shrouds the future, and covers the consequences of this tremendous step. They all tell us *how* we may secede, but not one has told us, not one can tell us, where we shall next find ourselves. No one has yet explained to us how the institution of slavery will be more efficiently protected, by making us and our children aliens upon this broad continent, than it is by the flag of the Republic. Shall we be more exempt from Northern fanaticism, when every check is

removed from its machinations and contrivances; from British interference, when we have nothing to lean on but our own arms? Will
slavery be safer when South Carolina can throw no shield but her own
around the institution, than when the Constitution protects us? We
confess that we cannot see how we shall gain in security from the prostration of the Union. A single State, like South Carolina, standing out
alone in the midst of a mighty nation, can only exist by sufferance.

But it is said she will not be alone. The other States, identified with
her in interests, will join with her in action. But what if the other
Southern States should happen to believe that their interests are better
promoted by the old Union, than by a new alliance with South Carolina?
They must judge for themselves, and if they should happen to have a
judgment of this sort, where shall we then be? Would it not be wise, at
least, to have some better proof than our own conjectures that they will
sustain us? They might leave us alone; and in that contingency, who
can say that our condition would be enviable. We should then have a
national government to maintain, an extensive post-office establishment
to organize, an army, a navy, foreign ambassadors, and all the appendages of independent States, to keep up. Has any one calculated our
resources for these things; and does any man believe that our population would stick to us for ten years, after their passions had subsided,
under the grinding system of taxation which it would be necessary to
institute? Then, again, we must be fully prepared for war, which is a
business less of arms than expense. Touching the United States in so
many points as we must necessarily do, however pacific the disposition
of the Federal Government might be towards us, hostilities would inevitably arise from our diplomatic relations to the other States, and that
speedily and suddenly. These are matters which ought to be well considered before we resolve upon so important a step as single-handed
secession. The truth is, we can see nothing in the measure but defeat
and disaster, insecurity to slavery, oppression to ourselves, ruin to the
State. There are other aspects in which the question might be treated,
but in every aspect of it we feel bound to express our solemn conviction
that, neither before God nor man, can we justify ourselves for the fearful hazard of forfeiting all our blessings, and all our influence for good,
by a hasty leap in the dark. We speak earnestly on the subject, because
we feel strongly. There may be great boldness in the enterprise, but
it should be remembered, as Lord Bacon has well expressed it, that boldness is blind; wherefore it is ill in counsel, but good in execution. For
in counsel, it is good to see dangers; in execution, not to see them except they be very great. Certainly, when we cannot see our way, we
should go softly. From present appearances, we think it likely that
South Carolina will secede alone. We expect to bear our full proportion of the consequent evils. We are not only in the State, but
of the State, and we have no thought but that of sharing her fortunes. If we were disposed, we are rather too heavily encumbered
to flee from the storm. Others may be noisy for revolution, whose

armour is light enough to admit of an easy transportation; who have come to us from abroad, and who can as easily depart. But for ourselves, we are linked to South Carolina, for weal or for woe. As long as our voice can be heard, we shall endeavour to avert calamity ; but if what we regard as rash counsels finally prevail, we have made up our mind, as God shall give us grace, to take what comes.

No. II.

OUR DANGER AND OUR DUTY.

The intense feelings under which Dr. Thornwell composed this appeal to his Southern countrymen are evinced in the headings of almost all the pages of the first draft: "The Crisis!—the Crisis!!—the Crisis!!!"

THE ravages of Louis XIV in the beautiful valleys of the Rhine, about the close of the seventeenth century, may be taken as a specimen of the appalling desolation which is likely to overspread the Confederate States if the Northern army should succeed in its schemes of subjugation and of plunder. Europe was then outraged by atrocities inflicted by Christians upon Christians, more fierce and cruel than even Mahometans could have had the heart to perpetrate. Private dwellings were razed to the ground, fields laid waste, cities burnt, churches demolished, and the fruits of industry wantonly and ruthlessly destroyed. But three days of grace were allowed to the wretched inhabitants to flee their country; and in a short time, the historian tells us, "the roads and fields, which then lay deep in snow, were blackened by innumerable multitudes of men, women, and children, flying from their homes. Many died of cold and hunger; but enough survived to fill the streets of all the cities of Europe with lean and squalid beggars, who had once been thriving farmers and shopkeepers." And what have we to expect if our enemies prevail? Our homes, too, are to be pillaged; our cities sacked and demolished; our property confiscated; our true men hanged, and those who escape the gibbet, to be driven as vagabonds and wanderers in foreign climes. This beautiful country is to pass out of our hands. The boundaries which mark our States are, in some instances, to be effaced; and the States that remain are to be converted into subject provinces, governed by Northern rulers and by Northern laws. Our property is to be ruthlessly seized, and turned over to mercenary strangers, in order to pay the enormous debt which our subjugation has cost. Our wives and daughters are to become the prey of brutal lust. The slave, too, will slowly pass away, as the red man did before him, under the protection of Northern philanthropy; and the whole country, now like the garden of Eden in beauty and fertility, will first be a blackened and smoking desert, and then the minister of Northern cupidity and avarice. Our history will be worse than that of Poland and Hungary. There is not a single redeeming feature in the picture of ruin which stares us in the face, if we permit ourselves to be conquered. It is a night of thick darkness that will settle upon us. Even sympathy, the last solace of the afflicted, will be denied to us. The civilized world will look coldly upon us, or even jeer us with the taunt that we have deservedly lost our own freedom in seeking to perpetuate the slavery of others. We shall perish under a cloud of reproach and of unjust suspicions, sedulously propagated by our enemies, which will be harder to bear than the loss of home and of goods. Such a fate never overtook any people before.

The case is as desperate with our enemies as with ourselves. They must succeed, or perish; they must conquer us, or be destroyed themselves. If they fail, national bankruptcy stares them in the face; divisions in their own ranks are inevitable, and their Government will fall to pieces under the weight of its own corruption. They know that they are a doomed people if they are defeated. Hence their madness. They must have our property to save them from insolvency. They must show that the Union cannot be dissolved, to save them from future secessions. The parties, therefore, in this conflict, can make no compromises. It is a matter of life and death with both; a struggle in which their *all* is involved.

But the consequences of success on our part will be very different from the consequences of success on the part of the North. If *they* prevail, the whole character of the Government will be changed, and, instead of a federal republic, the common agent of sovereign and independent States, we shall have a central despotism, with the notion of States for ever abolished, deriving its powers from the will, and shaping its policy according to the wishes, of a numerical majority of the people; we shall have, in other words, a supreme, irresponsible democracy. The will of the North will stand for law. The Government does not now recognize itself as an ordinance of God; and, when all the checks and balances of the Constitution are gone, we may easily figure to ourselves the career and the destiny of this godless monster of democratic absolutism. The progress of regulated liberty on this continent will be arrested, anarchy will soon succeed, and the end will be a military despotism, which preserves order by the sacrifice of the last vestige of liberty. We are fully persuaded that the triumph of the North in the present conflict will be as disastrous to the hopes of mankind as to our own fortunes. They are now fighting the battle of despotism. They have put their Constitution under their feet; they have annulled its most sacred provisions; and, in defiance of its solemn guaranties, they are now engaged, in the halls of Congress, in discussing and maturing bills which make Northern notions of necessity the paramount laws of the land. The avowed end of the present war is, to make the Government a government of force. It is to settle the principle that, whatever may be its corruptions and abuses, however unjust and tyrannical its legislation, there is no redress, except in vain petition or empty remonstrance. It was as a protest against this principle, which sweeps away the last security for liberty, that Virginia, North Carolina, Tennessee, and Missouri seceded ; and if the Government should be re-established, it must be re-established with this feature of remorseless despotism firmly and indelibly fixed.   The future fortunes of our children, and of this continent, would then be determined by a tyranny which has no parallel in history.

On the other hand, we are struggling for constitutional freedom.   We are upholding the great principles which our fathers bequeathed us ; and if we should succeed, and become, as we shall, the dominant nation of this continent, we shall perpetuate and diffuse the very liberty for which Washington bled, and which the heroes of the Revolution achieved.   We are not revolutionists ; we are resisting revolution.   We are upholding the true doctrines of the Federal Constitution.   We are conservative. Our success is the triumph of all that has been considered established in the past.   We can never become aggressive ; we may absorb, but we can never invade for conquest any neighbouring State.   The peace of the world is secured if our arms prevail.   We shall have a Government that acknowledges God, that reverences right, and that makes law supreme. We are therefore fighting, not for ourselves alone, but, when the struggle is rightly understood, for the salvation of this whole continent.   It is a noble cause in which we are engaged.   There is everything in it to rouse the heart and to nerve the arm of the freeman and the patriot ; and though it may now seem to be under a cloud, it is too big with the future of our race to be suffered to fail.   It cannot fail ; it must not fail.   Our people must not brook the infamy of betraying their sublime trust.   This beautiful land we must never suffer to pass into the hands of strangers.   Our fields, our homes, our firesides and sepulchres, our cities and temples, our wives and daughters, we must protect at every hazard.   The glorious inheritance which our fathers left us we must never betray.   The hopes with which they died, and which buoyed their spirits in the last conflict, of making their country a blessing to the world, we must not permit to be unrealized.   We must seize the torch from their hands, and transmit it with increasing brightness to distant generations.   The word failure must not be pronounced among us.   It is not a thing to be dreamed of.   We must settle it that we *must* succeed.   We must not sit down to count chances.   There is too much at stake to think of discussing probabilities.   We must make success a certainty ; and that, by the blessing of God, we can do.   If we are prepared to do our duty, and our whole duty, we have nothing to fear. But what is our duty ?   This is a question which we must gravely consider.   We shall briefly attempt to answer it.

In the first place, we must shake off all apathy, and become fully alive to the magnitude of the crisis.   We must look the danger in the face, and comprehend the real grandeur of the issue.   We shall not exert ourselves until we are sensible of the need of effort.   As long as we cherish a vague hope that help may come from abroad, or that there is something in our past history, or the genius of our institutions, to protect us from overthrow, we are hugging a fatal delusion to our bosoms. This apathy was the ruin of Greece at the time of the Macedonian invasion. This was the spell which Demosthenes laboured so earnestly to break. The Athenian was as devoted as ever to his native city, and the free institutions he inherited from his fathers; but somehow or other he could not believe that his country could be conquered. He read its safety in its ancient glory. He felt that it had a prescriptive right to live. The great orator saw and lamented the error; he poured forth his eloquence to dissolve the charm; but the fatal hour had come, and the spirit of Greece could not be roused. There was no more real patriotism at the time of the second Persian invasion than in the age of Philip; but, then, there was no apathy. Every man appreciated the danger; he saw the crash that was coming, and prepared himself to resist the blow. He knew that there was no safety except in courage and in desperate effort. Every man, too, felt identified with the State; a part of its weight rested on his shoulders. It was this sense of personal interest and personal responsibility; the profound conviction that every one had something to do, and that Greece expected him to do it. This was the public spirit which turned back the countless hordes of Xerxes, and saved Greece to liberty and man. This is the spirit which we must have, if we, too, would succeed. We must be brought to see that all, under God, depends on ourselves; and, looking away from all foreign alliances, we must make up our minds to fight desperately and fight long, if we would save the country from ruin, and ourselves from bondage. Every man should feel that he has an interest in the State, and that the State in a measure leans upon him; and he should rouse himself to efforts as bold and heroic as if all depended on his single right arm. Our courage should rise higher than the danger; and, whatever may be the odds against us, we must solemnly resolve, by God's blessing, that we will not be conquered. When, with a full knowledge of the danger, we are brought to this point, we are in the way of deliverance; but until this point is reached, it is idle to count on success.

It is implied in the spirit which the times demand, that all private interests are sacrificed to the public good. The State becomes everything, and the individual nothing. It is no time to be casting about for expedients to enrich ourselves. The man who is now intent upon money, who turns public necessity and danger into means of speculation, would, if very shame did not rebuke him, and he were allowed to follow the natural bent of his heart, go upon the field of battle, after an engagement, and strip the lifeless bodies of his brave countrymen of the few spoils they carried into the fight. Such men, unfit for anything generous or noble themselves, like the hyena, can only suck the blood of the lion. It ought to be a reproach to any man, that he is growing rich while his country is bleeding at every pore. If we had a Themistocles among us, he would not scruple to charge the miser and extortioner with stealing the Gorgon's head; he would search their stuff, and if he could not find that, he would find what would answer his country's needs much more effectually. This spirit must be rebuked; every man must forget himself, and think only of the public good.

The spirit of faction is even more to be dreaded than the spirit of avarice and plunder. It is equally selfish, and is, besides, distracting and divisive. The man who now labours to weaken the hands of the Government, that he may seize the reins of authority, or cavils at public measures and policy, that he may rise to distinction and office, has all the selfishness of a miser, and all the baseness of a traitor. Our rulers are not infallible; but their errors are to be reviewed with candour, and their authority sustained with unanimity. Whatever has a tendency to destroy public confidence in their prudence, their wisdom, their energy, and their patriotism, undermines the security of our cause. We must not be divided and distracted among ourselves. Our rulers have great responsibilities. They need the support of the whole country; and nothing short of a patriotism which buries all private differences, which is ready for compromises and concessions, which can make charitable allowances for differences of opinion, and even for errors of judgment, can save us from the consequences of party and faction. We must be united. If our views are not carried out, let us sacrifice private opinion to public safety. In the great conflict with Persia, Athens yielded to Sparta, and acquiesced in plans she could not approve, for the sake of the public good. Nothing could be more dangerous now than scrambles for office and power, and collisions among the different departments of the Government. We must present a united front.

It is further important that every man should be ready to work. It is no time to play the gentleman; no time for dignified leisure. All cannot serve in the field; but all can do something to help forward the common cause. The young and active, the stout and vigorous, should be prepared at a moment's warning for the ranks. The disposition should be one of eagerness to be employed; there should be no holding back, no counting the cost. The man who stands back from the ranks in these perilous times, because he is unwilling to serve his country as a private soldier, who loves his ease more than liberty, his luxuries more than his honour, that man is a dead fly in our precious ointment. In seasons of great calamity, the ancient pagans were accustomed to appease the anger of their gods by human sacrifices; and if they had gone upon the principle of selecting those whose moral insignificance rendered them alike offensive to heaven and useless to earth, they would always have selected these drones, and loafers, and exquisites. A Christian nation cannot offer them in sacrifice; but public contempt should whip them from their lurking holes, and compel them to share the common danger. The community that will cherish such men without rebuke, brings down wrath upon it. They must be forced to be useful, to avert the judgments of God from the patrons of cowardice and meanness.

Public spirit will not have reached the height which the exigency demands, until we shall have relinquished all fastidious notions of military etiquette, and have come to the point of expelling the enemy by any and every means that God has put in our power. We are not fighting for military glory; we are fighting for a home, and for a national existence. We are not aiming to display our skill in tactics and generalship; we are aiming to show ourselves a free people, worthy to possess and able to defend the institutions of our fathers. What signifies it to us how the foe is vanquished, provided it is done? Because we have not weapons of the most improved workmanship, are we to sit still and see our soil overrun, and our wives and children driven from their homes, while we have in our hands other weapons that can equally do the work of death? Are we to perish if we cannot conquer by the technical rules of scientific warfare? Are we to sacrifice our country to military punctilio? The thought is monstrous. We must be prepared to extemporize expedients. We must cease to be chary, either about our weapons or the means of using them. The end is to drive back our foes. If we cannot procure the best rifles, let us put up with the common guns of the country; if they cannot be had, with pikes, and axes, and tomahawks; anything that will do the work of death, is an effective instrument in a brave man's hand. We should be ready for the regular battle or the partisan skirmish. If we are too weak to stand an engagement in the open field, we can waylay the foe, and harass and annoy him. We must prepare ourselves for a guerilla war. The enemy must be conquered; and any method by which we can honourably do it must be resorted to. This is the kind of spirit which we want to see aroused among our people. With this spirit, they will never be subdued. If driven from the plains, they will retreat to the mountains; if beaten in the field, they will hide in swamps and marshes; and when their enemies are least expecting it, they will pounce down upon them in the dashing exploits of a Sumter, a Marion, and a Davie. It is only when we have reached this point that public spirit is commensurate with the danger.

In the second place, we must guard sacredly against cherishing a temper of presumptuous confidence. The cause is not ours, but God's; and if we measure its importance only by its accidental relation to ourselves, we may be suffered to perish for our pride. No nation ever yet achieved anything great, that did not regard itself as the instrument of Providence. The only lasting inspiration of lofty patriotism and exalted courage, is the inspiration of religion. The Greeks and Romans never ventured upon any important enterprise without consulting their gods. They felt that they were safe only as they were persuaded that they were in alliance with heaven. Man, though limited in space, limited in time, and limited in knowledge, is truly great, when he is linked to the Infinite as the means of accomplishing lasting ends. To be God's servant, that is his highest destiny, his sublimest calling. Nations are under the pupilage of Providence; they are in training themselves, that they may be the instruments of furthering the progress of the human race.

Polybius, the historian, traces the secret of Roman greatness to the profound sense of religion which constituted a striking feature of the national character. He calls it, expressly, the firmest pillar of the Roman State; and he does not hesitate to denounce, as enemies to public order and prosperity, those of his own contemporaries who sought to undermine the sacredness of these convictions. Even Napoleon sustained his vaulting ambition by a mysterious connection with the invisible world. He was a man of destiny. It is the relation to God, and His providential training of the race, that imparts true dignity to our struggle; and we must recognize ourselves as God's servants, working out His glorious ends, or we shall infallibly be left to stumble upon the dark mountains of error. Our trust in Him must be the real spring of our heroic resolution, to conquer or to die. A sentiment of honour, a momentary enthusiasm, may prompt and sustain spasmodic exertions of an extraordinary character; but a steady valour, a self-denying patriotism, protracted patience, a readiness to do, and dare, and suffer, through a generation or an age, this comes only from a sublime faith in God. The worst symptom that any people can manifest, is that of pride. With nations, as with individuals, it goes before a fall. Let us guard against it. Let us rise to the true grandeur of our calling, and go forth as servants of the Most High, to execute His purposes. In this spirit we are safe. By this spirit our principles are ennobled, and our cause translated from earth to heaven. An overweening confidence in the righteousness of our cause, as if that alone were sufficient to insure our success, betrays gross inattention to the Divine dealings with communities and States. In the issue betwixt ourselves and our enemies, we may be free from blame; but there may be other respects in which we have provoked the judgments of Heaven, and there may be other grounds on which God has a controversy with us, and the swords of our enemies may be His chosen instruments to execute His wrath. He may first use them as a rod, and then punish them in other forms for their own iniquities. Hence, it behooves us not only to have a righeous cause, but to be a righteous people. We must abandon all our sins, and put ourselves heartily and in earnest on the side of Providence.

Hence, this dependence upon Providence carries with it the necessity of removing from the midst of us whatever is offensive to a holy God. If the Government is His ordinance, and the people His instruments, they must see to it that they serve Him with no unwashed or defiled hands. We must cultivate a high standard of public virtue. We must renounce all personal and selfish aims, and we must rebuke every custom or institution that tends to deprave the public morals. Virtue is power, and vice is weakness. The same Polybius, to whom we have already referred, traces the influence of the religious sentiment at Rome in producing faithful and incorruptible magistrates, who were strangers alike to bribery and favour in executing the laws and dispensing the trusts of the State, and that high tone of public faith which made an oath an absolute security for faithfulness. This stern simplicity of manners we must cherish, if we hope to succeed. Bribery, corruption, favouritism, electioneering, flattery, and every species of double-dealing; drunkenness, profaneness, debauchery, selfishness, avarice, and extortion; all base material ends must be banished by a stern integrity, if we would become the fit instruments of a holy Providence in a holy cause. Sin is a reproach to any people. It is weakness; it is sure, though it may be slow, decay. Faith in God: that is the watchword of martyrs, whether in the cause of truth or of liberty. That alone ennobles and sanctifies.

"All other nations," except the French, as Burke has significantly remarked, in relation to the memorable revolution which was doomed to failure in consequence of this capital omission, " have begun the fabric of a new Government, or the reformation of an old, by establishing originally, or by enforcing with greater exactness, some rites or other of religion. All other people have laid the foundations of civil freedom in severer manners, and a system of more austere and masculine morality." To absolve the State, which is the society of rights, from a strict responsibility to the Author and Source of justice and of law, is to destroy the firmest security of public order, to convert liberty into license, and to impregnate the very being of the commonwealth with the seeds of dissolution and decay. France failed, because France forgot God; and if we tread in the footsteps of that infatuated people, and treat with equal contempt the holiest instincts of our nature, we, too, may be abandoned to our folly, and become the hissing and the scorn of all the nations of the earth. "Be wise, now, therefore, O ye kings! be instructed, ye judges of the earth. Kiss the Son, lest He be angry, and ye perish from the way, when His wrath is kindled but a little. Blessed are all they that put their trust in Him."

In the third place, let us endeavour rightly to interpret the reverses which have recently attended our arms. It is idle to make light of them. They are serious; they are disastrous. The whole end of Providence, in any dispensation, it were presumptuous for any one, independently of a special revelation, to venture to decipher. But there are tendencies which lie upon the surface, and these obvious tendencies are designed for our guidance and instruction. In the present case, we may humbly believe that one purpose aimed at has been to rebuke our confidence and our pride. We had begun to despise our enemy, and to prophesy safety without much hazard. We had laughed at his cowardice, and boasted of our superior prowess and skill. Is it strange that, while indulging such a temper, we ourselves should be made to turn our backs, and to become a jest to those whom we had jeered? We had grown licentious, intemperate, and profane: is it strange that, in the midst of our security, God should teach us that sin is a reproach to any people? Is it strange that He should remind us of the moral conditions upon which alone we are authorized to hope for success? The first lesson, therefore, is one of rebuke and repentance. It is a call to break off our sins by righteousness, and to turn our eyes to the real secret of national security and strength.

The second end may be one of trial. God has placed us in circumstances in which, if we show that we are equal to the emergency, all will

acknowledge our right to the freedom which we have so signally vindicated. We have now the opportunity for great exploits. We can now
demonstrate to the world what manner of spirit we are of. If our
courage and faith rise superior to the danger, we shall not only succeed,
but we shall succeed with a moral influence and character that shall
render our success doubly valuable. Providence seems to be against us;
disaster upon disaster has attended our arms; the enemy is in possession
of three States, and beleaguers us in all our coasts. His resources and
armaments are immense, and his energy and resolution desperate. His
numbers are so much superior, that we are like a flock of kids before
him. We have nothing to stand on but the eternal principles of truth
and right, and the protection and alliance of a just God. Can we look
the danger unflinchingly in the face, and calmly resolve to meet it and
subdue it? Can we say, in reliance upon Providence, that, were his
numbers and resources a thousand-fold greater, the interests at stake are
so momentous, that we will not be conquered? Do we feel the moral
power of courage, of resolution, of heroic will, rising and swelling within
us, until it towers above all the smoke and dust of the invasion? Then
we are in a condition to do great deeds. We are in the condition of
Greece when Xerxes hung upon the borders of Attica, with an army of
five millions that had never been conquered, and to which State after
State of northern Greece had yielded in its progress. Little Athens was
the object of his vengeance. Leonidas had fallen; four days more would
bring the destroyer to the walls of the devoted city. There the people
were—a mere handful. Their first step had been to consult the gods,
and the astounding reply which they received from Delphi would have
driven any other people to despair. "Wretched men!" said the oracle,
which they believed to be infallible, "why sit ye there? Quit your land
and city, and flee afar! Head, body, feet, and hands, are alike rotten;
fire and sword, in the train of the Syrian chariot, shall overwhelm you;
not only *your* city, but other cities also, as well as many even of the
temples of the gods, which are now sweating and trembling with fear,
and foreshadow, by drops of blood on their roofs, the hard calamities
impending. Get ye away from the sanctuary, with your souls steeped
in sorrow." *We* have had reverses, but no such oracle as this. It was
afterwards modified so as to give a ray of hope, in an ambiguous allusion
to wooden walls. But the soul of the Greek rose with the danger; and
we have a succession of events, from the desertion of Athens to the final
expulsion of the invader, which make that little spot of earth immortal.
Let us imitate, in Christian faith, this sublime example. Let our spirit
be loftier than that of the pagan Greek, and we can succeed in making
every pass a Thermopylæ, every strait a Salamis, and every plain a
Marathon. We can conquer, and we *must*. We must not suffer any
other thought to enter our minds. If we are overrun, we can at least
die; and if our enemies get possession of our land, we can leave it a
howling desert. But, under God, we shall not fail. If we are true to
Him, and true to ourselves, a glorious future is before us. We occupy

a sublime position. The eyes of the world are upon us; we are a spectacle to God, to angels, and to men. Can our hearts grow faint, or our hands feeble, in a cause like this? The spirits of our fathers call to us from their graves. The heroes of other ages and other countries are beckoning us on to glory. Let us seize the opportunity, and make to ourselves an immortal name, while we redeem a land from bondage and a continent from ruin.

No. III.

THE STATE OF THE COUNTRY.

DECLARATION OF THE IMMEDIATE CAUSES WHICH INDUCE AND JUSTIFY THE SECESSION OF SOUTH CAROLINA FROM THE FEDERAL UNION; AND THE ORDINANCE OF SECESSION. Printed by order of the Convention. Charleston: Evans & Cogswell, Printers to the Convention. pp. 13. 1860.

THE ADDRESS OF THE PEOPLE OF SOUTH CAROLINA, ASSEMBLED IN CONVENTION, TO THE PEOPLE OF THE SLAVEHOLDING STATES OF THE UNITED STATES. Printed by order of the Convention. Charleston: Evans & Cogswell, Printers to the Convention. pp. 16. 1860.

REPORT ON THE ADDRESS OF A PORTION OF THE MEMBERS OF THE GENERAL ASSEMBLY OF GEORGIA. Printed by order of the Convention. Charleston: Evans & Cogswell, Printers to the Convention. pp. 6. 1860.

IT is now universally known that, on the 20th day of last December, the people of South Carolina, in Convention assembled, solemnly annulled the ordinance by which they became members of the Federal Union, entitled the United States of America, and resumed to themselves the exercise of all the powers which they had delegated to the Federal Congress. South Carolina has now become a separate and independent State. She takes her place as an equal among the other nations of the earth. This is certainly one of the most grave and important events of modern times. It involves the destiny of a continent; and through that continent, the fortunes of the human race. As it is a matter of the utmost moment that the rest of the world, and especially that the people of the United States, should understand the causes which have brought about this astounding result, we propose, in a short article, and in a candid and dispassionate spirit, to explain them; and to make an appeal, both to the slaveholding and non-slaveholding States, touching their duty in the new and extraordinary aspect which affairs have assumed.

That there was a cause, and an adequate cause, might be presumed from the character of the Convention which passed the Ordinance of Secession, and the perfect unanimity with which it was done. That Convention was not a collection of demagogues and politicians. It was not a conclave of defeated place-hunters, who sought to avenge their disappointment by the ruin of their country. It was a body of sober, grave, and venerable men, selected from every pursuit in life, and distinguished, most of them, in their respective spheres, by every quality which can command confidence and respect. It embraced the wisdom, moderation, and integrity of the bench, the learning and prudence of the bar, and the eloquence and piety of the pulpit. It contained retired planters, scholars, and gentlemen, who had stood aloof from the turmoil and ambition of public life, and were devoting an elegant leisure, *otium cum dignitate*, to the culture of their minds, and to quiet and unobtrusive schemes of Christian philanthropy. There were men in that Convention who were utterly incapable of low and selfish schemes; who, in the calm serenity of their judgments, were as unmoved by the waves of popular passion and excitement as the everlasting granite by the billows that roll against it. There were men there who would have listened to no voice but what they believed to be the voice of reason; and would have bowed to no authority but what they believed to be the authority of God. There were men there who would not have been controlled by "uncertain opinion," nor betrayed into "sudden counsels;" men who could act from nothing, in the noble language of Milton, "but from mature wisdom, deliberate virtue, and dear affection to the public good." That Convention, in the character of its members, deserves every syllable of the glowing panegyric which Milton has pronounced upon the immortal Parliament of England, which taught the nations of the earth that resistance to tyrants is obedience to God. Were it not invidious, we might single out names, which, wherever they are known, are regarded as synonymous with purity, probity, magnanimity, and honour. It was a noble body, and all their proceedings were in harmony with their high character. In the midst of intense agitation and excitement, they were calm, cool, collected, and self-possessed. They deliberated without passion, and concluded without rashness. They sat with closed doors, that the tumult of the populace might not invade the sobriety of their minds. If a stranger could have passed from the stirring scenes with which the streets of Charleston were alive, into the calm and quiet sanctuary of this venerable council, he would have been impressed with the awe and veneration which subdued the rude Gaul, when he first beheld in senatorial dignity the Conscript Fathers of Rome. That, in such a body, there was not a single voice against the Ordinance of Secession, that there was not only no dissent, but that the assent was cordial and thorough-going, is a strong presumption that the measure was justified by the clearest and sternest necessities of justice and of right. That such an assembly should have inaugurated and completed a radical revolution in all the external relations of the State, in the face of acknowledged dangers, and at the risk of enormous sacrifices, and should have done it gravely, soberly, dispassionately, deliberately, and yet have done it without cause, transcends all the measures of probability. Whatever else may be said of it, it certainly must be admitted that this solemn act of South Carolina was well considered.

In her estimate of the magnitude of the danger, she has been seconded by every other slaveholding State. While we are writing, the telegraphic wires announce what the previous elections had prepared us to expect— that Florida, Alabama, and Mississippi have followed her example. They also have become separate and independent States. Three other States have taken the incipient steps for the consummation of the same result. And the rest of the slaveholding States are hanging by a single thread to the Union, the slender thread of hope, that guarantees may be divised which shall yet secure to them their rights. But even they proclaim, that without such guarantees, their wrongs are intolerable, and they will not longer endure them. Can any man believe that the secession of four sovereign States, under the most solemn circumstances, the determination of others to follow as soon as the constituted authorities can be called together, and the universal sentiment of all, that the Constitution of the United States has been virtually repealed, and that every slaveholding State has just ground for secession ; can any man believe that this is a factitious condition of the public mind of the South, produced by brawling politicians and disappointed demagogues, and not the calm, deliberate, profound utterance of a people who feel, in their inmost souls, that they have been deeply and flagrantly wronged? The presumption clearly is, that there is something in the attitude of the Government which portends danger, and demands resistance. There must be a cause for this intense and pervading sense of injustice and of injury.

It has been suggested, by those who know as little of the people of the South as they do of the Constitution of their country, that all this ferment is nothing but the result of a mercenary spirit on the part of the cotton-growing States, fed by Utopian dreams of aggrandizement and wealth, to be realized under the auspices of free trade, in a separate confederacy of their own. It has been gravely insinuated that they are willing to sell their faith for gold; that they have only made a pretext of recent events to accomplish a foregone scheme of deliberate treachery and fraud. That there is not the slightest ground in anything these States have ever said or done for this extraordinary slander, it is, of course, superfluous to add. The South has, indeed, complained of the unequal administration of the Government. Her best and purest statesmen have openly avowed the opinion that, in consequence of the partial legislation of Congress, she has borne burdens and experienced inconveniences which have retarded her own prosperity, while they have largely contributed to develope the resources of the North. But grievances of this kind, unless greatly exaggerated, never would have led to the dissolution of the Union. They would have been resisted within it, or patiently borne until they could be lawfully redressed. So far from contending for an arbitrary right to dissolve the Union, or the right to dissolve it on merely technical grounds, the South sets so high a value on good faith, that she would never have dissolved it for slight and temporary wrongs, even though they might involve such a violation, on the part of her confederates, of the terms of the compact, as released her from any further obligation of honour. It is, therefore, preposterous to say, that any dreams, however dazzling, of ambition and avarice, could have induced her to disregard her solemn engagements to her sister States, while they were faithfully fulfilling the conditions of the contract. We know the people of the South; and we can confidently affirm that, if they had been assured that all these golden visions could have been completely realized by setting up for themselves, as long as the Constitution of the United States continued to be sincerely observed, they would have spurned the temptation to purchase national greatness by perfidy. They would have preferred poverty, with honour, to the gain of the whole world by the loss of their integrity.

When it was perceived that the tendency of events was inevitably driving the South to disunion, a condition from which she at first recoiled with horror, then she began to cast about her for considerations to reconcile her to her destiny. Then, for the first time, was it maintained, that, instead of being a loser, she might be a gainer by the measure which the course of the Government was forcing upon her. It was alleged that good would spring from evil; that the prospect of independence was brighter and more cheering than her present condition; that she had much to anticipate, and little to dread, from the contemplated change. But these considerations were not invented to *justify* secession; they were only adduced as motives to reconcile the mind to its necessity. Apart from that necessity, they would have had as little weight in determining public opinion, as the small dust of the balance. We do not believe, when the present controversy began, that the advocates of what is called disunion *per se*, men who preferred a Southern Confederacy upon the grounds of its intrinsic superiority to the Constitutional Union of the United States, could have mustered a corporal's guard. The people of the South were loyal to the country, and if the country had been true to them, they would have been as ready to-day to defend its honour with their fortunes and their blood, as when they raised its triumphant flag upon the walls of Mexico.

It has also been asserted, as a ground of dissatisfaction with the present Government, and of desire to organize a separate government of their own, that the cotton-growing States are intent upon re-opening, as a means of fulfilling their magnificent visons of wealth, the African slave trade The agitation of this subject at the South has been grievously misunderstood. One extreme generates another. The violence of Northern abolitionists gave rise to a small party among ourselves, who were determined not to be outdone in extravagance. They wished to show that they could give a Rowland for an Oliver. Had abolitionists never denounced the domestic trade as plunder and robbery, not a whisper would ever have been breathed about disturbing the peace of Africa. The men who were loudest in their denunciations of the Government had, with very few exceptions, no more desire to have the trade reopened, than the rest of their countrymen; but they delighted in teasing their enemies. They took special satisfaction in providing hard nuts for abolitionists to crack. There were others, not at all in favour of the trade, who looked upon the law as unconstitutional which declared it to be piracy. But the great mass of the Southern people were content with the law as it stood. They were and are opposed to the trade. not because the traffic in slaves is immoral—that not a man among us believes—but because the traffic with Africa is *not* a traffic in slaves. It is a system of kidnapping and man-stealing, which is as abhorrent to the South as it is to the North; and we venture confidently to predict, that should a Southern Confederacy be formed, the African slave-trade is much more likely to be re-opened by the old Government than the new. The conscience of the North will be less tender when it has no Southern sins to bewail, and idle ships will naturally look to the Government to help them in finding employment.

The real cause of the intense excitement of the South, is not vain dreams of national glory in a separate confederacy, nor the love of the filthy lucre of the African slave-trade; it is the profound conviction that the Constitution, in its relations to slavery, has been virtually repealed; that the Government has assumed a new and dangerous attitude upon this subject; that we have, in short, new terms of union submitted to our acceptance or rejection. Here lies the evil. The election of Lincoln, when properly interpreted, is nothing more nor less than a proposition to the South to consent to a Government, fundamentally different upon the question of slavery, from that which our fathers established. If this point can be made out, secession becomes not only a right, but a bounden duty. Morally, it is only the abrogation of the forms of a contract, when its essential conditions have been abolished. Politically, it is a measure indispensable to the safety, if not to the very existence, of the South. It is needless to say that, in this issue, the personal character of Mr. Lincoln is not at all involved. There are no objections to him as a man, or as a citizen of the North. He is probably entitled, in the private relations of life, to all the commendations which his friends have bestowed upon him. We, at least, would be the last to detract from his personal worth. The issue has respect, not to the man, but to the principles upon which he is pledged to administer the Government, and which, we are significantly informed, are to be impressed upon it in all time to come. His election seals the triumph of those principles, and that triumph seals the subversion of the Constitution, in relation to a matter of paramount interest to the South.

This we shall proceed to show, by showing, first, the Constitutional attitude of the Government towards slavery, and then the attitude which, after the inauguration of Mr. Lincoln, it is to assume and maintain for ever:

I. What, now, is its Constitutional attitude? We affirm it to be *one of* ABSOLUTE INDIFFERENCE OR NEUTRALITY, with respect to all questions connected with the moral and political aspects of the subject. In the eye of the Constitution, slaveholding and non-slaveholding stand upon

a footing of perfect equality. The slaveholding State and the slaveholding citizen are the same to it as the non-slaveholding. It protects
both; it espouses the peculiarities of neither. It does not allow the
North to say the to South, "Your institutions are inferior to ours, and
should be changed;" neither does it allow the South to say to the North,
"You must accommodate yourselves to us." It says to both, "Enjoy your
own opinions upon your own soil, so that you do not interfere with the
rights of each other. To me there is no difference betwixt you." Formed
by parties whose divisive principle was this very subject of slavery, it
stands to reason, that the Constitution, without self-condemnation on the
part of one or the other, could not have been made the patron of either.
From the very nature of the case, its position must be one of complete
impartiality. This is what the South means by equality in the Union,
that the general Government shall make no difference betwixt its institutions and those of the North; that slaveholding shall be as good to it
as non-slaveholding. In other words, the Government is the organ of
neither party, but the common agent of both; and, as their common
agent, has no right to pronounce an opinion as to the merits of their
respective peculiarities. This, we contend, is the attitude fixed by the
Constitution. The Government is neither pro nor anti slavery. It is
simply neutral. Had it assumed any other attitude upon this subject, it
never would have been accepted by the slaveholding States. When Mr.
Pinckney could rise up in the Convention and declare, that "if slavery
be wrong, it is justified by the example of all the world;" when he could
boldly appeal to the unanimous testimony of ancient and modern times;
to Greece and Rome, to France, Holland, and England, in vindication of
its righteousness, it is not to be presumed that he ever would have joined
in the construction of a Government which was authorized to pronounce and treat it as an evil! It is not to be presumed that the slaveholding States, unless they seriously aimed at the ultimate extinction of
slavery, would have entered into an alliance which was confessedly to be
turned against them. That they did not aim at the extinction of slavery,
is clear from the pertinacity with which some of them clung to the continuance of the African slave-trade, until foreign supplies should be no
longer demanded. When Georgia and South Carolina made it a *sine
qua non* for entering the Union, that this traffic should be kept open for
a season, to say that these States meditated the abolition of slavery, is
grossly paradoxical. It is remarkable, too, that the time fixed for the
prohibition of this traffic, was a time within which the representatives
of those States were persuaded that the States themselves, if the question
were left to them, would prohibit it. These States conceded to the
Government the right to do, as their agent, only what they themselves
would do, as sovereign communities, under the same circumstances.
No presumption, therefore, of an attitude, on the part of the Constitution, hostile to slavery, can be deduced from the clause touching the
African slave-trade. On the contrary, the presumption is, that, as the
trade was kept open for a while—kept open, in fact, as long as the

African supply was needed—the slaveholding States never meant to abolish the institution, and never could have consented to set the face of the Government against it. No doubt, the fathers of the Republic were, many of them, not all, opposed to slavery. But they had to frame a government which should represent, not their personal and private opinions, but the interests of sovereign States. They had to adjust it to the institutions of South Carolina and Georgia, as well as those of New England. And they had the grace given them to impress upon it the only attitude which could conciliate and harmonize all parties, the attitude of perfect indifference.

This, at the same time, is the attitude of justice. We of the South have the same right to our opinions as the people of the North. They appear as true to us as theirs appear to them. We are as honest and sincere in forming and maintaining them. We unite to form a government. Upon what principle shall it be formed? Is it to be asked of us to renounce doctrines which we believe have come down to us from the earliest ages, and have the sanction of the oracles of God? Must we give up what we conscientiously believe to be the truth? The thing is absurd. The Government, in justice, can only say to both parties: I will protect you both, I will be the advocate of neither.

In order to exempt slavery from the operation of this plain principle of justice, it has been contended that the right of property in slaves is the creature of positive statute, and, consequently, of force only within the limits of the jurisdiction of the law; that it is a right not recognized by the Constitution of the United States, and, therefore, not to be protected where Congress is the local legislature. These two propositions contain everything that has any show of reason for the extraordinary revolution which the recent election has consummated in the Government of the United States.

They are both gratuitous:

(1.) In the first place, slavery has never, in any country, so far as we know, arisen under the operation of statute law. It is not a municipal institution; it is not the arbitrary creature of the State: it has not sprung from the mere force of legislation. Law defines, modifies, and regulates it, as it does every other species of property; but law never *created* it. The law found it in existence, and being in existence, the law subjects it to fixed rules. On the contrary, what is local and municipal is the *abolition* of slavery. The States that are now non-slaveholding, have been made so by positive statute. Slavery exists, of course, in every nation in which it is not prohibited. It arose, in the progress of human events, from the operation of moral causes; it has been grounded by philosophers in moral maxims; it has always been held to be moral by the vast majority of the race. No age has been without it. From the first dawn of authentic history, until the present period, it has come down to us through all the course of ages. We find it among nomadic tribes, barbarian hordes, and civilized States. Wherever communities have been organized, and any rights of property have been recognized at all, there slavery is seen. If, therefore, there can be any property which can be said to be founded in the common consent of the human race, it is the property in slaves. If there be any property that can be called natural, in the sense that it spontaneously springs up in the history of the species, it is the property in slaves. If there be any property which is founded in principles of universal operation, it is the property in slaves. To say of an institution, whose history is thus the history of man, which has always and everywhere existed, that it is a local and municipal relation, is of "all absurdities the motliest, the merest word that ever fooled the ear from out the schoolman's jargon." Mankind may have been wrong; that is not the question. The point is, whether the *law* made slavery; whether it is the police regulation of limited localities, or whether it is a property founded in natural causes, and causes of universal operation. We say nothing as to the moral character of the causes. We insist only upon the fact that slavery is rooted in a common law, wider and more pervading than the common law of England: THE UNIVERSAL CUSTOM OF MANKIND.

If, therefore, slavery is not municipal, but natural; if it is abolition which is municipal and local; then, upon the avowed doctrines of our opponents, two things follow: first, that slavery goes of right, and as a matter of course, into every territory from which it is not excluded by positive statute; and, second, that Congress is competent to forbid the Northern States from impressing their local peculiarity of non-slaveholding upon the common soil of the Union. If the Republican argument is good for anything, it goes the whole length of excluding for ever any additional non-slaveholding States from the Union. What would they think if the South had taken any such extravagant ground as this? What would they have done, if the South had taken advantage of a numerical majority, to legislate them and their institutions for ever out of the common territory? Would they have *submitted?* Would they have glorified the Union, and yielded to the triumph of slavery? We know that they would not. They would have scorned the crotchet about municipal and local laws which divested them of their dearest rights. Let them give the same measure to others which they expect from others. It is a noble maxim, commended by high authority, Do as you would be done by.

The South has neither asked for, nor does she desire, any exclusive benefits. All she demands is, that as South, as slaveholding, she shall be put upon the same footing with the North, as non-slaveholding; that the Government shall not undertake to say, one kind of States is better than the other; that it shall have no preference as to the character, in this respect, of any future States to be added to the Union. Non-slaveholding may be superior to slaveholding, but it is not the place of the Government to say so, much less to assume the right of saying so upon a principle which, properly applied, requires it to say the very reverse.

There is another sense in which municipal is opposed to international, and, in this sense, slavery is said to be municipal, because there is no obligation, by the law of nations, on the part of States in which

slavery is prohibited, to respect, within the limits of their own territory, the rights of the foreign slaveholder. This is the doctrine laid
down by Judge Story. No nation is bound to accord to a stranger a
right of property which it refuses to its own subjects. We cannot,
therefore, demand from the governments of France or England, or any
other foreign power, whose policy and interests are opposed to slavery,
the restoration of our fugitives from bondage. We are willing to concede, for the sake of argument, that the principle in question is an admitted principle of international law, though we are quite persuaded
that it is contrary to the whole current of Continental authorities, and is
intensely English. We doubt whether, even in England, it can be traced
beyond the famous decision of Lord Mansfield, in the case of Somerset.
But let us admit the principle. What then? The Constitution of the
United States has expressly provided that this principle shall not apply
within the limits of Federal jurisdiction. With reference to this country,
it has abrogated the law; every State is bound to respect the right of the
Southern master to his slave. The Constitution covers the whole territory of the Union, and throughout that territory has taken slavery under
the protection of law. However foreign nations may treat our fugitive
slaves, the States of this confederacy are bound to treat them as property, and to give them back to their lawful owners. How idle, therefore, to plead a principle of international law, which, in reference to the
relations of the States of this Union, is formally'abolished! Slavery is
clearly a part of the municipal law of the United States; and the whole
argument, from the local character of the institution, falls to the ground.
Slaveholding and non-slaveholding are both equally sectional, and both
equally national.

(2.) As to the allegation that the Constitution nowhere recognizes the
right of property in slaves, that is equally unfounded. We shall say nothing here of the decision of the Supreme Court, though that, one would
think, is entitled to some consideration. We shall appeal to the Constitution itself, and, if there is force in logic, we shall be able to make it
appear that the right is not only recognized, but recognized with a philosophical accuracy and precision that seize only on the essential, and
omit the variable and accidental. The subject, in the language of the
Constitution, is transferred from the technicalities of law, to the higher
sphere of abstract and speculative morality. Morally considered, to
what class does the slave belong? To the class of persons held to service. The two ideas that he is a person, and as a person, held to service,
constitute the generic conception of slavery. How is this obligation to
service fundamentally differenced from that of other labourers? By
this, as one essential circumstance, that it is independent of the for-
malities of contract. Add the circumstance that it is for life, and you
have a complete conception of the thing. You have the very definition,
almost in his own words, which a celebrated English philosopher gives
of slavery: "I define slavery," says Dr. Paley, "to be an obligation to

labour for the benefit of the master, without the contract or consent of the servant."*

Now, is such an obligation recognized in the Constitution of the United States? Are there persons spoken of in it who are held to service by a claim so sacred that the Government allows them, however anxious they may be to do so, to dissolve it neither by stratagem nor force? If they run away, they must be remanded to those who are entitled to their labour, even if they escape to a territory whose local laws would otherwise protect them. If they appeal to force, the whole power of the Union may be brought to crush them. Can any man say that the Constitution does not here recognize a right to the labour and service of men, of persons, which springs from no stipulations of their own, is entirely independent of their own consent, and which can never be annulled by any efforts, whether clandestine or open, on their part? *This is slavery;* it is the very essence and core of the institution. That upon which the right of property terminates in the slave, is his service or labour. It is not his soul, not his person, not his moral and intellectual nature; it is his *labour.* This is the thing which is bought and sold in the market; and it is, in consequence, of the right to regulate, control, and direct this, that the person comes under an obligation to obey. The ideas of a right on one side, and duty on the other, show that the slave, in this relation, is as truly a person as his master. The Constitution, therefore, does recognize and protect slavery, in every moral and ethical feature of it. The thing which, under that name, has commanded the approbation of mankind, is the very thing, among others analogous to it, included in the third clause of the second section of the fourth chapter of the Constitution. We see no way of getting round this argument. It is idle to say that slaves are not referred to; it is equally idle to say that the right of their labour is not respected and guarded. Let this right be acknowledged in the territories, and we are not disposed to wring changes upon words. Let the Government permit the South to carry her persons held to service, without their consent, into the territories, and let the right to their labour be protected, and there would be no quarrel about slavery. It is unworthy of statesmen, in a matter of this sort, to quibble about legal technicalities. That the law of slaveholding States classes slaves among chattels, and speaks of them as marketable commodities, does not imply that, morally and ethically, they are not persons; nor that the property is in them, rather than in their toil. These same laws treat them, in other respects, as persons; and speak of their service as obedience or duty. The meaning of chattel is relative, and is to be restricted to the relation which it implies.

We are happy to find that the Supreme Court of the United States has fully confirmed the interpretation which we have given to this clause of the Constitution. In the case of Priggs *vs.* the Common-

---

* Moral Philos. III., c. 3.

wealth of Pennsylvania,* it was asserted by every judge upon the bench that the design of the provision was "to secure to the citizens of the slaveholding States the complete right and title of ownership in their slaves, as property, in every State in the Union into which they might escape from the State where they were held in servitude." These are the very words of Mr. Justice Story, in delivering the opinion of the Court. He went on to add: "The full recognition of this right and title was indispensable to the security of this species of property in all the slaveholding States; and, indeed, was so vital to the preservation of the domestic interests and institutions, that it cannot be doubted that it constituted a fundamental article, without the adoption of which the Union could not have been formed."† Again: "We have said that the clause contains a positive and unqualified recognition of the right of the owner in the slave."‡ Chief Justice Taney held that, "by the national compact, this right of property is recognized as an existing right in every State of the Union."§ Judge Thompson said, the Constitution "affirms, in the most unequivocal manner, the right of the master to the service of his slave, according to the laws of the State under which he is so held."‖ Judge Wayne affirmed that all the judges concurred "in the declaration that the provision in the Constitution was a compromise between the slaveholding and the non-slaveholding States, to secure to the former fugitive slaves as property."¶ "The paramount authority of this clause in the Constitution," says Judge Daniel, "to guarantee to the owner the right of property in his slave, and the absolute nullity of any State power, directly or indirectly, openly or covertly, aimed to impair that right, or to obstruct its enjoyment, I admit—nay, insist upon—to the fullest extent."**

If, now, the Constitution recognizes slaves as property—that is, as persons to whose labour and service the master has a right—then, upon what principle shall Congress undertake to abolish this right upon a territory of which it is the local legislature? It will not permit the slave to cancel it, because the service is due. Upon what ground can it interpose between a man and his dues? Congress is as much the agent of the slaveholding as it is of the non-slaveholding States; and, as equally bound to protect both, and to hold the scales of justice even between them, it must guard the property of the one with the same care with which it guards the property of the other.

We have now refuted the postulates upon which the recent revolution in the Government is attempted to be justified. We have shown that slavery is not the creature of local and municipal law, and that the Constitution distinctly recognizes the right of the master to the labour or service of the slave; that is, the right of property in slaves. There is no conceivable pretext, then, for saying that the Government should resist the circulation of this kind of property more than any other.

That question it must leave to the providence of God, and to the natural and moral laws by which its solution is conditioned. All that the Government can do is to give fair play to both parties, the slaveholding and non-slaveholding States; protect the rights of both on their common soil, and as soon as a sovereign State emerges, to which the soil is henceforward to belong, remit the matter to its absolute discretion. This is justice ; this is the impartiality which becomes the agent of a great people, divided by two such great interests.

That the rights of the South, *as slaveholding*,—for it is in that relation only that she is politically a different section from the North,—and the rights of the North, as *non-slaveholding*, are absolutely equal, is so plain a proposition, that one wonders at the pertinacity with which it has been denied. Here let us expose a sophism whose only force consists in a play upon words. It is alleged that the equality of the sections is not disturbed by the exclusion of slavery from the territories, because the Southern man may take with him all that the Northern man can take. The plain English of which is this : if the Southern man will consent to become *as* a Northern man, and renounce what distinguishes him as a *Southern* man, he may go into the territories. But if he insists upon remaining a *Southern* man, he must stay at home. The geography is only an accident in this matter. The Southern man, politically, is the slaveholder; the Northern man, politically, is the non-slaveholder. The rights of the South are the rights of the South as slaveholding ; the rights of the North are the rights of the North as non-slaveholding. This is what makes the real difference betwixt the two sections. To exclude *slaveholding* is, therefore, to exclude the South. By the free-soil doctrine, therefore, she, as South, is utterly debarred from every foot of the soil which belongs of right as much to her as to her Northern confederates. The Constitution is made to treat her institutions as if they were a scandal and reproach. It becomes the patron of the North, and an enemy, instead of a protector, to her.

That this is the attitude which the Government is henceforward to assume, we shall now proceed to show :

(1.) In the first place, let it be distinctly understood that we do not charge the great body of the Northern people, who have accomplished the recent revolution, with being abolitionists, in the strict and technical sense. We are willing to concede that they have no design, for the present, to interfere directly with slavery in the slaveholding States. We shall give them credit for an honest purpose, under Mr. Lincoln's administration, to execute, as far as the hostility of the States will let them, the provisions of the fugitive slave law. All this may be admitted ; but it does not affect the real issue, nor mitigate the real danger. We know that there are various types of opinion at the North, with reference to the moral aspects of slavery ; and we have never apprehended that, under the Constitution as it stands, there was any likelihood of an attempt to interfere, by legislation, with our property on our own soil.

(2.) But, in the second place, it must likewise be conceded that the general, almost the universal, attitude of the Northern mind is one of hostility to slavery. Those who are not prepared to condemn it as a sin, nor to meddle with it where it is legally maintained, are yet opposed to it, as a natural and political evil, which every good man should desire to see extinguished. They all regard it as a calamity, an affliction, a misfortune. They regard it as an element of weakness, and as a draw-back upon the prosperity and glory of the country. They pity the South, as caught in the folds of a serpent, which is gradually squeezing out her life. And, even when they defend us from the reproach of sin in sustaining the relation, they make so many distinctions between the abstract notion of slavery and the system of our own laws, that their defence would hardly avail to save us, if there were any power competent to hang and quarter us. We are sure that we do not misrepresent the general tone of Northern sentiment. It is one of *hostility* to slavery; it is one which, while it might not be willing to break faith, under the present administration, with respect to the express injunctions of the Constitution, is utterly and absolutely opposed to any further extension of the system.

(3.) In the third place, let it be distinctly understood that we have no complaint to make of the opinions of the North, considered simply as their opinions. They have a right, so far as human authority is concerned, to think as they please. The South has never asked them to approve of slavery, or to change their own institutions, and to introduce it among themselves. The South has been willing to accord to them the most perfect and unrestricted right of private judgment.

(4.) But in the fourth place, what we *do* complain of, and what we have a right to complain of, is that they should not be content with thinking their own thoughts themselves, but should undertake to make the *Government* think them likewise. We of the South have, also, certain thoughts concerning slavery; and we cannot understand upon what principle the thinking of the South is totally excluded, and the thinking of the North made supreme. The Government is as much ours as theirs; and we cannot see why, in a matter that vitally concerns ourselves, we shall be allowed to do no effective thinking at all. This is the grievance. The Government is made to take the type of Northern sentiment; it is animated, in its relations to slavery, by the Northern mind; and the South, henceforward, is no longer *of* the Government, but only *under* the Government. The extension of slavery, in obedience to Northern prejudice, is to be for ever arrested. Congress is to treat it as an evil, an element of political weakness, and to restrain its influence within the limits which now circumscribe it. All this because the *North thinks* so; while the South, an equal party to the Government, has quite other thoughts. And when we indignantly complain of this absolute suppression of all right to think in and through our own Government, upon a subject that involves our homes and our firesides, we are coolly reminded that, as long as Congress does not usurp the rights of our own Legislatures, and abolish slavery on our own soil, nor harbour our fugitives when they attempt to escape from us, we have reason to be grateful for the indulgence accorded to us. The right to breathe is as much as we should venture to claim. You may exist, says free-soilism, as States, and manage your slaves at home; we will not abrogate your sovereignty. Your runaways we do not want, and we may occasionally send them back to you. But if you think you have a right to be heard at Washington upon this great subject, it is time that your presumption should be rebuked. The North is the thinking power, the soul of the Government. The life of the Government is Northern, not Southern; the type to be impressed upon all future States is Northern, not Southern. The North becomes the United States, and the South a subject province.

Now, we say that this is a state of things not to be borne. A free people can never consent to their own degradation. We say boldly, that the Government has no more right to adopt Northern thoughts on the subject of slavery than those of the South. It has no more right to presume that they are true. It has no right to arbitrate between them. It must treat them both with equal respect, and give them an equal chance. Upon no other footing can the South, with honour, remain in the Union. It is not to be endured for a moment, that fifteen sovereign States, embodying, in proportion to their population, as much intelligence, virtue, public spirit and patriotism, as any other people upon the globe, should be quietly reduced to zero, in a Government which they framed for their own protection. We put the question again to the North: "If the tables were turned, and it was your thoughts, your life, your institutions, that the Government was henceforward to discountenance; if non-slaveholding was hereafter to be prohibited in every territory, and the whole policy of the Government shaped by the principle that slavery is a blessing, would you endure it? Would not your blood boil, and would you not call upon your hungry millions to come to the rescue?" And yet, this is precisely what you have done to us, and think we ought not to resist. You have made us ciphers, and are utterly amazed that we should claim to be anything.

But, apart from the degradation which it inflicts upon the South, it may be asked, what real injury will result from putting the Government in an attitude of hostility to slavery?

The answer is, in the first place, that it will certainly lead to the extinction of the system. You may destroy the oak as effectually by girdling it as by cutting it down. The North are well assured that, if they can circumscribe the area of slavery, if they can surround it with a circle of non-slaveholding States, and prevent it from expanding, nothing more is required to secure its ultimate abolition. "Like the scorpion girt by fire," it will plunge its fangs into its own body, and perish. If, therefore, the South is not prepared to see her institutions surrounded by enemies, and wither and decay under these hostile influences, if she means to cherish and protect them, it is her bounden duty to resist the revolution which threatens them with ruin. The triumph of the principles which Mr. Lincoln is pledged to carry out, is the death-knell of slavery.

In the next place, the state of the Northern mind which has produced this revolution, cannot be expected to remain content with its present victory. It will hasten to other triumphs. The same spirit which has prevaricated with the express provisions of the Constitution, and resorted to expedients to evade the most sacred obligations, will not hesitate for a moment to change the Constitution when it finds itself in possession of the power. It will only be consistency to harmonize the fundamental law of the Government with its chosen policy, the real workings of its life. The same hostility to slavery which a numerical majority has impressed upon the Federal legislature, it will not scruple to impress upon the Federal Constitution. If the South could be induced to submit to Lincoln, the time, we confidently predict, will come when all grounds of controversy will be removed in relation to fugitive slaves, by expunging the provision under which they are claimed. The principle is at work, and enthroned in power, whose inevitable tendency is to secure this result. Let us crush the serpent in the egg.

From these considerations, it is obvious that nothing more nor less is at stake in this controversy than the very life of the South. The real question is, whether she shall be politically annihilated. We are not struggling for fleeting and temporary interests. We are struggling for our very being. And none know better than the Republican party itself that, if we submit to their new type of government, our fate as slave-holding States is for ever sealed. They have already exulted in the prospect of this glorious consummation. They boast that they have laid a mine which must ultimately explode in our utter ruin. They are singing songs of victory in advance, and are confidently anticipating the auspicious hour when they shall have nothing to do but to return to the field and bury the dead.

The sum of what we have said is briefly this: We have shown that the constitutional attitude of the Government toward slavery is one of absolute neutrality or indifference in relation to the moral and political aspects of the subject. We have shown, in the next place, that it is hereafter to take an attitude of hostility; that it is to represent the opinions and feelings exclusively of the North; that it is to become the Government of one section over another; and that the South, as South, is to sustain no other relation to it but the duty of obedience.

This is a thorough and radical revolution. It makes a new Government; it proposes new and extraordinary terms of union. The old Government is as completely abolished as if the people of the United States had met in convention and repealed the Constitution. It is frivolous to tell us that the change has been made through the forms of the Constitution. This is to add insult to injury. What signify forms, when the substance is gone? Of what value is the shell, when the kernel is extracted? Rights are *things*, and not words; and when the things are taken from us, it is no time to be nibbling at phrases. If a witness under oath designedly gives testimony, which, though literally true, conveys a false impression, is he not guilty of perjury? Is not his truth a lie? Temures kept the letter of his promise to the garrison of Sebastia, that, if they would surrender, no blood should be shed; but did that save him from the scandal of treachery in burying them alive? No man objects to the legality of the process of Mr. Lincoln's election. The objection is to the legality of that to which he is elected. He has been chosen, not to administer, but to revolutionize the Government. The very moment he goes into office, the Constitution of the United States, as touching the great question between North and South, is dead. The oath which makes him President, makes a new Union. The import of secession is simply the refusal, on the part of the South, to be parties to any such Union. She has not renounced, and, if it had been permitted to stand, she never would have renounced, the Constitution which our fathers framed. She would have stood by it for ever. But, as the North have substantially abolished it, and, taking advantage of their numbers, have substituted another in its place, which dooms the South to perdition, surely she has a right to say she will enter into no such conspiracy. The Government to which she consented was a Government under which she might hope to live. The new one presented in its place is one under which she can only die. Under these circumstances, we do not see how any man can question either the righteousness or the necessity of secession. The South is shut up to the duty of rejecting these new terms of union. No people on earth, without judicial infatuation, can organize a government to destroy them. It is too much to ask a man to sign his own death-warrant.

II. We wish to say a few words as to the policy of the slaveholding States in the present emergency.

We know it to be the fixed determination of them all not to acquiesce in the principles which have brought Mr. Lincoln into power. Several of them, however, have hesitated—and it is a sign of the scrupulous integrity of the South in maintaining her faith—whether the mere fact of his election, apart from any overt act of the Government, is itself a *casus belli*, and a sufficient reason for extreme measures of resistance. These States have also clung to the hope that there would yet be a returning sense of justice at the North, which shall give them satisfactory guarantees for the preservation of their rights, and restore peace without the necessity of schism. We respect the motives which have produced this hesitation. We have no sympathy with any taunting reflections upon the courage, magnanimity, public spirit, or patriotism of such a Commonwealth as Virginia. The mother of Washington is not to be insulted if, like her great hero, she takes counsel of moderation and prudence. We honour, too, the sentiment which makes it hard to give up the Union. It was a painful struggle to ourselves; the most painful struggle of our lives. There were precious memories and hallowed associations, connected with a glorious history, to which the heart cannot bid farewell without a pang. Few men, in all the South, brought themselves to pronounce the word DISUNION, without sadness of heart. Some States have not yet been able to pronounce it. But the tendency of events is irresistible. It is becoming every day clearer that the people of the North hate slavery more than they love the Union, and they are developing this spirit in a form which must soon bring every slaveholding State within the ranks of secession. The evil day may be put off, but it must come. The country must be divided into two people, and the point which we wish now to press upon the whole South is, the importance of preparing, at once, for this consummation.

The slaveholding interest is one, and it seems to us clear that the slaveholding States ought speedily to be organized under one general Government. United, they are strong enough to maintain themselves against the world. They have the territory, the resources, the population, the public spirit, the institutions, which, under a genial and fostering Constitution, would soon enable them to become one of the first people upon the globe. And if the North shall have wisdom to see her true policy, two Governments upon this continent may work out the problem of human liberty more successfully than one. Let the two people maintain the closest alliance for defence against a foreign foe; or, at least, let them be agreed that no European power shall ever set foot on American soil, and that no type of government but the republican shall ever be tolerated here; and what is to hinder the fullest and freest development of our noble institutions? The separation changes nothing but the external relations of the two sections. Such a dismemberment of the Union is not like the revolution of a State, where the internal system of government is subverted, where laws are suspended, and where anarchy reigns. The country might divide into two great nations to-morrow, without a jostle or a jar; the Government of each State might go on as regularly as before, the law be as supreme, and order as perfect, if the passions of the people could be kept from getting the better of their judgments. It is a great advantage, in the form of our Confederacy, that a radical revolution can take place without confusion and without anarchy. Every State has a perfect internal system at work already, and that undergoes no change, except in adjusting it to its altered external relations. Now, given this system of States, with every element of a perfect government in full and undisturbed operation, what is there in the circumstance of *one* Confederacy of *divided interests*, that shall secure a freer and safer development than *two Confederacies*, each representing an *undivided* interest? Are not two homogeneous Unions stronger than one that is heterogeneous? Should not the life of a Government be one? We do not see, therefore, that anything will be lost to freedom by the union of the South under a separate Government. She will carry into it every institution that she had before—her State constitutions, her legislatures, her courts of justice, her halls of learning—everything that she now possesses. She will put these precious interests under a Government embodying every principle which gave value to the old one, and amply adequate to protect. What will she lose of real freedom? We confess that we cannot understand the declamation that, with the American Union, American institutions are gone. Each section of the Union will preserve them and cherish them. Every principle that has ever made us glorious, and made our Government a wonder, will abide with us. The sections, separately, will not be as formidable to foreign powers as before. That is all. But each section will be strong enough to protect itself, and both together can save this continent for republicanism for ever.

Indeed, it is likely that both Governments will be purer, in consequence of their mutual rivalry, and the diminution of the extent of their patronage. They will both cherish intensely the American feeling, both maintain the pride of American character, and both try to make their Governments at home what they would desire to have them appear to be abroad. Once take away all pretext for meddling with one another's peculiar interests, and we do not see but that the magnificent visions of glory, which our imaginations have delighted to picture as the destiny of the Anglo-Saxon race on this North American continent, may yet be fully realized. They never can be, if we continue together, to bite and devour one another.

But, whether it be for weal for woe, the South has no election. She is driven to the wall, and the only question is, will she take care of herself in time? The sooner she can organize a general Government the better. That will be a centre of unity, and, once combined, we are safe.

We cannot close without saying a few words to the people of the North as to the policy which it becomes them to pursue. The whole question of peace or war is in their hands. The South is simply standing on the defensive, and has no notion of abandoning that attitude. Let the Northern people, then, seriously consider, and consider in the fear of God, how, under present circumstances, they can best conserve those great interests of freedom, of religion, and of order, which are equally dear to us both, and which they can fearfully jeopard. If their counsels incline to peace, the most friendly relations can speedily be restored, and the most favourable treaties entered into. We should feel ourselves the joint possessors of the continent, and should be drawn together by ties which unite no other people. We could, indeed, realize all the advantages of the Union, without any of its inconveniences. The cause of human liberty would not even be retarded, if the North can rise to a level with the exigencies of the occasion. If, on the other hand, their thoughts incline to war, we solemnly ask them what they expect to gain? What interest will be promoted? What end, worthy of a great people, will they be able to secure? They may gratify their bad passions, they may try to wreak their resentment upon the seceding States, and they may inflict a large amount of injury, disaster, and suffering. But what have they gained? Shall a free people be governed by their passions? Suppose they should conquer us, what will they do with us? How will they hold us in subjection? How many garrisons, and how many men, and how much treasure, will it take to keep the South in order as a conquered province? and where are these resources to come from? After they have subdued us, the hardest part of their task will remain. They will have the wolf by the ears.

But upon what grounds do they hope to conquer us? They know us well; they know our numbers, they know our spirit, and they know the value which we set upon our homes and firesides. We have fought for the glory of the Union, and the world admired us; but it was not such fighting as we shall do for our wives, our children, and our sacred honour. The very women of the South, like the Spartan matrons, will take hold of shield and buckler, and our boys at school will go to the field in all the determination of disciplined valour. Conquered we can never be. It would be madness to attempt it. And after years of blood and slaughter, the parties would be just where they began, except that they would have learned to hate one another with an intensity of hatred equalled only in hell. Freedom would suffer, religion would suffer, learning would suffer, every human interest would suffer, from such a war. But upon whose head would fall the responsibility? There can be but one answer. We solemnly believe that the South will be guiltless before the eyes of the Judge of all the earth. She has stood in her lot, and resisted aggression.

If the North could rise to the dignity of their present calling, this country would present to the world a spectacle of unparalleled grandeur. It would show how deeply the love of liberty and the influence of religion are rooted in our people, when a great empire can be divided without confusion, war, or disorder. Two great people united under one Government differ upon a question of vital importance to one. Neither can conscientiously give way. In the magnanimity of their souls, they say, let there be no strife between us, for we are brethren. The land is broad enough for us both. Let us part in peace; let us divide our common inheritance, adjust our common obligations; and, preserving as a sacred treasure our common principles, let each set up for himself, and let the Lord bless us both. A course like this—heroic, sublime, glorious—would be something altogether unexampled in the history of the world. It would be the wonder and astonishment of the nations. It would do more to command for American institutions the homage and respect of mankind than all the armies and fleets of the Republic. It would be a victory more august and imposing than any which can be achieved by the thunder of cannon and the shock of battle.

Peace is the policy of both North and South. Let peace prevail, and nothing really valuable is lost. To save the Union is impossible. The thing for Christian men and patriots to aim at now, is to save the country from war. That will be a scourge and a curse. But the South will emerge from it free as she was before. She is the invaded party, and her institutions are likely to gain strength from the conflict. Can the North, as the invading party, be assured that she will not fall into the hands of a military despot? The whole question is with her; and we calmly await her decision. We prefer peace; but if war must come, we are prepared to meet it with unshaken confidence in the God of battles. We lament the wide-spread mischief it will do, the arrest it will put upon every holy enterprise of the Church, and upon all the interests of life; but the South can boldly say to the bleeding, distracted country,

> "Shake not thy gory locks at me;
> Thou canst not say I did it."

INDEX.

A.

ABSTRACTION, early power of, 44.
ACADEMIC LIFE, occasional dissatisfaction with, 339; reasons for the same, 339–342.
ACT AND TESTIMONY, 206, 207.
ADDRESS to the Churches of Jesus Christ, 504.
ÆSTHETIC ELEMENT, not wanting in, 147–150.
AFFLICTION, unsanctified, 240; how to be improved, 241; fidelity to one sinking in, 419–422.
AMBITION, early, 20; anecdotes of, 42, 43.
AMERICA AND EUROPE, compared, 457.
ANDOVER SEMINARY, goes to and leaves, 113, 115.
ANCESTRY, pride of, 1, 2; on the paternal side, 3.
APOCRYPHA, essay on the, 226; discussion with Dr. Lynch on the, 245–247; book on the, 261.
AFRICAN SLAVE TRADE, opposition to revival of, 422, 423; Secession not caused by a purpose to re-open, 594.
ARKANSAS, admission of, 473.
ASPIRATIONS after fame, 94.
ASSEMBLY OF 1837, reform measures of, 207, 268; a member of, 212.
ASSEMBLY OF 1845, a member of, 245; its action on slavery, 285–287.
ASSEMBLY OF 1847, Moderator of, 297; his salutatory address, 297, 300.
ASSEMBLY OF 1848, his opening sermon before, 301; curious scene in, 304, 305.
ASSEMBLY OF 1852, criticism of its action on the Quorum question, &c., 369–371.
ASSEMBLY OF 1855, a member of, 389; discussion on subject of Boards, 389, 390.
ASSEMBLY OF 1856, a member of, 417; his sermon on Foreign Missions, 417.
ASSEMBLY OF 1857, a member of, 423.
ASSEMBLY OF 1859, a member of, 435; remarkable speech in, 436, 437; effect of sermon preached, 438, 439.
ASSEMBLY OF 1860, a member of, 445; debate on Boards, 446.
ASSEMBLY OF 1861, the Spring resolutions, 501.

B.

BALTIMORE, his call to, 267; this call accepted, 268; arrested for a year, 270; strictures on this, 271, 272; vindication of his course, 272–279; finally defeated by Presbytery, 282–284.
BAPTISMAL COVENANT, his views of, 416.

BARNWELL, Hon. R. W., notice of, 147.
BARNES, REV. A., trial of, 205.
BASLE, description of, 456.
BENEVOLENCE, disinterested, his views of, 124.
BENEFACTIONS, to young men, 319.
BETHEL PRESBYTERY, unites with, 128.
BENTHAM, criticism on, 87,
BIRTH, his, 2.
BOOKS, early fondness for, 20, 22.
BISHOP, REV. P. E., friendship with, 139; death of, 433; letter to widow of, 434.
BISHOP, MR. ROBERT, his relation to, and early death of, 320.
BIBLE SOCIETY, whether secular or religious, 344.
BOARDS, question of, 221; discussion on in Synod, 222; his views of, in letters, 223, 227, 228; his first article on, 224; his second article on, 229, 389, 390, 446, 447.
BRECKINRIDGE, REV. DR. R. J., sympathy with on death of his wife, 264, 265.
BROWNSON'S review of his work on the Apocrypha, 330, 331.
BRUSSELS, visit to, 462.
BUNSEN'S HIPPOLYTUS, criticism on, 373.
BUTLER'S ANALOGY, analysis of, 224.

C.

CALHOUN, MR., first interview with, 305, 306.
CALVIN, compared with, 532, 533.
CALIFORNIA, admission of. 475.
CAMBRIDGE PLATFORM, 189.
CAMBRIDGE UNIVERSITY, goes to, 116; visits later, 361–365.
CHAPLAIN in South Carolina College, elected, 155.
CHARACTER, his, when matured, 138.
CHANGE of political views, explained, 481–483.
CHERAW, removal to. 39; enters Cheraw Academy, 43; teaches in, 103
CHESTER, description of, 170–172.
CHILD, death of his first, 138.
CHILDREN, letters to his young, 294, 295, 350, 351.
CHRISTIAN EXPERIENCE, form of his, 562, 563.
CHURCH, union with the, 95; his views of the, as a spiritual agency, 225; demission of membership in, 304, 303; relation to voluntary societies, 303; secularization of the courts of the, 230, 291.
CLASSICS, fondness for the, 44.

611